Mathematics for Computer Science

A catalogue record for this book is available from the Hong Kong Public Libraries.

Published in Hong Kong by Samurai Media Limited.

Email: info@samuraimedia.org

ISBN 978-988-8407-06-4

Contents

II   *Structures*

III Counting

IV Probability

I   Proofs

Introduction

This text explains how to use mathematical models and methods to analyze problems that arise in computer science. Proofs play a central role in this work because the authors share a belief with most mathematicians that proofs are essential for genuine understanding. Proofs also play a growing role in computer science; they are used to certify that software and hardware will *always* behave correctly, something that no amount of testing can do.

Simply put, a proof is a method of establishing truth. Like beauty, "truth" sometimes depends on the eye of the beholder, and it should not be surprising that what constitutes a proof differs among fields. For example, in the judicial system, *legal* truth is decided by a jury based on the allowable evidence presented at trial. In the business world, *authoritative* truth is specified by a trusted person or organization, or maybe just your boss. In fields such as physics or biology, *scientific* truth is confirmed by experiment.[1] In statistics, *probable* truth is established by statistical analysis of sample data.

Philosophical proof involves careful exposition and persuasion typically based on a series of small, plausible arguments. The best example begins with "Cogito ergo sum," a Latin sentence that translates as "I think, therefore I am." This phrase comes from the beginning of a 17th century essay by the mathematician/philosopher, René Descartes, and it is one of the most famous quotes in the world: do a web search for it, and you will be flooded with hits.

Deducing your existence from the fact that you're thinking about your existence is a pretty cool and persuasive-sounding idea. However, with just a few more lines

---

[1] Actually, only scientific *falsehood* can be demonstrated by an experiment—when the experiment fails to behave as predicted. But no amount of experiment can confirm that the *next* experiment won't fail. For this reason, scientists rarely speak of truth, but rather of *theories* that accurately predict past, and anticipated future, experiments.

of argument in this vein, Descartes goes on to conclude that there is an infinitely beneficent God. Whether or not you believe in an infinitely beneficent God, you'll probably agree that any very short "proof" of God's infinite beneficence is bound to be far-fetched. So even in masterful hands, this approach is not reliable.

Mathematics has its own specific notion of "proof."

Definition. A *mathematical proof* of a *proposition* is a chain of *logical deductions* leading to the proposition from a base set of *axioms*.

The three key ideas in this definition are highlighted: *proposition*, *logical deduction*, and *axiom*. Chapter 1 examines these three ideas along with some basic ways of organizing proofs. Chapter 2 introduces the Well Ordering Principle, a basic method of proof; later, Chapter 5 introduces the closely related proof method of induction.

If you're going to prove a proposition, you'd better have a precise understanding of what the proposition means. To avoid ambiguity and uncertain definitions in ordinary language, mathematicians use language very precisely, and they often express propositions using logical formulas; these are the subject of Chapter 3.

The first three Chapters assume the reader is familiar with a few mathematical concepts like sets and functions. Chapters 4 and 8 offer a more careful look at such mathematical data types, examining in particular properties and methods for proving things about infinite sets. Chapter 7 goes on to examine recursively defined data types.

0.1 References

[12], [46], [1]

1 What is a Proof?

1.1 Propositions

Definition. A *proposition* is a statement (communication) that is either true or false.

For example, both of the following statements are propositions. The first is true, and the second is false.

Proposition 1.1.1. *2 + 3 = 5.*

Proposition 1.1.2. *1 + 1 = 3.*

Being true or false doesn't sound like much of a limitation, but it does exclude statements such as "Wherefore art thou Romeo?" and "Give me an *A*!" It also excludes statements whose truth varies with circumstance such as, "It's five o'clock," or "the stock market will rise tomorrow."

Unfortunately it is not always easy to decide if a claimed proposition is true or false:

Claim 1.1.3. *For every nonnegative integer n the value of $n^2 + n + 41$ is prime.*

(A *prime* is an integer greater than 1 that is not divisible by any other integer greater than 1. For example, 2, 3, 5, 7, 11, are the first five primes.) Let's try some numerical experimentation to check this proposition. Let

$$p(n) ::= n^2 + n + 41.^1 \qquad (1.1)$$

We begin with $p(0) = 41$, which is prime; then

$$p(1) = 43, p(2) = 47, p(3) = 53, \ldots, p(20) = 461$$

are each prime. Hmmm, starts to look like a plausible claim. In fact we can keep checking through $n = 39$ and confirm that $p(39) = 1601$ is prime.

But $p(40) = 40^2 + 40 + 41 = 41 \cdot 41$, which is not prime. So Claim 1.1.3 is false since it's not true that $p(n)$ is prime *for all* nonnegative integers n. In fact, it's not hard to show that *no* polynomial with integer coefficients can map all

---

[1] The symbol ::= means "equal by definition." It's always ok simply to write "=" instead of ::=, but reminding the reader that an equality holds by definition can be helpful.

nonnegative numbers into prime numbers, unless it's a constant (see Problem 1.26). But this example highlights the point that, in general, you can't check a claim about an infinite set by checking a finite sample of its elements, no matter how large the sample.

By the way, propositions like this about *all* numbers or all items of some kind are so common that there is a special notation for them. With this notation, Claim 1.1.3 would be

$$\forall n \in \mathbb{N}. \ p(n) \text{ is prime.} \tag{1.2}$$

Here the symbol $\forall$ is read "for all." The symbol $\mathbb{N}$ stands for the set of *nonnegative integers*: 0, 1, 2, 3, ... (ask your instructor for the complete list). The symbol "$\in$" is read as "is a member of," or "belongs to," or simply as "is in." The period after the $\mathbb{N}$ is just a separator between phrases.

Here are two even more extreme examples:

Conjecture. *[Euler] The equation*

$$a^4 + b^4 + c^4 = d^4$$

has no solution when a, b, c, d are positive integers.

Euler (pronounced "oiler") conjectured this in 1769. But the conjecture was proved false 218 years later by Noam Elkies at a liberal arts school up Mass Ave. The solution he found was $a = 95800, b = 217519, c = 414560, d = 422481$.

In logical notation, Euler's Conjecture could be written,

$$\forall a \in \mathbb{Z}^+ \ \forall b \in \mathbb{Z}^+ \ \forall c \in \mathbb{Z}^+ \ \forall d \in \mathbb{Z}^+. \ a^4 + b^4 + c^4 \neq d^4.$$

Here, $\mathbb{Z}^+$ is a symbol for the positive integers. Strings of $\forall$'s like this are usually abbreviated for easier reading:

$$\forall a, b, c, d \in \mathbb{Z}^+. \ a^4 + b^4 + c^4 \neq d^4.$$

Here's another claim which would be hard to falsify by sampling: the smallest possible x, y, z that satisfy the equality each have more than 1000 digits!

False Claim. $313(x^3 + y^3) = z^3$ *has no solution when $x, y, z \in \mathbb{Z}^+$.*

It's worth mentioning a couple of further famous propositions whose proofs were sought for centuries before finally being discovered:

Proposition 1.1.4 (Four Color Theorem)**.** *Every map can be colored with 4 colors so that adjacent[2] regions have different colors.*

---

[2]Two regions are adjacent only when they share a boundary segment of positive length. They are not considered to be adjacent if their boundaries meet only at a few points.

Several incorrect proofs of this theorem have been published, including one that stood for 10 years in the late 19th century before its mistake was found. A laborious proof was finally found in 1976 by mathematicians Appel and Haken, who used a complex computer program to categorize the four-colorable maps. The program left a few thousand maps uncategorized, which were checked by hand by Haken and his assistants—among them his 15-year-old daughter.

There was reason to doubt whether this was a legitimate proof—the proof was too big to be checked without a computer. No one could guarantee that the computer calculated correctly, nor was anyone enthusiastic about exerting the effort to recheck the four-colorings of thousands of maps that were done by hand. Two decades later a mostly intelligible proof of the Four Color Theorem was found, though a computer is still needed to check four-colorability of several hundred special maps.[3]

Proposition 1.1.5 (Fermat's Last Theorem). *There are no positive integers x, y and z such that*

$$x^n + y^n = z^n$$

for some integer n > 2.

In a book he was reading around 1630, Fermat claimed to have a proof for this proposition, but not enough space in the margin to write it down. Over the years, the Theorem was proved to hold for all *n* up to 4,000,000, but we've seen that this shouldn't necessarily inspire confidence that it holds for *all n*. There is, after all, a clear resemblance between Fermat's Last Theorem and Euler's false Conjecture. Finally, in 1994, British mathematician Andrew Wiles gave a proof, after seven years of working in secrecy and isolation in his attic. His proof did not fit in any margin.[4]

Finally, let's mention another simply stated proposition whose truth remains unknown.

Conjecture 1.1.6 (*Goldbach*). *Every even integer greater than 2 is the sum of two primes.*

Goldbach's Conjecture dates back to 1742. It is known to hold for all numbers up to 10^{18}, but to this day, no one knows whether it's true or false.

---

[3]The story of the proof of the Four Color Theorem is told in a well-reviewed popular (non-technical) book: "Four Colors Suffice. How the Map Problem was Solved." *Robin Wilson*. Princeton Univ. Press, 2003, 276pp. ISBN 0-691-11533-8.

[4]In fact, Wiles' original proof was wrong, but he and several collaborators used his ideas to arrive at a correct proof a year later. This story is the subject of the popular book, *Fermat's Enigma* by Simon Singh, Walker & Company, November, 1997.

For a computer scientist, some of the most important things to prove are the correctness of programs and systems—whether a program or system does what it's supposed to. Programs are notoriously buggy, and there's a growing community of researchers and practitioners trying to find ways to prove program correctness. These efforts have been successful enough in the case of CPU chips that they are now routinely used by leading chip manufacturers to prove chip correctness and avoid some notorious past mistakes.

Developing mathematical methods to verify programs and systems remains an active research area. We'll illustrate some of these methods in Chapter 5.

1.2   Predicates

A *predicate* can be understood as a proposition whose truth depends on the value of one or more variables. So "n is a perfect square" describes a predicate, since you can't say if it's true or false until you know what the value of the variable n happens to be. Once you know, for example, that n equals 4, the predicate becomes the true proposition "4 is a perfect square". Remember, nothing says that the proposition has to be true: if the value of n were 5, you would get the false proposition "5 is a perfect square."

Like other propositions, predicates are often named with a letter. Furthermore, a function-like notation is used to denote a predicate supplied with specific variable values. For example, we might use the name "P" for predicate above:

$$P(n) ::= \text{``}n \text{ is a perfect square''},$$

and repeat the remarks above by asserting that $P(4)$ is true, and $P(5)$ is false.

This notation for predicates is confusingly similar to ordinary function notation. If P is a predicate, then $P(n)$ is either *true* or *false*, depending on the value of n. On the other hand, if p is an ordinary function, like $n^2 + 1$, then $p(n)$ is a *numerical quantity*. **Don't confuse these two!**

1.3   The Axiomatic Method

The standard procedure for establishing truth in mathematics was invented by Euclid, a mathematician working in Alexandria, Egypt around 300 BC. His idea was to begin with five *assumptions* about geometry, which seemed undeniable based on direct experience. (For example, "There is a straight line segment between every pair of points".) Propositions like these that are simply accepted as true are called *axioms*.

Starting from these axioms, Euclid established the truth of many additional propositions by providing "proofs." A *proof* is a sequence of logical deductions from axioms and previously proved statements that concludes with the proposition in question. You probably wrote many proofs in high school geometry class, and you'll see a lot more in this text.

There are several common terms for a proposition that has been proved. The different terms hint at the role of the proposition within a larger body of work.

- Important true propositions are called *theorems*.

- A *lemma* is a preliminary proposition useful for proving later propositions.

- A *corollary* is a proposition that follows in just a few logical steps from a theorem.

These definitions are not precise. In fact, sometimes a good lemma turns out to be far more important than the theorem it was originally used to prove.

Euclid's axiom-and-proof approach, now called the *axiomatic method*, remains the foundation for mathematics today. In fact, just a handful of axioms, called the Zermelo-Fraenkel with Choice axioms (ZFC), together with a few logical deduction rules, appear to be sufficient to derive essentially all of mathematics. We'll examine these in Chapter 8.

1.4   Our Axioms

The ZFC axioms are important in studying and justifying the foundations of mathematics, but for practical purposes, they are much too primitive. Proving theorems in ZFC is a little like writing programs in byte code instead of a full-fledged programming language—by one reckoning, a formal proof in ZFC that $2 + 2 = 4$ requires more than 20,000 steps! So instead of starting with ZFC, we're going to take a *huge* set of axioms as our foundation: we'll accept all familiar facts from high school math.

This will give us a quick launch, but you may find this imprecise specification of the axioms troubling at times. For example, in the midst of a proof, you may start to wonder, "Must I prove this little fact or can I take it as an axiom?" There really is no absolute answer, since what's reasonable to assume and what requires proof depends on the circumstances and the audience. A good general guideline is simply to be up front about what you're assuming.

1.4.1   Logical Deductions

Logical deductions, or *inference rules*, are used to prove new propositions using previously proved ones.

A fundamental inference rule is *modus ponens*. This rule says that a proof of P together with a proof that P IMPLIES Q is a proof of Q.

Inference rules are sometimes written in a funny notation. For example, *modus ponens* is written:

Rule.

$$\frac{P, \quad P \text{ IMPLIES } Q}{Q}$$

When the statements above the line, called the *antecedents*, are proved, then we can consider the statement below the line, called the *conclusion* or *consequent*, to also be proved.

A key requirement of an inference rule is that it must be *sound*: an assignment of truth values to the letters P, Q, ..., that makes all the antecedents true must also make the consequent true. So if we start off with true axioms and apply sound inference rules, everything we prove will also be true.

There are many other natural, sound inference rules, for example:

Rule.

$$\frac{P \text{ IMPLIES } Q, \quad Q \text{ IMPLIES } R}{P \text{ IMPLIES } R}$$

Rule.

$$\frac{\text{NOT}(P) \text{ IMPLIES } \text{NOT}(Q)}{Q \text{ IMPLIES } P}$$

On the other hand,

Non-Rule.

$$\frac{\text{NOT}(P) \text{ IMPLIES } \text{NOT}(Q)}{P \text{ IMPLIES } Q}$$

is not sound: if P is assigned **T** and Q is assigned **F**, then the antecedent is true and the consequent is not.

As with axioms, we will not be too formal about the set of legal inference rules. Each step in a proof should be clear and "logical"; in particular, you should state what previously proved facts are used to derive each new conclusion.

1.4.2 Patterns of Proof

In principle, a proof can be *any* sequence of logical deductions from axioms and previously proved statements that concludes with the proposition in question. This freedom in constructing a proof can seem overwhelming at first. How do you even *start* a proof?

Here's the good news: many proofs follow one of a handful of standard templates. Each proof has it own details, of course, but these templates at least provide you with an outline to fill in. We'll go through several of these standard patterns, pointing out the basic idea and common pitfalls and giving some examples. Many of these templates fit together; one may give you a top-level outline while others help you at the next level of detail. And we'll show you other, more sophisticated proof techniques later on.

The recipes below are very specific at times, telling you exactly which words to write down on your piece of paper. You're certainly free to say things your own way instead; we're just giving you something you *could* say so that you're never at a complete loss.

1.5 Proving an Implication

Propositions of the form "If P, then Q" are called *implications*. This implication is often rephrased as "P IMPLIES Q."

Here are some examples:

- (Quadratic Formula) If $ax^2 + bx + c = 0$ and $a \neq 0$, then

$$x = \left(-b \pm \sqrt{b^2 - 4ac}\right)/2a.$$

- (Goldbach's Conjecture 1.1.6 rephrased) If n is an even integer greater than 2, then n is a sum of two primes.

- If $0 \leq x \leq 2$, then $-x^3 + 4x + 1 > 0$.

There are a couple of standard methods for proving an implication.

1.5.1 Method #1

In order to prove that P IMPLIES Q:

1. Write, "Assume P."

2. Show that Q logically follows.

Example

Theorem 1.5.1. *If $0 \leq x \leq 2$, then $-x^3 + 4x + 1 > 0$.*

Before we write a proof of this theorem, we have to do some scratchwork to figure out why it is true.

The inequality certainly holds for $x = 0$; then the left side is equal to 1 and $1 > 0$. As x grows, the $4x$ term (which is positive) initially seems to have greater magnitude than $-x^3$ (which is negative). For example, when $x = 1$, we have $4x = 4$, but $-x^3 = -1$ only. In fact, it looks like $-x^3$ doesn't begin to dominate until $x > 2$. So it seems the $-x^3 + 4x$ part should be nonnegative for all x between 0 and 2, which would imply that $-x^3 + 4x + 1$ is positive.

So far, so good. But we still have to replace all those "seems like" phrases with solid, logical arguments. We can get a better handle on the critical $-x^3 + 4x$ part by factoring it, which is not too hard:

$$-x^3 + 4x = x(2 - x)(2 + x)$$

Aha! For x between 0 and 2, all of the terms on the right side are nonnegative. And a product of nonnegative terms is also nonnegative. Let's organize this blizzard of observations into a clean proof.

Proof. Assume $0 \leq x \leq 2$. Then x, $2 - x$ and $2 + x$ are all nonnegative. Therefore, the product of these terms is also nonnegative. Adding 1 to this product gives a positive number, so:

$$x(2 - x)(2 + x) + 1 > 0$$

Multiplying out on the left side proves that

$$-x^3 + 4x + 1 > 0$$

as claimed.   ∎

There are a couple points here that apply to all proofs:

- You'll often need to do some scratchwork while you're trying to figure out the logical steps of a proof. Your scratchwork can be as disorganized as you like—full of dead-ends, strange diagrams, obscene words, whatever. But keep your scratchwork separate from your final proof, which should be clear and concise.

- Proofs typically begin with the word "Proof" and end with some sort of delimiter like □ or "QED." The only purpose for these conventions is to clarify where proofs begin and end.

1.5.2   Method #2 - Prove the Contrapositive

An implication ("P IMPLIES Q") is logically equivalent to its *contrapositive*

$$\text{NOT}(Q) \text{ IMPLIES NOT}(P).$$

Proving one is as good as proving the other, and proving the contrapositive is some-times easier than proving the original statement. If so, then you can proceed as follows:

1. Write, "We prove the contrapositive:" and then state the contrapositive.

2. Proceed as in Method #1.

Example

Theorem 1.5.2. *If r is irrational, then $\sqrt{r}$ is also irrational.*

A number is *rational* when it equals a quotient of integers —that is, if it equals m/n for some integers m and n. If it's not rational, then it's called *irrational*. So we must show that if r is *not* a ratio of integers, then $\sqrt{r}$ is also *not* a ratio of integers. That's pretty convoluted! We can eliminate both *not*'s and simplify the proof by using the contrapositive instead.

Proof. We prove the contrapositive: if $\sqrt{r}$ is rational, then r is rational.

Assume that $\sqrt{r}$ is rational. Then there exist integers m and n such that:

$$\sqrt{r} = \frac{m}{n}$$

Squaring both sides gives:

$$r = \frac{m^2}{n^2}$$

Since m^2 and n^2 are integers, r is also rational. ∎

1.6   Proving an "If and Only If"

Many mathematical theorems assert that two statements are logically equivalent; that is, one holds if and only if the other does. Here is an example that has been known for several thousand years:

> Two triangles have the same side lengths if and only if two side lengths and the angle between those sides are the same.

The phrase "if and only if" comes up so often that it is often abbreviated "iff."

1.6.1   Method #1: Prove Each Statement Implies the Other

The statement "P IFF Q" is equivalent to the two statements "P IMPLIES Q" and "Q IMPLIES P." So you can prove an "iff" by proving *two* implications:

1. Write, "We prove P implies Q and vice-versa."

2. Write, "First, we show P implies Q." Do this by one of the methods in Section 1.5.

3. Write, "Now, we show Q implies P." Again, do this by one of the methods in Section 1.5.

1.6.2   Method #2: Construct a Chain of Iffs

In order to prove that P is true iff Q is true:

1. Write, "We construct a chain of if-and-only-if implications."

2. Prove P is equivalent to a second statement which is equivalent to a third statement and so forth until you reach Q.

This method sometimes requires more ingenuity than the first, but the result can be a short, elegant proof.

Example

The *standard deviation* of a sequence of values $x_1, x_2, \ldots, x_n$ is defined to be:

$$\sqrt{\frac{(x_1 - \mu)^2 + (x_2 - \mu)^2 + \cdots + (x_n - \mu)^2}{n}} \tag{1.3}$$

where μ is the average or *mean* of the values:

$$\mu ::= \frac{x_1 + x_2 + \cdots + x_n}{n}$$

Theorem 1.6.1. *The standard deviation of a sequence of values $x_1, \ldots, x_n$ is zero iff all the values are equal to the mean.*

For example, the standard deviation of test scores is zero if and only if everyone scored exactly the class average.

Proof. We construct a chain of "iff" implications, starting with the statement that the standard deviation (1.3) is zero:

$$\sqrt{\frac{(x_1 - \mu)^2 + (x_2 - \mu)^2 + \cdots + (x_n - \mu)^2}{n}} = 0. \tag{1.4}$$

Now since zero is the only number whose square root is zero, equation (1.4) holds iff

$$(x_1 - \mu)^2 + (x_2 - \mu)^2 + \cdots + (x_n - \mu)^2 = 0. \qquad (1.5)$$

Squares of real numbers are always nonnegative, so every term on the left-hand side of equation (1.5) is nonnegative. This means that (1.5) holds iff

Every term on the left-hand side of (1.5) is zero.   (1.6)

But a term $(x_i - \mu)^2$ is zero iff $x_i = \mu$, so (1.6) is true iff

Every x_i equals the mean.

■

1.7   Proof by Cases

Breaking a complicated proof into cases and proving each case separately is a common, useful proof strategy. Here's an amusing example.

Let's agree that given any two people, either they have met or not. If every pair of people in a group has met, we'll call the group a *club*. If every pair of people in a group has not met, we'll call it a group of *strangers*.

Theorem. *Every collection of 6 people includes a club of 3 people or a group of 3 strangers.*

Proof. The proof is by case analysis[5]. Let x denote one of the six people. There are two cases:

1. Among 5 other people besides x, at least 3 have met x.

2. Among the 5 other people, at least 3 have not met x.

Now, we have to be sure that at least one of these two cases must hold,[6] but that's easy: we've split the 5 people into two groups, those who have shaken hands with x and those who have not, so one of the groups must have at least half the people.

    Case 1: Suppose that at least 3 people did meet x.

    This case splits into two subcases:

---

[5]Describing your approach at the outset helps orient the reader.

[6]Part of a case analysis argument is showing that you've covered all the cases. This is often obvious, because the two cases are of the form "P" and "not P." However, the situation above is not stated quite so simply.

Case 1.1: No pair among those people met each other. Then these people are a group of at least 3 strangers. The theorem holds in this subcase.

Case 1.2: Some pair among those people have met each other. Then that pair, together with x, form a club of 3 people. So the theorem holds in this subcase.

This implies that the theorem holds in Case 1.

Case 2: Suppose that at least 3 people did not meet x.

This case also splits into two subcases:

Case 2.1: Every pair among those people met each other. Then these people are a club of at least 3 people. So the theorem holds in this subcase.

Case 2.2: Some pair among those people have not met each other. Then that pair, together with x, form a group of at least 3 strangers. So the theorem holds in this subcase.

This implies that the theorem also holds in Case 2, and therefore holds in all cases. ∎

1.8   Proof by Contradiction

In a *proof by contradiction*, or *indirect proof*, you show that if a proposition were false, then some false fact would be true. Since a false fact by definition can't be true, the proposition must be true.

Proof by contradiction is *always* a viable approach. However, as the name suggests, indirect proofs can be a little convoluted, so direct proofs are generally preferable when they are available.

Method: In order to prove a proposition P by contradiction:

1. Write, "We use proof by contradiction."

2. Write, "Suppose P is false."

3. Deduce something known to be false (a logical contradiction).

4. Write, "This is a contradiction. Therefore, P must be true."

Example

We'll prove by contradiction that $\sqrt{2}$ is irrational. Remember that a number is *rational* if it is equal to a ratio of integers—for example, $3.5 = 7/2$ and $0.1111\cdots = 1/9$ are rational numbers.

Theorem 1.8.1. $\sqrt{2}$ *is irrational.*

Proof. We use proof by contradiction. Suppose the claim is false, and $\sqrt{2}$ is rational. Then we can write $\sqrt{2}$ as a fraction n/d in *lowest terms*.

Squaring both sides gives $2 = n^2/d^2$ and so $2d^2 = n^2$. This implies that n is a multiple of 2 (see Problems 1.15 and 1.16). Therefore n^2 must be a multiple of 4. But since $2d^2 = n^2$, we know $2d^2$ is a multiple of 4 and so d^2 is a multiple of 2. This implies that d is a multiple of 2.

So, the numerator and denominator have 2 as a common factor, which contradicts the fact that n/d is in lowest terms. Thus, $\sqrt{2}$ must be irrational. ∎

1.9 *Good* Proofs in Practice

One purpose of a proof is to establish the truth of an assertion with absolute certainty, and mechanically checkable proofs of enormous length or complexity can accomplish this. But humanly intelligible proofs are the only ones that help someone understand the subject. Mathematicians generally agree that important mathematical results can't be fully understood until their proofs are understood. That is why proofs are an important part of the curriculum.

To be understandable and helpful, more is required of a proof than just logical correctness: a good proof must also be clear. Correctness and clarity usually go together; a well-written proof is more likely to be a correct proof, since mistakes are harder to hide.

In practice, the notion of proof is a moving target. Proofs in a professional research journal are generally unintelligible to all but a few experts who know all the terminology and prior results used in the proof. Conversely, proofs in the first weeks of a beginning course like 6.042 would be regarded as tediously long-winded by a professional mathematician. In fact, what we accept as a good proof later in the term will be different from what we consider good proofs in the first couple of weeks of 6.042. But even so, we can offer some general tips on writing good proofs:

State your game plan. A good proof begins by explaining the general line of reasoning, for example, "We use case analysis" or "We argue by contradiction."

Keep a linear flow. Sometimes proofs are written like mathematical mosaics, with juicy tidbits of independent reasoning sprinkled throughout. This is not good. The steps of an argument should follow one another in an intelligible order.

A proof is an essay, not a calculation. Many students initially write proofs the way they compute integrals. The result is a long sequence of expressions without explanation, making it very hard to follow. This is bad. A good proof usually looks like an essay with some equations thrown in. Use complete sentences.

Avoid excessive symbolism. Your reader is probably good at understanding words, but much less skilled at reading arcane mathematical symbols. Use words where you reasonably can.

Revise and simplify. Your readers will be grateful.

Introduce notation thoughtfully. Sometimes an argument can be greatly simplified by introducing a variable, devising a special notation, or defining a new term. But do this sparingly, since you're requiring the reader to remember all that new stuff. And remember to actually *define* the meanings of new variables, terms, or notations; don't just start using them!

Structure long proofs. Long programs are usually broken into a hierarchy of smaller procedures. Long proofs are much the same. When your proof needed facts that are easily stated, but not readily proved, those fact are best pulled out as preliminary lemmas. Also, if you are repeating essentially the same argument over and over, try to capture that argument in a general lemma, which you can cite repeatedly instead.

Be wary of the "obvious." When familiar or truly obvious facts are needed in a proof, it's OK to label them as such and to not prove them. But remember that what's obvious to you may not be—and typically is not—obvious to your reader.

Most especially, don't use phrases like "clearly" or "obviously" in an attempt to bully the reader into accepting something you're having trouble proving. Also, go on the alert whenever you see one of these phrases in someone else's proof.

Finish. At some point in a proof, you'll have established all the essential facts you need. Resist the temptation to quit and leave the reader to draw the "obvious" conclusion. Instead, tie everything together yourself and explain why the original claim follows.

Creating a good proof is a lot like creating a beautiful work of art. In fact, mathematicians often refer to really good proofs as being "elegant" or "beautiful." It takes a practice and experience to write proofs that merit such praises, but to get you started in the right direction, we will provide templates for the most useful proof techniques.

Throughout the text there are also examples of *bogus proofs*—arguments that look like proofs but aren't. Sometimes a bogus proof can reach false conclusions because of missteps or mistaken assumptions. More subtle bogus proofs reach correct conclusions, but do so in improper ways such as circular reasoning, leaping to unjustified conclusions, or saying that the hard part of the proof is "left to the reader." Learning to spot the flaws in improper proofs will hone your skills at seeing how each proof step follows logically from prior steps. It will also enable you to spot flaws in your own proofs.

The analogy between good proofs and good programs extends beyond structure. The same rigorous thinking needed for proofs is essential in the design of critical computer systems. When algorithms and protocols only "mostly work" due to reliance on hand-waving arguments, the results can range from problematic to catastrophic. An early example was the Therac 25, a machine that provided radiation therapy to cancer victims, but occasionally killed them with massive overdoses due to a software race condition. A further example of a dozen years ago (August 2004) involved a single faulty command to a computer system used by United and American Airlines that grounded the entire fleet of both companies—and all their passengers!

It is a certainty that we'll all one day be at the mercy of critical computer systems designed by you and your classmates. So we really hope that you'll develop the ability to formulate rock-solid logical arguments that a system actually does what you think it should do!

1.10 References

[12], [1], [46], [16], [20]

Problems for Section 1.1

Class Problems

Problem 1.1.

Albert announces to his class that he plans to surprise them with a quiz sometime next week.

His students first wonder if the quiz could be on Friday of next week. They reason that it can't: if Albert didn't give the quiz *before* Friday, then by midnight Thursday, they would know the quiz had to be on Friday, and so the quiz wouldn't be a surprise any more.

Next the students wonder whether Albert could give the surprise quiz Thursday. They observe that if the quiz wasn't given *before* Thursday, it would have to be given *on* the Thursday, since they already know it can't be given on Friday. But having figured that out, it wouldn't be a surprise if the quiz was on Thursday either. Similarly, the students reason that the quiz can't be on Wednesday, Tuesday, or Monday. Namely, it's impossible for Albert to give a surprise quiz next week. All the students now relax, having concluded that Albert must have been bluffing. And since no one expects the quiz, that's why, when Albert gives it on Tuesday next week, it really is a surprise!

What, if anything, do you think is wrong with the students' reasoning?

Problem 1.2.

The Pythagorean Theorem says that if a and b are the lengths of the sides of a right triangle, and c is the length of its hypotenuse, then

$$a^2 + b^2 = c^2.$$

This theorem is so fundamental and familiar that we generally take it for granted. But just being familiar doesn't justify calling it "obvious"—witness the fact that people have felt the need to devise different proofs of it for milllenia.[7] In this problem we'll examine a particularly simple "proof without words" of the theorem.

Here's the strategy. Suppose you are given four different colored copies of a right triangle with sides of lengths a, b and c, along with a suitably sized square, as shown in Figure 1.1.

(a) You will first arrange the square and four triangles so they form a $c \times c$ square. From this arrangement you will see that the square is $(b - a) \times (b - a)$.

---

[7]Over a hundred different proofs are listed on the mathematics website http://www.cut-the-knot.org/pythagoras/.

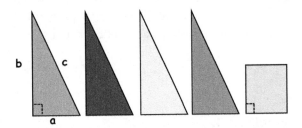

Figure 1.1   Right triangles and square.

(b) You will then arrange the same shapes so they form two squares, one $a \times a$ and the other $b \times b$.

You know that the area of an $s \times s$ square is s^2. So appealing to the principle that

Area is Preserved by Rearranging,

you can now conclude that $a^2 + b^2 = c^2$, as claimed.

This really is an elegant and convincing proof of the Pythagorean Theorem, but it has some worrisome features. One concern is that there might be something special about the shape of these particular triangles and square that makes the rearranging possible—for example, suppose $a = b$?

(c) How would you respond to this concern?

(d) Another concern is that a number of facts about right triangles, squares and lines are being *implicitly* assumed in justifying the rearrangements into squares. Enumerate some of these assumed facts.

Problem 1.3.
What's going on here?!

$$1 = \sqrt{1} = \sqrt{(-1)(-1)} = \sqrt{-1}\sqrt{-1} = \left(\sqrt{-1}\right)^2 = -1.$$

(a) Precisely identify and explain the mistake(s) in this *bogus* proof.

(b) Prove (correctly) that if $1 = -1$, then $2 = 1$.

(c) Every *positive* real number r has two square roots, one positive and the other negative. The standard convention is that the expression $\sqrt{r}$ refers to the *positive* square root of r. Assuming familiar properties of multiplication of real numbers, prove that for positive real numbers r and s,

$$\sqrt{rs} = \sqrt{r}\sqrt{s}.$$

Problem 1.4.
Identify exactly where the bugs are in each of the following bogus proofs.[8]
 (a) Bogus Claim: $1/8 > 1/4$.

Bogus proof.

$$3 > 2$$
$$3\log_{10}(1/2) > 2\log_{10}(1/2)$$
$$\log_{10}(1/2)^3 > \log_{10}(1/2)^2$$
$$(1/2)^3 > (1/2)^2,$$

and the claim now follows by the rules for multiplying fractions.   ∎

 (b) *Bogus proof*: $1\text{¢} = \$0.01 = (\$0.1)^2 = (10\text{¢})^2 = 100\text{¢} = \$1.$ ∎

 (c) Bogus Claim: If a and b are two equal real numbers, then $a = 0$.

Bogus proof.

$$a = b$$
$$a^2 = ab$$
$$a^2 - b^2 = ab - b^2$$
$$(a-b)(a+b) = (a-b)b$$
$$a+b = b$$
$$a = 0.$$

∎

---

[8] From [45], *Twenty Years Before the Blackboard* by Michael Stueben and Diane Sandford

Problem 1.5.
It's a fact that the Arithmetic Mean is at least as large as the Geometric Mean, namely,

$$\frac{a + b}{2} \geq \sqrt{ab}$$

for all nonnegative real numbers a and b. But there's something objectionable about the following proof of this fact. What's the objection, and how would you fix it?

Bogus proof.

$$\frac{a + b}{2} \overset{?}{\geq} \sqrt{ab}, \qquad\qquad \text{so}$$

$$a + b \overset{?}{\geq} 2\sqrt{ab}, \qquad\qquad \text{so}$$

$$a^2 + 2ab + b^2 \overset{?}{\geq} 4ab, \qquad\qquad \text{so}$$

$$a^2 - 2ab + b^2 \overset{?}{\geq} 0, \qquad\qquad \text{so}$$

$$(a - b)^2 \geq 0 \qquad\qquad \text{which we know is true.}$$

The last statement is true because $a - b$ is a real number, and the square of a real number is never negative. This proves the claim. ∎

Practice Problems

Problem 1.6.
Why does the "surprise" paradox of Problem 1.1 present a philosophical problem but not a mathematical one?

Problems for Section 1.5

Homework Problems

Problem 1.7.
Show that $\log_7 n$ is either an integer or irrational, where n is a positive integer. Use whatever familiar facts about integers and primes you need, but explicitly state such facts.

Problems for Section 1.7

Practice Problems

Problem 1.8.
Prove by cases that

$$\max(r, s) + \min(r, s) = r + s \tag{*}$$

for all real numbers r, s.

Class Problems

Problem 1.9.
If we raise an irrational number to an irrational power, can the result be rational?
Show that it can by considering $\sqrt{2}^{\sqrt{2}}$ and arguing by cases.

Problem 1.10.
Prove by cases that

$$|r + s| \leq |r| + |s| \tag{1}$$

for all real numbers r, s.[9]

Homework Problems

Problem 1.11. (a) Suppose that

$$a + b + c = d,$$

where a, b, c, d are nonnegative integers.

Let P be the assertion that d is even. Let W be the assertion that exactly one among a, b, c are even, and let T be the assertion that all three are even.

Prove by cases that

$$P \text{ IFF } [W \text{ OR } T].$$

(b) Now suppose that

$$w^2 + x^2 + y^2 = z^2,$$

---

[9]The *absolute value* $|r|$ of r equals whichever of r or $-r$ is not negative.

where w, x, y, z are nonnegative integers. Let P be the assertion that z is even, and let R be the assertion that all three of w, x, y are even. Prove by cases that

$$P \quad \text{IFF} \quad R.$$

Hint: An odd number equals $2m + 1$ for some integer m, so its square equals $4(m^2 + m) + 1$.

Exam Problems

Problem 1.12.
Prove that there is an irrational number a such that $a^{\sqrt{3}}$ is rational.
   Hint: Consider $\sqrt[3]{2}^{\sqrt{3}}$ and argue by cases.

Problems for Section 1.8

Practice Problems

Problem 1.13.
Prove that for any $n > 0$, if a^n is even, then a is even.
   Hint: Contradiction.

Problem 1.14.
Prove that if $a \cdot b = n$, then either a or b must be $\leq \sqrt{n}$, where a, b, and n are nonnegative real numbers. *Hint:* by contradiction, Section 1.8.

Problem 1.15.
Let n be a nonnegative integer.

 (a) Explain why if n^2 is even—that is, a multiple of 2—then n is even.

 (b) Explain why if n^2 is a multiple of 3, then n must be a multiple of 3.

Problem 1.16.
Give an example of two distinct positive integers m, n such that n^2 is a multiple of m, but n is not a multiple of m. How about having m be less than n?

Class Problems

Problem 1.17.
How far can you generalize the proof of Theorem 1.8.1 that $\sqrt{2}$ is irrational? For example, how about $\sqrt{3}$?

Problem 1.18.
Prove that $\log_4 6$ is irrational.

Problem 1.19.
Prove by contradiction that $\sqrt{3} + \sqrt{2}$ is irrational.
  Hint: $(\sqrt{3} + \sqrt{2})(\sqrt{3} - \sqrt{2})$

Problem 1.20.
Here is a generalization of Problem 1.17 that you may not have thought of:

Lemma. *Let the coefficients of the polynomial*

$$a_0 + a_1 x + a_2 x^2 + \cdots + a_{m-1} x^{m-1} + x^m$$

be integers. Then any real root of the polynomial is either integral or irrational.

 (a) Explain why the Lemma immediately implies that $\sqrt[m]{k}$ is irrational whenever k is not an mth power of some integer.

 (b) Carefully prove the Lemma.

You may find it helpful to appeal to:

Fact. If a prime p is a factor of some power of an integer, then it is a factor of that integer.

You may assume this Fact without writing down its proof, but see if you can explain why it is true.

Exam Problems

Problem 1.21.
Prove that $\log_9 12$ is irrational.

Problem 1.22.
Prove that $\log_{12} 18$ is irrational.

Problem 1.23.
A familiar proof that $\sqrt[3]{7^2}$ is irrational depends on the fact that a certain equation among those below is unsatisfiable by integers $a, b > 0$. Note that more than one is unsatisfiable. Indicate the equation that would appear in the proof, and explain why it is unsatisfiable. (Do *not* assume that $\sqrt[3]{7^2}$ is irrational.)

i. $a^2 = 7^2 + b^2$

ii. $a^3 = 7^2 + b^3$

iii. $a^2 = 7^2 b^2$

iv. $a^3 = 7^2 b^3$

v. $a^3 = 7^3 b^3$

vi. $(ab)^3 = 7^2$

Homework Problems

Problem 1.24.
The fact that that there are irrational numbers a, b such that a^b is rational was proved in Problem 1.9 by cases. Unfortunately, that proof was *nonconstructive*: it didn't reveal a specific pair a, b with this property. But in fact, it's easy to do this: let $a ::= \sqrt{2}$ and $b ::= 2 \log_2 3$.

We know $a = \sqrt{2}$ is irrational, and $a^b = 3$ by definition. Finish the proof that these values for a, b work, by showing that $2 \log_2 3$ is irrational.

Problem 1.25.
Here is a different proof that $\sqrt{2}$ is irrational, taken from the American Mathematical Monthly, v.116, #1, Jan. 2009, p.69:

Proof. Suppose for the sake of contradiction that $\sqrt{2}$ is rational, and choose the least integer $q > 0$ such that $\left(\sqrt{2} - 1\right) q$ is a nonnegative integer. Let $q' ::= \left(\sqrt{2} - 1\right) q$. Clearly $0 < q' < q$. But an easy computation shows that $\left(\sqrt{2} - 1\right) q'$ is a nonnegative integer, contradicting the minimality of q. ∎

(a) This proof was written for an audience of college teachers, and at this point it is a little more concise than desirable. Write out a more complete version which includes an explanation of each step.

(b) Now that you have justified the steps in this proof, do you have a preference for one of these proofs over the other? Why? Discuss these questions with your teammates for a few minutes and summarize your team's answers on your white-board.

Problem 1.26.

For $n = 40$, the value of polynomial $p(n) ::= n^2 + n + 41$ is not prime, as noted in Section 1.1. But we could have predicted based on general principles that no nonconstant polynomial can generate only prime numbers.

In particular, let $q(n)$ be a polynomial with integer coefficients, and let $c ::= q(0)$ be the constant term of q.

(a) Verify that $q(cm)$ is a multiple of c for all $m \in \mathbb{Z}$.

(b) Show that if q is nonconstant and $c > 1$, then as n ranges over the nonnegative integers $\mathbb{N}$ there are infinitely many $q(n) \in \mathbb{Z}$ that are not primes.

Hint: You may assume the familiar fact that the magnitude of any nonconstant polynomial $q(n)$ grows unboundedly as n grows.

(c) Conclude that for every nonconstant polynomial q there must be an $n \in \mathbb{N}$ such that $q(n)$ is not prime. *Hint:* Only one easy case remains.

2   The Well Ordering Principle

> Every *nonempty* set of *nonnegative integers* has a *smallest* element.

This statement is known as The *Well Ordering Principle*. Do you believe it? Seems sort of obvious, right? But notice how tight it is: it requires a *nonempty* set—it's false for the empty set which has *no* smallest element because it has no elements at all. And it requires a set of *nonnegative* integers—it's false for the set of *negative* integers and also false for some sets of nonnegative *rationals*—for example, the set of positive rationals. So, the Well Ordering Principle captures something special about the nonnegative integers.

While the Well Ordering Principle may seem obvious, it's hard to see offhand why it is useful. But in fact, it provides one of the most important proof rules in discrete mathematics. In this chapter, we'll illustrate the power of this proof method with a few simple examples.

2.1   Well Ordering Proofs

We actually have already taken the Well Ordering Principle for granted in proving that $\sqrt{2}$ is irrational. That proof assumed that for any positive integers m and n, the fraction m/n can be written in *lowest terms*, that is, in the form m'/n' where m' and n' are positive integers with no common prime factors. How do we know this is always possible?

Suppose to the contrary that there are positive integers m and n such that the fraction m/n cannot be written in lowest terms. Now let C be the set of positive integers that are numerators of such fractions. Then $m \in C$, so C is nonempty. Therefore, by Well Ordering, there must be a smallest integer $m_0 \in C$. So by definition of C, there is an integer $n_0 > 0$ such that

the fraction $\dfrac{m_0}{n_0}$ cannot be written in lowest terms.

This means that m_0 and n_0 must have a common prime factor, $p > 1$. But

$$\frac{m_0/p}{n_0/p} = \frac{m_0}{n_0},$$

so any way of expressing the left-hand fraction in lowest terms would also work for m_0/n_0, which implies

$$\text{the fraction } \frac{m_0/p}{n_0/p} \text{ cannot be in written in lowest terms either.}$$

So by definition of C, the numerator m_0/p is in C. But $m_0/p < m_0$, which contradicts the fact that m_0 is the smallest element of C.

Since the assumption that C is nonempty leads to a contradiction, it follows that C must be empty. That is, that there are no numerators of fractions that can't be written in lowest terms, and hence there are no such fractions at all.

We've been using the Well Ordering Principle on the sly from early on!

2.2   Template for Well Ordering Proofs

More generally, there is a standard way to use Well Ordering to prove that some property, $P(n)$ holds for every nonnegative integer n. Here is a standard way to organize such a well ordering proof:

To prove that "$P(n)$ is true for all $n \in \mathbb{N}$" using the Well Ordering Principle:

- Define the set C of *counterexamples* to P being true. Specifically, define

$$C ::= \{n \in \mathbb{N} \mid \text{NOT}(P(n)) \text{ is true}\}.$$

  (The notation $\{n \mid Q(n)\}$ means "the set of all elements n for which $Q(n)$ is true." See Section 4.1.4.)

- Assume for proof by contradiction that C is nonempty.

- By the Well Ordering Principle, there will be a smallest element n in C.

- Reach a contradiction somehow—often by showing that $P(n)$ is actually true or by showing that there is another member of C that is smaller than n. This is the open-ended part of the proof task.

- Conclude that C must be empty, that is, no counterexamples exist.   ∎

2.2.1   Summing the Integers

Let's use this template to prove

Theorem 2.2.1.

$$1 + 2 + 3 + \cdots + n = n(n+1)/2 \tag{2.1}$$

for all nonnegative integers n.

First, we'd better address a couple of ambiguous special cases before they trip us up:

- If $n = 1$, then there is only one term in the summation, and so $1 + 2 + 3 + \cdots + n$ is just the term 1. Don't be misled by the appearance of 2 and 3 or by the suggestion that 1 and n are distinct terms!

- If $n = 0$, then there are no terms at all in the summation. By convention, the sum in this case is 0.

So, while the three dots notation, which is called an *ellipsis*, is convenient, you have to watch out for these special cases where the notation is misleading. In fact, whenever you see an ellipsis, you should be on the lookout to be sure you understand the pattern, watching out for the beginning and the end.

We could have eliminated the need for guessing by rewriting the left side of (2.1) with *summation notation*:

$$\sum_{i=1}^{n} i \quad \text{or} \quad \sum_{1 \leq i \leq n} i.$$

Both of these expressions denote the sum of all values taken by the expression to the right of the sigma as the variable i ranges from 1 to n. Both expressions make it clear what (2.1) means when $n = 1$. The second expression makes it clear that when $n = 0$, there are no terms in the sum, though you still have to know the convention that a sum of no numbers equals 0 (the *product* of no numbers is 1, by the way).

OK, back to the proof:

Proof. By contradiction. Assume that Theorem 2.2.1 is *false*. Then, some nonnegative integers serve as *counterexamples* to it. Let's collect them in a set:

$$C ::= \{n \in \mathbb{N} \mid 1 + 2 + 3 + \cdots + n \neq \frac{n(n+1)}{2}\}.$$

Assuming there are counterexamples, C is a nonempty set of nonnegative integers. So, by the Well Ordering Principle, C has a minimum element, which we'll call c. That is, among the nonnegative integers, c is the *smallest counterexample* to equation (2.1).

Since c is the smallest counterexample, we know that (2.1) is false for $n = c$ but true for all nonnegative integers $n < c$. But (2.1) is true for $n = 0$, so $c > 0$. This means $c - 1$ is a nonnegative integer, and since it is less than c, equation (2.1) is true for $c - 1$. That is,

$$1 + 2 + 3 + \cdots + (c - 1) = \frac{(c - 1)c}{2}.$$

But then, adding c to both sides, we get

$$1 + 2 + 3 + \cdots + (c - 1) + c = \frac{(c - 1)c}{2} + c = \frac{c^2 - c + 2c}{2} = \frac{c(c + 1)}{2},$$

which means that (2.1) does hold for c, after all! This is a contradiction, and we are done. ∎

2.3   Factoring into Primes

We've previously taken for granted the *Prime Factorization Theorem*, also known as the *Unique Factorization Theorem* and the *Fundamental Theorem of Arithmetic*, which states that every integer greater than one has a unique[1] expression as a product of prime numbers. This is another of those familiar mathematical facts which are taken for granted but are not really obvious on closer inspection. We'll prove the uniqueness of prime factorization in a later chapter, but well ordering gives an easy proof that every integer greater than one can be expressed as *some* product of primes.

Theorem 2.3.1. *Every positive integer greater than one can be factored as a product of primes.*

Proof. The proof is by well ordering.

Let C be the set of all integers greater than one that cannot be factored as a product of primes. We assume C is not empty and derive a contradiction.

If C is not empty, there is a least element $n \in C$ by well ordering. The n can't be prime, because a prime by itself is considered a (length one) product of primes and no such products are in C.

So n must be a product of two integers a and b where $1 < a, b < n$. Since a and b are smaller than the smallest element in C, we know that $a, b \notin C$. In other words, a can be written as a product of primes $p_1 p_2 \cdots p_k$ and b as a product of

---

[1] . . . unique up to the order in which the prime factors appear

primes $q_1 \cdots q_l$. Therefore, $n = p_1 \cdots p_k q_1 \cdots q_l$ can be written as a product of primes, contradicting the claim that $n \in C$. Our assumption that C is not empty must therefore be false. ■

2.4   Well Ordered Sets

A set of numbers is *well ordered* when each of its nonempty subsets has a minimum element. The Well Ordering Principle says, of course, that the set of nonnegative integers is well ordered, but so are lots of other sets, such as every finite set, or the sets $r\mathbb{N}$ of numbers of the form rn, where r is a positive real number and $n \in \mathbb{N}$.

Well ordering commonly comes up in computer science as a method for proving that computations won't run forever. The idea is to assign a value to the successive steps of a computation so that the values get smaller at every step. If the values are all from a well ordered set, then the computation can't run forever, because if it did, the values assigned to its successive steps would define a subset with no minimum element. You'll see several examples of this technique applied in Chapter 6 to prove that various state machines will eventually terminate.

Notice that a set may have a minimum element but not be well ordered. The set of nonnegative rational numbers is an example: it has a minimum element zero, but it also has nonempty subsets that don't have minimum elements—the *positive* rationals, for example.

The following theorem is a tiny generalization of the Well Ordering Principle.

Theorem 2.4.1. *For any nonnegative integer n the set of integers greater than or equal to $-n$ is well ordered.*

This theorem is just as obvious as the Well Ordering Principle, and it would be harmless to accept it as another axiom. But repeatedly introducing axioms gets worrisome after a while, and it's worth noticing when a potential axiom can actually be proved. We can easily prove Theorem 2.4.1 using the Well Ordering Principle:

Proof. Let S be any nonempty set of integers $\geq -n$. Now add n to each of the elements in S; let's call this new set $S + n$. Now $S + n$ is a nonempty set of *nonnegative* integers, and so by the Well Ordering Principle, it has a minimum element m. But then it's easy to see that $m - n$ is the minimum element of S. ■

The definition of well ordering states that *every* subset of a well ordered set is well ordered, and this yields two convenient, immediate corollaries of Theorem 2.4.1:

Definition 2.4.2. A *lower bound* (respectively, *upper bound*) for a set S of real numbers is a number b such that $b \leq s$ (respectively, $b \geq s$) for every $s \in S$.

Note that a lower or upper bound of set S is not required to be in the set.

Corollary 2.4.3. *Any set of integers with a lower bound is well ordered.*

Proof. A set of integers with a lower bound $b \in \mathbb{R}$ will also have the integer $n = \lfloor b \rfloor$ as a lower bound, where $\lfloor b \rfloor$, called the floor of b, is gotten by rounding down b to the nearest integer. So Theorem 2.4.1 implies the set is well ordered. ■

Corollary 2.4.4. *Any nonempty set of integers with an upper bound has a maximum element.*

Proof. Suppose a set S of integers has an upper bound $b \in \mathbb{R}$. Now multiply each element of S by -1; let's call this new set of elements $-S$. Now, of course, $-b$ is a lower bound of $-S$. So $-S$ has a minimum element $-m$ by Corollary 2.4.3. But then it's easy to see that m is the maximum element of S. ■

2.4.1   A Different Well Ordered Set (Optional)

Another example of a well ordered set of numbers is the set $\mathbb{F}$ of fractions that can be expressed in the form $n/(n + 1)$:

$$\frac{0}{1}, \frac{1}{2}, \frac{2}{3}, \frac{3}{4}, \ldots, \frac{n}{n + 1}, \ldots.$$

The minimum element of any nonempty subset of $\mathbb{F}$ is simply the one with the minimum numerator when expressed in the form $n/(n + 1)$.

Now we can define a very different well ordered set by adding nonnegative integers to numbers in $\mathbb{F}$. That is, we take all the numbers of the form $n + f$ where n is a nonnegative integer and f is a number in $\mathbb{F}$. Let's call this set of numbers—you guessed it—$\mathbb{N} + \mathbb{F}$. There is a simple recipe for finding the minimum number in any nonempty subset of $\mathbb{N} + \mathbb{F}$, which explains why this set is well ordered:

Lemma 2.4.5. $\mathbb{N} + \mathbb{F}$ *is well ordered.*

Proof. Given any nonempty subset S of $\mathbb{N} + \mathbb{F}$, look at all the nonnegative integers n such that $n + f$ is in S for some $f \in \mathbb{F}$. This is a nonempty set nonnegative integers, so by the WOP, there is a minimum one; call it n_s.

By definition of n_s, there is some $f \in \mathbb{F}$ such that $n_S + f$ is in the set S. So the set all fractions f such that $n_S + f \in S$ is a nonempty subset of $\mathbb{F}$, and since $\mathbb{F}$ is well ordered, this nonempty set contains a minimum element; call it f_S. Now it easy to verify that $n_S + f_S$ is the minimum element of S (Problem 2.19). ■

The set $\mathbb{N} + \mathbb{F}$ is different from the earlier examples. In all the earlier examples, each element was greater than only a finite number of other elements. In $\mathbb{N} + \mathbb{F}$, every element greater than or equal to 1 can be the first element in strictly decreasing sequences of elements of arbitrary finite length. For example, the following decreasing sequences of elements in $\mathbb{N} + \mathbb{F}$ all start with 1:

$$1, 0.$$
$$1, \tfrac{1}{2}, 0.$$
$$1, \tfrac{2}{3}, \tfrac{1}{2}, 0.$$
$$1, \tfrac{3}{4}, \tfrac{2}{3}, \tfrac{1}{2}, 0.$$
$$\vdots$$

Nevertheless, since $\mathbb{N} + \mathbb{F}$ is well ordered, it is impossible to find an infinite decreasing sequence of elements in $\mathbb{N} + \mathbb{F}$, because the set of elements in such a sequence would have no minimum.

Problems for Section 2.2

Practice Problems

Problem 2.1.
For practice using the Well Ordering Principle, fill in the template of an easy to prove fact: every amount of postage that can be assembled using only 10 cent and 15 cent stamps is divisible by 5.

In particular, let the notation "$j \mid k$" indicate that integer j is a divisor of integer k, and let $S(n)$ mean that exactly n cents postage can be assembled using only 10 and 15 cent stamps. Then the proof shows that

$$S(n) \;\; \text{IMPLIES} \;\; 5 \mid n, \quad \text{for all nonnegative integers } n. \tag{2.2}$$

Fill in the missing portions (indicated by "…") of the following proof of (2.2).

Let C be the set of *counterexamples* to (2.2), namely

$$C ::= \{n \mid \ldots\}$$

Assume for the purpose of obtaining a contradiction that C is nonempty. Then by the WOP, there is a smallest number $m \in C$. This m must be positive because ….

But if $S(m)$ holds and m is positive, then $S(m - 10)$ or $S(m - 15)$ must hold, because . . . .

So suppose $S(m - 10)$ holds. Then $5 \mid (m - 10)$, because. . .

But if $5 \mid (m - 10)$, then obviously $5 \mid m$, contradicting the fact that m is a counterexample.

Next, if $S(m - 15)$ holds, we arrive at a contradiction in the same way.

Since we get a contradiction in both cases, we conclude that. . .

which proves that (2.2) holds.

Problem 2.2.

The Fibonacci numbers $F(0), F(1), F(2), \ldots$ are defined as follows:

$$F(n) ::= \begin{cases} 0 & \text{if } n = 0, \\ 1 & \text{if } n = 1, \\ F(n - 1) + F(n - 2) & \text{if } n > 1. \end{cases}$$

Exactly which sentence(s) in the following bogus proof contain logical errors? Explain.

False Claim. *Every Fibonacci number is even.*

Bogus proof. Let all the variables n, m, k mentioned below be nonnegative integer valued.

1. The proof is by the WOP.

2. Let $\text{EF}(n)$ mean that $F(n)$ is even.

3. Let C be the set of counterexamples to the assertion that $\text{EF}(n)$ holds for all $n \in \mathbb{N}$, namely,
$$C ::= \{n \in \mathbb{N} \mid \text{NOT}(\text{EF}(n))\}.$$

4. We prove by contradiction that C is empty. So assume that C is not empty.

5. By WOP, there is a least nonnegative integer $m \in C$.

6. Then $m > 0$, since $F(0) = 0$ is an even number.

7. Since m is the minimum counterexample, $F(k)$ is even for all $k < m$.

8. In particular, $F(m - 1)$ and $F(m - 2)$ are both even.

9. But by the definition, $F(m)$ equals the sum $F(m-1) + F(m-2)$ of two even numbers, and so it is also even.

10. That is, $EF(m)$ is true.

11. This contradicts the condition in the definition of m that $\text{NOT}(EF(m))$ holds.

12. This contradition implies that C must be empty. Hence, $F(n)$ is even for all $n \in \mathbb{N}$.

∎

Problem 2.3.

In Chapter 2, the Well Ordering Principle was used to show that all positive rational numbers can be written in "lowest terms," that is, as a ratio of positive integers with no common factor prime factor. Below is a different proof which also arrives at this correct conclusion, but this proof is bogus. Identify every step at which the proof makes an unjustified inference.

Bogus proof. Suppose to the contrary that there was positive rational q such that q cannot be written in lowest terms. Now let C be the set of such rational numbers that cannot be written in lowest terms. Then $q \in C$, so C is nonempty. So there must be a smallest rational $q_0 \in C$. So since $q_0/2 < q_0$, it must be possible to express $q_0/2$ in lowest terms, namely,

$$\frac{q_0}{2} = \frac{m}{n} \tag{2.3}$$

for positive integers m, n with no common prime factor. Now we consider two cases:

Case 1: [n is odd]. Then $2m$ and n also have no common prime factor, and therefore

$$q_0 = 2 \cdot \left(\frac{m}{n}\right) = \frac{2m}{n}$$

expresses q_0 in lowest terms, a contradiction.

Case 2: [n is even]. Any common prime factor of m and $n/2$ would also be a common prime factor of m and n. Therefore m and $n/2$ have no common prime factor, and so

$$q_0 = \frac{m}{n/2}$$

expresses q_0 in lowest terms, a contradiction.

Since the assumption that C is nonempty leads to a contradiction, it follows that C is empty—that is, there are no counterexamples. ∎

Class Problems

Problem 2.4.

Use the *Well Ordering Principle* [2] to prove that

$$\sum_{k=0}^{n} k^2 = \frac{n(n+1)(2n+1)}{6}. \tag{2.4}$$

for all nonnegative integers n.

Problem 2.5.

Use the Well Ordering Principle to prove that there is no solution over the positive integers to the equation:

$$4a^3 + 2b^3 = c^3.$$

Problem 2.6.

You are given a series of envelopes, respectively containing $1, 2, 4, \ldots, 2^m$ dollars. Define

> **Property** m: For any nonnegative integer less than 2^{m+1}, there is a selection of envelopes whose contents add up to *exactly* that number of dollars.

Use the Well Ordering Principle (WOP) to prove that Property m holds for all nonnegative integers m.

Hint: Consider two cases: first, when the target number of dollars is less than 2^m and second, when the target is at least 2^m.

Homework Problems

Problem 2.7.

Use the Well Ordering Principle to prove that any integer greater than or equal to 8 can be represented as the sum of nonnegative integer multiples of 3 and 5.

Problem 2.8.

Use the Well Ordering Principle to prove that any integer greater than or equal to 50 can be represented as the sum of nonnegative integer multiples of 7, 11, and 13.

---

[2]Proofs by other methods such as induction or by appeal to known formulas for similar sums will not receive full credit.

Problem 2.9.

Euler's Conjecture in 1769 was that there are no positive integer solutions to the equation

$$a^4 + b^4 + c^4 = d^4.$$

Integer values for a, b, c, d that do satisfy this equation were first discovered in 1986. So Euler guessed wrong, but it took more than two centuries to demonstrate his mistake.

Now let's consider Lehman's equation, similar to Euler's but with some coefficients:

$$8a^4 + 4b^4 + 2c^4 = d^4 \qquad (2.5)$$

Prove that Lehman's equation (2.5) really does not have any positive integer solutions.

Hint: Consider the minimum value of a among all possible solutions to (2.5).

Problem 2.10.

Use the Well Ordering Principle to prove that

$$n \le 3^{n/3} \qquad (2.6)$$

for every nonnegative integer n.

Hint: Verify (2.6) for $n \le 4$ by explicit calculation.

Problem 2.11.

A *winning configuration* in the game of Mini-Tetris is a complete tiling of a $2 \times n$ board using only the three shapes shown below:

For example, here are several possible winning configurations on a 2×5 board:

(a) Let T_n denote the number of different winning configurations on a $2 \times n$ board. Determine the values of T_1, T_2 and T_3.

(b) Express T_n in terms of T_{n-1} and T_{n-2} for $n > 2$.

(c) Use the Well Ordering Principle to prove that the number of winning configurations on a $2 \times n$ Mini-Tetris board is:[3]

$$T_n = \frac{2^{n+1} + (-1)^n}{3} \qquad\qquad (*)$$

Exam Problems

Problem 2.12.

Except for an easily repaired omission, the following proof using the Well Ordering Principle shows that every amount of postage that can be paid exactly using only 10 cent and 15 cent stamps, is divisible by 5.

Namely, let the notation "$j \mid k$" indicate that integer j is a divisor of integer k, and let $S(n)$ mean that exactly n cents postage can be assembled using only 10 and 15 cent stamps. Then the proof shows that

$$S(n) \ \text{IMPLIES} \ 5 \mid n, \quad \text{for all nonnegative integers } n. \qquad (2.7)$$

Fill in the missing portions (indicated by "...") of the following proof of (2.7), and at the end, identify the minor mistake in the proof and how to fix it.

Let C be the set of *counterexamples* to (2.7), namely

$$C ::= \{n \mid S(n) \text{ and } \text{NOT}(5 \mid n)\}$$

Assume for the purpose of obtaining a contradiction that C is nonempty. Then by the WOP, there is a smallest number $m \in C$. Then $S(m - 10)$ or $S(m - 15)$ must hold, because the m cents postage is made from 10 and 15 cent stamps, so we remove one.

So suppose $S(m - 10)$ holds. Then $5 \mid (m - 10)$, because...

But if $5 \mid (m - 10)$, then $5 \mid m$, because...

contradicting the fact that m is a counterexample.

Next suppose $S(m - 15)$ holds. Then the proof for $m - 10$ carries over directly for $m - 15$ to yield a contradiction in this case as well.

---

[3] A good question is how someone came up with equation $(*)$ in the first place. A simple Well Ordering proof gives no hint about this, but it should be absolutely convincing anyway.

Since we get a contradiction in both cases, we conclude that C must be empty. That is, there are no counterexamples to (2.7), which proves that (2.7) holds.

The proof makes an implicit assumption about the value of m. State the assumption and justify it in one sentence.

Problem 2.13. **(a)** Prove using the Well Ordering Principle that, using 6¢, 14¢, and 21¢ stamps, it is possible to make any amount of postage over 50¢. To save time, you may specify *assume without proof* that 50¢, 51¢, ... 100¢ are all makeable, but you should clearly indicate which of these assumptions your proof depends on.

(b) Show that 49¢ is not makeable.

Problem 2.14.
We'll use the Well Ordering Principle to prove that for every positive integer n, the sum of the first n odd numbers is n^2, that is,

$$\sum_{i=0}^{n-1}(2i+1) = n^2, \tag{2.8}$$

for all $n > 0$.

Assume to the contrary that equation (2.8) failed for some positive integer n. Let m be the least such number.

(a) Why must there be such an m?

(b) Explain why $m \geq 2$.

(c) Explain why part (b) implies that

$$\sum_{i=1}^{m-1}(2(i-1)+1) = (m-1)^2. \tag{2.9}$$

(d) What term should be added to the left-hand side of (2.9) so the result equals

$$\sum_{i=1}^{m}(2(i-1)+1)?$$

(e) Conclude that equation (2.8) holds for all positive integers n.

Problem 2.15.

Use the Well Ordering Principle (WOP) to prove that

$$2 + 4 + \cdots + 2n = n(n + 1) \tag{2.10}$$

for all $n > 0$.

Problem 2.16.

Prove by the Well Ordering Principle that for all nonnegative integers, n:

$$0^3 + 1^3 + 2^3 + \cdots + n^3 = \left(\frac{n(n + 1)}{2} \right)^2. \tag{2.11}$$

Problem 2.17.

Use the Well Ordering Principle to prove that

$$1 \cdot 2 + 2 \cdot 3 + 3 \cdot 4 + \cdots + n(n + 1) = \frac{n(n + 1)(n + 2)}{3} \tag{*}$$

for all integers $n \geq 1$.

Problem 2.18.

Say a number of cents is *makeable* if it is the value of some set of 6 cent and 15 cent stamps. Use the Well Ordering Principle to show that every integer that is a multiple of 3 and greater than or equal to twelve is makeable.

Problems for Section 2.4

Homework Problems

Problem 2.19.

Complete the proof of Lemma 2.4.5 by showing that the number $n_S + f_S$ is the minimum element in S.

Practice Problems

Problem 2.20.

Indicate which of the following sets of numbers have a minimum element and which are well ordered. For those that are not well ordered, give an example of a subset with no minimum element.

(a) The integers $\geq -\sqrt{2}$.

(b) The rational numbers $\geq \sqrt{2}$.

(c) The set of rationals of the form $1/n$ where n is a positive integer.

(d) The set G of rationals of the form m/n where $m, n > 0$ and $n \leq g$, where g is a *googol* 10^{100}.

(e) The set $\mathbb{F}$ of fractions of the form $n/(n+1)$:

$$\frac{0}{1}, \frac{1}{2}, \frac{2}{3}, \frac{3}{4}, \dots.$$

(f) Let $W ::= \mathbb{N} \cup \mathbb{F}$ be the set consisting of the nonnegative integers along with all the fractions of the form $n/(n+1)$. Describe a length 5 decreasing sequence of elements of W starting with $1, \dots$ length 50 decreasing sequence, ... length 500.

Problem 2.21.

Use the Well Ordering Principle to prove that every finite, nonempty set of real numbers has a minimum element.

Class Problems

Problem 2.22.

Prove that a set R of real numbers is well ordered iff there is no infinite decreasing sequence of numbers R. In other words, there is no set of numbers $r_i \in R$ such that

$$r_0 > r_1 > r_2 > \dots. \tag{2.12}$$

3   Logical Formulas

It is amazing that people manage to cope with all the ambiguities in the English language. Here are some sentences that illustrate the issue:

- "You may have cake, or you may have ice cream."

- "If pigs can fly, then your account won't get hacked."

- "If you can solve any problem we come up with, then you get an *A* for the course."

- "Every American has a dream."

What *precisely* do these sentences mean? Can you have both cake and ice cream or must you choose just one dessert? Pigs can't fly, so does the second sentence say anything about the security of your account? If you can solve some problems we come up with, can you get an *A* for the course? And if you can't solve a single one of the problems, does it mean you can't get an *A*? Finally, does the last sentence imply that all Americans have the same dream—say of owning a house—or might different Americans have different dreams—say, Eric dreams of designing a killer software application, Tom of being a tennis champion, Albert of being able to sing?

Some uncertainty is tolerable in normal conversation. But when we need to formulate ideas precisely—as in mathematics and programming—the ambiguities inherent in everyday language can be a real problem. We can't hope to make an exact argument if we're not sure exactly what the statements mean. So before we start into mathematics, we need to investigate the problem of how to talk about mathematics.

To get around the ambiguity of English, mathematicians have devised a special language for talking about logical relationships. This language mostly uses ordinary English words and phrases such as "or," "implies," and "for all." But mathematicians give these words precise and unambiguous definitions which don't always match common usage.

Surprisingly, in the midst of learning the language of logic, we'll come across the most important open problem in computer science—a problem whose solution could change the world.

3.1   Propositions from Propositions

In English, we can modify, combine, and relate propositions with words such as "not," "and," "or," "implies," and "if-then." For example, we can combine three propositions into one like this:

If all humans are mortal **and** all Greeks are human, **then** all Greeks are mortal.

For the next while, we won't be much concerned with the internals of propositions—whether they involve mathematics or Greek mortality—but rather with how propositions are combined and related. So, we'll frequently use variables such as P and Q in place of specific propositions such as "All humans are mortal" and "$2 + 3 = 5$." The understanding is that these *propositional variables*, like propositions, can take on only the values **T** (true) and **F** (false). Propositional variables are also called *Boolean variables* after their inventor, the nineteenth century mathematician George—you guessed it—Boole.

3.1.1   NOT, AND, and OR

Mathematicians use the words NOT, AND and OR for operations that change or combine propositions. The precise mathematical meaning of these special words can be specified by *truth tables*. For example, if P is a proposition, then so is "NOT(P)," and the truth value of the proposition "NOT(P)" is determined by the truth value of P according to the following truth table:

P	NOT(P)
T	**F**
F	**T**

The first row of the table indicates that when proposition P is true, the proposition "NOT(P)" is false. The second line indicates that when P is false, "NOT(P)" is true. This is probably what you would expect.

In general, a truth table indicates the true/false value of a proposition for each possible set of truth values for the variables. For example, the truth table for the proposition "P AND Q" has four lines, since there are four settings of truth values for the two variables:

P	Q	P AND Q
T	**T**	**T**
T	**F**	**F**
F	**T**	**F**
F	**F**	**F**

According to this table, the proposition "*P* AND *Q*" is true only when *P* and *Q* are both true. This is probably the way you ordinarily think about the word "and."

There is a subtlety in the truth table for "*P* OR *Q*":

P	*Q*	*P* OR *Q*
T	**T**	**T**
T	**F**	**T**
F	**T**	**T**
F	**F**	**F**

The first row of this table says that "*P* OR *Q*" is true even if *both* *P* and *Q* are true. This isn't always the intended meaning of "or" in everyday speech, but this is the standard definition in mathematical writing. So if a mathematician says, "You may have cake, or you may have ice cream," he means that you *could* have both.

If you want to exclude the possibility of having both cake *and* ice cream, you should combine them with the *exclusive-or* operation, XOR:

P	*Q*	*P* XOR *Q*
T	**T**	**F**
T	**F**	**T**
F	**T**	**T**
F	**F**	**F**

3.1.2 If and Only If

Mathematicians commonly join propositions in an additional way that doesn't arise in ordinary speech. The proposition "*P if and only if Q*" asserts that *P* and *Q* have the same truth value. Either both are true or both are false.

P	*Q*	*P* IFF *Q*
T	**T**	**T**
T	**F**	**F**
F	**T**	**F**
F	**F**	**T**

For example, the following if-and-only-if statement is true for every real number *x*:

$$x^2 - 4 \geq 0 \quad \text{IFF} \quad |x| \geq 2.$$

For some values of *x*, *both* inequalities are true. For other values of *x*, *neither* inequality is true. In every case, however, the IFF proposition as a whole is true.

3.1.3 IMPLIES

The combining operation whose technical meaning is least intuitive is "implies."
Here is its truth table, with the lines labeled so we can refer to them later.

P	Q	P IMPLIES Q	
T	**T**	**T**	(tt)
T	**F**	**F**	(tf)
F	**T**	**T**	(ft)
F	**F**	**T**	(ff)

The truth table for implications can be summarized in words as follows:

> An implication is true exactly when the if-part is false or the then-part is true.

This sentence is worth remembering; a large fraction of all mathematical statements
are of the if-then form!

Let's experiment with this definition. For example, is the following proposition
true or false?

> If Goldbach's Conjecture is true, then $x^2 \geq 0$ for every real number x.

We already mentioned that no one knows whether Goldbach's Conjecture, Proposition 1.1.6, is true or false. But that doesn't prevent us from answering the question!
This proposition has the form P IMPLIES Q where the *hypothesis* P is "Goldbach's Conjecture is true" and the *conclusion* Q is "$x^2 \geq 0$ for every real number
x." Since the conclusion is definitely true, we're on either line (tt) or line (ft) of the
truth table. Either way, the proposition as a whole is *true*!

Now let's figure out the truth of one of our original examples:

> If pigs fly, then your account won't get hacked.

Forget about pigs, we just need to figure out whether this proposition is true or
false. Pigs do not fly, so we're on either line (ft) or line (ff) of the truth table. In
both cases, the proposition is *true*!

False Hypotheses

This mathematical convention—that an implication as a whole is considered true
when its hypothesis is false—contrasts with common cases where implications are
supposed to have some *causal* connection between their hypotheses and conclusions.

For example, we could agree—or at least hope—that the following statement is
true:

If you followed the security protocal, then your account won't get hacked.

We regard this implication as unproblematical because of the clear *causal* connection between security protocols and account hackability.

On the other hand, the statement:

If pigs could fly, then your account won't get hacked,

would commonly be rejected as false—or at least silly—because porcine aeronautics have nothing to do with your account security. But mathematically, this implication counts as true.

It's important to accept the fact that mathematical implications ignore causal connections. This makes them a lot simpler than causal implications, but useful nevertheless. To illustrate this, suppose we have a system specification which consists of a series of, say, a dozen rules,[1]

> If the system sensors are in condition 1,
> then the system takes action 1.
> If the system sensors are in condition 2,
> then the system takes action 2.
> $$\vdots$$
> If the system sensors are in condition 12,
> then the system takes action 12.

Letting C_i be the proposition that the system sensors are in condition i, and A_i be the proposition that system takes action i, the specification can be restated more concisely by the logical formulas

$$C_1 \text{ IMPLIES } A_1,$$
$$C_2 \text{ IMPLIES } A_2,$$
$$\vdots$$
$$C_{12} \text{ IMPLIES } A_{12}.$$

Now the proposition that the system obeys the specification can be nicely expressed as a single logical formula by combining the formulas together with ANDs::

$$[C_1 \text{ IMPLIES } A_1] \text{ AND } [C_2 \text{ IMPLIES } A_2] \text{ AND } \cdots \text{ AND } [C_{12} \text{ IMPLIES } A_{12}]. \quad (3.1)$$

For example, suppose only conditions C_2 and C_5 are true, and the system indeed takes the specified actions A_2 and A_5. So in this case, the system is behaving

---

[1] Problem 3.15 concerns just such a system.

according to specification, and we accordingly want formula (3.1) to come out true. The implications C_2 IMPLIES A_2 and C_5 IMPLIES A_5 are both true because both their hypotheses and their conclusions are true. But in order for (3.1) to be true, we need all the other implications, all of whose hypotheses are false, to be true. This is exactly what the rule for mathematical implications accomplishes.

3.2   Propositional Logic in Computer Programs

Propositions and logical connectives arise all the time in computer programs. For example, consider the following snippet, which could be either C, C++, or Java:

```
if ( x > 0 || (x <= 0 && y > 100) )
    ⋮
```
(further instructions)

Java uses the symbol || for "OR," and the symbol && for "AND." The *further instructions* are carried out only if the proposition following the word if is true. On closer inspection, this big expression is built from two simpler propositions. Let A be the proposition that x > 0, and let B be the proposition that y > 100. Then we can rewrite the condition as

$$A \text{ OR } (\text{NOT}(A) \text{ AND } B). \tag{3.2}$$

3.2.1   Truth Table Calculation

A truth table calculation reveals that the more complicated expression 3.2 always has the same truth value as

$$A \text{ OR } B. \tag{3.3}$$

We begin with a table with just the truth values of A and B:

A	B	A OR (NOT(A) AND B)	A OR B
T	T		
T	F		
F	T		
F	F		

These values are enough to fill in two more columns:

A	B	A	OR	(NOT(A)	AND	B)	A OR B
T	T			F			**T**
T	F			F			**T**
F	T			T			**T**
F	F			T			**F**

Now we have the values needed to fill in the AND column:

A	B	A	OR	(NOT(A)	AND	B)	A OR B
T	T			F	F		**T**
T	F			F	F		**T**
F	T			T	T		**T**
F	F			T	F		**F**

and this provides the values needed to fill in the remaining column for the first OR:

A	B	A	OR	(NOT(A)	AND	B)	A OR B
T	T	**T**		F	F		**T**
T	F	**T**		F	F		**T**
F	T	**T**		T	T		**T**
F	F	**F**		T	F		**F**

Expressions whose truth values always match are called *equivalent*. Since the two emphasized columns of truth values of the two expressions are the same, they are equivalent. So we can simplify the code snippet without changing the program's behavior by replacing the complicated expression with an equivalent simpler one:

```
if ( x > 0 || y > 100 )
        ⋮
```

(further instructions)

The equivalence of (3.2) and (3.3) can also be confirmed reasoning by cases:

A is **T.** An expression of the form (**T** OR anything) is equivalent to **T.** Since A is **T** both (3.2) and (3.3) in this case are of this form, so they have the same truth value, namely, **T.**

A is **F.** An expression of the form (**F** OR *anything*) will have same truth value as *anything*. Since A is **F**, (3.3) has the same truth value as B.

An expression of the form (**T** AND *anything*) is equivalent to *anything*, as is any expression of the form **F** OR *anything*. So in this case A OR (NOT(A) AND B) is equivalent to (NOT(A) AND B), which in turn is equivalent to B.

Therefore both (3.2) and (3.3) will have the same truth value in this case, namely, the value of B.

Simplifying logical expressions has real practical importance in computer science. Expression simplification in programs like the one above can make a program easier to read and understand. Simplified programs may also run faster, since they require fewer operations. In hardware, simplifying expressions can decrease the number of logic gates on a chip because digital circuits can be described by logical formulas (see Problems 3.6 and 3.7). Minimizing the logical formulas corresponds to reducing the number of gates in the circuit. The payoff of gate minimization is potentially enormous: a chip with fewer gates is smaller, consumes less power, has a lower defect rate, and is cheaper to manufacture.

3.2.2   Cryptic Notation

Java uses symbols like "&&" and "||" in place of AND and OR. Circuit designers use "·" and "+," and actually refer to AND as a product and OR as a sum. Mathematicians use still other symbols, given in the table below.

English	Symbolic Notation
NOT(P)	$\neg P$ (alternatively, $\overline{P}$)
P AND Q	$P \wedge Q$
P OR Q	$P \vee Q$
P IMPLIES Q	$P \longrightarrow Q$
if P then Q	$P \longrightarrow Q$
P IFF Q	$P \longleftrightarrow Q$
P XOR Q	$P \oplus Q$

For example, using this notation, "If P AND NOT(Q), then R" would be written:

$$(P \wedge \overline{Q}) \longrightarrow R.$$

The mathematical notation is concise but cryptic. Words such as "AND" and "OR" are easier to remember and won't get confused with operations on numbers. We will often use $\overline{P}$ as an abbreviation for NOT(P), but aside from that, we mostly stick to the words—except when formulas would otherwise run off the page.

3.3   Equivalence and Validity

3.3.1   Implications and Contrapositives

Do these two sentences say the same thing?

> If I am hungry, then I am grumpy.
>
> If I am not grumpy, then I am not hungry.

We can settle the issue by recasting both sentences in terms of propositional logic. Let P be the proposition "I am hungry" and Q be "I am grumpy." The first sentence says "P IMPLIES Q" and the second says "NOT(Q) IMPLIES NOT(P)." Once more, we can compare these two statements in a truth table:

P	Q	$(P$ IMPLIES $Q)$	(NOT(Q)	IMPLIES	NOT(P))
T	T	T	F	T	F
T	F	F	T	F	F
F	T	T	F	T	T
F	F	T	T	T	T

Sure enough, the highlighted columns showing the truth values of these two statements are the same. A statement of the form "NOT(Q) IMPLIES NOT(P)" is called the *contrapositive* of the implication "P IMPLIES Q." The truth table shows that an implication and its contrapositive are equivalent—they are just different ways of saying the same thing.

In contrast, the *converse* of "P IMPLIES Q" is the statement "Q IMPLIES P." The converse to our example is:

> If I am grumpy, then I am hungry.

This sounds like a rather different contention, and a truth table confirms this suspicion:

P	Q	P IMPLIES Q	Q IMPLIES P
T	T	T	T
T	F	F	T
F	T	T	F
F	F	T	T

Now the highlighted columns differ in the second and third row, confirming that an implication is generally *not* equivalent to its converse.

One final relationship: an implication and its converse together are equivalent to an iff statement, specifically, to these two statements together. For example,

> If I am grumpy then I am hungry, and if I am hungry then I am grumpy.

are equivalent to the single statement:

> I am grumpy iff I am hungry.

Once again, we can verify this with a truth table.

P	Q	$(P$ IMPLIES $Q)$	AND	$(Q$ IMPLIES $P)$	P IFF Q
T	T	T	T	T	T
T	F	F	F	T	F
F	T	T	F	F	F
F	F	T	T	T	T

The fourth column giving the truth values of

$$(P \text{ IMPLIES } Q) \text{ AND } (Q \text{ IMPLIES } P)$$

is the same as the sixth column giving the truth values of P IFF Q, which confirms that the AND of the implications is equivalent to the IFF statement.

3.3.2   Validity and Satisfiability

A *valid* formula is one which is *always* true, no matter what truth values its variables may have. The simplest example is

$$P \text{ OR NOT}(P).$$

You can think about valid formulas as capturing fundamental logical truths. For example, a property of implication that we take for granted is that if one statement implies a second one, and the second one implies a third, then the first implies the third. The following valid formula confirms the truth of this property of implication.

$$[(P \text{ IMPLIES } Q) \text{ AND } (Q \text{ IMPLIES } R)] \text{ IMPLIES } (P \text{ IMPLIES } R).$$

Equivalence of formulas is really a special case of validity. Namely, statements F and G are equivalent precisely when the statement $(F$ IFF $G)$ is valid. For example, the equivalence of the expressions (3.3) and (3.2) means that

$$(A \text{ OR } B) \text{ IFF } (A \text{ OR } (\text{NOT}(A) \text{ AND } B))$$

is valid. Of course, validity can also be viewed as an aspect of equivalence. Namely, a formula is valid iff it is equivalent to **T**.

A *satisfiable* formula is one which can *sometimes* be true—that is, there is some assignment of truth values to its variables that makes it true. One way satisfiability comes up is when there are a collection of system specifications. The job of the system designer is to come up with a system that follows all the specs. This means that the AND of all the specs must be satisfiable or the designer's job will be impossible (see Problem 3.15).

There is also a close relationship between validity and satisfiability: a statement P is satisfiable iff its negation NOT(P) is *not* valid.

3.4 The Algebra of Propositions

3.4.1 Propositions in Normal Form

Every propositional formula is equivalent to a "sum-of-products" or *disjunctive form*. More precisely, a disjunctive form is simply an OR of AND-terms, where each AND-term is an AND of variables or negations of variables, for example,

$$(A \text{ AND } B) \text{ OR } (A \text{ AND } C). \tag{3.4}$$

You can read a disjunctive form for any propositional formula directly from its truth table. For example, the formula

$$A \text{ AND } (B \text{ OR } C) \tag{3.5}$$

has truth table:

A	B	C	A AND $(B$ OR $C)$
T	T	T	T
T	T	F	T
T	F	T	T
T	F	F	F
F	T	T	F
F	T	F	F
F	F	T	F
F	F	F	F

The formula (3.5) is true in the first row when A, B and C are all true, that is, where A AND B AND C is true. It is also true in the second row where A AND B AND $\overline{C}$ is true, and in the third row when A AND $\overline{B}$ AND C is true, and that's all. So (3.5) is true exactly when

$$(A \text{ AND } B \text{ AND } C) \text{ OR } (A \text{ AND } B \text{ AND } \overline{C}) \text{ OR } (A \text{ AND } \overline{B} \text{ AND } C) \tag{3.6}$$

is true.

The expression (3.6) is a disjunctive form where each AND-term is an AND of *every one* of the variables or their complements in turn. An expression of this form is called a *disjunctive normal form (DNF)*. A DNF formula can often be simplified into a smaller disjunctive form. For example, the DNF (3.6) further simplifies to the equivalent disjunctive form (3.4) above.

Applying the same reasoning to the **F** entries of a truth table yields a *conjunctive form* for any formula—an AND of OR-terms in which the OR-terms are OR's only of variables or their negations. For example, formula (3.5) is false in the fourth row of its truth table (3.4.1) where A is **T**, B is **F** and C is **F**. But this is exactly the one row where $(\overline{A} \text{ OR } B \text{ OR } C)$ is **F**! Likewise, the (3.5) is false in the fifth row which is exactly where $(A \text{ OR } \overline{B} \text{ OR } \overline{C})$ is **F**. This means that (3.5) will be **F** whenever the AND of these two OR-terms is false. Continuing in this way with the OR-terms corresponding to the remaining three rows where (3.5) is false, we get a *conjunctive normal form* (*CNF*) that is equivalent to (3.5), namely,

$$(\overline{A} \text{ OR } B \text{ OR } C) \text{ AND } (A \text{ OR } \overline{B} \text{ OR } \overline{C}) \text{ AND } (A \text{ OR } \overline{B} \text{ OR } C) \text{AND}$$
$$(A \text{ OR } B \text{ OR } \overline{C}) \text{ AND } (A \text{ OR } B \text{ OR } C)$$

The methods above can be applied to any truth table, which implies

Theorem 3.4.1. *Every propositional formula is equivalent to both a disjunctive normal form and a conjunctive normal form.*

3.4.2   Proving Equivalences

A check of equivalence or validity by truth table runs out of steam pretty quickly: a proposition with n variables has a truth table with 2^n lines, so the effort required to check a proposition grows exponentially with the number of variables. For a proposition with just 30 variables, that's already over a billion lines to check!

An alternative approach that *sometimes* helps is to use algebra to prove equivalence. A lot of different operators may appear in a propositional formula, so a useful first step is to get rid of all but three: AND, OR and NOT. This is easy because each of the operators is equivalent to a simple formula using only these three. For example, A IMPLIES B is equivalent to NOT(A) OR B. Formulas using onlyAND, OR and NOT for the remaining operators are left to Problem 3.16.

We list below a bunch of equivalence axioms with the symbol " $\longleftrightarrow$ " between equivalent formulas. These axioms are important because they are all that's needed to prove every possible equivalence. We'll start with some equivalences for AND's that look like the familiar ones for multiplication of numbers:

$$A \text{ AND } B \longleftrightarrow B \text{ AND } A \qquad \text{(commutativity of AND)}$$
$$(3.7)$$

$$(A \text{ AND } B) \text{ AND } C \longleftrightarrow A \text{ AND } (B \text{ AND } C) \qquad \text{(associativity of AND)}$$
$$(3.8)$$

$$\mathbf{T} \text{ AND } A \longleftrightarrow A \qquad \text{(identity for AND)}$$
$$\mathbf{F} \text{ AND } A \longleftrightarrow \mathbf{F} \qquad \text{(zero for AND)}$$
$$A \text{ AND } (B \text{ OR } C) \longleftrightarrow (A \text{ AND } B) \text{ OR } (A \text{ AND } C) \quad \text{(distributivity of AND over OR)}$$
$$(3.9)$$

Associativity (3.8) justifies writing A AND B AND C without specifying whether it is parenthesized as A AND (B AND C) or (A AND B) AND C. Both ways of inserting parentheses yield equivalent formulas.

Unlike arithmetic rules for numbers, there is also a distributivity law for "sums" over "products:"

$$A \text{ OR } (B \text{ AND } C) \longleftrightarrow (A \text{ OR } B) \text{ AND } (A \text{ OR } C) \quad \text{(distributivity of OR over AND)}$$
$$(3.10)$$

Three more axioms that don't directly correspond to number properties are

$$A \text{ AND } A \longleftrightarrow A \qquad \text{(idempotence for AND)}$$
$$A \text{ AND } \overline{A} \longleftrightarrow \mathbf{F} \qquad \text{(contradiction for AND)} \quad (3.11)$$
$$\text{NOT}(\overline{A}) \longleftrightarrow A \qquad \text{(double negation)} \quad (3.12)$$

There are a corresponding set of equivalences for OR which we won't bother to list, except for the OR rule corresponding to contradiction for AND (3.11):

$$A \text{ OR } \overline{A} \longleftrightarrow \mathbf{T} \qquad \text{(validity for OR)} \quad (3.13)$$

Finally, there are *DeMorgan's Laws* which explain how to distribute NOT's over AND's and OR's:

$$\text{NOT}(A \text{ AND } B) \longleftrightarrow \overline{A} \text{ OR } \overline{B} \qquad \text{(DeMorgan for AND)} \quad (3.14)$$
$$\text{NOT}(A \text{ OR } B) \longleftrightarrow \overline{A} \text{ AND } \overline{B} \qquad \text{(DeMorgan for OR)} \quad (3.15)$$

All of these axioms can be verified easily with truth tables.

These axioms are all that's needed to convert any formula to a disjunctive normal form. We can illustrate how they work by applying them to turn the negation of formula (3.5),

$$\text{NOT}((A \text{ AND } B) \text{ OR } (A \text{ AND } C)). \quad (3.16)$$

into disjunctive normal form.

We start by applying DeMorgan's Law for OR (3.15) to (3.16) in order to move the NOT deeper into the formula. This gives

$$\text{NOT}(A \text{ AND } B) \text{ AND } \text{NOT}(A \text{ AND } C).$$

Now applying DeMorgan's Law for AND (3.14) to the two innermost AND-terms, gives

$$(\overline{A} \text{ OR } \overline{B}) \text{ AND } (\overline{A} \text{ OR } \overline{C}). \quad (3.17)$$

At this point NOT only applies to variables, and we won't need Demorgan's Laws any further.

Now we will repeatedly apply (3.9), distributivity of AND over OR, to turn (3.17) into a disjunctive form. To start, we'll distribute $(\overline{A}$ OR $\overline{B})$ over AND to get

$$((\overline{A} \text{ OR } \overline{B}) \text{ AND } \overline{A}) \text{ OR } ((\overline{A} \text{ OR } \overline{B}) \text{ AND } \overline{C}).$$

Using distributivity over both AND's we get

$$((\overline{A} \text{ AND } \overline{A}) \text{ OR } (\overline{B} \text{ AND } \overline{A})) \text{ OR } ((\overline{A} \text{ AND } \overline{C}) \text{ OR } (\overline{B} \text{ AND } \overline{C})).$$

By the way, we've implicitly used commutativity (3.7) here to justify distributing over an AND from the right. Now applying idempotence to remove the duplicate occurrence of $\overline{A}$ we get

$$(\overline{A} \text{ OR } (\overline{B} \text{ AND } \overline{A})) \text{ OR } ((\overline{A} \text{ AND } \overline{C}) \text{ OR } (\overline{B} \text{ AND } \overline{C})).$$

Associativity now allows dropping the parentheses around the terms being OR'd to yield the following disjunctive form for (3.16):

$$\overline{A} \text{ OR } (\overline{B} \text{ AND } \overline{A}) \text{ OR } (\overline{A} \text{ AND } \overline{C}) \text{ OR } (\overline{B} \text{ AND } \overline{C}). \tag{3.18}$$

The last step is to turn each of these AND-terms into a disjunctive normal form with all three variables A, B and C. We'll illustrate how to do this for the second AND-term $(\overline{B}$ AND $\overline{A})$. This term needs to mention C to be in normal form. To introduce C, we use validity for OR and identity for AND to conclude that

$$(\overline{B} \text{ AND } \overline{A}) \longleftrightarrow (\overline{B} \text{ AND } \overline{A}) \text{ AND } (C \text{ OR } \overline{C}).$$

Now distributing $(\overline{B}$ AND $\overline{A})$ over the OR yields the disjunctive normal form

$$(\overline{B} \text{ AND } \overline{A} \text{ AND } C) \text{ OR } (\overline{B} \text{ AND } \overline{A} \text{ AND } \overline{C}).$$

Doing the same thing to the other AND-terms in (3.18) finally gives a disjunctive normal form for (3.5):

$$\begin{aligned}
&(\overline{A} \text{ AND } B \text{ AND } C) \text{ OR } (\overline{A} \text{ AND } B \text{ AND } \overline{C}) \text{ OR}\\
&(\overline{A} \text{ AND } \overline{B} \text{ AND } C) \text{ OR } (\overline{A} \text{ AND } \overline{B} \text{ AND } \overline{C}) \text{ OR}\\
&(\overline{B} \text{ AND } \overline{A} \text{ AND } C) \text{ OR } (\overline{B} \text{ AND } \overline{A} \text{ AND } \overline{C}) \text{ OR}\\
&(\overline{A} \text{ AND } \overline{C} \text{ AND } B) \text{ OR } (\overline{A} \text{ AND } \overline{C} \text{ AND } \overline{B}) \text{ OR}\\
&(\overline{B} \text{ AND } \overline{C} \text{ AND } A) \text{ OR } (\overline{B} \text{ AND } \overline{C} \text{ AND } \overline{A}).
\end{aligned}$$

Using commutativity to sort the term and OR-idempotence to remove duplicates, finally yields a unique sorted DNF:

$$(A \text{ AND } \overline{B} \text{ AND } \overline{C}) \text{ OR}$$
$$(\overline{A} \text{ AND } B \text{ AND } C) \text{ OR}$$
$$(\overline{A} \text{ AND } B \text{ AND } \overline{C}) \text{ OR}$$
$$(\overline{A} \text{ AND } \overline{B} \text{ AND } C) \text{ OR}$$
$$(\overline{A} \text{ AND } \overline{B} \text{ AND } \overline{C}).$$

This example illustrates a strategy for applying these equivalences to convert any formula into disjunctive normal form, and conversion to conjunctive normal form works similarly, which explains:

Theorem 3.4.2. *Any propositional formula can be transformed into disjunctive normal form or a conjunctive normal form using the equivalences listed above.*

What has this got to do with equivalence? That's easy: to prove that two formulas are equivalent, convert them both to disjunctive normal form over the set of variables that appear in the terms. Then use commutativity to sort the variables and AND-terms so they all appear in some standard order. We claim the formulas are equivalent iff they have the same sorted disjunctive normal form. This is obvious if they do have the same disjunctive normal form. But conversely, the way we read off a disjunctive normal form from a truth table shows that two different sorted DNF's over the same set of variables correspond to different truth tables and hence to inequivalent formulas. This proves

Theorem 3.4.3 (Completeness of the propositional equivalence axioms). *Two propositional formula are equivalent iff they can be proved equivalent using the equivalence axioms listed above.*

The benefit of the axioms is that they leave room for ingeniously applying them to prove equivalences with less effort than the truth table method. Theorem 3.4.3 then adds the reassurance that the axioms are guaranteed to prove every equivalence, which is a great punchline for this section. But we don't want to mislead you: it's important to realize that using the strategy we gave for applying the axioms involves essentially the same effort it would take to construct truth tables, and there is no guarantee that applying the axioms will generally be any easier than using truth tables.

3.5   The SAT Problem

Determining whether or not a more complicated proposition is satisfiable is not so easy. How about this one?

$$(P \text{ OR } Q \text{ OR } R) \text{ AND } (\overline{P} \text{ OR } \overline{Q}) \text{ AND } (\overline{P} \text{ OR } \overline{R}) \text{ AND } (\overline{R} \text{ OR } \overline{Q})$$

The general problem of deciding whether a proposition is satisfiable is called *SAT*. One approach to SAT is to construct a truth table and check whether or not a **T** ever appears, but as with testing validity, this approach quickly bogs down for formulas with many variables because truth tables grow exponentially with the number of variables.

Is there a more efficient solution to SAT? In particular, is there some brilliant procedure that determines SAT in a number of steps that grows *polynomially*—like n^2 or n^{14}—instead of *exponentially*—2^n—whether any given proposition of size n is satisfiable or not? No one knows. And an awful lot hangs on the answer.

The general definition of an "efficient" procedure is one that runs in *polynomial time*, that is, that runs in a number of basic steps bounded by a polynomial in s, where s is the size of an input. It turns out that an efficient solution to SAT would immediately imply efficient solutions to many other important problems involving scheduling, routing, resource allocation, and circuit verification across multiple disciplines including programming, algebra, finance, and political theory. This would be wonderful, but there would also be worldwide chaos. Decrypting coded messages would also become an easy task, so online financial transactions would be insecure and secret communications could be read by everyone. Why this would happen is explained in Section 9.12.

Of course, the situation is the same for validity checking, since you can check for validity by checking for satisfiability of a negated formula. This also explains why the simplification of formulas mentioned in Section 3.2 would be hard—validity testing is a special case of determining if a formula simplifies to **T**.

Recently there has been exciting progress on *SAT-solvers* for practical applications like digital circuit verification. These programs find satisfying assignments with amazing efficiency even for formulas with millions of variables. Unfortunately, it's hard to predict which kind of formulas are amenable to SAT-solver methods, and for formulas that are *un*satisfiable, SAT-solvers generally get nowhere.

So no one has a good idea how to solve SAT in polynomial time, or how to prove that it can't be done—researchers are completely stuck. The problem of determining whether or not SAT has a polynomial time solution is known as the

"**P** vs. **NP**" problem.[2] It is the outstanding unanswered question in theoretical computer science. It is also one of the seven Millenium Problems: the Clay Institute will award you $1,000,000 if you solve the **P** vs. **NP** problem.

3.6 Predicate Formulas

3.6.1 Quantifiers

The "for all" notation $\forall$ has already made an early appearance in Section 1.1. For example, the predicate

$$\text{``}x^2 \geq 0\text{''}$$

is always true when x is a real number. That is,

$$\forall x \in \mathbb{R}.\, x^2 \geq 0$$

is a true statement. On the other hand, the predicate

$$\text{``}5x^2 - 7 = 0\text{''}$$

is only sometimes true; specifically, when $x = \pm\sqrt{7/5}$. There is a "there exists" notation $\exists$ to indicate that a predicate is true for at least one, but not necessarily all objects. So

$$\exists x \in \mathbb{R}.\, 5x^2 - 7 = 0$$

is true, while

$$\forall x \in \mathbb{R}.\, 5x^2 - 7 = 0$$

is not true.

There are several ways to express the notions of "always true" and "sometimes true" in English. The table below gives some general formats on the left and specific examples using those formats on the right. You can expect to see such phrases hundreds of times in mathematical writing!

---

[2]**P** stands for problems whose instances can be solved in time that grows polynomially with the size of the instance. **NP** stands for *nondeterministtic polynomial time*, but we'll leave an explanation of what that is to texts on the theory of computational complexity.

Always True

For all $x \in D$, $P(x)$ is true.   For all $x \in \mathbb{R}$, $x^2 \geq 0$.
$P(x)$ is true for every x in the set D. $x^2 \geq 0$ for every $x \in \mathbb{R}$.

Sometimes True

There is an $x \in D$ such that $P(x)$ is true.   There is an $x \in \mathbb{R}$ such that $5x^2 - 7 = 0$.
$P(x)$ is true for some x in the set D. $5x^2 - 7 = 0$ for some $x \in \mathbb{R}$.
$P(x)$ is true for at least one $x \in D$. $5x^2 - 7 = 0$ for at least one $x \in \mathbb{R}$.

All these sentences "quantify" how often the predicate is true. Specifically, an assertion that a predicate is always true is called a *universal quantification*, and an assertion that a predicate is sometimes true is an *existential quantification*. Sometimes the English sentences are unclear with respect to quantification:

If you can solve any problem we come up with,

then you get an A for the course.   (3.19)

The phrase "you can solve any problem we can come up with" could reasonably be interpreted as either a universal or existential quantification:

you can solve *every* problem we come up with,   (3.20)

or maybe

you can solve *at least one* problem we come up with.   (3.21)

To be precise, let Probs be the set of problems we come up with, Solves(x) be the predicate "You can solve problem x," and G be the proposition, "You get an A for the course." Then the two different interpretations of (3.19) can be written as follows:

$$(\forall x \in \text{Probs}. \text{Solves}(x)) \text{ IMPLIES } G, \qquad \text{for (3.20)},$$
$$(\exists x \in \text{Probs}. \text{Solves}(x)) \text{ IMPLIES } G. \qquad \text{for (3.21)}.$$

3.6.2   Mixing Quantifiers

Many mathematical statements involve several quantifiers. For example, we already described

> Goldbach's Conjecture 1.1.6: Every even integer greater than 2 is the sum of two primes.

Let's write this out in more detail to be precise about the quantification:

For every even integer n greater than 2, there exist primes p and q such that $n = p + q$.

Let Evens be the set of even integers greater than 2, and let Primes be the set of primes. Then we can write Goldbach's Conjecture in logic notation as follows:

$$\underbrace{\forall n \in \text{Evens}}_{\substack{\text{for every even} \\ \text{integer } n > 2}} \underbrace{\exists p \in \text{Primes } \exists q \in \text{Primes.}}_{\substack{\text{there exist primes} \\ p \text{ and } q \text{ such that}}} n = p + q.$$

3.6.3 Order of Quantifiers

Swapping the order of different kinds of quantifiers (existential or universal) usually changes the meaning of a proposition. For example, let's return to one of our initial, confusing statements:

"Every American has a dream."

This sentence is ambiguous because the order of quantifiers is unclear. Let A be the set of Americans, let D be the set of dreams, and define the predicate $H(a, d)$ to be "American a has dream d." Now the sentence could mean there is a single dream that every American shares—such as the dream of owning their own home:

$$\exists d \in D \; \forall a \in A. \; H(a, d)$$

Or it could mean that every American has a personal dream:

$$\forall a \in A \; \exists d \in D. \; H(a, d)$$

For example, some Americans may dream of a peaceful retirement, while others dream of continuing practicing their profession as long as they live, and still others may dream of being so rich they needn't think about work at all.

Swapping quantifiers in Goldbach's Conjecture creates a patently false statement that every even number ≥ 2 is the sum of *the same* two primes:

$$\underbrace{\exists p \in \text{Primes } \exists q \in \text{Primes.}}_{\substack{\text{there exist primes} \\ p \text{ and } q \text{ such that}}} \underbrace{\forall n \in \text{Evens}}_{\substack{\text{for every even} \\ \text{integer } n > 2}} n = p + q.$$

3.6.4 Variables Over One Domain

When all the variables in a formula are understood to take values from the same nonempty set D it's conventional to omit mention of D. For example, instead of $\forall x \in D \; \exists y \in D. \; Q(x, y)$ we'd write $\forall x \exists y. \; Q(x, y)$. The unnamed nonempty set that x and y range over is called the *domain of discourse*, or just plain *domain*, of the formula.

It's easy to arrange for all the variables to range over one domain. For example, Goldbach's Conjecture could be expressed with all variables ranging over the domain $\mathbb{N}$ as

$$\forall n. n \in \text{Evens IMPLIES } (\exists p \, \exists q. \ p \in \text{Primes AND } q \in \text{Primes AND } n = p + q).$$

3.6.5   Negating Quantifiers

There is a simple relationship between the two kinds of quantifiers. The following two sentences mean the same thing:

> Not everyone likes ice cream.

> There is someone who does not like ice cream.

The equivalence of these sentences is a instance of a general equivalence that holds between predicate formulas:

$$\text{NOT}(\forall x. \ P(x)) \quad \text{is equivalent to} \quad \exists x. \ \text{NOT}(P(x)). \tag{3.22}$$

Similarly, these sentences mean the same thing:

> There is no one who likes being mocked.

> Everyone dislikes being mocked.

The corresponding predicate formula equivalence is

$$\text{NOT}(\exists x. \ P(x)) \quad \text{is equivalent to} \quad \forall x. \ \text{NOT}(P(x)). \tag{3.23}$$

Note that the equivalence (3.23) follows directly by negating both sides the equivalence (3.22).

The general principle is that *moving a* NOT *across a quantifier changes the kind of quantifier.*

These equivalences are called *De Morgan's Laws for Quantifiers* because they correspond directly to De Morgan's Laws for propositional formulas if we rewrite $\forall x. P(x)$ as a (possibly infinite) conjunction $\text{AND}_x. P(x)$ and $\exists x. \text{NOT}(P(x))$ as the disjunction $\text{OR}_x. \text{NOT}(P(x))$.

3.6.6 Validity for Predicate Formulas

The idea of validity extends to predicate formulas, but to be valid, a formula now must evaluate to true no matter what the domain of discourse may be, no matter what values its variables may take over the domain, and no matter what interpretations its predicate variables may be given. For example, the equivalence (3.22) that gives the rule for negating a universal quantifier means that the following formula is valid:

$$\text{NOT}(\forall x.\ P(x))\ \text{IFF}\ \exists x.\ \text{NOT}(P(x)). \tag{3.24}$$

Another useful example of a valid assertion is

$$\exists x \forall y.\ P(x, y)\ \text{IMPLIES}\ \forall y \exists x.\ P(x, y). \tag{3.25}$$

Here's an explanation why this is valid:

Let D be the domain for the variables and P_0 be some binary predicate[3] on D. We need to show that if

$$\exists x \in D.\ \forall y \in D.\ P_0(x, y) \tag{3.26}$$

holds under this interpretation, then so does

$$\forall y \in D\ \exists x \in D.\ P_0(x, y). \tag{3.27}$$

So suppose (3.26) is true. Then by definition of $\exists$, this means that some element $d_0 \in D$ has the property that

$$\forall y \in D.\ P_0(d_0, y).$$

By definition of $\forall$, this means that

$$P_0(d_0, d)$$

is true for all $d \in D$. So given any $d \in D$, there is an element in D, namely d_0, such that $P_0(d_0, d)$ is true. But that's exactly what (3.27) means, so we've proved that (3.27) holds under this interpretation, as required.

We hope this is helpful as an explanation, but we don't really want to call it a "proof." The problem is that with something as basic as (3.25), it's hard to see what more elementary axioms are ok to use in proving it. What the explanation

---

[3]That is, a predicate that depends on two variables.

above did was translate the logical formula (3.25) into English and then appeal to the meaning, in English, of "for all" and "there exists" as justification.

In contrast to (3.25), the formula

$$\forall y \exists x.\, P(x, y) \text{ IMPLIES } \exists x \forall y.\, P(x, y). \tag{3.28}$$

is *not* valid. We can prove this just by describing an interpretation where the hypothesis $\forall y \exists x.\, P(x, y)$ is true but the conclusion $\exists x \forall y.\, P(x, y)$ is not true. For example, let the domain be the integers and $P(x, y)$ mean $x > y$. Then the hypothesis would be true because, given a value n for y we could choose the value of x to be $n + 1$, for example. But under this interpretation the conclusion asserts that there is an integer that is bigger than all integers, which is certainly false. An interpretation like this that falsifies an assertion is called a *counter-model* to that assertion.

3.7   References

[19]

Problems for Section 3.1

Practice Problems

Problem 3.1.
Some people are uncomfortable with the idea that from a false hypothesis you can prove everything, and instead of having P IMPLIES Q be true when P is false, they want P IMPLIES Q to be false when P is false. This would lead to IMPLIES having the same truth table as what propositional connective?

Problem 3.2.
Your class has a textbook and a final exam. Let P, Q and R be the following propositions:

$P ::=$ You get an A on the final exam.

$Q ::=$ You do every exercise in the book.

$R ::=$ You get an A in the class.

Translate following assertions into propositional formulas using P, Q, R and the propositional connectives AND, NOT, IMPLIES.

(a) You get an A in the class, but you do not do every exercise in the book.

(b) You get an A on the final, you do every exercise in the book, and you get an A in the class.

(c) To get an A in the class, it is necessary for you to get an A on the final.

(d) You get an A on the final, but you don't do every exercise in this book; nevertheless, you get an A in this class.

Class Problems

Problem 3.3.

When the mathematician says to his student, "If a function is not continuous, then it is not differentiable," then letting D stand for "differentiable" and C for continuous, the only proper translation of the mathematician's statement would be

$$\text{NOT}(C) \text{ IMPLIES NOT}(D),$$

or equivalently,

$$D \text{ IMPLIES } C.$$

But when a mother says to her son, "If you don't do your homework, then you can't watch TV," then letting T stand for "can watch TV" and H for "do your homework," a reasonable translation of the mother's statement would be

$$\text{NOT}(H) \text{ IFF NOT}(T),$$

or equivalently,

$$H \text{ IFF } T.$$

Explain why it is reasonable to translate these two IF-THEN statements in different ways into propositional formulas.

Homework Problems

Problem 3.4.

Describe a simple procedure which, given a positive integer argument, n, produces a width n array of truth-values whose rows would be all the possible truth-value assignments for n propositional variables. For example, for $n = 2$, the array would be:

$$
\begin{array}{cc}
\textbf{T} & \textbf{T} \\
\textbf{T} & \textbf{F} \\
\textbf{F} & \textbf{T} \\
\textbf{F} & \textbf{F}
\end{array}
$$

Your description can be in English, or a simple program in some familiar language such as Python or Java. If you do write a program, be sure to include some sample output.

Problem 3.5.

Sloppy Sam is trying to prove a certain proposition P. He defines two related propositions Q and R, and then proceeds to prove three implications:

$$P \text{ IMPLIES } Q, \qquad Q \text{ IMPLIES } R, \qquad R \text{ IMPLIES } P.$$

He then reasons as follows:

> If Q is true, then since I proved (Q IMPLIES R), I can conclude that R is true. Now, since I proved (R IMPLIES P), I can conclude that P is true. Similarly, if R is true, then P is true and so Q is true. Likewise, if P is true, then so are Q and R. So any way you look at it, all three of P, Q and R are true.

(a) Exhibit truth tables for

$$(P \text{ IMPLIES } Q) \text{ AND } (Q \text{ IMPLIES } R) \text{ AND } (R \text{ IMPLIES } P) \qquad (*)$$

and for

$$P \text{ AND } Q \text{ AND } R. \qquad (**)$$

Use these tables to find a truth assignment for P, Q, R so that ($*$) is **T** and ($**$) is **F**.

(b) You show these truth tables to Sloppy Sam and he says "OK, I'm wrong that P, Q and R all have to be true, but I still don't see the mistake in my reasoning. Can you help me understand my mistake?" How would you explain to Sammy where the flaw lies in his reasoning?

Problems for Section 3.2

Class Problems

Problem 3.6.
Propositional logic comes up in digital circuit design using the convention that **T** corresponds to 1 and **F** to 0. A simple example is a 2-bit *half-adder* circuit. This circuit has 3 binary inputs, a_1, a_0 and b, and 3 binary outputs, c, s_1, s_0. The 2-bit word $a_1 a_0$ gives the binary representation of an integer k between 0 and 3. The 3-bit word $c s_1 s_0$ gives the binary representation of $k + b$. The third output bit c is called the final *carry bit*.

So if k and b were both 1, then the value of $a_1 a_0$ would be 01 and the value of the output $c s_1 s_0$ would 010, namely, the 3-bit binary representation of $1 + 1$.

In fact, the final carry bit equals 1 only when all three binary inputs are 1, that is, when $k = 3$ and $b = 1$. In that case, the value of $c s_1 s_0$ is 100, namely, the binary representation of $3 + 1$.

This 2-bit half-adder could be described by the following formulas:

$$c_0 = b$$
$$s_0 = a_0 \text{ XOR } c_0$$
$$c_1 = a_0 \text{ AND } c_0 \qquad\qquad \text{the carry into column 1}$$
$$s_1 = a_1 \text{ XOR } c_1$$
$$c_2 = a_1 \text{ AND } c_1 \qquad\qquad \text{the carry into column 2}$$
$$c = c_2.$$

(a) Generalize the above construction of a 2-bit half-adder to an $n + 1$ bit half-adder with inputs $a_n, \ldots, a_1, a_0$ and b and outputs $c, s_n, \ldots, s_1, s_0$. That is, give simple formulas for s_i and c_i for $0 \le i \le n + 1$, where c_i is the carry into column $i + 1$, and $c = c_{n+1}$.

(b) Write similar definitions for the digits and carries in the sum of two $n + 1$-bit binary numbers $a_n \ldots a_1 a_0$ and $b_n \ldots b_1 b_0$.

Visualized as digital circuits, the above adders consist of a sequence of single-digit half-adders or adders strung together in series. These circuits mimic ordinary pencil-and-paper addition, where a carry into a column is calculated directly from the carry into the previous column, and the carries have to ripple across all the columns before the carry into the final column is determined. Circuits with this design are called *ripple-carry* adders. Ripple-carry adders are easy to understand and remember and require a nearly minimal number of operations. But the higher-order output bits and the final carry take time proportional to n to reach their final values.

(c) How many of each of the propositional operations does your adder from part (b) use to calculate the sum?

Homework Problems

Problem 3.7.

As in Problem 3.6, a digital circuit is called an $(n + 1)$-bit *half-adder* when it has with $n + 2$ inputs

$$a_n, \ldots, a_1, a_0, b$$

and $n + 2$ outputs

$$c, s_n, \ldots, s_1, s_0.$$

The input-output specification of the half-adder is that, if the 0-1 values of inputs $a_n, \ldots, a_1, a_0$ are taken to be the $(n + 1)$-bit binary representation of an integer k then the 0-1 values of the outputs $c, s_n, \ldots, s_1, s_0$ are supposed to be the $(n+2)$-bit binary representation of $k + b$.

For example suppose $n = 2$ and the values of $a_2 a_1 a_0$ were 101. This is the binary representation of $k = 5$. Now if the value of b was 1, then the output should be the 4-bit representation of $5 + 1 = 6$. Namely, the values of $c s_2 s_1 s_0$ would be 0110.

There are many different circuit designs for half adders. The most straighforward one is the "ripple carry" design described in Problem 3.6. We will now develop a different design for a half-adder circuit called a *parallel-design* or "look-ahead carry" half-adder. This design works by computing the values of higher-order digits for both a carry of 0 and a carry of 1, *in parallel*. Then, when the carry from the low-order digits finally arrives, the pre-computed answer can be quickly selected.

We'll illustrate this idea by working out a parallel design for an $(n + 1)$-bit half-adder.

Parallel-design half-adders are built out of parallel-design circuits called *add1-modules*. The input-output behavior of an add1-module is just a special case of a half-adder, where instead of an adding an input b to the input, the add1-module *always* adds 1. That is, an $(n + 1)$-bit add1-module has $(n + 1)$ binary inputs

$$a_n, \ldots, a_1, a_0,$$

and $n + 2$ binary outputs

$$c\, p_n, \ldots, p_1, p_0.$$

If $a_n \ldots a_1 a_0$ are taken to be the $(n + 1)$-bit representation of an integer k then $cp_n \ldots p_1 p_0$ is supposed to be the $(n + 2)$-bit binary representation of $k + 1$.

So a 1-bit add1-module just has input a_0 and outputs c, p_0 where

$$p_0 ::= a_0 \text{ XOR } 1, \text{(or more simply, } p_0 ::= \text{NOT}(a_0)\text{)},$$

$$c ::= a_0.$$

In the ripple-carry design, a double-size half-adder with $2(n + 1)$ inputs takes twice as long to produce its output values as an $(n + 1)$-input ripple-carry circuit. With parallel-design add1-modules, a double-size add1-module produces its output values nearly as fast as a single-size add1-modules. To see how this works, suppose the inputs of the double-size module are

$$a_{2n+1}, \ldots, a_1, a_0$$

and the outputs are

$$c, p_{2n+1}, \ldots, p_1, p_0.$$

We will build the double-size add1-module by having two single-size add1-modules work in parallel. The setup is illustrated in Figure 3.1.

Namely, the first single-size add1-module handles the first $n + 1$ inputs. The inputs to this module are the low-order $n + 1$ input bits $a_n, \ldots, a_1, a_0$, and its outputs will serve as the first $n + 1$ outputs $p_n, \ldots, p_1, p_0$ of the double-size module. Let $c_{(1)}$ be the remaining carry output from this module.

The inputs to the second single-size module are the higher-order $n + 1$ input bits $a_{2n+1}, \ldots, a_{n+2}, a_{n+1}$. Call its first $n + 1$ outputs $r_n, \ldots, r_1, r_0$ and let $c_{(2)}$ be its carry.

(a) Write a formula for the carry c of the double-size add1-module *solely* in terms of carries $c_{(1)}$ and $c_{(2)}$ of the single-size add1-modules.

(b) Complete the specification of the double-size add1-module by writing propositional formulas for the remaining outputs p_{n+i} for $1 \le i \le n + 1$. The formula for p_{n+i} should only involve the variables a_{n+i}, r_{i-1} and $c_{(1)}$.

(c) Explain how to build an $(n + 1)$-bit parallel-design half-adder from an $(n + 1)$-bit add1-module by writing a propositional formula for the half-adder output s_i using only the variables a_i, p_i and b.

(d) The speed or *latency* of a circuit is determined by the largest number of gates on any path from an input to an output. In an n-bit ripple carry circuit(Problem 3.6), there is a path from an input to the final carry output that goes through about $2n$ gates. In contrast, parallel half-adders are exponentially faster than ripple-carry half-adders. Confirm this by determining the largest number of propositional operations, that is, gates, on any path from an input to an output of an n-bit add1-module. (You may assume n is a power of 2.)

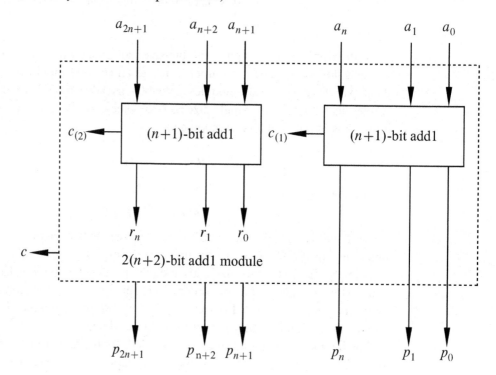

Figure 3.1   Structure of a Double-size *add1* Module.

Exam Problems

Problem 3.8.

Claim. *There are exactly two truth environments (assignments) for the variables M, N, P, Q, R, S that satisfy the following formula:*

$$\underbrace{(\overline{P} \text{ OR } Q)}_{\text{clause (1)}} \text{ AND } \underbrace{(\overline{Q} \text{ OR } R)}_{\text{clause (2)}} \text{ AND } \underbrace{(\overline{R} \text{ OR } S)}_{\text{clause (3)}} \text{ AND } \underbrace{(\overline{S} \text{ OR } P)}_{\text{clause (4)}} \text{ AND } M \text{ AND } \overline{N}$$

(a) This claim could be proved by truth-table. How many rows would the truth table have?

(b) Instead of a truth-table, prove this claim with an argument by cases according to the truth value of P.

Problem 3.9.
An n-bit AND-circuit has 0-1 valued inputs $a_0, a_1, \ldots, a_{n-1}$ and one output c whose value will be

$$c = a_0 \text{ AND } a_1 \text{ AND} \cdots \text{AND } a_{n-1}.$$

There are various ways to design an n-bit AND-circuit. A *serial* design is simply a series of AND-gates, each with one input being a circuit input a_i and the other input being the output of the previous gate as shown in Figure 3.2.

We can also use a *tree* design. A 1-bit tree design is just a wire, that is $c ::= a_1$. Assuming for simplicity that n is a power of two, an n-input tree circuit for $n > 1$ simply consists of two $n/2$-input tree circuits whose outputs are AND'd to produce output c, as in Figure 3.3. For example, a 4-bit tree design circut is shown in Figure 3.4.

(a) How many AND-gates are in the n-input serial circuit?

(b) The "speed" or *latency* of a circuit is the largest number of gates on any path from an input to an output. Briefly explain why the tree circuit is *exponentially faster* than the serial circuit.

(c) Assume n is a power of two. Prove that the n-input tree circuit has $n - 1$ AND-gates.

Problems for Section 3.3

Practice Problems

Problem 3.10.
Indicate whether each of the following propositional formulas is valid (V), satisfiable but not valid (S), or not satisfiable (N). For the satisfiable ones, indicate a satisfying truth assignment.

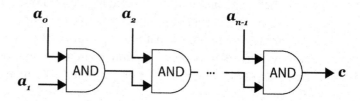

Figure 3.2   A serial AND-circuit.

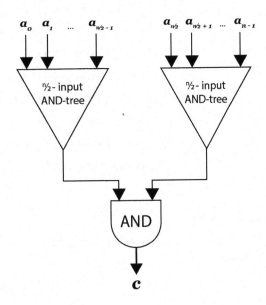

Figure 3.3 An *n*-bit AND-tree circuit.

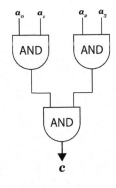

Figure 3.4 A 4-bit AND-tree circuit.

$$M \text{ IMPLIES } Q$$

$$M \text{ IMPLIES } (\overline{P} \text{ OR } \overline{Q})$$

$$M \text{ IMPLIES } [M \text{ AND } (P \text{ IMPLIES } M)]$$

$$(P \text{ OR } Q) \text{ IMPLIES } Q$$

$$(P \text{ OR } Q) \text{ IMPLIES } (\overline{P} \text{ AND } \overline{Q})$$

$$(P \text{ OR } Q) \text{ IMPLIES } [M \text{ AND } (P \text{ IMPLIES } M)]$$

$$(P \text{ XOR } Q) \text{ IMPLIES } Q$$

$$(P \text{ XOR } Q) \text{ IMPLIES } (\overline{P} \text{ OR } \overline{Q})$$

$$(P \text{ XOR } Q) \text{ IMPLIES } [M \text{ AND } (P \text{ IMPLIES } M)]$$

Problem 3.11.
Show truth tables that verify the equivalence of the following two propositional formulas

$$(P \text{ XOR } Q),$$
$$\text{NOT}(P \text{ IFF } Q).$$

Problem 3.12.
Prove that the propositional formulas

$$P \text{ OR } Q \text{ OR } R$$

and

$$(P \text{ AND NOT}(Q)) \text{ OR } (Q \text{ AND NOT}(R)) \text{ OR } (R \text{ AND NOT}(P)) \text{ OR } (P \text{ AND } Q \text{ AND } R).$$

are equivalent.

Problem 3.13.
Prove by truth table that OR distributes over AND, namely,

$$P \text{ OR } (Q \text{ AND } R) \quad \text{is equivalent to} \quad (P \text{ OR } Q) \text{ AND } (P \text{ OR } R) \qquad (3.29)$$

Class Problems

Problem 3.14. (a) Verify by truth table that

$$(P \text{ IMPLIES } Q) \text{ OR } (Q \text{ IMPLIES } P)$$

is valid.

(b) Let P and Q be propositional formulas. Describe a single formula R using only AND's, OR's, NOT's, and copies of P and Q, such that R is valid iff P and Q are equivalent.

(c) A propositional formula is *satisfiable* iff there is an assignment of truth values to its variables—an *environment*—that makes it true. Explain why

$$P \text{ is valid} \quad \text{iff} \quad \text{NOT}(P) \text{ is } not \text{ satisfiable.}$$

(d) A set of propositional formulas $P_1, \ldots, P_k$ is *consistent* iff there is an environment in which they are all true. Write a formula S such that the set $P_1, \ldots, P_k$ is *not* consistent iff S is valid.

Problem 3.15.

This problem[4] examines whether the following specifications are *satisfiable*:

1. If the file system is not locked, then

   (a) new messages will be queued.

   (b) new messages will be sent to the messages buffer.

   (c) the system is functioning normally, and conversely, if the system is functioning normally, then the file system is not locked.

2. If new messages are not queued, then they will be sent to the messages buffer.

3. New messages will not be sent to the message buffer.

(a) Begin by translating the five specifications into propositional formulas using four propositional variables:

$$L ::= \text{file system locked,}$$
$$Q ::= \text{new messages are queued,}$$
$$B ::= \text{new messages are sent to the message buffer,}$$
$$N ::= \text{system functioning normally.}$$

---

[4]Revised from Rosen, 5th edition, Exercise 1.1.36

(b) Demonstrate that this set of specifications is satisfiable by describing a single truth assignment for the variables L, Q, B, N and verifying that under this assignment, all the specifications are true.

(c) Argue that the assignment determined in part (b) is the only one that does the job.

Problems for Section 3.4

Practice Problems

Problem 3.16.
A half dozen different operators may appear in propositional formulas, but just AND, OR, and NOT are enough to do the job. That is because each of the operators is equivalent to a simple formula using only these three operators. For example, A IMPLIES B is equivalent to NOT(A) OR B. So all occurences of IMPLIES in a formula can be replaced using just NOT and OR.

(a) Write formulas using only AND, OR, NOT that are equivalent to each of A IFF B and A XOR B. Conclude that every propositional formula is equivalent to an AND-OR-NOT formula.

(b) Explain why you don't even need AND.

(c) Explain how to get by with the single operator NAND where A NAND B is equivalent by definition to NOT(A AND B).

Class Problems

Problem 3.17.
The propositional connective NOR is defined by the rule

$$P \text{ NOR } Q ::= (\text{NOT}(P) \text{ AND } \text{NOT}(Q)).$$

Explain why every propositional formula—possibly involving any of the usual operators such as IMPLIES, XOR, ...—is equivalent to one whose only connective is NOR.

Problem 3.18.
Explain how to read off a conjunctive form for a propositional formula directly from a disjunctive form for its complement.

Problem 3.19.

Let P be the proposition depending on propositional variable A, B, C, D whose truth values for each truth assignment to A, B, C, D are given in the table below. Write out both a disjunctive and a conjunctive normal form for P.

A	B	C	D	P
T	T	T	T	T
T	T	T	F	F
T	T	F	T	T
T	T	F	F	F
T	F	T	T	T
T	F	T	F	T
T	F	F	T	T
T	F	F	F	T
F	T	T	T	T
F	T	T	F	F
F	T	F	T	T
F	T	F	F	F
F	F	T	T	F
F	F	T	F	F
F	F	F	T	T
F	F	F	F	T

Homework Problems

Problem 3.20.

Use the equivalence axioms of Section 3.4.2 to convert the formula

$$A \text{ XOR } B \text{ XOR } C$$

(a) ... to disjunctive (OR of AND's) form,

(b) ... to conjunctive (AND of OR's) form.

Problems for Section 3.5

Class Problems

Problem 3.21.

The circuit-SAT problem is the problem of determining, for any given digital circuit with one output wire, whether there are truth values that can be fed into the circuit input wires which will lead the circuit to give output **T**.

It's easy to see that any efficient way of solving the circuit-SAT problem would yield an efficient way to solve the usual SAT problem for propositional formulas (Section 3.5). Namely, for any formula F, just construct a circuit C_F using that computes the values of the formula. Then there are inputs for which C_F gives output true iff F is satisfiable. Constructing C_F from F is easy, using a binary gate in C_F for each propositional connective in F. So an efficient circuit-SAT procedure leads to an efficient SAT procedure.

Conversely, there is a simple recursive procedure that will construct, given C, a formula E_C that is equivalent to C in the sense that the truth value E_C and the output of C are the same for every truth assignment of the variables. The difficulty is that, in general, the "equivalent" formula E_C, will be *exponentially larger* than C. For the purposes of showing that satifiability of circuits and satisfiability of formulas take roughly the same effort to solve, spending an exponential time translating one problem to the other swamps any benefit in switching from one problem to the other.

So instead of a formula E_C that is equivalent to C, we aim instead for a formula F_C that is "equisatisfiable" with C. That is, there will be input values that make C output **True iff** there is a truth assignment that satisfies F_C. (In fact, F_C and C need not even use the same variables.) But now we make sure that the amount of computation needed to construct F_C is not much larger than the size of the circuit C. In particular, the size of F_C will also not be much larger than C.

The idea behind the construction of F_C is that, given any digital circuit C with binary gates and one output, we can assign a distinct variable to each wire of C. Then for each gate of C, we can set up a propositional formula that represents the constraints that the gate places on the values of its input and output wires. For example, for an AND gate with input wire variables P and Q and output wire variable R, the constraint proposition would be

$$(P \text{ AND } Q) \text{ IFF } R. \tag{3.30}$$

(a) Given a circuit C, explain how to easily find a formula F_C of size proportional to the number of wires in C such that F_C is satisfiable iff C gives output **T** for some set of input values.

(b) Conclude that any efficient way of solving SAT would yield an efficient way to solve circuit-SAT.

Homework Problems

Problem 3.22.

A 3-conjunctive form (3CF) formula is a conjunctive form formula in which each OR-term is an OR of at most 3 variables or negations of variables. Although it may be hard to tell if a propositional formula F is satisfiable, it is always easy to construct a formula $C(F)$ that is

- in 3-conjunctive form,

- has at most 24 times as many occurrences of variables as F, and

- is satisfiable iff F is satisfiable.

To construct $C(F)$, introduce a different new variables for each operator that occurs in F. For example, if F was

$$((P \text{ XOR } Q) \text{ XOR } R) \text{ OR } (\overline{P} \text{ AND } S) \tag{3.31}$$

we might use new variables X_1, X_2 O and A corresponding to the operator occurrences as follows:

$$((P \underbrace{\text{ XOR }}_{X_1} Q) \underbrace{\text{ XOR }}_{X_2} R) \underbrace{\text{ OR }}_{O} (\overline{P} \underbrace{\text{ AND }}_{A} S).$$

Next we write a formula that constrains each new variable to have the same truth value as the subformula determined by its corresponding operator. For the example above, these constraining formulas would be

$$X_1 \text{ IFF } (P \text{ XOR } Q),$$
$$X_2 \text{ IFF } (X_1 \text{ XOR } R),$$
$$A \text{ IFF } (\overline{P} \text{ AND } S),$$
$$O \text{ IFF } (X_2 \text{ OR } A)$$

(a) Explain why the AND of the four constraining formulas above along with a fifth formula consisting of just the variable O will be satisfiable iff (3.31) is satisfiable.

(b) Explain why each constraining formula will be equivalent to a 3CF formula with at most 24 occurrences of variables.

(c) Using the ideas illustrated in the previous parts, explain how to construct $C(F)$ for an arbitrary propositional formula F.

Problems for Section 3.6

Practice Problems

Problem 3.23.
For each of the following propositions:

    1. $\forall x \, \exists y. \, 2x - y = 0$

    2. $\forall x \, \exists y. \, x - 2y = 0$

    3. $\forall x. \, x < 10$ IMPLIES $(\forall y. \, y < x$ IMPLIES $y < 9)$

    4. $\forall x \, \exists y. \, [y > x \wedge \exists z. \, y + z = 100]$

determine which propositions are true when the variables range over:

 (a) the nonnegative integers.

 (b) the integers.

 (c) the real numbers.

Problem 3.24.
Let $Q(x, y)$ be the statement

"x has been a contestant on television show y."

The universe of discourse for x is the set of all students at your school and for y is the set of all quiz shows that have ever been on television.

    Determine whether or not each of the following expressions is logically equivalent to the sentence:

"No student at your school has ever been a contestant on a television quiz show."

 (a) $\forall x \, \forall y. \, \text{NOT}(Q(x, y))$

 (b) $\exists x \, \exists y. \, \text{NOT}(Q(x, y))$

 (c) $\text{NOT}(\forall x \, \forall y. \, Q(x, y))$

 (d) $\text{NOT}(\exists x \, \exists y. \, Q(x, y))$

Problem 3.25.

Find a counter-model showing the following is not valid.

$$\exists x.P(x) \text{ IMPLIES } \forall x.P(x)$$

(Just define your counter-model. You do not need to verify that it is correct.)

Problem 3.26.

Find a counter-model showing the following is not valid.

$$[\exists x.\, P(x) \text{ AND } \exists x.Q(x)] \text{ IMPLIES } \exists x.[P(x) \text{ AND } Q(x)]$$

(Just define your counter-model. You do not need to verify that it is correct.)

Problem 3.27.

Which of the following are *valid*? For those that are not valid, desribe a counter-model.

(a) $\exists x \exists y.\ P(x, y)$ IMPLIES $\exists y \exists x.\ P(x, y)$

(b) $\forall x \exists y.\ Q(x, y)$ IMPLIES $\exists y \forall x.\ Q(x, y)$

(c) $\exists x \forall y.\ R(x, y)$ IMPLIES $\forall y \exists x.\ R(x, y)$

(d) NOT$(\exists x\ S(x))$ IFF $\forall x$ NOT$(S(x))$

Problem 3.28. (a) Verify that the propositional formula

$$(P \text{ IMPLIES } Q) \text{ OR } (Q \text{ IMPLIES } P)$$

is valid.

(b) The valid formula of part (a) leads to sound proof method: to prove that an implication is true, just prove that its converse is false.[5] For example, from elementary calculus we know that the assertion

If a function is continuous, then it is differentiable

is false. This allows us to reach at the correct conclusion that its converse,

---

[5]This problem was stimulated by the discussion of the fallacy in [3].

If a function is differentiable, then it is continuous

is true, as indeed it is.

But wait a minute! The implication

If a function is differentiable, then it is not continuous

is completely false. So we could conclude that its converse

If a function is not continuous, then it is differentiable,

should be true, but in fact the converse is also completely false.

So something has gone wrong here. Explain what.

Class Problems

Problem 3.29.

A media tycoon has an idea for an all-news television network called LNN: The Logic News Network. Each segment will begin with a definition of the domain of discourse and a few predicates. The day's happenings can then be communicated concisely in logic notation. For example, a broadcast might begin as follows:

THIS IS LNN. The domain of discourse is

{Albert, Ben, Claire, David, Emily}.

Let $D(x)$ be a predicate that is true if x is deceitful. Let $L(x, y)$ be a predicate that is true if x likes y. Let $G(x, y)$ be a predicate that is true if x gave gifts to y.

Translate the following broadcasts in logic notation into (English) statements.

(a)

$$\text{NOT}(D(\text{Ben}) \text{ OR } D(\text{David})) \text{ IMPLIES}$$
$$(L(\text{Albert}, \text{Ben}) \text{ AND } L(\text{Ben}, \text{Albert})).$$

(b)

$\forall x.\ ((x = \text{Claire AND NOT}(L(x, \text{Emily}))) \text{ OR } (x \neq \text{Claire AND } L(x, \text{Emily})))$

AND

$\forall x.\ ((x = \text{David AND } L(x, \text{Claire})) \text{ OR } (x \neq \text{David AND NOT}(L(x, \text{Claire}))))$

(c)

$$\text{NOT}(D(\text{Claire})) \text{ IMPLIES } (G(\text{Albert, Ben}) \text{ AND } \exists x. \, G(\text{Ben}, x))$$

(d)

$$\forall x \exists y \exists z \, (y \neq z) \text{ AND } L(x, y) \text{ AND } \text{NOT}(L(x, z)).$$

(e) How could you express "Everyone except for Claire likes Emily" using just propositional connectives *without* using any quantifiers ($\forall, \exists$)? Can you generalize to explain how *any* logical formula over this domain of discourse can be expressed without quantifiers? How big would the formula in the previous part be if it was expressed this way?

Problem 3.30.

The goal of this problem is to translate some assertions about binary strings into logic notation. The domain of discourse is the set of all finite-length binary strings: λ, 0, 1, 00, 01, 10, 11, 000, 001, ... (Here λ denotes the empty string.) In your translations, you may use all the ordinary logic symbols (including =), variables, and the binary symbols 0, 1 denoting 0, 1.

A string like $01x0y$ of binary symbols and variables denotes the *concatenation* of the symbols and the binary strings represented by the variables. For example, if the value of x is 011 and the value of y is 1111, then the value of $01x0y$ is the binary string 0101101111.

Here are some examples of formulas and their English translations. Names for these predicates are listed in the third column so that you can reuse them in your solutions (as we do in the definition of the predicate NO-1S below).

Meaning	Formula	Name
x is a prefix of y	$\exists z \, (xz = y)$	PREFIX(x, y)
x is a substring of y	$\exists u \exists v \, (uxv = y)$	SUBSTRING(x, y)
x is empty or a string of 0's	NOT(SUBSTRING$(1, x)$)	NO-1S(x)

(a) x consists of three copies of some string.

(b) x is an even-length string of 0's.

(c) x does not contain both a 0 and a 1.

(d) x is the binary representation of $2^k + 1$ for some integer $k \geq 0$.

(e) An elegant, slightly trickier way to define NO-1S(x) is:

$$\text{PREFIX}(x, 0x). \qquad\qquad (*)$$

Explain why $(*)$ is true only when x is a string of 0's.

Problem 3.31.

For each of the logical formulas, indicate whether or not it is true when the domain of discourse is $\mathbb{N}$, (the nonnegative integers 0, 1, 2, ...), $\mathbb{Z}$ (the integers), $\mathbb{Q}$ (the rationals), $\mathbb{R}$ (the real numbers), and $\mathbb{C}$ (the complex numbers). Add a brief explanation to the few cases that merit one.

$$\exists x.\, x^2 = 2$$
$$\forall x. \exists y.\, x^2 = y$$
$$\forall y. \exists x.\, x^2 = y$$
$$\forall x \neq 0. \exists y.\, xy = 1$$
$$\exists x. \exists y.\, x + 2y = 2 \text{ AND } 2x + 4y = 5$$

Problem 3.32.
Show that

$$(\forall x \exists y.\, P(x, y)) \longrightarrow \forall z.\, P(z, z)$$

is not valid by describing a counter-model.

Homework Problems

Problem 3.33.
Express each of the following predicates and propositions in formal logic notation. The domain of discourse is the nonnegative integers, $\mathbb{N}$. Moreover, in addition to the propositional operators, variables and quantifiers, you may define predicates using addition, multiplication, and equality symbols, and nonnegative integer *constants* $(0, 1, ...)$, but no *exponentiation* (like x^y). For example, the predicate "n is an even number" could be defined by either of the following formulas:

$$\exists m.\, (2m = n), \qquad \exists m.\, (m + m = n).$$

(a) m is a divisor of n.

(b) *n* is a prime number.

(c) *n* is a power of a prime.

Problem 3.34.
Translate the following sentence into a predicate formula:

> There is a student who has e-mailed at most two other people in the class, besides possibly himself.

The domain of discourse should be the set of students in the class; in addition, the only predicates that you may use are

- equality, and
- $E(x, y)$, meaning that "*x* has sent e-mail to *y*."

Problem 3.35. (a) Translate the following sentence into a predicate formula:

> There is a student who has e-mailed at most *n* other people in the class, besides possibly himself.

The domain of discourse should be the set of students in the class; in addition, the only predicates that you may use are

- equality,
- $E(x, y)$, meaning that "*x* has sent e-mail to *y*."

(b) Explain how you would use your predicate formula (or some variant of it) to express the following two sentences.

1. There is a student who has emailed at least *n* other people in the class, besides possibly himself.
2. There is a student who has emailed exactly *n* other people in the class, besides possibly himself.

Exam Problems

Problem 3.36.
For each of the logic formulas below, indicate the smallest domain in which it is true, among

$\mathbb{N}$(nonnegative integers), $\mathbb{Z}$(integers), $\mathbb{Q}$(rationals), $\mathbb{R}$(reals), $\mathbb{C}$(complex numbers), or state "**none**" if it is not true in any of them.

i. $\forall x \exists y.\, y = 3x$

ii. $\forall x \exists y.\, 3y = x$

iii. $\forall x \exists y.\, y^2 = x$

iv. $\forall x \exists y.\, y < x$

v. $\forall x \exists y.\, y^3 = x$

vi. $\forall x \neq 0.\, \exists y, z.\, y \neq z \text{ AND } y^2 = x = z^2$

Problem 3.37.

The following predicate logic formula is invalid:

$$\forall x, \exists y.\, P(x, y) \longrightarrow \exists y, \forall x.\, P(x, y)$$

Which of the following are counter models for it?

1. The predicate $P(x, y) = \text{`}y \cdot x = 1\text{'}$ where the domain of discourse is $\mathbb{Q}$.

2. The predicate $P(x, y) = \text{`}y < x\text{'}$ where the domain of discourse is $\mathbb{R}$.

3. The predicate $P(x, y) = \text{`}y \cdot x = 2\text{'}$ where the domain of discourse is $\mathbb{R}$ without 0.

4. The predicate $P(x, y) = \text{`}yxy = x\text{'}$ where the domain of discourse is the set of all binary strings, including the empty string.

Problem 3.38.
Some students from a large class will be lined up left to right. There will be at least two students in the line. Translate each of the following assertions into predicate formulas with the set of students in the class as the domain of discourse. The only predicates you may use are

- equality and,

- $F(x, y)$, meaning that "x is somewhere to the left of y in the line." For example, in the line "CDA", both $F(C, A)$ and $F(C, D)$ are true.

Once you have defined a formula for a predicate P you may use the abbreviation "P" in further formulas.

(a) Student x is in the line.

(b) Student x is first in line.

(c) Student x is immediately to the right of student y.

(d) Student x is second.

Problem 3.39.

We want to find predicate formulas about the nonnegative integers $\mathbb{N}$ in which $\leq$ is the only predicate that appears, and no constants appear.

For example, there is such a formula defining the equality predicate:

$$[x = y] ::= [x \leq y \text{ AND } y \leq x].$$

Once predicate is shown to be expressible solely in terms of $\leq$, it may then be used in subsequent translations. For example,

$$[x > 0] ::= \exists y. \text{ NOT}(x = y) \text{ AND } y \leq x.$$

(a) $[x = 0]$.

(b) $[x = y + 1]$.

Hint: If an integer is bigger than y, then it must be $\geq x$.

(c) $x = 3$.

Problem 3.40.

Predicate Formulas whose only predicate symbol is equality are called "pure equality" formulas. For example,

$$\forall x \, \forall y. \, x = y \qquad \qquad \text{(1-element)}$$

is a pure equality formula. Its meaning is that there is exactly one element in the domain of discourse.[6] Another such formula is

$$\exists a \, \exists b \, \forall x. \, x = a \text{ OR } x = b. \qquad \qquad (\leq \text{2-elements})$$

---

[6]Remember, a domain of discourse is not allowed to be empty.

Its meaning is that there are at most two elements in the domain of discourse.

A formula that is not a pure equality formula is

$$x \leq y. \qquad \textbf{(not-pure)}$$

Formula (**not**-pure) uses the less-than-or-equal predicate $\leq$ which is *not* allowed.[7]

(a) Describe a pure equality formula that means that there are *exactly* two elements in the domain of discourse.

(b) Describe a pure equality formula that means that there are *exactly* three elements in the domain of discourse.

---

[7]In fact, formula (**not**-pure) only makes sense when the domain elements are ordered, while pure equality formulas make sense over every domain.

4 Mathematical Data Types

We have assumed that you've already been introduced to the concepts of sets, sequences, and functions, and we've used them informally several times in previous sections. In this chapter, we'll now take a more careful look at these mathematical data types. We'll quickly review the basic definitions, add a few more such as "images" and "inverse images" that may not be familiar, and end the chapter with some methods for comparing the sizes of sets.

4.1 Sets

Informally, a *set* is a bunch of objects, which are called the *elements* of the set. The elements of a set can be just about anything: numbers, points in space, or even other sets. The conventional way to write down a set is to list the elements inside curly-braces. For example, here are some sets:

$$A = \{\text{Alex, Tippy, Shells, Shadow}\} \qquad \text{dead pets}$$
$$B = \{\text{red, blue, yellow}\} \qquad \text{primary colors}$$
$$C = \{\{a, b\}, \{a, c\}, \{b, c\}\} \qquad \text{a set of sets}$$

This works fine for small finite sets. Other sets might be defined by indicating how to generate a list of them:

$$D ::= \{1, 2, 4, 8, 16, \ldots\} \qquad \text{the powers of 2}$$

The order of elements is not significant, so $\{x, y\}$ and $\{y, x\}$ are the same set written two different ways. Also, any object is, or is not, an element of a given set—there is no notion of an element appearing more than once in a set.[1] So, writing $\{x, x\}$ is just indicating the same thing twice: that x is in the set. In particular, $\{x, x\} = \{x\}$.

The expression "$e \in S$" asserts that e is an element of set S. For example, $32 \in D$ and blue $\in B$, but Tailspin $\notin A$—yet.

Sets are simple, flexible, and everywhere. You'll find some set mentioned in nearly every section of this text.

---

[1] It's not hard to develop a notion of *multisets* in which elements can occur more than once, but multisets are not ordinary sets and are not covered in this text.

4.1.1 Some Popular Sets

Mathematicians have devised special symbols to represent some common sets.

symbol	set	elements
$\emptyset$	the empty set	none
$\mathbb{N}$	nonnegative integers	$\{0, 1, 2, 3, \ldots\}$
$\mathbb{Z}$	integers	$\{\ldots, -3, -2, -1, 0, 1, 2, 3, \ldots\}$
$\mathbb{Q}$	rational numbers	$\frac{1}{2}$, $-\frac{5}{3}$, 16, etc.
$\mathbb{R}$	real numbers	π, e, -9, $\sqrt{2}$, etc.
$\mathbb{C}$	complex numbers	i, $\frac{19}{2}$, $\sqrt{2} - 2i$, etc.

A superscript "$+$" restricts a set to its positive elements; for example, $\mathbb{R}^+$ denotes the set of positive real numbers. Similarly, $\mathbb{Z}^-$ denotes the set of negative integers.

4.1.2 Comparing and Combining Sets

The expression $S \subseteq T$ indicates that set S is a *subset* of set T, which means that every element of S is also an element of T. For example, $\mathbb{N} \subseteq \mathbb{Z}$ because every nonnegative integer is an integer; $\mathbb{Q} \subseteq \mathbb{R}$ because every rational number is a real number, but $\mathbb{C} \not\subseteq \mathbb{R}$ because not every complex number is a real number.

As a memory trick, think of the "$\subseteq$" symbol as like the "$\leq$" sign with the smaller set or number on the left-hand side. Notice that just as $n \leq n$ for any number n, also $S \subseteq S$ for any set S.

There is also a relation $\subset$ on sets like the "less than" relation $<$ on numbers. $S \subset T$ means that S is a subset of T, but the two are *not* equal. So just as $n \not< n$ for every number n, also $A \not\subset A$, for every set A. "$S \subset T$" is read as "S is a *strict subset* of T."

There are several basic ways to combine sets. For example, suppose

$$X ::= \{1, 2, 3\},$$
$$Y ::= \{2, 3, 4\}.$$

Definition 4.1.1.

- The *union* of sets A and B, denoted $A \cup B$, includes exactly the elements appearing in A or B or both. That is,

$$x \in A \cup B \quad \text{IFF} \quad x \in A \text{ OR } x \in B.$$

So $X \cup Y = \{1, 2, 3, 4\}$.

- The *intersection* of A and B, denoted $A \cap B$, consists of all elements that appear in *both* A and B. That is,

$$x \in A \cap B \quad \text{IFF} \quad x \in A \text{ AND } x \in B.$$

So, $X \cap Y = \{2, 3\}$.

- The *set difference* of A and B, denoted $A - B$, consists of all elements that are in A, but not in B. That is,

$$x \in A - B \quad \text{IFF} \quad x \in A \text{ AND } x \notin B.$$

So, $X - Y = \{1\}$ and $Y - X = \{4\}$.

Often all the sets being considered are subsets of a known domain of discourse D. Then for any subset A of D, we define $\overline{A}$ to be the set of all elements of D *not* in A. That is,

$$\overline{A} ::= D - A.$$

The set $\overline{A}$ is called the *complement* of A. So

$$\overline{A} = \emptyset \quad \text{IFF} \quad A = D.$$

For example, if the domain we're working with is the integers, the complement of the nonnegative integers is the set of negative integers:

$$\overline{\mathbb{N}} = \mathbb{Z}^-.$$

We can use complement to rephrase subset in terms of equality

$$A \subseteq B \text{ is equivalent to } A \cap \overline{B} = \emptyset.$$

4.1.3 Power Set

The set of all the subsets of a set A is called the *power set* pow(A) of A. So

$$B \in \text{pow}(A) \quad \text{IFF} \quad B \subseteq A.$$

For example, the elements of pow($\{1, 2\}$) are $\emptyset, \{1\}, \{2\}$ and $\{1, 2\}$.

More generally, if A has n elements, then there are 2^n sets in pow(A)—see Theorem 4.5.5. For this reason, some authors use the notation 2^A instead of pow(A).

4.1.4   Set Builder Notation

An important use of predicates is in *set builder notation*. We'll often want to talk about sets that cannot be described very well by listing the elements explicitly or by taking unions, intersections, etc., of easily described sets. Set builder notation often comes to the rescue. The idea is to define a *set* using a *predicate*; in particular, the set consists of all values that make the predicate true. Here are some examples of set builder notation:

$$A ::= \{n \in \mathbb{N} \mid n \text{ is a prime and } n = 4k + 1 \text{ for some integer } k\},$$
$$B ::= \{x \in \mathbb{R} \mid x^3 - 3x + 1 > 0\},$$
$$C ::= \{a + bi \in \mathbb{C} \mid a^2 + 2b^2 \le 1\},$$
$$D ::= \{L \in \text{books} \mid L \text{ is cited in this text}\}.$$

The set A consists of all nonnegative integers n for which the predicate

"n is a prime and $n = 4k + 1$ for some integer k"

is true. Thus, the smallest elements of A are:

$$5, 13, 17, 29, 37, 41, 53, 61, 73, \ldots.$$

Trying to indicate the set A by listing these first few elements wouldn't work very well; even after ten terms, the pattern is not obvious. Similarly, the set B consists of all real numbers x for which the predicate

$$x^3 - 3x + 1 > 0$$

is true. In this case, an explicit description of the set B in terms of intervals would require solving a cubic equation. Set C consists of all complex numbers $a + bi$ such that:

$$a^2 + 2b^2 \le 1$$

This is an oval-shaped region around the origin in the complex plane. Finally, the members of set D can be determined by filtering out journal articles in from the list of references in the Bibliography 22.5.

4.1.5   Proving Set Equalities

Two sets are defined to be equal if they have exactly the same elements. That is, $X = Y$ means that $z \in X$ if and only if $z \in Y$, for all elements z.[2] So, set equalities can be formulated and proved as "iff" theorems. For example:

---

[2]This is actually the first of the ZFC axioms for set theory mentioned at the end of Section 1.3 and discussed further in Section 8.3.2.

Theorem 4.1.2. *[Distributive Law for Sets] Let A, B and C be sets. Then:*

$$A \cap (B \cup C) = (A \cap B) \cup (A \cap C) \tag{4.1}$$

Proof. The equality (4.1) is equivalent to the assertion that

$$z \in A \cap (B \cup C) \quad \text{iff} \quad z \in (A \cap B) \cup (A \cap C) \tag{4.2}$$

for all z. Now we'll prove (4.2) by a chain of iff's.
  Now we have

$z \in A \cap (B \cup C)$

iff	$(z \in A)$ AND $(z \in B \cup C)$	(def of $\cap$)
iff	$(z \in A)$ AND $(z \in B$ OR $z \in C)$	(def of $\cup$)
iff	$(z \in A$ AND $z \in B)$ OR $(z \in A$ AND $z \in C)$	(AND distributivity (3.9))
iff	$(z \in A \cap B)$ OR $(z \in A \cap C)$	(def of $\cap$)
iff	$z \in (A \cap B) \cup (A \cap C)$	(def of $\cup$)

∎

The proof of Theorem 4.1.2 illustrates a general method for proving a set equality involving the basic set operations by checking that a corresponding propositional formula is valid. As a further example, from De Morgan's Law (3.14) for propositions

$$\text{NOT}(P \text{ AND } Q) \text{ is equivalent to } \overline{P} \text{ OR } \overline{Q}$$

we can derive (Problem 4.5) a corresponding De Morgan's Law for set equality:

$$\overline{A \cap B} = \overline{A} \cup \overline{B}. \tag{4.3}$$

Despite this correspondence between two kinds of operations, it's important not to confuse propositional operations with set operations. For example, if X and Y are sets, then it is wrong to write "X AND Y" instead of "$X \cap Y$." Applying AND to sets will cause your compiler—or your grader—to throw a type error, because an operation that is only supposed to be applied to truth values has been applied to sets. Likewise, if P and Q are propositions, then it is a type error to write "$P \cup Q$" instead of "P OR Q."

4.2   Sequences

Sets provide one way to group a collection of objects. Another way is in a *sequence*, which is a list of objects called its *components*, members, or elements. Short sequences are commonly described by listing the elements between parentheses; for example, the sequence (a, b, c) has three components. It would also be referred to as a three element sequence or a sequence of length three. These phrases are all synonyms—sequences are so basic that they appear everywhere and there are a lot of ways to talk about them.

While both sets and sequences perform a gathering role, there are several differences.

- The elements of a set are required to be distinct, but elements in a sequence can be the same. Thus, (a, b, a) is a valid sequence of length three, but $\{a, b, a\}$ is a set with two elements, not three.

- The elements in a sequence have a specified order, but the elements of a set do not. For example, (a, b, c) and (a, c, b) are different sequences, but $\{a, b, c\}$ and $\{a, c, b\}$ are the same set.

- Texts differ on notation for the *empty sequence*; we use λ for the empty sequence.

The product operation is one link between sets and sequences. A *Cartesian product* of sets, $S_1 \times S_2 \times \cdots \times S_n$, is a new set consisting of all sequences where the first component is drawn from S_1, the second from S_2, and so forth. Length two sequences are called *pairs*.[3] For example, $\mathbb{N} \times \{a, b\}$ is the set of all pairs whose first element is a nonnegative integer and whose second element is an a or a b:

$$\mathbb{N} \times \{a, b\} = \{(0, a), (0, b), (1, a), (1, b), (2, a), (2, b), \ldots\}$$

A product of n copies of a set S is denoted S^n. For example, $\{0, 1\}^3$ is the set of all 3-bit sequences:

$$\{0, 1\}^3 = \{(0, 0, 0), (0, 0, 1), (0, 1, 0), (0, 1, 1), (1, 0, 0), (1, 0, 1), (1, 1, 0), (1, 1, 1)\}$$

---

[3] Some texts call them *ordered pairs*.

4.3 Functions

4.3.1 Domains and Images

A *function* assigns an element of one set, called the *domain*, to an element of another set, called the *codomain*. The notation

$$f : A \rightarrow B$$

indicates that f is a function with domain A and codomain B. The familiar notation "$f(a) = b$" indicates that f assigns the element $b \in B$ to a. Here b would be called the *value* of f at *argument a*.

Functions are often defined by formulas, as in:

$$f_1(x) ::= \frac{1}{x^2}$$

where x is a real-valued variable, or

$$f_2(y, z) ::= y10yz$$

where y and z range over binary strings, or

$$f_3(x, n) ::= \text{ the length } n \text{ sequence } \underbrace{(x, \ldots, x)}_{n \ x\text{'s}}$$

where n ranges over the nonnegative integers.

A function with a finite domain could be specified by a table that shows the value of the function at each element of the domain. For example, a function $f_4(P, Q)$ where P and Q are propositional variables is specified by:

P	Q	$f_4(P, Q)$
T	T	T
T	F	F
F	T	T
F	F	T

Notice that f_4 could also have been described by a formula:

$$f_4(P, Q) ::= [P \text{ IMPLIES } Q].$$

A function might also be defined by a procedure for computing its value at any element of its domain, or by some other kind of specification. For example, define

$f_5(y)$ to be the length of a left to right search of the bits in the binary string y until a 1 appears, so

$$
\begin{aligned}
f_5(0010) &= 3, \\
f_5(100) &= 1, \\
f_5(0000) &\quad \text{is} \quad \text{undefined.}
\end{aligned}
$$

Notice that f_5 does not assign a value to any string of just 0's. This illustrates an important fact about functions: they need not assign a value to every element in the domain. In fact this came up in our first example $f_1(x) = 1/x^2$, which does not assign a value to 0. So in general, functions may be *partial functions*, meaning that there may be domain elements for which the function is not defined. If a function is defined on every element of its domain, it is called a *total function*.

It's often useful to find the set of values a function takes when applied to the elements in *a set* of arguments. So if $f : A \to B$, and S is a subset of A, we define $f(S)$ to be the set of all the values that f takes when it is applied to elements of S. That is,

$$
f(S) ::= \{b \in B \mid f(s) = b \text{ for some } s \in S\}.
$$

For example, if we let $[r, s]$ denote set of numbers in the interval from r to s on the real line, then $f_1([1, 2]) = [1/4, 1]$.

For another example, let's take the "search for a 1" function f_5. If we let X be the set of binary words which start with an even number of 0's followed by a 1, then $f_5(X)$ would be the odd nonnegative integers.

Applying f to a set S of arguments is referred to as "applying f *pointwise* to S", and the set $f(S)$ is referred to as the *image* of S under f.[4] The set of values that arise from applying f to all possible arguments is called the *range* of f. That is,

$$
\text{range}(f) ::= f(\text{domain}(f)).
$$

Some authors refer to the codomain as the range of a function, but they shouldn't. The distinction between the range and codomain will be important later in Sections 4.5 when we relate sizes of sets to properties of functions between them.

4.3.2   Function Composition

Doing things step by step is a universal idea. Taking a walk is a literal example, but so is cooking from a recipe, executing a computer program, evaluating a formula, and recovering from substance abuse.

---

[4]There is a picky distinction between the function f which applies to elements of A and the function which applies f pointwise to subsets of A, because the domain of f is A, while the domain of pointwise-f is $\text{pow}(A)$. It is usually clear from context whether f or pointwise-f is meant, so there is no harm in overloading the symbol f in this way.

Abstractly, taking a step amounts to applying a function, and going step by step corresponds to applying functions one after the other. This is captured by the operation of *composing* functions. Composing the functions f and g means that first f is applied to some argument, x, to produce $f(x)$, and then g is applied to that result to produce $g(f(x))$.

Definition 4.3.1. For functions $f : A \rightarrow B$ and $g : B \rightarrow C$, the *composition*, $g \circ f$, of g with f is defined to be the function from A to C defined by the rule:

$$(g \circ f)(x) ::= g(f(x)),$$

for all $x \in A$.

Function composition is familiar as a basic concept from elementary calculus, and it plays an equally basic role in discrete mathematics.

4.4 Binary Relations

Binary relations define relations between two objects. For example, "less-than" on the real numbers relates every real number a to a real number b, precisely when $a < b$. Similarly, the subset relation relates a set A to another set B precisely when $A \subseteq B$. A function $f : A \rightarrow B$ is a special case of binary relation in which an element $a \in A$ is related to an element $b \in B$ precisely when $b = f(a)$.

In this section we'll define some basic vocabulary and properties of binary relations.

Definition 4.4.1. A *binary relation* R consists of a set A, called the *domain* of R, a set B called the *codomain* of R, and a subset of $A \times B$ called the *graph of R*.

A relation whose domain is A and codomain is B is said to be "between A and B", or "from A to B." As with functions, we write $R : A \rightarrow B$ to indicate that R is a relation from A to B. When the domain and codomain are the same set A we simply say the relation is "on A." It's common to use "$a \ R \ b$" to mean that the pair (a, b) is in the graph of R.[5]

Notice that Definition 4.4.1 is exactly the same as the definition in Section 4.3 of a *function*, except that it doesn't require the functional condition that, for each

---

[5]Writing the relation or operator symbol between its arguments is called *infix notation*. Infix expressions like "$m < n$" or "$m + n$" are the usual notation used for things like the less-then relation or the addition operation rather than prefix notation like "$< (m, n)$" or "$+(m, n)$."

domain element a, there is *at most* one pair in the graph whose first coordinate is a. As we said, a function is a special case of a binary relation.

The "in-charge of" relation *Chrg* for MIT in Spring '10 subjects and instructors is a handy example of a binary relation. Its domain Fac is the names of all the MIT faculty and instructional staff, and its codomain is the set SubNums of subject numbers in the Fall '09–Spring '10 MIT subject listing. The graph of *Chrg* contains precisely the pairs of the form

$$(\langle\text{instructor-name}\rangle , \langle\text{subject-num}\rangle)$$

such that the faculty member named ⟨instructor-name⟩ is in charge of the subject with number ⟨subject-num⟩ that was offered in Spring '10. So graph(*Chrg*) contains pairs like

```
(T. Eng,        6.UAT)
(G. Freeman,    6.011)
(G. Freeman,    6.UAT)
(G. Freeman,    6.881)
(G. Freeman,    6.882)
(J. Guttag,     6.00)
(A. R. Meyer,   6.042)                        (4.4)
(A. R. Meyer,   18.062)
(A. R. Meyer,   6.844)
(T. Leighton,   6.042)
(T. Leighton,   18.062)
                  ⋮
```

Some subjects in the codomain SubNums do not appear among this list of pairs— that is, they are not in range(*Chrg*). These are the Fall term-only subjects. Similarly, there are instructors in the domain Fac who do not appear in the list because they are not in charge of any Spring term subjects.

4.4.1   Relation Diagrams

Some standard properties of a relation can be visualized in terms of a diagram. The diagram for a binary relation R has points corresponding to the elements of the domain appearing in one column (a very long column if domain(R) is infinite). All the elements of the codomain appear in another column which we'll usually picture as being to the right of the domain column. There is an arrow going from a point a in the left-hand, domain column to a point b in the right-hand, codomain column, precisely when the corresponding elements are related by R. For example, here are diagrams for two functions:

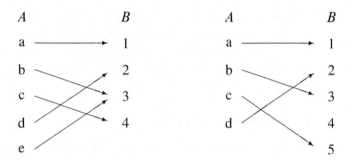

Being a function is certainly an important property of a binary relation. What it means is that every point in the domain column has *at most one arrow coming out of it*. So we can describe being a function as the "≤ 1 arrow out" property. There are four more standard properties of relations that come up all the time. Here are all five properties defined in terms of arrows:

Definition 4.4.2. A binary relation R is:

- a *function* when it has the [≤ 1 arrow **out**] property.

- *surjective* when it has the [≥ 1 arrows **in**] property. That is, every point in the right-hand, codomain column has at least one arrow pointing to it.

- *total* when it has the [≥ 1 arrows **out**] property.

- *injective* when it has the [≤ 1 arrow **in**] property.

- *bijective* when it has both the [= 1 arrow **out**] and the [= 1 arrow **in**] property.

From here on, we'll stop mentioning the arrows in these properties and for example, just write [≤ 1 in] instead of [≤ 1 arrows in].

So in the diagrams above, the relation on the left has the [= 1 out] and [≥ 1 in] properties, which means it is a total, surjective function. But it does not have the [≤ 1 in] property because element 3 has two arrows going into it; it is not injective.

The relation on the right has the [= 1 out] and [≤ 1 in] properties, which means it is a total, injective function. But it does not have the [≥ 1 in] property because element 4 has no arrow going into it; it is not surjective.

The arrows in a diagram for R correspond, of course, exactly to the pairs in the graph of R. Notice that the arrows alone are not enough to determine, for example, if R has the [≥ 1 out], total, property. If all we knew were the arrows, we wouldn't know about any points in the domain column that had no arrows out. In other words, graph(R) alone does not determine whether R is total: we also need to know what domain(R) is.

Example 4.4.3. The function defined by the formula $1/x^2$ has the [≥ 1 out] property if its domain is $\mathbb{R}^+$, but not if its domain is some set of real numbers including 0. It has the [$= 1$ in] and [$= 1$ out] property if its domain and codomain are both $\mathbb{R}^+$, but it has neither the [≤ 1 in] nor the [≥ 1 out] property if its domain and codomain are both $\mathbb{R}$.

4.4.2   Relational Images

The idea of the image of a set under a function extends directly to relations.

Definition 4.4.4. The *image* of a set Y under a relation R written $R(Y)$, is the set of elements of the codomain B of R that are related to some element in Y. In terms of the relation diagram, $R(Y)$ is the set of points with an arrow coming in that starts from some point in Y.

For example, the set of subject numbers that Meyer is in charge of in Spring '10 is exactly *Chrg*(A. Meyer). To figure out what this is, we look for all the arrows in the *Chrg* diagram that start at "A. Meyer," and see which subject-numbers are at the other end of these arrows. Looking at the list (4.4) of pairs in graph(*Chrg*), we see that these subject-numbers are {6.042, 18.062, 6.844}. Similarly, to find the subject numbers that either Freeman or Eng are in charge of, we can collect all the arrows that start at either "G. Freeman," or "T. Eng" and, again, see which subject-numbers are at the other end of these arrows. This is *Chrg*({G. Freeman, T. Eng}). Looking again at the list (4.4), we see that

$$Chrg(\{\text{G. Freeman, T. Eng}\}) = \{6.011, 6.881, 6.882, 6.\text{UAT}\}$$

Finally, Fac is the set of all in-charge instructors, so *Chrg*(Fac) is the set of all the subjects listed for Spring '10.

Inverse Relations and Images

Definition 4.4.5. The *inverse*, R^{-1} of a relation $R : A \to B$ is the relation from B to A defined by the rule

$$b \; R^{-1} \; a \quad \text{IFF} \quad a \; R \; b.$$

In other words, R^{-1} is the relation you get by reversing the direction of the arrows in the diagram of R.

Definition 4.4.6. The image of a set under the relation R^{-1} is called the *inverse image* of the set. That is, the inverse image of a set X under the relation R is defined to be $R^{-1}(X)$.

Continuing with the in-charge example above, the set of instructors in charge of 6.UAT in Spring '10 is exactly the inverse image of {6.UAT} under the *Chrg* relation. From the list (4.4), we see that Eng and Freeman are both in charge of 6.UAT, that is,

$$\{\text{T. Eng, D. Freeman}\} \subseteq Chrg^{-1}(\{6.\text{UAT}\}).$$

We can't assert equality here because there may be additional pairs further down the list showing that additional instructors are co-incharge of 6.UAT.

Now let Intro be the set of introductory course 6 subject numbers. These are the subject numbers that start with "6.0." So the set of names of the instructors who were in-charge of introductory course 6 subjects in Spring '10, is $Chrg^{-1}(\text{Intro})$. From the part of the *Chrg* list shown in (4.4), we see that Meyer, Leighton, Freeman, and Guttag were among the instructors in charge of introductory subjects in Spring '10. That is,

$$\{\text{Meyer, Leighton, Freeman, Guttag}\} \subseteq Chrg^{-1}(\text{Intro}).$$

Finally, $Chrg^{-1}(\text{SubNums})$ is the set of all instructors who were in charge of a subject listed for Spring '10.

4.5   Finite Cardinality

A finite set is one that has only a finite number of elements. This number of elements is the "size" or *cardinality* of the set:

Definition 4.5.1. If A is a finite set, the *cardinality* $|A|$ of A is the number of elements in A.

A finite set may have no elements (the empty set), or one element, or two elements,..., so the cardinality of finite sets is always a nonnegative integer.

Now suppose $R : A \rightarrow B$ is a function. This means that every element of A contributes at most one arrow to the diagram for R, so the number of arrows is at most the number of elements in A. That is, if R is a function, then

$$|A| \geq \#\text{arrows}.$$

If R is also surjective, then every element of B has an arrow into it, so there must be at least as many arrows in the diagram as the size of B. That is,

$$\#\text{arrows} \geq |B|.$$

Combining these inequalities implies that if R is a surjective function, then $|A| \geq |B|$.

In short, if we write A surj B to mean that there is a surjective function from A to B, then we've just proved a lemma: if A surj B for finite sets A, B, then $|A| \geq |B|$. The following definition and lemma lists this statement and three similar rules relating domain and codomain size to relational properties.

Definition 4.5.2. Let A, B be (not necessarily finite) sets. Then

1. A surj B iff there is a surjective *function* from A to B.

2. A inj B iff there is an injective *total* relation from A to B.

3. A bij B iff there is a bijection from A to B.

Lemma 4.5.3. *For finite sets A, B:*

1. If A surj B, then $|A| \geq |B|$.

2. If A inj B, then $|A| \leq |B|$.

3. If A bij B, then $|A| = |B|$.

Proof. We've already given an "arrow" proof of implication 1. Implication 2. follows immediately from the fact that if R has the $[\leq 1 \text{ out}]$, function property, and the $[\geq 1 \text{ in}]$, surjective property, then R^{-1} is total and injective, so A surj B iff B inj A. Finally, since a bijection is both a surjective function and a total injective relation, implication 3. is an immediate consequence of the first two. ∎

Lemma 4.5.3.1. has a converse: if the size of a finite set A is greater than or equal to the size of another finite set B then it's always possible to define a surjective function from A to B. In fact, the surjection can be a total function. To see how this works, suppose for example that

$$A = \{a_0, a_1, a_2, a_3, a_4, a_5\}$$
$$B = \{b_0, b_1, b_2, b_3\}.$$

Then define a total function $f : A \to B$ by the rules

$$f(a_0) ::= b_0, \ f(a_1) ::= b_1, \ f(a_2) ::= b_2, \ f(a_3) = f(a_4) = f(a_5) ::= b_3.$$

More concisely,

$$f(a_i) ::= b_{\min(i,3)},$$

for $0 \leq i \leq 5$. Since $5 \geq 3$, this f is a surjection.

So we have figured out that if A and B are finite sets, then $|A| \geq |B|$ *if and only if* A surj B. All told, this argument wraps up the proof of a theorem that summarizes the whole finite cardinality story:

Theorem 4.5.4. *[Mapping Rules]* *For* finite *sets* A, B,

$$|A| \geq |B| \quad \textit{iff} \quad A \text{ surj } B, \tag{4.5}$$

$$|A| \leq |B| \quad \textit{iff} \quad A \text{ inj } B, \tag{4.6}$$

$$|A| = |B| \quad \textit{iff} \quad A \text{ bij } B, \tag{4.7}$$

4.5.1 How Many Subsets of a Finite Set?

As an application of the bijection mapping rule (4.7), we can give an easy proof of:

Theorem 4.5.5. *There are* 2^n *subsets of an n-element set. That is,*

$$|A| = n \quad \textit{implies} \quad |\text{pow}(A)| = 2^n.$$

For example, the three-element set $\{a_1, a_2, a_3\}$ has eight different subsets:

$$\emptyset \qquad \{a_1\} \qquad \{a_2\} \qquad \{a_1, a_2\}$$
$$\{a_3\} \quad \{a_1, a_3\} \quad \{a_2, a_3\} \quad \{a_1, a_2, a_3\}$$

Theorem 4.5.5 follows from the fact that there is a simple bijection from subsets of A to $\{0, 1\}^n$, the n-bit sequences. Namely, let $a_1, a_2, \ldots, a_n$ be the elements of A. The bijection maps each subset of $S \subseteq A$ to the bit sequence $(b_1, \ldots, b_n)$ defined by the rule that

$$b_i = 1 \quad \text{iff} \quad a_i \in S.$$

For example, if $n = 10$, then the subset $\{a_2, a_3, a_5, a_7, a_{10}\}$ maps to a 10-bit sequence as follows:

subset:	{	a_2,	a_3,		a_5,		a_7,			a_{10}	}
sequence:	(	0,	1,	1,	0,	1,	0,	1,	0,	0,	1	)

Now by bijection case of the Mapping Rules 4.5.4.(4.7),

$$|\text{pow}(A)| = |\{0, 1\}^n|.$$

But every computer scientist knows[6] that there are 2^n n-bit sequences! So we've proved Theorem 4.5.5!

---

[6]In case you're someone who doesn't know how many n-bit sequences there are, you'll find the 2^n explained in Section 15.2.2.

Problems for Section 4.1

Practice Problems

Problem 4.1.
For any set A, let pow(A) be its *power set*, the set of all its subsets; note that A is itself a member of pow(A). Let $\emptyset$ denote the empty set.

(a) The elements of pow($\{1, 2\}$) are:

(b) The elements of pow($\{\emptyset, \{\emptyset\}\}$) are:

(c) How many elements are there in pow($\{1, 2, \ldots, 8\}$)?

Problem 4.2.
Express each of the following assertions about sets by a formula of set theory.[7] Expressions may use abbreviations introduced earlier (so it is now legal to use "=" because we just defined it).

(a) $x = \emptyset$.

(b) $x = \{y, z\}$.

(c) $x \subseteq y$. (x is a subset of y that might equal y.)

Now we can explain how to express "x is a proper subset of y" as a set theory formula using things we already know how to express. Namely, letting "$x \neq y$" abbreviate NOT($x = y$), the expression

$$(x \subseteq y \text{ AND } x \neq y),$$

describes a formula of set theory that means $x \subset y$.

From here on, feel free to use any previously expressed property in describing formulas for the following:

(d) $x = y \cup z$.

(e) $x = y - z$.

(f) $x = \text{pow}(y)$.

---

[7]See Section 8.3.2.

(g) $x = \bigcup_{z \in y} z.$

This means that y is supposed to be a collection of sets, and x is the union of all of them. A more concise notation for "$\bigcup_{z \in y} z$' is simply "$\bigcup y$."

Class Problems

Problem 4.3.
Set Formulas and Propositional Formulas.

(a) Verify that the propositional formula $(P \text{ AND } \overline{Q}) \text{ OR } (P \text{ AND } Q)$ is equivalent to P.

(b) Prove that

$$A = (A - B) \cup (A \cap B)$$

for all sets, A, B, by showing

$$x \in A \text{ IFF } x \in (A - B) \cup (A \cap B)$$

for all elements x using the equivalence of part (a) in a chain of IFF's.

Problem 4.4.
Prove

Theorem (Distributivity of union over intersection).

$$A \cup (B \cap C) = (A \cup B) \cap (A \cup C) \tag{4.8}$$

for all sets, A, B, C, by using a chain of iff's to show that

$$x \in A \cup (B \cap C) \text{ IFF } x \in (A \cup B) \cap (A \cup C)$$

for all elements x. You may assume the corresponding propositional equivalence 3.10.

Problem 4.5.
Prove De Morgan's Law for set equality

$$\overline{A \cap B} = \overline{A} \cup \overline{B}. \tag{4.9}$$

by showing with a chain of IFF's that $x \in$ the left-hand side of (4.9) iff $x \in$ the right-hand side. You may assume the propositional version (3.14) of De Morgan's Law.

Problem 4.6.

Powerset Properties.

Let A and B be sets.

(a) Prove that
$$\text{pow}(A \cap B) = \text{pow}(A) \cap \text{pow}(B).$$

(b) Prove that
$$(\text{pow}(A) \cup \text{pow}(B)) \subseteq \text{pow}(A \cup B),$$

with equality holding iff one of A or B is a subset of the other.

Problem 4.7.

Subset take-away[8] is a two player game played with a finite set A of numbers. Players alternately choose nonempty subsets of A with the conditions that a player may not choose

- the whole set A, or

- any set containing a set that was named earlier.

The first player who is unable to move loses the game.

For example, if the size of A is one, then there are no legal moves and the second player wins. If A has exactly two elements, then the only legal moves are the two one-element subsets of A. Each is a good reply to the other, and so once again the second player wins.

The first interesting case is when A has three elements. This time, if the first player picks a subset with one element, the second player picks the subset with the other two elements. If the first player picks a subset with two elements, the second player picks the subset whose sole member is the third element. In both cases, these moves lead to a situation that is the same as the start of a game on a set with two elements, and thus leads to a win for the second player.

Verify that when A has four elements, the second player still has a winning strategy.[9]

---

[8]From Christenson & Tilford, *David Gale's Subset Takeaway Game, American Mathematical Monthly, Oct. 1997*

[9]David Gale worked out some of the properties of this game and conjectured that the second player wins the game for any set A. This remains an open problem.

Homework Problems

Problem 4.8.
Let A, B and C be sets. Prove that

$$A \cup B \cup C = (A - B) \cup (B - C) \cup (C - A) \cup (A \cap B \cap C) \qquad (4.10)$$

using a chain of IFF's as Section 4.1.5.

Problem 4.9.
Union distributes over the intersection of two sets:

$$A \cup (B \cap C) = (A \cup B) \cap (A \cup C) \qquad (4.11)$$

(see Problem 4.4).

Use (4.11) and the Well Ordering Principle to prove the Distributive Law of union over the intersection of n sets:

$$A \cup (B_1 \cap \cdots \cap B_{n-1} \cap B_n)$$
$$= (A \cup B_1) \cap \cdots \cap (A \cup B_{n-1}) \cap (A \cup B_n) \qquad (4.12)$$

Extending formulas to an arbitrary number of terms is a common (if mundane) application of the WOP.

Exam Problems

Problem 4.10.
You've seen how certain set identities follow from corresponding propositional equivalences. For example, you proved by a chain of iff's that

$$(A - B) \cup (A \cap B) = A$$

using the fact that the propositional formula $(P \text{ AND } \overline{Q}) \text{ OR } (P \text{ AND } Q)$ is equivalent to P.

State a similar propositional equivalence that would justify the key step in a proof for the following set equality organized as a chain of iff's:

$$\overline{A - B} = \left(\overline{A} - \overline{C}\right) \cup (B \cap C) \cup \left(\left(\overline{A} \cup B\right) \cap \overline{C}\right) \qquad (4.13)$$

(You are *not* being asked to write out an iff-proof of the equality or to write out a proof of the propositional equivalence. Just state the equivalence.)

Problem 4.11.

You've seen how certain set identities follow from corresponding propositional equivalences. For example, you proved by a chain of iff's that

$$(A - B) \cup (A \cap B) = A$$

using the fact that the propositional formula $(P \text{ AND } \overline{Q}) \text{ OR } (P \text{ AND } Q)$ is equivalent to P.

State a similar propositional equivalence that would justify the key step in a proof for the following set equality organized as a chain of iff's:

$$\overline{A \cap B \cap C} = \overline{A} \cup (\overline{B} - \overline{A}) \cup \overline{C}.$$

(You are *not* being asked to write out an iff-proof of the equality or to write out a proof of the propositional equivalence. Just state the equivalence.)

Problem 4.12.

The set equation

$$\overline{A \cap B} = \overline{A} \cup \overline{B}$$

follows from a certain equivalence between propositional formulas.

(a) What is the equivalence?

(b) Show how to derive the equation from this equivalence.

Problems for Section 4.2

Homework Problems

Problem 4.13.

Prove that for any sets A, B, C and D, if the Cartesian products $A \times B$ and $C \times D$ are disjoint, then either A and C are disjoint or B and D are disjoint.

Problem 4.14. (a) Give a simple example where the following result fails, and briefly explain why:

False Theorem. *For sets A, B, C and D, let*

$$L ::= (A \cup B) \times (C \cup D),$$
$$R ::= (A \times C) \cup (B \times D).$$

Then $L = R$.

(b) Identify the mistake in the following proof of the False Theorem.

Bogus proof. Since L and R are both sets of pairs, it's sufficient to prove that $(x, y) \in L \longleftrightarrow (x, y) \in R$ for all x, y.

The proof will be a chain of iff implications:

$$
\begin{array}{ll}
& (x, y) \in R \\
\text{iff} & (x, y) \in (A \times C) \cup (B \times D) \\
\text{iff} & (x, y) \in A \times C, \text{ or } (x, y) \in B \times D \\
\text{iff} & (x \in A \text{ and } y \in C) \text{ or else } (x \in B \text{ and } y \in D) \\
\text{iff} & \text{either } x \in A \text{ or } x \in B, \text{ and either } y \in C \text{ or } y \in D \\
\text{iff} & x \in A \cup B \text{ and } y \in C \cup D \\
\text{iff} & (x, y) \in L.
\end{array}
$$

$\blacksquare$

(c) Fix the proof to show that $R \subseteq L$.

Problems for Section 4.4

Practice Problems

Problem 4.15.
The *inverse* R^{-1} of a binary relation R from A to B is the relation from B to A defined by:

$$b \, R^{-1} \, a \quad \text{iff} \quad a \, R \, b.$$

In other words, you get the diagram for R^{-1} from R by "reversing the arrows" in the diagram describing R. Now many of the relational properties of R correspond to different properties of R^{-1}. For example, R is *total* iff R^{-1} is a *surjection*.

Fill in the remaining entries is this table:

R is	iff R^{-1} is
total	a surjection
a function	
a surjection	
an injection	
a bijection	

Hint: Explain what's going on in terms of "arrows" from A to B in the diagram for R.

Problem 4.16.
Describe a total injective function [$= 1$ out], [≤ 1 in,] from $\mathbb{R} \rightarrow \mathbb{R}$ that is not a bijection.

Problem 4.17.
For a binary relation $R : A \rightarrow B$, some properties of R can be determined from just the arrows of R, that is, from graph(R), and others require knowing if there are elements in the domain A or the codomain B that don't show up in graph(R). For each of the following possible properties of R, indicate whether it is always determined by

1. graph(R) alone,

2. graph(R) and A alone,

3. graph(R) and B alone,

4. all three parts of R.

Properties:

(a) surjective

(b) injective

(c) total

(d) function

(e) bijection

Problem 4.18.
For each of the following real-valued functions on the real numbers, indicate whether it is a bijection, a surjection but not a bijection, an injection but not a bijection, or neither an injection nor a surjection.

(a) $x \rightarrow x + 2$

(b) $x \rightarrow 2x$

(c) $x \to x^2$

(d) $x \to x^3$

(e) $x \to \sin x$

(f) $x \to x \sin x$

(g) $x \to e^x$

Problem 4.19.
Let $f : A \to B$ and $g : B \to C$ be functions and $h : A \to C$ be their composition, namely, $h(a) ::= g(f(a))$ for all $a \in A$.
(a) Prove that if f and g are surjections, then so is h.

(b) Prove that if f and g are bijections, then so is h.

(c) If f is a bijection, then so is f^{-1}.

Problem 4.20.
Give an example of a relation R that is a total injective function from a set A to itself but is not a bijection.

Problem 4.21.
Let $R : A \to B$ be a binary relation. Each of the following formulas expresses the fact that R has a familiar relational "arrow" property such as being surjective or being a function.

Identify the relational property expressed by each of the following relational expressions. Explain your reasoning.

(a) $R \circ R^{-1} \subseteq \mathrm{Id}_B$

(b) $R^{-1} \circ R \subseteq \mathrm{Id}_A$

(c) $R^{-1} \circ R \supseteq \mathrm{Id}_A$

(d) $R \circ R^{-1} \supseteq \mathrm{Id}_B$

Class Problems

Problem 4.22. (a) Prove that if A surj B and B surj C, then A surj C.

(b) Explain why A surj B iff B inj A.

(c) Conclude from (a) and (b) that if A inj B and B inj C, then A inj C.

(d) Explain why A inj B iff there is a total injective *function* ($[= 1$ out, ≤ 1 in]) from A to B. [10]

Problem 4.23.
Five basic properties of binary relations $R : A \to B$ are:

1. R is a surjection [≥ 1 in]

2. R is an injection [≤ 1 in]

3. R is a function [≥ 1 out]

4. R is total [≥ 1 out]

5. R is empty [$= 0$ out]

Below are some assertions about a relation R. For each assertion, write the numbers of all the properties above that the relation R must have; write "none" if R might not have any of these properties. For example, you should write "(1), (4)" next to the first assertion.

Variables $a, a_1, \ldots$ range over A and $b, b_1, \ldots$ range over B.

(a) $\forall a \, \forall b. \, a \, R \, b$.   (1), (4)

(b) NOT($\forall a \, \forall b. \, a \, R \, b$).

(c) $\forall a \, \forall b. \, QNOT(a \, R \, b)$.

(d) $\forall a \, \exists b. \, a \, R \, b$.

(e) $\forall b \, \exists a. \, a \, R \, b$.

(f) R is a bijection.

(g) $\forall a \, \exists b_1 \, a \, R \, b_1 \bigwedge \forall b. \, a \, R \, b$ IMPLIES $b = b_1$.

(h) $\forall a, b. \, a \, R \, b$ OR $a \neq b$.

(i) $\forall b_1, b_2, a. \, (a \, R \, b_1$ AND $a \, R \, b_2)$ IMPLIES $b_1 = b_2$.

---

[10]The official definition of inj is with a total injective *relation* ($[\geq 1$ out, ≤ 1 in])

(j) $\forall a_1, a_2, b.\ (a_1\ R\ b\ \text{AND}\ a_2\ R\ b)\ \text{IMPLIES}\ a_1 = a_2.$

(k) $\forall a_1, a_2, b_1, b_2.\ (a_1\ R\ b_1\ \text{AND}\ a_2\ R\ b_2\ \text{AND}\ a_1 \neq a_2)\ \text{IMPLIES}\ b_1 \neq b_2.$

(l) $\forall a_1, a_2, b_1, b_2.\ (a_1\ R\ b_1\ \text{AND}\ a_2\ R\ b_2\ \text{AND}\ b_1 \neq b_2)\ \text{IMPLIES}\ a_1 \neq a_2.$

Homework Problems

Problem 4.24.
Let $f : A \to B$ and $g : B \to C$ be functions.

(a) Prove that if the composition $g \circ f$ is a bijection, then f is a total injection and g is a surjection.

(b) Show there is a total injection f and a bijection, g, such that $g \circ f$ is not a bijection.

Problem 4.25.
Let A, B and C be nonempty sets, and let $f : B \to C$ and $g : A \to B$ be functions. Let $h ::= f \circ g$ be the composition function of f and g, namely, the function with domain A and codomain C such that $h(x) = f(g(x))$.

(a) Prove that if h is surjective and f is total and injective, then g must be surjective.

Hint: contradiction.

(b) Suppose that h is injective and f is total. Prove that g must be injective and provide a counterexample showing how this claim could fail if f was *not* total.

Problem 4.26.
Let A, B and C be sets, and let $f : B \to C$ and $g : A \to B$ be functions. Let $h : A \to C$ be the composition $f \circ g$; that is, $h(x) ::= f(g(x))$ for $x \in A$. Prove or disprove the following claims:

(a) If h is surjective, then f must be surjective.

(b) If h is surjective, then g must be surjective.

(c) If h is injective, then f must be injective.

(d) If h is injective and f is total, then g must be injective.

Problem 4.27.

Let R be a binary relation on a set D. Let x, y be variables ranging over D. Indicate the expressions below whose meaning is that R is an *injection* [≤ 1 in]. Remember R is a not necessarily total or a function.

1. $R(x) = R(y)$ IMPLIES $x = y$

2. $R(x) \cap R(y) = \emptyset$ IMPLIES $x \neq y$

3. $R(x) \cap R(y) \neq \emptyset$ IMPLIES $x \neq y$

4. $R(x) \cap R(y) \neq \emptyset$ IMPLIES $x = y$

5. $R^{-1}(R(x)) = \{x\}$

6. $R^{-1}(R(x)) \subseteq \{x\}$

7. $R^{-1}(R(x)) \supseteq \{x\}$

8. $R(R^{-1}(x)) = x$

Problem 4.28.

The language of sets and relations may seem remote from the practical world of programming, but in fact there is a close connection to *relational databases*, a very popular software application building block implemented by such software packages as MySQL. This problem explores the connection by considering how to manipulate and analyze a large data set using operators over sets and relations. Systems like MySQL are able to execute very similar high-level instructions efficiently on standard computer hardware, which helps programmers focus on high-level design.

Consider a basic Web search engine, which stores information on Web pages and processes queries to find pages satisfying conditions provided by users. At a high level, we can formalize the key information as:

- A set P of *pages* that the search engine knows about

- A binary relation L (for *link*) over pages, defined such that p_1 L p_2 iff page p_1 links to p_2

- A set E of *endorsers*, people who have recorded their opinions about which pages are high-quality

- A binary relation R (for *recommends*) between endorsers and pages, such that $e\ R\ p$ iff person e has recommended page p

- A set W of *words* that may appear on pages

- A binary relation M (for *mentions*) between pages and words, where $p\ M\ w$ iff word w appears on page p

Each part of this problem describes an intuitive, informal query over the data, and your job is to produce a single expression using the standard set and relation operators, such that the expression can be interpreted as answering the query correctly, for any data set. Your answers should use only the set and relation symbols given above, in addition to terms standing for constant elements of E or W, plus the following operators introduced in the text:

- set union $\cup$.

- set intersection $\cap$.

- set difference $-$.

- relational image—for example, $R(A)$ for some set A, or $R(a)$ for some specific element a.

- relational inverse $^{-1}$.

- ...and one extra: *relational composition* which generalizes composition of functions

$$a\ (R \circ S)\ c ::= \exists b \in B.\,(a\ S\ b)\ \text{AND}\ (b\ R\ c).$$

In other words, a is related to c in $R \circ S$ if starting at a you can follow an S arrow to the start of an R arrow and then follow the R arrow to get to c.[11]

Here is one worked example to get you started:

- **Search description:** The set of pages containing the word "logic"

- **Solution expression:** M^{-1}("logic")

Find similar solutions for each of the following searches:

(a) The set of pages containing the word "logic" but not the word "predicate"

---

[11] Note the reversal of R and S in the definition; this is to make relational composition work like function composition. For functions, $f \circ g$ means you apply g first. That is, if we let h be $f \circ g$, then $h(x) = f(g(x))$.

(b) The set of pages containing the word "set" that have been recommended by "Meyer"

(c) The set of endorsers who have recommended pages containing the word "algebra"

(d) The relation that relates endorser e and word w iff e has recommended a page containing w

(e) The set of pages that have at least one incoming or outgoing link

(f) The relation that relates word w and page p iff w appears on a page that links to p

(g) The relation that relates word w and endorser e iff w appears on a page that links to a page that e recommends

(h) The relation that relates pages p_1 and p_2 iff p_2 can be reached from p_1 by following a sequence of exactly 3 links

Exam Problems

Problem 4.29.
Let A be the set containing the five sets: $\{a\}, \{b, c\}, \{b, d\}, \{a, e\}, \{e, f\}$, and let B be the set containing the three sets: $\{a, b\}, \{b, c, d\}, \{e, f\}$. Let R be the "is subset of" binary relation from A to B defined by the rule:

$$X \, R \, Y \quad \text{IFF} \quad X \subseteq Y.$$

(a) Fill in the arrows so the following figure describes the graph of the relation, R:

A	arrows	*B*
{*a*}		
		{*a*, *b*}
{*b*, *c*}		
		{*b*, *c*, *d*}
{*b*, *d*}		
		{*e*, *f*}
{*a*, *e*}		
{*e*, *f*}		

(b) Circle the properties below possessed by the relation *R*:

  function   total   injective   surjective   bijective

(c) Circle the properties below possessed by the relation R^{-1}:

  function   total   injective   surjective   bijective

Problem 4.30. (a) Five assertions about a binary relation $R : A \to B$ are bulleted below. There are nine predicate formulas that express some of these assertions. Write the numbers of the formulas next to the assertions they express. For example, you should write "4" next to the last assertion, since formula (4) expresses the assertion that *R* is the identity relation.

Variables $a, a_1, \ldots$ range over the domain *A* and $b, b_1, \ldots$ range over the codomain *B*. More than one formula may express one assertion.

- *R* is a surjection
- *R* is an injection

- R is a function
- R is total
- R is the identity relation.

1. $\forall b.\, \exists a.\, a\, R\, b.$
2. $\forall a.\, \exists b.\, a\, R\, b.$
3. $\forall a.\, a\, R\, a.$
4. $\forall a, b.\, a\, R\, b$ IFF $a = b.$
5. $\forall a, b.\, a\, R\, b$ OR $a \neq b.$
6. $\forall b_1, b_2, a.\, (a\, R\, b_1$ AND $a\, R\, b_2)$ IMPLIES $b_1 = b_2.$
7. $\forall a_1, a_2, b.\, (a_1\, R\, b$ AND $a_2\, R\, b)$ IMPLIES $a_1 = a_2.$
8. $\forall a_1, a_2, b_1, b_2.\, (a_1\, R\, b_1$ AND $a_2\, R\, b_2$ AND $a_1 \neq a_2)$ IMPLIES $b_1 \neq b_2.$
9. $\forall a_1, a_2, b_1, b_2.\, (a_1\, R\, b_1$ AND $a_2\, R\, b_2$ AND $b_1 \neq b_2)$ IMPLIES $a_1 \neq a_2.$

(b) Give an example of a relation R that satisfies three of the properties surjection, injection, total, and function (you indicate which) but is not a bijection.

Problem 4.31.
Prove that if relation $R : A \to B$ is a total injection, $[\geq 1$ out$], [\leq 1$ in$]$, then

$$R^{-1} \circ R = \mathrm{Id}_A,$$

where Id_A is the identity function on A.
   (A simple argument in terms of "arrows" will do the job.)

Problem 4.32.
Let $R : A \to B$ be a binary relation.
 (a) Prove that R is a function iff $R \circ R^{-1} \subseteq \mathrm{Id}_B$.
Write similar containment formulas involving $R^{-1} \circ R$, $R \circ R^{-1}$, Id_a, Id_B equivalent to the assertion that R has each of the following properties. No proof is required.
 (b) total.

 (c) a surjection.

 (d) a injection.

Problem 4.33.

Let $R : A \to B$ and $S : B \to C$ be binary relations such that $S \circ R$ is a bijection and $|A| = 2$.

Give an example of such R, S where neither R nor S is a function. Indicate exactly which properties—total, surjection, function, and injection—your examples of R and S have.

Hint: Let $|B| = 4$.

Problem 4.34.

The set $\{1, 2, 3\}^{\omega}$ consists of the **infinite** sequences of the digits 1,2, and 3, and likewise $\{4, 5\}^{\omega}$ is the set of infinite sequences of the digits 4,5. For example

$$
\begin{aligned}
123123123\ldots \quad &\in \{1, 2, 3\}^{\omega}, \\
222222222222\ldots \quad &\in \{1, 2, 3\}^{\omega}, \\
4554445554444\ldots \quad &\in \{4, 5\}^{\omega}.
\end{aligned}
$$

(a) Give an example of a total injective function

$$f : \{1, 2, 3\}^{\omega} \to \{4, 5\}^{\omega}.$$

(b) Give an example of a bijection $g : (\{1, 2, 3\}^{\omega} \times \{1, 2, 3\}^{\omega}) \to \{1, 2, 3\}^{\omega}$.

(c) Explain why there is a bijection between $\{1, 2, 3\}^{\omega} \times \{1, 2, 3\}^{\omega}$ and $\{4, 5\}^{\omega}$. (You need not explicitly define the bijection.)

Problems for Section 4.5

Practice Problems

Problem 4.35.

Assume $f : A \to B$ is total function, and A is finite. Replace the $\star$ with one of $\leq, =, \geq$ to produce the *strongest* correct version of the following statements:

(a) $|f(A)| \star |B|$.

(b) If f is a surjection, then $|A| \star |B|$.

(c) If f is a surjection, then $|f(A)| \star |B|$.

(d) If f is an injection, then $|f(A)| \star |A|$.

(e) If f is a bijection, then $|A| \star |B|$.

Class Problems

Problem 4.36.

Let $A = \{a_0, a_1, \ldots, a_{n-1}\}$ be a set of size n, and $B = \{b_0, b_1, \ldots, b_{m-1}\}$ a set of size m. Prove that $|A \times B| = mn$ by defining a simple bijection from $A \times B$ to the nonnegative integers from 0 to $mn - 1$.

Problem 4.37.

Let $R : A \to B$ be a binary relation. Use an arrow counting argument to prove the following generalization of the Mapping Rule 1.

Lemma. *If R is a function, and $X \subseteq A$, then*

$$|X| \geq |R(X)|.$$

5 Induction

Induction is a powerful method for showing a property is true for all nonnegative integers. Induction plays a central role in discrete mathematics and computer science. In fact, its use is a defining characteristic of *discrete*—as opposed to *continuous*—mathematics. This chapter introduces two versions of induction, Ordinary and Strong, and explains why they work and how to use them in proofs. It also introduces the Invariant Principle, which is a version of induction specially adapted for reasoning about step-by-step processes.

5.1 Ordinary Induction

To understand how induction works, suppose there is a professor who brings a bottomless bag of assorted miniature candy bars to her large class. She offers to share the candy in the following way. First, she lines the students up in order. Next she states two rules:

1. The student at the beginning of the line gets a candy bar.

2. If a student gets a candy bar, then the following student in line also gets a candy bar.

Let's number the students by their order in line, starting the count with 0, as usual in computer science. Now we can understand the second rule as a short description of a whole sequence of statements:

- If student 0 gets a candy bar, then student 1 also gets one.

- If student 1 gets a candy bar, then student 2 also gets one.

- If student 2 gets a candy bar, then student 3 also gets one.

$$\vdots$$

Of course, this sequence has a more concise mathematical description:

If student n gets a candy bar, then student $n + 1$ gets a candy bar, for all nonnegative integers n.

So suppose you are student 17. By these rules, are you entitled to a miniature candy bar? Well, student 0 gets a candy bar by the first rule. Therefore, by the second rule, student 1 also gets one, which means student 2 gets one, which means student 3 gets one as well, and so on. By 17 applications of the professor's second rule, you get your candy bar! Of course the rules really guarantee a candy bar to *every* student, no matter how far back in line they may be.

5.1.1   A Rule for Ordinary Induction

The reasoning that led us to conclude that every student gets a candy bar is essentially all there is to induction.

The Induction Principle.

Let P be a predicate on nonnegative integers. If

- $P(0)$ is true, and

- $P(n)$ IMPLIES $P(n + 1)$ for all nonnegative integers n

then

- $P(m)$ is true for all nonnegative integers m.

Since we're going to consider several useful variants of induction in later sections, we'll refer to the induction method described above as *ordinary induction* when we need to distinguish it. Formulated as a proof rule as in Section 1.4.1, this would be

Rule. *Induction Rule*

$$\frac{P(0), \quad \forall n \in \mathbb{N}.\ P(n) \text{ IMPLIES } P(n + 1)}{\forall m \in \mathbb{N}.\ P(m)}$$

This Induction Rule works for the same intuitive reason that all the students get candy bars, and we hope the explanation using candy bars makes it clear why the soundness of ordinary induction can be taken for granted. In fact, the rule is so obvious that it's hard to see what more basic principle could be used to justify it.[1] What's not so obvious is how much mileage we get by using it.

---

[1]But see Section 5.3.

5.1.2   A Familiar Example

Below is the formula (5.1) for the sum of the nonnegative integers up to n. The formula holds for all nonnegative integers, so it is the kind of statement to which induction applies directly. We've already proved this formula using the Well Ordering Principle (Theorem 2.2.1), but now we'll prove it *by induction*, that is, using the Induction Principle.

Theorem 5.1.1. *For all $n \in \mathbb{N}$,*

$$1 + 2 + 3 + \cdots + n = \frac{n(n+1)}{2} \qquad (5.1)$$

To prove the theorem by induction, define predicate $P(n)$ to be the equation (5.1). Now the theorem can be restated as the claim that $P(n)$ is true for all $n \in \mathbb{N}$. This is great, because the Induction Principle lets us reach precisely that conclusion, provided we establish two simpler facts:

- $P(0)$ is true.

- For all $n \in \mathbb{N}$, $P(n)$ IMPLIES $P(n+1)$.

So now our job is reduced to proving these two statements.

The first statement follows because of the convention that a sum of zero terms is equal to 0. So $P(0)$ is the true assertion that a sum of zero terms is equal to $0(0+1)/2 = 0$.

The second statement is more complicated. But remember the basic plan from Section 1.5 for proving the validity of any implication: *assume* the statement on the left and then *prove* the statement on the right. In this case, we assume $P(n)$—namely, equation (5.1)—in order to prove $P(n+1)$, which is the equation

$$1 + 2 + 3 + \cdots + n + (n+1) = \frac{(n+1)(n+2)}{2}. \qquad (5.2)$$

These two equations are quite similar; in fact, adding $(n+1)$ to both sides of equation (5.1) and simplifying the right side gives the equation (5.2):

$$1 + 2 + 3 + \cdots + n + (n+1) = \frac{n(n+1)}{2} + (n+1)$$
$$= \frac{(n+2)(n+1)}{2}$$

Thus, if $P(n)$ is true, then so is $P(n+1)$. This argument is valid for every nonnegative integer n, so this establishes the second fact required by the induction proof. Therefore, the Induction Principle says that the predicate $P(m)$ is true for all nonnegative integers, m. The theorem is proved.

5.1.3   A Template for Induction Proofs

The proof of equation (5.1) was relatively simple, but even the most complicated induction proof follows exactly the same template. There are five components:

1. **State that the proof uses induction.** This immediately conveys the overall structure of the proof, which helps your reader follow your argument.

2. **Define an appropriate predicate $P(n)$.** The predicate $P(n)$ is called the *induction hypothesis*. The eventual conclusion of the induction argument will be that $P(n)$ is true for all nonnegative n. A clearly stated induction hypothesis is often the most important part of an induction proof, and its omission is the largest source of confused proofs by students.

   In the simplest cases, the induction hypothesis can be lifted straight from the proposition you are trying to prove, as we did with equation (5.1). Sometimes the induction hypothesis will involve several variables, in which case you should indicate which variable serves as n.

3. **Prove that $P(0)$ is true.** This is usually easy, as in the example above. This part of the proof is called the *base case* or *basis step*.

4. **Prove that $P(n)$ implies $P(n + 1)$ for every nonnegative integer n.** This is called the *inductive step*. The basic plan is always the same: assume that $P(n)$ is true and then use this assumption to prove that $P(n + 1)$ is true. These two statements should be fairly similar, but bridging the gap may require some ingenuity. Whatever argument you give must be valid for every nonnegative integer n, since the goal is to prove that *all* the following implications are true:

$$P(0) \to P(1), \ P(1) \to P(2), \ P(2) \to P(3), \ldots.$$

5. **Invoke induction.** Given these facts, the induction principle allows you to conclude that $P(n)$ is true for all nonnegative n. This is the logical capstone to the whole argument, but it is so standard that it's usual not to mention it explicitly.

Always be sure to explicitly label the *base case* and the *inductive step*. Doing so will make your proofs clearer and will decrease the chance that you forget a key step—like checking the base case.

5.1.4 A Clean Writeup

The proof of Theorem 5.1.1 given above is perfectly valid; however, it contains a lot of extraneous explanation that you won't usually see in induction proofs. The writeup below is closer to what you might see in print and should be prepared to produce yourself.

Revised proof of Theorem 5.1.1. We use induction. The induction hypothesis $P(n)$ will be equation (5.1).

Base case: $P(0)$ is true, because both sides of equation (5.1) equal zero when $n = 0$.

Inductive step: Assume that $P(n)$ is true, that is equation (5.1) holds for some nonnegative integer n. Then adding $n + 1$ to both sides of the equation implies that

$$1 + 2 + 3 + \cdots + n + (n + 1) = \frac{n(n + 1)}{2} + (n + 1)$$
$$= \frac{(n + 1)(n + 2)}{2} \qquad \text{(by simple algebra)}$$

which proves $P(n + 1)$.

So it follows by induction that $P(n)$ is true for all nonnegative n. ∎

It probably bothers you that induction led to a proof of this summation formula but did not provide an intuitive way to understand it nor did it explain where the formula came from in the first place.[2] This is both a weakness and a strength. It is a weakness when a proof does not provide insight. But it is a strength that a proof can provide a reader with a reliable guarantee of correctness without *requiring* insight.

5.1.5 A More Challenging Example

During the development of MIT's famous Stata Center, as costs rose further and further beyond budget, some radical fundraising ideas were proposed. One rumored plan was to install a big square courtyard divided into unit squares. The big square would be 2^n units on a side for some undetermined nonnegative integer n, and one of the unit squares in the center[3] occupied by a statue of a wealthy potential donor—whom the fund raisers privately referred to as "Bill." The $n = 3$ case is shown in Figure 5.1.

A complication was that the building's unconventional architect, Frank Gehry, was alleged to require that only special L-shaped tiles (shown in Figure 5.2) be

---

[2]Methods for finding such formulas are covered in Part III of the text.

[3]In the special case $n = 0$, the whole courtyard consists of a single central square; otherwise, there are four central squares.

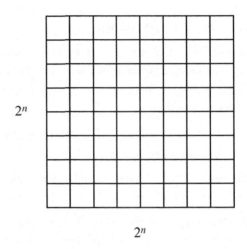

2^n

2^n

Figure 5.1   A $2^n \times 2^n$ courtyard for $n = 3$.

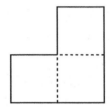

Figure 5.2   The special L-shaped tile.

used for the courtyard. For $n = 2$, a courtyard meeting these constraints is shown in Figure 5.3. But what about for larger values of n? Is there a way to tile a $2^n \times 2^n$ courtyard with L-shaped tiles around a statue in the center? Let's try to prove that this is so.

Theorem 5.1.2. *For all $n \geq 0$ there exists a tiling of a $2^n \times 2^n$ courtyard with Bill in a central square.*

Proof. (doomed attempt) The proof is by induction. Let $P(n)$ be the proposition that there exists a tiling of a $2^n \times 2^n$ courtyard with Bill in the center.

Base case: $P(0)$ is true because Bill fills the whole courtyard.

Inductive step: Assume that there is a tiling of a $2^n \times 2^n$ courtyard with Bill in the center for some $n \geq 0$. We must prove that there is a way to tile a $2^{n+1} \times 2^{n+1}$ courtyard with Bill in the center . . . . ∎

Now we're in trouble! The ability to tile a smaller courtyard with Bill in the

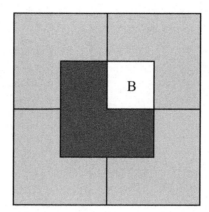

Figure 5.3   A tiling using L-shaped tiles for $n = 2$ with Bill in a center square.

center isn't much help in tiling a larger courtyard with Bill in the center. We haven't figured out how to bridge the gap between $P(n)$ and $P(n + 1)$.

So if we're going to prove Theorem 5.1.2 by induction, we're going to need some *other* induction hypothesis than simply the statement about n that we're trying to prove.

When this happens, your first fallback should be to look for a *stronger* induction hypothesis; that is, one which implies your previous hypothesis. For example, we could make $P(n)$ the proposition that for *every* location of Bill in a $2^n \times 2^n$ courtyard, there exists a tiling of the remainder.

This advice may sound bizarre: "If you can't prove something, try to prove something grander!" But for induction arguments, this makes sense. In the inductive step, where you have to prove $P(n)$ IMPLIES $P(n + 1)$, you're in better shape because you can *assume* $P(n)$, which is now a more powerful statement. Let's see how this plays out in the case of courtyard tiling.

Proof (successful attempt). The proof is by induction. Let $P(n)$ be the proposition that for every location of Bill in a $2^n \times 2^n$ courtyard, there exists a tiling of the remainder.

Base case: $P(0)$ is true because Bill fills the whole courtyard.

Inductive step: Assume that $P(n)$ is true for some $n \geq 0$; that is, for every location of Bill in a $2^n \times 2^n$ courtyard, there exists a tiling of the remainder. Divide the $2^{n+1} \times 2^{n+1}$ courtyard into four quadrants, each $2^n \times 2^n$. One quadrant contains Bill (**B** in the diagram below). Place a temporary Bill (**X** in the diagram) in each of the three central squares lying outside this quadrant as shown in Figure 5.4.

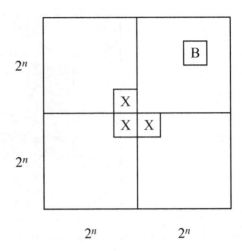

Figure 5.4   Using a stronger inductive hypothesis to prove Theorem 5.1.2.

Now we can tile each of the four quadrants by the induction assumption. Replacing the three temporary Bills with a single L-shaped tile completes the job. This proves that $P(n)$ implies $P(n + 1)$ for all $n \geq 0$. Thus $P(m)$ is true for all $m \in \mathbb{N}$, and the theorem follows as a special case where we put Bill in a central square.   ∎

This proof has two nice properties. First, not only does the argument guarantee that a tiling exists, but also it gives an algorithm for finding such a tiling. Second, we have a stronger result: if Bill wanted a statue on the edge of the courtyard, away from the pigeons, we could accommodate him!

Strengthening the induction hypothesis is often a good move when an induction proof won't go through. But keep in mind that the stronger assertion must actually be *true*; otherwise, there isn't much hope of constructing a valid proof. Sometimes finding just the right induction hypothesis requires trial, error, and insight. For example, mathematicians spent almost twenty years trying to prove or disprove the conjecture that every planar graph is 5-choosable.[4] Then, in 1994, Carsten Thomassen gave an induction proof simple enough to explain on a napkin. The key turned out to be finding an extremely clever induction hypothesis; with that in hand, completing the argument was easy!

---

[4]5-choosability is a slight generalization of 5-colorability. Although every planar graph is 4-colorable and therefore 5-colorable, not every planar graph is 4-choosable. If this all sounds like nonsense, don't panic. We'll discuss graphs, planarity, and coloring in Part II of the text.

5.1.6   A Faulty Induction Proof

If we have done a good job in writing this text, right about now you should be thinking, "Hey, this induction stuff isn't so hard after all—just show $P(0)$ is true and that $P(n)$ implies $P(n + 1)$ for any number n." And, you would be right, although sometimes when you start doing induction proofs on your own, you can run into trouble. For example, we will now use induction to "prove" that all horses are the same color—just when you thought it was safe to skip class and work on your robot program instead. Sorry!

False Theorem. *All horses are the same color.*

Notice that no n is mentioned in this assertion, so we're going to have to reformulate it in a way that makes an n explicit. In particular, we'll (falsely) prove that

False Theorem 5.1.3. *In every set of $n \geq 1$ horses, all the horses are the same color.*

This is a statement about all integers $n \geq 1$ rather ≥ 0, so it's natural to use a slight variation on induction: prove $P(1)$ in the base case and then prove that $P(n)$ implies $P(n + 1)$ for all $n \geq 1$ in the inductive step. This is a perfectly valid variant of induction and is *not* the problem with the proof below.

Bogus proof. The proof is by induction on n. The induction hypothesis $P(n)$ will be

$$\text{In every set of } n \text{ horses, all are the same color.} \tag{5.3}$$

Base case: ($n = 1$). $P(1)$ is true, because in a size-1 set of horses, there's only one horse, and this horse is definitely the same color as itself.

Inductive step: Assume that $P(n)$ is true for some $n \geq 1$. That is, assume that in every set of n horses, all are the same color. Now suppose we have a set of $n + 1$ horses:

$$h_1, \ h_2, \ \ldots, \ h_n, \ h_{n+1}.$$

We need to prove these $n + 1$ horses are all the same color.

By our assumption, the first n horses are the same color:

$$\underbrace{h_1, \ h_2, \ \ldots, \ h_n}_{\text{same color}}, h_{n+1}$$

Also by our assumption, the last n horses are the same color:

$$h_1, \ \underbrace{h_2, \ \ldots, \ h_n, \ h_{n+1}}_{\text{same color}}$$

So h_1 is the same color as the remaining horses besides h_{n+1} —that is, $h_2, \ldots, h_n$. Likewise, h_{n+1} is the same color as the remaining horses besides h_1—that is, $h_2, \ldots, h_n$, again. Since h_1 and h_{n+1} are the same color as $h_2, \ldots, h_n$, all $n + 1$ horses must be the same color, and so $P(n + 1)$ is true. Thus, $P(n)$ implies $P(n + 1)$.

By the principle of induction, $P(n)$ is true for all $n \geq 1$.   ∎

We've proved something false! Does this mean that math broken and we should all take up poetry instead? Of course not! It just means that this proof has a mistake.

The mistake in this argument is in the sentence that begins "So h_1 is the same color as the remaining horses besides h_{n+1}—that is $h_2, \ldots, h_n, \ldots$." The ellipsis notation ("$\ldots$") in the expression "$h_1, h_2, \ldots, h_n, h_{n+1}$" creates the impression that there are some remaining horses—namely $h_2, \ldots, h_n$ —besides h_1 and h_{n+1}. However, this is not true when $n = 1$. In that case, $h_1, h_2, \ldots, h_n, h_{n+1}$ is just h_1, h_2 and *there are no "remaining" horses* for h_1 to share a color with. And of course, in this case h_1 and h_2 really don't need to be the same color.

This mistake knocks a critical link out of our induction argument. We proved $P(1)$ and we *correctly* proved $P(2) \longrightarrow P(3)$, $P(3) \longrightarrow P(4)$, etc. But we failed to prove $P(1) \longrightarrow P(2)$, and so everything falls apart: we cannot conclude that $P(2), P(3)$, etc., are true. And naturally, these propositions are all false; there are sets of n horses of different colors for all $n \geq 2$.

Students sometimes explain that the mistake in the proof is because $P(n)$ is false for $n \geq 2$, and the proof assumes something false, $P(n)$, in order to prove $P(n+1)$. You should think about how to help such a student understand why this explanation would get no credit on a Math for Computer Science exam.

5.2   Strong Induction

A useful variant of induction is called *strong induction*. Strong induction and ordinary induction are used for exactly the same thing: proving that a predicate is true for all nonnegative integers. Strong induction is useful when a simple proof that the predicate holds for $n + 1$ does not follow just from the fact that it holds at n, but from the fact that it holds for other values $\leq n$.

5.2.1 A Rule for Strong Induction

Principle of Strong Induction.

Let P be a predicate on nonnegative integers. If

- $P(0)$ is true, and

- for all $n \in \mathbb{N}$, $P(0)$, $P(1)$, ..., $P(n)$ *together* imply $P(n+1)$,

then $P(m)$ is true for all $m \in \mathbb{N}$.

The only change from the ordinary induction principle is that strong induction allows you make more assumptions in the inductive step of your proof! In an ordinary induction argument, you assume that $P(n)$ is true and try to prove that $P(n+1)$ is also true. In a strong induction argument, you may assume that $P(0)$, $P(1)$, ..., and $P(n)$ are *all* true when you go to prove $P(n+1)$. So you can assume a *stronger* set of hypotheses which can make your job easier.

Formulated as a proof rule, strong induction is

Rule. *Strong Induction Rule*

$$\frac{P(0), \quad \forall n \in \mathbb{N}. \ \big(P(0) \text{ AND } P(1) \text{ AND} \ldots \text{ AND } P(n)\big) \text{ IMPLIES } P(n+1)}{\forall m \in \mathbb{N}. \ P(m)}$$

Stated more succinctly, the rule is

Rule.

$$\frac{P(0), \quad [\forall k \leq n \in \mathbb{N}. \ P(k)] \text{ IMPLIES } P(n+1)}{\forall m \in \mathbb{N}. \ P(m)}$$

The template for strong induction proofs is identical to the template given in Section 5.1.3 for ordinary induction except for two things:

- you should state that your proof is by strong induction, and

- you can assume that $P(0)$, $P(1)$, ..., $P(n)$ are all true instead of only $P(n)$ during the inductive step.

5.2.2 Fibonacci numbers

The numbers that bear his name arose out of the Italian mathematician Fibonacci's models of population growth at the beginning of the thirteenth century. Fibonacci numbers turn out to describe the growth of lots of interesting biological quantities such as the shape of pineapple sprouts or pine cones, and they also come up regularly in Computer Science where they describe the growth of various data structures and computation times of algorithms.

To generate the list of successive Fibonacci numbers, you start by writing 0, 1 and then keep adding another element to the list by summing the two previous ones:

$$0, 1, 1, 2, 3, 5, 8, 13, 21, \ldots.$$

Another way to describe this process is to define nth Fibonacci number $F(n)$ by the equations:

$$F(0) ::= 0,$$
$$F(1) ::= 1,$$
$$F(n) ::= F(n-1) + F(n-2) \qquad\qquad \text{for } n \geq 2.$$

Note that because the general rule for finding the Fibonacci $F(n)$ refers to the two previous values $F(n-1)$ and $F(n-2)$, we needed to know the two values $F(0)$ and $F(1)$ in order to get started.

One simple property of Fibonacci numbers is that the even/odd pattern of Fibonacci numbers repeats in a cycle of length three. A nice way to say this is that for all $n \geq 0$,

$$F(n) \text{ is even IFF } F(n+3) \text{ is even.} \qquad\qquad (5.4)$$

We will verify the equivalence (5.4) by induction, but strong induction is called for because properties of $F(n)$ depend not just on $F(n-1)$ but also on $F(n-2)$.

Proof. The (strong) induction hypothesis $P(n)$ will be (5.4).

Base cases:

- ($n = 0$). $F(0) = 0$ and $F(3) = 2$ are both even.

- ($n = 1$). $F(1) = 1$ and $F(4) = 3$ are both not even.

Induction step: For $n \geq 1$, we want to prove $P(n+1)$ is true assuming by strong induction that $P(n)$ and $P(n-1)$ are true.

Now it is easy to verify that for all integers k, m,

$$m + k \text{ is even IFF } [m \text{ is even IFF } k \text{ is even}]. \qquad\qquad (*)$$

So for $n \geq 1$,

$F(n + 1)$ is even

    IFF $F(n) + F(n - 1)$ is even   (def of $F(n + 1)$)

    IFF $[F(n)$ is even IFF $F(n - 1)$ is even$]$ (by (*))

    IFF $[F(n + 3)$ is even IFF $F(n + 2)$ is even$]$

           (by strong ind. hyp. $P(n), P(n - 1)$)

    IFF $F(n + 3) + F(n + 2)$ is even   (by (*))

    IFF $F(n + 4)$ is even   (by def of $F(n + 4)$).

This shows that

$$F(n + 1) \text{ is even } \text{IFF } F(n + 4) \text{ is even,}$$

which means that $P(n + 1)$ is true, as required.   ■

There is a long standing community of Fibonacci number enthusiasts who have been captivated by the many extraordinary properties of these number—a few further illustrative properties appear in Problems 5.8, 5.25, and 5.30.

5.2.3 Products of Primes

We can use strong induction to re-prove Theorem 2.3.1 which we previously proved using Well Ordering.

Theorem. *Every integer greater than 1 is a product of primes.*

Proof. We will prove the Theorem by strong induction, letting the induction hypothesis $P(n)$ be

$$n \text{ is a product of primes.}$$

So the Theorem will follow if we prove that $P(n)$ holds for all $n \geq 2$.

Base Case: ($n = 2$): $P(2)$ is true because 2 is prime, so it is a length one product of primes by convention.

Inductive step: Suppose that $n \geq 2$ and that every number from 2 to n is a product of primes. We must show that $P(n + 1)$ holds, namely, that $n + 1$ is also a product of primes. We argue by cases:

If $n + 1$ is itself prime, then it is a length one product of primes by convention, and so $P(n + 1)$ holds in this case.

Otherwise, $n + 1$ is not prime, which by definition means $n + 1 = k \cdot m$ for some integers k, m between 2 and n. Now by the strong induction hypothesis, we know that both k and m are products of primes. By multiplying these products, it follows

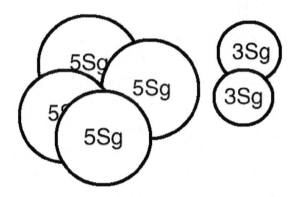

Figure 5.5   One way to make 26 Sg using Strongian currency

immediately that $k \cdot m = n + 1$ is also a product of primes. Therefore, $P(n + 1)$ holds in this case as well.

So $P(n + 1)$ holds in any case, which completes the proof by strong induction that $P(n)$ holds for all $n \geq 2$.

■

5.2.4   Making Change

The country Inductia, whose unit of currency is the Strong, has coins worth 3Sg (3 Strongs) and 5Sg. Although the Inductians have some trouble making small change like 4Sg or 7Sg, it turns out that they can collect coins to make change for any number that is at least 8 Strongs.

Strong induction makes this easy to prove for $n + 1 \geq 11$, because then $(n + 1) - 3 \geq 8$, so by strong induction the Inductians can make change for exactly $(n + 1) - 3$ Strongs, and then they can add a 3Sg coin to get $(n + 1)$Sg. So the only thing to do is check that they can make change for all the amounts from 8 to 10Sg, which is not too hard to do.

Here's a detailed writeup using the official format:

Proof. We prove by strong induction that the Inductians can make change for any amount of at least 8Sg. The induction hypothesis $P(n)$ will be:

There is a collection of coins whose value is $n + 8$ Strongs.

We now proceed with the induction proof:

Base case: $P(0)$ is true because a 3Sg coin together with a 5Sg coin makes 8Sg.

Inductive step: We assume $P(k)$ holds for all $k \leq n$, and prove that $P(n + 1)$ holds. We argue by cases:

Case $(n + 1 = 1)$: We have to make $(n + 1) + 8 = 9$Sg. We can do this using three 3Sg coins.

Case $(n + 1 = 2)$: We have to make $(n + 1) + 8 = 10$Sg. Use two 5Sg coins.

Case $(n + 1 \geq 3)$: Then $0 \leq n - 2 \leq n$, so by the strong induction hypothesis, the Inductians can make change for $(n - 2) + 8$Sg. Now by adding a 3Sg coin, they can make change for $(n + 1) + 8$Sg, so $P(n + 1)$ holds in this case.

Since $n \geq 0$, we know that $n + 1 \geq 1$ and thus that the three cases cover every possibility. Since $P(n + 1)$ is true in every case, we can conclude by strong induction that for all $n \geq 0$, the Inductians can make change for $n + 8$ Strong. That is, they can make change for any number of eight or more Strong. ∎

5.2.5 The Stacking Game

Here is another exciting game that's surely about to sweep the nation!

You begin with a stack of n boxes. Then you make a sequence of moves. In each move, you divide one stack of boxes into two nonempty stacks. The game ends when you have n stacks, each containing a single box. You earn points for each move; in particular, if you divide one stack of height $a + b$ into two stacks with heights a and b, then you score ab points for that move. Your overall score is the sum of the points that you earn for each move. What strategy should you use to maximize your total score?

As an example, suppose that we begin with a stack of $n = 10$ boxes. Then the game might proceed as shown in Figure 5.6. Can you find a better strategy?

Analyzing the Game

Let's use strong induction to analyze the unstacking game. We'll prove that your score is determined entirely by the number of boxes—your strategy is irrelevant!

Theorem 5.2.1. *Every way of unstacking n blocks gives a score of $n(n - 1)/2$ points.*

There are a couple technical points to notice in the proof:

- The template for a strong induction proof mirrors the one for ordinary induction.

- As with ordinary induction, we have some freedom to adjust indices. In this case, we prove $P(1)$ in the base case and prove that $P(1), \ldots, P(n)$ imply $P(n + 1)$ for all $n \geq 1$ in the inductive step.

Stack Heights   **Score**

Stack Heights										Score
10										
5	5									25 points
5	3	2								6
4	3	2	1							4
2	3	2	1	2						4
2	2	2	1	2	1					2
1	2	2	1	2	1	1				1
1	1	2	1	2	1	1	1			1
1	1	1	1	2	1	1	1	1		1
1	1	1	1	1	1	1	1	1	1	1

Total Score   =   45 points

Figure 5.6   An example of the stacking game with $n = 10$ boxes. On each line, the underlined stack is divided in the next step.

Proof. The proof is by strong induction. Let $P(n)$ be the proposition that every way of unstacking n blocks gives a score of $n(n-1)/2$.

Base case: If $n = 1$, then there is only one block. No moves are possible, and so the total score for the game is $1(1-1)/2 = 0$. Therefore, $P(1)$ is true.

Inductive step: Now we must show that $P(1), \ldots, P(n)$ imply $P(n+1)$ for all $n \geq 1$. So assume that $P(1), \ldots, P(n)$ are all true and that we have a stack of $n+1$ blocks. The first move must split this stack into substacks with positive sizes a and b where $a + b = n + 1$ and $0 < a, b \leq n$. Now the total score for the game is the sum of points for this first move plus points obtained by unstacking the two resulting substacks:

$$
\begin{aligned}
\text{total score} = \ &(\text{score for 1st move}) \\
&+ (\text{score for unstacking } a \text{ blocks}) \\
&+ (\text{score for unstacking } b \text{ blocks}) \\
= \ &ab + \frac{a(a-1)}{2} + \frac{b(b-1)}{2} \qquad \text{by } P(a) \text{ and } P(b) \\
= \ &\frac{(a+b)^2 - (a+b)}{2} = \frac{(a+b)((a+b)-1)}{2} \\
= \ &\frac{(n+1)n}{2}
\end{aligned}
$$

This shows that $P(1), P(2), \ldots, P(n)$ imply $P(n+1)$.

Therefore, the claim is true by strong induction. ∎

5.3 Strong Induction vs. Induction vs. Well Ordering

Strong induction looks genuinely "stronger" than ordinary induction —after all, you can assume a lot more when proving the induction step. Since ordinary induction is a special case of strong induction, you might wonder why anyone would bother with the ordinary induction.

But strong induction really isn't any stronger, because a simple text manipulation program can automatically reformat any proof using strong induction into a proof using ordinary induction—just by decorating the induction hypothesis with a universal quantifier in a standard way. Still, it's worth distinguishing these two kinds of induction, since which you use will signal whether the inductive step for $n + 1$ follows directly from the case for n or requires cases smaller than n, and that is generally good for your reader to know.

The template for the two kinds of induction rules looks nothing like the one for the Well Ordering Principle, but this chapter included a couple of examples where induction was used to prove something already proved using well ordering. In fact, this can always be done. As the examples may suggest, any well ordering proof can automatically be reformatted into an induction proof. So theoretically, no one need bother with the Well Ordering Principle either.

But it's equally easy to go the other way, and automatically reformat any strong induction proof into a Well Ordering proof. The three proof methods—well ordering, induction, and strong induction—are simply different formats for presenting the same mathematical reasoning!

So why three methods? Well, sometimes induction proofs are clearer because they don't require proof by contradiction. Also, induction proofs often provide recursive procedures that reduce large inputs to smaller ones. On the other hand, well ordering can come out slightly shorter and sometimes seem more natural and less worrisome to beginners.

So which method should you use? There is no simple recipe. Sometimes the only way to decide is to write up a proof using more than one method and compare how they come out. But whichever method you choose, be sure to state the method up front to help a reader follow your proof.

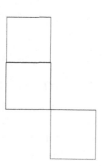

Figure 5.7   Gehry's new tile.

Problems for Section 5.1

Practice Problems

Problem 5.1.
Prove by induction that every nonempty finite set of real numbers has a minimum element.

Problem 5.2.
Frank Gehry has changed his mind. Instead of the L-shaped tiles shown in figure 5.3, he wants to use an odd offset pattern of tiles (or its mirror-image reflection), as shown in 5.7. To prove this is possible, he uses reasoning similar to the proof in 5.1.5. However, unlike the proof in the text, this proof is flawed. Which part of the proof below contains a logical error?

False Claim.   *The proof is by induction. Let $P(n)$ be the proposition that for every location of Bill in a $2^n \times 2^n$ courtyard, there exists a tiling of the remainder with the offset tile pattern.*

False proof.   **Base case**: $P(0)$ is true because Bill fills the whole courtyard.

Inductive step: Assume that $P(n)$ is true for some $n \geq 0$; that is, for every location of Bill in a $2^n \times 2^n$ courtyard, there exists a tiling of the remainder. Divide the $2^{n+1} \times 2^{n+1}$ courtyard into four quadrants, each $2^n \times 2^n$. One quadrant contains

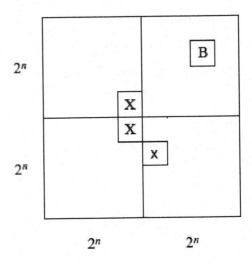

Figure 5.8   The induction hypothesis for the false theorem.

Bill (**B** in the diagram below). Place a temporary Bill (**X** in the diagram) in each of the three squares lying near this quadrant as shown in Figure 5.8.

We can tile each of the four quadrants by the induction assumption. Replacing the three temporary Bills with a single offset tile completes the job. This proves that $P(n)$ implies $P(n + 1)$ for all $n \geq 0$. Thus $P(m)$ is true for all $m \in \mathbb{N}$, and the ability to place Bill in the center of the courtyard follows as a special case where we put Bill in a central square. ∎

Class Problems

Problem 5.3.

Use induction to prove that

$$1^3 + 2^3 + \cdots + n^3 = \left(\frac{n(n+1)}{2} \right)^2 . \tag{5.5}$$

for all $n \geq 1$.

Remember to formally

1. Declare proof by induction.

2. Identify the induction hypothesis $P(n)$.

3. Establish the base case.

4. Prove that $P(n) \Rightarrow P(n+1)$.

5. Conclude that $P(n)$ holds for all $n \geq 1$.

as in the five part template.

Problem 5.4.
Prove by induction on n that

$$1 + r + r^2 + \cdots + r^n = \frac{r^{n+1} - 1}{r - 1} \tag{5.6}$$

for all $n \in \mathbb{N}$ and numbers $r \neq 1$.

Problem 5.5.
Prove by induction:

$$1 + \frac{1}{4} + \frac{1}{9} + \cdots + \frac{1}{n^2} < 2 - \frac{1}{n}, \tag{5.7}$$

for all $n > 1$.

Problem 5.6. (a) Prove by induction that a $2^n \times 2^n$ courtyard with a 1×1 statue of Bill in *a corner* can be covered with L-shaped tiles. (Do not assume or reprove the (stronger) result of Theorem 5.1.2 that Bill can be placed anywhere. The point of this problem is to show a different induction hypothesis that works.)

 (b) Use the result of part (a) to prove the original claim that there is a tiling with Bill in the middle.

Problem 5.7.
We've proved in two different ways that

$$1 + 2 + 3 + \cdots + n = \frac{n(n+1)}{2}$$

But now we're going to prove a *contradictory* theorem!

False Theorem. *For all $n \geq 0$,*

$$2 + 3 + 4 + \cdots + n = \frac{n(n+1)}{2}$$

Proof. We use induction. Let $P(n)$ be the proposition that $2 + 3 + 4 + \cdots + n = n(n+1)/2$.

Base case: $P(0)$ is true, since both sides of the equation are equal to zero. (Recall that a sum with no terms is zero.)

Inductive step: Now we must show that $P(n)$ implies $P(n+1)$ for all $n \geq 0$. So suppose that $P(n)$ is true; that is, $2 + 3 + 4 + \cdots + n = n(n+1)/2$. Then we can reason as follows:

$$
\begin{aligned}
2 + 3 + 4 + \cdots + n + (n+1) &= [2 + 3 + 4 + \cdots + n] + (n+1) \\
&= \frac{n(n+1)}{2} + (n+1) \\
&= \frac{(n+1)(n+2)}{2}
\end{aligned}
$$

Above, we group some terms, use the assumption $P(n)$, and then simplify. This shows that $P(n)$ implies $P(n+1)$. By the principle of induction, $P(n)$ is true for all $n \in \mathbb{N}$. ∎

Where exactly is the error in this proof?

Homework Problems

Problem 5.8.
The Fibonacci numbers $F(n)$ are described in Section 5.2.2.

Prove by induction that for all $n \geq 1$,

$$
F(n-1) \cdot F(n+1) - F(n)^2 = (-1)^n. \tag{5.8}
$$

Problem 5.9.
For any binary string α let num (α) be the nonnegative integer it represents in binary notation. For example, num $(10) = 2$, and num $(0101) = 5$.

An $n + 1$-*bit adder* adds two $n + 1$-bit binary numbers. More precisely, an $n + 1$-bit adder takes two length $n + 1$ binary strings

$$
\begin{aligned}
\alpha_n &::= a_n \ldots a_1 a_0, \\
\beta_n &::= b_n \ldots b_1 b_0,
\end{aligned}
$$

and a binary digit c_0 as inputs, and produces a length-$(n+1)$ binary string

$$
\sigma_n ::= s_n \ldots s_1 s_0,
$$

and a binary digit c_{n+1} as outputs, and satisfies the specification:

$$\text{num}\,(\alpha_n) + \text{num}\,(\beta_n) + c_0 = 2^{n+1} c_{n+1} + \text{num}\,(\sigma_n)\,. \tag{5.9}$$

There is a straightforward way to implement an $n+1$-bit adder as a digital circuit: an $n + 1$-bit *ripple-carry circuit* has $1 + 2(n + 1)$ binary inputs

$$a_n, \ldots, a_1, a_0, b_n, \ldots, b_1, b_0, c_0,$$

and $n + 2$ binary outputs,

$$c_{n+1}, s_n, \ldots, s_1, s_0.$$

As in Problem 3.6, the ripple-carry circuit is specified by the following formulas:

$$s_i ::= a_i \;\; \text{XOR} \;\; b_i \;\; \text{XOR} \;\; c_i \tag{5.10}$$

$$c_{i+1} ::= (a_i \;\; \text{AND} \;\; b_i) \;\; \text{OR} \;\; (a_i \;\; \text{AND} \;\; c_i) \;\; \text{OR} \;\; (b_i \;\; \text{AND} \;\; c_i),\,. \tag{5.11}$$

for $0 \leq i \leq n$.

(a) Verify that definitions (5.10) and (5.11) imply that

$$a_n + b_n + c_n = 2c_{n+1} + s_n. \tag{5.12}$$

for all $n \in \mathbb{N}$.

(b) Prove by induction on n that an $n+1$-bit ripple-carry circuit really is an $n+1$-bit adder, that is, its outputs satisfy (5.9).

Hint: You may assume that, by definition of binary representation of integers,

$$\text{num}\,(\alpha_{n+1}) = a_{n+1} 2^{n+1} + \text{num}\,(\alpha_n)\,. \tag{5.13}$$

Problem 5.10.
Divided Equilateral Triangles[5] (DETs) can be built up as follows:

- A single equilateral triangle counts as a DET whose only subtriangle is itself.

- If $T ::=$ is a DET, then the equilateral triangle T' built out of four copies of T as shown in in Figure 5.9 is also a DET, and the subtriangles of T' are exactly the subtriangles of each of the copies of T.

---

[5] Adapted from [46].

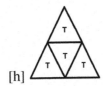

Figure 5.9   DET T' from Four Copies of DET T

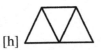

Figure 5.10   Trapezoid from Three Triangles

(a) Define the *length* of a DET to be the number of subtriangles with an edge on its base. Prove **by induction on length** that the total number of subtriangles of a DET is the square of its length.

(b) Show that a DET with one of its corner subtriangles removed can be tiled with trapezoids built out of three subtriangles as in Figure 5.10.

Problem 5.11.

The Math for Computer Science mascot, Theory Hippotamus, made a startling discovery while playing with his prized collection of unit squares over the weekend. Here is what happened.

First, Theory Hippotamus put his favorite unit square down on the floor as in Figure 5.11 (a). He noted that the length of the periphery of the resulting shape was 4, an even number. Next, he put a second unit square down next to the first so that the two squares shared an edge as in Figure 5.11 (b). He noticed that the length of the periphery of the resulting shape was now 6, which is also an even number. (The periphery of each shape in the figure is indicated by a thicker line.) Theory Hippotamus continued to place squares so that each new square shared an edge with at least one previously-placed square and no squares overlapped. Eventually, he arrived at the shape in Figure 5.11 (c). He realized that the length of the periphery of this shape was 36, which is again an even number.

Our plucky porcine pal is perplexed by this peculiar pattern. Use induction on the number of squares to prove that the length of the periphery is always even, no matter how many squares Theory Hippotamus places or how he arranges them.

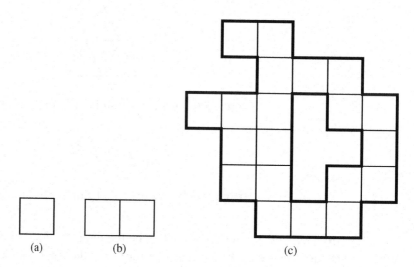

Figure 5.11   Some shapes that Theory Hippotamus created.

Problem 5.12.
Prove the Distributive Law of intersection over the union of n sets by induction:

$$A \cap \bigcup_{i=1}^{n} B_i = \bigcup_{i=1}^{n} (A \cap B_i). \tag{5.14}$$

Hint: Theorem 4.1.2 gives the $n = 2$ case.

Problem 5.13.
Here is an interesting construction of a geometric object known as the *Koch snowflake*. Define a sequence of polygons S_0, S_1 recursively, starting with S_0 equal to an equilateral triangle with unit sides. We construct S_{n+1} by removing the middle third of each edge of S_n and replacing it with two line segments of the same length, as illustrated in Figure 5.12.

Let a_n be the area of S_n. Observe that a_0 is just the area of the unit equilateral triangle which by elementary geometry is $\sqrt{3}/4$.

Prove by induction that for $n \geq 0$, the area of the nth snowflake is given by:

$$a_n = a_0 \left(\frac{8}{5} - \frac{3}{5} \left(\frac{4}{9} \right)^n \right). \tag{5.15}$$

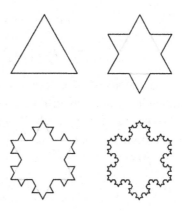

Figure 5.12 S_0, S_1, S_2 and S_3.

Exam Problems

Problem 5.14.
Prove by induction that

$$\sum_{1}^{n} k \cdot k! = (n+1)! - 1. \tag{5.16}$$

Problem 5.15.
Prove by induction:

$$0^3 + 1^3 + 2^3 + \cdots + n^3 = \left(\frac{n(n+1)}{2}\right)^2, \forall n \geq 0.$$

using the equation itself as the induction hypothesis $P(n)$.

(a) Prove the

base case $(n = 0)$.

(b) Now prove the

inductive step.

Problem 5.16.

Suppose $P(n)$ is a predicate on nonnegative numbers, and suppose

$$\forall k.\ P(k)\ \text{IMPLIES}\ P(k+2). \tag{5.17}$$

For P's that satisfy (5.17), some of the assertions below **Can** hold for some, but not all, such P, other assertions **Always** hold no matter what the P may be, and some **Never** hold for any such P. Indicate which case applies for each of the assertions and briefly explain why.

(a) $\forall n \geq 0.\ P(n)$

(b) $\text{NOT}(P(0))\ \text{AND}\ \forall n \geq 1.\ P(n)$

(c) $\forall n \geq 0.\ \text{NOT}(P(n))$

(d) $(\forall n \leq 100.\ P(n))\ \text{AND}\ (\forall n > 100.\ \text{NOT}(P(n)))$

(e) $(\forall n \leq 100.\ \text{NOT}(P(n)))\ \text{AND}\ (\forall n > 100.\ P(n))$

(f) $P(0)\ \text{IMPLIES}\ \forall n.\ P(n+2)$

(g) $[\exists n.\ P(2n)]\ \text{IMPLIES}\ \forall n.\ P(2n+2)$

(h) $P(1)\ \text{IMPLIES}\ \forall n.\ P(2n+1)$

(i) $[\exists n.\ P(2n)]\ \text{IMPLIES}\ \forall n.\ P(2n+2)$

(j) $\exists n.\ \exists m > n.\ [P(2n)\ \text{AND}\ \text{NOT}(P(2m))]$

(k) $[\exists n.\ P(n)]\ \text{IMPLIES}\ \forall n.\ \exists m > n.\ P(m)$

(l) $\text{NOT}(P(0))\ \text{IMPLIES}\ \forall n.\ \text{NOT}(P(2n))$

Problem 5.17.

Consider the following sequence of predicates:

$$
\begin{aligned}
Q_1(x_1) &::= x_1 \\
Q_2(x_1, x_2) &::= x_1\ \text{IMPLIES}\ x_2 \\
Q_3(x_1, x_2, x_3) &::= (x_1\ \text{IMPLIES}\ x_2)\ \text{IMPLIES}\ x_3 \\
Q_4(x_1, x_2, x_3, x_4) &::= ((x_1\ \text{IMPLIES}\ x_2)\ \text{IMPLIES}\ x_3)\ \text{IMPLIES}\ x_4 \\
Q_5(x_1, x_2, x_3, x_4, x_5) &::= (((x_1\ \text{IMPLIES}\ x_2)\ \text{IMPLIES}\ x_3)\ \text{IMPLIES}\ x_4)\ \text{IMPLIES}\ x_5 \\
&\vdots
\end{aligned}
$$

Let T_n be the number of different true/false settings of the variables $x_1, x_2, \ldots, x_n$ for which $Q_n(x_1, x_2, \ldots, x_n)$ is true. For example, $T_2 = 3$ since $Q_2(x_1, x_2)$ is true for 3 different settings of the variables x_1 and x_2:

x_1	x_2	$Q_2(x_1, x_2)$
T	T	T
T	F	F
F	T	T
F	F	T

(a) Express T_{n+1} in terms of T_n, assuming $n \geq 1$.

(b) Use induction to prove that $T_n = \frac{1}{3}(2^{n+1} + (-1)^n)$ for $n \geq 1$. You may assume your answer to the previous part without proof.

Problem 5.18.
You are given n envelopes, numbered $0, 1, \ldots, n-1$. Envelope 0 contains $2^0 = 1$ dollar, Envelope 1 contains $2^1 = 2$ dollars, ..., and Envelope $n-1$ contains 2^{n-1} dollars. Let $P(n)$ be the assertion that:

> For all nonnegative integers $k < 2^n$, there is a subset of the n envelopes whose contents total to exactly k dollars.

Prove by induction that $P(n)$ holds for all integers $n \geq 1$.

Problem 5.19.
Prove by induction that

$$1 \cdot 2 + 2 \cdot 3 + 3 \cdot 4 + \cdots + n(n+1) = \frac{n(n+1)(n+2)}{3} \qquad (5.18)$$

for all integers $n \geq 1$.

Problem 5.20.
A k-bit AND-circuit is a digital circuit that has k 0-1 valued inputs[6] $d_0, d_1, \ldots, d_{k-1}$ and one 0-1-valued output variable whose value will be

$$d_0 \text{ AND } d_1 \text{ AND } \cdots \text{ AND } d_{k-1}.$$

---

[6]Following the usual conventions for digital circuits, we're using 1 for the truth value **T** and 0 for **F**.

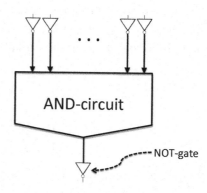

Figure 5.13   OR-circuit from AND-circuit.

OR-circuits are defined in the same way, with "OR" replacing "AND."

(a) Suppose we want an OR-circuit but only have a supply of AND-circuits and some NOT-gates ("inverters") that have one 0-1 valued input and one 0-1 valued output. We can turn an AND-circuit into an OR-circuit by attaching a NOT-gate to each input of the AND-circuit and also attaching a NOT-gate to the output of the AND-circuit. This is illustrated in Figure 5.13. Briefly explain why this works.

Large digital circuits are built by connecting together smaller digital circuits as components. One of the most basic components is a two-input/one-output AND-gate that produces an output value equal to the AND of its two input values. So according the definition in part (a), a single AND-*gate* is a 1-bit AND-*circuit*.

We can build up larger AND-circuits out of a collection of AND-gates in several ways. For example, one way to build a 4-bit AND-circuit is to connect three AND-gates as illustrated in Figure 5.14.

More generally, a *depth-n tree-design* AND-*circuit*—"depth-n circuit" for short—has 2^n inputs and is built from two depth-$(n-1)$ circuits by using the outputs of the two depth-$(n-1)$ circuits as inputs to a single AND-gate. This is illustrated in Figure 5.15. So the 4-bit AND-circuit in Figure 5.14 is a depth-2 circuit. A depth-1 circuit is defined simply to be a single AND-gate.

(b) Let gate#(n) be the number of AND-gates in a depth-n circuit. Prove by induction that

$$\text{gate\#}(n) = 2^n - 1 \tag{5.19}$$

for all $n \geq 1$.

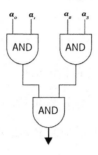

Figure 5.14 A 4-bit AND-circuit.

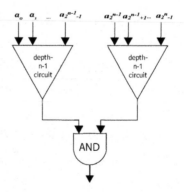

Figure 5.15 An n-bit tree-design AND-circuit.

Problems for Section 5.2

Practice Problems

Problem 5.21.

Some fundamental principles for reasoning about nonnegative integers are:

1. The Induction Principle,

2. The Strong Induction Principle,

3. The Well Ordering Principle.

Identify which, if any, of the above principles is captured by each of the following inference rules.

(a)

$$\frac{P(0), \forall m. \, (\forall k \le m. \, P(k)) \text{ IMPLIES } P(m+1)}{\forall n. \, P(n)}$$

(b)

$$\frac{P(b), \forall k \ge b. \, P(k) \text{ IMPLIES } P(k+1)}{\forall k \ge b. \, P(k)}$$

(c)

$$\frac{\exists n. \, P(n)}{\exists m. \, [P(m) \text{ AND } (\forall k. \, P(k) \text{ IMPLIES } k \ge m)]}$$

(d)

$$\frac{P(0), \forall k > 0. \, P(k) \text{ IMPLIES } P(k+1)}{\forall n. \, P(n)}$$

(e)

$$\frac{\forall m. \, (\forall k < m. \, P(k)) \text{ IMPLIES } P(m)}{\forall n. \, P(n)}$$

Problem 5.22.

The Fibonacci numbers $F(n)$ are described in Section 5.2.2.

Indicate exactly which sentence(s) in the following bogus proof contain logical errors? Explain.

False Claim. *Every Fibonacci number is even.*

Bogus proof. Let all the variables n, m, k mentioned below be nonnegative integer valued. Let Even(n) mean that $F(n)$ is even. The proof is by strong induction with induction hypothesis Even(n).

base case: $F(0) = 0$ is an even number, so Even(0) is true.

inductive step: We assume may assume the strong induction hypothesis

$$\text{Even}(k) \text{ for } 0 \leq k \leq n,$$

and we must prove Even($n + 1$).

Then by strong induction hypothesis, Even(n) and Even($n - 1$) are true, that is, $F(n)$ and $F(n - 1)$ are both even. But by the definition, $F(n + 1)$ equals the sum $F(n) + F(n - 1)$ of two even numbers, and so it is also even. This proves Even($n + 1$) as required.

Hence, $F(m)$ is even for all $m \in \mathbb{N}$ by the Strong Induction Principle.

■

Problem 5.23.

Alice wants to prove by induction that a predicate P holds for certain nonnegative integers. She has proven that for all nonnegative integers $n = 0, 1, \ldots$

$$P(n) \text{ IMPLIES } P(n + 3).$$

(a) Suppose Alice also proves that $P(5)$ holds. Which of the following propositions can she infer?

   1. $P(n)$ holds for all $n \geq 5$

   2. $P(3n)$ holds for all $n \geq 5$

   3. $P(n)$ holds for $n = 8, 11, 14, \ldots$

   4. $P(n)$ does not hold for $n < 5$

   5. $\forall n.\ P(3n + 5)$

   6. $\forall n > 2.\ P(3n - 1)$

   7. $P(0)$ IMPLIES $\forall n.\ P(3n + 2)$

   8. $P(0)$ IMPLIES $\forall n.\ P(3n)$

(b) Which of the following could Alice prove in order to conclude that $P(n)$ holds for all $n \geq 5$?

   1. $P(0)$

2. $P(5)$

3. $P(5)$ and $P(6)$

4. $P(0)$, $P(1)$ and $P(2)$

5. $P(5)$, $P(6)$ and $P(7)$

6. $P(2)$, $P(4)$ and $P(5)$

7. $P(2)$, $P(4)$ and $P(6)$

8. $P(3)$, $P(5)$ and $P(7)$

Problem 5.24.
Prove that every amount of postage of 12 cents or more can be formed using just 4-cent and 5-cent stamps.

Class Problems

Problem 5.25.
The Fibonacci numbers are described in Section 5.2.2.

Prove, using strong induction, the following closed-form formula for the Fibonacci numbers.[7]

$$F(n) = \frac{p^n - q^n}{\sqrt{5}}$$

where $p = \frac{1+\sqrt{5}}{2}$ and $q = \frac{1-\sqrt{5}}{2}$.

Hint: Note that p and q are the roots of $x^2 - x - 1 = 0$, and so $p^2 = p + 1$ and $q^2 = q + 1$.

Problem 5.26.
A sequence of numbers is *weakly decreasing* when each number in the sequence is $\geq$ the numbers after it. (This implies that a sequence of just one number is weakly decreasing.)

Here's a bogus proof of a very important true fact, every integer greater than 1 is a *product of a unique weakly decreasing sequence of primes*—a pusp, for short.

Explain what's bogus about the proof.

Lemma. *Every integer greater than 1 is a pusp.*

---

[7]This mind-boggling formula is known as *Binet's formula*. We'll explain in Chapter 16, and again in Chapter 22, how it comes about.

For example, $252 = 7 \cdot 3 \cdot 3 \cdot 2 \cdot 2$, and no other weakly decreasing sequence of primes will have a product equal to 252.

Bogus proof. We will prove the lemma by strong induction, letting the induction hypothesis $P(n)$ be

$$n \text{ is a pusp.}$$

So the lemma will follow if we prove that $P(n)$ holds for all $n \geq 2$.

Base Case $(n = 2)$: $P(2)$ is true because 2 is prime, and so it is a length one product of primes, and this is obviously the only sequence of primes whose product can equal 2.

Inductive step: Suppose that $n \geq 2$ and that i is a pusp for every integer i where $2 \leq i < n + 1$. We must show that $P(n + 1)$ holds, namely, that $n + 1$ is also a pusp. We argue by cases:

If $n + 1$ is itself prime, then it is the product of a length one sequence consisting of itself. This sequence is unique, since by definition of prime, $n + 1$ has no other prime factors. So $n + 1$ is a pusp, that is $P(n + 1)$ holds in this case.

Otherwise, $n + 1$ is not prime, which by definition means $n + 1 = km$ for some integers k, m such that $2 \leq k, m < n + 1$. Now by the strong induction hypothesis, we know that k and m are pusps. It follows that by merging the unique prime sequences for k and m, in sorted order, we get a unique weakly decreasing sequence of primes whose product equals $n + 1$. So $n + 1$ is a pusp, in this case as well.

So $P(n + 1)$ holds in any case, which completes the proof by strong induction that $P(n)$ holds for all $n \geq 2$.

∎

Problem 5.27.
Define the *potential* $p(S)$ of a stack of blocks S to be $k(k-1)/2$ where k is the number of blocks in S. Define the potential $p(A)$ of a set of stacks A to be the sum of the potentials of the stacks in A.

Generalize Theorem 5.2.1 about scores in the stacking game to show that for any set of stacks A if a sequence of moves starting with A leads to another set of stacks B then $p(A) \geq p(B)$, and the score for this sequence of moves is $p(A) - p(B)$.

Hint: Try induction on the number of moves to get from A to B.

Homework Problems

Problem 5.28.

A group of $n \geq 1$ people can be divided into teams, each containing either 4 or 7 people. What are all the possible values of n? Use induction to prove that your answer is correct.

Problem 5.29.

The following Lemma is true, but the *proof* given for it below is defective. Pinpoint *exactly* where the proof first makes an unjustified step and explain why it is unjustified.

Lemma. *For any prime p and positive integers $n, x_1, x_2, \ldots, x_n$, if $p \mid x_1 x_2 \ldots x_n$, then $p \mid x_i$ for some $1 \leq i \leq n$.*

Bogus proof. Proof by strong induction on n. The induction hypothesis $P(n)$ is that Lemma holds for n.

Base case $n = 1$: When $n = 1$, we have $p \mid x_1$, therefore we can let $i = 1$ and conclude $p \mid x_i$.

Induction step: Now assuming the claim holds for all $k \leq n$, we must prove it for $n + 1$.

So suppose $p \mid x_1 x_2 \cdots x_{n+1}$. Let $y_n = x_n x_{n+1}$, so $x_1 x_2 \cdots x_{n+1} = x_1 x_2 \cdots x_{n-1} y_n$. Since the right-hand side of this equality is a product of n terms, we have by induction that p divides one of them. If $p \mid x_i$ for some $i < n$, then we have the desired i. Otherwise $p \mid y_n$. But since y_n is a product of the two terms x_n, x_{n+1}, we have by strong induction that p divides one of them. So in this case $p \mid x_i$ for $i = n$ or $i = n + 1$. ∎

Exam Problems

Problem 5.30.

The Fibonacci numbers $F(n)$ are described in Section 5.2.2.

These numbers satisfy many unexpected identities, such as

$$F(0)^2 + F(1)^2 + \cdots + F(n)^2 = F(n)F(n + 1). \qquad (5.20)$$

Equation (5.20) can be proved to hold for all $n \in \mathbb{N}$ by induction, using the equation itself as the induction hypothesis $P(n)$.

(a) Prove the

base case $(n = 0)$.

(b) Now prove the

inductive step.

Problem 5.31.
Use strong induction to prove that $n \leq 3^{n/3}$ for every integer $n \geq 0$.

Problem 5.32.
A class of any size of 18 or more can be assembled from student teams of sizes 4 and 7. Prove this by **induction** (of some kind), using the induction hypothesis:

$S(n) ::=$ a class of $n + 18$ students can be assembled from teams of sizes 4 and 7.

Problem 5.33.
Any amount of ten or more cents postage that is a multiple of five can be made using only 10¢ and 15¢ stamps. Prove this *by induction* (ordinary or strong, but say which) using the induction hypothesis

$S(n) ::= (5n + 10)$¢ postage can be made using only 10¢ and 15¢ stamps.

6   State Machines

State machines are a simple, abstract model of step-by-step processes. Since computer programs can be understood as defining step-by-step computational processes, it's not surprising that state machines come up regularly in computer science. They also come up in many other settings such as designing digital circuits and modeling probabilistic processes. This section introduces *Floyd's Invariant Principle* which is a version of induction tailored specifically for proving properties of state machines.

One of the most important uses of induction in computer science involves proving one or more desirable properties continues to hold at every step in a process. A property that is preserved through a series of operations or steps is known as a *preserved invariant*.

Examples of desirable invariants include properties such as a variable never exceeding a certain value, the altitude of a plane never dropping below 1,000 feet without the wingflaps being deployed, and the temperature of a nuclear reactor never exceeding the threshold for a meltdown.

6.1   States and Transitions

Formally, a *state machine* is nothing more than a binary relation on a set, except that the elements of the set are called "states," the relation is called the transition relation, and an arrow in the graph of the transition relation is called a *transition*. A transition from state q to state r will be written $q \longrightarrow r$. The transition relation is also called the *state graph* of the machine. A state machine also comes equipped with a designated *start state*.

A simple example is a bounded counter, which counts from 0 to 99 and overflows at 100. This state machine is pictured in Figure 6.1, with states pictured as circles, transitions by arrows, and with start state 0 indicated by the double circle. To be

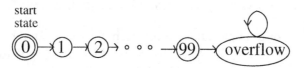

Figure 6.1   *State transitions for the 99-bounded counter.*

precise, what the picture tells us is that this bounded counter machine has

$$\text{states} ::= \{0, 1, \ldots, 99, \text{overflow}\},$$
$$\text{start state} ::= 0,$$
$$\text{transitions} ::= \{n \longrightarrow n + 1 \mid 0 \le n < 99\}$$
$$\cup \{99 \longrightarrow \text{overflow}, \text{overflow} \longrightarrow \text{overflow}\}.$$

This machine isn't much use once it overflows, since it has no way to get out of its overflow state.

State machines for digital circuits and string pattern matching algorithms, for instance, usually have only a finite number of states. Machines that model continuing computations typically have an infinite number of states. For example, instead of the 99-bounded counter, we could easily define an "unbounded" counter that just keeps counting up without overflowing. The unbounded counter has an infinite state set, the nonnegative integers, which makes its state diagram harder to draw.

State machines are often defined with labels on states and/or transitions to indicate such things as input or output values, costs, capacities, or probabilities. Our state machines don't include any such labels because they aren't needed for our purposes. We do name states, as in Figure 6.1, so we can talk about them, but the names aren't part of the state machine.

6.2   The Invariant Principle

6.2.1   A Diagonally-Moving Robot

Suppose we have a robot that starts at the origin and moves on an infinite 2-dimensional integer grid. The *state* of the robot at any time can be specified by the integer coordinates (x, y) of the robot's current position. So the *start state* is $(0, 0)$. At each step, the robot may move to a diagonally adjacent grid point, as illustrated in Figure 6.2.

To be precise, the robot's transitions are:

$$\{(m, n) \longrightarrow (m \pm 1, n \pm 1) \mid m, n \in \mathbb{Z}\}.$$

For example, after the first step, the robot could be in states $(1, 1)$, $(1, -1)$, $(-1, 1)$ or $(-1, -1)$. After two steps, there are 9 possible states for the robot, including $(0, 0)$. The question is, can the robot ever reach position $(1, 0)$?

If you play around with the robot a bit, you'll probably notice that the robot can only reach positions (m, n) for which $m + n$ is even, which of course means that it

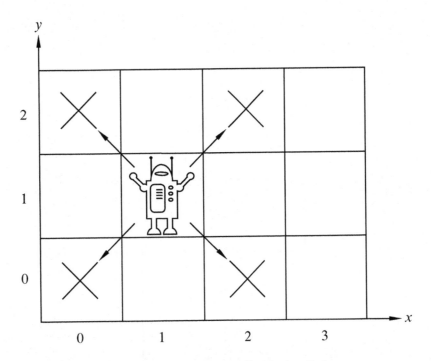

Figure 6.2 *The Diagonally Moving Robot.*

can't reach $(1, 0)$. This follows because the evenness of the sum of the coordinates is a property that is *preserved* by transitions. This is an example of a *preserved invariant*.

This once, let's go through this preserved invariant argument, carefully highlighting where induction comes in. Specifically, define the even-sum property of states to be:

$$\text{Even-sum}((m, n)) ::= [m + n \text{ is even}].$$

Lemma 6.2.1. *For any transition* $q \longrightarrow r$ *of the diagonally-moving robot, if Even-sum(q), then Even-sum(r).*

This lemma follows immediately from the definition of the robot's transitions: $(m, n) \longrightarrow (m \pm 1, n \pm 1)$. After a transition, the sum of coordinates changes by $(\pm 1) + (\pm 1)$, that is, by 0, 2, or -2. Of course, adding 0, 2 or -2 to an even number gives an even number. So by a trivial induction on the number of transitions, we can prove:

Theorem 6.2.2. *The sum of the coordinates of any state reachable by the diagonally-moving robot is even.*

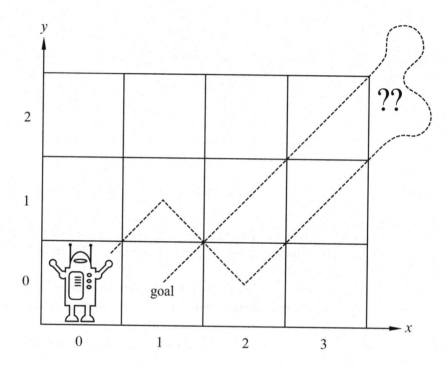

Figure 6.3   *Can the Robot get to (1, 0)?*

Proof. The proof is induction on the number of transitions the robot has made. The induction hypothesis is

$P(n) ::=$ if q is a state reachable in n transitions, then Even-sum(q).

Base case: $P(0)$ is true since the only state reachable in 0 transitions is the start state $(0, 0)$, and $0 + 0$ is even.

Inductive step: Assume that $P(n)$ is true, and let r be any state reachable in $n + 1$ transitions. We need to prove that Even-sum(r) holds.

Since r is reachable in $n + 1$ transitions, there must be a state q reachable in n transitions such that $q \longrightarrow r$. Since $P(n)$ is assumed to be true, Even-sum(q) holds, and so by Lemma 6.2.1, Even-sum(r) also holds. This proves that $P(n)$ IMPLIES $P(n + 1)$ as required, completing the proof of the inductive step.

We conclude by induction that for all $n \geq 0$, if q is reachable in n transitions, then Even-sum(q). This implies that every reachable state has the Even-sum property. $\blacksquare$

Corollary 6.2.3. *The robot can never reach position* $(1, 0)$.

Proof. By Theorem 6.2.2, we know the robot can only reach positions with coordinates that sum to an even number, and thus it cannot reach position $(1, 0)$. $\blacksquare$

6.2.2 Statement of the Invariant Principle

Using the Even-sum invariant to understand the diagonally-moving robot is a simple example of a basic proof method called The Invariant Principle. The Principle summarizes how induction on the number of steps to reach a state applies to invariants.

A state machine *execution* describes a possible sequence of steps a machine might take.

Definition 6.2.4. An *execution* of the state machine is a (possibly infinite) sequence of states with the property that

- it begins with the start state, and

- if q and r are consecutive states in the sequence, then $q \longrightarrow r$.

A state is called *reachable* if it appears in some execution.

Definition 6.2.5. A *preserved invariant* of a state machine is a predicate P on states, such that whenever $P(q)$ is true of a state q and $q \longrightarrow r$ for some state r then $P(r)$ holds.

The Invariant Principle

If a preserved invariant of a state machine is true for the start state,
then it is true for all reachable states.

The Invariant Principle is nothing more than the Induction Principle reformulated in a convenient form for state machines. Showing that a predicate is true in the start state is the base case of the induction, and showing that a predicate is a preserved invariant corresponds to the inductive step.[1]

---

[1] Preserved invariants are commonly just called "invariants" in the literature on program correctness, but we decided to throw in the extra adjective to avoid confusion with other definitions. For example, other texts (as well as another subject at MIT) use "invariant" to mean "predicate true of all reachable states." Let's call this definition "invariant-2." Now invariant-2 seems like a reasonable definition, since unreachable states by definition don't matter, and all we want to show is that a desired property is invariant-2. But this confuses the *objective* of demonstrating that a property is invariant-2 with the *method* of finding a *preserved* invariant—which is preserved even at unreachable states—to *show* that it is invariant-2.

Robert W. Floyd

The Invariant Principle was formulated by Robert W. Floyd at Carnegie Tech in 1967. (Carnegie Tech was renamed Carnegie-Mellon University the following year.) Floyd was already famous for work on the formal grammars that transformed the field of programming language parsing; that was how he got to be a professor even though he never got a Ph.D. (He had been admitted to a PhD program as a teenage prodigy, but flunked out and never went back.)

In that same year, Albert R. Meyer was appointed Assistant Professor in the Carnegie Tech Computer Science Department, where he first met Floyd. Floyd and Meyer were the only theoreticians in the department, and they were both delighted to talk about their shared interests. After just a few conversations, Floyd's new junior colleague decided that Floyd was the smartest person he had ever met.

Naturally, one of the first things Floyd wanted to tell Meyer about was his new, as yet unpublished, Invariant Principle. Floyd explained the result to Meyer, and Meyer wondered (privately) how someone as brilliant as Floyd could be excited by such a trivial observation. Floyd had to show Meyer a bunch of examples before Meyer understood Floyd's excitement —not at the truth of the utterly obvious Invariant Principle, but rather at the insight that such a simple method could be so widely and easily applied in verifying programs.

Floyd left for Stanford the following year. He won the Turing award—the "Nobel prize" of computer science—in the late 1970's, in recognition of his work on grammars and on the foundations of program verification. He remained at Stanford from 1968 until his death in September, 2001. You can learn more about Floyd's life and work by reading the eulogy at

http://oldwww.acm.org/pubs/membernet/stories/floyd.pdf

written by his closest colleague, Don Knuth.

6.2.3   The Die Hard Example

The movie *Die Hard 3: With a Vengeance* includes an amusing example of a state machine. The lead characters played by Samuel L. Jackson and Bruce Willis have to disarm a bomb planted by the diabolical Simon Gruber:

Simon: On the fountain, there should be 2 jugs, do you see them? A 5-gallon and a 3-gallon. Fill one of the jugs with exactly 4 gallons of water and place it on the scale and the timer will stop. You must be precise; one ounce more or less will result in detonation. If you're still alive in 5 minutes, we'll speak.

Bruce: Wait, wait a second. I don't get it. Do you get it?

Samuel: No.

Bruce: Get the jugs. Obviously, we can't fill the 3-gallon jug with 4 gallons of water.

Samuel: Obviously.

Bruce: All right. I know, here we go. We fill the 3-gallon jug exactly to the top, right?

Samuel: Uh-huh.

Bruce: Okay, now we pour this 3 gallons into the 5-gallon jug, giving us exactly 3 gallons in the 5-gallon jug, right?

Samuel: Right, then what?

Bruce: All right. We take the 3-gallon jug and fill it a third of the way...

Samuel: No! He said, "Be precise." Exactly 4 gallons.

Bruce: Sh - -. Every cop within 50 miles is running his a - - off and I'm out here playing kids games in the park.

Samuel: Hey, you want to focus on the problem at hand?

Fortunately, they find a solution in the nick of time. You can work out how.

The Die Hard 3 State Machine

The jug-filling scenario can be modeled with a state machine that keeps track of the amount b of water in the big jug, and the amount l in the little jug. With the 3 and 5 gallon water jugs, the states formally will be pairs (b, l) of real numbers such that $0 \le b \le 5, 0 \le l \le 3$. (We can prove that the reachable values of b and l will be nonnegative integers, but we won't assume this.) The start state is $(0,0)$, since both jugs start empty.

Since the amount of water in the jug must be known exactly, we will only consider moves in which a jug gets completely filled or completely emptied. There are several kinds of transitions:

1. Fill the little jug: $(b,l) \longrightarrow (b,3)$ for $l < 3$.

2. Fill the big jug: $(b,l) \longrightarrow (5,l)$ for $b < 5$.

3. Empty the little jug: $(b,l) \longrightarrow (b,0)$ for $l > 0$.

4. Empty the big jug: $(b,l) \longrightarrow (0,l)$ for $b > 0$.

5. Pour from the little jug into the big jug: for $l > 0$,

$$(b,l) \longrightarrow \begin{cases} (b+l,0) & \text{if } b+l \le 5, \\ (5, l-(5-b)) & \text{otherwise.} \end{cases}$$

6. Pour from big jug into little jug: for $b > 0$,

$$(b,l) \longrightarrow \begin{cases} (0, b+l) & \text{if } b+l \le 3, \\ (b-(3-l), 3) & \text{otherwise.} \end{cases}$$

Note that in contrast to the 99-counter state machine, there is more than one possible transition out of states in the Die Hard machine. Machines like the 99-counter with at most one transition out of each state are called *deterministic*. The Die Hard machine is *nondeterministic* because some states have transitions to several different states.

The Die Hard 3 bomb gets disarmed successfully because the state $(4,3)$ is reachable.

Die Hard Permanently

The *Die Hard* series is getting tired, so we propose a final *Die Hard Permanently*. Here, Simon's brother returns to avenge him, posing the same challenge, but with the 5 gallon jug replaced by a 9 gallon one. The state machine has the same specification as the Die Hard 3 version, except all occurrences of "5" are replaced by "9."

Now, reaching any state of the form $(4,l)$ is impossible. We prove this using the Invariant Principle. Specifically, we define the preserved invariant predicate $P((b,l))$ to be that b and l are nonnegative integer multiples of 3.

To prove that P is a preserved invariant of Die-Hard-Once-and-For-All machine, we assume $P(q)$ holds for some state $q ::= (b, l)$ and that $q \longrightarrow r$. We have to show that $P(r)$ holds. The proof divides into cases, according to which transition rule is used.

One case is a "fill the little jug" transition. This means $r = (b, 3)$. But $P(q)$ implies that b is an integer multiple of 3, and of course 3 is an integer multiple of 3, so $P(r)$ still holds.

Another case is a "pour from big jug into little jug" transition. For the subcase when there isn't enough room in the little jug to hold all the water, that is, when $b + l > 3$, we have $r = (b - (3 - l), 3)$. But $P(q)$ implies that b and l are integer multiples of 3, which means $b - (3 - l)$ is too, so in this case too, $P(r)$ holds.

We won't bother to crank out the remaining cases, which can all be checked just as easily. Now by the Invariant Principle, we conclude that every reachable state satisifies P. But since no state of the form $(4, l)$ satisifies P, we have proved rigorously that Bruce dies once and for all!

By the way, notice that the state (1,0), which satisfies NOT(P), has a transition to (0,0), which satisfies P. So the negation of a preserved invariant may not be a preserved invariant.

6.3   Partial Correctness & Termination

Floyd distinguished two required properties to verify a program. The first property is called *partial correctness*; this is the property that the final results, if any, of the process must satisfy system requirements.

You might suppose that if a result was only partially correct, then it might also be partially incorrect, but that's not what Floyd meant. The word "partial" comes from viewing a process that might not terminate as computing a *partial relation*. Partial correctness means that *when there is a result*, it is correct, but the process might not always produce a result, perhaps because it gets stuck in a loop.

The second correctness property, called *termination*, is that the process does always produce some final value.

Partial correctness can commonly be proved using the Invariant Principle. Termination can commonly be proved using the Well Ordering Principle. We'll illustrate this by verifying a Fast Exponentiation procedure.

6.3.1 Fast Exponentiation

Exponentiating

The most straightforward way to compute the bth power of a number a is to multiply a by itself $b-1$ times. But the solution can be found in considerably fewer multiplications by using a technique called *Fast Exponentiation*. The register machine program below defines the fast exponentiation algorithm. The letters x, y, z, r denote registers that hold numbers. An *assignment statement* has the form "$z := a$" and has the effect of setting the number in register z to be the number a.

A Fast Exponentiation Program

Given inputs $a \in \mathbb{R}, b \in \mathbb{N}$, initialize registers x, y, z to $a, 1, b$ respectively, and repeat the following sequence of steps until termination:

- if $z = 0$ **return** y and terminate

- $r := \text{remainder}(z, 2)$

- $z := \text{quotient}(z, 2)$

- if $r = 1$, then $y := xy$

- $x := x^2$

We claim this program always terminates and leaves $y = a^b$.

To begin, we'll model the behavior of the program with a state machine:

1. states $::= \mathbb{R} \times \mathbb{R} \times \mathbb{N}$,

2. start state $::= (a, 1, b)$,

3. transitions are defined by the rule

$$(x, y, z) \longrightarrow \begin{cases} (x^2, y, \text{quotient}(z, 2)) & \text{if } z \text{ is nonzero and even,} \\ (x^2, xy, \text{quotient}(z, 2)) & \text{if } z \text{ is nonzero and odd.} \end{cases}$$

The preserved invariant $P((x, y, z))$ will be

$$z \in \mathbb{N} \text{ AND } yx^z = a^b. \tag{6.1}$$

To prove that P is preserved, assume $P((x, y, z))$ holds and that $(x, y, z) \longrightarrow (x_t, y_t, z_t)$. We must prove that $P((x_t, y_t, z_t))$ holds, that is,

$$z_t \in \mathbb{N} \text{ AND } y_t x_t^{z_t} = a^b. \tag{6.2}$$

Since there is a transition from (x, y, z), we have $z \neq 0$, and since $z \in \mathbb{N}$ by (6.1), we can consider just two cases:

If z is even, then we have that $x_t = x^2, y_t = y, z_t = z/2$. Therefore, $z_t \in \mathbb{N}$ and

$$
\begin{aligned}
y_t x_t^{z_t} &= y(x^2)^{z/2} \\
&= yx^{2 \cdot z/2} \\
&= yx^z \\
&= a^b \qquad\qquad\qquad \text{(by (6.1))}
\end{aligned}
$$

If z is odd, then we have that $x_t = x^2, y_t = xy, z_t = (z-1)/2$. Therefore, $z_t \in \mathbb{N}$ and

$$
\begin{aligned}
y_t x_t^{z_t} &= xy(x^2)^{(z-1)/2} \\
&= yx^{1+2 \cdot (z-1)/2} \\
&= yx^{1+(z-1)} \\
&= yx^z \\
&= a^b \qquad\qquad\qquad \text{(by (6.1))}
\end{aligned}
$$

So in both cases, (6.2) holds, proving that P is a preserved invariant.

Now it's easy to prove partial correctness: if the Fast Exponentiation program terminates, it does so with a^b in register y. This works because $1 \cdot a^b = a^b$, which means that the start state $(a, 1, b)$ satisifies P. By the Invariant Principle, P holds for all reachable states. But the program only stops when $z = 0$. If a terminated state $(x, y, 0)$ is reachable, then $y = yx^0 = a^b$ as required.

Ok, it's partially correct, but what's fast about it? The answer is that the number of multiplications it performs to compute a^b is roughly the length of the binary representation of b. That is, the Fast Exponentiation program uses roughly $\log b$[2] multiplications, compared to the naive approach of multiplying by a a total of $b-1$ times.

More precisely, it requires at most $2(\lceil \log b \rceil + 1)$ multiplications for the Fast Exponentiation algorithm to compute a^b for $b > 1$. The reason is that the number in register z is initially b, and gets at least halved with each transition. So it can't be halved more than $\lceil \log b \rceil + 1$ times before hitting zero and causing the program to terminate. Since each of the transitions involves at most two multiplications, the total number of multiplications until $z = 0$ is at most $2(\lceil \log b \rceil + 1)$ for $b > 0$ (see Problem 6.6).

---

[2]As usual in computer science, $\log b$ means the base two logarithm $\log_2 b$. We use, $\ln b$ for the natural logarithm $\log_e b$, and otherwise write the logarithm base explicitly, as in $\log_{10} b$.

6.3.2 Derived Variables

The preceding termination proof involved finding a nonnegative integer-valued measure to assign to states. We might call this measure the "size" of the state. We then showed that the size of a state decreased with every state transition. By the Well Ordering Principle, the size can't decrease indefinitely, so when a minimum size state is reached, there can't be any transitions possible: the process has terminated.

More generally, the technique of assigning values to states—not necessarily nonnegative integers and not necessarily decreasing under transitions—is often useful in the analysis of algorithms. *Potential functions* play a similar role in physics. In the context of computational processes, such value assignments for states are called *derived variables*.

For example, for the Die Hard machines we could have introduced a derived variable f : states $\rightarrow \mathbb{R}$ for the amount of water in both buckets, by setting $f((a, b)) ::= a + b$. Similarly, in the robot problem, the position of the robot along the x-axis would be given by the derived variable x-coord, where x-coord$((i, j)) ::= i$.

There are a few standard properties of derived variables that are handy in analyzing state machines.

Definition 6.3.1. A derived variable f : states $\rightarrow \mathbb{R}$ is *strictly decreasing* iff

$$q \longrightarrow q' \text{ IMPLIES } f(q') < f(q).$$

It is *weakly decreasing* iff

$$q \longrightarrow q' \text{ IMPLIES } f(q') \leq f(q).$$

Strictly increasingweakly increasing derived variables are defined similarly.[3]

We confirmed termination of the Fast Exponentiation procedure by noticing that the derived variable z was nonnegative-integer-valued and strictly decreasing. We can summarize this approach to proving termination as follows:

Theorem 6.3.2. *If f is a strictly decreasing $\mathbb{N}$-valued derived variable of a state machine, then the length of any execution starting at state q is at most $f(q)$.*

Of course, we could prove Theorem 6.3.2 by induction on the value of $f(q)$, but think about what it says: "If you start counting down at some nonnegative integer $f(q)$, then you can't count down more than $f(q)$ times." Put this way, it's obvious.

---

[3]Weakly increasing variables are often also called *nondecreasing*. We will avoid this terminology to prevent confusion between nondecreasing variables and variables with the much weaker property of *not* being a decreasing variable.

6.3.3   Termination with Well ordered Sets (Optional)

Theorem 6.3.2 generalizes straightforwardly to derived variables taking values in a well ordered set (Section 2.4.

Theorem 6.3.3. *If there exists a strictly decreasing derived variable whose range is a well ordered set, then every execution terminates.*

Theorem 6.3.3 follows immediately from the observation that a set of numbers is well ordered iff it has no infinite decreasing sequences (Problem 2.22).

Note that the existence of a *weakly* decreasing derived variable does not guarantee that every execution terminates. An infinite execution could proceed through states in which a weakly decreasing variable remained constant.

6.3.4   A Southeast Jumping Robot (Optional)

Here's a simple, contrived example of a termination proof based on a variable that is strictly decreasing over a well ordered set. Let's think about a robot that travels around the nonnegative integer quadrant $\mathbb{N}^2$.

If the robot is at some position (x, y) different from the origin $(0, 0)$, the robot must make a move, which may be

- a unit distance West—that is, $(x, y) \longrightarrow (x - 1, y)$ for $x > 0$, or

- a unit distance South combined with an arbitrary jump East—that is, $(x, y) \longrightarrow (z, y - 1)$ for $z \geq x$,

providing the move does not leave the quadrant.

Claim 6.3.4. *The robot will always get stuck at the origin.*

If we think of the robot as a nondeterministic state machine, then Claim 6.3.4 is a termination assertion. The Claim may seem obvious, but it really has a different character than termination based on nonnegative integer-valued variables. That's because, even knowing that the robot is at position $(0, 1)$, for example, there is no way to bound the time it takes for the robot to get stuck. It can delay getting stuck for as many seconds as it wants by making its next move to a distant point in the Far East. This rules out proving termination using Theorem 6.3.2.

So does Claim 6.3.4 still seem obvious?

Well it is if you see the trick. Define a derived variable v mapping robot states to the numbers in the well ordered set $\mathbb{N} + \mathbb{F}$ of Lemma 2.4.5. In particular, define $v : \mathbb{N}^2 \to \mathbb{N} + \mathbb{F}$ as follows

$$v(x, y) ::= y + \frac{x}{x + 1}.$$

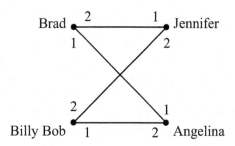

Figure 6.4 Preferences for four people. Both men like Angelina best and both women like Brad best.

Now it's easy to check that if $(x, y) \longrightarrow (x', y')$ is a legitimate robot move, then $v((x', y')) < v((x, y))$. In particular, v is a strictly decreasing derived variable, so Theorem 6.3.3 implies that the robot always get stuck—even though we can't say how many moves it will take until it does.

6.4 The Stable Marriage Problem

Suppose we have a population of men and women in which each person has preferences of the opposite-gender person they would like to marry: each man has his preference list of all the women, and each woman has her preference list of all of the men.

The preferences don't have to be symmetric. That is, Jennifer might like Brad best, but Brad doesn't necessarily like Jennifer best. The goal is to marry everyone: every man must marry exactly one woman and *vice versa*—no polygamy and heterosexual marriages only.[4] Moreover, we would like to find a matching between men and women that is *stable* in the sense that there is no pair of people who prefer one another to their spouses.

For example, suppose Brad likes Angelina best, and Angelina likes Brad best, but Brad and Angelina are married to other people, say Jennifer and Billy Bob. Now *Brad and Angelina prefer each other to their spouses*, which puts their marriages at risk. Pretty soon, they're likely to start spending late nights together working on problem sets!

This unfortunate situation is illustrated in Figure 6.4, where the digits "1" and "2" near a man shows which of the two women he ranks first and second, respectively, and similarly for the women.

---

[4]Same-sex marriage is an interesting but separate case.

More generally, in any matching, a man and woman who are not married to each other and who like each other better than their spouses is called a *rogue couple*. In the situation shown in Figure 6.4, Brad and Angelina would be a rogue couple.

Having a rogue couple is not a good thing, since it threatens the stability of the marriages. On the other hand, if there are no rogue couples, then for any man and woman who are not married to each other, at least one likes their spouse better than the other, and so there won't be any mutual temptation to start an affair.

Definition 6.4.1. A *stable matching* is a matching with no rogue couples.

The question is, given everybody's preferences, can you find a stable set of marriages? In the example consisting solely of the four people in Figure 6.4, we could let Brad and Angelina both have their first choices by marrying each other. Now neither Brad nor Angelina prefers anybody else to their spouse, so neither will be in a rogue couple. This leaves Jen not-so-happily married to Billy Bob, but neither Jen nor Billy Bob can entice somebody else to marry them, and so this is a stable matching.

It turns out there *always* is a stable matching among a group of men and women. We don't know of any immediate way to recognize this, and it seems surprising. In fact, in the apparently similar same-sex or "buddy" matching problem where people are supposed to be paired off as buddies, regardless of gender, a stable matching *may not* be possible. An example of preferences among four people where there is no stable buddy match is given in Problem 6.23. But when men are only allowed to marry women, and *vice versa*, then there is a simple procedure to produce a stable matching and the concept of preserved invariants provides an elegant way to understand and verify the procedure.

6.4.1 The Mating Ritual

The procedure for finding a stable matching can be described in a memorable way as a *Mating Ritual* that takes place over several days. On the starting day, each man has his full preference list of all the women, and likewise each woman has her full preference list of all the men. Then following events happen each day:

Morning: Each man stands under the balcony of the woman on the top of his list, that is the woman he prefers above all the other remaining women. The he serenades her. He is said to be her *suitor*. If a man has no women left on his list, he stays home and does his math homework.

Afternoon: Each woman who has one or more suitors says to her favorite among them, "We might get engaged. Please stay around." To the other suitors, she says, "No. I will never marry you! Take a hike!"

Evening: Any man who is told by a woman to take a hike crosses that woman off his preference list.

Termination condition: When a day arrives in which every woman has at most one suitor, the ritual ends with each woman marrying her suitor, if she has one.

There are a number of facts about this Mating Ritual that we would like to prove:

- The Ritual eventually reaches the termination condition.

- Everybody ends up married.

- The resulting marriages are stable.

To prove these facts, it will be helpful to recognize the Ritual as the description of a state machine. The state at the start of any day is determined by knowing for each man, which woman, if any, he will serenade that day—that is, the woman at the top of his preference list after he has crossed out all the women who have rejected him on earlier days.

Mating Ritual at Akamai

The Internet infrastructure company Akamai, cofounded by Tom Leighton, also uses a variation of the Mating Ritual to assign web traffic to its servers.

In the early days, Akamai used other combinatorial optimization algorithms that got to be too slow as the number of servers (over 65,000 in 2010) and requests (over 800 billion per day) increased. Akamai switched to a Ritual-like approach, since a Ritual is fast and can be run in a distributed manner. In this case, web requests correspond to women and web servers correspond to men. The web requests have preferences based on latency and packet loss, and the web servers have preferences based on cost of bandwidth and co-location.

6.4.2   There is a Marriage Day

It's easy to see why the Mating Ritual has a terminal day when people finally get married. Every day on which the ritual hasn't terminated, at least one man crosses a woman off his list. (If the ritual hasn't terminated, there must be some woman serenaded by at least two men, and at least one of them will have to cross her off his list). If we start with n men and n women, then each of the n men's lists initially has n women on it, for a total of n^2 list entries. Since no women ever gets added to a list, the total number of entries on the lists decreases every day that the Ritual continues, and so the Ritual can continue for at most n^2 days.

6.4.3   They All Live Happily Ever After...

We will prove that the Mating Ritual leaves everyone in a stable marriage. To do this, we note one very useful fact about the Ritual: if on some morning a woman has any suitor, then her favorite suitor will still be serenading her the next morning—his list won't have changed. So she is sure to have today's favorite suitor among her suitors tomorrow. That means she will be able to choose a favorite suitor tomorrow who is at least as desirable to her as today's favorite. So day by day, her favorite suitor can stay the same or get better, never worse. This sounds like an invariant, and it is. Namely, let P be the predicate

> For every woman w and man m, if w is crossed off m's list, then w has a suitor whom she prefers over m.

Lemma 6.4.2. *P is a preserved invariant for The Mating Ritual.*

Proof. Woman w gets crossed off m's list only when w has a suitor she prefers to m. Thereafter, her favorite suitor doesn't change until one she likes better comes along. So if her favorite suitor was preferable to m, then any new favorite suitor will be as well.

■

Notice that the invariant P holds vacuously at the beginning since no women are crossed off to start. So by the Invariant Principle, P holds throughout the Ritual. Now we can prove:

Theorem 6.4.3. *Everyone is married at the end of the Mating Ritual.*

Proof. Assume to the contrary that on the last day of the Mating Ritual, some man—call him Bob—is not married. This means Bob can't be serenading anybody, that is, his list must be empty. So every woman must have been crossed off his list and, since P is true, every woman has a suitor whom she prefers to Bob. In particular, every woman has *some* suitor, and since it is the last day, they have only one suitor, and this is who they marry. But there are an equal number of men and women, so if all women are married, so are all men, contradicting the assumption that Bob is not married. ∎

Theorem 6.4.4. *The Mating Ritual produces a stable matching.*

Proof. Let Brad and Jen be any man and woman, respectively, that are *not* married to each other on the last day of the Mating Ritual. We will prove that Brad and Jen are not a rogue couple, and thus that all marriages on the last day are stable. There are two cases to consider.

Case 1: Jen is not on Brad's list by the end. Then by invariant P, we know that Jen has a suitor (and hence a husband) whom she prefers to Brad. So she's not going to run off with Brad—Brad and Jen cannot be a rogue couple.

Case 2: Jen is on Brad's list. Since Brad picks women to serenade by working down his list, his wife must be higher on his preference list than Jen. So he's not going to run off with Jen—once again, Brad and Jen are not a rogue couple. ∎

6.4.4 ...Especially the Men

Who is favored by the Mating Ritual, the men or the women? The women *seem* to have all the power: each day they choose their favorite suitor and reject the rest. What's more, we know their suitors can only change for the better as the Ritual progresses. Similarly, a man keeps serenading the woman he most prefers among those on his list until he must cross her off, at which point he serenades the next most preferred woman on his list. So from the man's perspective, the woman he is serenading can only change for the worse. Sounds like a good deal for the women.

But it's not! We will show that the men are by far the favored gender under the Mating Ritual.

While the Mating Ritual produces one stable matching, stable matchings need not be unique. For example, reversing the roles of men and women will often yield a different stable matching among them. So a man may have different wives in different sets of stable marriages. In some cases, a man can stably marry every one of the women, but in most cases, there are some women who cannot be a man's wife in any stable matching. For example, given the preferences shown in Figure 6.4, Jennifer cannot be Brad's wife in any stable matching because if he was married to her, then he and Angelina would be a rogue couple. It is not feasible for Jennifer to be stably married to Brad.

Definition 6.4.5. Given a set of preferences for the men and women, one person is a *feasible spouse* for another person when there is a stable matching in which these two people are married.

Definition 6.4.6. Let Q be the predicate: for every woman w and man m, if w is crossed off m's list, then w is not a feasible spouse for m.

Lemma 6.4.7. Q *is a preserved invariant*[5] *for The Mating Ritual.*

Proof. Suppose Q holds at some point in the Ritual and some woman Alice is about to be crossed off some man's, Bob's, list. We claim that Alice must not be feasible for Bob. Therefore Q will still hold after Alice is crossed off, proving that Q is invariant.

To verify the claim, notice that when Alice gets crossed of Bob's list, it's because Alice has a suitor, Ted, she prefers to Bob. What's more, since Q holds, all Ted's feasible wives are still on his list, and Alice is at the top. So Ted likes Alice better than all his other feasible spouses. Now if Alice could be married to Bob in some set of stable marriages, then Ted must be married to a wife he likes less than Alice, making Alice and Ted a rogue couple and contradicting stability. So Alice can't be married to Bob, that is, Alice is not a feasible wife for Bob, as claimed. ∎

Definition 6.4.8. A person's *optimal spouse* is their most preferred feasible spouse. A person's *pessimal spouse* is their least preferred feasible spouse.

Everybody has an optimal and a pessimal spouse, since we know there is at least one stable matching, namely, the one produced by the Mating Ritual. Lemma 6.4.7 implies a key property the Mating Ritual:

Theorem 6.4.9. *The Mating Ritual marries every man to his optimal spouse and every woman to her pessimal spouse.*

Proof. If Bob is married to Alice on the final day of the Ritual, then everyone above Alice on Bob's preference list was crossed off, and by property Q, all these crossed off women were infeasible for Bob. So Alice is Bob's highest ranked feasible spouse, that is, his optimal spouse.

Further, since Bob likes Alice better than any other feasible wife, Alice and Bob would be a rogue couple if Alice was married to a husband she liked less than Bob. So Bob must be Alice's least preferred feasible husband. ∎

---

[5]We appeal to P in justifying Q, so technically it is P AND Q which is actually the preserved invariant. But let's not be picky.

6.4.5 Applications

The Mating Ritual was first announced in a paper by D. Gale and L.S. Shapley in 1962, but ten years before the Gale-Shapley paper was published, and unknown to them, a similar algorithm was being used to assign residents to hospitals by the National Resident Matching Program (NRMP). The NRMP has, since the turn of the twentieth century, assigned each year's pool of medical school graduates to hospital residencies (formerly called "internships"), with hospitals and graduates playing the roles of men and women.[6] Before the Ritual-like algorithm was adopted, there were chronic disruptions and awkward countermeasures taken to preserve unstable assignments of graduates to residencies. The Ritual resolved these problems so successfully, that it was used essentially without change at least through 1989.[7] For this and related work, Shapley was awarded the 2012 Nobel prize in Economics.

Not surprisingly, the Mating Ritual is also used by at least one large online dating agency. Of course there is no serenading going on—everything is handled by computer.

Problems for Section 6.3

Practice Problems

Problem 6.1.
Which states of the Die Hard 3 machine below have transitions to exactly two states?

Die Hard Transitions

1. Fill the little jug: $(b, l) \longrightarrow (b, 3)$ for $l < 3$.

2. Fill the big jug: $(b, l) \longrightarrow (5, l)$ for $b < 5$.

3. Empty the little jug: $(b, l) \longrightarrow (b, 0)$ for $l > 0$.

4. Empty the big jug: $(b, l) \longrightarrow (0, l)$ for $b > 0$.

---

[6]In this case there may be multiple women married to one man, but this is a minor complication, see Problem 6.24.

[7]Much more about the Stable Marriage Problem can be found in the very readable mathematical monograph by Dan Gusfield and Robert W. Irving, [25].

5. Pour from the little jug into the big jug: for $l > 0$,

$$(b, l) \longrightarrow \begin{cases} (b + l, 0) & \text{if } b + l \leq 5, \\ (5, l - (5 - b)) & \text{otherwise.} \end{cases}$$

6. Pour from big jug into little jug: for $b > 0$,

$$(b, l) \longrightarrow \begin{cases} (0, b + l) & \text{if } b + l \leq 3, \\ (b - (3 - l), 3) & \text{otherwise.} \end{cases}$$

Homework Problems

Problem 6.2.

In the late 1960s, the military junta that ousted the government of the small republic of Nerdia completely outlawed built-in multiplication operations, and also forbade division by any number other than 3. Fortunately, a young dissident found a way to help the population multiply any two nonnegative integers without risking persecution by the junta. The procedure he taught people is:

procedure *multiply*(x, y: nonnegative integers)
$r := x$;
$s := y$;
$a := 0$;
while $s \neq 0$ **do**
    if $3 \mid s$ **then**
        $r := r + r + r$;
        $s := s/3$;
    else if $3 \mid (s - 1)$ **then**
        $a := a + r$;
        $r := r + r + r$;
        $s := (s - 1)/3$;
    else
        $a := a + r + r$;
        $r := r + r + r$;
        $s := (s - 2)/3$;
return a;

We can model the algorithm as a state machine whose states are triples of nonnegative integers (r, s, a). The initial state is $(x, y, 0)$. The transitions are given by the rule that for $s > 0$:

$$(r, s, a) \rightarrow \begin{cases} (3r, s/3, a) & \text{if } 3 \mid s \\ (3r, (s-1)/3, a+r) & \text{if } 3 \mid (s-1) \\ (3r, (s-2)/3, a+2r) & \text{otherwise.} \end{cases}$$

(a) List the sequence of steps that appears in the execution of the algorithm for inputs $x = 5$ and $y = 10$.

(b) Use the Invariant Method to prove that the algorithm is partially correct—that is, if $s = 0$, then $a = xy$.

(c) Prove that the algorithm terminates after at most $1 + \log_3 y$ executions of the body of the **do** statement.

Problem 6.3.
A robot named Wall-E wanders around a two-dimensional grid. He starts out at $(0, 0)$ and is allowed to take four different types of steps:

1. $(+2, -1)$

2. $(+1, -2)$

3. $(+1, +1)$

4. $(-3, 0)$

Thus, for example, Wall-E might walk as follows. The types of his steps are listed above the arrows.

$$(0, 0) \xrightarrow{1} (2, -1) \xrightarrow{3} (3, 0) \xrightarrow{2} (4, -2) \xrightarrow{4} (1, -2) \rightarrow \cdots$$

Wall-E's true love, the fashionable and high-powered robot, Eve, awaits at $(0, 2)$.

(a) Describe a state machine model of this problem.

(b) Will Wall-E ever find his true love? Either find a path from Wall-E to Eve, or use the Invariant Principle to prove that no such path exists.

Problem 6.4.
A hungry ant is placed on an unbounded grid. Each square of the grid either contains a crumb or is empty. The squares containing crumbs form a path in which,

except at the ends, every crumb is adjacent to exactly two other crumbs. The ant is placed at one end of the path and on a square containing a crumb. For example, the figure below shows a situation in which the ant faces North, and there is a trail of food leading approximately Southeast. The ant has already eaten the crumb upon which it was initially placed.

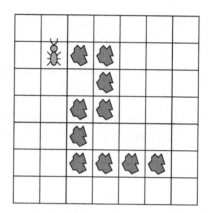

The ant can only smell food directly in front of it. The ant can only remember a small number of things, and what it remembers after any move only depends on what it remembered and smelled immediately before the move. Based on smell and memory, the ant may choose to move forward one square, or it may turn right or left. It eats a crumb when it lands on it.

The above scenario can be nicely modelled as a state machine in which each state is a pair consisting of the "ant's memory" and "everything else"—for example, information about where things are on the grid. Work out the details of such a model state machine; design the ant-memory part of the state machine so the ant will eat all the crumbs on *any* finite path at which it starts and then signal when it is done. Be sure to clearly describe the possible states, transitions, and inputs and outputs (if any) in your model. Briefly explain why your ant will eat all the crumbs.

Note that the last transition is a self-loop; the ant signals done for eternity. One could also add another end state so that the ant signals done only once.

Problem 6.5.

Suppose that you have a regular deck of cards arranged as follows, from top to bottom:

$$A\heartsuit \ 2\heartsuit \ldots K\heartsuit \ A\spadesuit \ 2\spadesuit \ldots K\spadesuit \ A\clubsuit \ 2\clubsuit \ldots K\clubsuit \ A\diamondsuit \ 2\diamondsuit \ldots K\diamondsuit$$

Only two operations on the deck are allowed: *inshuffling* and *outshuffling*. In both, you begin by cutting the deck exactly in half, taking the top half into your right-hand and the bottom into your left. Then you shuffle the two halves together so that the cards are perfectly interlaced; that is, the shuffled deck consists of one card from the left, one from the right, one from the left, one from the right, etc. The top card in the shuffled deck comes from the right-hand in an outshuffle and from the left-hand in an inshuffle.

(a) Model this problem as a state machine.

(b) Use the Invariant Principle to prove that you cannot make the entire first half of the deck black through a sequence of inshuffles and outshuffles.

Note: Discovering a suitable invariant can be difficult! This is the part of a correctness proof that generally requires some insight, and there is no simple recipe for finding invariants. A standard initial approach is to identify a bunch of reachable states and then look for a pattern—some feature that they all share.

Problem 6.6.
Prove that the fast exponentiation state machine of Section 6.3.1 will halt after

$$\lceil \log_2 n \rceil + 1 \tag{6.3}$$

transitions starting from any state where the value of z is $n \in \mathbb{Z}^+$.
  Hint: Strong induction.

Problem 6.7.
Nim is a two-person game that starts with some piles of stones. A player's move consists of removing one or more stones from a single pile. Players alternate moves, and the loser is the one who is left with no stones to remove.

  It turns out there is a winning strategy for one of the players that is easy to carry out but is not so obvious.

  To explain the winning strategy, we need to think of a number in two ways: as a nonnegative integer and as the bit string equal to the binary representation of the number—possibly with leading zeroes.

  For example, the XOR of *numbers r, s, ...* is defined in terms of their binary representations: combine the corresponding bits of the binary representations of $r, s, ...$ using XOR, and then interpret the resulting bit-string as a number. For example,

$$2 \text{ XOR } 7 \text{ XOR } 9 = 12$$

because, taking XOR's down the columns, we have

$$
\begin{array}{cccc}
0 & 0 & 1 & 0 \quad \text{(binary rep of 2)} \\
0 & 1 & 1 & 1 \quad \text{(binary rep of 7)} \\
1 & 0 & 0 & 1 \quad \text{(binary rep of 9)} \\
\hline
1 & 1 & 0 & 0 \quad \text{(binary rep of 12)}
\end{array}
$$

This is the same as doing binary addition of the numbers, but throwing away the carries (see Problem 3.6).

The XOR of the numbers of stones in the piles is called their *Nim sum*. In this problem we will verify that if the Nim sum is not zero on a player's turn, then the player has a winning strategy. For example, if the game starts with five piles of equal size, then the first player has a winning strategy, but if the game starts with four equal-size piles, then the second player can force a win.

 (a) Prove that if the Nim sum of the piles is zero, then any one move will leave a nonzero Nim sum.

 (b) Prove that if there is a pile with more stones than the Nim sum of all the other piles, then there is a move that makes the Nim sum equal to zero.

 (c) Prove that if the Nim sum is not zero, then one of the piles is bigger than the Nim sum of the all the other piles.

Hint: Notice that the largest pile may not be the one that is bigger than the Nim sum of the others; three piles of sizes 2,2,1 is an example.

 (d) Conclude that if the game begins with a nonzero Nim sum, then the first player has a winning strategy.

Hint: Describe a preserved invariant that the first player can maintain.

 (e) (Extra credit) Nim is sometimes played with winners and losers reversed, that is, the person who takes the last stone *loses*. This is called the *misère* version of the game. Use ideas from the winning strategy above for regular play to find one for *misère* play.

Class Problems

Problem 6.8.

In this problem you will establish a basic property of a puzzle toy called the *Fifteen Puzzle* using the method of invariants. The Fifteen Puzzle consists of sliding square tiles numbered $1, \ldots, 15$ held in a 4×4 frame with one empty square. Any tile adjacent to the empty square can slide into it.

The standard initial position is

1	2	3	4
5	6	7	8
9	10	11	12
13	14	15	

We would like to reach the target position (known in the oldest author's youth as "the impossible"):

15	14	13	12
11	10	9	8
7	6	5	4
3	2	1	

A state machine model of the puzzle has states consisting of a 4×4 matrix with 16 entries consisting of the integers $1, \ldots, 15$ as well as one "empty" entry—like each of the two arrays above.

The state transitions correspond to exchanging the empty square and an adjacent numbered tile. For example, an empty at position $(2, 2)$ can exchange position with tile above it, namely, at position $(1, 2)$:

n_1	n_2	n_3	n_4
n_5		n_6	n_7
n_8	n_9	n_{10}	n_{11}
n_{12}	n_{13}	n_{14}	n_{15}

$\longrightarrow$

n_1		n_3	n_4
n_5	n_2	n_6	n_7
n_8	n_9	n_{10}	n_{11}
n_{12}	n_{13}	n_{14}	n_{15}

We will use the invariant method to prove that there is no way to reach the target state starting from the initial state.

We begin by noting that a state can also be represented as a pair consisting of two things:

1. a list of the numbers $1, \ldots, 15$ in the order in which they appear—reading rows left-to-right from the top row down, ignoring the empty square, and

2. the coordinates of the empty square—where the upper left square has coordinates $(1, 1)$, the lower right $(4, 4)$.

(a) Write out the "list" representation of the start state and the "impossible" state.

Let L be a list of the numbers $1, \ldots, 15$ in some order. A pair of integers is an *out-of-order pair* in L when the first element of the pair both comes *earlier* in the list and *is larger*, than the second element of the pair. For example, the list $1, 2, 4, 5, 3$ has two out-of-order pairs: $(4,3)$ and $(5,3)$. The increasing list $1, 2 \ldots n$ has no out-of-order pairs.

Let a state S be a pair $(L, (i, j))$ described above. We define the *parity* of S to be 0 or 1 depending on whether the sum of the number of out-of-order pairs in L and the row-number of the empty square is even or odd. that is

$$\text{parity}(S) ::= \begin{cases} 0 & \text{if } p(L) + i \text{ is even,} \\ 1 & \text{otherwise.} \end{cases}$$

(b) Verify that the parity of the start state and the target state are different.

(c) Show that the parity of a state is preserved under transitions. Conclude that "the impossible" is impossible to reach.

By the way, if two states have the same parity, then in fact there *is* a way to get from one to the other. If you like puzzles, you'll enjoy working this out on your own.

Problem 6.9.

The Massachusetts Turnpike Authority is concerned about the integrity of the new Zakim bridge. Their consulting architect has warned that the bridge may collapse if more than 1000 cars are on it at the same time. The Authority has also been warned by their traffic consultants that the rate of accidents from cars speeding across bridges has been increasing.

Both to lighten traffic and to discourage speeding, the Authority has decided to make the bridge *one-way* and to put tolls at *both* ends of the bridge (don't laugh, this is Massachusetts). So cars will pay tolls both on entering and exiting the bridge, but the tolls will be different. In particular, a car will pay $3 to enter onto the bridge and will pay $2 to exit. To be sure that there are never too many cars on the bridge, the Authority will let a car onto the bridge only if the difference between the amount of money currently at the entry toll booth and the amount at the exit toll booth is strictly less than a certain threshold amount of T_0.

The consultants have decided to model this scenario with a state machine whose states are triples (A, B, C) of nonnegative integers, where

- A is an amount of money at the entry booth,

- B is an amount of money at the exit booth, and

- C is a number of cars on the bridge.

Any state with $C > 1000$ is called a *collapsed* state, which the Authority dearly hopes to avoid. There will be no transition out of a collapsed state.

Since the toll booth collectors may need to start off with some amount of money in order to make change, and there may also be some number of "official" cars already on the bridge when it is opened to the public, the consultants must be ready to analyze the system started at *any* uncollapsed state. So let A_0 be the initial number of dollars at the entrance toll booth, B_0 the initial number of dollars at the exit toll booth, and $C_0 \leq 1000$ the number of official cars on the bridge when it is opened. You should assume that even official cars pay tolls on exiting or entering the bridge after the bridge is opened.

(a) Give a mathematical model of the Authority's system for letting cars on and off the bridge by specifying a transition relation between states of the form (A, B, C) above.

(b) Characterize each of the following derived variables

$$A, B, A+B, A-B, 3C-A, 2A-3B, B+3C, 2A-3B-6C, 2A-2B-3C$$

as one of the following

constant	C
strictly increasing	SI
strictly decreasing	SD
weakly increasing but not constant	WI
weakly decreasing but not constant	WD
none of the above	N

and briefly explain your reasoning.

The Authority has asked their engineering consultants to determine T and to verify that this policy will keep the number of cars from exceeding 1000.

The consultants reason that if C_0 is the number of official cars on the bridge when it is opened, then an additional $1000 - C_0$ cars can be allowed on the bridge. So as long as $A - B$ has not increased by $3(1000 - C_0)$, there shouldn't more than 1000 cars on the bridge. So they recommend defining

$$T_0 ::= 3(1000 - C_0) + (A_0 - B_0), \tag{6.4}$$

where A_0 is the initial number of dollars at the entrance toll booth, B_0 is the initial number of dollars at the exit toll booth.

(c) Use the results of part (b) to define a simple predicate P on states of the transition system which is satisfied by the start state—that is $P(A_0, B_0, C_0)$ holds—is not satisfied by any collapsed state, and is a preserved invariant of the system. Explain why your P has these properties. Conclude that the traffic won't cause the bridge to collapse.

(d) A clever MIT intern working for the Turnpike Authority agrees that the Turnpike's bridge management policy will be *safe*: the bridge will not collapse. But she warns her boss that the policy will lead to *deadlock*—a situation where traffic can't move on the bridge even though the bridge has not collapsed.

Explain more precisely in terms of system transitions what the intern means, and briefly, but clearly, justify her claim.

Problem 6.10.
Start with 102 coins on a table, 98 showing heads and 4 showing tails. There are two ways to change the coins:

   (i) flip over any ten coins, or

  (ii) let n be the number of heads showing. Place $n + 1$ additional coins, all showing tails, on the table.

For example, you might begin by flipping nine heads and one tail, yielding 90 heads and 12 tails, then add 91 tails, yielding 90 heads and 103 tails.

(a) Model this situation as a state machine, carefully defining the set of states, the start state, and the possible state transitions.

(b) Explain how to reach a state with exactly one tail showing.

(c) Define the following derived variables:

C	::=	the number of coins on the table,	H	::=	the number of heads,
T	::=	the number of tails,	C_2	::=	remainder($C/2$),
H_2	::=	remainder($H/2$),	T_2	::=	remainder($T/2$).

Which of these variables is

  1. strictly increasing

  2. weakly increasing

  3. strictly decreasing

  4. weakly decreasing

  5. constant

(d) Prove that it is not possible to reach a state in which there is exactly one head showing.

Problem 6.11.

A classroom is designed so students sit in a square arrangement. An outbreak of beaver flu sometimes infects students in the class; beaver flu is a rare variant of bird flu that lasts forever, with symptoms including a yearning for more quizzes and the thrill of late night problem set sessions.

Here is an illustration of a 6×6-seat classroom with seats represented by squares. The locations of infected students are marked with an asterisk.

*				*	
	*				
		*	*		
			*		
				*		*

Outbreaks of infection spread rapidly step by step. A student is infected after a step if either

- the student was infected at the previous step (since beaver flu lasts forever), or

- the student was adjacent to *at least two* already-infected students at the previous step.

Here *adjacent* means the students' individual squares share an edge (front, back, left or right); they are not adjacent if they only share a corner point. So each student is adjacent to 2, 3 or 4 others.

In the example, the infection spreads as shown below.

In this example, over the next few time-steps, all the students in class become infected.

Theorem. *If fewer than n students among those in an $n \times n$ arrangment are initially infected in a flu outbreak, then there will be at least one student who never gets infected in this outbreak, even if students attend all the lectures.*

Prove this theorem.

Hint: Think of the state of an outbreak as an $n \times n$ square above, with asterisks indicating infection. The rules for the spread of infection then define the transitions of a state machine. Find a weakly decreasing derived variable that leads to a proof of this theorem.

Exam Problems

Problem 6.12.

Token replacing-1-2 is a single player game using a set of tokens, each colored black or white. Except for color, the tokens are indistinguishable. In each move, a player can replace one black token with two white tokens, or replace one white token with two black tokens.

We can model this game as a state machine whose states are pairs (n_b, n_w) where $n_b \geq 0$ equals the number of black tokens, and $n_w \geq 0$ equals the number of white tokens.

(a) List the numbers of the following predicates that are preserved invariants.

$$n_b + n_w \ \mathrm{rem}(n_b + n_w, \ 3) \neq 2 \tag{6.5}$$

$$n_w - n_b \ \mathrm{rem}(n_w - n_b, \ 3) = 2 \tag{6.6}$$

$$n_b - n_w \ \mathrm{rem}(n_b - n_2, \ 3) = 2 \tag{6.7}$$

$$n_b + n_w > 5 \tag{6.8}$$

$$n_b + n_w < 5 \tag{6.9}$$

Now assume the game starts with a single black token, that is, the start state is $(1, 0)$.

(b) List the numbers of the predicates above are true for all reachable states:

(c) Define the predicate $T(n_b, n_w)$ by the rule:

$$T(n_b, n_w) ::= \ \mathrm{rem}(n_w - n_b, \ 3) = 2.$$

We will now prove the following:

Claim. *If $T(n_b, n_w)$, then state (n_b, n_w) is reachable.*

Note that this claim is different from the claim that T is a preserved invariant.

The proof of the Claim will be by induction in n using induction hypothesis $P(n)::=$

$$\forall (n_b, n_w). \, [(n_b + n_w = n) \text{ AND } T(n_b, n_w)] \text{ IMPLIES } (n_b, n_w) \text{ is reachable.}$$

The base cases will be when $n \leq 2$.

- Assuming that the base cases have been verified, complete the **Inductive Step**.
- Now verify the **Base Cases**: $P(n)$ for $n \leq 2$.

Problem 6.13.

Token Switching is a process for updating a set of black and white tokens. The process starts with a single black token. At each step,

(i) one black token can be replaced with two white tokens, or

(ii) if the numbers of white and black tokens are not the same, the colors of all the tokens can be switched: all the black tokens become white, and the white tokens become black.

We can model Token Switching as a state machine whose states are pairs (b, w) of nonnegative integers, where b equals the number of black tokens, and w equals the number of white tokens. So the start state is $(1, 0)$.

(a) Indicate which of the following states can be reached from the start state in *exactly* two steps:

$$(0, 0), \; (1, 0), \; (0, 1), \; (1, 1), \; (0, 2), \; (2, 0), \; (2, 1), \; (1, 2), \; (0, 3), \; (3, 0)$$

(b) Define the predicate $F(b, w)$ by the rule:

$$F(b, w) ::= \; (b - w) \text{is not a multiple of 3.}$$

Prove the following

Claim. *If $F(b, w)$, then state (b, w) is reachable from the start state.*

(c) Explain why state $(11^{6^{7777}}, 5^{10^{88}})$ is *not* a reachable state.

Hint: Do not assume F is a preserved invariant without proving it.

Problem 6.14.

Token replacing-1-3 is a single player game using a set of tokens, each colored black or white. In each move, a player can replace a black token with three white tokens, or replace a white token with three black tokens. We can model this game as a state machine whose states are pairs (b, w) of nonnegative integers, where b is the number of black tokens and w the number of white ones.

The game has two possible start states: $(5, 4)$ or $(4, 3)$.

We call a state (b, w) *eligible* when

$$\text{rem}(b - w, \ 4) = 1, \text{ AND} \tag{6.10}$$
$$\min\{b, w\} \geq 3. \tag{6.11}$$

This problem examines the connection between eligible states and states that are *reachable* from either of the possible start states.

(a) Give an example of a reachable state that is not eligible.

(b) Show that the derived variable $b + w$ is strictly increasing. Conclude that state $(3, 2)$ is not reachable.

(c) Suppose (b, w) is eligible and $b \geq 6$. Verify that $(b - 3, w + 1)$ is eligible.

For the rest of the problem, you may—and should—**assume** the following Fact:

Fact. If $\max\{b, w\} \leq 5$ and (b, w) is eligible, then (b, w) is reachable.

(This is easy to verify since there are only nine states with $b, w \in \{3, 4, 5\}$, but don't waste time doing this.)

(d) Define the predicate $P(n)$ to be:

$$\forall (b, w).[b + w = n \text{ AND } (b, w) \text{ is eligible}] \text{ IMPLIES } (b, w) \text{ is reachable}.$$

Prove that $P(n - 1)$ IMPLIES $P(n + 1)$ for all $n \geq 1$.

(e) Conclude that all eligible states are reachable.

(f) Prove that $(4^7 + 1, 4^5 + 2)$ is *not* reachable.

(g) Verify that $\text{rem}(3b - w, \ 8)$ is a derived variable that is constant. Conclude that no state is reachable from both start states.

Problem 6.15.

There is a bucket containing more blue balls than red balls. As long as there are more blues than reds, any one of the following rules may be applied to add and/or remove balls from the bucket:

(i) Add a red ball.

(ii) Remove a blue ball.

(iii) Add two reds and one blue.

(iv) Remove two blues and one red.

(a) Starting with 10 reds and 16 blues, what is the largest number of balls the bucket will contain by applying these rules?

Let b be the number of blue balls and r be the number of red balls in the bucket at any given time.

(b) Prove that $b - r \geq 0$ is a preserved invariant of the process of adding and removing balls according to rules (i)–(iv).

(c) Prove that no matter how many balls the bucket contains, repeatedly applying rules (i)–(iv) will eventually lead to a state where no further rule can be applied.

Problem 6.16.

The following problem is a twist on the Fifteen-Puzzle analyzed in Problem 6.8.

Let A be a sequence consisting of the numbers $1, \ldots, n$ in some order. A pair of integers in A is called an *out-of-order pair* when the first element of the pair both comes *earlier* in the sequence, and *is larger*, than the second element of the pair. For example, the sequence $(1, 2, 4, 5, 3)$ has two out-of-order pairs: $(4, 3)$ and $(5, 3)$. We let $t(A)$ equal the number of out-of-order pairs in A. For example, $t((1, 2, 4, 5, 3)) = 2$.

The elements in A can be rearranged using the *Rotate-Triple* operation, in which three consecutive elements of A are rotated to move the smallest of them to be first.

For example, in the sequence $(2, 4, 1, 5, 3)$, the *Rotate-Triple* operation could rotate the consecutive numbers $4, 1, 5$, into $1, 5, 4$ so that

$$(2, 4, 1, 5, 3) \longrightarrow (2, 1, 5, 4, 3).$$

The *Rotate-Triple* could also rotate the consecutive numbers $2, 4, 1$ into $1, 2, 4$ so that

$$(2, 4, 1, 5, 3) \longrightarrow (1, 2, 4, 5, 3).$$

We can think of a sequence A as a state of a state machine whose transitions correspond to possible applications of the *Rotate-Triple* operation.

(a) Argue that the derived variable t is *weakly decreasing*.

(b) Prove that having an even number of out-of-order pairs is a preserved invariant of this machine.

(c) Starting with

$$S ::= (2014, 2013, 2012, \ldots, 2, 1),$$

explain why it is impossible to reach

$$T ::= (1, 2, \ldots, 2012, 2013, 2014).$$

Problems for Section 6.4

Practice Problems

Problem 6.17.

Four Students want separate assignments to four VI-A Companies. Here are their preference rankings:

Student	Companies
Albert:	HP, Bellcore, AT&T, Draper
Sarah:	AT&T, Bellcore, Draper, HP
Tasha:	HP, Draper, AT&T, Bellcore
Elizabeth:	Draper, AT&T, Bellcore, HP

Company	Students
AT&T:	Elizabeth, Albert, Tasha, Sarah
Bellcore:	Tasha, Sarah, Albert, Elizabeth
HP:	Elizabeth, Tasha, Albert, Sarah
Draper:	Sarah, Elizabeth, Tasha, Albert

(a) Use the Mating Ritual to find *two* stable assignments of Students to Companies.

(b) Describe a simple procedure to determine whether any given stable marriage problem has a unique solution, that is, only one possible stable matching. Briefly explain why it works.

Problem 6.18.

Suppose that Harry is one of the boys and Alice is one of the girls in the *Mating Ritual*. Which of the properties below are preserved invariants? Why?

a. Alice is the only girl on Harry's list.

b. There is a girl who does not have any boys serenading her.

c. If Alice is not on Harry's list, then Alice has a suitor that she prefers to Harry.

d. Alice is crossed off Harry's list, and Harry prefers Alice to anyone he is serenading.

e. If Alice is on Harry's list, then she prefers Harry to any suitor she has.

Problem 6.19.

Prove that in a stable set of marriages, every man is the pessimal husband of his optimal wife.

Hint: Follows directly from the definition of "rogue couple."

Problem 6.20.

In the Mating Ritual for stable marriages between an equal number of boys and girls, explain why there must be a girl to whom no boy proposes (serenades) until the last day.

Class Problems

Problem 6.21.

The preferences among 4 boys and 4 girls are partially specified in the following table:

B1:	G1	G2	–	–
B2:	G2	G1	–	–
B3:	–	–	G4	G3
B4:	–	–	G3	G4
G1:	B2	B1	–	–
G2:	B1	B2	–	–
G3:	–	–	B3	B4
G4:	–	–	B4	B3

(a) Verify that

$$(B1, G1), (B2, G2), (B3, G3), (B4, G4)$$

will be a stable matching whatever the unspecified preferences may be.

(b) Explain why the stable matching above is neither boy-optimal nor boy-pessimal and so will not be an outcome of the Mating Ritual.

(c) Describe how to define a set of marriage preferences among n boys and n girls which have at least $2^{n/2}$ stable assignments.

Hint: Arrange the boys into a list of $n/2$ pairs, and likewise arrange the girls into a list of $n/2$ pairs of girls. Choose preferences so that the kth pair of boys ranks the kth pair of girls just below the previous pairs of girls, and likewise for the kth pair of girls. Within the kth pairs, make sure each boy's first choice girl in the pair prefers the other boy in the pair.

Problem 6.22.

The Mating Ritual of Section 6.4.1 for finding stable marriages works even when the numbers of men and women are not equal. As before, a set of (monogamous) marriages between men and women is called stable when it has no "rogue couples."

(a) Extend the definition of *rogue couple* so it covers the case of unmarried men and women. Verify that in a stable set of marriages, either all the men are married or all the women are married.

(b) Explain why even in the case of unequal numbers of men and women, applying the Mating Ritual will yield a stable matching.

Homework Problems

Problem 6.23.

Suppose we want to assign pairs of "buddies," who may be of the sex, where each person has a preference rank for who they would like to be buddies with. For the preference ranking given in Figure 6.5, show that there is no stable buddy assignment. In this figure Mergatroid's preferences aren't shown because they don't even matter.

Problem 6.24.

The most famous application of stable matching was in assigning graduating medical students to hospital residencies. Each hospital has a preference ranking of

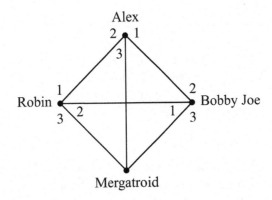

Figure 6.5   Some preferences with no stable buddy matching.

students, and each student has a preference ranking of hospitals, but unlike finding stable marriages between an equal number of boys and girls, hospitals generally have differing numbers of available residencies, and the total number of residencies may not equal the number of graduating students.

Explain how to adapt the Stable Matching problem with an equal number of boys and girls to this more general situation. In particular, modify the definition of stable matching so it applies in this situation, and explain how to adapt the Mating Ritual to handle it.

Problem 6.25.
Give an example of a stable matching between 3 boys and 3 girls where no person gets their first choice. Briefly explain why your matching is stable. Can your matching be obtained from the Mating Ritual or the Ritual with boys and girls reversed?

Problem 6.26.
In a stable matching between an equal number of boys and girls produced by the Mating Ritual, call a person *lucky* if they are matched up with someone in the top half of their preference list. Prove that there must be at least one lucky person.

Hint: The average number of times a boy gets rejected by girls.

Problem 6.27.
Suppose there are two stable sets of marriages. So each man has a first wife and a

second wife , and likewise each woman has a first husband and a second husband.

Someone in a given marriage is a *winner* when they prefer their current spouse to their other spouse, and they are a *loser* when they prefer their other spouse to their current spouse. (If someone has the same spouse in both of their marriages, then they will be neither a winner nor a loser.)

We will show that

> In every marriage, someone is a winner iff their spouse is a loser.   (WL)

This will lead to an alternative proof of Theorem 6.4.9 that when men are married to their optimal spouses, women must be married to their pessimal spouses. This alternative proof does not depend on the Mating Ritual of Section 6.4.1.

(a) The left to right direction of (WL) is equivalent to the assertion that married partners cannot both be winners. Explain why this follows directly from the definition of rogue couple.

The right to left direction of (WL) is equivalent to the assertion that a married couple cannot both be losers. This will follow by comparing the number of winners and losers among the marriages.

(b) Explain why the number of winners must equal the number of losers among the two sets of marriages.

(c) Complete the proof of (WL) by showing that if some married couple were both losers, then there must be another couple who were both winners.

(d) Conclude that in a stable set of marriages, someone's spouse is optimal iff they are pessimal for their spouse.

Problem 6.28.
Suppose there are two stable sets of marriages, a first set and a second set. So each man has a first wife and a second wife (they may be the same), and likewise each woman has a first husband and a second husband. We can form a third set of marriages by matching each man with the wife he prefers among his first and second wives.

(a) Prove that this third set of marriages is an exact matching: no woman is married to two men.

(b) Prove that this third marriage set is stable.

Hint: You may assume the following fact from Problem 6.27.

> In every marriage, someone is a winner iff their spouse is a loser.   (SL)

Problem 6.29.

A state machine has *commuting transitions* if for any states p, q, r

$$(p \longrightarrow q \text{ AND } p \longrightarrow r) \text{ IMPLIES } \exists t. q \longrightarrow t \text{ AND } r \longrightarrow t.$$

The state machine is *confluent* if

$$(p \longrightarrow^* q \text{ AND } p \longrightarrow^* r) \text{ IMPLIES } \exists t. q \longrightarrow^* t \text{ AND } r \longrightarrow^* t.$$

(a) Prove that if a state machine has commuting transitions, then it is confluent.

Hint: By induction on the number of moves from p to q plus the number from p to r.

(b) A *final state* of a state machine is one from which no transition is possible. Explain why, if a state machine is confluent, then at most one final state is reachable from the start state.

Problem 6.30.

According to the day-by-day description of the Mating Ritual of Section 6.4.1, at the end of each day, *every* the man's list is updated to remove the name of the woman he who rejected him. But it's easier, and more flexible, simply to let one women reject one suitor at a time.

In particular, the states of this Flexible Mating Ritual state machine will be the same as for the day-by-day Ritual: a state will be a list, for each man, of the women who have not rejected him. But now a transition will be to choose two men who are serenading the same woman—that is, who have the same woman at the top of their current lists—and then have the woman reject whichever of the two she likes less. So the only change in state is that the name of the serenaded woman gets deleted from the top of the list of the man she liked less among two of her serenaders—everything else stays the same.

It's a worthwhile review to verify that the same preserved invariants used to establish the properties of the Mating Ritual will apply to the Flexible Mating Ritual. This ensures that the Flexible Ritual will also terminate with a stable set of marriages.

But now a new issue arises: we know that there can be many sets of possible sets of stable marriages for the same set of men/women preferences. So it seems possible that the Flexible Ritual might terminate with different stable marriage sets, depending on which choice of transition was made at each state. But this does not happen: the Flexible Ritual will always terminate with the same set of stable marriages as the day-by-day Ritual.

To prove this, we begin with a definition: a state machine has *commuting transitions* if for any states p, q, r,

$$(p \longrightarrow q \text{ AND } p \longrightarrow r) \text{ IMPLIES } \exists t. q \longrightarrow t \text{ AND } r \longrightarrow t.$$

(a) Verify that the Flexible Mating Ritual has commuting transitions.

(b) Now conclude from Problem 6.29 that the Flexible Mating Ritual always terminate with the same set of stable marriages as the day-by-day Ritual.

Exam Problems

Problem 6.31.

Four unfortunate children want to be adopted by four foster families of ill repute. A child can only be adopted by one family, and a family can only adopt one child. Here are their preference rankings (most-favored to least-favored):

Child	Families
Bottlecap:	Hatfields, McCoys, Grinches, Scrooges
Lucy:	Grinches, Scrooges, McCoys, Hatfields
Dingdong:	Hatfields, Scrooges, Grinches, McCoys
Zippy:	McCoys, Grinches, Scrooges, Hatfields

Family	Children
Grinches:	Zippy, Dingdong, Bottlecap, Lucy
Hatfields:	Zippy, Bottlecap, Dingdong, Lucy
Scrooges:	Bottlecap, Lucy, Dingdong, Zippy
McCoys:	Lucy, Zippy, Bottlecap, Dingdong

(a) Exhibit two different stable matching of Children and Families.

Family	Child in 1st match	Child in 2nd match
Grinches:		
Hatfields:		
Scrooges:		
McCoys:		

(b) Examine the matchings from part a, and explain why these matchings are the only two possible stable matchings between Children and Families.

Hint: In general, there may be many more than two stable matchings for the same set of preferences.

Problem 6.32.
The Mating Ritual 6.4.1 for finding stable marriages works without change when there are at least as many, and possibly more, men than women. You may assume this. So the Ritual ends with all the women married and no rogue couples for these marriages, where an unmarried man and a married woman who prefers him to her spouse is also considered to be a "rogue couple."

Let Alice be one of the women, and Bob be one of the men. Indicate which of the properties below that are preserved invariants of the Mating Ritual 6.4 when there are **at least as many** men as women. Briefly explain your answers.

(a) Alice has a suitor (man who is serenading her) whom she prefers to Bob.

(b) Alice is the only woman on Bob's list.

(c) Alice has no suitor.

(d) Bob prefers Alice to the women he is serenading.

(e) Bob is serenading Alice.

(f) Bob is not serenading Alice.

(g) Bob's list of women to serenade is empty.

Problem 6.33.
We want a stable matching between n boys and n girls for a positive integer n.

(a) Explain how to define preference rankings for the boys and the girls that allow only *one* possible stable matching. Briefly justify your answer.

(b) Mark each of the following predicates about the Stable Marriage Ritual **P** if it is a **P**reserved Invariant, **N** if it is **n**ot, and "U" if you are very unsure. "Bob's list" refers to the list of the women he has not crossed off.

  (i) Alice is not on Bob's list.

 (ii) No girl is on Bob's list.

(iii) Bob is the only boy serenading Alice.

 (iv) Bob has fewer than 5 girls on his list.

  (v) Bob prefers Alice to his favorite remaining girl.

 (vi) Alice prefers her favorite current suitor to Bob.

(vii) Bob is serenading his optimal spouse.

(viii) Bob is serenading his pessimal spouse.

(ix) Alice's optimal spouse is serenading her.

(x) Alice's pessimal spouse is serenading her.

7   Recursive Data Types

Recursive data types play a central role in programming, and induction is really all about them.

Recursive data types are specified by *recursive definitions*, which say how to construct new data elements from previous ones. Along with each recursive data type there are recursive definitions of properties or functions on the data type. Most importantly, based on a recursive definition, there is a *structural induction* method for proving that all data of the given type have some property.

This chapter examines a few examples of recursive data types and recursively defined functions on them:

- strings of characters,

- "balanced" strings of brackets,

- the nonnegative integers, and

- arithmetic expressions.

7.1   Recursive Definitions and Structural Induction

We'll start off illustrating recursive definitions and proofs using the example of character strings. Normally we'd take strings of characters for granted, but it's informative to treat them as a recursive data type. In particular, strings are a nice first example because you will see recursive definitions of things that are easy to understand, or that you already know, so you can focus on how the definitions work without having to figure out what they are supposed to mean.

Definitions of recursive data types have two parts:

- **Base case(s)** specifying that some known mathematical elements are in the data type, and

- **Constructor case(s)** that specify how to construct new data elements from previously constructed elements or from base elements.

The definition of strings over a given character set A follows this pattern:

Definition 7.1.1. Let A be a nonempty set called an *alphabet*, whose elements are referred to as *characters* (also called *letters*, *symbols*, or *digits*). The recursive data type A^* of strings over alphabet A is defined as follows:

- **Base case**: the empty string λ is in A^*.

- **Constructor case**: If $a \in A$ and $s \in A^*$, then the pair $\langle a, s \rangle \in A^*$.

So $\{0, 1\}^*$ are the binary strings.

The usual way to treat binary strings is as sequences of 0's and 1's. For example, we have identified the length-4 binary string 1011 as a sequence of bits, the 4-tuple $(1, 0, 1, 1)$. But according to the recursive Definition 7.1.1, this string would be represented by nested pairs, namely

$$\langle 1, \langle 0, \langle 1, \langle 1, \lambda \rangle \rangle \rangle \rangle .$$

These nested pairs are definitely cumbersome and may also seem bizarre, but they actually reflect the way that such lists of characters would be represented in programming languages like Scheme or Python, where $\langle a, s \rangle$ would correspond to cons(a, s).

Notice that we haven't said exactly how the empty string is represented. It really doesn't matter, as long as we can recognize the empty string and not confuse it with any nonempty string.

Continuing the recursive approach, let's define the length of a string.

Definition 7.1.2. The length $|s|$ of a string s is defined recursively based on Definition 7.1.1.

Base case: $|\lambda| ::= 0$.

Constructor case: $|\langle a, s \rangle| ::= 1 + |s|$.

This definition of length follows a standard pattern: functions on recursive data types can be defined recursively using the same cases as the data type definition. Specifically, to define a function f on a recursive data type, define the value of f for the base cases of the data type definition, then define the value of f in each constructor case in terms of the values of f on the component data items.

Let's do another example: the *concatenation* $s \cdot t$ of the strings s and t is the string consisting of the letters of s followed by the letters of t. This is a perfectly clear mathematical definition of concatenation (except maybe for what to do with the empty string), and in terms of Scheme/Python lists, $s \cdot t$ would be the list append(s, t). Here's a recursive definition of concatenation.

Definition 7.1.3. The *concatenation* $s \cdot t$ of the strings $s, t \in A^*$ is defined recursively based on Definition 7.1.1:

Base case:
$$\lambda \cdot t ::= t.$$

Constructor case:
$$\langle a, s \rangle \cdot t ::= \langle a, s \cdot t \rangle.$$

7.1.1 Structural Induction

Structural induction is a method for proving that all the elements of a recursively defined data type have some property. A structural induction proof has two parts corresponding to the recursive definition:

- Prove that each base case element has the property.

- Prove that each constructor case element has the property, when the constructor is applied to elements that have the property.

For example, in the base case of the definition of concatenation 7.1.3, we *defined* concatenation so the empty string was a "left identity," namely, $\lambda \cdot s ::= s$. We want the empty string also to be "right identity," namely, $s \cdot \lambda = s$. Being a right identity is not part of Definition 7.1.3, but we can prove it easily by structural induction:

Lemma 7.1.4.
$$s \cdot \lambda = s$$

for all $s \in A^*$.

Proof. The proof is by structural induction on the recursive definition 7.1.3 of concatenation. The induction hypothesis will be

$$P(s) ::= [s \cdot \lambda = s].$$

Base case: $(s = \lambda)$.

$$
\begin{aligned}
s \cdot \lambda &= \lambda \cdot \lambda \\
&= \lambda \qquad (\lambda \text{ is a left identity by Def } 7.1.3) \\
&= s.
\end{aligned}
$$

Constructor case: $(s = a \cdot t)$.

$$
\begin{aligned}
s \cdot \lambda &= (a \cdot t) \cdot \lambda \\
&= a \cdot (t \cdot \lambda) && \text{(Constructor case of Def 7.1.3)} \\
&= a \cdot t && \text{by induction hypothesis } P(t) \\
&= s.
\end{aligned}
$$

So $P(s)$ holds. This completes the proof of the constructor case, and we conclude by structural induction that equation (7.1.4) holds for all $s \in A^*$.   ∎

We can also verify properties of recursive functions by structural induction on their definitions. For example, let's verify the familiar fact that the length of the concatenation of two strings is the sum of their lengths:

Lemma.

$$
|s \cdot t| = |s| + |t|
$$

for all $s, t \in A^*$.

Proof. By structural induction on the definition of $s \in A^*$. The induction hypothesis is

$$
P(s) ::= \ \forall t \in A^*. |s \cdot t| = |s| + |t|.
$$

Base case $(s = \lambda)$:

$$
\begin{aligned}
|s \cdot t| &= |\lambda \cdot t| \\
&= |t| && \text{(base case of Def 7.1.3 of concatenation)} \\
&= 0 + |t| \\
&= |s| + |t| && \text{(Def of } |\lambda|).
\end{aligned}
$$

Constructor case: $(s ::= \langle a, r \rangle)$.

$$
\begin{aligned}
|s \cdot t| &= |\langle a, r \rangle \cdot t| \\
&= |\langle a, r \cdot t \rangle| && \text{(constructor case of Def of concat)} \\
&= 1 + |r \cdot t| && \text{(constructor case of def length)} \\
&= 1 + (|r| + |t|) && \text{(ind. hyp. } P(r)) \\
&= (1 + |r|) + |t| \\
&= |\langle a, r \rangle| + |t| && \text{(constructor case, def of length)} \\
&= |s| + |t|.
\end{aligned}
$$

This proves that $P(s)$ holds, completing the constructor case. By structural induction, we conclude that $P(s)$ holds for all strings $s \in A^*$.   ∎

These proofs illustrate the general principle:

The Principle of Structural Induction.

Let P be a predicate on a recursively defined data type R. If

- $P(b)$ is true for each base case element $b \in R$, and

- for all two-argument constructors **c**,

$$[P(r) \text{ AND } P(s)] \text{ IMPLIES } P(\mathbf{c}(r, s))$$

  for all $r, s \in R$,
  and likewise for all constructors taking other numbers of arguments,

then

$$P(r) \text{ is true for all } r \in R.$$

7.2 Strings of Matched Brackets

Let $\{], [\}^*$ be the set of all strings of square brackets. For example, the following two strings are in $\{], [\}^*$:

$$[\,]\,][\,[\,[\,[\,[\,]\,]\quad \text{and} \quad [\,[\,[\,]\,][\,]\,][\,] \qquad (7.1)$$

A string $s \in \{], [\}^*$ is called a *matched string* if its brackets "match up" in the usual way. For example, the left-hand string above is not matched because its second right bracket does not have a matching left bracket. The string on the right is matched.

We're going to examine several different ways to define and prove properties of matched strings using recursively defined sets and functions. These properties are pretty straightforward, and you might wonder whether they have any particular relevance in computer science. The honest answer is "not much relevance *any more*." The reason for this is one of the great successes of computer science, as explained in the text box below.

Expression Parsing

During the early development of computer science in the 1950's and 60's, creation of effective programming language compilers was a central concern. A key aspect in processing a program for compilation was expression parsing. One significant problem was to take an expression like

$$x + y * z^2 \div y + 7$$

and *put in* the brackets that determined how it should be evaluated—should it be

$$[[x + y] * z^2 \div y] + 7, \text{ or,}$$
$$x + [y * z^2 \div [y + 7]], \text{ or,}$$
$$[x + [y * z^2]] \div [y + 7], \text{ or} \ldots?$$

The Turing award (the "Nobel Prize" of computer science) was ultimately bestowed on Robert W. Floyd, for, among other things, discovering simple procedures that would insert the brackets properly.

In the 70's and 80's, this parsing technology was packaged into high-level compiler-compilers that automatically generated parsers from expression grammars. This automation of parsing was so effective that the subject no longer demanded attention. It had largely disappeared from the computer science curriculum by the 1990's.

The matched strings can be nicely characterized as a recursive data type:

Definition 7.2.1. Recursively define the set RecMatch of strings as follows:

- **Base case**: $\lambda \in$ RecMatch.

- **Constructor case**: If $s, t \in$ RecMatch, then

$$[s]t \in \text{RecMatch}.$$

Here $[s]t$ refers to the concatenation of strings which would be written in full as

$$[\cdot(s\cdot(]\cdot t)).$$

From now on, we'll usually omit the "·'s."

Using this definition, $\lambda \in$ RecMatch by the base case, so letting $s = t = \lambda$ in the constructor case implies

$$[\lambda]\lambda = [\,] \in \text{RecMatch}.$$

Now,

$$[\lambda][\,] = [\,][\,] \in \text{RecMatch} \qquad (\text{letting } s = \lambda, t = [\,])$$
$$[[\,]]\lambda = [[\,]] \in \text{RecMatch} \qquad (\text{letting } s = [\,], t = \lambda)$$
$$[[\,]][\,] \in \text{RecMatch} \qquad (\text{letting } s = [\,], t = [\,])$$

are also strings in RecMatch by repeated applications of the constructor case; and so on.

It's pretty obvious that in order for brackets to match, there had better be an equal number of left and right ones. For further practice, let's carefully prove this from the recursive definitions, beginning with a recursive definition of the number $\#_c(s)$ of occurrences of the character $c \in A$ in a string s:

Definition 7.2.2.

Base case: $\#_c(\lambda) ::= 0.$

Constructor case:

$$\#_c(\langle a, s \rangle) ::= \begin{cases} \#_c(s) & \text{if } a \neq c, \\ 1 + \#_c(s) & \text{if } a = c. \end{cases}$$

The following Lemma follows directly by structural induction on Definition 7.2.2. We'll leave the proof for practice (Problem 7.9).

Lemma 7.2.3.

$$\#_c(s \cdot t) = \#_c(s) + \#_c(t).$$

Lemma. *Every string in RecMatch has an equal number of left and right brackets.*

Proof. The proof is by structural induction with induction hypothesis

$$P(s) ::= \left[\#_{[}(s) = \#_{]}(s) \right].$$

Base case: $P(\lambda)$ holds because

$$\#_{[}(\lambda) = 0 = \#_{]}(\lambda)$$

by the base case of Definition 7.2.2 of $\#_c()$.

Constructor case: By structural induction hypothesis, we assume $P(s)$ and $P(t)$ and must show $P([s]t)$:

$$\#_{[}\ ([s]t) = \#_{[}\ ([) + \#_{[}\ (s) + \#_{[}\ (]) + \#_{[}\ (t) \qquad \text{(Lemma 7.2.3)}$$
$$= 1 + \#_{[}\ (s) + 0 + \#_{[}\ (t) \qquad \text{(def } \#_{[}\ ())$$
$$= 1 + \#_{]}\ (s) + 0 + \#_{]}\ (t) \qquad \text{(by } P(s) \text{ and } P(t))$$
$$= 0 + \#_{]}\ (s) + 1 + \#_{]}\ (t)$$
$$= \#_{]}\ ([) + \#_{]}\ (s) + \#_{]}\ (]) + \#_{]}\ (t) \qquad \text{(def } \#_{]}\ ())$$
$$= \#_{]}\ ([s]t) \qquad \text{(Lemma 7.2.3)}$$

This completes the proof of the constructor case. We conclude by structural induction that $P(s)$ holds for all $s \in \mathrm{RecMatch}$. ■

Warning: When a recursive definition of a data type allows the same element to be constructed in more than one way, the definition is said to be *ambiguous*. We were careful to choose an *un*ambiguous definition of RecMatch to ensure that functions defined recursively on its definition would always be well-defined. Recursively defining a function on an ambiguous data type definition usually will not work. To illustrate the problem, here's another definition of the matched strings.

Definition 7.2.4. Define the set, AmbRecMatch $\subseteq \{], [\}^*$ recursively as follows:

- **Base case**: $\lambda \in \mathrm{AmbRecMatch}$,

- **Constructor cases**: if $s, t \in \mathrm{AmbRecMatch}$, then the strings $[s]$ and st are also in AmbRecMatch.

It's pretty easy to see that the definition of AmbRecMatch is just another way to define RecMatch, that is AmbRecMatch = RecMatch (see Problem 7.19). The definition of AmbRecMatch is arguably easier to understand, but we didn't use it because it's ambiguous, while the trickier definition of RecMatch is unambiguous. Here's why this matters. Let's define the number of operations $f(s)$ to construct a matched string s recursively on the definition of $s \in \mathrm{AmbRecMatch}$:

$$f(\lambda) ::= 0, \qquad (f \text{ base case})$$
$$f([s]) ::= 1 + f(s),$$
$$f(st) ::= 1 + f(s) + f(t). \qquad (f \text{ concat case})$$

This definition may seem ok, but it isn't: $f(\lambda)$ winds up with two values, and consequently:

$$
\begin{aligned}
0 &= f(\lambda) && (f \text{ base case})) \\
&= f(\lambda \cdot \lambda) && (\text{concat def, base case}) \\
&= 1 + f(\lambda) + f(\lambda) && (f \text{ concat case}), \\
&= 1 + 0 + 0 = 1 && (f \text{ base case}).
\end{aligned}
$$

This is definitely not a situation we want to be in!

7.3   Recursive Functions on Nonnegative Integers

The nonnegative integers can be understood as a recursive data type.

Definition 7.3.1. The set $\mathbb{N}$ is a data type defined recursively as:

- $0 \in \mathbb{N}$.

- If $n \in \mathbb{N}$, then the *successor* $n + 1$ of n is in $\mathbb{N}$.

The point here is to make it clear that ordinary induction is simply the special case of structural induction on the recursive Definition 7.3.1. This also justifies the familiar recursive definitions of functions on the nonnegative integers.

7.3.1   Some Standard Recursive Functions on $\mathbb{N}$

Example 7.3.2. *The factorial function.* This function is often written "$n!$." You will see a lot of it in later chapters. Here, we'll use the notation $\text{fac}(n)$:

- $\text{fac}(0) ::= 1$.

- $\text{fac}(n + 1) ::= (n + 1) \cdot \text{fac}(n)$ for $n \geq 0$.

Example 7.3.3. *Summation notation.* Let "$S(n)$" abbreviate the expression "$\sum_{i=1}^{n} f(i)$." We can recursively define $S(n)$ with the rules

- $S(0) ::= 0$.

- $S(n + 1) ::= f(n + 1) + S(n)$ for $n \geq 0$.

7.3.2   Ill-formed Function Definitions

There are some other blunders to watch out for when defining functions recursively. The main problems come when recursive definitions don't follow the recursive definition of the underlying data type. Below are some function specifications that resemble good definitions of functions on the nonnegative integers, but really aren't.

$$f_1(n) ::= 2 + f_1(n-1). \tag{7.2}$$

This "definition" has no base case. If some function f_1 satisfied (7.2), so would a function obtained by adding a constant to the value of f_1. So equation (7.2) does not uniquely define an f_1.

$$f_2(n) ::= \begin{cases} 0, & \text{if } n = 0, \\ f_2(n+1) & \text{otherwise.} \end{cases} \tag{7.3}$$

This "definition" has a base case, but still doesn't uniquely determine f_2. Any function that is 0 at 0 and constant everywhere else would satisfy the specification, so (7.3) also does not uniquely define anything.

In a typical programming language, evaluation of $f_2(1)$ would begin with a recursive call of $f_2(2)$, which would lead to a recursive call of $f_2(3)$, ... with recursive calls continuing without end. This "operational" approach interprets (7.3) as defining a *partial* function f_2 that is undefined everywhere but 0.

$$f_3(n) ::= \begin{cases} 0, & \text{if } n \text{ is divisible by 2,} \\ 1, & \text{if } n \text{ is divisible by 3,} \\ 2, & \text{otherwise.} \end{cases} \tag{7.4}$$

This "definition" is inconsistent: it requires $f_3(6) = 0$ and $f_3(6) = 1$, so (7.4) doesn't define anything.

Mathematicians have been wondering about this function specification, known as the Collatz conjecture for a while:

$$f_4(n) ::= \begin{cases} 1, & \text{if } n \leq 1, \\ f_4(n/2) & \text{if } n > 1 \text{ is even,} \\ f_4(3n+1) & \text{if } n > 1 \text{ is odd.} \end{cases} \tag{7.5}$$

For example, $f_4(3) = 1$ because

$$f_4(3) ::= f_4(10) ::= f_4(5) ::= f_4(16) ::= f_4(8) ::= f_4(4) ::= f_4(2) ::= f_4(1) ::= 1.$$

The constant function equal to 1 will satisfy (7.5), but it's not known if another function does as well. The problem is that the third case specifies $f_4(n)$ in terms of f_4 at arguments larger than n, and so cannot be justified by induction on $\mathbb{N}$. It's known that any f_4 satisfying (7.5) equals 1 for all n up to over 10^{18}.

A final example is the Ackermann function, which is an extremely fast-growing function of two nonnegative arguments. Its inverse is correspondingly slow-growing— it grows slower than $\log n$, $\log \log n$, $\log \log \log n$, ..., but it does grow unboundly. This inverse actually comes up analyzing a useful, highly efficient procedure known as the *Union-Find algorithm*. This algorithm was conjectured to run in a number of steps that grew linearly in the size of its input, but turned out to be "linear" but with a slow growing coefficient nearly equal to the inverse Ackermann function. This means that pragmatically, *Union-Find* is linear, since the theoretically growing coefficient is less than 5 for any input that could conceivably come up.

The Ackermann function can be defined recursively as the function A given by the following rules:

$$A(m, n) = 2n \qquad\qquad \text{if } m = 0 \text{ or } n \le 1, \qquad (7.6)$$
$$A(m, n) = A(m - 1, A(m, n - 1)) \qquad \text{otherwise.} \qquad (7.7)$$

Now these rules are unusual because the definition of $A(m, n)$ involves an evaluation of A at arguments that may be a lot bigger than m and n. The definitions of f_2 above showed how definitions of function values at small argument values in terms of larger one can easily lead to nonterminating evaluations. The definition of the Ackermann function is actually ok, but proving this takes some ingenuity (see Problem 7.25).

7.4 Arithmetic Expressions

Expression evaluation is a key feature of programming languages, and recognition of expressions as a recursive data type is a key to understanding how they can be processed.

To illustrate this approach we'll work with a toy example: arithmetic expressions like $3x^2 + 2x + 1$ involving only one variable, "x." We'll refer to the data type of such expressions as Aexp. Here is its definition:

Definition 7.4.1.

- **Base cases:**

- The variable x is in Aexp.

- The arabic numeral k for any nonnegative integer k is in Aexp.

- **Constructor cases**: If $e, f \in$ Aexp, then

   - $[e + f] \in$ Aexp. The expression $[e + f]$ is called a *sum*. The Aexp's e and f are called the *components* of the sum; they're also called the *summands*.

   - $[e * f] \in$ Aexp. The expression $[e * f]$ is called a *product*. The Aexp's e and f are called the *components* of the product; they're also called the *multiplier* and *multiplicand*.

   - $-[e] \in$ Aexp. The expression $-[e]$ is called a *negative*.

Notice that Aexp's are fully bracketed, and exponents aren't allowed. So the Aexp version of the polynomial expression $3x^2 + 2x + 1$ would officially be written as

$$[[3 * [x * x]] + [[2 * x] + 1]]. \qquad (7.8)$$

These brackets and $*$'s clutter up examples, so we'll often use simpler expressions like "$3x^2 + 2x + 1$" instead of (7.8). But it's important to recognize that $3x^2 + 2x + 1$ is not an Aexp; it's an *abbreviation* for an Aexp.

7.4.1   Evaluation and Substitution with Aexp's

Evaluating Aexp's

Since the only variable in an Aexp is x, the value of an Aexp is determined by the value of x. For example, if the value of x is 3, then the value of $3x^2 + 2x + 1$ is 34. In general, given any Aexp e and an integer value n for the variable x we can evaluate e to finds its value $\mathrm{eval}(e, n)$. It's easy, and useful, to specify this evaluation process with a recursive definition.

Definition 7.4.2. The *evaluation function*, eval : Aexp $\times \mathbb{Z} \to \mathbb{Z}$, is defined recursively on expressions $e \in$ Aexp as follows. Let n be any integer.

- **Base cases**:

$$\mathrm{eval}(x, n) ::= n \qquad \text{(value of variable } x \text{ is } n\text{)}, \qquad (7.9)$$
$$\mathrm{eval}(\mathrm{k}, n) ::= k \qquad \text{(value of numeral k is } k, \text{ regardless of } x.) \qquad (7.10)$$

- **Constructor cases**:

$$\text{eval}([\, e_1 + e_2 \,], n) ::= \text{eval}(e_1, n) + \text{eval}(e_2, n), \tag{7.11}$$

$$\text{eval}([\, e_1 * e_2 \,], n) ::= \text{eval}(e_1, n) \cdot \text{eval}(e_2, n), \tag{7.12}$$

$$\text{eval}(\text{-}[\, e_1 \,], n) ::= -\,\text{eval}(e_1, n). \tag{7.13}$$

For example, here's how the recursive definition of eval would arrive at the value of $3 + x^2$ when x is 2:

$$
\begin{aligned}
\text{eval}([\, 3 + [\, x * x \,] \,], 2) &= \text{eval}(3, 2) + \text{eval}([\, x * x \,], 2) &&\text{(by Def 7.4.2.7.11)}\\
&= 3 + \text{eval}([\, x * x \,], 2) &&\text{(by Def 7.4.2.7.10)}\\
&= 3 + (\text{eval}(x, 2) \cdot \text{eval}(x, 2)) &&\text{(by Def 7.4.2.7.12)}\\
&= 3 + (2 \cdot 2) &&\text{(by Def 7.4.2.7.9)}\\
&= 3 + 4 = 7.
\end{aligned}
$$

Substituting into Aexp's

Substituting expressions for variables is a standard operation used by compilers and algebra systems. For example, the result of substituting the expression $3x$ for x in the expression $x(x - 1)$ would be $3x(3x - 1)$. We'll use the general notation $\text{subst}(f, e)$ for the result of substituting an Aexp f for each of the x's in an Aexp e. So as we just explained,

$$\text{subst}(3x, x(x - 1)) = 3x(3x - 1).$$

This substitution function has a simple recursive definition:

Definition 7.4.3. The *substitution function* from Aexp $\times$ Aexp to Aexp is defined recursively on expressions $e \in$ Aexp as follows. Let f be any Aexp.

- **Base cases**:

$$\text{subst}(f, x) ::= f \qquad \text{(subbing } f \text{ for variable } x \text{ just gives } f,) \tag{7.14}$$

$$\text{subst}(f, \text{k}) ::= \text{k} \qquad \text{(subbing into a numeral does nothing.)} \tag{7.15}$$

- **Constructor cases**:

$$\text{subst}(f, [\, e_1 + e_2 \,]) ::= [\, \text{subst}(f, e_1) + \text{subst}(f, e_2) \,] \tag{7.16}$$

$$\text{subst}(f, [\, e_1 * e_2 \,]) ::= [\, \text{subst}(f, e_1) * \text{subst}(f, e_2) \,] \tag{7.17}$$

$$\text{subst}(f, \text{-}[\, e_1 \,]) ::= \text{-}[\, \text{subst}(f, e_1) \,] . \tag{7.18}$$

Here's how the recursive definition of the substitution function would find the result of substituting $3x$ for x in the expression $x(x - 1)$:

$$
\begin{aligned}
&\text{subst}(3x, x(x-1)) \\
&= \text{subst}([\, 3 * x \,], [\, x * [\, x + \text{-}[\, 1 \,] \,] \,]) && \text{(unabbreviating)} \\
&= [\, \text{subst}([\, 3 * x \,], x) * \\
&\qquad \text{subst}([\, 3 * x \,], [\, x + \text{-}[\, 1 \,] \,])] && \text{(by Def 7.4.3 7.17)} \\
&= [\, [\, 3 * x \,] * \text{subst}([\, 3 * x \,], [\, x + \text{-}[\, 1 \,] \,])] && \text{(by Def 7.4.3 7.14)} \\
&= [\, [\, 3 * x \,] * [\, \text{subst}([\, 3 * x \,], x) \\
&\qquad\qquad + \text{subst}([\, 3 * x \,], \text{-}[\, 1 \,])]] && \text{(by Def 7.4.3 7.16)} \\
&= [\, [\, 3 * x \,] * [\, [\, 3 * x \,] + \text{-}[\, \text{subst}([\, 3 * x \,], 1)]]] && \text{(by Def 7.4.3 7.14 \& 7.18)} \\
&= [\, [\, 3 * x \,] * [\, [\, 3 * x \,] + \text{-}[\, 1 \,]]] && \text{(by Def 7.4.3 7.15)} \\
&= 3x(3x - 1) && \text{(abbreviation)}
\end{aligned}
$$

Now suppose we have to find the value of $\text{subst}(3x, x(x - 1))$ when $x = 2$. There are two approaches. First, we could actually do the substitution above to get $3x(3x - 1)$, and then we could evaluate $3x(3x - 1)$ when $x = 2$, that is, we could recursively calculate $\text{eval}(3x(3x - 1), 2)$ to get the final value 30. This approach is described by the expression

$$\text{eval}(\text{subst}(3x, x(x - 1)), 2). \tag{7.19}$$

In programming jargon, this would be called evaluation using the *Substitution Model*. With this approach, the formula $3x$ appears twice after substitution, so the multiplication $3 \cdot 2$ that computes its value gets performed twice.

The second approach is called evaluation using the *Environment Model*. Here, to compute the value of (7.19), we evaluate $3x$ when $x = 2$ using just 1 multiplication to get the value 6. Then we evaluate $x(x - 1)$ when x has this value 6 to arrive at the value $6 \cdot 5 = 30$. This approach is described by the expression

$$\text{eval}(x(x - 1), \text{eval}(3x, 2)). \tag{7.20}$$

The Environment Model only computes the value of $3x$ once, and so it requires one fewer multiplication than the Substitution model to compute (7.20).

This is a good place to stop and work this example out yourself (Problem 7.26).

The fact that the final integer values of (7.19) and (7.20) agree is no surprise. The substitution model and environment models will *always* produce the same final. We can prove this by structural induction directly following the definitions of the two approaches. More precisely, what we want to prove is

Theorem 7.4.4. *For all expressions $e, f \in Aexp$ and $n \in \mathbb{Z}$,*

$$\mathrm{eval}(\mathrm{subst}(f, e), n) = \mathrm{eval}(e, \mathrm{eval}(f, n)). \qquad (7.21)$$

Proof. The proof is by structural induction on e.[1]

Base cases:

- Case[x]

  The left-hand side of equation (7.21) equals $\mathrm{eval}(f, n)$ by this base case in Definition 7.4.3 of the substitution function; the right-hand side also equals $\mathrm{eval}(f, n)$ by this base case in Definition 7.4.2 of eval.

- Case[k].

  The left-hand side of equation (7.21) equals k by this base case in Definitions 7.4.3 and 7.4.2 of the substitution and evaluation functions. Likewise, the right-hand side equals k by two applications of this base case in the Definition 7.4.2 of eval.

Constructor cases:

- Case[[$e_1 + e_2$]]

  By the structural induction hypothesis (7.21), we may assume that for all $f \in Aexp$ and $n \in \mathbb{Z}$,

  $$\mathrm{eval}(\mathrm{subst}(f, e_i), n) = \mathrm{eval}(e_i, \mathrm{eval}(f, n)) \qquad (7.22)$$

  for $i = 1, 2$. We wish to prove that

  $$\mathrm{eval}(\mathrm{subst}(f, [\, e_1 + e_2 \,]), n) = \mathrm{eval}([\, e_1 + e_2 \,], \mathrm{eval}(f, n)). \qquad (7.23)$$

  The left-hand side of (7.23) equals

  $$\mathrm{eval}([\, \mathrm{subst}(f, e_1) + \mathrm{subst}(f, e_2) \,], n)$$

---

[1] This is an example of why it's useful to notify the reader what the induction variable is—in this case it isn't n.

by Definition 7.4.3.7.16 of substitution into a sum expression. But this equals

$$\text{eval}(\text{subst}(f, e_1), n) + \text{eval}(\text{subst}(f, e_2), n)$$

by Definition 7.4.2.(7.11) of eval for a sum expression. By induction hypothesis (7.22), this in turn equals

$$\text{eval}(e_1, \text{eval}(f, n)) + \text{eval}(e_2, \text{eval}(f, n)).$$

Finally, this last expression equals the right-hand side of (7.23) by Definition 7.4.2.(7.11) of eval for a sum expression. This proves (7.23) in this case.

- Case[[$e_1 * e_2$]] Similar.

- Case[−[e_1]] Even easier.

This covers all the constructor cases, and so completes the proof by structural induction.

∎

7.5   Induction in Computer Science

Induction is a powerful and widely applicable proof technique, which is why we've devoted two entire chapters to it. Strong induction and its special case of ordinary induction are applicable to any kind of thing with nonnegative integer sizes—which is an awful lot of things, including all step-by-step computational processes.

Structural induction then goes beyond number counting, and offers a simple, natural approach to proving things about recursive data types and recursive computation.

In many cases, a nonnegative integer size can be defined for a recursively defined datum, such as the length of a string, or the number of operations in an Aexp. It is then possible to prove properties of data by ordinary induction on their size. But this approach often produces more cumbersome proofs than structural induction.

In fact, structural induction is theoretically more powerful than ordinary induction. However, it's only more powerful when it comes to reasoning about infinite data types—like infinite trees, for example—so this greater power doesn't matter in practice. What does matter is that for recursively defined data types, structural induction is a simple and natural approach. This makes it a technique every computer scientist should embrace.

Problems for Section 7.1

Practice Problems

Problem 7.1.
The set OBT of *Ordered Binary Trees* is defined recursively as follows:

Base case: $\langle \textbf{leaf} \rangle$ is an OBT, and

Constructor case: if R and S are OBT's, then $\langle \textbf{node}, R, S \rangle$ is an OBT.

If T is an OBT, let n_T be the number of **node** labels in T and l_T be the number of **leaf** labels in T.

Prove by structural induction that for all $T \in$ OBT,

$$l_T = n_T + 1. \tag{7.24}$$

Class Problems

Problem 7.2.
Prove by structural induction on the recursive definition(7.1.1) of A^* that concatenation is *associative*:
$$(r \cdot s) \cdot t = r \cdot (s \cdot t) \tag{7.25}$$
for all strings $r, s, t \in A^*$.

Problem 7.3.
The *reversal* of a string is the string written backwards, for example, $\text{rev}(abcde) = edcba$.

(a) Give a simple recursive definition of $\text{rev}(s)$ based on the recursive definitions 7.1.1 of $s \in A^*$ and of the concatenation operation 7.1.3.

(b) Prove that
$$\text{rev}(s \cdot t) = \text{rev}(t) \cdot \text{rev}(s), \tag{7.26}$$
for all strings $s, t \in A^*$. You may assume that concatenation is associative:
$$(r \cdot s) \cdot t = r \cdot (s \cdot t)$$
for all strings $r, s, t \in A^*$ (Problem 7.2).

Problem 7.4.
The Elementary 18.01 Functions (F18's) are the set of functions of one real variable defined recursively as follows:

Base cases:

- The identity function $id(x) ::= x$ is an F18,

- any constant function is an F18,

- the sine function is an F18,

Constructor cases:
If f, g are F18's, then so are

1. $f + g\ fg\ 2^g$,

2. the inverse function f^{-1},

3. the composition $f \circ g$.

(a) Prove that the function $1/x$ is an F18.

Warning: Don't confuse $1/x = x^{-1}$ with the inverse id^{-1} of the identity function $id(x)$. The inverse id^{-1} is equal to id.

(b) Prove by Structural Induction on this definition that the Elementary 18.01 Functions are *closed under taking derivatives*. That is, show that if $f(x)$ is an F18, then so is $f' ::= df/dx$. (Just work out 2 or 3 of the most interesting constructor cases; you may skip the less interesting ones.)

Problem 7.5.
Here is a simple recursive definition of the set E of even integers:

Definition. Base case: $0 \in E$.
  Constructor cases: If $n \in E$, then so are $n + 2$ and $-n$.

Provide similar simple recursive definitions of the following sets:
(a) The set $S ::= \{2^k 3^m 5^n \in \mathbb{N} \mid k, m, n \in \mathbb{N}\}$.

(b) The set $T ::= \{2^k 3^{2k+m} 5^{m+n} \in \mathbb{N} \mid k, m, n \in \mathbb{N}\}$.

(c) The set $L ::= \{(a, b) \in \mathbb{Z}^2 \mid (a - b) \text{ is a multiple of 3}\}$.

Let L' be the set defined by the recursive definition you gave for L in the previous part. Now if you did it right, then $L' = L$, but maybe you made a mistake. So let's check that you got the definition right.

(d) Prove by structural induction on your definition of L' that

$$L' \subseteq L.$$

(e) Confirm that you got the definition right by proving that

$$L \subseteq L'.$$

(f) See if you can give an *unambiguous* recursive definition of L.

Problem 7.6.

Definition. The recursive data type binary-2PG of *binary trees* with leaf labels L is defined recursively as follows:

- **Base case:** $\langle \texttt{leaf}, l \rangle \in$ binary-2PG, for all labels $l \in L$.

- **Constructor case:** If $G_1, G_2 \in$ binary-2PG, then

$$\langle \texttt{bintree}, G_1, G_2 \rangle \in \text{binary-2PG}.$$

The *size* $|G|$ of $G \in$ binary-2PG is defined recursively on this definition by:

- **Base case:**
$$|\langle \texttt{leaf}, l \rangle| ::= 1, \quad \text{for all } l \in L.$$

- **Constructor case:**
$$|\langle \texttt{bintree}, G_1, G_2 \rangle| ::= |G_1| + |G_2| + 1.$$

For example, the size of the binary-2PG G pictured in Figure 7.1, is 7.

(a) Write out (using angle brackets and labels $\texttt{bintree}, \texttt{leaf}$, etc.) the binary-2PG G pictured in Figure 7.1.

The value of flatten(G) for $G \in$ binary-2PG is the sequence of labels in L of the leaves of G. For example, for the binary-2PG G pictured in Figure 7.1,

$$\text{flatten}(G) = (\texttt{win}, \texttt{lose}, \texttt{win}, \texttt{win}).$$

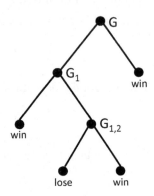

Figure 7.1   A picture of a binary tree G.

(b) Give a recursive definition of flatten. (You may use the operation of *concatenation* (append) of two sequences.)

(c) Prove by structural induction on the definitions of flatten and size that

$$2 \cdot \text{length(flatten}(G)) = |G| + 1. \tag{7.27}$$

Homework Problems

Problem 7.7.
The string *reversal* function, rev : $A^* \to A^*$ has a simple recursive definition.

Base case: rev(λ) ::= λ.

Constructor case: rev(as) ::= rev(s)a for $s \in A^*$ and $a \in A$.

A string s is a *palindrome* when rev(s) $=s$. The *palindromes* also have a simple recursive definition as the set RecPal.

Base cases: $\lambda \in$ RecPal and $a \in$ RecPal for $a \in A$.

Constructor case: If $s \in$ RecPal, then $asa \in$ RecPal for $a \in A$.

Verifying that the two definitions agree offers a nice exercise in structural induction and also induction on length of strings. The verification rests on three basic properties of concatenation and reversal proved in separate problems 7.2 and 7.3.

Fact.

$$(rs = uv \text{ AND } |r| = |u|) \text{ IFF } (r = u \text{ AND } s = v) \tag{7.28}$$

$$r \cdot (s \cdot t) = (r \cdot s) \cdot t \tag{7.29}$$

$$\text{rev}(st) = \text{rev}(t)\,\text{rev}(s) \tag{7.30}$$

(a) Prove that $s = \text{rev}(s)$ for all $s \in \text{RecPal}$.

(b) Prove conversely that if $s = \text{rev}(s)$, then $s \in \text{RecPal}$.

Hint: By induction on $n = |s|$.

Problem 7.8.
Let m, n be integers, not both zero. Define a set of integers, $L_{m,n}$, recursively as follows:

- **Base cases**: $m, n \in L_{m,n}$.

- **Constructor cases**: If $j, k \in L_{m,n}$, then

    1. $-j \in L_{m,n}$,
    2. $j + k \in L_{m,n}$.

Let L be an abbreviation for $L_{m,n}$ in the rest of this problem.

(a) Prove *by structural induction* that every common divisor of m and n also divides every member of L.

(b) Prove that any integer multiple of an element of L is also in L.

(c) Show that if $j, k \in L$ and $k \neq 0$, then $\text{rem}(j, k) \in L$.

(d) Show that there is a positive integer $g \in L$ that divides every member of L. *Hint:* The least positive integer in L.

(e) Conclude that g from part (d) is $\gcd(m, n)$, the greatest common divisor, of m and n.

Problem 7.9.

Figure 7.2   Constructing the Koch Snowflake.

Definition. Define the number $\#_c(s)$ of occurrences of the character $c \in A$ in the string s recursively on the definition of $s \in A^*$:

   base case: $\#_c(\lambda) ::= 0$.
   constructor case:

$$\#_c(\langle a, s \rangle) ::= \begin{cases} \#_c(s) & \text{if } a \neq c, \\ 1 + \#_c(s) & \text{if } a = c. \end{cases}$$

Prove by structural induction that for all $s, t \in A^*$ and $c \in A$

$$\#_c(s \cdot t) = \#_c(s) + \#_c(t).$$

Problem 7.10.
Fractals are an example of mathematical objects that can be defined recursively. In this problem, we consider the Koch snowflake. Any Koch snowflake can be constructed by the following recursive definition.

- **Base case**: An equilateral triangle with a positive integer side length is a Koch snowflake.

- **Constructor case**: Let K be a Koch snowflake, and let l be a line segment on the snowflake. Remove the middle third of l, and replace it with two line segments of the same length $|l|$, as is done in Figure 7.2

  The resulting figure is also a Koch snowflake.

Prove by structural induction that the area inside any Koch snowflake is of the form $q\sqrt{3}$, where q is a rational number.

Problem 7.11.
The set RBT of *Red-Black Trees* is defined recursively as follows:

Base cases:

- $\langle \textbf{red} \rangle \in$ RBT, and

- $\langle \mathbf{black} \rangle \in$ RBT.

Constructor cases: A, B are RBT's, then

- if A, B start with **black**, then $\langle \mathbf{red}, A, B \rangle$ is an RBT.

- if A, B start with **red**, then $\langle \mathbf{black}, A, B \rangle$ is an RBT.

For any RBT T, let

- r_T be the number of **red** labels in T,

- b_T be the number of **black** labels in T, and

- $n_T ::= r_T + b_T$ be the total number of labels in T.

Prove that

$$\text{If } T \text{ starts with a } \mathbf{red} \text{ label, then } \frac{n_T}{3} \leq r_T \leq \frac{2n_T + 1}{3}, \qquad (7.31)$$

Hint:

$$n/3 \leq r \quad \text{IFF} \quad (2/3)n \geq n - r$$

Exam Problems

Problem 7.12.
The Arithmetic Trig Functions (*Atrig*'s) are the set of functions of one real variable defined recursively as follows:

Base cases:

- The identity function $\mathrm{id}(x) ::= x$ is an *Atrig*,

- any constant function is an *Atrig*,

- the sine function is an *Atrig*,

Constructor cases:
If f, g are *Atrig*'s, then so are

1. $f + g$

2. $f \cdot g$

3. the composition $f \circ g$.

Prove by structural induction on this definition that if $f(x)$ is an *Atrig*, then so is $f' ::= df/dx$.

Problem 7.13.

Definition. The set RAF of *rational functions* of one real variable is the set of functions defined recursively as follows:

Base cases:

- The identity function, $\text{id}(r) ::= r$ for $r \in \mathbb{R}$ (the real numbers), is an RAF,

- any constant function on $\mathbb{R}$ is an RAF.

Constructor cases: If f, g are RAF's, then so is $f \circledast g$, where $\circledast$ is one of the operations

1. addition $+$,

2. multiplication $\cdot$ or

3. division $/$.

(a) Describe how to construct functions $e, f, g \in \text{RAF}$ such that

$$e \circ (f + g) \neq (e \circ f) + (e \circ g). \tag{7.32}$$

(b) Prove that for all real-valued functions e, f, g (not just those in RAF):

$$(e \circledast f) \circ g = (e \circ g) \circledast (f \circ g), \tag{7.33}$$

Hint: $(e \circledast f)(x) ::= e(x) \circledast f(x)$.

(c) Let predicate $P(h)$ be the following predicate on functions $h \in \text{RAF}$:

$$P(h) ::= \forall g \in \text{RAF}. \ h \circ g \in \text{RAF}.$$

Prove by structural induction on the definition of RAF that $P(h)$ holds for all $h \in$ RAF.

Make sure to indicate explicitly

- each of the base cases, and
- each of the constructor cases.

Problem 7.14.

The *2-3-averaged numbers* are a subset, N23, of the real interval $[0, 1]$ defined recursively as follows:

Base cases: $0, 1 \in$ N23.

Constructor case: If a, b are in N23, then so is $L(a, b)$ where

$$L(a, b) ::= \frac{2a + 3b}{5}.$$

(a) Use ordinary induction or the Well-Ordering Principle to prove that

$$\left(\frac{3}{5}\right)^n \in \text{N23}$$

for all nonnegative integers n.

(b) Prove by Structural Induction that the product of two 2-3-averaged numbers is also a 2-3-averaged number.

Hint: Prove by structural induction on c that, if $d \in$ N23, then $cd \in$ N23.

Problem 7.15.

This problem is about binary strings $s \in \{0, 1\}^*$.

Let's call a recursive definition of a set of strings cat-OK when all its constructors are defined as concatenations of strings.[2]

For example, the set, One1, of strings with exactly one 1 has the cat-OK definition:

Base case: The length-one string 1 is in One1.

Constructor case: If s is in One1, then so is $0s$ and $s0$.

(a) Give a cat-OK definition of the set E of even length strings consisting solely of 0's.

---

[2] The concatenation of two strings x and y, written xy, is the string obtained by appending x to the left end of y. For example, the concatenation of 01 and 101 is 01101.

(b) Let rev(s) be the reversal of the string s. For example, rev(001) = 100. A *palindrome* is a string s such that $s = $ rev(s). For example, 11011 and 010010 are palindromes.

Give a cat-OK definition of the *palindromes*.

(c) Give a cat-OK definition of the set P of strings consisting solely of 0's whose length is a power of two.

Problems for Section 7.2

Practice Problems

Problem 7.16.
Define the sets F_1 and F_2 recursively:

- F_1:

  - $5 \in F_1$,
  - if $n \in F_1$, then $5n \in F_1$.

- F_2:

  - $5 \in F_2$,
  - if $n, m \in F_1$, then $nm \in F_2$.

(a) Show that one of these definitions is technically *ambiguous*. (Remember that "ambiguous recursive definition" has a technical mathematical meaning which does not imply that the ambiguous definition is unclear.)

(b) Briefly explain what advantage unambiguous recursive definitions have over ambiguous ones.

(c) A way to prove that $F_1 = F_2$, is to show first that $F_1 \subseteq F_2$ and second that $F_2 \subseteq F_1$. One of these containments follows easily by structural induction. Which one? What would be the induction hypothesis? (You do not need to complete a proof.)

Problem 7.17. (a) To prove that the set RecMatch, of matched strings of Definition 7.2.1 equals the set AmbRecMatch of ambiguous matched strings of Definition 7.2.4, you could first prove that

$$\forall r \in \text{RecMatch. } r \in \text{AmbRecMatch},$$

and then prove that

$$\forall u \in \text{AmbRecMatch. } u \in \text{RecMatch}.$$

Of these two statements, indicate the one that would be simpler to prove by structural induction directly from the definitions.

(b) Suppose structural induction was being used to prove that AmbRecMatch $\subseteq$ RecMatch. Indicate the one predicate below that would fit the format for a structural induction hypothesis in such a proof.

- $P_0(n) ::= |s| \leq n$ IMPLIES $s \in$ RecMatch.
- $P_1(n) ::= |s| \leq n$ IMPLIES $s \in$ AmbRecMatch.
- $P_2(s) ::= s \in$ RecMatch.
- $P_3(s) ::= s \in$ AmbRecMatch.
- $P_4(s) ::= (s \in$ RecMatch IMPLIES $s \in$ AmbRecMatch).

(c) The recursive definition AmbRecMatch is ambiguous because it allows the $s \cdot t$ constructor to apply when s or t is the empty string. But even fixing that, ambiguity remains. Demonstrate this by giving two different derivations for the string "[ ][ ][ ] according to AmbRecMatch but only using the $s \cdot t$ constructor when $s \neq \lambda$ and $t \neq \lambda$.

Class Problems

Problem 7.18.

Let p be the string [ ]. A string of brackets is said to be *erasable* iff it can be reduced to the empty string by repeatedly erasing occurrences of p. For example, to erase the string

$$[[[ ]] [ ]] [ ],$$

start by erasing the three occurrences of p to obtain

$$[[ ]].$$

Then erase the single occurrence of p to obtain,

$$[ ],$$

which can now be erased to obtain the empty string λ.

On the other hand the string

$$[\,]\,[\,[\,[\,[\,[\,]\,] \tag{7.34}$$

is not erasable, because when we try to erase, we get stuck. Namely, start by erasing the two occurrences of p in (7.34) to obtain

$$]\,[\,[\,[\,[\,]\,.$$

The erase the one remaining occurrence of p to obtain.

$$]\,[\,[\,[\,.$$

At this point we are stuck with no remaining occurrences of p. [3]

Let Erasable be the set of erasable strings of brackets. Let RecMatch be the recursive data type of strings of *matched* brackets given in Definition 7.2.1

(a) Use structural induction to prove that

$$\text{RecMatch} \subseteq \text{Erasable}.$$

(b) Supply the missing parts (labeled by "(*)") of the following proof that

$$\text{Erasable} \subseteq \text{RecMatch}.$$

Proof. We prove by strong induction that every length n string in Erasable is also in RecMatch. The induction hypothesis is

$$P(n) ::= \forall x \in \text{Erasable}.\ |x| = n \text{ IMPLIES } x \in \text{RecMatch}.$$

Base case:

(*) What is the base case? Prove that P is true in this case.

Inductive step: To prove $P(n + 1)$, suppose $|x| = n + 1$ and $x \in$ Erasable. We need to show that $x \in$ RecMatch.

Let's say that a string y is an *erase* of a string z iff y is the result of erasing a *single* occurrence of p in z.

---

[3] Notice that there are many ways to erase a string, depending on when and which occurrences of p are chosen to be erased. It turns out that given any initial string, the final string reached after performing all possible erasures will be the same, no matter how erasures are performed. We take this for granted here, although it is not altogether obvious. (See Problem 6.29 for a proof).

Since $x \in$ Erasable and has positive length, there must be an erase, $y \in$ Erasable, of x. So $|y| = n - 1 \geq 0$, and since $y \in$ Erasable, we may assume by induction hypothesis that $y \in$ RecMatch.

Now we argue by cases:

Case (y is the empty string):

(*) Prove that $x \in$ RecMatch in this case.

Case ($y = [\, s\,]\, t$ for some strings $s, t \in$ RecMatch): Now we argue by subcases.

- **Subcase**($x = py$):

  (*) Prove that $x \in$ RecMatch in this subcase.

- **Subcase** (x is of the form $[\, s'\,]\, t$ where s is an erase of s'):

  Since $s \in$ RecMatch, it is erasable by part (b), which implies that $s' \in$ Erasable. But $|s'| < |x|$, so by induction hypothesis, we may assume that $s' \in$ RecMatch. This shows that x is the result of the constructor step of RecMatch, and therefore $x \in$ RecMatch.

- **Subcase** (x is of the form $[\, s\,]\, t'$ where t is an erase of t'):

  (*) Prove that $x \in$ RecMatch in this subcase.

(*) Explain why the above cases are sufficient.

This completes the proof by strong induction on n, so we conclude that $P(n)$ holds for all $n \in \mathbb{N}$. Therefore $x \in$ RecMatch for every string $x \in$ Erasable. That is, Erasable $\subseteq$ RecMatch. Combined with part (a), we conclude that

$$\text{Erasable} = \text{RecMatch}.$$

∎

Problem 7.19. **(a)** Prove that the set RecMatch of matched strings of Definition 7.2.1 is closed under string concatenation. Namely, if $s, t \in$ RecMatch, then $s \cdot t \in$ RecMatch.

(b) Prove AmbRecMatch $\subseteq$ RecMatch, where AmbRecMatch is the set of ambiguous matched strings of Definition 7.2.4.

(c) Prove that RecMatch $=$ AmbRecMatch.

Homework Problems

Problem 7.20.

One way to determine if a string has matching brackets, that is, if it is in the set, RecMatch, of Definition 7.2.1 is to start with 0 and read the string from left to right, adding 1 to the count for each left bracket and subtracting 1 from the count for each right bracket. For example, here are the counts for two sample strings:

$$
\begin{array}{ccccccccccccc}
[&] &] & [& [& [& [& [&] &] &] &] \\
0 & 1 & 0 & -1 & 0 & 1 & 2 & 3 & 4 & 3 & 2 & 1 & 0
\end{array}
$$

$$
\begin{array}{cccccccccccc}
[& [& & [&] &] & [&] &] & [&] \\
0 & 1 & 2 & 3 & 2 & 1 & 2 & 1 & 0 & 1 & 0
\end{array}
$$

A string has a *good count* if its running count never goes negative and ends with 0. So the second string above has a good count, but the first one does not because its count went negative at the third step. Let

$$
\text{GoodCount} ::= \{s \in \{\,],[\,\}^* \mid s \text{ has a good count}\}.
$$

The empty string has a length 0 running count we'll take as a good count by convention, that is, $\lambda \in \text{GoodCount}$. The matched strings can now be characterized precisely as this set of strings with good counts.

(a) Prove that GoodCount contains RecMatch by structural induction on the definition of RecMatch.

(b) Conversely, prove that RecMatch contains GoodCount.

Hint: By induction on the length of strings in GoodCount. Consider when the running count equals 0 for the second time.

Problem 7.21.

Divided Equilateral Triangles (DETs) were defined in Problem 5.10 as follows:

- **Base case:** A single equilateral triangle is a DET whose only subtriangle is itself.

- If $T ::=$  is a DET, then the equilateral triangle T' built out of four copies of T as shown in in Figure 7.3 is also a DET, and the subtriangles of T' are exactly the subtriangles of each of the copies of T.

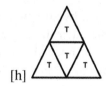

[h]

Figure 7.3 DET T' from Four Copies of DET T

[h]

Figure 7.4 Trapezoid from Three Triangles

Properties of DETs were proved earlier by induction on the length of a side of the triangle. Recognizing that the definition of DETs is recursive, we can instead prove properties of DETs by structural induction.

(a) Prove by structural induction that a DET with one of its corner subtriangles removed can be tiled with trapezoids built out of three subtriangles as in Figure 7.4.

(b) Explain why a DET with a triangle removed from the middle of one side can also be tiled by trapezoids.

(c) In tiling a large square using L-shaped blocks as described in Section 5.1.5, there was a tiling with any single subsquare removed. Part (b) indicates that trapezoid-tilings are possible for DETs with a non-corner subtriangle removed, so it's natural to make the mistaken guess that DETs have a corresponding property:

False Claim. *A DET with any single subtriangle removed can be trapezoid-tiled.*

We can try to prove the claim by structural induction as in part (a).

Bogus proof. The claim holds vacuously in the base case of a DET with a single subtriangle.

Now let T' be a DET made of four copies of a DET T, and suppose we remove an arbitrary subtriangle from T'.

The removed subtriangle must be a subtriangle of one of the copies of T. The copies are the same, so for definiteness we assume the subtriangle was removed from copy 1. Then by structural induction hypothesis, copy 1 can be trapezoid-tiled, and then the other three copies of T can be trapezoid-tiled exactly as in the solution to part(a). This yields a complete trapezoid-tiling of T' with the arbitrary subtriangle removed.

We conclude by structural induction that any DET with any subtriangle removed can be trapezoid-tiled.   ∎

What's wrong with the proof?

Hint: Find a counter-example and show where the proof breaks down.

We don't know if there is a simple characterization of exactly which subtriangles can be removed to allow a trapezoid tiling.

Problem 7.22.

A *binary word* is a finite sequence of 0's and 1's. In this problem, we'll simply call them "words." For example, $(1, 1, 0)$ and (1) are words of length three and one, respectively. We usually omit the parentheses and commas in the descriptions of words, so the preceding binary words would just be written as 110 and 1.

The basic operation of placing one word immediately after another is called *concatenation*. For example, the concatenation of 110 and 1 is 1101, and the concatenation of 110 with itself is 110110.

We can extend this basic operation on words to an operation on *sets* of words. To emphasize the distinction between a word and a set of words, from now on we'll refer to a set of words as a *language*. Now if R and S are languages, then $R \cdot S$ is the language consisting of all the words you can get by concatenating a word from R with a word from S. That is,

$$R \cdot S ::= \{rs \mid r \in R \text{ AND } s \in S\}.$$

For example,

$$\{0, 00\} \cdot \{00, 000\} = \{000, 0000, 00000\}$$

Another example is $D \cdot D$, abbreviated as D^2, where $D ::= \{1, 0\}$.

$$D^2 = \{00, 01, 10, 11\}.$$

In other words, D^2 is the language consisting of all the length-two words. More generally, D^n will be the language of length-n words.

If S is a language, the language you can get by concatenating any number of copies of words in S is called S^*—pronounced "S star." (By convention, the empty word λ always included in S^*.) For example, $\{0, 11\}^*$ is the language consisting of all the words you can make by stringing together 0's and 11's. This language could also be described as consisting of the words whose blocks of 1's are always of even length. Another example is $(D^2)^*$, which consists of all the even length words. Finally, the language B of *all* binary words is just D^*.

The *Concatenation-Definable (C-D)* languages are defined recursively:

- **Base case**: Every finite language is a C-D.

- **Constructor cases**: If L and M are C-D's, then

$$L \cdot M, \quad L \cup M, \quad \text{and} \ \overline{L}$$

are C-D's.

Note that the *-operation is *not* allowed. For this reason, the C-D languages are also called the "star-free languages," [33].

Lots of interesting languages turn out to be concatenation-definable, but some very simple languages are not. This problem ends with the conclusion that the language $\{00\}^*$ of even length words whose bits are all 0's is not a C-D language.

(a) Show that the set B of all binary words is C-D. *Hint:* The empty set is finite.

Now a more interesting example of a C-D set is the language of all binary words that include three consecutive 1's:

$$B111B.$$

Notice that the proper expression here is "$B \cdot \{111\} \cdot B$." But it causes no confusion and helps readability to omit the dots in concatenations and the curly braces for sets with only one element.

(b) Show that the language consisting of the binary words that start with 0 and end with 1 is C-D.

(c) Show that 0^* is C-D.

(d) Show that if R and S are C-D, then so is $R \cap S$.

(e) Show that $\{01\}^*$ is C-D.

Let's say a language S is 0-*finite* when it includes only a finite number of words whose bits are all 0's, that is, when $S \cap 0^*$ is a finite set of words. A langauge S is 0-*boring*—boring, for short—when either S or $\overline{S}$ is 0-finite.

(f) Explain why $\{00\}^*$ is not boring.

(g) Verify that if R and S are boring, then so is $R \cup S$.

(h) Verify that if R and S are boring, then so is $R \cdot S$.

Hint: By cases: whether R and S are both 0-finite, whether R or S contains no all-0 words at all (including the empty word λ), and whether neither of these cases hold.

(i) Conclude by structural induction that all C-D languages are boring.

So we have proved that the set $(00)^*$ of even length all-0 words is not a C-D language.

Problem 7.23.

We can explain in a simple and precise way how digital circuits work, and gain the powerful proof method of structural induction to verify their properties, by defining digital circuits as a recursive data type DigCirc. The definition is a little easier to state if all the gates in the circuit take two inputs, so we will use the two-input NOR gate rather than a one-input NOT, and let the set of gates be

$$\text{Gates} ::= \{\text{NOR}, \text{AND}, \text{OR}, \text{XOR}\}.$$

A digital circuit will be a recursively defined list of *gate connections* of the form (x, y, G, I) where G is a gate, x and y are the input wires, and I is the set of wires that the gate output feeds into as illustrated in Figure 7.5.

Formally, we let W be a set $w_0, w_1, \ldots$ whose elements are called *wires*, and $\mathbf{O} \notin W$ be an object called the *output*.

Definition. The set of digital circuit DigCirc, and their inputs and internal wires, are defined recursively as follows:

Base case: If $x, y \in W$, then $C \in \text{DigCirc}$, where

$$C = \text{list}((x, y, G, \{\mathbf{O}\})) \text{ for some } G \in \text{Gates},$$
$$\text{inputs}(C) ::= \{x, y\},$$
$$\text{internal}(C) ::= \emptyset.$$

Constructor cases: If

$$C \in \text{DigCirc},$$
$$I \subseteq \text{inputs}(C), I \neq \emptyset,$$
$$x, y \in W - (I \cup \text{internal}(C))$$

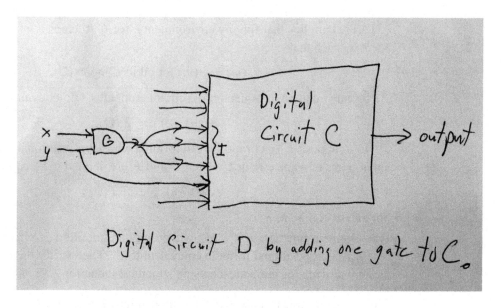

Figure 7.5 Digital Circuit Constructor Step

then $D \in \text{DigCirc}$, where

$$D = \text{cons}((\text{x}, \text{y}, \text{G}, \text{I}), \text{C}) \text{ for some } G \in \text{Gates},$$
$$\text{inputs}(\text{D}) ::= \{x, y\} \cup (\text{inputs}(\text{C}) - I),$$
$$\text{internal}(\text{D}) ::= \text{internal}(\text{C}) \cup I.$$

For any circuit C define

$$\text{wires}(\text{C}) ::= \text{inputs}(\text{C}) \cup \text{internal}(\text{C}) \cup \{\mathbf{O}\}.$$

A *wire assignment* for C is a function

$$\alpha : \text{wires}(\text{C}) \to \{\mathbf{T}, \mathbf{F}\}$$

such that for each gate connection $(x, y, G, I) \in C$,

$$\alpha(i) = (\alpha(x) \, G \, \alpha(y)) \text{ for all } i \in I.$$

(a) Define an *environment* for C to be a function $e : \text{inputs}(\text{C}) \to \{\mathbf{T}, \mathbf{F}\}$. Prove that if two wire assignments for C are equal for each wire in $\text{inputs}(\text{C})$, then the wire assignments are equal for all wires.

Part (a) implies that for any environment e for C, there is a *unique* wire assignment α_e such that

$$\alpha_e(w) = e(w) \text{ for all } w \in \text{inputs}(C).$$

So for any input environment e, the circuit computes a unique *output*

$$\text{eval}(C, e) ::= \alpha_e(\mathbf{O}).$$

Now suppose F is a propositional formula whose propositional variables are the input wires of some circuit C. Then C and F are defined to be *equivalent* iff

$$\text{eval}(C, e) = \text{eval}(F, e)$$

for all environments e for C.

(b) Define a function $E(C)$ recursively on the definition of circuit C, such that $E(C)$ is a propositional formula equivalent to C. Then verify the recursive definition by proving the equivalence using structural induction.

(c) Give examples where $E(C)$ is exponentially larger than C.

Exam Problems

Problem 7.24.
Let P be a propositional variable.

(a) Show how to express $\text{NOT}(P)$ using P and a selection from among the constant **True**, and the connectives XOR and AND.

The use of the constant **True** above is essential. To prove this, we begin with a recursive definition of XOR-AND formulas that do not use **True**, called the PXA formulas.

Definition. Base case: The propositional variable P is a PXA formula.

Constructor cases If $R, S \in \text{PXA}$, then

- R XOR S,

- R AND S

are PXA's.

For example,

$$(((P \text{ XOR } P) \text{ AND } P) \text{ XOR } (P \text{ AND } P)) \text{ XOR } (P \text{ XOR } P)$$

is a PXA.

(b) Prove by structural induction on the definition of PXA that every PXA formula A is equivalent to P or to **False**.

Problems for Section 7.3

Homework Problems

Problem 7.25.
One version of the the Ackermann function $A : \mathbb{N}^2 \to \mathbb{N}$ is defined recursively by the following rules:

$$A(m, n) ::= 2n \qquad\qquad \text{if } m = 0 \text{ or } n \leq 1, \qquad \text{(A-base)}$$

$$A(m, n) ::= A(m - 1, A(m, n - 1)) \qquad\qquad \text{otherwise.} \qquad \text{(AA)}$$

Prove that if $B : \mathbb{N}^2 \to \mathbb{N}$ is a partial function that satisfies this same definition, then B is total and $B = A$.

Problems for Section 7.4

Practice Problems

Problem 7.26. (a) Write out the evaluation of

$$\text{eval}(\text{subst}(3x, x(x - 1)), 2)$$

according to the Environment Model and the Substitution Model, indicating where the rule for each case of the recursive definitions of eval(,) and [:=] or substitution is first used. Compare the number of arithmetic operations and variable lookups.

(b) Describe an example along the lines of part (a) where the Environment Model would perform 6 fewer multiplications than the Substitution model. You need *not* carry out the evaluations.

(c) Describe an example along the lines of part (a) where the Substitution Model would perform 6 fewer multiplications than the Environment model. You need *not* carry out the evaluations.

Class Problems

Problem 7.27.
In this problem we'll need to be careful about the propositional *operations* on truth values and connective *symbols* that appear in formulas. We'll restrict ourselves to formulas with connective *symbols* **And** and **Not**, since we know every propositional

formula is equivalent to one with only these connectives. We will also allow the constant symbols **True** and **False**.

(a) Give a simple recursive definition of *propositional formula* F and the set $\text{pvar}(F)$ of propositional *variables that appear* in it.

Let V be a set of propositional variables. A *truth environment e* over V assigns truth values to all these variables. In other words, e is a total function,

$$e : V \to \{\mathbf{T}, \mathbf{F}\}.$$

(b) Give a recursive definition of the *truth value*, $\text{eval}(F, e)$, of propositional formula F in an environment e over a set of variables $V \supseteq \text{pvar}(F)$.

Clearly the truth value of a propositional formula only depends on the truth values of the variables in it. How could it be otherwise? But it's good practice to work out a rigorous definition and proof of this assumption.

(c) Give an example of a propositional formula containing the variable P but whose truth value does not depend on P. Now give a rigorous definition of the assertion that "the truth value of propositional formula F does not depend on propositional variable P."

Hint: Let e_1, e_2 be two environments whose values agree on all variables other than P.

(d) Give a rigorous definition of the assertion that "the truth value of a propositional formula only depends on the truth values of the variables that appear in it," and then prove it by structural induction on the definition of propositional formula.

(e) Now we can formally define F being *valid*. Namely, F is valid iff

$$\forall e. \ \text{eval}(F, e) = \mathbf{T}.$$

Give a similar formal definition of formula G being *unsatisfiable*. Then use the definition of eval to prove that a formula F is valid iff $\textbf{Not}(F)$ is unsatisfiable.

Homework Problems

Problem 7.28. (a) Give a recursive definition of a function $\text{erase}(e)$ that erases all the symbols in $e \in \text{Aexp}$ but the brackets. For example

$$\text{erase}([\,[\,3*[\,x*x\,]\,]+[\,[\,2*x\,]+1\,]\,]) = [\,[\,[\,]\,]\,[\,[\,2*x\,]+1\,]\,].$$

(b) Prove that $\text{erase}(e) \in \text{RecMatch}$ for all $e \in \text{Aexp}$.

(c) Give an example of a small string $s \in$ RecMatch such that $[\![s]\!] \neq$ erase(e) for any $e \in$ Aexp.

Problem 7.29.
We're going to characterize a large category of games as a recursive data type and then prove, by structural induction, a fundamental theorem about game strategies. The games we'll consider are known as *deterministic games of perfect information*. Checkers, chess, and GO, for example, all fit this description. It's useful to regard each game situation as a game in its own right. For example, after five moves in a chess game, we think of the players as being at the start of a new "chess" game determined by the current board position.

It's also useful to define the "payoff" of a chess game to be 1 if White wins, -1 if Black wins, and 0 if the game ends in stalement (a draw). Now we can describe White's objective as maximizing the payoff, and Black's objective is minimizing it. This leads to an elegant abstraction of this kind of game.

We suppose there are two players, called the *max-player* and the *min-player*, whose aim is, respectively, to maximize and minimize the final score. A game will specify its set of possible first moves, each of which will simply be another game. A game with no possible moves is called a *finish* that determines the payoff. An unfinished game will have a label max or min indicating which player is supposed to move next.

Here's the formal definition:

Definition. Let V be a nonempty set of real numbers. The class VG of *V-valued deterministic max-min games of perfect information* is defined recursively as follows:

Base case: A value $v \in V$ is a VG known as a *finish*.

Constructor case: If $\mathcal{M}$ is a nonempty set of VG's, and a is a label equal to max or min, then
$$G ::= (a, \mathcal{M})$$
is a VG. Each game $M \in \mathcal{M}$ is called a possible *first move* of G.

In Chess, the White player moves first and has 20 possible first moves, so the game of Chess would be represented by a VG of the form

$$(\text{max}, \{(\text{min}, B_1), (\text{min}, B_2), \ldots,, (\text{min}, B_{20})\}),$$

where (min, B_i) is White's ith possible opening move.

B_i in turn is the set of moves that Black can make if White opens with its ith move. Since Black has 20 possible second moves after White's first, each B_i is of the form

$$(\min, \{(\max, W_1), (\max, W_2), \ldots, (\max, W_{20})\}),$$

where W_j is the set of second moves White can make after Black makes its jth possible first move. Now the size of the W_j's is no longer the same but depends on the previous two moves.

A *play* of a game is sequence of legal moves that either comes to a finish, or goes on forever without finishing. More formally:

Definition. A *play* of a VG G is defined recursively on the definition of VG:

Base case: ($G = v \in V$ is a finish.) Then the sequence (v) of length one is a *play* of G. Its *payoff* is defined to be v.

Constructor case: ($G = (a, \mathcal{M})$) Then a *play* of G is a sequence that starts with a possible first move $M \in \mathcal{M}$ of G and continues with the elements of a play of M. Its *payoff* is the payoff of the play in M.

The basic rules of some games do allow plays that go on forever. In Chess for example, a player might just keep moving the same piece back and forth, and if his opponent did the same, the play could go on forever.[4] But the recursive definition of VG's actually rules out the possibility of infinite play.

(a) Prove that every play of a VG is finite and has a payoff.

Hint: By structural induction assume that each possible first move has a payoff.

A *strategy* for a player is a rule that tells the player which move to make when it's their turn. Matching up any `max`-player strategy with a `min`-player strategy will determine a unique play of a VG.

The Fundamental Theorem for deterministic games of perfect information says that in any game, each player has an optimal strategy, and these strategies lead to the same payoff. For example in Checkers or Chess, the Fundamental Theorem implies that

- there is winning strategy for one of the players, or

- both players have strategies that guarantee them at worst a draw.

Theorem (Fundamental Theorem for VG's). *Let V be a finite set of real numbers and G be a V-valued VG. Then there is a value $v \in V$ is called the value of G such that*

---

[4]Real chess tournaments rule this out by setting an advance limit on the number of moves, or by forbidding repetitions of the same position more than twice.

- *the max-player has a strategy that, matched with* any *min-player strategy, will define a play of G that finishes with a value of at least v,*

- *the min-player has a strategy that, matched with* any *max-player strategy, will define a play of G that finishes with a value of at most v.*

(b) Prove the Fundamental Theorem for VG's.

Hint: Assume by induction that each first move M in a game G has a value v_M.

Supplemental Part (optional)

(c) State some reasonable generalization of the Fundamental Theorem to games with an infinite set V of possible payoffs. Prove your generalization.

8 Infinite Sets

This chapter is about infinite sets and some challenges in proving things about them.

Wait a minute! Why bring up infinity in a Mathematics for *Computer Science* text? After all, any data set in a computer is limited by the size of the computer's memory, and there is a bound on the possible size of computer memory, for the simple reason that the universe is (or at least appears to be) bounded. So why not stick with *finite* sets of some large, but bounded, size? This is a good question, but let's see if we can persuade you that dealing with infinite sets is inevitable.

You may not have noticed, but up to now you've already accepted the routine use of the integers, the rationals and irrationals, and sequences of them—infinite sets all. Further, do you really want Physics or the other sciences to give up the real numbers on the grounds that only a bounded number of bounded measurements can be made in a bounded universe? It's pretty convincing—and a lot simpler—to ignore such big and uncertain bounds (the universe seems to be getting bigger all the time) and accept theories using real numbers.

Likewise in computer science, it's implausible to think that writing a program to add nonnegative integers with up to as many digits as, say, the stars in the sky—billions of galaxies each with billions of stars—would be different from writing a program that would add *any* two integers, no matter how many digits they had. The same is true in designing a compiler: it's neither useful nor sensible to make use of the fact that in a bounded universe, only a bounded number of programs will ever be compiled.

Infinite sets also provide a nice setting to practice proof methods, because it's harder to sneak in unjustified steps under the guise of intuition. And there has been a truly astonishing outcome of studying infinite sets. Their study led to the discovery of fundamental, logical limits on what computers can possibly do. For example, in Section 8.2, we'll use reasoning developed for infinite sets to prove that it's impossible to have a perfect type-checker for a programming language.

So in this chapter, we ask you to bite the bullet and start learning to cope with infinity.

8.1   Infinite Cardinality

In the late nineteenth century, the mathematician Georg Cantor was studying the convergence of Fourier series and found some series that he wanted to say converged "most of the time," even though there were an infinite number of points where they didn't converge. As a result, Cantor needed a way to compare the size of infinite sets. To get a grip on this, he got the idea of extending the Mapping Rule Theorem 4.5.4 to infinite sets: he regarded two infinite sets as having the "same size" when there was a bijection between them. Likewise, an infinite set A should be considered "as big as" a set B when A surj B. So we could consider A to be "strictly smaller" than B, which we abbreviate as A strict B, when A is *not* "as big as" B:

Definition 8.1.1. A strict B iff   NOT(A surj B).

On finite sets, this strict relation really does mean "strictly smaller." This follows immediately from the Mapping Rule Theorem 4.5.4.

Corollary 8.1.2. *For finite sets A, B,*

$$A \text{ strict } B \quad \textit{iff} \quad |A| < |B|.$$

Proof.

$$
\begin{aligned}
A \text{ strict } B \quad &\text{iff} \quad \text{NOT}(A \text{ surj } B) & \text{(Def 8.1.1)} \\
&\text{iff} \quad \text{NOT}(|A| \geq |B|) & \text{(Theorem 4.5.4.(4.5))} \\
&\text{iff} \quad |A| < |B|.
\end{aligned}
$$

∎

Cantor got diverted from his study of Fourier series by his effort to develop a theory of infinite sizes based on these ideas. His theory ultimately had profound consequences for the foundations of mathematics and computer science. But Cantor made a lot of enemies in his own time because of his work: the general mathematical community doubted the relevance of what they called "Cantor's paradise" of unheard-of infinite sizes.

A nice technical feature of Cantor's idea is that it avoids the need for a definition of what the "size" of an infinite set might be—all it does is compare "sizes."

Warning: We haven't, and won't, define what the "size" of an infinite set is. The definition of infinite "sizes" requires the definition of some infinite sets called *ordinals* with special well-ordering properties. The theory of ordinals requires getting deeper into technical set theory than we want to go, and we can get by just fine without defining infinite sizes. All we need are the "as big as" and "same size" relations, surj and bij, between sets.

But there's something else to watch out for: we've referred to surj as an "as big as" relation and bij as a "same size" relation on sets. Of course, most of the "as big as" and "same size" properties of surj and bij on finite sets do carry over to infinite sets, but *some important ones don't*—as we're about to show. So you have to be careful: don't assume that surj has any particular "as big as" property on *infinite* sets until it's been proved.

Let's begin with some familiar properties of the "as big as" and "same size" relations on finite sets that do carry over exactly to infinite sets:

Lemma 8.1.3. *For any sets A, B, C,*

1. *A surj B iff B inj A.*

2. *If A surj B and B surj C, then A surj C.*

3. *If A bij B and B bij C, then A bij C.*

4. *A bij B iff B bij A.*

Part 1. follows from the fact that R has the $[\leq 1 \text{ out}, \geq 1 \text{ in}]$ surjective function property iff R^{-1} has the $[\geq 1 \text{ out}, \leq 1 \text{ in}]$ total, injective property. Part 2. follows from the fact that compositions of surjections are surjections. Parts 3. and 4. follow from the first two parts because R is a bijection iff R and R^{-1} are surjective functions. We'll leave verification of these facts to Problem 4.22.

Another familiar property of finite sets carries over to infinite sets, but this time some real ingenuity is needed to prove it:

Theorem 8.1.4. *[Schröder-Bernstein] For any sets A, B, if A surj B and B surj A, then A bij B.*

That is, the Schröder-Bernstein Theorem says that if A is at least as big as B and conversely, B is at least as big as A, then A is the same size as B. Phrased this way, you might be tempted to take this theorem for granted, but that would be a mistake. For infinite sets A and B, the Schröder-Bernstein Theorem is actually pretty technical. Just because there is a surjective function $f : A \to B$—which need not be a bijection—and a surjective function $g : B \to A$—which also need not be a bijection—it's not at all clear that there must be a bijection $e : A \to B$. The idea is to construct e from parts of both f and g. We'll leave the actual construction to Problem 8.10.

Another familiar set property is that for any two sets, either the first is at least as big as the second, or vice-versa. For finite sets this follows trivially from the Mapping Rule. It's actually still true for infinite sets, but assuming it was obvious would be mistaken again.

Theorem 8.1.5. *For all sets A, B,*

$$A \text{ surj } B \quad \text{OR} \quad B \text{ surj } A.$$

Theorem 8.1.5 lets us prove that another basic property of finite sets carries over to infinite ones:

Lemma 8.1.6.

$$A \text{ strict } B \quad \text{AND} \quad B \text{ strict } C \tag{8.1}$$

implies

$$A \text{ strict } C$$

for all sets A, B, C.

Proof. (of Lemma 8.1.6)

Suppose 8.1 holds, and assume for the sake of contradiction that NOT(A strict C), which means that A surj C. Now since B strict C, Theorem 8.1.5 lets us conclude that C surj B. So we have

$$A \text{ surj } C \quad \text{AND} \quad C \text{ surj } B,$$

and Lemma 8.1.3.2 lets us conclude that A surj B, contradicting the fact that A strict B. ∎

We're omitting a proof of Theorem 8.1.5 because proving it involves technical set theory—typically the theory of ordinals again—that we're not going to get into. But since proving Lemma 8.1.6 is the only use we'll make of Theorem 8.1.5, we hope you won't feel cheated not to see a proof.

8.1.1   Infinity is different

A basic property of finite sets that does *not* carry over to infinite sets is that adding something new makes a set bigger. That is, if A is a finite set and $b \notin A$, then $|A \cup \{b\}| = |A| + 1$, and so A and $A \cup \{b\}$ are not the same size. But if A is infinite, then these two sets *are* the same size!

Lemma 8.1.7. *Let A be a set and $b \notin A$. Then A is infinite iff A bij $A \cup \{b\}$.*

Proof. Since A is *not* the same size as $A \cup \{b\}$ when A is finite, we only have to show that $A \cup \{b\}$ *is* the same size as A when A is infinite.

That is, we have to find a bijection between $A \cup \{b\}$ and A when A is infinite. Here's how: since A is infinite, it certainly has at least one element; call it a_0. But since A is infinite, it has at least two elements, and one of them must not equal to a_0; call this new element a_1. But since A is infinite, it has at least three elements, one of which must not equal both a_0 and a_1; call this new element a_2. Continuing in this way, we conclude that there is an infinite sequence $a_0, a_1, a_2, \ldots, a_n, \ldots$ of different elements of A. Now it's easy to define a bijection $e : A \cup \{b\} \rightarrow A$:

$$
\begin{aligned}
e(b) &::= a_0, \\
e(a_n) &::= a_{n+1} && \text{for } n \in \mathbb{N}, \\
e(a) &::= a && \text{for } a \in A - \{b, a_0, a_1, \ldots\}.
\end{aligned}
$$

∎

8.1.2 Countable Sets

A set C is *countable* iff its elements can be listed in order, that is, the elements in C are precisely the elements in the sequence

$$c_0, c_1, \ldots, c_n, \ldots.$$

Assuming no repeats in the list, saying that C can be listed in this way is formally the same as saying that the function, $f : \mathbb{N} \rightarrow C$ defined by the rule that $f(i) ::= c_i$, is a bijection.

Definition 8.1.8. A set C is *countably infinite* iff $\mathbb{N}$ bij C. A set is *countable* iff it is finite or countably infinite. A set is *uncountable* iff it is not countable.

We can also make an infinite list using just a finite set of elements if we allow repeats. For example, we can list the elements in the three-element set $\{2, 4, 6\}$ as

$$2, 4, 6, 6, 6, \ldots.$$

This simple observation leads to an alternative characterization of countable sets that does not make separate cases of finite and infinite sets. Namely, a set C is countable iff there is a list

$$c_0, c_1, \ldots, c_n, \ldots$$

of the elements of C, possibly with repeats.

Lemma 8.1.9. *A set C is countable iff $\mathbb{N}$ surj C. In fact, a nonempty set C is countable iff there is a total surjective function $g : \mathbb{N} \rightarrow C$.*

The proof is left to Problem 8.11.

The most fundamental countably infinite set is the set $\mathbb{N}$ itself. But the set $\mathbb{Z}$ of *all* integers is also countably infinite, because the integers can be listed in the order:

$$0, -1, 1, -2, 2, -3, 3, \ldots . \tag{8.2}$$

In this case, there is a simple formula for the nth element of the list (8.2). That is, the bijection $f : \mathbb{N} \to \mathbb{Z}$ such that $f(n)$ is the nth element of the list can be defined as:

$$f(n) ::= \begin{cases} n/2 & \text{if } n \text{ is even,} \\ -(n+1)/2 & \text{if } n \text{ is odd.} \end{cases}$$

There is also a simple way to list all *pairs* of nonnegative integers, which shows that $(\mathbb{N} \times \mathbb{N})$ is also countably infinite (Problem 8.17). From this, it's a small step to reach the conclusion that the set $\mathbb{Q}^{\geq 0}$ of nonnegative rational numbers is countable. This may be a surprise—after all, the rationals densely fill up the space between integers, and for any two, there's another in between. So it might seem as though you couldn't write out all the rationals in a list, but Problem 8.9 illustrates how to do it. More generally, it is easy to show that countable sets are closed under unions and products (Problems 8.16 and 8.17) which implies the countability of a bunch of familiar sets:

Corollary 8.1.10. *The following sets are countably infinite:*

$$\mathbb{Z}^+, \mathbb{Z}, \mathbb{N} \times \mathbb{N}, \mathbb{Q}^+, \mathbb{Z} \times \mathbb{Z}, \mathbb{Q}.$$

A small modification of the proof of Lemma 8.1.7 shows that countably infinite sets are the "smallest" infinite sets. Namely,

Lemma 8.1.11. *If A is an infinite set, and B is countable, then A surj B.*

We leave the proof to Problem 8.8.

Also, since adding one new element to an infinite set doesn't change its size, you can add any *finite* number of elements without changing the size by simply adding one element after another. Something even stronger is true: you can add a *countably* infinite number of new elements to an infinite set and still wind up with just a set of the same size (Problem 8.13).

By the way, it's a common mistake to think that, because you can add any finite number of elements to an infinite set and have a bijection with the original set, that you can also throw in infinitely many new elements. In general it isn't true that just because it's OK to do something any finite number of times, it's also OK to do it an infinite number of times. For example, starting from 3, you can increment by 1 any finite number of times, and the result will be some integer greater than or equal to 3. But if you increment an infinite number of times, you don't get an integer at all.

8.1.3 Power sets are strictly bigger

Cantor's astonishing discovery was that *not all infinite sets are the same size*. In particular, he proved that for any set A the power set $\mathrm{pow}(A)$ is "strictly bigger" than A. That is,

Theorem 8.1.12. *[Cantor] For any set A,*

$$A \text{ strict } \mathrm{pow}(A).$$

Proof. To show that A is strictly smaller than $\mathrm{pow}(A)$, we have to show that if g is a function from A to $\mathrm{pow}(A)$, then g is *not* a surjection. To do this, we'll simply find a subset $A_g \subseteq A$ that is not in the range of g. The idea is, for any element $a \in A$, to look at the set $g(a) \subseteq A$ and ask whether or not a happens to be in $g(a)$. First, define

$$A_g ::= \{a \in A \mid a \notin g(a)\}.$$

A_g is now a well-defined subset of A, which means it is a member of $\mathrm{pow}(A)$. But A_g can't be in the range of g, because if it were, we would have

$$A_g = g(a_0)$$

for some $a_0 \in A$, so by definition of A_g,

$$a \in g(a_0) \quad \text{iff} \quad a \in A_g \quad \text{iff} \quad a \notin g(a)$$

for all $a \in A$. Now letting $a = a_0$ yields the contradiction

$$a_0 \in g(a_0) \quad \text{iff} \quad a_0 \notin g(a_0).$$

So g is not a surjection, because there is an element in the power set of A, specifically the set A_g, that is not in the range of g. ∎

Cantor's Theorem immediately implies:

Corollary 8.1.13. $\mathrm{pow}(\mathbb{N})$ *is uncountable.*

Proof. By Lemma 8.1.9, U is uncountable iff $\mathbb{N}$ strict U. ∎

The bijection between subsets of an n-element set and the length n bit-strings $\{0, 1\}^n$ used to prove Theorem 4.5.5, carries over to a bijection between subsets of a countably infinite set and the infinite bit-strings, $\{0, 1\}^\omega$. That is,

$$\mathrm{pow}(\mathbb{N}) \text{ bij } \{0, 1\}^\omega.$$

This immediately implies

Corollary 8.1.14. $\{0, 1\}^\omega$ *is uncountable.*

More Countable and Uncountable Sets

Once we have a few sets we know are countable or uncountable, we can get lots more examples using Lemma 8.1.3. In particular, we can appeal to the following immediate corollary of the Lemma:

Corollary 8.1.15.

(a) If U is an uncountable set and A surj *U, then A is uncountable.*

(b) If C is a countable set and C surj *A, then A is countable.*

For example, now that we know that the set $\{0, 1\}^\omega$ of infinite bit strings is uncountable, it's a small step to conclude that

Corollary 8.1.16. *The set $\mathbb{R}$ of real numbers is uncountable.*

To prove this, think about the infinite decimal expansion of a real number:

$$\sqrt{2} = 1.4142\ldots,$$
$$5 = 5.000\ldots,$$
$$1/10 = 0.1000\ldots,$$
$$1/3 = 0.333\ldots,$$
$$1/9 = 0.111\ldots,$$
$$4\frac{1}{99} = 4.010101\ldots.$$

Let's map any real number r to the infinite bit string $b(r)$ equal to the sequence of bits in the decimal expansion of r, starting at the decimal point. If the decimal expansion of r happens to contain a digit other than 0 or 1, leave $b(r)$ undefined. For example,

$$b(5) = 000\ldots,$$
$$b(1/10) = 1000\ldots,$$
$$b(1/9) = 111\ldots,$$
$$b(4\frac{1}{99}) = 010101\ldots$$
$$b(\sqrt{2}), b(1/3) \text{ are undefined.}$$

Now b is a function from real numbers to infinite bit strings.[1] It is not a total function, but it clearly is a surjection. This shows that

$$\mathbb{R} \text{ surj } \{0, 1\}^\omega,$$

and the uncountability of the reals now follows by Corollary 8.1.15.(a).

For another example, let's prove

Corollary 8.1.17. *The set $(\mathbb{Z}^+)^*$ of all finite sequences of positive integers is countable.*

To prove this, think about the prime factorization of a nonnegative integer:

$$20 = 2^2 \cdot 3^0 \cdot 5^1 \cdot 7^0 \cdot 11^0 \cdot 13^0 \cdots,$$
$$6615 = 2^0 \cdot 3^3 \cdot 5^1 \cdot 7^2 \cdot 11^0 \cdot 13^0 \cdots.$$

Let's map any nonnegative integer n to the finite sequence $e(n)$ of nonzero exponents in its prime factorization. For example,

$$e(20) = (2, 1),$$
$$e(6615) = (3, 1, 2),$$
$$e(5^{13} \cdot 11^9 \cdot 47^{817} \cdot 103^{44}) = (13, 9, 817, 44),$$
$$e(1) = \lambda, \qquad\qquad \text{(the empty string)}$$
$$e(0) \text{ is undefined.}$$

Now e is a function from $\mathbb{N}$ to $(\mathbb{Z}^+)^*$. It is defined on all positive integers, and it clearly is a surjection. This shows that

$$\mathbb{N} \text{ surj } (\mathbb{Z}^+)^*,$$

and the countability of the finite strings of positive integers now follows by Corollary 8.1.15.(b).

---

[1] Some rational numbers can be expanded in two ways—as an infinite sequence ending in all 0's or as an infinite sequence ending in all 9's. For example,

$$5 = 5.000 \cdots = 4.999 \ldots,$$
$$\frac{1}{10} = 0.1000 \cdots = 0.0999 \ldots.$$

In such cases, define $b(r)$ to be the sequence that ends with all 0's.

Larger Infinities

There are lots of different sizes of infinite sets. For example, starting with the infinite set $\mathbb{N}$ of nonnegative integers, we can build the infinite sequence of sets

$$\mathbb{N} \text{ strict } \text{pow}(\mathbb{N}) \text{ strict } \text{pow}(\text{pow}(\mathbb{N})) \text{ strict } \text{pow}(\text{pow}(\text{pow}(\mathbb{N}))) \text{ strict } \ldots.$$

By Cantor's Theorem 8.1.12, each of these sets is strictly bigger than all the preceding ones. But that's not all: the union of all the sets in the sequence is strictly bigger than each set in the sequence (see Problem 8.24). In this way you can keep going indefinitely, building "bigger" infinities all the way.

8.1.4 Diagonal Argument

Theorem 8.1.12 and similar proofs are collectively known as "diagonal arguments" because of a more intuitive version of the proof described in terms of on an infinite square array. Namely, suppose there was a bijection between $\mathbb{N}$ and $\{0, 1\}^{\omega}$. If such a relation existed, we would be able to display it as a list of the infinite bit strings in some countable order or another. Once we'd found a viable way to organize this list, any given string in $\{0, 1\}^{\omega}$ would appear in a finite number of steps, just as any integer you can name will show up a finite number of steps from 0. This hypothetical list would look something like the one below, extending to infinity both vertically and horizontally:

A_0	$=$	1	0	0	0	1	1	$\cdots$
A_1	$=$	0	1	1	1	0	1	$\cdots$
A_2	$=$	1	1	1	1	1	1	$\cdots$
A_3	$=$	0	1	0	0	1	0	$\cdots$
A_4	$=$	0	0	1	0	0	0	$\cdots$
A_5	$=$	1	0	0	1	1	1	$\cdots$
$\vdots$		$\vdots$	$\vdots$	$\vdots$	$\vdots$	$\vdots$	$\vdots$	$\ddots$

But now we can exhibit a sequence that's missing from our allegedly complete list of all the sequences. Look at the diagonal in our sample list:

A_0	$=$	**1**	0	0	0	1	1	$\cdots$
A_1	$=$	0	**1**	1	1	0	1	$\cdots$
A_2	$=$	1	1	**1**	1	1	1	$\cdots$
A_3	$=$	0	1	0	**0**	1	0	$\cdots$
A_4	$=$	0	0	1	0	**0**	0	$\cdots$
A_5	$=$	1	0	0	1	1	**1**	$\cdots$
$\vdots$		$\vdots$	$\vdots$	$\vdots$	$\vdots$	$\vdots$	$\vdots$	$\ddots$

Here is why the diagonal argument has its name: we can form a sequence D consisting of the bits on the diagonal.

$$D = \quad 1 \quad 1 \quad 1 \quad 0 \quad 0 \quad 1 \quad \cdots,$$

Then, we can form another sequence by switching the 1's and 0's along the diagonal. Call this sequence C:

$$C = \quad 0 \quad 0 \quad 0 \quad 1 \quad 1 \quad 0 \quad \cdots.$$

Now if nth term of A_n is **1** then the nth term of C is **0**, and *vice versa*, which guarantees that C differs from A_n. In other words, C has at least one bit different from *every* sequence on our list. So C is an element of $\{0, 1\}^\omega$ that does not appear in our list—our list can't be complete!

This diagonal sequence C corresponds to the set $\{a \in A \mid a \notin g(a)\}$ in the proof of Theorem 8.1.12. Both are defined in terms of a countable subset of the uncountable infinity in a way that excludes them from that subset, thereby proving that no countable subset can be as big as the uncountable set.

8.2 The Halting Problem

Although towers of larger and larger infinite sets are at best a romantic concern for a computer scientist, the *reasoning* that leads to these conclusions plays a critical role in the theory of computation. Diagonal arguments are used to show that lots of problems can't be solved by computation, and there is no getting around it.

This story begins with a reminder that having procedures operate on programs is a basic part of computer science technology. For example, *compilation* refers to taking any given program text written in some "high level" programming language like Java, C++, Python, ..., and then generating a program of low-level instructions that does the same thing but is targeted to run well on available hardware. Similarly, *interpreters* or *virtual machines* are procedures that take a program text designed to be run on one kind of computer and simulate it on another kind of computer. Routine features of compilers involve "type-checking" programs to ensure that certain kinds of run-time errors won't happen, and "optimizing" the generated programs so they run faster or use less memory.

The fundamental thing that just can't be done by computation is a *perfect* job of type-checking, optimizing, or any kind of analysis of the overall run time behavior of programs. In this section, we'll illustrate this with a basic example known as the *Halting Problem*. The general Halting Problem for some programming language is, given an arbitrary program, to determine whether the program will run forever if it is not interrupted. If the program does not run forever, it is said to halt. Real programs may halt in many ways, for example, by returning some final value, aborting with some kind of error, or by awaiting user input. But it's easy to detect when any given program will halt: just run it on a virtual machine and wait till it stops. The problem comes when the given program does *not* halt—you may wind up waiting indefinitely without realizing that the wait is fruitless. So how could you detect that the program does *not* halt? We will use a diagonal argument to prove that if an analysis program tries to recognize the non-halting programs, it is bound to give wrong answers, or no answers, for an infinite number of the programs it is supposed to be able to analyze!

To be precise about this, let's call a programming procedure—written in your favorite programming language—C++, or Java, or Python—a *string procedure* when it is applicable to strings in the set ASCII* of strings over the 256 character ASCII alphabet.

As a simple example, you might think about how to write a string procedure that halts precisely when it is applied to a *double letter* string in ASCII*, namely, a string in which every character occurs twice in a row. For example, `aaCC33`, and `zz++ccBB` are double letter strings, but `aa;bb`, `b33`, and `AAAAA` are not.

If the computation that happens when a procedure applied to a string eventually comes to a halt, the procedure is said to *recognize* the string. In this context, a set of strings a commonly called a (formal) *language*. We let lang(P) to be the language recognized by procedure P:

$$\text{lang}(P) ::= \{s \in \text{ASCII}^* \mid P \text{ applied to } s \text{ halts}\}.$$

A language is called *recognizable* when it equals lang(P) for some string procedure P. For example, we've just agreed that the set of double letter strings is recognizable.

There is no harm in assuming that every program can be written as a string in ASCII*; they usually are. When a string $s \in \text{ASCII}^*$ is actually the ASCII description of some string procedure, we'll refer to that string procedure as P_s. You can think of P_s as the result of compiling s into something executable.[2] It's technically helpful to treat *every* string in ASCII* as a program for a string procedure. So when a string $s \in \text{ASCII}^*$ doesn't parse as a proper string procedure, we'll define P_s to

---

[2]The string $s \in \text{ASCII}^*$ and the procedure P_s have to be distinguished to avoid a type error: you can't apply a string to string. For example, let s be the string that you wrote as your program to recognize the double letter strings. Applying s to a string argument, say `aabbccdd`, should throw a type exception; what you need to do is compile s to the procedure P_s and then apply P_s to `aabbccdd`.

be some default string procedure—say one that never halts on anything it is applied to.

Focusing just on string procedures, the general Halting Problem is to decide, given strings s and t, whether or not the procedure P_s recognizes t. We'll show that the general problem can't be solved by showing that a special case can't be solved, namely, whether or not P_s recognizes s.

Definition 8.2.1.

$$\text{No-halt} ::= \{s \mid P_s \text{ applied to } s \text{ does not halt}\} = \{s \notin \text{lang}(P_s)\}. \tag{8.3}$$

We're going to prove

Theorem 8.2.2. *No-halt is not recognizable.*

We'll use an argument just like Cantor's in the proof of Theorem 8.1.12.

Proof. By definition,

$$s \in \text{No-halt} \text{ IFF } s \notin \text{lang}(P_s), \tag{8.4}$$

for all strings $s \in \text{ASCII}^*$.

Now suppose to the contrary that No-halt was recognizable. This means there is some procedure P_{s_0} that recognizes No-halt, that is,

$$\text{No-halt} = \text{lang}(P_{s_0}).$$

Combined with (8.4), we get

$$s \in \text{lang}(P_{s_0}) \quad \text{iff} \quad s \notin \text{lang}(P_s) \tag{8.5}$$

for all $s \in \text{ASCII}^*$. Now letting $s = s_0$ in (8.5) yields the immediate contradiction

$$s_0 \in \text{lang}(P_{s_0}) \quad \text{iff} \quad s_0 \notin \text{lang}(P_{s_0}).$$

This contradiction implies that No-halt cannot be recognized by any string procedure. ∎

So that does it: it's logically impossible for programs in any particular language to solve just this special case of the general Halting Problem for programs in that language. And having proved that it's impossible to have a procedure that figures out whether an arbitrary program halts, it's easy to show that it's impossible to have a procedure that is a perfect recognizer for *any* overall run time property.[3]

---

[3]The weasel word "overall" creeps in here to rule out some run time properties that are easy to recognize because they depend only on part of the run time behavior. For example, the set of programs that halt after executing at most 100 instructions is recognizable.

For example, most compilers do "static" type-checking at compile time to ensure that programs won't make run-time type errors. A program that type-checks is guaranteed not to cause a run-time type-error. But since it's impossible to recognize perfectly when programs won't cause type-errors, it follows that the type-checker must be rejecting programs that really wouldn't cause a type-error. The conclusion is that no type-checker is perfect—you can always do better!

It's a different story if we think about the *practical* possibility of writing programming analyzers. The fact that it's logically impossible to analyze perfectly arbitrary programs does not mean that you can't do a very good job analyzing interesting programs that come up in practice. In fact, these "interesting" programs are commonly *intended* to be analyzable in order to confirm that they do what they're supposed to do.

In the end, it's not clear how much of a hurdle this theoretical limitation implies in practice. But the theory does provide some perspective on claims about general analysis methods for programs. The theory tells us that people who make such claims either

- are exaggerating the power (if any) of their methods, perhaps to make a sale or get a grant, or

- are trying to keep things simple by not going into technical limitations they're aware of, or

- perhaps most commonly, are so excited about some useful practical successes of their methods that they haven't bothered to think about the limitations which must be there.

So from now on, if you hear people making claims about having general program analysis/verification/optimization methods, you'll know they can't be telling the whole story.

One more important point: there's no hope of getting around this by switching programming languages. Our proof covered programs written in some given programming language like Java, for example, and concluded that no Java program can perfectly analyze all Java programs. Could there be a C++ analysis procedure that successfully takes on all Java programs? After all, C++ does allow more intimate manipulation of computer memory than Java does. But there is no loophole here: it's possible to write a virtual machine for C++ in Java, so if there were a C++ procedure that analyzed Java programs, the Java virtual machine would be able to do it too, and that's impossible. These logical limitations on the power of computation apply no matter what kinds of programs or computers you use.

8.3 The Logic of Sets

8.3.1 Russell's Paradox

Reasoning naively about sets turns out to be risky. In fact, one of the earliest attempts to come up with precise axioms for sets in the late nineteenth century by the logician Gotlob Frege, was shot down by a three line argument known as *Russell's Paradox*[4] which reasons in nearly the same way as the proof of Cantor's Theorem 8.1.12. This was an astonishing blow to efforts to provide an axiomatic foundation for mathematics:

Russell's Paradox

Let S be a variable ranging over all sets, and define

$$W ::= \{S \mid S \notin S\}.$$

So by definition,

$$S \in W \text{ iff } S \notin S,$$

for every set S. In particular, we can let S be W, and obtain the contradictory result that

$$W \in W \text{ iff } W \notin W.$$

The simplest reasoning about sets crashes mathematics! Russell and his colleague Whitehead spent years trying to develop a set theory that was not contradictory, but would still do the job of serving as a solid logical foundation for all of mathematics.

Actually, a way out of the paradox was clear to Russell and others at the time: *it's unjustified to assume that W is a set*. The step in the proof where we let S be W has no justification, because S ranges over sets, and W might not be a set. In fact, the paradox implies that W had better not be a set!

---

[4]Bertrand Russell was a mathematician/logician at Cambridge University at the turn of the Twentieth Century. He reported that when he felt too old to do mathematics, he began to study and write about philosophy, and when he was no longer smart enough to do philosophy, he began writing about politics. He was jailed as a conscientious objector during World War I. For his extensive philosophical and political writing, he won a Nobel Prize for Literature.

But denying that W is a set means we must *reject* the very natural axiom that every mathematically well-defined collection of sets is actually a set. The problem faced by Frege, Russell and their fellow logicians was how to specify *which* well-defined collections are sets. Russell and his Cambridge University colleague Whitehead immediately went to work on this problem. They spent a dozen years developing a huge new axiom system in an even huger monograph called *Principia Mathematica*, but for all intents and purposes, their approach failed. It was so cumbersome no one ever used it, and it was subsumed by a much simpler, and now widely accepted, axiomatization of set theory by the logicians Zermelo and Fraenkel.

8.3.2   The ZFC Axioms for Sets

A *formula of set theory*[5] is a predicate formula that only talks about membership in sets. That is, a first-order formula of set theory is built using logical connectives and quantifiers starting *solely* from expressions of the form "$x \in y$." The domain of discourse is the collection of sets, and "$x \in y$" is interpreted to mean that x and y are variables that range over sets, and x is one of the elements in y.

Formulas of set theory are not even allowed to have the equality symbol "$=$," but sets are equal iff they have the same elements, so there is an easy way to express equality of sets purely in terms of membership:

$$(x = y) ::= \quad \forall z. \, (z \in x \text{ IFF } z \in y). \qquad (8.6)$$

Similarly, the subset symbol "$\subseteq$" is not allowed in formulas of set theory, but we can also express subset purely in terms of membership:

$$(x \subseteq y) ::= \quad \forall z. \, (z \in x \text{ IMPLIES } z \in y). \qquad (8.7)$$

So formulas using symbols "$=, \subseteq$," in addition to "$\in$" can be understood as *abbreviations* for formulas only using "$\in$." We won't worry about this distinction between formulas and abbreviations for formulas—we'll now just call them all "formulas of set theory." For example,

$$x = y \text{ IFF } [x \subseteq y \text{ AND } y \subseteq x]$$

is a formula of set theory that explains a basic connection between set equality and set containment.

It's generally agreed that essentially *all of mathematics* can be derived from a few formulas of set theory, called the Axioms of *Zermelo-Fraenkel Set Theory* with Choice (ZFC), using a few simple logical deduction rules.

---

[5]Technically this is called a *pure first-order formula* of set theory

We're *not* going to be studying the axioms of ZFC in this text, but we thought you might like to see them—and while you're at it, get some more practice reading and writing quantified formulas:

Extensionality. Two sets are equal iff they are members of the same sets:

$$x = y \text{ IFF } (\forall z.\ z \in x \text{ IFF } z \in y).$$

Pairing. For any two sets x and y, there is a set $\{x, y\}$ with x and y as its only elements:

$$\forall x, y \exists u \forall z.\ [z \in u \text{ IFF } (z = x \text{ OR } z = y)]$$

Union. The union u of a collection z of sets is also a set:

$$\forall z \exists u \forall x.\ (x \in u) \text{ IFF } (\exists y.\ x \in y \text{ AND } y \in z)$$

Infinity. There is an infinite set. Specifically, there is a nonempty set x such that for any set $y \in x$, the set $\{y\}$ is also a member of x.

Subset. Given any set x and any definable property of sets, there is a set y containing precisely those elements in x that have the property.

$$\forall x \exists y \forall z.\ z \in y \text{ IFF } [z \in x \text{ AND } \phi(z)]$$

where $\phi(z)$ is a formula of set theory.[6]

Power Set. All the subsets of a set form another set:

$$\forall x \exists p \forall u.\ u \subseteq x \text{ IFF } u \in p.$$

Replacement. Suppose a formula ϕ of set theory defines the graph of a total function on a set s, that is,

$$\forall x \in s\ \exists y.\ \phi(x, y),$$

and

$$\forall x \in s\ \forall y, z.\ [\phi(x, y) \text{ AND } \phi(x, z)] \text{ IMPLIES } y = z.$$

Then the image of s under that function is also a set t. Namely,

$$\exists t \forall y.\ y \in t \text{ IFF } [\exists x \in s.\ \phi(x, y)].$$

---

[6]This axiom is more commonly called the *Comprehension Axiom*.

Foundation. The aim is to forbid any infinite sequence of sets of the form

$$\cdots \in x_n \in \cdots \in x_1 \in x_0$$

in which each set is a member of the next one. This can be captured by saying every nonempty set has a "member-minimal" element. Namely, define

$$\text{member-minimal}(m, x) ::= [m \in x \text{ AND } \forall y \in x.\ y \notin m].$$

Then the Foundation Axiom[7] is

$$\forall x.\ x \neq \emptyset \text{ IMPLIES } \exists m.\ \text{member-minimal}(m, x).$$

Choice. Let s be a set of nonempty, disjoint sets. Then there is a set c consisting of exactly one element from each set in s. The formula is given in Problem 8.30.

8.3.3   Avoiding Russell's Paradox

These modern ZFC axioms for set theory are much simpler than the system Russell and Whitehead first came up with to avoid paradox. In fact, the ZFC axioms are as simple and intuitive as Frege's original axioms, with one technical addition: the Foundation axiom. Foundation captures the intuitive idea that sets must be built up from "simpler" sets in certain standard ways. And in particular, Foundation implies that no set is ever a member of itself. So the modern resolution of Russell's paradox goes as follows: since $S \notin S$ for all sets S, it follows that W, defined above, contains every set. This means W can't be a set—or it would be a member of itself.

8.4   Does All This Really Work?

So this is where mainstream mathematics stands today: there is a handful of ZFC axioms from which virtually everything else in mathematics can be logically derived. This sounds like a rosy situation, but there are several dark clouds, suggesting that the essence of truth in mathematics is not completely resolved.

- The ZFC axioms weren't etched in stone by God. Instead, they were mostly made up by Zermelo, who may have been a brilliant logician, but was also a fallible human being—probably some days he forgot his house keys. So

---

[7]This axiom is also called the *Regularity Axiom*.

maybe Zermelo, just like Frege, didn't get his axioms right and will be shot down by some successor to Russell who will use his axioms to prove a proposition P and its negation $\overline{P}$. Then math as we understand it would be broken—this may sound crazy, but it has happened before.

In fact, while there is broad agreement that the ZFC axioms are capable of proving all of standard mathematics, the axioms have some further consequences that sound paradoxical. For example, the Banach-Tarski Theorem says that, as a consequence of the *axiom of choice*, a solid ball can be divided into six pieces and then the pieces can be rigidly rearranged to give *two* solid balls of the same size as the original!

- Some basic questions about the nature of sets remain unresolved. For example, Cantor raised the question whether there is a set whose size is strictly between the smallest infinite set $\mathbb{N}$ (see Problem 8.8) and the strictly larger set $\mathrm{pow}(\mathbb{N})$? Cantor guessed not:

  Cantor's *Contiuum Hypothesis*: There is no set A such that

$$\mathbb{N} \text{ strict } A \text{ strict pow}(\mathbb{N}).$$

The Continuum Hypothesis remains an open problem a century later. Its difficulty arises from one of the deepest results in modern Set Theory—discovered in part by Gödel in the 1930's and Paul Cohen in the 1960's—namely, the ZFC axioms are not sufficient to settle the Continuum Hypothesis: there are two collections of sets, each obeying the laws of ZFC, and in one collection the Continuum Hypothesis is true, and in the other it is false. Until a mathematician with a deep understanding of sets can extend ZFC with persuasive new axioms, the Continuum Hypothesis will remain undecided.

- But even if we use more or different axioms about sets, there are some unavoidable problems. In the 1930's, Gödel proved that, assuming that an axiom system like ZFC is consistent—meaning you can't prove both P and $\overline{P}$ for any proposition, P—then the very proposition that the system is consistent (which is not too hard to express as a logical formula) cannot be proved in the system. In other words, no consistent system is strong enough to verify itself.

8.4.1 Large Infinities in Computer Science

If the romance of different-size infinities and continuum hypotheses doesn't appeal to you, not knowing about them is not going to limit you as a computer scientist.

These abstract issues about infinite sets rarely come up in mainstream mathematics, and they don't come up at all in computer science, where the focus is generally on "countable," and often just finite, sets. In practice, only logicians and set theorists have to worry about collections that are "too big" to be sets. That's part of the reason that the 19th century mathematical community made jokes about "Cantor's paradise" of obscure infinities. But the challenge of reasoning correctly about this far-out stuff led directly to the profound discoveries about the logical limits of computation described in Section 8.2, and that really is something every computer scientist should understand.

Problems for Section 8.1

Practice Problems

Problem 8.1.
Show that the set $\{0, 1\}^*$ of finite binary strings is countable.

Problem 8.2.
Describe an example of two **un**countable sets A and B such that there is no bijection between A and B.

Problem 8.3.
Indicate which of the following assertions (there may be more than one) are equivalent to

$$A \text{ strict } \mathbb{N}.$$

- $|A|$ is undefined.

- A is countably infinite.

- A is uncountable.

- A is finite.

- $\mathbb{N} \text{ surj } A$.

- $\forall n \in \mathbb{N}, |A| \leq n$.

- $\forall n \in \mathbb{N}, |A| \geq n$.

- $\exists n \in \mathbb{N}. |A| \leq n.$

- $\exists n \in \mathbb{N}. |A| < n.$

Problem 8.4.
Prove that if there is a total injective ($[\geq 1$ out, ≤ 1 in$]$) relation from S to $\mathbb{N}$, then S is countable.

Problem 8.5.
Prove that if S is an infinite set, then pow S is uncountable.

Problem 8.6.
Let A to be some infinite set and B to be some countable set. We know from Lemma 8.1.7 that

$$A \text{ bij } (A \cup \{b_0\})$$

for any element $b_0 \in B$. An easy induction implies that

$$A \text{ bij } (A \cup \{b_0, b_1, \ldots, b_n\}) \tag{8.8}$$

for any finite subset $\{b_0, b_1, \ldots, b_n\} \subset B$.

Students sometimes think that (8.8) shows that A bij $(A \cup B)$. Now it's true that A bij $(A \cup B)$ for all such A and B for any countable set B (Problem 8.13), but the facts above do not prove it.

To explain this, let's say that a predicate $P(C)$ is *finitely discontinuous* when $P(A \cup F)$ is true for every *finite* subset $F \subset B$, but $P(A \cup B)$ is false. The hole in the claim that (8.8) implies A bij $(A \cup B)$ is the assumption (without proof) that the predicate

$$P_0(C) ::= [A \text{ bij } C]$$

is not finitely discontinuous. This assumption about P_0 is correct, but it's not completely obvious and takes some proving.

To illustrate this point, let A be the nonnegative integers and B be the nonnegative rational numbers, and remember that both A and B are countably infinite. Some of the predicates $P(C)$ below are finitely **d**iscontinuous and some are **not**. Indicate which is which.

1. C is finite.

2. C is countable.

3. C is uncountable.

4. C contains only finitely many non-integers.

5. C contains the rational number 2/3.

6. There is a maximum non-integer in C.

7. There is an $\epsilon > 0$ such that any two elements of C are ϵ apart.

8. C is countable.

9. C is uncountable.

10. C has no infinite decreasing sequence $c_0 > c_1 > \cdots$.

11. Every nonempty subset of C has a minimum element.

12. C has a maximum element.

13. C has a minimum element.

Class Problems

Problem 8.7.
Show that the set $\mathbb{N}^*$ of finite sequences of nonnegative integers is countable.

Problem 8.8. (a) Several students felt the proof of Lemma 8.1.7 was worrisome, if not circular. What do you think?

(b) Use the proof of Lemma 8.1.7 to show that if A is an infinite set, then A surj $\mathbb{N}$, that is, every infinite set is "at least as big as" the set of nonnegative integers.

Problem 8.9.
The rational numbers fill the space between integers, so a first thought is that there must be more of them than the integers, but it's not true. In this problem you'll show that there are the same number of positive rationals as positive integers. That is, the positive rationals are countable.

(a) Define a bijection between the set $\mathbb{Z}^+$ of positive integers, and the set $(\mathbb{Z}^+ \times \mathbb{Z}^+)$ of all pairs of positive integers:

$$(1,1), (1,2), (1,3), (1,4), (1,5), \ldots$$
$$(2,1), (2,2), (2,3), (2,4), (2,5), \ldots$$
$$(3,1), (3,2), (3,3), (3,4), (3,5), \ldots$$
$$(4,1), (4,2), (4,3), (4,4), (4,5), \ldots$$
$$(5,1), (5,2), (5,3), (5,4), (5,5), \ldots$$
$$\vdots$$

(b) Conclude that the set $\mathbb{Q}^+$ of all positive rational numbers is countable.

Problem 8.10.

This problem provides a proof of the [Schröder-Bernstein] Theorem:

If A inj B and B inj A, then A bij B. (8.9)

Since A inj B and B inj A, there are are total injective functions $f : A \to B$ and $g : B \to A$.

Assume for simplicity that A and B have no elements in common. Let's picture the elements of A arranged in a column, and likewise B arranged in a second column to the right, with left-to-right arrows connecting a to $f(a)$ for each $a \in A$ and likewise right-to-left arrows for g. Since f and g are total functions, there is *exactly one* arrow *out* of each element. Also, since f and g are injections, there is *at most one* arrow *into* any element.

So starting at any element, there is a unique and unending path of arrows going forwards (it might repeat). There is also a unique path of arrows going backwards, which might be unending, or might end at an element that has no arrow into it. These paths are completely separate: if two ran into each other, there would be two arrows into the element where they ran together.

This divides all the elements into separate paths of four kinds:

 (i) paths that are infinite in both directions,

 (ii) paths that are infinite going forwards starting from some element of A.

 (iii) paths that are infinite going forwards starting from some element of B.

 (iv) paths that are unending but finite.

(a) What do the paths of the last type (iv) look like?

(b) Show that for each type of path, either

  (i) the f-arrows define a bijection between the A and B elements on the path, or

  (ii) the g-arrows define a bijection between B and A elements on the path, or

 (iii) both sets of arrows define bijections.

For which kinds of paths do both sets of arrows define bijections?

(c) Explain how to piece these bijections together to form a bijection between A and B.

(d) Justify the assumption that A and B are disjoint.

Problem 8.11. **(a)** Prove that if a nonempty set C is countable, then there is a *total* surjective function $f : \mathbb{N} \to C$.

(b) Conversely, suppose that $\mathbb{N}$ surj D, that is, there is a not necessarily total surjective function $f : \mathbb{N}D$. Prove that D is countable.

Problem 8.12. **(a)** For each of the following sets, indicate whether it is finite, countably infinite, or uncountable.

  (i) The set of even integers greater than 10^{100}.

 (ii) The set of "pure" complex numbers of the form ri for nonzero real numbers r.

(iii) The powerset of the integer interval $[10..10^{10}]$.

(iv) The complex numbers c such that $\exists m, n \in \mathbb{Z}. \, (m + nc)c = 0$.

     Let $\mathcal{U}$ be an uncountable set, $\mathcal{C}$ be a countably infinite subset of $\mathcal{U}$, and $\mathcal{D}$ be a countably infinite set.

 (v) $\mathcal{U} \cup \mathcal{D}$.

 (vi) $\mathcal{U} \cap \mathcal{C}$

(vii) $\mathcal{U} - \mathcal{D}$

(b) Given examples of sets A and B such that

$$\mathbb{R} \text{ strict } A \text{ strict } B.$$

Recall that A strict B means that A is not "as big as" B.

Homework Problems

Problem 8.13.

Prove that if A is an infinite set and B is a countably infinite set that has no elements in common with A, then

$$A \text{ bij } (A \cup B).$$

Reminder: You may assume any of the results from class or text as long as you state them explicitly.

Problem 8.14.

In this problem you will prove a fact that may surprise you—or make you even more convinced that set theory is nonsense: the half-open unit interval is actually the "*same size*" as the nonnegative quadrant of the real plane![8] Namely, there is a bijection from $(0, 1]$ to $[0, \infty) \times [0, \infty)$.

 (a) Describe a bijection from $(0, 1]$ to $[0, \infty)$.

Hint: $1/x$ almost works.

 (b) An infinite sequence of the decimal digits $\{0, 1, \ldots, 9\}$ will be called *long* if it does not end with all 0's. An equivalent way to say this is that a long sequence is one that has infinitely many occurrences of nonzero digits. Let L be the set of all such long sequences. Describe a bijection from L to the half-open real interval $(0, 1]$.

Hint: Put a decimal point at the beginning of the sequence.

 (c) Describe a surjective function from L to L^2 that involves alternating digits from two long sequences. *Hint*: The surjection need not be total.

 (d) Prove the following lemma and use it to conclude that there is a bijection from L^2 to $(0, 1]^2$.
Lemma 8.4.1. *Let A and B be nonempty sets. If there is a bijection from A to B, then there is also a bijection from $A \times A$ to $B \times B$.*

 (e) Conclude from the previous parts that there is a surjection from $(0, 1]$ to $(0, 1]^2$. Then appeal to the Schröder-Bernstein Theorem to show that there is actually a bijection from $(0, 1]$ to $(0, 1]^2$.

 (f) Complete the proof that there is a bijection from $(0, 1]$ to $[0, \infty)^2$.

---

[8]The half-open unit interval $(0, 1]$ is $\{r \in \mathbb{R} \mid 0 < r \le 1\}$. Similarly, $[0, \infty) ::= \{r \in \mathbb{R} \mid r \ge 0\}$.

Exam Problems

Problem 8.15. (a) For each of the following sets, indicate whether it is finite, countably infinite, or uncountable.

(i) The set of even integers greater than 10^{100}.

(ii) The set of "pure" complex numbers of the form ri for nonzero real numbers r.

(iii) The powerset of the integer interval $[10..10^{10}]$.

(iv) The complex numbers c such that c is the root of a quadratic with integer coefficients, that is,

$$\exists m, n, p \in \mathbb{Z}, m \neq 0. \ mc^2 + nc + p = 0.$$

Let $\mathcal{U}$ be an uncountable set, $\mathcal{C}$ be a countably infinite subset of $\mathcal{U}$, and $\mathcal{D}$ be a countably infinite set.

(v) $\mathcal{U} \cup \mathcal{D}$.

(vi) $\mathcal{U} \cap \mathcal{C}$

(vii) $\mathcal{U} - \mathcal{D}$

(b) Give an example of sets A and B such that

$$\mathbb{R} \text{ strict } A \text{ strict } B.$$

Problem 8.16.
Prove that if $A_0, A_1, \ldots, A_n, \ldots$ is an infinite sequence of countable sets, then so is

$$\bigcup_{n=0}^{\infty} A_n$$

Problem 8.17.
Let A and B be countably infinite sets:

$$A = \{a_0, a_1, a_2, a_3, \ldots\}$$
$$B = \{b_0, b_1, b_2, b_3, \ldots\}$$

Show that their product $A \times B$ is also a countable set by showing how to list the elements of $A \times B$. You need only show enough of the initial terms in your sequence to make the pattern clear—a half dozen or so terms usually suffice.

Problem 8.18.

Let $\{0, 1\}^*$ be the set of finite binary sequences, $\{0, 1\}^\omega$ be the set of infinite binary sequences, and F be the set of sequences in $\{0, 1\}^\omega$ that contain only a finite number of occurrences of 1's.

(a) Describe a simple surjective function from $\{0, 1\}^*$ to F.

(b) The set $\overline{F} ::= \{0, 1\}^\omega - F$ consists of all the infinite binary sequences with *infinitely* many 1's. Use the previous problem part to prove that $\overline{F}$ is uncountable.

Hint: We know that $\{0, 1\}^*$ is countable and $\{0, 1\}^\omega$ is not.

Problem 8.19.

Let $\{0, 1\}^\omega$ be the set of infinite binary strings, and let $B \subset \{0, 1\}^\omega$ be the set of infinite binary strings containing infinitely many occurrences of 1's. Prove that B is uncountable. (We have already shown that $\{0, 1\}^\omega$ is uncountable.)

Hint: Define a suitable function from $\{0, 1\}^\omega$ to B.

Problem 8.20.

A real number is called *quadratic* when it is a root of a degree two polynomial with integer coefficients. Explain why there are only countably many quadratic reals.

Problem 8.21.

Describe which of the following sets have bijections between them:

$\mathbb{Z}$ (integers),	$\mathbb{R}$ (real numbers),
$\mathbb{C}$ (complex numbers),	$\mathbb{Q}$ (rational numbers),
$\text{pow}(\mathbb{Z})$ (all subsets of integers),	$\text{pow}(\emptyset)$,
$\text{pow}(\text{pow}(\emptyset))$,	$\{0, 1\}^*$ (finite binary sequences),
$\{0, 1\}^\omega$ (infinite binary sequences)	$\{\mathbf{T}, \mathbf{F}\}$ (truth values)
$\text{pow}(\{\mathbf{T}, \mathbf{F}\})$,	$\text{pow}(\{0, 1\}^\omega)$

Problem 8.22.

Prove that the set $\left(\mathbb{Z}^+\right)^*$ of all finite sequences of positive integers is countable.

Hint: If $s \in \left(\mathbb{Z}^+\right)^*$, let $\text{sum}(s)$ be the sum of the successive integers in s.

Problems for Section 8.2

Class Problems

Problem 8.23.
Let $\mathbb{N}^\omega$ be the set of infinite sequences of nonnegative integers. For example, some sequences of this kind are:

$$(0, 1, 2, 3, 4, \ldots),$$
$$(2, 3, 5, 7, 11, \ldots),$$
$$(3, 1, 4, 5, 9, \ldots).$$

Prove that this set of sequences is uncountable.

Problem 8.24.
There are lots of different sizes of infinite sets. For example, starting with the infinite set $\mathbb{N}$ of nonnegative integers, we can build the infinite sequence of sets

$$\mathbb{N} \text{ strict } \mathrm{pow}(\mathbb{N}) \text{ strict } \mathrm{pow}(\mathrm{pow}(\mathbb{N})) \text{ strict } \mathrm{pow}(\mathrm{pow}(\mathrm{pow}(\mathbb{N}))) \text{ strict } \ldots.$$

where each set is "strictly smaller" than the next one by Theorem 8.1.12. Let $\mathrm{pow}^n(\mathbb{N})$ be the nth set in the sequence, and

$$U ::= \bigcup_{n=0}^{\infty} \mathrm{pow}^n(\mathbb{N}).$$

(a) Prove that

$$U \text{ surj } \mathrm{pow}^n(\mathbb{N}), \tag{8.10}$$

for all $n > 0$.

(b) Prove that

$$\mathrm{pow}^n(\mathbb{N}) \text{ strict } U$$

for all $n \in \mathbb{N}$.

Now of course, we could take $U, \mathrm{pow}(U), \mathrm{pow}(\mathrm{pow}(U)), \ldots$ and keep on in this way building still bigger infinities indefinitely.

Homework Problems

Problem 8.25.
For any sets A and B, let $[A \to B]$ be the set of total functions from A to B. Prove that if A is not empty and B has more than one element, then $\text{NOT}(A \text{ surj } [A \to B])$.

Hint: Suppose that σ is a function from A to $[A \to B]$ mapping each element $a \in A$ to a function $\sigma_a : A \to B$. Pick any two elements of B; call them 0 and 1. Then define

$$\text{diag}(a) ::= \begin{cases} 0 \text{ if } \sigma_a(a) = 1, \\ 1 \text{ otherwise.} \end{cases}$$

Problem 8.26.
String procedures are one-argument procedures that apply to strings over the ASCII alphabet. If application of procedure P to string s results in a computation that eventually halts, we say that P *recognizes* s. We define $\text{lang}(P)$ to be the set of strings or *language* recognized by P:

$$\text{lang}(P) ::= \{s \in \text{ASCII}^* \mid P \text{ recognizes } s\}.$$

A language is *unrecognizable* when it is not equal to $\text{lang}(P)$ for any procedure P.

A string procedure declaration is a text $s \in \text{ASCII}^*$ that conforms to the grammatical rules for programs. The declaration defines a procedure P_s, which we can think of as the result of compiling s into an executable object. If $s \in \text{ASCII}^*$ is not a grammatically well-formed procedure declaration, we arbitrarily define P_s to be the string procedure that fails to halt when applied to any string. Now every string defines a string procedure, and every string procedure is P_s for some $s \in \text{ASCII}^*$.

An easy diagonal argument in Section 8.2 showed that

$$\text{No-halt} ::= \{s \mid P_s \text{ applied to } s \text{ does not halt}\} = \{s \mid s \notin \text{lang}(P_s)\}$$

is not recognizable.

It may seem pretty weird to apply a procedure to its own declaration. Are there any less weird examples of unrecognizable set? The answer is "many more." In this problem, we'll show three more:

$$\text{No-halt-}\lambda ::= \{s \mid P_s \text{ applied to } \lambda \text{ does not halt}\} = \{s \mid \lambda \notin \text{lang}(P_s)\},$$
$$\text{Finite-halt} ::= \{s \mid \text{lang}(P_s) \text{ is finite}\},$$
$$\text{Always-halt} ::= \{s \mid \text{lang}(P_s) = \text{ASCII}^*\}.$$

Let's begin by showing how we could use a recognizer for No-halt-λ to define a recognizer for No-halt. That is, we will "reduce" the weird problem of recognizing No-halt to the more understandable problem of recognizing No-halt-λ. Since there is no recognizer for No-halt, it follows that there can't be one for No-halt-λ either.

Here's how this reduction would work: suppose we want to recognize when a given string s is in No-halt. Revise s to be the declaration of a slightly modified procedure $P_{s'}$ which behaves as follows:

> $P_{s'}$ applied to argument $t \in \text{ASCII}^*$, ignores t, and simulates P_s applied to s.

So, if P_s applied to s halts, then $P_{s'}$ halts on every string it is applied to, and if P_s applied to s does not halt, then $P_{s'}$ does not halt on any string it is applied to. That is,

$$s \in \text{No-halt IMPLIES } \text{lang}(P_{s'}) = \emptyset$$
$$\text{IMPLIES } \lambda \notin \text{lang}(P_{s'})$$
$$\text{IMPLIES } s' \in \text{No-halt-}\lambda,$$
$$s \notin \text{No-halt IMPLIES } \text{lang}(P_{s'}) = \text{ASCII}^*$$
$$\text{IMPLIES } \lambda \in \text{lang}(P_{s'})$$
$$\text{IMPLIES } s' \notin \text{No-halt-}\lambda.$$

In short,

$$s \in \text{No-halt IFF } s' \in \text{No-halt-}\lambda.$$

So to recognize when $s \in$ No-halt all you need to do is recognize when $s' \in$ No-halt-λ. As already noted above (but we know that remark got by several students, so we're repeating the explanation), this means that if No-halt-λ was recognizable, then No-halt would be as well. Since we know that No-halt is unrecognizable, then No-halt-λ must also be unrecognizable, as claimed.

(a) Conclude that Finite-halt is unrecognizable.

Hint: Same s'.

Next, let's see how a reduction of No-halt to Always-halt would work. Suppose we want to recognize when a given string s is in No-halt. Revise s to be the declaration of a slightly modified procedure $P_{s''}$ which behaves as follows:

> When $P_{s''}$ is applied to argument $t \in \text{ASCII}^*$, it simulates P_s applied to s for up to $|t|$ "steps" (executions of individual machine instructions). If P_s applied to s has *not* halted in $|t|$ steps, then the application of $P_{s''}$ to t halts. If P_s applied to s *has* halted within $|t|$ steps, then the application of $P_{s''}$ to t runs forever.

(b) Conclude that Always-halt is unrecognizable.

Hint: Explain why

$$s \in \text{No-halt IFF } s'' \in \text{Always-halt}.$$

(c) Explain why $\overline{\text{Finite-halt}}$ is unrecognizable.

Hint: Same s''.

Note that it's easy to recognize when P_s does halt on s: just simulate the application of P_s to s until it halts. This shows that $\overline{\text{No-halt}}$ *is* recognizable. We've just concluded that Finite-halt is nastier: neither it nor its complement is recognizable.

Problem 8.27.

There is a famous paradox about describing numbers which goes as follows:

There are only so many possible definitions of nonnegative integers that can be written out in English using no more than 161 characters from the Roman alphabet, punctuation symbols, and spaces. So there have to be an infinite number of nonnegative integers that don't have such short definitions. By the Well Ordering Principle, there must be a *least* nonnegative integer n that has no such short definition. But wait a minute,

> "The *least* nonnegative integer that cannot be defined in English using at most 161 characters from the Roman alphabet, punctuation symbols, and spaces."

is a definition of n that uses 161 characters (count 'em). So n can't exist, and the Well Ordering Principle is unsound!

Now this "paradox" doesn't stand up to reason because it rests on the decidedly murky concept of a "definition in English." As usual, when you don't know what you're talking about, reaching contradictory conclusions is to be expected.

But we can extract from this paradox a well-defined and interesting theorem about definability in predicate logic. The method we use is essentialy the same as the one used to prove Cantor's Theorem 8.1.12, and it leads to many other important results about the logical limits of mathematics and computer science. In particular, we'll present a simple and precise description of a set of binary strings that can't be described by ordinary logical formulas. In other words, we will give a precise description of an undescribable set of strings, which sounds paradoxical, but won't be when we look at it more closely.

Let's start by illustrating how a logical formula can describe the set of binary strings that do not contain a 1:

$$\text{NOT}[\exists y. \exists z. s = y1z]. \tag{no-1s}$$

So the strings s described by formula (no-1s) are exactly the strings consisting solely of 0's.

Formula (no-1s) is an example of a "string formula" of the kind we will use to describe properties of binary strings. More precisely, an *atomic* string formula is a formula, like "$s = y1z$" above, that is of the general form

$$\text{"}xy \ldots z = uv \ldots w\text{"}$$

where $x, y, \ldots, z, u, v, \ldots, w$ may be the constants $0,1$, or may be variables ranging over the set, $\{0, 1\}^*$, of finite binary strings. A string formula in general is one like (no-1s), built up from atomic formulas using quantifiers and propositional connectives.

When $G(s)$ is a string formula, we'll use the notation $\text{desc}(G)$ for the set of binary strings s that satisfy G. That is,

$$\text{desc}(G) ::= \{s \in \{0, 1\}^* \mid G(s)\}.$$

A set of binary strings is *describable* if it equals $\text{desc}(G)$ for some string formula G. For example, the set 0^* of finite strings of 0's is describable because

$$\text{desc}((\text{no-1s})) = 0^*.$$

The next important idea comes from the observation that a string formula itself is a syntactic object, consisting of a string of characters over some standard character alphabet. Now coding characters of an alphabet into binary strings is a familiar idea. For example, the characters of the ASCII alphabet have a standard coding into the length eight binary strings. Once its individual characters are coded into binary, a complete string formula can be coded into a binary string by concatenating the binary codes of its consecutive characters—a very familiar idea to a computer scientist.

Now suppose x is a binary string that codes some formula G_x. The details of how we extract G_x from its code x don't matter much—we only require that there is some procedure to actually display the string formula G_x given its code x.

It's technically convenient to treat every string as the code of a string formula, so if x is not a binary string we would get from a string formula, we'll arbitrarily define G_x to be the formula (no-1s).

Now we have just the kind of situation where a Cantor-style diagonal argument can be applied, namely, we'll ask whether a string describes a property of *itself*! That may sound like a mind-bender, but all we're asking is whether

$$G_x(x)$$

is true, or equivalently whether

$$x \in \mathrm{desc}(G_x).$$

For example, using character-by-character translations of formulas into binary, neither the string 0000 nor the string 10 would be the binary representation of a formula, so our convention implies that

$$G_{0000} = G_{10} ::= \text{formula (no-1s)}.$$

So

$$\mathrm{desc}(G_{0000}) = \mathrm{desc}(G_{10}) = 0^*.$$

This means that

$$0000 \in \mathrm{desc}(G_{0000}) \quad \text{and} \quad 10 \notin \mathrm{desc}(G_{10}).$$

Now we are in a position to give a precise mathematical description of an "undescribable" set of binary strings, namely:

Theorem. *Define*

$$U ::= \{x \in \{0,1\}^* \mid x \notin \mathrm{desc}(G_x)\}. \tag{8.11}$$

The set U is not describable.

Use reasoning similar to Cantor's Theorem 8.1.12 to prove this Theorem.
Hint: Suppose $U = \mathrm{desc}(G_{x_U})$.

Exam Problems

Problem 8.28.

Let $\{1, 2, 3\}^\omega$ be the set of infinite sequences containing only the numbers 1, 2, and 3. For example, some sequences of this kind are:

$$(1, 1, 1, 1...),$$
$$(2, 2, 2, 2...),$$
$$(3, 2, 1, 3...).$$

Prove that $\{1, 2, 3\}^\omega$ is uncountable.
Hint: One approach is to define a surjective function from $\{1, 2, 3\}^\omega$ to the power set $\mathrm{pow}(\mathbb{N})$.

Problems for Section 8.3

Class Problems

Problem 8.29.

Forming a pair (a, b) of items a and b is a mathematical operation that we can safely take for granted. But when we're trying to show how all of mathematics can be reduced to set theory, we need a way to represent the pair (a, b) as a set.

(a) Explain why representing (a, b) by $\{a, b\}$ won't work.

(b) Explain why representing (a, b) by $\{a, \{b\}\}$ won't work either. *Hint:* What pair does $\{\{1\}, \{2\}\}$ represent?

(c) Define

$$\text{pair}(a, b) ::= \{a, \{a, b\}\}.$$

Explain why representing (a, b) as pair(a, b) uniquely determines a and b. *Hint:* Sets can't be indirect members of themselves: $a \in a$ never holds for any set a, and neither can $a \in b \in a$ hold for any b.

Problem 8.30.

The axiom of choice says that if s is a set whose members are nonempty sets that are *pairwise disjoint*—that is, no two sets in s have an element in common—then there is a set c consisting of exactly one element from each set in s.

In formal logic, we could describe s with the formula,

$$\text{pairwise-disjoint}(s) ::= \forall x \in s.\, x \neq \emptyset \text{ AND}$$
$$\forall x, y \in s.\, x \neq y \text{ IMPLIES } x \cap y = \emptyset.$$

Similarly we could describe c with the formula

$$\text{choice-set}(c, s) ::= \quad \forall x \in s.\, \exists! z.\, z \in c \cap x.$$

Here "$\exists!\, z$." is fairly standard notation for "there exists a *unique* z."

Now we can give the formal definition:

Definition (Axiom of Choice).

$$\forall s.\, \text{pairwise-disjoint}(s) \text{ IMPLIES } \exists c.\, \text{choice-set}(c, s).$$

The only issue here is that set theory is technically supposed to be expressed in terms of *pure* formulas in the language of sets, which means formula that uses only the membership relation $\in$ propositional connectives, the two quantifies $\forall$ and $\exists$, and variables ranging over all sets. Verify that the axiom of choice can be expressed as a pure formula, by explaining how to replace all impure subformulas above with equivalent pure formulas.

For example, the formula $x = y$ could be replaced with the pure formula $\forall z.\, z \in x$ IFF $z \in y$.

Problem 8.31.
Let $R : A \to A$ be a binary relation on a set A. If $a_1\ R\ a_0$, we'll say that a_1 is "R-smaller" than a_0. R is called *well founded* when there is no infinite "R-decreasing" sequence:

$$\cdots R\ a_n\ R \cdots R\ a_1\ R\ a_0, \tag{8.12}$$

of elements $a_i \in A$.

For example, if $A = \mathbb{N}$ and R is the $<$-relation, then R is well founded because if you keep counting down with nonnegative integers, you eventually get stuck at zero:

$$0 < \cdots < n - 1 < n.$$

But you can keep counting up forever, so the $>$-relation is not well founded:

$$\cdots > n > \cdots > 1 > 0.$$

Also, the $\leq$-relation on $\mathbb{N}$ is not well founded because a *constant* sequence of, say, 2's, gets $\leq$-smaller forever:

$$\cdots \leq 2 \leq \cdots \leq 2 \leq 2.$$

(a) If B is a subset of A, an element $b \in B$ is defined to be *R-minimal in B* iff there is no R-smaller element in B. Prove that $R : A \to A$ is well founded iff every nonempty subset of A has an R-minimal element.

A logic *formula of set theory* has only predicates of the form "$x \in y$" for variables x, y ranging over sets, along with quantifiers and propositional operations. For example,

$$\text{isempty}(x) ::= \forall w.\ \text{NOT}(w \in x)$$

is a formula of set theory that means that "x is empty."

(b) Write a formula member-minimal(u, v) of set theory that means that u is $\in$-minimal in v.

(c) The Foundation axiom of set theory says that $\in$ is a well founded relation on sets. Express the Foundation axiom as a formula of set theory. You may use "member-minimal" and "isempty" in your formula as abbreviations for the formulas defined above.

(d) Explain why the Foundation axiom implies that no set is a member of itself.

Homework Problems

Problem 8.32.

In writing formulas, it is OK to use abbreviations introduced earlier (so it is now legal to use "=" because we just defined it).

(a) Explain how to write a formula, $\text{Subset}_n(x, y_1, y_2, \ldots, y_n)$, of set theory [9] that means $x \subseteq \{y_1, y_2, \ldots, y_n\}$.

(b) Now use the formula Subset_n to write a formula, $\text{Atmost}_n(x)$, of set theory that means that x has at most n elements.

(c) Explain how to write a formula Exactly_n of set theory that means that x has exactly n elements. Your formula should only be about twice the length of the formula Atmost_n.

(d) The direct way to write a formula $D_n(y_1, \ldots, y_n)$ of set theory that means that $y_1, \ldots, y_n$ are distinct elements is to write an AND of subformulas "$y_i \neq y_j$" for $1 \leq i < j \leq n$. Since there are $n(n-1)/2$ such subformulas, this approach leads to a formula D_n whose length grows proportional to n^2. Describe how to write such a formula $D_n(y_1, \ldots, y_n)$ whose length only grows proportional to n.

Hint: Use Subset_n and Exactly_n.

Exam Problems

Problem 8.33. (a) Explain how to write a formula $\text{Members}(p, a, b)$ of set theory [10] that means $p = \{a, b\}$.

Hint: Say that everything in p is either a or b. It's OK to use subformulas of the form "$x = y$," since we can regard "$x = y$" as an abbreviation for a genuine set theory formula.

A *pair* (a, b) is simply a sequence of length two whose first item is a and whose second is b. Sequences are a basic mathematical data type we take for granted, but when we're trying to show how all of mathematics can be reduced to set theory, we

---

[9] See Section 8.3.2.
[10] See Section 8.3.2.

need a way to represent the ordered pair (a, b) as a set. One way that will work[11] is to represent (a, b) as

$$\text{pair}(a, b) ::= \{a, \{a, b\}\}.$$

(b) Explain how to write a formula $\text{Pair}(p, a, b)$, of set theory [12] that means $p = \text{pair}(a, b)$.

Hint: Now it's OK to use subformulas of the form "Members(p, a, b)."

(c) Explain how to write a formula $\text{Second}(p, b)$, of set theory that means p is a pair whose second item is b.

Problems for Section 8.4

Homework Problems

Problem 8.34.
In this problem, structural induction and the Foundation Axiom of set theory provide simple proofs about some utterly infinite objects.

Definition. The class of 'recursive-set-like" objects, Recs, is defined recursively as follows:

Base case: The empty set $\emptyset$ is a Recs.

Constructor step: If P is a property of Recs's that is not identically false, then

$$\{s \in \text{Recs} \mid P(s)\}$$

is a Recs.

(a) Prove that Recs satisfies the Foundation Axiom: there is no infinite sequence of Recs, $r_o, r_1, \ldots, r_{n-1}, r_n, \ldots$ such that

$$\ldots r_n \in r_{n-1} \in \ldots r_1 \in r_0. \tag{8.13}$$

Hint: Structural induction.

(b) Prove that *every* set is a Recs.[13]

Hint: Use the Foundation axiom.

---

[11]Some similar ways that don't work are described in problem 8.29.

[12]See Section 8.3.2.

[13]Remember that in the context of set theory, every mathematical datum is a set. For example, we think of the nonnegative integers, 0,1,2,..., as a basic mathematical data type, but this data type could be understood as just referring to the sets $\emptyset, \{\emptyset\}, \{\{\emptyset\}\}, \ldots$.

(c) Every Recs R defines a special kind of two-person game of perfect information called a *uniform* game. The initial "board position" of the game is R itself. A player's move consists of choosing any member R. The two players alternate moves, with the player whose turn it is to move called the *Next* player. The Next player's move determines a game in which the other player, called the *Previous* player, moves first.

The game is called "uniform" because the two players have the *same* objective: to leave the other player stuck with no move to make. That is, whoever moves to the empty set is a winner, because then the next player has no move.

Prove that in every uniform game, either the Previous player or the Next player has a winning strategy.

Problem 8.35.

For any set x, define next(x) to be the set consisting of all the elements of x, along with x itself:

$$\text{next}(x) ::= x \cup \{x\}.$$

So by definition,

$$x \in \text{next}(x) \text{ and } x \subset \text{next}(x). \tag{8.14}$$

Now we give a recursive definition of a collection Ord of sets called *ordinals* that provide a way to count infinite sets. Namely,

Definition.

$$\emptyset \in \text{Ord},$$
$$\text{if } v \in \text{Ord, then next}(v) \in \text{Ord},$$
$$\text{if } S \subset \text{Ord, then } \bigcup_{v \in S} v \in \text{Ord}.$$

There is a method for proving things about ordinals that follows directly from the way they are defined. Namely, let $P(x)$ be some property of sets. The *Ordinal Induction Rule* says that to prove that $P(v)$ is true for all ordinals v, you need only show two things

- If P holds for all the members of next(x), then it holds for next(x), and

- if P holds for all members of some set S, then it holds for their union.

That is:

Rule. *Ordinal Induction*

$$\frac{\forall x.\ (\forall y \in next(x).\ P(y))\ \text{IMPLIES}\ P(next(x)),}{\forall v \in Ord.\ P(v)}$$
$$\frac{\forall S.\ (\forall x \in S.\ P(x))\ \text{IMPLIES}\ P(\bigcup_{x \in S} x)}{\forall v \in Ord.\ P(v)}$$

The intuitive justification for the Ordinal Induction Rule is similar to the justification for strong induction. We will accept the soundness of the Ordinal Induction Rule as a basic axiom.

(a) A set x is *closed under membership* if every element of x is also a subset of x, that is

$$\forall y \in x.\ y \subset x.$$

Prove that every ordinal v is closed under membership.

(b) A sequence

$$\cdots \in v_{n+1} \in v_n \in \cdots \in v_1 \in v_0 \tag{8.15}$$

of ordinals v_i is called a *member-decreasing* sequence starting at v_0. Use Ordinal Induction to prove that no ordinal starts an infinite member-decreasing sequence.[14]

---

[14]Do not assume the Foundation Axiom of ZFC (Section 8.3.2) which says that there isn't *any* set that starts an infinite member-decreasing sequence. Even in versions of set theory in which the Foundation Axiom does not hold, there cannot be any infinite member-decreasing sequence of ordinals.

II Structures

Introduction

The properties of the set of integers are the subject of Number Theory. This part of the text starts with a chapter on this topic because the integers are a very familiar mathematical structure that have lots of easy-to-state and interesting-to-prove properties. This makes Number Theory a good place to start serious practice with the methods of proof outlined in Part 1. Moreover, Number Theory has turned out to have multiple applications in computer science. For example, most modern data encryption methods are based on Number theory.

We study numbers as a "*structure*" that has multiple parts of different kinds. One part is, of course, the set of all the integers. A second part is the collection of basic integer operations: addition, multiplication, exponentiation,.... Other parts are the important subsets of integers—like the prime numbers—out of which all integers can be built using multiplication.

Structured objects more generally are fundamental in computer science. Whether you are writing code, solving an optimization problem, or designing a network, you will be dealing with structures.

Graphs, also known as *networks*, are a fundamental structure in computer science. Graphs can model associations between pairs of objects; for example, two exams that cannot be given at the same time, two people that like each other, or two subroutines that can be run independently. In Chapter 10, we study *directed graphs* which model *one-way* relationships such as being bigger than, loving (sadly, it's often not mutual), and being a prerequisite for. A highlight is the special case of acyclic digraphs (*DAGs*) that correspond to a class of relations called *partial orders*. Partial orders arise frequently in the study of scheduling and concurrency. Digraphs as models for data communication and routing problems are the topic of Chapter 11.

In Chapter 12 we focus on *simple graphs* that represent mutual or *symmetric* relationships, such as being in conflict, being compatible, being independent, being capable of running in parallel. Planar Graphs—simple graphs that can be drawn in the plane—are examined in Chapter 13, the final chapter of Part II. The impossibility of placing 50 geocentric satellites in orbit so that they *uniformly* blanket the globe will be one of the conclusions reached in this chapter.

9 Number Theory

Number theory is the study of the integers. *Why* anyone would want to study the integers may not be obvious. First of all, what's to know? There's 0, there's 1, 2, 3, and so on, and, oh yeah, -1, -2, ... Which one don't you understand? What practical value is there in it?

The mathematician G. H. Hardy delighted at its impracticality. He wrote:

> [Number theorists] may be justified in rejoicing that there is one science, at any rate, and that their own, whose very remoteness from ordinary human activities should keep it gentle and clean.

Hardy was especially concerned that number theory not be used in warfare; he was a pacifist. You may applaud his sentiments, but he got it wrong: number theory underlies modern cryptography, which is what makes secure online communication possible. Secure communication is of course crucial in war—leaving poor Hardy spinning in his grave. It's also central to online commerce. Every time you buy a book from Amazon, use a certificate to access a web page, or use a PayPal account, you are relying on number theoretic algorithms.

Number theory also provides an excellent environment for us to practice and apply the proof techniques that we developed in previous chapters. We'll work out properties of greatest common divisors (gcd's) and use them to prove that integers factor uniquely into primes. Then we'll introduce modular arithmetic and work out enough of its properties to explain the RSA public key crypto-system.

Since we'll be focusing on properties of the integers, we'll adopt the default convention in this chapter that *variables range over the set $\mathbb{Z}$ of integers*.

9.1 Divisibility

The nature of number theory emerges as soon as we consider the *divides* relation.

Definition 9.1.1. *a divides b* (notation $a \mid b$) iff there is an integer k such that

$$ak = b.$$

The divides relation comes up so frequently that multiple synonyms for it are used all the time. The following phrases all say the same thing:

- $a \mid b$,

- a divides b,

- a is a *divisor* of b,

- a is a *factor* of b,

- b is *divisible* by a,

- b is a *multiple* of a.

Some immediate consequences of Definition 9.1.1 are that for all n

$$n \mid 0, \qquad n \mid n, \text{ and} \qquad \pm 1 \mid n.$$

Also,

$$0 \mid n \text{ IMPLIES } n = 0.$$

Dividing seems simple enough, but let's play with this definition. The Pythagoreans, an ancient sect of mathematical mystics, said that a number is *perfect* if it equals the sum of its positive integral divisors, excluding itself. For example, $6 = 1 + 2 + 3$ and $28 = 1 + 2 + 4 + 7 + 14$ are perfect numbers. On the other hand, 10 is not perfect because $1 + 2 + 5 = 8$, and 12 is not perfect because $1 + 2 + 3 + 4 + 6 = 16$. Euclid characterized all the *even* perfect numbers around 300 BC (Problem 9.2). But is there an *odd* perfect number? More than two thousand years later, we still don't know! All numbers up to about 10^{300} have been ruled out, but no one has proved that there isn't an odd perfect number waiting just over the horizon.

So a half-page into number theory, we've strayed past the outer limits of human knowledge. This is pretty typical; number theory is full of questions that are easy to pose, but incredibly difficult to answer. We'll mention a few more such questions in later sections.[1]

9.1.1   Facts about Divisibility

The following lemma collects some basic facts about divisibility.

Lemma 9.1.2.

1. If $a \mid b$ and $b \mid c$, then $a \mid c$.

---

[1]*Don't Panic*—we're going to stick to some relatively benign parts of number theory. These super-hard unsolved problems rarely get put on problem sets.

2. *If $a \mid b$ and $a \mid c$, then $a \mid sb + tc$ for all s and t.*

3. *For all $c \neq 0$, $a \mid b$ if and only if $ca \mid cb$.*

Proof. These facts all follow directly from Definition 9.1.1. To illustrate this, we'll prove just part 2:

Given that $a \mid b$, there is some $k_1 \in \mathbb{Z}$ such that $ak_1 = b$. Likewise, $ak_2 = c$, so

$$sb + tc = s(k_1 a) + t(k_2 a) = (sk_1 + tk_2)a.$$

Therefore $sb + tc = k_3 a$ where $k_3 ::= (sk_1 + tk_2)$, which means that

$$a \mid sb + tc.$$

∎

A number of the form $sb + tc$ is called an *integer linear combination* of b and c, or, since in this chapter we're only talking about integers, just a *linear combination*. So Lemma 9.1.2.2 can be rephrased as

If a divides b and c, then a divides every linear combination of b and c.

We'll be making good use of linear combinations, so let's get the general definition on record:

Definition 9.1.3. An integer n is a *linear combination* of numbers $b_0, \ldots, b_k$ iff

$$n = s_0 b_0 + s_1 b_1 + \cdots + s_k b_k$$

for some integers $s_0, \ldots, s_k$.

9.1.2 When Divisibility Goes Bad

As you learned in elementary school, if one number does *not* evenly divide another, you get a "quotient" and a "remainder" left over. More precisely:

Theorem 9.1.4. *[Division Theorem][2] Let n and d be integers such that $d \neq 0$. Then there exists a unique pair of integers q and r, such that*

$$n = q \cdot d + r \text{ AND } 0 \leq r < |d|. \tag{9.1}$$

---

[2]This theorem is often called the "Division Algorithm," but we prefer to call it a theorem since it does not actually describe a division procedure for computing the quotient and remainder.

The number q is called the *quotient* and the number r is called the *remainder* of n divided by d. We use the notation qcnt(n, d) for the quotient and rem(n, d) for the remainder.

The absolute value notation $|d|$ used above is probably familiar from introductory calculus, but for the record, let's define it.

Definition 9.1.5. For any real number r, the *absolute value* $|r|$ of r is:[3]

$$|r| ::= \begin{cases} r & \text{if } r \geq 0, \\ -r & \text{if } r < 0. \end{cases}$$

So by definition, the *remainder* rem(n, d) *is nonnegative* regardless of the sign of n and d. For example, rem$(-11, 7) = 3$, since $-11 = (-2) \cdot 7 + 3$.

"Remainder" operations built into many programming languages can be a source of confusion. For example, the expression "32 % 5" will be familiar to programmers in Java, C, and C++; it evaluates to rem$(32, 5) = 2$ in all three languages. On the other hand, these and other languages are inconsistent in how they treat remainders like "32 % -5" or "-32 % 5" that involve negative numbers. So don't be distracted by your familiar programming language's behavior on remainders, and stick to the mathematical convention that *remainders are nonnegative*.

The remainder on division by d by definition is a number in the (integer) *interval* from 0 to $|d| - 1$. Such integer intervals come up so often that it is useful to have a simple notation for them. For $k \leq n \in \mathbb{Z}$,

$$\begin{aligned} (k..n) &::= & \{i \mid k < i < n\}, \\ (k..n] &::= & (k, n) \cup \{n\}, \\ [k..n) &::= & \{k\} \cup (k, n), \\ [k..n] &::= & \{k\} \cup (k, n) \cup \{n\} = \{i \mid k \leq i \leq n\}. \end{aligned}$$

9.1.3   Die Hard

Die Hard 3 is just a B-grade action movie, but we think it has an inner message: everyone should learn at least a little number theory. In Section 6.2.3, we formalized a state machine for the Die Hard jug-filling problem using 3 and 5 gallon jugs,

---

[3]The absolute value of r could be defined as $\sqrt{r^2}$, which works because of the convention that square root notation always refers to the *nonnegative* square root (see Problem 1.3). Absolute value generalizes to complex numbers where it is called the *norm*. For $a, b \in \mathbb{R}$,

$$|a + bi| ::= \sqrt{a^2 + b^2}.$$

and also with 3 and 9 gallon jugs, and came to different conclusions about bomb explosions. What's going on in general? For example, how about getting 4 gallons from 12- and 18-gallon jugs, getting 32 gallons with 899- and 1147-gallon jugs, or getting 3 gallons into a jug using just 21- and 26-gallon jugs?

It would be nice if we could solve all these silly water jug questions at once. This is where number theory comes in handy.

A Water Jug Invariant

Suppose that we have water jugs with capacities a and b with $b \geq a$. Let's carry out some sample operations of the state machine and see what happens, assuming the b-jug is big enough:

$$
\begin{array}{lll}
(0,0) \rightarrow (a,0) & & \text{fill first jug} \\
\rightarrow (0,a) & & \text{pour first into second} \\
\rightarrow (a,a) & & \text{fill first jug} \\
\rightarrow (2a-b,b) & & \text{pour first into second (assuming } 2a \geq b) \\
\rightarrow (2a-b,0) & & \text{empty second jug} \\
\rightarrow (0,2a-b) & & \text{pour first into second} \\
\rightarrow (a,2a-b) & & \text{fill first} \\
\rightarrow (3a-2b,b) & & \text{pour first into second (assuming } 3a \geq 2b)
\end{array}
$$

What leaps out is that at every step, the amount of water in each jug is a linear combination of a and b. This is easy to prove by induction on the number of transitions:

Lemma 9.1.6 (Water Jugs). *In the* Die Hard *state machine of Section 6.2.3 with jugs of sizes a and b, the amount of water in each jug is always a linear combination of a and b.*

Proof. The induction hypothesis $P(n)$ is the proposition that after n transitions, the amount of water in each jug is a linear combination of a and b.

Base case ($n = 0$): $P(0)$ is true, because both jugs are initially empty, and $0 \cdot a + 0 \cdot b = 0$.

Inductive step: Suppose the machine is in state (x, y) after n steps, that is, the little jug contains x gallons and the big one contains y gallons. There are two cases:

- If we fill a jug from the fountain or empty a jug into the fountain, then that jug is empty or full. The amount in the other jug remains a linear combination of a and b. So $P(n + 1)$ holds.

- Otherwise, we pour water from one jug to another until one is empty or the other is full. By our assumption, the amount x and y in each jug is a linear combination of a and b before we begin pouring. After pouring, one jug is either empty (contains 0 gallons) or full (contains a or b gallons). Thus, the other jug contains either $x + y$, $x + y - a$ or $x + y - b$ gallons, all of which are linear combinations of a and b since x and y are. So $P(n + 1)$ holds in this case as well.

Since $P(n + 1)$ holds in any case, this proves the inductive step, completing the proof by induction. ∎

So we have established that the jug problem has a preserved invariant, namely, the amount of water in every jug is a linear combination of the capacities of the jugs. Lemma 9.1.6 has an important corollary:

Corollary. *In trying to get 4 gallons from 12- and 18-gallon jugs, and likewise to get 32 gallons from 899- and 1147-gallon jugs,*

Bruce will die!

Proof. By the Water Jugs Lemma 9.1.6, with 12- and 18-gallon jugs, the amount in any jug is a linear combination of 12 and 18. This is always a multiple of 6 by Lemma 9.1.2.2, so Bruce can't get 4 gallons. Likewise, the amount in any jug using 899- and 1147-gallon jugs is a multiple of 31, so he can't get 32 either. ∎

But the Water Jugs Lemma doesn't tell the complete story. For example, it leaves open the question of getting 3 gallons into a jug using just 21- and 26-gallon jugs: the only positive factor of both 21 and 26 is 1, and of course 1 divides 3, so the Lemma neither rules out nor confirms the possibility of getting 3 gallons.

A bigger issue is that we've just managed to recast a pretty understandable question about water jugs into a technical question about linear combinations. This might not seem like a lot of progress. Fortunately, linear combinations are closely related to something more familiar, greatest common divisors, and will help us solve the general water jug problem.

9.2   The Greatest Common Divisor

A *common divisor* of a and b is a number that divides them both. The *greatest common divisor* of a and b is written $\gcd(a, b)$. For example, $\gcd(18, 24) = 6$.

As long as a and b are not both 0, they will have a gcd. The gcd turns out to be very valuable for reasoning about the relationship between a and b and for reasoning about integers in general. We'll be making lots of use of gcd's in what follows.

Some immediate consequences of the definition of gcd are that for $n > 0$,

$$\gcd(n, n) = n, \qquad \gcd(n, 1) = 1, \qquad \gcd(n, 0) = n,$$

where the last equality follows from the fact that everything is a divisor of 0.

9.2.1 Euclid's Algorithm

The first thing to figure out is how to find gcd's. A good way called *Euclid's algorithm* has been known for several thousand years. It is based on the following elementary observation.

Lemma 9.2.1. *For $b \neq 0$,*

$$\gcd(a, b) = \gcd(b, \text{rem}(a, b)).$$

Proof. By the Division Theorem 9.1.4,

$$a = qb + r \tag{9.2}$$

where $r = \text{rem}(a, b)$. So a is a linear combination of b and r, which implies that any divisor of b and r is a divisor of a by Lemma 9.1.2.2. Likewise, r is a linear combination $a - qb$ of a and b, so any divisor of a and b is a divisor of r. This means that a and b have the same common divisors as b and r, and so they have the same *greatest* common divisor. ∎

Lemma 9.2.1 is useful for quickly computing the greatest common divisor of two numbers. For example, we could compute the greatest common divisor of 1147 and 899 by repeatedly applying it:

$$\gcd(1147, 899) = \gcd(899, \underbrace{\text{rem}(1147, 899)}_{=248})$$

$$= \gcd(248, \text{rem}(899, 248) = 155)$$
$$= \gcd(155, \text{rem}(248, 155) = 93)$$
$$= \gcd(93, \text{rem}(155, 93) = 62)$$
$$= \gcd(62, \text{rem}(93, 62) = 31)$$
$$= \gcd(31, \text{rem}(62, 31) = 0)$$
$$= 31$$

This calculation that $\gcd(1147, 899) = 31$ was how we figured out that with water jugs of sizes 1147 and 899, Bruce dies trying to get 32 gallons.

On the other hand, applying Euclid's algorithm to 26 and 21 gives

$$\gcd(26, 21) = \gcd(21, 5) = \gcd(5, 1) = 1,$$

so we can't use the reasoning above to rule out Bruce getting 3 gallons into the big jug. As a matter of fact, because the gcd here is 1, Bruce *will* be able to get any number of gallons into the big jug up to its capacity. To explain this, we will need a little more number theory.

Euclid's Algorithm as a State Machine

Euclid's algorithm can easily be formalized as a state machine. The set of states is $\mathbb{N}^2$ and there is one transition rule:

$$(x, y) \longrightarrow (y, \text{rem}(x, y)), \tag{9.3}$$

for $y > 0$. By Lemma 9.2.1, the gcd stays the same from one state to the next. That means the predicate

$$\gcd(x, y) = \gcd(a, b)$$

is a preserved invariant on the states (x, y). This preserved invariant is, of course, true in the start state (a, b). So by the Invariant Principle, if y ever becomes 0, the invariant will be true and so

$$x = \gcd(x, 0) = \gcd(a, b).$$

Namely, the value of x will be the desired gcd.

What's more x and therefore also y, gets to be 0 pretty fast. To see why, note that starting from (x, y), two transitions leads to a state whose the first coordinate is $\text{rem}(x, y)$, which is at most half the size of x.[4] Since x starts off equal to a and gets halved or smaller every two steps, it will reach its minimum value—which is $\gcd(a, b)$—after at most $2 \log a$ transitions. After that, the algorithm takes at most one more transition to terminate. In other words, Euclid's algorithm terminates after at most $1 + 2 \log a$ transitions.[5]

---

[4]In other words,
$$\text{rem}(x, y) \leq x/2 \qquad \text{for } 0 < y \leq x. \tag{9.4}$$
This is immediate if $y \leq x/2$, since the remainder of x divided by y is less than y by definition. On the other hand, if $y > x/2$, then $\text{rem}(x, y) = x - y < x/2$.

[5]A tighter analysis shows that at most $\log_\varphi(a)$ transitions are possible where φ is the golden ratio $(1 + \sqrt{5})/2$, see Problem 9.14.

9.2.2 The Pulverizer

We will get a lot of mileage out of the following key fact:

Theorem 9.2.2. *The greatest common divisor of a and b is a linear combination of a and b. That is,*

$$\gcd(a, b) = sa + tb,$$

for some integers s and t.[6]

We already know from Lemma 9.1.2.2 that every linear combination of a and b is divisible by any common factor of a and b, so it is certainly divisible by the greatest of these common divisors. Since any constant multiple of a linear combination is also a linear combination, Theorem 9.2.2 implies that any multiple of the gcd is a linear combination, giving:

Corollary 9.2.3. *An integer is a linear combination of a and b iff it is a multiple of* $\gcd(a, b)$.

We'll prove Theorem 9.2.2 directly by explaining how to find s and t. This job is tackled by a mathematical tool that dates back to sixth-century India, where it was called *kuttaka*, which means "the Pulverizer." Today, the Pulverizer is more commonly known as the "Extended Euclidean Gcd Algorithm," because it is so close to Euclid's algorithm.

For example, following Euclid's algorithm, we can compute the gcd of 259 and 70 as follows:

$$
\begin{aligned}
\gcd(259, 70) &= \gcd(70, 49) && \text{since rem}(259, 70) = 49 \\
&= \gcd(49, 21) && \text{since rem}(70, 49) = 21 \\
&= \gcd(21, 7) && \text{since rem}(49, 21) = 7 \\
&= \gcd(7, 0) && \text{since rem}(21, 7) = 0 \\
&= 7.
\end{aligned}
$$

The Pulverizer goes through the same steps, but requires some extra bookkeeping along the way: as we compute $\gcd(a, b)$, we keep track of how to write each of the remainders (49, 21, and 7, in the example) as a linear combination of a and b. This is worthwhile, because our objective is to write the last nonzero remainder,

---

[6]This result is often referred to as *Bezout's lemma*, which is a misattribution since it was first published in the West 150 years earlier by someone else, and was described a thousand years before that by Indian mathematicians Aryabhata and Bhaskara.

which is the gcd, as such a linear combination. For our example, here is this extra bookkeeping:

x	y	$(\text{rem}(x,\ y))$	$=$	$x - q \cdot y$
259	70	49	$=$	$a - 3 \cdot b$
70	49	21	$=$	$b - 1 \cdot 49$
			$=$	$b - 1 \cdot (a - 3 \cdot b)$
			$=$	$-1 \cdot a + 4 \cdot b$
49	21	7	$=$	$49 - 2 \cdot 21$
			$=$	$(a - 3 \cdot b) - 2 \cdot (-1 \cdot a + 4 \cdot b)$
			$=$	$\boxed{3 \cdot a - 11 \cdot b}$
21	7	0		

We began by initializing two variables, $x = a$ and $y = b$. In the first two columns above, we carried out Euclid's algorithm. At each step, we computed $\text{rem}(x,\ y)$ which equals $x - \text{qcnt}(x, y) \cdot y$. Then, in this linear combination of x and y, we replaced x and y by equivalent linear combinations of a and b, which we already had computed. After simplifying, we were left with a linear combination of a and b equal to $\text{rem}(x,\ y)$, as desired. The final solution is boxed.

This should make it pretty clear how and why the Pulverizer works. If you have doubts, you may work through Problem 9.13, where the Pulverizer is formalized as a state machine and then verified using an invariant that is an extension of the one used for Euclid's algorithm.

Since the Pulverizer requires only a little more computation than Euclid's algorithm, you can "pulverize" very large numbers very quickly by using this algorithm. As we will soon see, its speed makes the Pulverizer a very useful tool in the field of cryptography.

Now we can restate the Water Jugs Lemma 9.1.6 in terms of the greatest common divisor:

Corollary 9.2.4. *Suppose that we have water jugs with capacities a and b. Then the amount of water in each jug is always a multiple of* $\gcd(a, b)$.

For example, there is no way to form 4 gallons using 3- and 6-gallon jugs, because 4 is not a multiple of $\gcd(3, 6) = 3$.

9.2.3   One Solution for All Water Jug Problems

Corollary 9.2.3 says that 3 can be written as a linear combination of 21 and 26, since 3 is a multiple of $\gcd(21, 26) = 1$. So the Pulverizer will give us integers s and t such that

$$3 = s \cdot 21 + t \cdot 26 \tag{9.5}$$

The coefficient s could be either positive or negative. However, we can readily transform this linear combination into an equivalent linear combination

$$3 = s' \cdot 21 + t' \cdot 26 \tag{9.6}$$

where the coefficient s' is positive. The trick is to notice that if in equation (9.5) we increase s by 26 and decrease t by 21, then the value of the expression $s \cdot 21 + t \cdot 26$ is unchanged overall. Thus, by repeatedly increasing the value of s (by 26 at a time) and decreasing the value of t (by 21 at a time), we get a linear combination $s' \cdot 21 + t' \cdot 26 = 3$ where the coefficient s' is positive. (Of course t' must then be negative; otherwise, this expression would be much greater than 3.)

Now we can form 3 gallons using jugs with capacities 21 and 26: We simply repeat the following steps s' times:

1. Fill the 21-gallon jug.

2. Pour all the water in the 21-gallon jug into the 26-gallon jug. If at any time the 26-gallon jug becomes full, empty it out, and continue pouring the 21-gallon jug into the 26-gallon jug.

At the end of this process, we must have emptied the 26-gallon jug exactly $-t'$ times. Here's why: we've taken $s' \cdot 21$ gallons of water from the fountain, and we've poured out some multiple of 26 gallons. If we emptied fewer than $-t'$ times, then by (9.6), the big jug would be left with at least $3 + 26$ gallons, which is more than it can hold; if we emptied it more times, the big jug would be left containing at most $3 - 26$ gallons, which is nonsense. But once we have emptied the 26-gallon jug exactly $-t'$ times, equation (9.6) implies that there are exactly 3 gallons left.

Remarkably, we don't even need to know the coefficients s' and t' in order to use this strategy! Instead of repeating the outer loop s' times, we could just repeat *until we obtain 3 gallons*, since that must happen eventually. Of course, we have to keep track of the amounts in the two jugs so we know when we're done. Here's the solution using this approach starting with empty jugs, that is, at $(0,0)$:

$\xrightarrow{\text{fill 21}}$ $(21,0)$ $\xrightarrow{\text{pour 21 into 26}}$ $(0,21)$

$\xrightarrow{\text{fill 21}}$ $(21,21)$ $\xrightarrow{\text{pour 21 to 26}}$ $(16,26)$ $\xrightarrow{\text{empty 26}}$ $(16,0)$ $\xrightarrow{\text{pour 21 to 26}}$ $(0,16)$

$\xrightarrow{\text{fill 21}}$ $(21,16)$ $\xrightarrow{\text{pour 21 to 26}}$ $(11,26)$ $\xrightarrow{\text{empty 26}}$ $(11,0)$ $\xrightarrow{\text{pour 21 to 26}}$ $(0,11)$

$\xrightarrow{\text{fill 21}}$ $(21,11)$ $\xrightarrow{\text{pour 21 to 26}}$ $(6,26)$ $\xrightarrow{\text{empty 26}}$ $(6,0)$ $\xrightarrow{\text{pour 21 to 26}}$ $(0,6)$

$\xrightarrow{\text{fill 21}}$ $(21,6)$ $\xrightarrow{\text{pour 21 to 26}}$ $(1,26)$ $\xrightarrow{\text{empty 26}}$ $(1,0)$ $\xrightarrow{\text{pour 21 to 26}}$ $(0,1)$

$\xrightarrow{\text{fill 21}}$ $(21,1)$ $\xrightarrow{\text{pour 21 to 26}}$ $(0,22)$

$\xrightarrow{\text{fill 21}}$ $(21,22)$ $\xrightarrow{\text{pour 21 to 26}}$ $(17,26)$ $\xrightarrow{\text{empty 26}}$ $(17,0)$ $\xrightarrow{\text{pour 21 to 26}}$ $(0,17)$

$\xrightarrow{\text{fill 21}}$ $(21,17)$ $\xrightarrow{\text{pour 21 to 26}}$ $(12,26)$ $\xrightarrow{\text{empty 26}}$ $(12,0)$ $\xrightarrow{\text{pour 21 to 26}}$ $(0,12)$

$\xrightarrow{\text{fill 21}}$ $(21,12)$ $\xrightarrow{\text{pour 21 to 26}}$ $(7,26)$ $\xrightarrow{\text{empty 26}}$ $(7,0)$ $\xrightarrow{\text{pour 21 to 26}}$ $(0,7)$

$\xrightarrow{\text{fill 21}}$ $(21,7)$ $\xrightarrow{\text{pour 21 to 26}}$ $(2,26)$ $\xrightarrow{\text{empty 26}}$ $(2,0)$ $\xrightarrow{\text{pour 21 to 26}}$ $(0,2)$

$\xrightarrow{\text{fill 21}}$ $(21,2)$ $\xrightarrow{\text{pour 21 to 26}}$ $(0,23)$

$\xrightarrow{\text{fill 21}}$ $(21,23)$ $\xrightarrow{\text{pour 21 to 26}}$ $(18,26)$ $\xrightarrow{\text{empty 26}}$ $(18,0)$ $\xrightarrow{\text{pour 21 to 26}}$ $(0,18)$

$\xrightarrow{\text{fill 21}}$ $(21,18)$ $\xrightarrow{\text{pour 21 to 26}}$ $(13,26)$ $\xrightarrow{\text{empty 26}}$ $(13,0)$ $\xrightarrow{\text{pour 21 to 26}}$ $(0,13)$

$\xrightarrow{\text{fill 21}}$ $(21,13)$ $\xrightarrow{\text{pour 21 to 26}}$ $(8,26)$ $\xrightarrow{\text{empty 26}}$ $(8,0)$ $\xrightarrow{\text{pour 21 to 26}}$ $(0,8)$

$\xrightarrow{\text{fill 21}}$ $(21,8)$ $\xrightarrow{\text{pour 21 to 26}}$ $(3,26)$ $\xrightarrow{\text{empty 26}}$ $(3,0)$ $\xrightarrow{\text{pour 21 to 26}}$ $(0,3)$

The same approach works regardless of the jug capacities and even regardless of the amount we're trying to produce! Simply repeat these two steps until the desired amount of water is obtained:

1. Fill the smaller jug.

2. Pour all the water in the smaller jug into the larger jug. If at any time the larger jug becomes full, empty it out, and continue pouring the smaller jug into the larger jug.

By the same reasoning as before, this method eventually generates every multiple—up to the size of the larger jug—of the greatest common divisor of the jug capacities, all the quantities we can possibly produce. No ingenuity is needed at all!

So now we have the complete water jug story:

Theorem 9.2.5. *Suppose that we have water jugs with capacities a and b. For any $c \in [0..a]$, it is possible to get c gallons in the size a jug iff c is a multiple of $\gcd(a, b)$.*

9.2.4 Properties of the Greatest Common Divisor

It can help to have some basic gcd facts on hand:

Lemma 9.2.6.

a) $\gcd(ka, kb) = k \cdot \gcd(a, b)$ *for all $k > 0$.*

b) $(d \mid a$ AND $d \mid b)$ IFF $d \mid \gcd(a, b)$.

c) *If $\gcd(a, b) = 1$ and $\gcd(a, c) = 1$, then $\gcd(a, bc) = 1$.*

d) *If $a \mid bc$ and $\gcd(a, b) = 1$, then $a \mid c$.*

Showing how all these facts follow from Theorem 9.2.2 that gcd is a linear combination is a good exercise (Problem 9.11).

These properties are also simple consequences of the fact that integers factor into primes in a unique way (Theorem 9.4.1). But we'll need some of these facts to prove unique factorization in Section 9.4, so proving them by appeal to unique factorization would be circular.

9.3 Prime Mysteries

Some of the greatest mysteries and insights in number theory concern properties of prime numbers:

Definition 9.3.1. A *prime* is a number greater than 1 that is divisible only by itself and 1. A number other than 0, 1, and -1 that is not a prime is called *composite*.[7]

Here are three famous mysteries:

Twin Prime Conjecture There are infinitely many primes p such that $p + 2$ is also a prime.

In 1966, Chen showed that there are infinitely many primes p such that $p + 2$ is the product of at most two primes. So the conjecture is known to be *almost true*!

Conjectured Inefficiency of Factoring Given the product of two large primes $n = pq$, there is no efficient procedure to recover the primes p and q. That is, no *polynomial time* procedure (see Section 3.5) is guaranteed to find p and

---

[7]So 0, 1, and -1 are the only integers that are neither prime nor composite.

q in a number of steps bounded by a polynomial in the length of the binary representation of n (not n itself). The length of the binary representation at most $1 + \log_2 n$.

The best algorithm known is the "number field sieve," which runs in time proportional to:

$$e^{1.9(\ln n)^{1/3}(\ln \ln n)^{2/3}}.$$

This number grows more rapidly than any polynomial in $\log n$ and is infeasible when n has 300 digits or more.

Efficient factoring is a mystery of particular importance in computer science, as we'll explain later in this chapter.

Goldbach's Conjecture   We've already mentioned Goldbach's Conjecture 1.1.6 several times: every even integer greater than two is equal to the sum of two primes. For example, $4 = 2 + 2$, $6 = 3 + 3$, $8 = 3 + 5$, etc.

In 1939, Schnirelman proved that every even number can be written as the sum of not more than 300,000 primes, which was a start. Today, we know that every even number is the sum of at most 6 primes.

Primes show up erratically in the sequence of integers. In fact, their distribution seems almost random:

$$2, 3, 5, 7, 11, 13, 17, 19, 23, 29, 31, 37, 41, 43, \ldots.$$

One of the great insights about primes is that their density among the integers has a precise limit. Namely, let $\pi(n)$ denote the number of primes up to n:

Definition 9.3.2.

$$\pi(n) ::= |\{p \in [2..n] \mid p \text{ is prime}\}|.$$

For example, $\pi(1) = 0$, $\pi(2) = 1$ and $\pi(10) = 4$, because 2, 3, 5, and 7 are the primes less than or equal to 10. Step by step, π grows erratically according to the erratic spacing between successive primes, but its overall growth rate is known to smooth out to be the same as the growth of the function $n/\ln n$:

Theorem 9.3.3 (Prime Number Theorem).

$$\lim_{n \to \infty} \frac{\pi(n)}{n/\ln n} = 1.$$

Thus, primes gradually taper off. As a rule of thumb, about 1 integer out of every $\ln n$ in the vicinity of n is a prime.

The Prime Number Theorem was conjectured by Legendre in 1798 and proved a century later by de la Vallée Poussin and Hadamard in 1896. However, after his death, a notebook of Gauss was found to contain the same conjecture, which he apparently made in 1791 at age 15. (You have to feel sorry for all the otherwise "great" mathematicians who had the misfortune of being contemporaries of Gauss.)

A proof of the Prime Number Theorem is beyond the scope of this text, but there is a manageable proof (see Problem 9.22) of a related result that is sufficient for our applications:

Theorem 9.3.4 (Chebyshev's Theorem on Prime Density). *For $n > 1$,*

$$\pi(n) > \frac{n}{3 \ln n}.$$

9.4 The Fundamental Theorem of Arithmetic

There is an important fact about primes that you probably already know: every positive integer number has a *unique* prime factorization. So every positive integer can be built up from primes in *exactly one way*. These quirky prime numbers are the building blocks for the integers.

Since the value of a product of numbers is the same if the numbers appear in a different order, there usually isn't a unique way to express a number as a product of primes. For example, there are three ways to write 12 as a product of primes:

$$12 = 2 \cdot 2 \cdot 3 = 2 \cdot 3 \cdot 2 = 3 \cdot 2 \cdot 2.$$

What's unique about the prime factorization of 12 is that any product of primes equal to 12 will have exactly one 3 and two 2's. This means that if we *sort* the primes by size, then the product really will be unique.

Let's state this more carefully. A sequence of numbers is *weakly decreasing* when each number in the sequence is at least as big as the numbers after it. Note that a sequence of just one number as well as a sequence of no numbers—the empty sequence—is weakly decreasing by this definition.

Theorem 9.4.1. *[Fundamental Theorem of Arithmetic] Every positive integer is a product of a* unique *weakly decreasing sequence of primes.*

A Prime for Google

In late 2004 a billboard appeared in various locations around the country:

$$\left\{ \begin{array}{l} \text{first 10-digit prime found} \\ \text{in consecutive digits of } e \end{array} \right\} \cdot \textbf{com}$$

Substituting the correct number for the expression in curly-braces produced the URL for a Google employment page. The idea was that Google was interested in hiring the sort of people that could and would solve such a problem.

How hard is this problem? Would you have to look through thousands or millions or billions of digits of e to find a 10-digit prime? The rule of thumb derived from the Prime Number Theorem says that among 10-digit numbers, about 1 in

$$\ln 10^{10} \approx 23$$

is prime. This suggests that the problem isn't really so hard! Sure enough, the first 10-digit prime in consecutive digits of e appears quite early:

$e =$2.7182818284590452353602874713526624977572470936999595749669676277240766303535475945713821785251664274274663919320030599218174135966290435729003342952605956307381323286279434...

For example, 75237393 is the product of the weakly decreasing sequence of primes

$$23, 17, 17, 11, 7, 7, 7, 3,$$

and no other weakly decreasing sequence of primes will give 75237393.[8]

Notice that the theorem would be false if 1 were considered a prime; for example, 15 could be written as $5 \cdot 3$, or $5 \cdot 3 \cdot 1$, or $5 \cdot 3 \cdot 1 \cdot 1, \ldots$.

There is a certain wonder in unique factorization, especially in view of the prime number mysteries we've already mentioned. It's a mistake to take it for granted, even if you've known it since you were in a crib. In fact, unique factorization actually fails for many integer-like sets of numbers, such as the complex numbers of the form $n + m\sqrt{-5}$ for $m, n \in \mathbb{Z}$ (see Problem 9.25).

The Fundamental Theorem is also called the *Unique Factorization Theorem*, which is a more descriptive and less pretentious, name—but we really want to get your attention to the importance and non-obviousness of unique factorization.

9.4.1 Proving Unique Factorization

The Fundamental Theorem is not hard to prove, but we'll need a couple of preliminary facts.

Lemma 9.4.2. *If p is a prime and $p \mid ab$, then $p \mid a$ or $p \mid b$.*

Lemma 9.4.2 follows immediately from Unique Factorization: the primes in the product ab are exactly the primes from a and from b. But proving the lemma this way would be cheating: we're going to need this lemma to prove Unique Factorization, so it would be circular to assume it. Instead, we'll use the properties of gcd's and linear combinations to give an easy, noncircular way to prove Lemma 9.4.2.

Proof. One case is if $\gcd(a, p) = p$. Then the claim holds, because a is a multiple of p.

Otherwise, $\gcd(a, p) \neq p$. In this case $\gcd(a, p)$ must be 1, since 1 and p are the only positive divisors of p. Now $\gcd(a, p)$ is a linear combination of a and p, so we have $1 = sa + tp$ for some s, t. Then $b = s(ab) + (tb)p$, that is, b is a linear combination of ab and p. Since p divides both ab and p, it also divides their linear combination b. ∎

A routine induction argument extends this statement to:

---

[8]The "product" of just one number is defined to be that number, and the product of no numbers is by convention defined to be 1. So each prime p is uniquely the product of the primes in the length-one sequence consisting solely of p, and 1, which you will remember is not a prime, is uniquely the product of the empty sequence.

Lemma 9.4.3. *Let p be a prime. If $p \mid a_1 a_2 \cdots a_n$, then p divides some a_i.*

Now we're ready to prove the Fundamental Theorem of Arithmetic.

Proof. Theorem 2.3.1 showed, using the Well Ordering Principle, that every positive integer can be expressed as a product of primes. So we just have to prove this expression is unique. We will use Well Ordering to prove this too.

The proof is by contradiction: assume, contrary to the claim, that there exist positive integers that can be written as products of primes in more than one way. By the Well Ordering Principle, there is a smallest integer with this property. Call this integer n, and let

$$n = p_1 \cdot p_2 \cdots p_j,$$
$$= q_1 \cdot q_2 \cdots q_k,$$

where both products are in weakly decreasing order and $p_1 \leq q_1$.

If $q_1 = p_1$, then n/q_1 would also be the product of different weakly decreasing sequences of primes, namely,

$$p_2 \cdots p_j,$$
$$q_2 \cdots q_k.$$

Since $n/q_1 < n$, this can't be true, so we conclude that $p_1 < q_1$.

Since the p_i's are weakly decreasing, all the p_i's are less than q_1. But

$$q_1 \mid n = p_1 \cdot p_2 \cdots p_j,$$

so Lemma 9.4.3 implies that q_1 divides one of the p_i's, which contradicts the fact that q_1 is bigger than all them.   ∎

9.5   Alan Turing

The man pictured in Figure 9.1 is Alan Turing, the most important figure in the history of computer science. For decades, his fascinating life story was shrouded by government secrecy, societal taboo, and even his own deceptions.

At age 24, Turing wrote a paper entitled *On Computable Numbers, with an Application to the Entscheidungsproblem.* The crux of the paper was an elegant way to model a computer in mathematical terms. This was a breakthrough, because it allowed the tools of mathematics to be brought to bear on questions of computation. For example, with his model in hand, Turing immediately proved that there exist

Figure 9.1 Alan Turing

problems that no computer can solve—no matter how ingenious the programmer. Turing's paper is all the more remarkable because he wrote it in 1936, a full decade before any electronic computer actually existed.

The word "Entscheidungsproblem" in the title refers to one of the 28 mathematical problems posed by David Hilbert in 1900 as challenges to mathematicians of the 20th century. Turing knocked that one off in the same paper. And perhaps you've heard of the "Church-Turing thesis"? Same paper. So Turing was a brilliant guy who generated lots of amazing ideas. But this lecture is about one of Turing's less-amazing ideas. It involved codes. It involved number theory. And it was sort of stupid.

Let's look back to the fall of 1937. Nazi Germany was rearming under Adolf Hitler, world-shattering war looked imminent, and—like us —Alan Turing was pondering the usefulness of number theory. He foresaw that preserving military secrets would be vital in the coming conflict and proposed a way *to encrypt communications using number theory*. This is an idea that has ricocheted up to our own time. Today, number theory is the basis for numerous public-key cryptosystems, digital signature schemes, cryptographic hash functions, and electronic payment systems. Furthermore, military funding agencies are among the biggest investors in cryptographic research. Sorry, Hardy!

Soon after devising his code, Turing disappeared from public view, and half a century would pass before the world learned the full story of where he'd gone and what he did there. We'll come back to Turing's life in a little while; for now, let's investigate the code Turing left behind. The details are uncertain, since he never formally published the idea, so we'll consider a couple of possibilities.

9.5.1   Turing's Code (Version 1.0)

The first challenge is to translate a text message into an integer so we can perform mathematical operations on it. This step is not intended to make a message harder to read, so the details are not too important. Here is one approach: replace each letter of the message with two digits ($A = 01$, $B = 02$, $C = 03$, etc.) and string all the digits together to form one huge number. For example, the message "victory" could be translated this way:

$$\begin{array}{ccccccc} \text{v} & \text{i} & \text{c} & \text{t} & \text{o} & \text{r} & \text{y} \\ \rightarrow \quad 22 & 09 & 03 & 20 & 15 & 18 & 25 \end{array}$$

Turing's code requires the message to be a prime number, so we may need to pad the result with some more digits to make a prime. The Prime Number Theorem indicates that padding with relatively few digits will work. In this case, appending the digits 13 gives the number 2209032015182513, which is prime.

Here is how the encryption process works. In the description below, m is the unencoded message (which we want to keep secret), $\widehat{m}$ is the encrypted message (which the Nazis may intercept), and k is the key.

Beforehand   The sender and receiver agree on a *secret key*, which is a large prime k.

Encryption   The sender encrypts the message m by computing:

$$\widehat{m} = m \cdot k$$

Decryption   The receiver decrypts $\widehat{m}$ by computing:

$$\frac{\widehat{m}}{k} = m.$$

For example, suppose that the secret key is the prime number $k = 22801763489$ and the message m is "victory." Then the encrypted message is:

$$\begin{aligned} \widehat{m} &= m \cdot k \\ &= 2209032015182513 \cdot 22801763489 \\ &= 50369825549820718594667857 \end{aligned}$$

There are a couple of basic questions to ask about Turing's code.

1. How can the sender and receiver ensure that m and k are prime numbers, as required?

   The general problem of determining whether a large number is prime or composite has been studied for centuries, and tests for primes that worked well in practice were known even in Turing's time. In the past few decades, very fast primality tests have been found as described in the text box below.

Primality Testing

It's easy to see that an integer n is prime iff it is not divisible by any number from 2 to $\lfloor \sqrt{n} \rfloor$ (see Problem 1.14). Of course this naive way to test if n is prime takes more than $\sqrt{n}$ steps, which is exponential in the *size* of n measured by the number of digits in the decimal or binary representation of n. Through the early 1970's, no prime testing procedure was known that would never blow up like this.

In 1974, Volker Strassen invented a simple, fast *probabilistic* primality test. Strassens's test gives the right answer when applied to any prime number, but has some probability of giving a wrong answer on a nonprime number. However, the probability of a wrong answer on any given number is so tiny that relying on the answer is the best bet you'll ever make.

Still, the theoretical possibility of a wrong answer was intellectually bothersome—even if the probability of being wrong was a lot less than the probability of an undetectable computer hardware error leading to a wrong answer. Finally in 2002, in a breakthrough paper beginning with a quote from Gauss emphasizing the importance and antiquity of primality testing, Manindra Agrawal, Neeraj Kayal, and Nitin Saxena presented an amazing, thirteen line description of a polynomial time primality test.

This definitively places primality testing way below the exponential effort apparently needed for SAT and similar problems. The polynomial bound on the Agrawal *et al.* test had degree 12, and subsequent research has reduced the degree to 5, but this is still too large to be practical, and probabilistic primality tests remain the method used in practice today. It's plausible that the degree bound can be reduced a bit more, but matching the speed of the known probabilistic tests remains a daunting challenge.

---

2. Is Turing's code secure?

   The Nazis see only the encrypted message $\widehat{m} = m \cdot k$, so recovering the original message m requires factoring $\widehat{m}$. Despite immense efforts, no really efficient factoring algorithm has ever been found. It appears to be a fundamentally difficult problem. So, although a breakthrough someday can't be ruled out, the conjecture that there is no efficient way to factor is widely accepted. In effect, Turing's code puts to practical use his discovery that there are limits to the power of computation. Thus, provided m and k are sufficiently large, the Nazis seem to be out of luck!

This all sounds promising, but there is a major flaw in Turing's code.

9.5.2   Breaking Turing's Code (Version 1.0)

Let's consider what happens when the sender transmits a *second* message using Turing's code and the same key. This gives the Nazis two encrypted messages to look at:

$$\widehat{m_1} = m_1 \cdot k \qquad \text{and} \qquad \widehat{m_2} = m_2 \cdot k$$

The greatest common divisor of the two encrypted messages, $\widehat{m_1}$ and $\widehat{m_2}$, is the secret key k. And, as we've seen, the gcd of two numbers can be computed very efficiently. So after the second message is sent, the Nazis can recover the secret key and read *every* message!

A mathematician as brilliant as Turing is not likely to have overlooked such a glaring problem, and we can guess that he had a slightly different system in mind, one based on *modular* arithmetic.

9.6   Modular Arithmetic

On the first page of his masterpiece on number theory, *Disquisitiones Arithmeticae*, Gauss introduced the notion of "*congruence*." Now, Gauss is another guy who managed to cough up a half-decent idea every now and then, so let's take a look at this one. Gauss said that *a is congruent to b modulo n* iff $n \mid (a - b)$. This is written

$$a \equiv b \pmod{n}.$$

For example:

$$29 \equiv 15 \pmod{7} \quad \text{because } 7 \mid (29 - 15).$$

It's not useful to allow a modulus $n \le 1$, and so we will assume from now on that moduli are greater than 1.

There is a close connection between congruences and remainders:

Lemma 9.6.1 (Remainder).

$$a \equiv b \pmod{n} \quad \textit{iff} \quad \text{rem}(a, n) = \text{rem}(b, n).$$

Proof. By the Division Theorem 9.1.4, there exist unique pairs of integers q_1, r_1 and q_2, r_2 such that:

$$a = q_1 n + r_1$$
$$b = q_2 n + r_2,$$

where $r_1, r_2 \in [0..n)$. Subtracting the second equation from the first gives:

$$a - b = (q_1 - q_2)n + (r_1 - r_2),$$

where $r_1 - r_2$ is in the interval $(-n, n)$. Now $a \equiv b \pmod{n}$ if and only if n divides the left-hand side of this equation. This is true if and only if n divides the right-hand side, which holds if and only if $r_1 - r_2$ is a multiple of n. But the only multiple of n in $(-n, n)$ is 0, so $r_1 - r_2$ must in fact equal 0, that is, when $r_1 ::= \text{rem}(a, n) = r_2 ::= \text{rem}(b, n)$. ∎

So we can also see that

$$29 \equiv 15 \pmod{7} \quad \text{because rem}(29, 7) = 1 = \text{rem}(15, 7).$$

Notice that even though "(mod 7)" appears on the end, the $\equiv$ symbol isn't any more strongly associated with the 15 than with the 29. It would probably be clearer to write $29 \equiv_{\text{mod } 7} 15$, for example, but the notation with the modulus at the end is firmly entrenched, and we'll just live with it.

The Remainder Lemma 9.6.1 explains why the congruence relation has properties like an equality relation. In particular, the following properties[9] follow immediately:

Lemma 9.6.2.

$$a \equiv a \pmod{n} \qquad \text{(reflexivity)}$$
$$a \equiv b \text{ IFF } b \equiv a \pmod{n} \qquad \text{(symmetry)}$$
$$(a \equiv b \text{ AND } b \equiv c) \text{ IMPLIES } a \equiv c \pmod{n} \qquad \text{(transitivity)}$$

We'll make frequent use of another immediate corollary of the Remainder Lemma 9.6.1:

Corollary 9.6.3.
$$a \equiv \text{rem}(a, n) \pmod{n}$$

---

[9] Binary relations with these properties are called *equivalence relations*, see Section 10.10.

Still another way to think about congruence modulo n is that it *defines a partition of the integers into n sets so that congruent numbers are all in the same set.* For example, suppose that we're working modulo 3. Then we can partition the integers into 3 sets as follows:

$$\{ \ \ldots, \ -6, \ -3, \ 0, \ 3, \ 6, \ 9, \ \ldots \ \}$$
$$\{ \ \ldots, \ -5, \ -2, \ 1, \ 4, \ 7, \ 10, \ \ldots \ \}$$
$$\{ \ \ldots, \ -4, \ -1, \ 2, \ 5, \ 8, \ 11, \ \ldots \ \}$$

according to whether their remainders on division by 3 are 0, 1, or 2. The upshot is that when arithmetic is done modulo n, there are really only n different kinds of numbers to worry about, because there are only n possible remainders. In this sense, modular arithmetic is a simplification of ordinary arithmetic.

The next most useful fact about congruences is that they are *preserved* by addition and multiplication:

Lemma 9.6.4 (Congruence). *If $a \equiv b$ (mod n) and $c \equiv d$ (mod n), then*

$$a + c \equiv b + d \quad (\text{mod } n), \tag{9.7}$$

$$ac \equiv bd \quad (\text{mod } n). \tag{9.8}$$

Proof. Let's start with 9.7. Since $a \equiv b$ (mod n), we have by definition that $n \mid (b - a) = (b + c) - (a + c)$, so

$$a + c \equiv b + c \quad (\text{mod } n).$$

Since $c \equiv d$ (mod n), the same reasoning leads to

$$b + c \equiv b + d \quad (\text{mod } n).$$

Now transitivity (Lemma 9.6.2) gives

$$a + c \equiv b + d \quad (\text{mod } n).$$

The proof for 9.8 is virtually identical, using the fact that if n divides $(b - a)$, then it certainly also divides $(bc - ac)$.   ■

9.7   Remainder Arithmetic

The Congruence Lemma 9.6.1 says that two numbers are congruent iff their remainders are equal, so we can understand congruences by working out arithmetic with remainders. And if all we want is the remainder modulo n of a series of additions, multiplications, subtractions applied to some numbers, we can take remainders at every step so that the entire computation only involves number in the range $[0..n)$.

General Principle of Remainder Arithmetic

To find the remainder on division by n of the result of a series of additions and multiplications, applied to some integers

- replace each integer operand by its remainder on division by n,

- keep each result of an addition or multiplication in the range $[0..n)$ by immediately replacing any result outside that range by its remainder on division by n.

For example, suppose we want to find

$$\text{rem}((44427^{3456789} + 15555858^{5555})403^{6666666}, 36). \qquad (9.9)$$

This looks really daunting if you think about computing these large powers and then taking remainders. For example, the decimal representation of $44427^{3456789}$ has about 20 million digits, so we certainly don't want to go that route. But remembering that integer exponents specify a series of multiplications, we follow the General Principle and replace the numbers being multiplied by their remainders. Since $\text{rem}(44427, 36) = 3, \text{rem}(15555858, 36) = 6$, and $\text{rem}(403, 36) = 7$, we find that (9.9) equals the remainder on division by 36 of

$$(3^{3456789} + 6^{5555})7^{6666666}. \qquad (9.10)$$

That's a little better, but $3^{3456789}$ has about a million digits in its decimal representation, so we still don't want to compute that. But let's look at the remainders of the first few powers of 3:

$$\text{rem}(3, 36) = 3$$
$$\text{rem}(3^2, 36) = 9$$
$$\text{rem}(3^3, 36) = 27$$
$$\text{rem}(3^4, 36) = 9.$$

We got a repeat of the second step, $\text{rem}(3^2, 36)$ after just two more steps. This means means that starting at 3^2, the sequence of remainders of successive powers of 3 will keep repeating every 2 steps. So a product of an odd number of at least three 3's will have the same remainder on division by 36 as a product of just three 3's. Therefore,

$$\text{rem}(3^{3456789}, 36) = \text{rem}(3^3, 36) = 27.$$

What a win!

Powers of 6 are even easier because $\text{rem}(6^2, 36) = 0$, so 0's keep repeating after the second step. Powers of 7 repeat after six steps, but on the fifth step you get a 1, that is $\text{rem}(7^6, 36) = 1$, so (9.10) successively simplifies to be the remainders of the following terms:

$$(3^{3456789} + 6^{5555})7^{6666666}$$
$$(3^3 + 6^2 \cdot 6^{5553})(7^6)^{1111111}$$
$$(3^3 + 0 \cdot 6^{5553})1^{1111111}$$
$$= 27.$$

Notice that *it would be a disastrous blunder to replace an exponent by its remainder.* The general principle applies to numbers that are *operands* of plus and times, whereas the exponent is a number that controls how many multiplications to perform. Watch out for this.

9.7.1   The ring $\mathbb{Z}_n$

It's time to be more precise about the general principle and why it works. To begin, let's introduce the notation $+_n$ for doing an addition and then immediately taking a remainder on division by n, as specified by the general principle; likewise for multiplying:

$$i +_n j ::= \text{rem}(i + j, n),$$
$$i \cdot_n j ::= \text{rem}(ij, n).$$

Now the General Principle is simply the repeated application of the following lemma.

Lemma 9.7.1.

$$\text{rem}(i + j, n) = \text{rem}(i, n) +_n \text{rem}(j, n), \qquad (9.11)$$
$$\text{rem}(ij, n) = \text{rem}(i, n) \cdot_n \text{rem}(j, n). \qquad (9.12)$$

Proof. By Corollary 9.6.3, $i \equiv \text{rem}(i, n)$ and $j \equiv \text{rem}(j, n)$, so by the Congruence Lemma 9.6.4

$$i + j \equiv \text{rem}(i, n) + \text{rem}(j, n) \pmod{n}.$$

By Corollary 9.6.3 again, the remainders on each side of this congruence are equal, which immediately gives (9.11). An identical proof applies to (9.12). ∎

The set of integers in the range $[0..n)$ together with the operations $+_n$ and $\cdot_n$ is referred to as $\mathbb{Z}_n$, the *ring of integers modulo n*. As a consequence of Lemma 9.7.1, the familiar rules of arithmetic hold in $\mathbb{Z}_n$, for example:

$$(i \cdot_n j) \cdot_n k = i \cdot_n (j \cdot_n k).$$

These subscript-n's on arithmetic operations really clog things up, so instead we'll just write "$(\mathbb{Z}_n)$" on the side to get a simpler looking equation:

$$(i \cdot j) \cdot k = i \cdot (j \cdot k) \quad (\mathbb{Z}_n).$$

In particular, all of the following equalities[10] are true in $\mathbb{Z}_n$:

$$
\begin{aligned}
(i \cdot j) \cdot k &= i \cdot (j \cdot k) & \text{(associativity of $\cdot$)}, \\
(i + j) + k &= i + (j + k) & \text{(associativity of $+$)}, \\
1 \cdot k &= k & \text{(identity for $\cdot$)}, \\
0 + k &= k & \text{(identity for $+$)}, \\
k + (-k) &= 0 & \text{(inverse for $+$)}, \\
i + j &= j + i & \text{(commutativity of $+$)} \\
i \cdot (j + k) &= (i \cdot j) + (i \cdot k) & \text{(distributivity)}, \\
i \cdot j &= j \cdot i & \text{(commutativity of $\cdot$)}
\end{aligned}
$$

Associativity implies the familiar fact that it's safe to omit the parentheses in products:

$$k_1 \cdot k_2 \cdots k_m$$

comes out the same in $\mathbb{Z}_n$ no matter how it is parenthesized.

The overall theme is that remainder arithmetic is a lot like ordinary arithmetic. But there are a couple of exceptions we're about to examine.

9.8 Turing's Code (Version 2.0)

In 1940, France had fallen before Hitler's army, and Britain stood alone against the Nazis in western Europe. British resistance depended on a steady flow of sup-

---

[10] A set with addition and multiplication operations that satisfy these equalities is known as a *commutative ring*. In addition to $\mathbb{Z}_n$, the integers, rationals, reals, and polynomials with integer coefficients are all examples of commutative rings. On the other hand, the set $\{\mathbf{T}, \mathbf{F}\}$ of truth values with OR for addition and AND for multiplication is *not* a commutative ring because it fails to satisfy one of these equalities. The $n \times n$ matrices of integers are not a commutative ring because they fail to satisfy another one of these equalities.

plies brought across the north Atlantic from the United States by convoys of ships. These convoys were engaged in a cat-and-mouse game with German "U-boats" —submarines—which prowled the Atlantic, trying to sink supply ships and starve Britain into submission. The outcome of this struggle pivoted on a balance of information: could the Germans locate convoys better than the Allies could locate U-boats, or vice versa?

Germany lost.

A critical reason behind Germany's loss was not made public until 1974: Germany's naval code, *Enigma*, had been broken by the Polish Cipher Bureau,[11] and the secret had been turned over to the British a few weeks before the Nazi invasion of Poland in 1939. Throughout much of the war, the Allies were able to route convoys around German submarines by listening in to German communications. The British government didn't explain *how* Enigma was broken until 1996. When the story was finally released (by the US), it revealed that Alan Turing had joined the secret British codebreaking effort at Bletchley Park in 1939, where he became the lead developer of methods for rapid, bulk decryption of German Enigma messages. Turing's Enigma deciphering was an invaluable contribution to the Allied victory over Hitler.

Governments are always tight-lipped about cryptography, but the half-century of official silence about Turing's role in breaking Enigma and saving Britain may be related to some disturbing events after the war—more on that later. Let's get back to number theory and consider an alternative interpretation of Turing's code. Perhaps we had the basic idea right (multiply the message by the key), but erred in using *conventional* arithmetic instead of *modular* arithmetic. Maybe this is what Turing meant:

Beforehand The sender and receiver agree on a large number n, which may be made public. (This will be the modulus for all our arithmetic.) As in Version 1.0, they also agree that some prime number $k < n$ will be the secret key.

Encryption As in Version 1.0, the message m should be another prime in $[0..n)$. The sender encrypts the message m to produce $\widehat{m}$ by computing mk, but this time modulo n:

$$\widehat{m} ::= m \cdot k \ (\mathbb{Z}_n) \tag{9.13}$$

Decryption (Uh-oh.)

The decryption step is a problem. We might hope to decrypt in the same way as before by dividing the encrypted message $\widehat{m}$ by the key k. The difficulty is that $\widehat{m}$

---

[11] See http://en.wikipedia.org/wiki/Polish_Cipher_Bureau.

is the *remainder* when mk is divided by n. So dividing $\widehat{m}$ by k might not even give us an integer!

This decoding difficulty can be overcome with a better understanding of when it is ok to divide by k in modular arithmetic.

9.9 Multiplicative Inverses and Cancelling

The *multiplicative inverse* of a number x is another number x^{-1} such that

$$x^{-1} \cdot x = 1.$$

From now on, when we say "inverse," we mean *multiplicative* (not relational) inverse.

For example, over the rational numbers, $1/3$ is, of course, an inverse of 3, since,

$$\frac{1}{3} \cdot 3 = 1.$$

In fact, with the sole exception of 0, every rational number n/m has an inverse, namely, m/n. On the other hand, over the integers, only 1 and -1 have inverses. Over the ring $\mathbb{Z}_n$, things get a little more complicated. For example, 2 is a multiplicative inverse of 8 in $\mathbb{Z}_{15}$, since

$$2 \cdot 8 = 1 \ (\mathbb{Z}_{15}).$$

On the other hand, 3 does not have a multiplicative inverse in $\mathbb{Z}_{15}$. We can prove this by contradiction: suppose there was an inverse j for 3, that is

$$1 = 3 \cdot j \ (\mathbb{Z}_{15}).$$

Then multiplying both sides of this equality by 5 leads directly to the contradiction $5 = 0$:

$$
\begin{aligned}
5 &= 5 \cdot (3 \cdot j) \\
&= (5 \cdot 3) \cdot j \\
&= 0 \cdot j = 0 \ (\mathbb{Z}_{15}).
\end{aligned}
$$

So there can't be any such inverse j.

So some numbers have inverses modulo 15 and others don't. This may seem a little unsettling at first, but there's a simple explanation of what's going on.

9.9.1   Relative Primality

Integers that have no prime factor in common are called *relatively prime*.[12] This is the same as having no common divisor (prime or not) greater than 1. It's also equivalent to saying $\gcd(a, b) = 1$.

For example, 8 and 15 are relatively prime, since $\gcd(8, 15) = 1$. On the other hand, 3 and 15 are not relatively prime, since $\gcd(3, 15) = 3 \neq 1$. This turns out to explain why 8 has an inverse over $\mathbb{Z}_{15}$ and 3 does not.

Lemma 9.9.1. *If $k \in [0..n)$ is relatively prime to n, then k has an inverse in $\mathbb{Z}_n$.*

Proof. If k is relatively prime to n, then $\gcd(n, k) = 1$ by definition of gcd. This means we can use the Pulverizer from section 9.2.2 to find a linear combination of n and k equal to 1:

$$sn + tk = 1.$$

So applying the General Principle of Remainder Arithmetic (Lemma 9.7.1), we get

$$(\text{rem}(s,\ n) \cdot \text{rem}(n,\ n)) + (\text{rem}(t,\ n) \cdot \text{rem}(k,\ n)) = 1 \ (\mathbb{Z}_n).$$

But $\text{rem}(n,\ n) = 0$, and $\text{rem}(k,\ n) = k$ since $k \in [0..n)$, so we get

$$\text{rem}(t,\ n) \cdot k = 1 \ (\mathbb{Z}_n).$$

Thus, $\text{rem}(t,\ n)$ is a multiplicative inverse of k. ∎

By the way, it's nice to know that when they exist, inverses are unique. That is,

Lemma 9.9.2. *If i and j are both inverses of k in $\mathbb{Z}_n$, then $i = j$.*

Proof.

$$i = i \cdot 1 = i \cdot (k \cdot j) = (i \cdot k) \cdot j = 1 \cdot j = j \ (\mathbb{Z}_n).$$

∎

So the proof of Lemma 9.9.1 shows that for any k relatively prime to n, the inverse of k in $\mathbb{Z}_n$ is simply the remainder of a coefficient we can easily find using the Pulverizer.

Working with a prime modulus is attractive here because, like the rational and real numbers, when p is prime, every nonzero number has an inverse in $\mathbb{Z}_p$. But arithmetic modulo a composite is really only a little more painful than working modulo a prime—though you may think this is like the doctor saying, "This is only going to hurt a little," before he jams a big needle in your arm.

---

[12]Other texts call them *coprime*.

9.9.2 Cancellation

Another sense in which real numbers are nice is that it's ok to cancel common factors. In other words, if we know that $tr = ts$ for real numbers r, s, t, then as long as $t \neq 0$, we can cancel the t's and conclude that $r = s$. In general, cancellation is *not* valid in $\mathbb{Z}_n$. For example,

$$3 \cdot 10 = 3 \cdot 5 \ (\mathbb{Z}_{15}), \tag{9.14}$$

but cancelling the 3's leads to the absurd conclusion that 10 equals 5.

The fact that multiplicative terms cannot be cancelled is the most significant way in which $\mathbb{Z}_n$ arithmetic differs from ordinary integer arithmetic.

Definition 9.9.3. A number k is *cancellable* in $\mathbb{Z}_n$ iff

$$k \cdot a = k \cdot b \quad \text{implies} \quad a = b \ (\mathbb{Z}_n)$$

for all $a, b \in [0..n)$.

If a number is relatively prime to 15, it can be cancelled by multiplying by its inverse. So cancelling works for numbers that have inverses:

Lemma 9.9.4. *If k has an inverse in $\mathbb{Z}_n$, then it is cancellable.*

But 3 is not relatively prime to 15, and that's why it is not cancellable. More generally, if k is not relatively prime to n, then we can show it isn't cancellable in $\mathbb{Z}_n$ in the same way we showed that 3 is not cancellable in (9.14).

To summarize, we have

Theorem 9.9.5. *The following are equivalent for $k \in [0..n)$:*

$$\gcd(k, n) = 1,$$
$$k \text{ has an inverse in } \mathbb{Z}_n,$$
$$k \text{ is cancellable in } \mathbb{Z}_n.$$

9.9.3 Decrypting (Version 2.0)

Multiplicative inverses are the key to decryption in Turing's code. Specifically, we can recover the original message by multiplying the encoded message by the $\mathbb{Z}_n$-inverse j of the key:

$$\widehat{m} \cdot j = (m \cdot k) \cdot j = m \cdot (k \cdot j) = m \cdot 1 = m \ (\mathbb{Z}_n).$$

So all we need to decrypt the message is to find an inverse of the secret key k, which will be easy using the Pulverizer—providing k has an inverse. But k is positive and less than the modulus n, so one simple way to ensure that k is relatively prime to the modulus is to have n be a prime number.

9.9.4   Breaking Turing's Code (Version 2.0)

The Germans didn't bother to encrypt their weather reports with the highly-secure Enigma system. After all, so what if the Allies learned that there was rain off the south coast of Iceland? But amazingly, this practice provided the British with a critical edge in the Atlantic naval battle during 1941.

The problem was that some of those weather reports had originally been transmitted using Enigma from U-boats out in the Atlantic. Thus, the British obtained both unencrypted reports and the same reports encrypted with Enigma. By comparing the two, the British were able to determine which key the Germans were using that day and could read all other Enigma-encoded traffic. Today, this would be called a *known-plaintext attack*.

Let's see how a known-plaintext attack would work against Turing's code. Suppose that the Nazis know both the plain text m and its

$$\widehat{m} = m \cdot k \ (\mathbb{Z}_n),$$

and since m is positive and less than the prime n, the Nazis can use the Pulverizer to find the $\mathbb{Z}_n$-inverse j of m. Now

$$j \cdot \widehat{m} = j \cdot (m \cdot k) = (j \cdot m) \cdot k = 1 \cdot k = k \ (\mathbb{Z}_n).$$

So by computing $j \cdot \widehat{m} = k \ (\mathbb{Z}_n)$, the Nazis get the secret key and can then decrypt any message!

This is a huge vulnerability, so Turing's hypothetical Version 2.0 code has no practical value. Fortunately, Turing got better at cryptography after devising this code; his subsequent deciphering of Enigma messages surely saved thousands of lives, if not the whole of Britain.

9.9.5   Turing Postscript

A few years after the war, Turing's home was robbed. Detectives soon determined that a former homosexual lover of Turing's had conspired in the robbery. So they arrested him—that is, they arrested Alan Turing—because at that time in Britain, homosexuality was a crime punishable by up to two years in prison. Turing was sentenced to a hormonal "treatment" for his homosexuality: he was given estrogen injections. He began to develop breasts.

Three years later, Alan Turing, the founder of computer science, was dead. His mother explained what happened in a biography of her own son. Despite her repeated warnings, Turing carried out chemistry experiments in his own home. Apparently, her worst fear was realized: by working with potassium cyanide while eating an apple, he poisoned himself.

However, Turing remained a puzzle to the very end. His mother was a devout woman who considered suicide a sin. And, other biographers have pointed out, Turing had previously discussed committing suicide by eating a poisoned apple. Evidently, Alan Turing, who founded computer science and saved his country, took his own life in the end, and in just such a way that his mother could believe it was an accident.

Turing's last project before he disappeared from public view in 1939 involved the construction of an elaborate mechanical device to test a mathematical conjecture called the Riemann Hypothesis. This conjecture first appeared in a sketchy paper by Bernhard Riemann in 1859 and is now one of the most famous unsolved problems in mathematics.

9.10   Euler's Theorem

The RSA cryptosystem examined in the next section, and other current schemes for encoding secret messages, involve computing remainders of numbers raised to large powers. A basic fact about remainders of powers follows from a theorem due to Euler about congruences.

Definition 9.10.1. For $n > 0$, define[13]

$$\phi(n) ::= \text{the number of integers in } [0..n), \text{ that are relatively prime to } n.$$

This function ϕ is known as Euler's ϕ function.[14]

¡For example, $\phi(7) = 6$ because all 6 positive numbers in $[0..7)$ are relatively prime to the prime number 7. Only 0 is not relatively prime to 7. Also, $\phi(12) = 4$ since 1, 5, 7, and 11 are the only numbers in $[0..12)$ that are relatively prime to 12.

More generally, if p is prime, then $\phi(p) = p - 1$ since every positive number in $[0..p)$ is relatively prime to p. When n is composite, however, the ϕ function gets a little complicated. We'll get back to it in the next section.

Euler's Theorem is traditionally stated in terms of congruence:

Theorem (*Euler's Theorem*). *If n and k are relatively prime, then*

$$k^{\phi(n)} \equiv 1 \pmod{n}. \tag{9.15}$$

---

[13]Since 0 is not relatively prime to anything, $\phi(n)$ could equivalently be defined using the interval $(0..n)$ instead of $[0..n)$.

[14]Some texts call it Euler's *totient function*.

The Riemann Hypothesis

The formula for the sum of an infinite geometric series says:

$$1 + x + x^2 + x^3 + \cdots = \frac{1}{1-x}.$$

Substituting $x = \frac{1}{2^s}$, $x = \frac{1}{3^s}$, $x = \frac{1}{5^s}$, and so on for each prime number gives a sequence of equations:

$$1 + \frac{1}{2^s} + \frac{1}{2^{2s}} + \frac{1}{2^{3s}} + \cdots = \frac{1}{1 - 1/2^s}$$

$$1 + \frac{1}{3^s} + \frac{1}{3^{2s}} + \frac{1}{3^{3s}} + \cdots = \frac{1}{1 - 1/3^s}$$

$$1 + \frac{1}{5^s} + \frac{1}{5^{2s}} + \frac{1}{5^{3s}} + \cdots = \frac{1}{1 - 1/5^s}$$

$$\vdots$$

Multiplying together all the left-hand sides and all the right-hand sides gives:

$$\sum_{n=1}^{\infty} \frac{1}{n^s} = \prod_{p \in \text{primes}} \left(\frac{1}{1 - 1/p^s} \right).$$

The sum on the left is obtained by multiplying out all the infinite series and applying the Fundamental Theorem of Arithmetic. For example, the term $1/300^s$ in the sum is obtained by multiplying $1/2^{2s}$ from the first equation by $1/3^s$ in the second and $1/5^{2s}$ in the third. Riemann noted that every prime appears in the expression on the right. So he proposed to learn about the primes by studying the equivalent, but simpler expression on the left. In particular, he regarded s as a complex number and the left side as a function $\zeta(s)$. Riemann found that the distribution of primes is related to values of s for which $\zeta(s) = 0$, which led to his famous conjecture:

Definition 9.9.6. The *Riemann Hypothesis*: Every nontrivial zero of the zeta function $\zeta(s)$ lies on the line $s = 1/2 + ci$ in the complex plane.

A proof would immediately imply, among other things, a strong form of the Prime Number Theorem.

Researchers continue to work intensely to settle this conjecture, as they have for over a century. It is another of the Millennium Problems whose solver will earn $1,000,000 from the Clay Institute.

Things get simpler when we rephrase Euler's Theorem in terms of $\mathbb{Z}_n$.

Definition 9.10.2. Let $\mathbb{Z}_n^*$ be the integers in $(0..n)$, that are relatively prime to n:[15]

$$\mathbb{Z}_n^* ::= \{k \in (0..n) \mid \gcd(k, n) = 1\}. \tag{9.16}$$

Consequently,

$$\phi(n) = \left| \mathbb{Z}_n^* \right|.$$

Theorem 9.10.3 (Euler's Theorem for $\mathbb{Z}_n$). *For all* $k \in \mathbb{Z}_n^*$,

$$k^{\phi(n)} = 1 \ (\mathbb{Z}_n). \tag{9.17}$$

Theorem 9.10.3 will follow from two very easy lemmas.

Let's start by observing that $\mathbb{Z}_n^*$ is closed under multiplication in $\mathbb{Z}_n$:

Lemma 9.10.4. *If* $j, k \in \mathbb{Z}_n^*$, *then* $j \cdot_n k \in \mathbb{Z}_n^*$.

There are lots of easy ways to prove this (see Problem 9.67).

Definition 9.10.5. For any element k and subset S of $\mathbb{Z}_n$, let

$$kS ::= \{k \cdot_n s \mid s \in S\}.$$

Lemma 9.10.6. *If* $k \in \mathbb{Z}_n^*$ *and* $S \subseteq \mathbb{Z}_n$, *then*

$$|kS| = |S|.$$

Proof. Since $k \in \mathbb{Z}_n^*$, by Theorem 9.9.5 it is cancellable. Therefore,

$$[ks = kt \ (\mathbb{Z}_n)] \quad \text{implies} \quad s = t.$$

So mulitplying by k in $\mathbb{Z}_n$ maps all the elements of S to distinct elements of kS, which implies S and kS are the same size. ∎

Corollary 9.10.7. *If* $k \in \mathbb{Z}_n^*$, *then*

$$k\mathbb{Z}_n^* = \mathbb{Z}_n^*.$$

Proof. A product of elements in $\mathbb{Z}_n^*$ remains in $\mathbb{Z}_n^*$ by Lemma 9.10.4. So if $k \in \mathbb{Z}_n^*$, then $k\mathbb{Z}_n^* \subseteq \mathbb{Z}_n^*$. But by Lemma 9.10.6, $k\mathbb{Z}_n^*$ and $\mathbb{Z}_n^*$ are the same size, so they must be equal. ∎

Now we can complete the proof of Euler's Theorem 9.10.3 for $\mathbb{Z}_n$):

---

[15]Some other texts use the notation n^* for $\mathbb{Z}_n^*$.

Proof. Let

$$P ::= k_1 \cdot k_2 \cdots k_{\phi(n)} \ (\mathbb{Z}_n)$$

be the product in $\mathbb{Z}_n$ of all the numbers in $\mathbb{Z}_n^*$. Let

$$Q ::= (k \cdot k_1) \cdot (k \cdot k_2) \cdots (k \cdot k_{\phi(n)}) \ (\mathbb{Z}_n)$$

for some $k \in \mathbb{Z}_n^*$. Factoring out k's immediately gives

$$Q = k^{\phi(n)} P \ (\mathbb{Z}_n).$$

But Q is the same as the product of the numbers in $k\mathbb{Z}_n^*$, and $k\mathbb{Z}_n^* = \mathbb{Z}_n^*$, so we realize that Q is the product of the same numbers as P, just in a different order. Altogether, we have

$$P = Q = k^{\phi(n)} P \ (\mathbb{Z}_n).$$

Furthermore, $P \in \mathbb{Z}_n^*$ by Lemma 9.10.4, and so it can be cancelled from both sides of this equality, giving

$$1 = k^{\phi(n)} \ (\mathbb{Z}_n).$$

■

Euler's theorem offers another way to find inverses modulo n: if k is relatively prime to n, then $k^{\phi(n)-1}$ is a $\mathbb{Z}_n$-inverse of k, and we can compute this power of k efficiently using fast exponentiation. However, this approach requires computing $\phi(n)$. In the next section, we'll show that computing $\phi(n)$ is easy *if* we know the prime factorization of n. But we know that finding the factors of n is generally hard to do when n is large, and so the Pulverizer remains the best approach to computing inverses modulo n.

Fermat's Little Theorem

For the record, we mention a famous special case of Euler's Theorem that was known to Fermat a century earlier.

Corollary 9.10.8 (*Fermat's Little Theorem*). *Suppose p is a prime and k is not a multiple of p. Then*

$$k^{p-1} \equiv 1 \pmod{p}.$$

9.10.1   Computing Euler's ϕ Function

RSA works using arithmetic modulo the product of two large primes, so we begin with an elementary explanation of how to compute $\phi(pq)$ for primes p and q:

Lemma 9.10.9.

$$\phi(pq) = (p-1)(q-1)$$

for primes $p \neq q$.

Proof. Since p and q are prime, any number that is not relatively prime to pq must be a multiple of p or a multiple of q. Among the pq numbers in $[0..pq)$, there are precisely q multiples of p and p multiples of q. Since p and q are relatively prime, the only number in $[0..pq)$ that is a multiple of both p and q is 0. Hence, there are $p + q - 1$ numbers in $[0..pq)$ that are *not* relatively prime to n. This means that

$$\phi(pq) = pq - (p + q - 1)$$
$$= (p-1)(q-1),$$

as claimed.[16]   ∎

The following theorem provides a way to calculate $\phi(n)$ for arbitrary n.

Theorem 9.10.10.

(a) *If p is a prime, then $\phi(p^k) = p^k - p^{k-1}$ for $k \geq 1$.*

(b) *If a and b are relatively prime, then $\phi(ab) = \phi(a)\phi(b)$.*

Here's an example of using Theorem 9.10.10 to compute $\phi(300)$:

$$\begin{aligned}
\phi(300) &= \phi(2^2 \cdot 3 \cdot 5^2) \\
&= \phi(2^2) \cdot \phi(3) \cdot \phi(5^2) && \text{(by Theorem 9.10.10.(b))} \\
&= (2^2 - 2^1)(3^1 - 3^0)(5^2 - 5^1) && \text{(by Theorem 9.10.10.(a))} \\
&= 80.
\end{aligned}$$

Note that Lemma 9.10.9 also follows as a special case of Theorem 9.10.10.(b), since we know that $\phi(p) = p - 1$ for any prime p.

To prove Theorem 9.10.10.(a), notice that every pth number among the p^k numbers in $[0..p^k)$ is divisible by p, and only these are divisible by p. So $1/p$ of these numbers are divisible by p and the remaining ones are not. That is,

$$\phi(p^k) = p^k - (1/p)p^k = p^k - p^{k-1}.$$

We'll leave a proof of Theorem 9.10.10.(b) to Problem 9.61.

As a consequence of Theorem 9.10.10, we have

---

[16]This proof previews a kind of counting argument that we will explore more fully in Part III.

Corollary 9.10.11. *For any number n, if p_1, p_2, ..., p_j are the (distinct) prime factors of n, then*

$$\phi(n) = n \left(1 - \frac{1}{p_1}\right) \left(1 - \frac{1}{p_2}\right) \cdots \left(1 - \frac{1}{p_j}\right).$$

We'll give another proof of Corollary 9.10.11 based on rules for counting in Section 15.9.5.

9.11   RSA Public Key Encryption

Turing's code did not work as he hoped. However, his essential idea—using number theory as the basis for cryptography—succeeded spectacularly in the decades after his death.

In 1977, Ronald Rivest, Adi Shamir, and Leonard Adleman at MIT proposed a highly secure cryptosystem, called **RSA**, based on number theory. The purpose of the RSA scheme is to transmit secret messages over public communication channels. As with Turing's codes, the messages transmitted are nonnegative integers of some fixed size.

Moreover, RSA has a major advantage over traditional codes: the sender and receiver of an encrypted message need not meet beforehand to agree on a secret key. Rather, the receiver has both a *private key*, which they guard closely, and a *public key*, which they distribute as widely as possible. A sender wishing to transmit a secret message to the receiver encrypts their message using the receiver's widely-distributed public key. The receiver can then decrypt the received message using their closely held private key. The use of such a *public key cryptography* system allows you and Amazon, for example, to engage in a secure transaction without meeting up beforehand in a dark alley to exchange a key.

Interestingly, RSA does not operate modulo a prime, as Turing's hypothetical Version 2.0 may have, but rather modulo the product of *two* large primes—typically primes that are hundreds of digits long. Also, instead of encrypting by multiplication with a secret key, RSA exponentiates to a secret power—which is why Euler's Theorem is central to understanding RSA.

The scheme for RSA public key encryption appears in the box.

If the message m is relatively prime to n, then a simple application of Euler's Theorem implies that this way of decoding the encrypted message indeed reproduces the original unencrypted message. In fact, the decoding always works—even in (the highly unlikely) case that m is not relatively prime to n. The details are worked out in Problem 9.81.

The RSA Cryptosystem

A **Receiver** who wants to be able to receive secret numerical messages creates a *private key*, which they keep secret, and a *public key*, which they make publicly available. Anyone with the public key can then be a **Sender** who can publicly send secret messages to the **Receiver**—even if they have never communicated or shared any information besides the public key.
Here is how they do it:

Beforehand The **Receiver** creates a public key and a private key as follows.

1. Generate two distinct primes, p and q. These are used to generate the private key, and they must be kept hidden. (In current practice, p and q are chosen to be hundreds of digits long.)

2. Let $n ::= pq$.

3. Select an integer $e \in [0..n)$ such that $\gcd(e, (p-1)(q-1)) = 1$. The *public key* is the pair (e, n). This should be distributed widely.

4. Let the *private key* $d \in [0..n)$ be the inverse of e in the ring $\mathbb{Z}_{(p-1)(q-1)}$. This private key can be found using the Pulverizer. The private key d should be kept hidden!

Encoding To transmit a message $m \in [0..n)$ to **Receiver**, a **Sender** uses the public key to encrypt m into a numerical message

$$\widehat{m} ::= m^e \ (\mathbb{Z}_n).$$

The **Sender** can then publicly transmit $\widehat{m}$ to the **Receiver**.

Decoding The **Receiver** decrypts message $\widehat{m}$ back to message m using the private key:

$$m = \widehat{m}^d \ (\mathbb{Z}_n).$$

Why is RSA thought to be secure? It would be easy to figure out the private key d if you knew p and q—you could do it the same way the **Receiver** does using the Pulverizer. But assuming the conjecture that it is hopelessly hard to factor a number that is the product of two primes with hundreds of digits, an effort to factor n is not going to break RSA.

Could there be another approach to reverse engineer the private key d from the public key that did not involve factoring n? Not really. It turns out that given just the private and the public keys, it is easy to factor n[17] (a proof of this is sketched in Problem 9.83). So if we are confident that factoring is hopelessly hard, then we can be equally confident that finding the private key just from the public key will be hopeless.

But even if we are confident that an RSA private key won't be found, this doesn't rule out the possibility of decoding RSA messages in a way that sidesteps the private key. It is an important unproven conjecture in cryptography that *any* way of cracking RSA—not just by finding the secret key—would imply the ability to factor. This would be a much stronger theoretical assurance of RSA security than is presently known.

But the real reason for confidence is that RSA has withstood all attacks by the world's most sophisticated cryptographers for nearly 40 years. Despite decades of these attacks, no significant weakness has been found. That's why the mathematical, financial, and intelligence communities are betting the family jewels on the security of RSA encryption.

You can hope that with more studying of number theory, you will be the first to figure out how to do factoring quickly and, among other things, break RSA. But be further warned that even Gauss worked on factoring for years without a lot to show for his efforts—and if you do figure it out, you might wind up meeting some humorless fellows working for a Federal agency in charge of security....

9.12   What has SAT got to do with it?

So why does society, or at least everybody's secret codes, fall apart if there is an efficient test for satisfiability (SAT), as we claimed in Section 3.5? To explain this, remember that RSA can be managed computationally because multiplication of two primes is fast, but factoring a product of two primes seems to be overwhelmingly demanding.

---

[17]In practice, for this reason, the public and private keys should be randomly chosen so that neither is "too small."

Let's begin with the observation from Section 3.2 that a digital circuit can be described by a bunch of propositional formulas of about the same total size as the circuit. So testing circuits for satisfiability is equivalent to the SAT problem for propositional formulas (see Problem 3.21).

Now designing digital multiplication circuits is completely routine. We can easily build a digital "product checker" circuit out of AND, OR, and NOT gates with 1 output wire and $4n$ digital input wires. The first n inputs are for the binary representation of an integer i, the next n inputs for the binary representation of an integer j, and the remaining $2n$ inputs for the binary representation of an integer k. The output of the circuit is 1 iff $ij = k$ and $i, j > 1$. A straightforward design for such a product checker uses proportional to n^2 gates.

Now here's how to factor any number m with a length $2n$ binary representation using a SAT solver. First, fix the last $2n$ digital inputs—the ones for the binary representation of k—so that k equals m.

Next, set the first of the n digital inputs for the representation of i to be 1. Do a SAT test to see if there is a satisfying assignment of values for the remaining $2n - 1$ inputs used for the i and j representations. That is, see if the remaining inputs for i and j can be filled in to cause the circuit to give output 1. If there is such an assignment, fix the first i-input to be 1, otherwise fix it to be 0. So now we have set the first i-input equal to the first digit of the binary representations of an i such that $ij = m$.

Now do the same thing to fix the second of the n digital inputs for the representation of i, and then third, proceeding in this way through all the n inputs for the number i. At this point, we have the complete n-bit binary representation of an $i > 1$ such $ij = m$ for some $j > 1$. In other words, we have found an integer i that is a factor of m. We can now find j by dividing m by i.

So after n SAT tests, we have factored m. This means that if SAT for digital circuits with $4n$ inputs and about n^2 gates could be determined by a procedure taking a number of steps bounded above by a degree d polynomial in n, then $2n$ digit numbers can be factored in n times this many steps, that is, with a number of steps bounded by a polynomial of degree $d + 1$ in n. So if SAT could be solved in polynomial time, then so could factoring, and consequently RSA would be "easy" to break.

9.13 References

[2], [42]

Problems for Section 9.1

Practice Problems

Problem 9.1.
Prove that a linear combination of linear combinations of integers $a_0, \ldots, a_n$ is a linear combination of $a_0, \ldots, a_n$.

Class Problems

Problem 9.2.
A number is *perfect* if it is equal to the sum of its positive divisors, other than itself. For example, 6 is perfect, because $6 = 1 + 2 + 3$. Similarly, 28 is perfect, because $28 = 1 + 2 + 4 + 7 + 14$. Explain why $2^{k-1}(2^k - 1)$ is perfect when $2^k - 1$ is prime.[18]

Problems for Section 9.2

Practice Problems

Problem 9.3.
Let

$$x ::= 21212121,$$
$$y ::= 12121212.$$

Use the Euclidean algorithm to find the GCD of x and y. *Hint:* Looks scary, but it's not.

Problem 9.4.

---

[18]Euclid proved this 2300 years ago. About 250 years ago, Euler proved the converse: *every* even perfect number is of this form (for a simple proof see http://primes.utm.edu/notes/proofs/EvenPerfect.html). It is not known if there are *any* odd perfect numbers at all. It is also not known if there are an infinite number of even perfect numbers. One of the charms of number theory is that simple results like those given in this problem lie at the brink of the unknown.

Let

$$x ::= 17^{88} \cdot 31^5 \cdot 37^2 \cdot 59^{1000}$$
$$y ::= 19^{(9^{22})} \cdot 37^{12} \cdot 53^{3678} \cdot 59^{29}.$$

(a) What is $\gcd(x, y)$?

(b) What is $\text{lcm}(x, y)$? ("lcm" is *least common multiple*.)

Problem 9.5.
Show that there is an integer x such that

$$ax \equiv b \pmod{n}$$

iff

$$\gcd(a, n) \mid b.$$

Problem 9.6.
Prove that
$$\gcd(a^5, b^5) = \gcd(a, b)^5$$
for all $a, b \in \mathbb{Z}$.

Class Problems

Problem 9.7.
Use the Euclidean Algorithm to prove that

$$\gcd(13a + 8b, 5a + 3b) = \gcd(a, b).$$

Problem 9.8.

(a) Use the Pulverizer to find integers x, y such that

$$x30 + y22 = \gcd(30, 22).$$

(b) Now find integers x', y' with $0 \le y' < 30$ such that

$$x'30 + y'22 = \gcd(30, 22)$$

Problem 9.9. (a) Use the Pulverizer to find $\gcd(84, 108)$

(b) Find integers x, y with $0 \leq y < 84$ such that

$$x \cdot 84 + y \cdot 108 = \gcd(84, 108).$$

(c) Is there a multiplicative inverse of 84 in $\mathbb{Z}_{108}$? If not briefly explain why, otherwise find it.

Problem 9.10.

Indicate true or false for the following statements about the greatest common divisor, and *provide counterexamples* for those that are false.

(a) If $\gcd(a, b) \neq 1$ and $\gcd(b, c) \neq 1$, then $\gcd(a, c) \neq 1$.   **true**   **false**

(b) If $a \mid bc$ and $\gcd(a, b) = 1$, then $a \mid c$.   **true**   **false**

(c) $\gcd(a^n, b^n) = (\gcd(a, b))^n$ **true**   **false**

(d) $\gcd(ab, ac) = a \gcd(b, c)$.   **true**   **false**

(e) $\gcd(1 + a, 1 + b) = 1 + \gcd(a, b)$.   **true**   **false**

(f) If an integer linear combination of a and b equals 1, then so does some integer linear combination of a and b^2.   **true**   **false**

(g) If no integer linear combination of a and b equals 2, then neither does any integer linear combination of a^2 and b^2.   **true**   **false**

Problem 9.11.
For nonzero integers a, b, prove the following properties of divisibility and GCD'S. You may use Theorem 9.2.2 that $\gcd(a, b)$ is an integer linear combination of a and b. You may *not* appeal to uniqueness of prime factorization Theorem 9.4.1, because some of these properties are needed to *prove* unique factorization.)

(a) Every common divisor of a and b divides $\gcd(a, b)$.

(b) $\gcd(ka, kb) = k \cdot \gcd(a, b)$ for all $k > 0$.

(c) If $a \mid bc$ and $\gcd(a, b) = 1$, then $a \mid c$.

(d) If $p \mid bc$ for some prime p then $p \mid b$ or $p \mid c$.

(e) Let m be the smallest integer linear combination of a and b that is positive. Show that $m = \gcd(a, b)$.

Homework Problems

Problem 9.12.

Here is a game you can analyze with number theory and always beat me. We start with two distinct, positive integers written on a blackboard. Call them a and b. Now we take turns. (I'll let you decide who goes first.) On each turn, the player must write a new positive integer on the board that is the difference of two numbers that are already there. If a player cannot play, then they lose.

For example, suppose that 12 and 15 are on the board initially. Your first play must be 3, which is $15 - 12$. Then I might play 9, which is $12 - 3$. Then you might play 6, which is $15 - 9$. Then I can't play, so I lose.

(a) Show that every number on the board at the end of the game is a multiple of $\gcd(a, b)$.

(b) Show that every positive multiple of $\gcd(a, b)$ up to $\max(a, b)$ is on the board at the end of the game.

(c) Describe a strategy that lets you win this game every time.

Problem 9.13.

Define the Pulverizer State machine to have:

$$\text{states} ::= \mathbb{N}^6$$

$$\text{start state} ::= (a, b, 0, 1, 1, 0) \qquad\qquad \text{(where } a \geq b > 0\text{)}$$

$$\text{transitions} ::= (x, y, s, t, u, v) \longrightarrow$$

$$(y, \text{rem}(x, y), u - sq, v - tq, s, t) \quad \text{(for } q = \text{qcnt}(x, y), y > 0\text{)}.$$

(a) Show that the following properties are preserved invariants of the Pulverizer machine:

$$\gcd(x, y) = \gcd(a, b), \qquad\qquad\qquad (\text{Inv1})$$
$$sa + tb = y, \text{ and} \qquad\qquad\qquad\qquad (\text{Inv2})$$
$$ua + vb = x. \qquad\qquad\qquad\qquad\qquad (\text{Inv3})$$

(b) Conclude that the Pulverizer machine is partially correct.

(c) Explain why the machine terminates after at most the same number of transitions as the Euclidean algorithm.

Problem 9.14.

Prove that the smallest positive integers $a \geq b$ for which, starting in state (a, b), the Euclidean state machine will make n transitions are $F(n + 1)$ and $F(n)$, where $F(n)$ is the nth Fibonacci number.

Hint: Induction.

In a later chapter, we'll show that $F(n) \leq \varphi^n$ where φ is the golden ratio $(1 + \sqrt{5})/2$. This implies that the Euclidean algorithm halts after at most $\log_\varphi(a)$ transitions. This is a somewhat smaller than the $2\log_2 a$ bound derived from equation (9.4).

Problem 9.15.

Let's extend the jug filling scenario of Section 9.1.3 to three jugs and a receptacle. Suppose the jugs can hold a, b and c gallons of water, respectively.

The receptacle can be used to store an unlimited amount of water, but has no measurement markings. Excess water can be dumped into the drain. Among the possible moves are:

1. fill a bucket from the hose,

2. pour from the receptacle to a bucket until the bucket is full or the receptacle is empty, whichever happens first,

3. empty a bucket to the drain,

4. empty a bucket to the receptacle, and

5. pour from one bucket to another until either the first is empty or the second is full.

(a) Model this scenario with a state machine. (What are the states? How does a state change in response to a move?)

(b) Prove that Bruce can get $k \in \mathbb{N}$ gallons of water into the receptacle using the above operations if $\gcd(a, b, c) \mid k$.

Problem 9.16.

The *Binary GCD* state machine computes the GCD of integers $a, b > 0$ using only division by 2 and subtraction, which makes it run very efficiently on hardware that uses binary representation of numbers. In practice, it runs more quickly than the more famous Euclidean algorithm described in Section 9.2.1.

$$\text{states}::=\mathbb{N}^3$$

$$\text{start state}::=(a, b, 1)$$

$$\text{transitions}::= \text{ if } \min(x, y) > 0, \text{ then } (x, y, e) \longrightarrow$$

$(x/2, y/2, 2e)$	(if $2 \mid x$ and $2 \mid y$)	(i1)
$(x/2, y, e)$	(else if $2 \mid x$)	(i2)
$(x, y/2, e)$	(else if $2 \mid y$)	(i3)
$(x - y, y, e)$	(else if $x > y$)	(i4)
$(y - x, x, e)$	(else if $y > x$)	(i5)
$(1, 0, ex)$	(otherwise ($x = y$)).	(i6)

(a) Use the Invariant Principle to prove that if this machine stops, that is, reaches a state (x, y, e) in which no transition is possible, then $e = \gcd(a, b)$.

(b) Prove that rule (i1)

$$(x, y, e) \rightarrow (x/2, y/2, 2e)$$

is never executed after any of the other rules is executed.

(c) Prove that the machine reaches a final state in at most $1 + 3(\log a + \log b)$ transitions. (This is a coarse bound; you may be able to get a better one.)

Problem 9.17.

Extend the binary gcd procedure of Problem 9.16 to obtain a new pulverizer that uses only division by 2 and subtraction.

Hint: After the binary gcd procedure has factored out 2's, it starts computing the $\gcd(a, b)$ for numbers a, b at least one of which is odd. It does this by successively updating a pair of numbers (x, y) such that $\gcd(x, y) = \gcd(a, b)$. Extend the procedure to find and update coefficients u_x, v_x, u_y, v_y such that

$$u_x a + v_x b = x \text{ and } u_y a + v_y b = y.$$

To see how to update the coefficients when at least one of a and b is odd and $ua + vb$ is even, show that either u and v are both even, or else $u - b$ and $v + a$ are both even.

Problem 9.18.

For any set A of integers,

$$\gcd(A) ::= \text{the greatest common divisor of the elements of } A.$$

The following useful property of gcd's of sets is easy to take for granted:

Theorem.

$$\gcd(A \cup B) = \gcd(\gcd(A), \gcd(B)), \qquad \text{(AuB)}$$

for all finite sets $A, B \subset \mathbb{Z}$.

The theorem has an easy proof as a Corollary of the Unique Factorization Theorem. In this problem we develop a proof by induction of Theorem (AuB) just making repeated use of Lemma 9.2.6.b :

$$(d \mid a \text{ AND } d \mid b) \text{ IFF } d \mid \gcd(a, b). \qquad \text{(gcddiv)}$$

The key to proving (AuB) will be generalizing (gcddiv) to finite sets.

Definition. For any subset $A \subseteq \mathbb{Z}$,

$$d \mid A ::= \forall a \in A. \, d \mid a. \qquad \text{(divdef)}$$

Lemma.

$$d \mid A \text{ IFF } d \mid \gcd(A). \qquad \text{(dAdgA)}$$

for all $d \in \mathbb{Z}$ and finite sets $A \subset \mathbb{Z}$.

(a) Prove that

$$\gcd(a, \gcd(b, c)) = \gcd(\gcd(a, b), c) \qquad \text{(gcd-associativity)}$$

for all integers a, b, c.

From here on we write "$a \cup A$" as an abbreviation for "$\{a\} \cup A$."

(b) Prove that

$$d \mid (a \cup b \cup C) \text{ IFF } d \mid (\gcd(a, b) \cup C) \qquad \text{(abCgcd)}$$

for all $a, b, d \in \mathbb{Z}$, and $C \subseteq \mathbb{Z}$.

Proof.

$$d \mid (a \cup b \cup C) \text{ IFF } (d \mid a) \text{ AND } (d \mid b) \text{ AND } (d \mid C) \quad \text{(def (divdef) of divides)}$$
$$\text{IFF } (d \mid \gcd(a,b)) \text{ AND } (d \mid C) \qquad \text{by (gcddiv)}$$
$$\text{IFF } d \mid (\gcd(a,b) \cup C) \qquad \text{(def (divdef) of divides).}$$

∎

(c) Using parts (a) and (b), prove by induction on the size of A, that

$$d \mid (a \cup A) \quad \text{IFF} \quad d \mid \gcd(a, \gcd(A)), \qquad \text{(divauA)}$$

for all integers a, d and finite sets $A \subset \mathbb{Z}$. Explain why this proves Lemma (dAdgA).

(d) Prove Theorem (AuB).

(e) Conclude that $\gcd(A)$ is an integer linear combination of the elements in A.

Exam Problems

Problem 9.19.
Prove that $\gcd(mb + r, b) = \gcd(b, r)$ for all integers m, b, r.

Problem 9.20.
The Stata Center's delicate balance depends on two buckets of water hidden in a secret room. The big bucket has a volume of 25 gallons, and the little bucket has a volume of 10 gallons. If at any time a bucket contains exactly 13 gallons, the Stata Center will collapse. There is an interactive display where tourists can remotely fill and empty the buckets according to certain rules. We represent the buckets as a state machine.

The state of the machine is a pair (b, l), where b is the volume of water in big bucket, and l is the volume of water in little bucket.

(a) We informally describe some of the legal operations tourists can perform below. Represent each of the following operations as a transition of the state machine. The first is done for you as an example.

1. Fill the big bucket.

$$(b, l) \longrightarrow (25, l).$$

2. Empty the little bucket.

3. Pour the big bucket into the little bucket. You should have two cases defined in terms of the state (b, l): if all the water from the big bucket fits in the little bucket, then pour all the water. If it doesn't, pour until the little jar is full, leaving some water remaining in the big jar.

(b) Use the Invariant Principle to show that, starting with empty buckets, the Stata Center will never collapse. That is, the state $(13, x)$ in unreachable. (In verifying your claim that the invariant is preserved, you may restrict to the representative transitions of part (a).)

Problem 9.21.

Let

$$m = 2^9 5^{24} 7^4 11^7,$$
$$n = 2^3 7^{22} 11^{211} 19^7,$$
$$p = 2^5 3^4 7^{6042} 19^{30}.$$

(a) What is the $\gcd(m, n, p)$?

(b) What is the *least common multiple* $\operatorname{lcm}(m, n, p)$?

Let $v_k(n)$ be the largest power of k that divides n, where $k > 1$. That is,

$$v_k(n) ::= \max\{i \mid k^i \text{ divides } n\}.$$

If A is a nonempty set of nonnegative integers, define

$$v_k(A) ::= \{v_k(a) \mid a \in A\}.$$

(c) Express $v_k(\gcd(A))$ in terms of $v_k(A)$.

(d) Let p be a prime number. Express $v_p(\operatorname{lcm}(A))$ in terms of $v_p(A)$.

(e) Give an example of integers a, b where $v_6(\operatorname{lcm}(a, b)) > \max(v_6(a), v_6(b))$.

(f) Let $\prod A$ be the product of all the elements in A. Express $v_p(n)(\prod A)$ in terms of $v_p(A)$.

(g) Let B also be a nonempty set of nonnegative integers. Conclude that

$$\gcd(A \cup B) = \gcd(\gcd(A), \gcd(B)). \qquad (9.18)$$

Hint: Consider $v_p()$ of the left and right-hand sides of (9.18). You may assume

$$\min(A \cup B) = \min(\min(A), \min(B)). \qquad (9.19)$$

Problems for Section 9.3

Homework Problems

Problem 9.22.
TBA: Chebyshvev lower bound in prime density, based on Shoup pp.75–76

Problems for Section 9.4

Practice Problems

Problem 9.23.
Let p be a prime number and $a_1, \ldots, a_n$ integers. Prove the following Lemma *by induction*:

Lemma.

$$\text{If } p \text{ divides a product } a_1 \cdot a_2 \cdots a_n, \text{ then } p \text{ divides some } a_i. \qquad (*)$$

You may assume the case for $n = 2$ which was given by Lemma 9.4.2.

Be sure to clearly state and label your Induction Hypothesis, Base case(s), and Induction step.

Class Problems

Problem 9.24. (a) Let $m = 2^9 5^{24} 11^7 17^{12}$ and $n = 2^3 7^{22} 11^{211} 13^1 17^9 19^2$. What is the $\gcd(m, n)$? What is the *least common multiple* $\text{lcm}(m, n)$ of m and n? Verify that

$$\gcd(m, n) \cdot \text{lcm}(m, n) = mn. \qquad (9.20)$$

(b) Describe in general how to find the $\gcd(m, n)$ and $\text{lcm}(m, n)$ from the prime factorizations of m and n. Conclude that equation (9.20) holds for all positive integers m, n.

Homework Problems

Problem 9.25.
The set of complex numbers that are equal to $m + n\sqrt{-5}$ for some integers m, n is called $\mathbb{Z}[\sqrt{-5}]$. It will turn out that in $\mathbb{Z}[\sqrt{-5}]$, not all numbers have unique factorizations.

A sum or product of numbers in $\mathbb{Z}[\sqrt{-5}]$ is in $\mathbb{Z}[\sqrt{-5}]$, and since $\mathbb{Z}[\sqrt{-5}]$ is a subset of the complex numbers, all the usual rules for addition and multiplication are true for it. But some weird things do happen. For example, the prime 29 has factors:

   (a) Find $x, y \in \mathbb{Z}[\sqrt{-5}]$ such that $xy = 29$ and $x \neq \pm 1 \neq y$.

   On the other hand, the number 3 is still a "prime" even in $\mathbb{Z}[\sqrt{-5}]$. More precisely, a number $p \in \mathbb{Z}[\sqrt{-5}]$ is called *irreducible* over $\mathbb{Z}[\sqrt{-5}]$ iff when $xy = p$ for some $x, y \in \mathbb{Z}[\sqrt{-5}]$, either $x = \pm 1$ or $y = \pm 1$.

Claim. *The numbers* $3, 2 + \sqrt{-5}$, *and* $2 - \sqrt{-5}$ *are irreducible over* $\mathbb{Z}[\sqrt{-5}]$.

   In particular, this Claim implies that the number 9 factors into irreducibles over $\mathbb{Z}[\sqrt{-5}]$ in two different ways:

$$3 \cdot 3 = 9 = (2 + \sqrt{-5})(2 - \sqrt{-5}).$$

So $\mathbb{Z}[\sqrt{-5}]$ is an example of what is called a *non-unique factorization* domain.

   To verify the Claim, we'll appeal (without proof) to a familiar technical property of complex numbers given in the following Lemma.

Definition. For a complex number $c = r + si$ where $r, s \in \mathbb{R}$ and i is $\sqrt{-1}$, the *norm* $|c|$ of c is $\sqrt{r^2 + s^2}$.

Lemma. *For* $c, d \in \mathbb{C}$,

$$|cd| = |c| \, |d|.$$

   (b) Prove that $|x|^2 \neq 3$ for all $x \in \mathbb{Z}[\sqrt{-5}]$.

   (c) Prove that if $x \in \mathbb{Z}[\sqrt{-5}]$ and $|x| = 1$, then $x = \pm 1$.

   (d) Prove that if $|xy| = 3$ for some $x, y \in \mathbb{Z}[\sqrt{-5}]$, then $x = \pm 1$ or $y = \pm 1$.
Hint: $|z|^2 \in \mathbb{N}$ for $z \in \mathbb{Z}[\sqrt{-5}]$.

   (e) Complete the proof of the Claim.

Problems for Section 9.6

Practice Problems

Problem 9.26.
Prove that if $a \equiv b \pmod{14}$ and $a \equiv b \pmod 5$, then $a \equiv b \pmod{70}$.

Class Problems

Problem 9.27. (a) Prove if n is not divisible by 3, then $n^2 \equiv 1 \pmod 3$.

(b) Show that if n is odd, then $n^2 \equiv 1 \pmod 8$.

(c) Conclude that if p is a prime greater than 3, then $p^2 - 1$ is divisible by 24.

Problem 9.28.
The values of polynomial $p(n) ::= n^2 + n + 41$ are prime for all the integers from 0 to 39 (see Section 1.1). Well, p didn't work, but are there any other polynomials whose values are always prime? No way! In fact, we'll prove a much stronger claim.

Definition. The set P of integer polynomials can be defined recursively:

Base cases:

- the identity function $\mathrm{Id}_{\mathbb{Z}}(x) ::= x$ is in P.

- for any integer m the constant function $c_m(x) ::= m$ is in P.

Constructor cases. If $r, s \in P$, then $r + s$ and $r \cdot s \in P$.

(a) Using the recursive definition of integer polynomials given above, prove by structural induction that for all $q \in P$,

$$j \equiv k \pmod n \quad \text{IMPLIES} \quad q(j) \equiv q(k) \pmod n,$$

for all integers j, k, n where $n > 1$.

Be sure to clearly state and label your Induction Hypothesis, Base case(s), and Constructor step.

(b) We'll say that q *produces multiples* if, for every integer greater than one in the range of q, there are infinitely many different multiples of that integer in the range. For example, if $q(4) = 7$ and q produces multiples, then there are infinitely many different multiples of 7 in the range of q, and of course, except for 7 itself, none of these multiples is prime.

Prove that if q has positive degree and positive leading coefficient, then q produces multiples. You may assume that every such polynomial is strictly increasing for large arguments.

Part (b) implies that an integer polynomial with positive leading coefficient and degree has infinitely many nonprimes in its range. This fact no longer holds true for multivariate polynomials. An amazing consequence of Matiyasevich's [32] solution to Hilbert's Tenth Problem is that multivariate polynomials can be understood as *general purpose* programs for generating sets of integers. If a set of nonnegative integers can be generated by *any* program, then it equals the set of nonnegative integers in the range of a multivariate integer polynomial! In particular, there is an integer polynomial $p(x_1, \ldots, x_7)$ whose nonnegative values as $x_1, \ldots, x_7$ range over $\mathbb{N}$ are precisely the set of all prime numbers!

Problems for Section 9.7

Practice Problems

Problem 9.29.
List the numbers of all statements below that are *equivalent* to

$$a \equiv b \pmod{n},$$

where $n > 1$ and a and b are integers. Briefly explain your reasoning.

i) $2a \equiv 2b \pmod{n}$

ii) $2a \equiv 2b \pmod{2n}$

iii) $a^3 \equiv b^3 \pmod{n}$

iv) $\operatorname{rem}(a, n) = \operatorname{rem}(b, n)$

v) $\operatorname{rem}(n, a) = \operatorname{rem}(n, b)$

vi) $\gcd(a, n) = \gcd(b, n)$

vii) $\gcd(n, a - b) = n$

viii) $(a - b)$ is a multiple of n

ix) $\exists k \in \mathbb{Z}. \, a = b + nk$

Problem 9.30.

What is remainder$(3^{101}, 21)$?

Homework Problems

Problem 9.31.

Prove that congruence is preserved by arithmetic expressions. Namely, prove that

$$a \equiv b \quad (\text{mod } n), \tag{9.21}$$

then

$$\text{eval}(e, a) \equiv \text{eval}(e, b) \quad (\text{mod } n), \tag{9.22}$$

for all $e \in$ Aexp (see Section 7.4).

Problem 9.32.

A commutative ring is a set R of elements along with two binary operations $\oplus$ and $\otimes$ from $R \times R$ to R. There is an element in R called the zero-element, $\mathbf{0}$, and another element called the unit-element, $\mathbf{1}$. The operations in a commutative ring satisfy the following *ring axioms* for $r, s, t \in R$:

$$\begin{array}{ll}
(r \otimes s) \otimes t = r \otimes (s \otimes t) & \text{(associativity of } \otimes), \\
(r \oplus s) \oplus t = r \oplus (s \oplus t) & \text{(associativity of } \oplus), \\
r \oplus s = s \oplus r & \text{(commutativity of } \oplus) \\
r \otimes s = s \otimes r & \text{(commutativity of } \otimes), \\
\mathbf{0} \oplus r = r & \text{(identity for } \oplus), \\
\mathbf{1} \otimes r = r & \text{(identity for } \otimes), \\
\exists r' \in R. \, r \oplus r' = \mathbf{0} & \text{(inverse for } \oplus), \\
r \otimes (s \oplus t) = (r \otimes s) \oplus (r \otimes t) & \text{(distributivity).}
\end{array}$$

(a) Show that the zero-element is unique, that is, show that if $z \in R$ has the property that

$$z \oplus r = r, \tag{9.23}$$

then $z = \mathbf{0}$.

(b) Show that additive inverses are unique, that is, show that

$$r \oplus r_1 = \mathbf{0} \quad \text{and} \tag{9.24}$$

$$r \oplus r_2 = \mathbf{0} \tag{9.25}$$

implies $r_1 = r_2$.

(c) Show that multiplicative inverses are unique, that is, show that

$$r \otimes r_1 = 1$$
$$r \otimes r_2 = 1$$

implies $r_1 = r_2$.

Problem 9.33.
This problem will use elementary properties of congruences to prove that every positive integer divides infinitely many Fibonacci numbers.
   A function $f : \mathbb{N} \to \mathbb{N}$ that satisifies

$$f(n) = c_1 f(n-1) + c_2 f(n-2) + \cdots + c_d f(n-d) \qquad (9.26)$$

for some $c_i \in \mathbb{N}$ and all $n \geq d$ is called a *degree d linear-recursive*.
   A function $f : \mathbb{N} \to \mathbb{N}$ *has a degree d repeat modulo m at n and k* when it satisfies the following *repeat congruences*:

$$
\begin{aligned}
f(n) &\equiv f(k) &&(\mathrm{mod}\ m), \\
f(n-1) &\equiv f(k-1) &&(\mathrm{mod}\ m), \\
&\ \ \vdots \\
f(n-(d-1)) &\equiv f(k-(d-1)) &&(\mathrm{mod}\ m).
\end{aligned}
$$

for $k > n \geq d - 1$.
   For the rest of this problem, assume linear-recursive functions and repeats are degree $d > 0$.

(a) Prove that if a linear-recursive function has a repeat modulo m at n and k, then it has one at $n + 1$ and $k + 1$.

(b) Prove that for all $m > 1$, every linear-recursive function repeats modulo m at n and k for some $n, k \in [d - 1, d + m^d)$.

(c) A linear-recursive function is *reverse-linear* if its dth coefficient $c_d = \pm 1$. Prove that if a reverse-linear function repeats modulo m at n and k for some $n \geq d$, then it repeats modulo m at $n - 1$ and $k - 1$.

(d) Conclude that every reverse-linear function must repeat modulo m at $d - 1$ and $(d - 1) + j$ for some $j > 0$.

(e) Conclude that if f is an reverse-linear function and $f(k) = 0$ for some $k \in [0, d)$, then every positive integer is a divisor of $f(n)$ for infinitely many n.

(f) Conclude that every positive integer is a divisor of infinitely many Fibonacci numbers.

Hint: Start the Fibonacci sequence with the values 0,1 instead of 1, 1.

Class Problems

Problem 9.34.
Find
$$\text{remainder}\left(9876^{3456789}\left(9^{99}\right)^{5555} - 6789^{3414259}, 14\right). \tag{9.27}$$

Problem 9.35.
The following properties of equivalence mod n follow directly from its definition and simple properties of divisibility. See if you can prove them without looking up the proofs in the text.

(a) If $a \equiv b \pmod{n}$, then $ac \equiv bc \pmod{n}$.

(b) If $a \equiv b \pmod{n}$ and $b \equiv c \pmod{n}$, then $a \equiv c \pmod{n}$.

(c) If $a \equiv b \pmod{n}$ and $c \equiv d \pmod{n}$, then $ac \equiv bd \pmod{n}$.

(d) $\text{rem}(a, n) \equiv a \pmod{n}$.

Problem 9.36. (a) Why is a number written in decimal evenly divisible by 9 if and only if the sum of its digits is a multiple of 9? *Hint:* $10 \equiv 1 \pmod 9$.

(b) Take a big number, such as 37273761261. Sum the digits, where every other one is negated:

$$3 + (-7) + 2 + (-7) + 3 + (-7) + 6 + (-1) + 2 + (-6) + 1 = -11$$

Explain why the original number is a multiple of 11 if and only if this sum is a multiple of 11.

Problem 9.37.
At one time, the Guinness Book of World Records reported that the "greatest human

calculator" was a guy who could compute 13th roots of 100-digit numbers that were 13th powers. What a curious choice of tasks....

In this problem, we prove

$$n^{13} \equiv n \pmod{10} \tag{9.28}$$

for all n.

(a) Explain why (9.28) does not follow immediately from Euler's Theorem.

(b) Prove that

$$d^{13} \equiv d \pmod{10} \tag{9.29}$$

for $0 \le d < 10$.

(c) Now prove the congruence (9.28).

Problem 9.38. (a) Ten pirates find a chest filled with gold and silver coins. There are twice as many silver coins in the chest as there are gold. They divide the gold coins in such a way that the difference in the number of coins given to any two pirates is not divisible by 10. They will only take the silver coins if it is possible to divide them the same way. Is this possible, or will they have to leave the silver behind? Prove your answer.

(b) There are also 3 sacks in the chest, containing 5, 49, and 51 rubies respectively. The treasurer of the pirate ship is bored and decides to play a game with the following rules:

- He can merge any two piles together into one pile, and
- he can divide a pile with an even number of rubies into two piles of equal size.

He makes one move every day, and he will finish the game when he has divided the rubies into 105 piles of one. Is it possible for him to finish the game?

Exam Problems

Problem 9.39.
The sum of the digits of the base 10 representation of an integer is congruent modulo 9 to that integer. For example,

$$763 \equiv 7 + 6 + 3 \pmod{9}.$$

We can say that "9 is a *good modulus for base* 10."

More generally, we'll say "k is a good modulus for base b" when, for any non-negative integer n, the sum of the digits of the base b representation of n is congruent to n modulo k. So 2 is *not* a good modulus for base 10 because

$$763 \not\equiv 7 + 6 + 3 \pmod 2.$$

(a) What integers $k > 1$ are good moduli for base 10?

(b) Show that if $b \equiv 1 \pmod k$, then k is good for base b.

(c) Prove conversely, that if k is good for some base $b \geq 2$, then $b \equiv 1 \pmod k$. *Hint:* The base b representation of b.

(d) Exactly which integers $k > 1$ are good moduli for base 106?

Problem 9.40.
We define the sequence of numbers

$$a_n = \begin{cases} 1, & \text{for } n \leq 3, \\ a_{n-1} + a_{n-2} + a_{n-3} + a_{n-4}, & \text{for } n > 3. \end{cases}$$

Use *strong induction* to prove that $\text{remainder}(a_n, 3) = 1$ for all $n \geq 0$.

Problems for Section 9.8

Exam Problems

Problem 9.41.

Definition. The set P of single variable integer polynomials can be defined recursively:

Base cases:

- the identity function, $\text{Id}_{\mathbb{Z}}(x) ::= x$ is in P.

- for any integer m the constant function, $c_m(x) ::= m$ is in P.

Constructor cases. If $r, s \in P$, then $r + s$ and $r \cdot s \in P$.

Prove by structural induction that for all $q \in P$,

$$j \equiv k \pmod{n} \quad \text{IMPLIES} \quad q(j) \equiv q(k) \pmod{n},$$

for all integers j, k, n where $n > 1$.

Be sure to clearly state and label your Induction Hypothesis, Base case(s), and Constructor step.

Problems for Section 9.9

Practice Problems

Problem 9.42.

(a) Given inputs $m, n \in \mathbb{Z}^+$, the Pulverizer will produce $x, y \in \mathbb{Z}$ such that:

(b) Assume $n > 1$. Explain how to use the numbers x, y to find the inverse of m modulo n when there is an inverse.

Problem 9.43.

What is the multiplicative inverse (mod 7) of 2? *Reminder:* by definition, your answer must be an integer between 0 and 6.

Problem 9.44. (a) Find integer coefficients x, y such that $25x + 32y = \gcd(25, 32)$.

(b) What is the inverse (mod 25) of 32?

Problem 9.45. (a) Use the Pulverizer to find integers s, t such that

$$40s + 7t = \gcd(40, 7).$$

(b) Adjust your answer to part (a) to find an inverse modulo 40 of 7 in $[1, 40)$.

Class Problems

Problem 9.46.

Two nonparallel lines in the real plane intersect at a point. Algebraically, this means that the equations

$$y = m_1 x + b_1$$
$$y = m_2 x + b_2$$

have a unique solution (x, y), provided $m_1 \neq m_2$. This statement would be false if we restricted x and y to the integers, since the two lines could cross at a noninteger point:

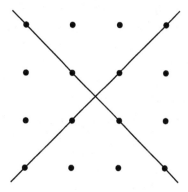

However, an analogous statement holds if we work over the integers *modulo a prime p*. Find a solution to the congruences

$$y \equiv m_1 x + b_1 \quad (\text{mod } p)$$
$$y \equiv m_2 x + b_2 \quad (\text{mod } p)$$

when $m_1 \not\equiv m_2$ (mod p). Express your solution in the form $x \equiv ?$ (mod p) and $y \equiv ?$ (mod p) where the ?'s denote expressions involving m_1, m_2, b_1 and b_2. You may find it helpful to solve the original equations over the reals first.

Problems for Section 9.10

Practice Problems

Problem 9.47.

Prove that $k \in [0, n)$ has an inverse modulo n iff it has an inverse in $\mathbb{Z}_n$.

Problem 9.48.

What is $\text{rem}(24^{79},\ 79)$?

   Hint: You should not need to do any actual multiplications!

Problem 9.49. (a) Prove that 22^{12001} has a multiplicative inverse modulo 175.

  (b) What is the value of $\phi(175)$, where ϕ is Euler's function?

  (c) What is the remainder of 22^{12001} divided by 175?

Problem 9.50.

How many numbers between 1 and 6042 (inclusive) are relatively prime to 3780?
Hint: 53 is a factor.

Problem 9.51.

How many numbers between 1 and 3780 (inclusive) are relatively prime to 3780?

Problem 9.52.

  (a) What is the probability that an integer from 1 to 360 selected with uniform probability is relatively prime to 360?

  (b) What is the value of $\text{rem}(7^{98},\ 360)$?

Class Problems

Problem 9.53.

Find the remainder of $26^{1818181}$ divided by 297.

   Hint: $1818181 = (180 \cdot 10101) + 1$; use Euler's theorem.

Problem 9.54.

Find the last digit of $7^{7^{7^7}}$.

Problem 9.55.
Prove that n and n^5 have the same last digit. For example:

$$2^5 = 3\underline{2} \qquad\qquad 7\underline{9}^5 = 307705639\underline{9}$$

Problem 9.56.
Use Fermat's theorem to find the inverse i of 13 modulo 23 with $1 \le i < 23$.

Problem 9.57.
Let ϕ be Euler's function.

(a) What is the value of $\phi(2)$?

(b) What are three nonnegative integers $k > 1$ such that $\phi(k) = 2$?

(c) Prove that $\phi(k)$ is even for $k > 2$.

Hint: Consider whether k has an odd prime factor or not.

(d) Briefly explain why $\phi(k) = 2$ for exactly three values of k.

Problem 9.58.
Suppose a, b are relatively prime and greater than 1. In this problem you will prove the *Chinese Remainder Theorem*, which says that for all m, n, there is an x such that

$$x \equiv m \bmod a, \tag{9.30}$$
$$x \equiv n \ \bmod b. \tag{9.31}$$

Moreover, x is unique up to congruence modulo ab, namely, if x' also satisfies (9.30) and (9.31), then

$$x' \equiv x \bmod ab.$$

(a) Prove that for any m, n, there is some x satisfying (9.30) and (9.31).

Hint: Let b^{-1} be an inverse of b modulo a and define $e_a ::= b^{-1}b$. Define e_b similarly. Let $x = me_a + ne_b$.

(b) Prove that

$$[x \equiv 0 \bmod a \ \text{AND} \ x \equiv 0 \bmod b] \quad \text{implies} \quad x \equiv 0 \bmod ab.$$

(c) Conclude that

$$\left[x \equiv x' \bmod a \ \text{ AND } \ x \equiv x' \bmod b \right] \quad \text{implies} \quad x \equiv x' \bmod ab.$$

(d) Conclude that the Chinese Remainder Theorem is true.

(e) What about the converse of the implication in part (c)?

Problem 9.59.

The *order* of $k \in \mathbb{Z}_n$ is the smallest positive m such that $k^m = 1 \ (\mathbb{Z}_n)$.

(a) Prove that

$$k^m = 1 \ (\mathbb{Z}_n) \ \text{ IMPLIES } \ \text{ord}(k, n) \mid m.$$

Hint: Take the remainder of m divided by the order.

Now suppose $p > 2$ is a prime of the form $2^s + 1$. For example, $2^1 + 1, 2^2 + 1, 2^4 + 1$ are such primes.

(b) Conclude from part (a) that if $0 < k < p$, then $\text{ord}(k, p)$ is a power of 2.

(c) Prove that $\text{ord}(2, p) = 2s$ and conclude that s is a power of 2.[19]

Hint: $2^k - 1$ for $k \in [1..r]$ is positive but too small to equal 0 $(\mathbb{Z}_p)$.

Homework Problems

Problem 9.60.

This problem is about finding square roots modulo a prime p.

(a) Prove that $x^2 \equiv y^2 \pmod{p}$ if and only if $x \equiv y \pmod{p}$ or $x \equiv -y \pmod{p}$. *Hint:* $x^2 - y^2 = (x + y)(x - y)$

An integer x is called a *square root* of $n \bmod p$ when

$$x^2 \equiv n \pmod{p}.$$

An integer with a square root is called a *square* mod p. For example, if n is congruent to 0 or 1 mod p, then n is a square and it is it's own square root.

So let's assume that p is an odd prime and $n \not\equiv 0 \pmod{p}$. It turns out there is a simple test we can perform to see if n is a square mod p:

---

[19]Numbers of the form $2^{2^k} + 1$ are called *Fermat numbers*, so we can rephrase this conclusion as saying that any prime of the form $2^s + 1$ must actually be a Fermat number. The Fermat numbers are prime for $k = 1, 2, 3, 4$, but not for $k = 5$. In fact, it is not known if any Fermat number with $k > 4$ is prime.

Euler's Criterion

i. If n is a square modulo p, then $n^{(p-1)/2} \equiv 1 \pmod{p}$.

ii. If n is not a square modulo p then $n^{(p-1)/2} \equiv -1 \pmod{p}$.

(b) Prove Case (i) of Euler's Criterion. *Hint:* Use Fermat's theorem.

(c) Prove Case (ii) of Euler's Criterion. *Hint:* Use part (a)

(d) Suppose that $p \equiv 3 \pmod 4$, and n is a square mod p. Find a simple expression in terms of n and p for a square root of n. *Hint:* Write p as $p = 4k + 3$ and use Euler's Criterion. You might have to multiply two sides of an equation by n at one point.

Problem 9.61.
Suppose a, b are relatively prime integers greater than 1. In this problem you will prove that Euler's function is *multiplicative*, that is, that

$$\phi(ab) = \phi(a)\phi(b).$$

The proof is an easy consequence of the Chinese Remainder Theorem (Problem 9.58).

(a) Conclude from the Chinese Remainder Theorem that the function $f : [0..ab) \to [0..a) \times [0..b)$ defined by

$$f(x) ::= (\text{rem}(x, a), \text{rem}(x, b))$$

is a bijection.

(b) For any positive integer k let $\mathbb{Z}_k^*$ be the integers in $[0..k)$ that are relatively prime to k. Prove that the function f from part (a) also defines a bijection from $\mathbb{Z}_{ab}^*$ to $\mathbb{Z}_a^* \times \mathbb{Z}_b^*$.

(c) Conclude from the preceding parts of this problem that

$$\phi(ab) = \phi(a)\phi(b). \tag{9.32}$$

(d) Prove Corollary 9.10.11: for any number $n > 1$, if $p_1, p_2, \ldots, p_j$ are the (distinct) prime factors of n, then

$$\phi(n) = n\left(1 - \frac{1}{p_1}\right)\left(1 - \frac{1}{p_2}\right)\cdots\left(1 - \frac{1}{p_j}\right).$$

Problem 9.62.

Definition. Define the *order* of k over $\mathbb{Z}_n$ to be

$$\operatorname{ord}(k, n) ::= \min\{m > 0 \mid k^m = 1 \ (\mathbb{Z}_n)\}.$$

If no positive power of k equals 1 in $\mathbb{Z}_n$, then $\operatorname{ord}(k, n) ::= \infty$.

 (a) Show that $k \in \mathbb{Z}_n^*$ iff k has finite order in $\mathbb{Z}_n$.

 (b) Prove that for every $k \in \mathbb{Z}_n^*$, the order of k over $\mathbb{Z}_n$ divides $\phi(n)$.

Hint: Let $m = \operatorname{ord}(k, n)$. Consider the quotient and remainder of $\phi(n)$ divided by m.

Problem 9.63.

The general version of the Chinese Remainder Theorem (see Problem 9.58) extends to more than two relatively prime moduli. Namely,

Theorem (General Chinese Remainder). *Suppose $a_1, \ldots, a_k$ are integers greater than 1 and each is relatively prime to the others. Let $n ::= a_1 \cdot a_2 \cdots a_k$. Then for any integers $m_1, m_2, \ldots, m_k$, there is a unique $x \in [0..n)$ such that*

$$x \equiv m_i \quad (\bmod \ a_i),$$

for $1 \le i \le k$.

The proof is a routine induction on k using a fact that follows immediately from unique factorization: if a number is relatively prime to some other numbers, then it is relatively prime to their product.

The General Chinese Remainder Theorem is the basis for an efficient approach to performing a long series of additions and multiplications on "large" numbers.

Namely, suppose n was large, but each of the factors a_i was small enough to be handled by cheap and available arithmetic hardware units. Suppose a calculation requiring many additions and multiplications needs to be performed. To do a single multiplication or addition of two large numbers x and y in the usual way in this setting would involve breaking up the x and y into pieces small enough to be handled by the arithmetic units, using the arithmetic units to perform additions and multiplications on (many) pairs of small pieces, and then reassembling the pieces into an answer. Moreover, the order in which these operations on pieces can be performed is contrained by dependence among the pieces—because of "carries," for example. And this process of breakup and reassembly has to be performed for each addition and multiplication that needs to be performed on large numbers.

Explain how the General Chinese Remainder Theorem can be applied to perform a long series of additions and multiplications on "large" numbers much more efficiently than the usual way described above.

Problem 9.64.

In this problem we'll prove that for all integers a, m where $m > 1$,

$$a^m \equiv a^{m-\phi(m)} \pmod{m}. \tag{9.33}$$

Note that a and m need not be relatively prime.

Assume $m = p_1^{k_1} \cdots p_n^{k_n}$ for distinct primes, $p_1, \ldots, p_n$ and positive integers $k_1, \ldots, k_n$.

(a) Show that if p_i does not divide a, then

$$a^{\phi(m)} \equiv 1 \pmod{p_i^{k_i}}.$$

(b) Show that if $p_i \mid a$ then

$$a^{m-\phi(m)} \equiv 0 \pmod{p_i^{k_i}}. \tag{9.34}$$

(c) Conclude (9.33) from the facts above.

Hint: $a^m - a^{m-\phi(m)} = a^{m-\phi(m)}(a^{\phi(m)} - 1)$.

Problem 9.65.

The Generalized Postage Problem

Several other problems (2.7, 2.1, 5.32) work out which amounts of postage can be formed using two stamps of given denominations. In this problem, we generalize this to two stamps with arbitrary positive integer denominations a and b cents. Let's call an amount of postage that can be made from a and b cent stamps a *makeable* amount.

Lemma. *(Generalized Postage) If a and b are relatively prime positive integers, then any integer greater than $ab - a - b$ is makeable.*

To prove the Lemma, consider the following array with a infinite rows:

$$
\begin{array}{cccc}
0 & a & 2a & 3a \quad \ldots \\
b & b+a & b+2a & b+3a \quad \ldots \\
2b & 2b+a & 2b+2a & 2b+3a \quad \ldots \\
3b & 3b+a & 3b+2a & 3b+3a \quad \ldots \\
\vdots & \vdots & \vdots & \vdots \quad \ldots \\
(a-1)b & (a-1)b+a & (a-1)b+2a & (a-1)b+3a \quad \ldots
\end{array}
$$

Note that every element in this array is clearly makeable.

(a) Suppose that n is at least as large as, and also congruent mod a to, the first element in some row of this array. Explain why n must appear in the array.

(b) Prove that every integer from 0 to $a-1$ is congruent modulo a to one of the integers in the first column of this array.

(c) Complete the proof of the Generalized Postage Lemma by using parts (a) and (b) to conclude that every integer $n > ab - a - b$ appears in the array, and hence is makeable.

Hint: Suppose n is congruent mod a to the first element in some row. Assume n is less than that element, and then show that $n \leq ab - a - b$.

(d) (Optional) What's more, $ab - a - b$ is not makeable. Prove it.

(e) Explain why the following even more general lemma follows directly from the Generalized Lemma and part (d).

Lemma. (Generalized^2 Postage) If m and n are positive integers and $g ::= \gcd(m, n) > 1$, then with m and n cent stamps, you can only make amounts of postage that are multiples of g. You can actually make any amount of postage greater than $(mn/g) - m - n$ that is a multiple of g, but you cannot make $(mn/g) - m - n$ cents postage.

(f) Optional and possibly unknown. Suppose you have three denominations of stamps, a, b, c and $\gcd(a, b, c) = 1$. Give a formula for the smallest number n_{abc} such that you can make every amount of postage $\geq n_{abc}$.

Exam Problems

Problem 9.66.
What is the remainder of 63^{9601} divided by 220?

Problem 9.67.
Prove that if k_1 and k_2 are relatively prime to n, then so is $k_1 \cdot_n k_2$,

(a) ...using the fact that k is relatively prime to n iff k has an inverse modulo n.
Hint: Recall that $k_1 k_2 \equiv k_1 \cdot_n k_2 \pmod{n}$.

(b) ...using the fact that k is relatively prime to n iff k is cancellable modulo n.

(c) ...using the Unique Factorization Theorem and the basic GCD properties such as Lemma 9.2.1.

Problem 9.68.

Circle **true** or **false** for the statements below, and *provide counterexamples* for those that are **false**. Variables, a, b, c, m, n range over the integers and $m, n > 1$.

(a) $\gcd(1 + a, 1 + b) = 1 + \gcd(a, b)$.   **true**   **false**

(b) If $a \equiv b \pmod{n}$, then $p(a) \equiv p(b) \pmod{n}$
for any polynomial $p(x)$ with integer coefficients.   **true**   **false**

(c) If $a \mid bc$ and $\gcd(a, b) = 1$, then $a \mid c$.   **true**   **false**

(d) $\gcd(a^n, b^n) = (\gcd(a, b))^n$ **true**   **false**

(e) If $\gcd(a, b) \neq 1$ and $\gcd(b, c) \neq 1$, then $\gcd(a, c) \neq 1$.   **true**   **false**

(f) If an integer linear combination of a and b equals 1,
then so does some integer linear combination of a^2 and b^2.   **true**   **false**

(g) If no integer linear combination of a and b equals 2,
then neither does any integer linear combination of a^2 and b^2. **true**   **false**

(h) If $ac \equiv bc \pmod{n}$ and n does not divide c,
then $a \equiv b \pmod{n}$.   **true**   **false**

(i) Assuming a, b have inverses modulo n,
if $a^{-1} \equiv b^{-1} \pmod{n}$, then $a \equiv b \pmod{n}$.   **true**   **false**

(j) If $ac \equiv bc \pmod{n}$ and n does not divide c,
then $a \equiv b \pmod{n}$.   **true**   **false**

(k) If $a \equiv b \pmod{\phi(n)}$ for $a, b > 0$, then $c^a \equiv c^b \pmod{n}$.   **true**   **false**

(l) If $a \equiv b \pmod{nm}$, then $a \equiv b \pmod{n}$.   **true**   **false**

(m) If $\gcd(m, n) = 1$, then

$[a \equiv b \pmod{m}$ AND $a \equiv b \pmod{n}]$ iff $[a \equiv b \pmod{mn}]$ **true**   **false**

(n) If $\gcd(a, n) = 1$, then $a^{n-1} \equiv 1 \pmod{n}$ **true**   **false**

(o) If $a, b > 1$, then

$[a$ has a inverse mod b iff b has an inverse mod $a]$.   **true**   **false**

Problem 9.69.
Find an integer $k > 1$ such that n and n^k agree in their last three digits whenever n is divisible by neither 2 nor 5. *Hint:* Euler's theorem.

Problem 9.70.

(a) Explain why $(-12)^{482}$ has a multiplicative inverse modulo 175.

(b) What is the value of $\phi(175)$, where ϕ is Euler's function?

(c) Call a number from 0 to 174 *powerful* iff some positive power of the number is congruent to 1 modulo 175. What is the probability that a random number from 0 to 174 is powerful?

(d) What is the remainder of $(-12)^{482}$ divided by 175?

Problem 9.71. (a) Calculate the remainder of 35^{86} divided by 29.

(b) Part (a) implies that the remainder of 35^{86} divided by 29 is not equal to 1. So there there must be a mistake in the following proof, where all the congruences are taken with modulus 29:

$$1 \not\equiv 35^{86} \qquad \text{(by part (a))} \qquad (9.35)$$
$$\equiv 6^{86} \qquad \text{(since } 35 \equiv 6 \pmod{29}) \qquad (9.36)$$
$$\equiv 6^{28} \qquad \text{(since } 86 \equiv 28 \pmod{29}) \qquad (9.37)$$
$$\equiv 1 \qquad \text{(by Fermat's Little Theorem)} \qquad (9.38)$$

Identify the exact line containing the mistake and explain the logical error.

Problem 9.72.
Indicate whether the following statements are **true** or **false**. For each of the false statements, **give counterexamples**. All variables range over the integers, $\mathbb{Z}$.

(a) For all a and b, there are x and y such that: $ax + by = 1$.

(b) $\gcd(mb + r, b) = \gcd(r, b)$ for all m, r and b.

(c) $k^{p-1} \equiv 1 \pmod{p}$ for every prime p and every k.

(d) For primes $p \neq q$, $\phi(pq) = (p-1)(q-1)$, where ϕ is Euler's totient function.

(e) If a and b are relatively prime to d, then

$$[ac \equiv bc \bmod d] \quad \text{IMPLIES} \quad [a \equiv b \bmod d].$$

Problem 9.73. (a) Show that if $p \mid n$ for some prime p and integer $n > 0$, then $(p - 1) \mid \phi(n)$.

(b) Conclude that $\phi(n)$ is even for all $n > 2$.

Problem 9.74. (a) Calculate the value of $\phi(6042)$.

Hint: 53 is a factor of 6042.

(b) Consider an integer $k > 0$ that is relatively prime to 6042. Explain why $k^{9361} \equiv k \pmod{6042}$.

Hint: Use your solution to part (a).

Problem 9.75.

Let

$$S_k = 1^k + 2^k + \cdots + p^k,$$

where p is an odd prime and k is a positive multiple of $p - 1$. Find $a \in [0..p)$ and $b \in (-p..0]$ such that

$$S_k \equiv a \equiv b \pmod{p}.$$

Problems for Section 9.11

Practice Problems

Problem 9.76.

Suppose a cracker knew how to factor the RSA modulus n into the product of distinct primes p and q. Explain how the cracker could use the public key-pair (e, n) to find a private key-pair (d, n) that would allow him to read any message encrypted with the public key.

Problem 9.77.

Suppose the RSA modulus $n = pq$ is the product of distinct 200 digit primes p and q. A message $m \in [0..n)$ is called *dangerous* if $\gcd(m, n) = p$, because such an m can be used to factor n and so crack RSA. Circle the best estimate of the fraction of messages in $[0..n)$ that are dangerous.

$$\frac{1}{200} \qquad \frac{1}{400} \qquad \frac{1}{200^{10}} \qquad \frac{1}{10^{200}} \qquad \frac{1}{400^{10}} \qquad \frac{1}{10^{400}}$$

Problem 9.78.

Ben Bitdiddle decided to encrypt all his data using RSA. Unfortunately, he lost his private key. He has been looking for it all night, and suddenly a genie emerges from his lamp. He offers Ben a quantum computer that can perform exactly one procedure on large numbers e, d, n. Which of the following procedures should Ben choose to recover his data?

- Find $\gcd(e, d)$.

- Find the prime factorization of n.

- Determine whether n is prime.

- Find $\mathrm{rem}(e^d, n)$.

- Find the inverse of e modulo n (the inverse of e in $\mathbb{Z}_n$).

- Find the inverse of e modulo $\phi(n)$.

Class Problems

Problem 9.79.

Let's try out RSA!

(a) Go through the **beforehand** steps.

- Choose primes p and q to be relatively small, say in the range 10–40. In practice, p and q might contain hundreds of digits, but small numbers are easier to handle with pencil and paper.
- Try $e = 3, 5, 7, \ldots$ until you find something that works. Use Euclid's algorithm to compute the gcd.
- Find d (using the Pulverizer).

When you're done, put your public key on the board prominentally labelled "Public Key." This lets another team send you a message.

(b) Now send an encrypted message to another team using their public key. Select your message m from the codebook below:

- 2 = Greetings and salutations!
- 3 = Yo, wassup?
- 4 = You guys are slow!
- 5 = All your base are belong to us.
- 6 = Someone on *our* team thinks someone on *your* team is kinda cute.
- 7 = You *are* the weakest link. Goodbye.

(c) Decrypt the message sent to you and verify that you received what the other team sent!

Problem 9.80. (a) Just as RSA would be trivial to crack knowing the factorization into two primes of n in the public key, explain why RSA would also be trivial to crack knowing $\phi(n)$.

(b) Show that if you knew n, $\phi(n)$, and that n was the product of two primes, then you could easily factor n.

Problem 9.81.

A critical fact about RSA is, of course, that decrypting an encrypted message always gives back the original message m. Namely, if $n = pq$ where p and q are distinct primes, $m \in [0..pq)$, and

$$d \cdot e \equiv 1 \quad (\mathrm{mod}\ (p-1)(q-1)),$$

then

$$\widehat{m}^d ::= \left(m^e\right)^d = m\ (\mathbb{Z}_n). \tag{9.39}$$

We'll now prove this.

(a) Explain why (9.39) follows very simply from Euler's theorem when m is *relatively prime to n*.

All the rest of this problem is about removing the restriction that m be relatively prime to n. That is, we aim to prove that equation (9.39) holds for *all $m \in [0..n)$*.

It is important to realize that there is no practical reason to worry about—or to bother to check for—this relative primality condition before sending a message m using RSA. That's because the whole RSA enterprise is predicated on the difficulty of factoring. If an m ever came up that wasn't relatively prime to n, then we could factor n by computing $\gcd(m,n)$. So believing in the security of RSA implies believing that the liklihood of a message m turning up that was not relatively prime to n is negligible.

But let's be pure, impractical mathematicians and get rid of this technically unnecessary relative primality side condition, even if it is harmless. One gain for doing this is that statements about RSA will be simpler without the side condition. More important, the proof below illustrates a useful general method of proving things about a number n by proving them separately for the prime factors of n.

(b) Prove that if p is prime and $a \equiv 1 \pmod{p-1}$, then

$$m^a = m\ (\mathbb{Z}_p). \tag{9.40}$$

(c) Give an elementary proof[20] that if $a \equiv b \pmod{p_i}$ for distinct primes p_i, then $a \equiv b$ modulo the product of these primes.

(d) Note that (9.39) is a special case of

---

[20]There is no need to appeal to the Chinese Remainder Theorem.

Claim. *If n is a product of distinct primes and $a \equiv 1 \pmod{\phi(n)}$, then*

$$m^a = m \ (\mathbb{Z}_n).$$

Use the previous parts to prove the Claim.

Homework Problems

Problem 9.82.

Although RSA has successfully withstood cryptographic attacks for a more than a quarter century, it is not known that breaking RSA would imply that factoring is easy.

In this problem we will examine the *Rabin cryptosystem* that does have such a security certification. Namely, if someone has the ability to break the Rabin cryptosystem efficiently, then they also have the ability to factor numbers that are products of two primes.

Why should that convince us that it is hard to break the cryptosystem efficiently? Well, mathematicians have been trying to factor efficiently for centuries, and they still haven't figured out how to do it.

What is the Rabin cryptosystem? The public key will be a number N that is a product of two very large primes p, q such that $p \equiv q \equiv 3 \pmod 4$. To send the message m, send $\text{rem}(m^2, \ N)$.[21]

The private key is the factorization of N, namely, the primes p, q. We need to show that if the person being sent the message knows p, q, then they can decode the message. On the other hand, if an eavesdropper who doesn't know p, q listens in, then we must show that they are very unlikely to figure out this message.

Say that s is a *square modulo N* if there is an $m \in [0, N)$ such that $s \equiv m^2 \pmod N$. Such an m is a *square root of s modulo N*.

(a) What are the squares modulo 5? For each square in the interval $[0, 5)$, how many square roots does it have?

(b) For each integer in $[1, 15)$ that is relatively prime to 15, how many square roots (modulo 15) does it have? Note that all the square roots are *also* relatively prime to 15. We won't go through why this is so here, but keep in mind that this is a general phenomenon!

(c) Suppose that p is a prime such that $p \equiv 3 \pmod 4$. It turns out that squares modulo p have exactly 2 square roots. First show that $(p + 1)/4$ is an integer.

---

[21] We will see soon, that there are other numbers that would be encrypted by $\text{rem}(m^2, \ N)$, so we'll have to disallow those other numbers as possible messages in order to make it possible to decode this cryptosystem, but let's ignore that for now.

Next figure out the two square roots of 1 modulo p. Then show that you can find a "square root mod a prime p" of a number by raising the number to the $(p + 1)/4$th power. That is, given s, to find m such that $s \equiv m^2 \pmod{p}$, you can compute $\text{rem}(s^{(p+1)/4}, p)$.

(d) The Chinese Remainder Theorem (Problem 9.58) implies that if p, q are distinct primes, then s is a square modulo pq if and only if s is a square modulo p and s is a square modulo q. In particular, if $s \equiv x^2 \equiv (x')^2 \pmod{p}$ where $x \neq x'$, and likewise $s \equiv y^2 \equiv (y')^2 \pmod{q}$ then s has exactly four square roots modulo N, namely,

$$s \equiv (xy)^2 \equiv (x'y)^2 \equiv (xy')^2 \equiv (x'y')^2 \pmod{pq}.$$

So, if you know p, q, then using the solution to part (c), you can efficiently find the square roots of s! Thus, given the private key, decoding is easy.

But what if you don't know p, q?

Let's assume that the evil message interceptor claims to have a program that can find all four square roots of any number modulo N. Show that he can actually use this program to efficiently find the factorization of N. Thus, unless this evil message interceptor is extremely smart and has figured out something that the rest of the scientific community has been working on for years, it is very unlikely that this efficient square root program exists!

Hint: Pick r arbitrarily from $[1, N)$. If $gcd(N, r) > 1$, then you are done (why?) so you can halt. Otherwise, use the program to find all four square roots of r, call them $r, -r, r', -r'$. Note that $r^2 \equiv r'^2 \pmod{N}$. How can you use these roots to factor N?

(e) If the evil message interceptor knows that the message is the encoding one of two possible candidate messages (that is, either "meet at dome at dusk" or "meet at dome at dawn") and is just trying to figure out which of the two, then can he break this cryptosystem?

Problem 9.83.

You've seen how the RSA encryption scheme works, but why is it hard to break? In this problem, you will see that finding private keys is as hard as finding the prime factorizations of integers. Since there is a general consensus in the crypto community (enough to persuade many large financial institutions, for example) that factoring numbers with a few hundred digits requires astronomical computing resources, we can therefore be sure it will take the same kind of overwhelming effort to find RSA private keys of a few hundred digits. This means we can be confident the private RSA keys are not somehow revealed by the public keys[22].

For this problem, assume that $n = p \cdot q$ where p, q are both *odd* primes and that e is the public key and d the private key of the RSA protocol.. Let $c ::= e \cdot d - 1$.

(a) Show that $\phi(n)$ divides c.

(b) Conclude that 4 divides c.

(c) Show that if $\gcd(r, n) = 1$, then $r^c \equiv 1 \pmod{n}$.

A *square root* of m modulo n is an integer $s \in [0.n)$ such that $s^2 \equiv m \pmod{n}$. Here is a nice fact to know: when n is a product of two odd primes, then every number m such that $\gcd(m, n) = 1$ has 4 square roots modulo n.

In particular, the number 1 has four square roots modulo n. The two trivial ones are 1 and $n - 1$ (which is $\equiv -1 \pmod{n}$). The other two are called the *nontrivial* square roots of 1.

(d) Since you know c, then for any integer r you can also compute the remainder y of $r^{c/2}$ divided by n. So $y^2 \equiv r^c \pmod{n}$. Now if r is relatively prime to n, then y will be a square root of 1 modulo n by part (c).

Show that if y turns out to be a *nontrivial* root of 1 modulo n, then you can factor n. *Hint:* From the fact that $y^2 - 1 = (y + 1)(y - 1)$, show that $y + 1$ must be divisible by exactly one of q and p.

(e) It turns out that at least half the positive integers $r < n$ that are relatively prime to n will yield y's in part (d) that are nontrivial roots of 1. Conclude that if, in addition to n and the public key e you also knew the private key d, then you can be sure of being able to factor n.

Exam Problems

Problem 9.84.
Suppose Alice and Bob are using the RSA cryptosystem to send secure messages. Each of them has a public key visible to everyone and a private key known only to themselves, and using RSA in the usual way, they are able to send secret messages to each other over public channels.

But a concern for Bob is how he knows that a message he gets is actually from Alice—as opposed to some imposter claiming to be Alice. This concern can be met by using RSA to add unforgeable "signatures" to messages. To send a message m

---

[22]This is a very weak kind of "security" property, because it doesn't even rule out the possibility of deciphering RSA encoded messages by some method that did not require knowing the private key. Nevertheless, over twenty years experience supports the security of RSA in practice.

to Bob with an unforgeable signature, Alice uses RSA encryption on her message m, but instead using Bob's public key to encrypt m, she uses her own *private* key to obtain a message m_1. She then sends m_1 as her "signed" message to Bob.

(a) Explain how Bob can read the original message m from Alice's signed message m_1. (Let (n_A, e_A) be Alice's public key and d_A her private key. Assume $m \in [0..n_A)$.)

(b) Briefly explain why Bob can be confident, assuming RSA is secure, that m_1 came from Alice rather than some imposter.

(c) Notice that not only Bob, but *anyone* can use Alice's public key to reconstruct her message m from its signed version m_1. So how can Alice send a secret signed message to Bob over public channels?

10   Directed graphs & Partial Orders

Directed graphs, called *digraphs* for short, provide a handy way to represent how things are connected together and how to get from one thing to another by following those connections. They are usually pictured as a bunch of dots or circles with arrows between some of the dots, as in Figure 10.1. The dots are called *nodes* or *vertices* and the lines are called *directed edges* or *arrows*; the digraph in Figure 10.1 has 4 nodes and 6 directed edges.

Digraphs appear everywhere in computer science. For example, the digraph in Figure 10.2 represents a communication net, a topic we'll explore in depth in Chapter 11. Figure 10.2 has three "in" nodes (pictured as little squares) representing locations where packets may arrive at the net, the three "out" nodes representing destination locations for packets, and the remaining six nodes (pictured with little circles) represent switches. The 16 edges indicate paths that packets can take through the router.

Another place digraphs emerge in computer science is in the hyperlink structure of the World Wide Web. Letting the vertices $x_1, \ldots, x_n$ correspond to web pages, and using arrows to indicate when one page has a hyperlink to another, results in a digraph like the one in Figure 10.3—although the graph of the real World Wide Web would have n be a number in the billions and probably even the trillions. At first glance, this graph wouldn't seem to be very interesting. But in 1995, two students at Stanford, Larry Page and Sergey Brin, ultimately became multibillionaires from the realization of how useful the structure of this graph could be in building a search engine. So pay attention to graph theory, and who knows what might happen!

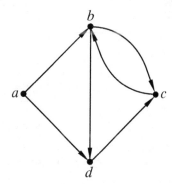

Figure 10.1   A 4-node directed graph with 6 edges.

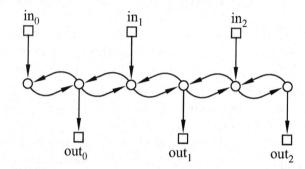

Figure 10.2   A 6-switch packet routing digraph.

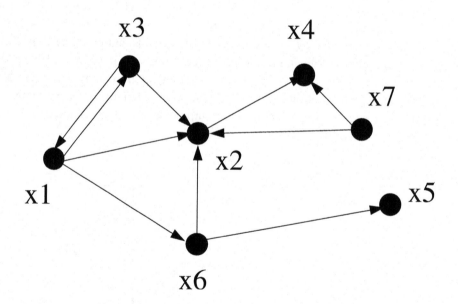

Figure 10.3   Links among Web Pages.

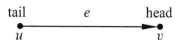

Figure 10.4 A directed edge $e = \langle u \to v \rangle$. The edge e starts at the tail vertex u and ends at the head vertex v.

Definition 10.0.1. A *directed graph G* consists of a nonempty set $V(G)$, called the *vertices* of G, and a set $E(G)$, called the *edges* of G. An element of $V(G)$ is called a *vertex*. A vertex is also called a *node*; the words "vertex" and "node" are used interchangeably. An element of $E(G)$ is called a *directed edge*. A directed edge is also called an "arrow" or simply an "edge." A directed edge *starts* at some vertex u called the *tail* of the edge, and *ends* at some vertex v called the *head* of the edge, as in Figure 10.4. Such an edge can be represented by the ordered pair (u, v). The notation $\langle u \to v \rangle$ denotes this edge.

There is nothing new in Definition 10.0.1 except for a lot of vocabulary. Formally, a digraph G is the same as a binary relation on the set, $V = V(G)$—that is, a digraph is just a binary relation whose domain and codomain are the same set V. In fact, we've already referred to the arrows in a relation G as the "graph" of G. For example, the divisibility relation on the integers in the interval [1..12] could be pictured by the digraph in Figure 10.5.

10.1 Vertex Degrees

The *in-degree* of a vertex in a digraph is the number of arrows coming into it, and similarly its *out-degree* is the number of arrows out of it. More precisely,

Definition 10.1.1. If G is a digraph and $v \in V(G)$, then

$$\text{indeg}(v) ::= |\{e \in E(G) \mid \text{head}(e) = v\}|$$
$$\text{outdeg}(v) ::= |\{e \in E(G) \mid \text{tail}(e) = v\}|$$

An immediate consequence of this definition is

Lemma 10.1.2.
$$\sum_{v \in V(G)} \text{indeg}(v) = \sum_{v \in V(G)} \text{outdeg}(v).$$

Proof. Both sums are equal to $|E(G)|$. ∎

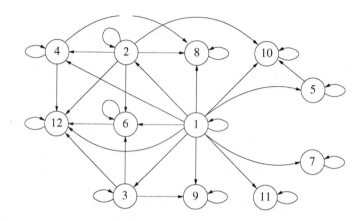

Figure 10.5   The Digraph for Divisibility on $\{1, 2, \ldots, 12\}$.

10.2   Walks and Paths

Picturing digraphs with points and arrows makes it natural to talk about following successive edges through the graph. For example, in the digraph of Figure 10.5, you might start at vertex 1, successively follow the edges from vertex 1 to vertex 2, from 2 to 4, from 4 to 12, and then from 12 to 12 twice (or as many times as you like). The sequence of edges followed in this way is called a *walk* through the graph. A *path* is a walk which never visits a vertex more than once. So following edges from 1 to 2 to 4 to 12 is a path, but it stops being a path if you go to 12 again.

The natural way to represent a walk is with the sequence of sucessive vertices it went through, in this case:

$$1 \;\; 2 \;\; 4 \;\; 12 \;\; 12 \;\; 12.$$

However, it is conventional to represent a walk by an alternating sequence of successive vertices and edges, so this walk would formally be

$$1 \;\; \langle 1 \to 2 \rangle \;\; 2 \;\; \langle 2 \to 4 \rangle \;\; 4 \;\; \langle 4 \to 12 \rangle \;\; 12 \;\; \langle 12 \to 12 \rangle \;\; 12 \;\; \langle 12 \to 12 \rangle \;\; 12. \qquad (10.1)$$

The redundancy of this definition is enough to make any computer scientist cringe, but it does make it easy to talk about how many times vertices and edges occur on the walk. Here is a formal definition:

Definition 10.2.1. A *walk in a digraph* is an alternating sequence of vertices and edges that begins with a vertex, ends with a vertex, and such that for every edge $\langle u \to v \rangle$ in the walk, vertex u is the element just before the edge, and vertex v is the next element after the edge.

So a walk **v** is a sequence of the form

$$\mathbf{v} ::= v_0 \ \langle v_0 \to v_1 \rangle \ v_1 \ \langle v_1 \to v_2 \rangle \ v_2 \ \ldots \ \langle v_{k-1} \to v_k \rangle \ v_k$$

where $\langle v_i \to v_{i+1} \rangle \in E(G)$ for $i \in [0..k)$. The walk is said to *start* at v_0, to *end* at v_k, and the *length* $|\mathbf{v}|$ of the walk is defined to be k.

The walk is a *path* iff all the v_i's are different, that is, if $i \neq j$, then $v_i \neq v_j$.

A *closed walk* is a walk that begins and ends at the same vertex. A *cycle* is a positive length closed walk whose vertices are distinct except for the beginning and end vertices.

Note that a single vertex counts as a length zero path that begins and ends at itself. It also is a closed walk, but does not count as a cycle, since cycles by definition must have positive length. Length one cycles are possible when a node has an arrow leading back to itself. The graph in Figure 10.1 has none, but every vertex in the divisibility relation digraph of Figure 10.5 is in a length one cycle. Length one cycles are sometimes called *self-loops*.

Although a walk is officially an alternating sequence of vertices and edges, it is completely determined just by the sequence of successive vertices on it, or by the sequence of edges on it. We will describe walks in these ways whenever it's convenient. For example, for the graph in Figure 10.1,

- (a, b, d), or simply abd, is a (vertex-sequence description of a) length two path,

- $(\langle a \to b \rangle, \langle b \to d \rangle)$, or simply $\langle a \to b \rangle \langle b \to d \rangle$, is (an edge-sequence description of) the same length two path,

- $abcbd$ is a length four walk,

- $dcbcbd$ is a length five closed walk,

- $bdcb$ is a length three cycle,

- $\langle b \to c \rangle \langle c \to b \rangle$ is a length two cycle, and

- $\langle c \to b \rangle \langle b \leftarrow a \rangle \langle a \to d \rangle$ is *not* a walk. A walk is not allowed to follow edges in the wrong direction.

If you walk for a while, stop for a rest at some vertex, and then continue walking, you have broken a walk into two parts. For example, stopping to rest after following two edges in the walk (10.1) through the divisibility graph breaks the walk into the first part of the walk

$$1 \ \langle 1 \to 2 \rangle \ 2 \ \langle 2 \to 4 \rangle \ 4 \tag{10.2}$$

from 1 to 4, and the rest of the walk

$$4 \; \langle 4 \to 12 \rangle \; 12 \; \langle 12 \to 12 \rangle \; 12 \; \langle 12 \to 12 \rangle \; 12. \qquad (10.3)$$

from 4 to 12, and we'll say the whole walk (10.1) is the *merge* walks (10.2) and (10.3). In general, if a walk $\mathbf{f}$ ends with a vertex v and a walk $\mathbf{r}$ starts with the same vertex v we'll say that their *merge* $\mathbf{f} \mathbf{\hat{\ }} \mathbf{r}$ is the walk that starts with $\mathbf{f}$ and continues with $\mathbf{r}$.[1] Two walks can only be merged if the first walk ends at the same vertex v with which the second one walk starts. Sometimes it's useful to name the node v where the walks merge; we'll use the notation $\mathbf{f} \, \widehat{v} \, \mathbf{r}$ to describe the merge of a walk $\mathbf{f}$ that ends at v with a walk $\mathbf{r}$ that begins at v.

A consequence of this definition is that

Lemma 10.2.2.

$$|\mathbf{f} \mathbf{\hat{\ }} \mathbf{r}| = |\mathbf{f}| + |\mathbf{r}|.$$

In the next section we'll get mileage out of walking this way.

10.2.1   Finding a Path

If you were trying to walk somewhere quickly, you'd know you were in trouble if you came to the same place twice. This is actually a basic theorem of graph theory.

Theorem 10.2.3. *The shortest walk from one vertex to another is a path.*

Proof. If there is a walk from vertex u to another vertex $v \neq u$, then by the Well Ordering Principle, there must be a minimum length walk $\mathbf{w}$ from u to v. We claim $\mathbf{w}$ is a path.

To prove the claim, suppose to the contrary that $\mathbf{w}$ is not a path, meaning that some vertex x occurs twice on this walk. That is,

$$\mathbf{w} = \mathbf{e} \, \widehat{x} \, \mathbf{f} \, \widehat{x} \, \mathbf{g}$$

for some walks $\mathbf{e}, \mathbf{f}, \mathbf{g}$ where the length of $\mathbf{f}$ is positive. But then "deleting" $\mathbf{f}$ yields a strictly shorter walk

$$\mathbf{e} \, \widehat{x} \, \mathbf{g}$$

from u to v, contradicting the minimality of $\mathbf{w}$.   ■

Definition 10.2.4. The *distance*, dist (u, v), in a graph from vertex u to vertex v is the length of a shortest path from u to v.

---

[1] It's tempting to say the *merge* is the concatenation of the two walks, but that wouldn't quite be right because if the walks were concatenated, the vertex v would appear twice in a row where the walks meet.

As would be expected, this definition of distance satisfies:

Lemma 10.2.5. *[The Triangle Inequality]*

$$dist\,(u,v) \le dist\,(u,x) + dist\,(x,v)$$

for all vertices u,v,x with equality holding iff x is on a shortest path from u to v.

Of course, you might expect this property to be true, but distance has a technical definition and its properties can't be taken for granted. For example, unlike ordinary distance in space, the distance from u to v is typically different from the distance from v to u. So, let's prove the Triangle Inequality

Proof. To prove the inequality, suppose **f** is a shortest path from u to x and **r** is a shortest path from x to v. Then by Lemma 10.2.2, $\mathbf{f}\,\widehat{x}\,\mathbf{r}$ is a walk of length $dist\,(u,x) + dist\,(x,v)$ from u to v, so this sum is an upper bound on the length of the shortest path from u to v by Theorem 10.2.3.

Proof of the "iff" is in Problem 10.3. ∎

Finally, the relationship between walks and paths extends to closed walks and cycles:

Lemma 10.2.6. *The shortest positive length closed walk through a vertex is a cycle through that vertex.*

The proof of Lemma 10.2.6 is essentially the same as for Theorem 10.2.3; see Problem 10.4.

10.3 Adjacency Matrices

If a graph G has n vertices $v_0, v_1, \ldots, v_{n-1}$, a useful way to represent it is with an $n \times n$ matrix of zeroes and ones called its *adjacency matrix* A_G. The ijth entry of the adjacency matrix, $(A_G)_{ij}$, is 1 if there is an edge from vertex v_i to vertex v_j and 0 otherwise. That is,

$$(A_G)_{ij} ::= \begin{cases} 1 & \text{if } \langle v_i \to v_j \rangle \in E(G), \\ 0 & \text{otherwise.} \end{cases}$$

For example, let H be the 4-node graph shown in Figure 10.1. Its adjacency matrix A_H is the 4×4 matrix:

$$
A_H = \begin{array}{c|cccc}
 & a & b & c & d \\
\hline
a & 0 & 1 & 0 & 1 \\
b & 0 & 0 & 1 & 1 \\
c & 0 & 1 & 0 & 0 \\
d & 0 & 0 & 1 & 0
\end{array}
$$

A payoff of this representation is that we can use matrix powers to count numbers of walks between vertices. For example, there are two length two walks between vertices a and c in the graph H:

$$a \ \langle a \to b \rangle \ b \ \langle b \to c \rangle \ c$$
$$a \ \langle a \to d \rangle \ d \ \langle d \to c \rangle \ c$$

and these are the only length two walks from a to c. Also, there is exactly one length two walk from b to c and exactly one length two walk from c to c and from d to b, and these are the only length two walks in H. It turns out we could have read these counts from the entries in the matrix $(A_H)^2$:

$$
(A_H)^2 = \begin{array}{c|cccc}
 & a & b & c & d \\
\hline
a & 0 & 0 & 2 & 1 \\
b & 0 & 1 & 1 & 0 \\
c & 0 & 0 & 1 & 1 \\
d & 0 & 1 & 0 & 0
\end{array}
$$

More generally, the matrix $(A_G)^k$ provides a count of the number of length k walks between vertices in any digraph G as we'll now explain.

Definition 10.3.1. The length-k *walk counting matrix* for an n-vertex graph G is the $n \times n$ matrix C such that

$$C_{uv} ::= \text{the number of length-}k \text{ walks from } u \text{ to } v. \tag{10.4}$$

Notice that the adjacency matrix A_G is the length-1 walk counting matrix for G, and that $(A_G)^0$, which by convention is the identity matrix, is the length-0 walk counting matrix.

Theorem 10.3.2. *If C is the length-k walk counting matrix for a graph G, and D is the length-m walk counting matrix, then CD is the length $k + m$ walk counting matrix for G.*

According to this theorem, the square $(A_G)^2$ of the adjacency matrix is the length two walk counting matrix for G. Applying the theorem again to $(A_G)^2 A_G$ shows that the length-3 walk counting matrix is $(A_G)^3$. More generally, it follows by induction that

Corollary 10.3.3. *The length-k counting matrix of a digraph G is $(A_G)^k$, for all $k \in \mathbb{N}$.*

In other words, you can determine the number of length k walks between any pair of vertices simply by computing the kth power of the adjacency matrix!

That may seem amazing, but the proof uncovers this simple relationship between matrix multiplication and numbers of walks.

Proof of Theorem 10.3.2. Any length $(k+m)$ walk between vertices u and v begins with a length k walk starting at u and ending at some vertex w followed by a length m walk starting at w and ending at v. So the number of length $(k+m)$ walks from u to v that go through w at the kth step equals the number C_{uw} of length k walks from u to w, times the number D_{wv} of length m walks from w to v. We can get the total number of length $(k+m)$ walks from u to v by summing, over all possible vertices w, the number of such walks that go through w at the kth step. In other words,

$$\#\text{length } (k+m) \text{ walks from } u \text{ to } v = \sum_{w \in V(G)} C_{uw} \cdot D_{wv} \qquad (10.5)$$

But the right-hand side of (10.5) is precisely the definition of $(CD)_{uv}$. Thus, CD is indeed the length-$(k+m)$ walk counting matrix. ∎

10.3.1 Shortest Paths

The relation between powers of the adjacency matrix and numbers of walks is cool—to us math nerds at least—but a much more important problem is finding shortest paths between pairs of nodes. For example, when you drive home for vacation, you generally want to take the shortest-time route.

One simple way to find the lengths of all the shortest paths in an n-vertex graph G is to compute the successive powers of A_G one by one up to the $n - 1$st, watching for the first power at which each entry becomes positive. That's because Theorem 10.3.2 implies that the length of the shortest path, if any, between u and v, that is, the distance from u to v, will be the smallest value k for which $(A_G)_{uv}^k$ is nonzero, and if there is a shortest path, its length will be $\leq n - 1$. Refinements of this idea lead to methods that find shortest paths in reasonably efficient ways. The methods apply as well to weighted graphs, where edges are labelled with weights or costs and the objective is to find least weight, cheapest paths. These refinements are typically covered in introductory algorithm courses, and we won't go into them any further.

10.4 Walk Relations

A basic question about a digraph is whether there is a way to get from one particular vertex to another. So for any digraph G we are interested in a binary relation G^*, called the *walk relation* on $V(G)$, where

$$u \; G^* \; v ::= \text{there is a walk in } G \text{ from } u \text{ to } v. \qquad (10.6)$$

Similarly, there is a *positive walk relation*

$$u \; G^+ \; v ::= \text{there is a positive length walk in } G \text{ from } u \text{ to } v. \qquad (10.7)$$

Definition 10.4.1. When there is a walk from vertex v to vertex w, we say that w is *reachable* from v, or equivalently, that v is *connected* to w.

10.4.1 Composition of Relations

There is a simple way to extend composition of functions to composition of relations, and this gives another way to talk about walks and paths in digraphs.

Definition 10.4.2. Let $R : B \to C$ and $S : A \to B$ be binary relations. Then the composition of R with S is the binary relation $(R \circ S) : A \to C$ defined by the rule

$$a \; (R \circ S) \; c ::= \exists b \in B. \, (a \; S \; b) \text{ AND } (b \; R \; c). \qquad (10.8)$$

This agrees with the Definition 4.3.1 of composition in the special case when R and S are functions.[2]

Remembering that a digraph is a binary relation on its vertices, it makes sense to compose a digraph G with itself. Then if we let G^n denote the composition of G with itself n times, it's easy to check (see Problem 10.11) that G^n is the *length-n walk relation*:

$$a \; G^n \; b \quad \text{iff} \quad \text{there is a length } n \text{ walk in } G \text{ from } a \text{ to } b.$$

---

[2]The reversal of the order of R and S in (10.8) is not a typo. This is so that relational composition generalizes function composition. The value of function f composed with function g at an argument x is $f(g(x))$. So in the composition $f \circ g$, the function g is applied first.

This even works for $n = 0$, with the usual convention that G^0 is the *identity relation* $\mathrm{Id}_{V(G)}$ on the set of vertices.[3] Since there is a walk iff there is a path, and every path is of length at most $|V(G)| - 1$, we now have[4]

$$G^* = G^0 \cup G^1 \cup G^2 \cup \ldots \cup G^{|V(G)|-1} = (G \cup G^0)^{|V(G)|-1}. \qquad (10.9)$$

The final equality points to the use of repeated squaring as a way to compute G^* with $\log n$ rather than $n - 1$ compositions of relations.

10.5 Directed Acyclic Graphs & Scheduling

Some of the prerequisites of MIT computer science subjects are shown in Figure 10.6. An edge going from subject s to subject t indicates that s is listed in the catalogue as a direct prerequisite of t. Of course, before you can take subject t, you have to take not only subject s, but also all the prerequisites of s, and any prerequisites of those prerequisites, and so on. We can state this precisely in terms of the positive walk relation: if D is the direct prerequisite relation on subjects, then subject u has to be completed before taking subject v iff $u \; D^+ \; v$.

Of course it would take forever to graduate if this direct prerequisite graph had a positive length closed walk. We need to forbid such closed walks, which by Lemma 10.2.6 is the same as forbidding cycles. So, the direct prerequisite graph among subjects had better be *acyclic*:

Definition 10.5.1. A *directed acyclic graph (DAG)* is a directed graph with no cycles.

DAGs have particular importance in computer science. They capture key concepts used in analyzing task scheduling and concurrency control. When distributing a program across multiple processors, we're in trouble if one part of the program needs an output that another part hasn't generated yet! So let's examine DAGs and their connection to scheduling in more depth.

---

[3]The *identity relation* Id_A on a set A is the equality relation:

$$a \; \mathrm{Id}_A \; b \quad \text{iff} \quad a = b,$$

for $a, b \in A$.

[4]Equation (10.9) involves a harmless abuse of notation: we should have written

$$\mathrm{graph}(G^*) = \mathrm{graph}(G^0) \cup \mathrm{graph}(G^1)\ldots.$$

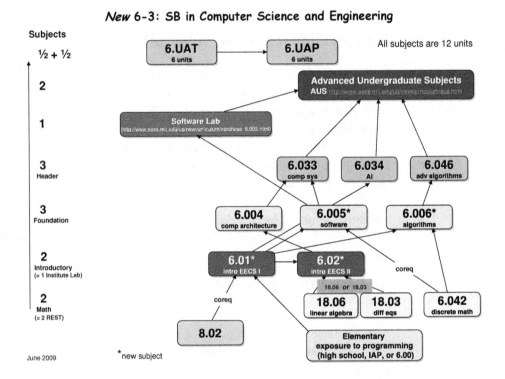

Figure 10.6   Subject prerequisites for MIT Computer Science (6-3) Majors.

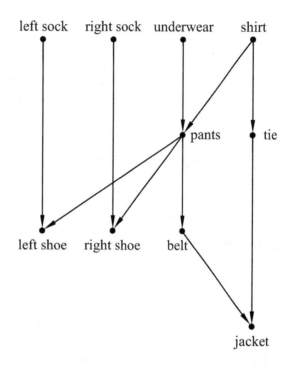

Figure 10.7 DAG describing which clothing items have to be put on before others.

10.5.1 Scheduling

In a scheduling problem, there is a set of tasks, along with a set of constraints specifying that starting certain tasks depends on other tasks being completed beforehand. We can map these sets to a digraph, with the tasks as the nodes and the direct prerequisite constraints as the edges.

For example, the DAG in Figure 10.7 describes how a man might get dressed for a formal occasion. As we describe above, vertices correspond to garments and the edges specify which garments have to be put on before which others.

When faced with a set of prerequisites like this one, the most basic task is finding an order in which to perform all the tasks, one at a time, while respecting the dependency constraints. Ordering tasks in this way is known as *topological sorting*.

Definition 10.5.2. A *topological sort* of a finite DAG is a list of all the vertices such that each vertex v appears earlier in the list than every other vertex reachable from v.

There are many ways to get dressed one item at a time while obeying the constraints of Figure 10.7. We have listed two such topological sorts in Figure 10.8. In

underwear	left sock
shirt	shirt
pants	tie
belt	underwear
tie	right sock
jacket	pants
left sock	right shoe
right sock	belt
left shoe	jacket
right shoe	left shoe
(a)	(b)

Figure 10.8   Two possible topological sorts of the prerequisites described in Figure 10.7

.

fact, we can prove that *every* finite DAG has a topological sort. You can think of this as a mathematical proof that you can indeed get dressed in the morning.

Topological sorts for finite DAGs are easy to construct by starting from *minimal* elements:

Definition 10.5.3. An vertex v of a DAG D is *minimum* iff every other vertex is reachable from v.

A vertex v is *minimal* iff v is not reachable from any other vertex.

It can seem peculiar to use the words "minimum" and "minimal" to talk about vertices that start paths. These words come from the perspective that a vertex is "smaller" than any other vertex it connects to. We'll explore this way of thinking about DAGs in the next section, but for now we'll use these terms because they are conventional.

One peculiarity of this terminology is that a DAG may have no minimum element but lots of minimal elements. In particular, the clothing example has four minimal elements: leftsock, rightsock, underwear, and shirt.

To build an order for getting dressed, we pick one of these minimal elements—say, shirt. Now there is a new set of minimal elements; the three elements we didn't chose as step 1 are still minimal, and once we have removed shirt, tie becomes minimal as well. We pick another minimal element, continuing in this way until all elements have been picked. The sequence of elements in the order they were picked will be a topological sort. This is how the topological sorts above were constructed.

So our construction shows:

Theorem 10.5.4. *Every finite DAG has a topological sort.*

There are many other ways of constructing topological sorts. For example, instead of starting from the minimal elements at the beginning of paths, we could build a topological sort starting from *maximal* elements at the end of paths. In fact, we could build a topological sort by picking vertices arbitrarily from a finite DAG and simply inserting them into the list wherever they will fit.[5]

10.5.2 Parallel Task Scheduling

For task dependencies, topological sorting provides a way to execute tasks one after another while respecting those dependencies. But what if we have the ability to execute more than one task at the same time? For example, say tasks are programs, the DAG indicates data dependence, and we have a parallel machine with lots of processors instead of a sequential machine with only one. How should we schedule the tasks? Our goal should be to minimize the total *time* to complete all the tasks. For simplicity, let's say all the tasks take the same amount of time and all the processors are identical.

So given a finite set of tasks, how long does it take to do them all in an optimal parallel schedule? We can use walk relations on acyclic graphs to analyze this problem.

In the first unit of time, we should do all minimal items, so we would put on our left sock, our right sock, our underwear, and our shirt.[6] In the second unit of time, we should put on our pants and our tie. Note that we cannot put on our left or right shoe yet, since we have not yet put on our pants. In the third unit of time, we should put on our left shoe, our right shoe, and our belt. Finally, in the last unit of time, we can put on our jacket. This schedule is illustrated in Figure 10.9.

The total time to do these tasks is 4 units. We cannot do better than 4 units of time because there is a sequence of 4 tasks that must each be done before the next. We have to put on a shirt before pants, pants before a belt, and a belt before a jacket. Such a sequence of items is known as a *chain*.

Definition 10.5.5. Two vertices in a DAG are *comparable* when one of them is reachable from the other. A *chain* in a DAG is a set of vertices such that any two of them are comparable. A vertex in a chain that is reachable from all other vertices in the chain is called a *maximum element* of the chain. A finite chain is said to *end at* its maximum element.

---

[5]In fact, the DAG doesn't even need to be finite, but you'll be relieved to know that we have no need to go into this.

[6]Yes, we know that you can't actually put on both socks at once, but imagine you are being dressed by a bunch of robot processors and you are in a big hurry. Still not working for you? Ok, forget about the clothes and imagine they are programs with the precedence constraints shown in Figure 10.7.

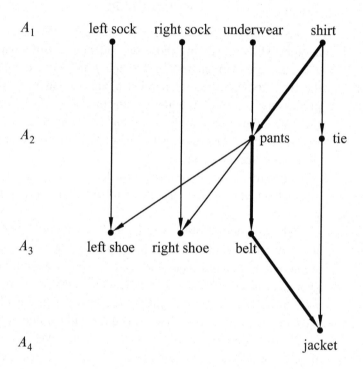

Figure 10.9 A parallel schedule for the tasks-getting-dressed digraph in Figure 10.7. The tasks in A_i can be performed in step i for $1 \leq i \leq 4$. A chain of 4 tasks (the critical path in this example) is shown with bold edges.

The time it takes to schedule tasks, even with an unlimited number of processors, is at least as large as the number of vertices in any chain. That's because if we used less time than the size of some chain, then two items from the chain would have to be done at the same step, contradicting the precedence constraints. For this reason, a *largest* chain is also known as a *critical path*. For example, Figure 10.9 shows the critical path for the getting-dressed digraph.

In this example, we were able to schedule all the tasks with t steps, where t is the size of the largest chain. A nice feature of DAGs is that this is always possible! In other words, for any DAG, there is a legal parallel schedule that runs in t total steps.

In general, a *schedule* for performing tasks specifies which tasks to do at successive steps. Every task a has to be scheduled at some step, and all the tasks that have to be completed before task a must be scheduled for an earlier step. Here's a rigorous definition of schedule.

Definition 10.5.6. A *partition* of a set A is a set of nonempty subsets of A called the *blocks*[7] of the partition, such that every element of A is in exactly one block.

For example, one possible partition of the set $\{a, b, c, d, e\}$ into three blocks is

$$\{a, c\} \qquad \{b, e\} \qquad \{d\}.$$

Definition 10.5.7. A *parallel schedule* for a DAG D is a partition of $V(D)$ into blocks $A_0, A_1, \ldots,$ such that when $j < k$, no vertex in A_j is reachable from any vertex in A_k. The block A_k is called the set of elements *scheduled at step k*, and the *time* of the schedule is the number of blocks. The maximum number of elements scheduled at any step is called the *number of processors* required by the schedule.

A *largest* chain ending at an element a is called a *critical path* to a, and the number of elements less than a in the chain is called the *depth* of a. So in any possible parallel schedule, there must be at least depth (a) steps before task a can be started. In particular, the minimal elements are precisely the elements with depth 0.

There is a very simple schedule that completes every task in its minimum number of steps: just use a "greedy" strategy of performing tasks as soon as possible. Schedule all the elements of depth k at step k. That's how we found the above schedule for getting dressed.

---

[7] We think it would be nicer to call them the *parts* of the partition, but "blocks" is the standard terminology.

Theorem 10.5.8. *A minimum time schedule for a finite DAG D consists of the sets* $A_0, A_1, \ldots,$ *where*

$$A_k ::= \{a \in V(D) \mid \text{depth}\,(a) = k\}.$$

We'll leave to Problem 10.24 the proof that the sets A_k are a parallel schedule according to Definition 10.5.7. We can summarize the story above in this way: with an unlimited number of processors, the parallel time to complete all tasks is simply the size of a critical path:

Corollary 10.5.9. *Parallel time = size of critical path.*

Things get more complex when the number of processors is bounded; see Problem 10.25 for an example.

10.5.3   Dilworth's Lemma

Definition 10.5.10. An *antichain* in a DAG is a set of vertices such that *no* two elements in the set are comparable—no walk exists between any two different vertices in the set.

Our conclusions about scheduling also tell us something about antichains.

Corollary 10.5.11. *In a DAG D if the size of the largest chain is t, then V(D) can be partitioned into t antichains.*

Proof. Let the antichains be the sets $A_k ::= \{a \in V(D) \mid \text{depth}\,(a) = k\}$. It is an easy exercise to verify that each A_k is an antichain (Problem 10.24).   ∎

Corollary 10.5.11 implies[8] a famous result about acyclic digraphs:

Lemma 10.5.12 (Dilworth). *For all $t > 0$, every DAG with n vertices must have either a chain of size greater than t or an antichain of size at least n/t.*

Proof. Assume that there is no chain of size greater than t. Let ℓ be the size of the largest antichain. If we make a parallel schedule according to the proof of Corollary 10.5.11, we create a number of antichains equal to the size of the largest chain, which is less than or equal t. Each element belongs to exactly one antichain, none of which are larger than ℓ. So the total number of elements at most ℓ times t—that is, $\ell t \geq n$. Simple division implies that $\ell \geq n/t$.   ∎

---

[8]Lemma 10.5.12 also follows from a more general result known as Dilworth's Theorem, which we will not discuss.

Corollary 10.5.13. *Every DAG with n vertices has a chain of size greater than $\sqrt{n}$ or an antichain of size at least $\sqrt{n}$.*

Proof. Set $t = \sqrt{n}$ in Lemma 10.5.12. ∎

Example 10.5.14. When the man in our example is getting dressed, $n = 10$.
   Try $t = 3$. There is a chain of size 4.
   Try $t = 4$. There is no chain of size 5, but there is an antichain of size $4 \geq 10/4$.

10.6 Partial Orders

After mapping the "direct prerequisite" relation onto a digraph, we were then able to use the tools for understanding computer scientists' graphs to make deductions about something as mundane as getting dressed. This may or may not have impressed you, but we can do better. In the introduction to this chapter, we mentioned a useful fact that bears repeating: any digraph is formally the same as a binary relation whose domain and codomain are its vertices. This means that *any* binary relation whose domain is the same as its codomain can be translated into a digraph! Talking about the edges of a binary relation or the image of a set under a digraph may seem odd at first, but doing so will allow us to draw important connections between different types of relations. For instance, we can apply Dilworth's lemma to the "direct prerequisite" relation for getting dressed, because the graph of that relation was a DAG.

But how can we tell if a binary relation is a DAG? And once we know that a relation is a DAG, what exactly can we conclude? In this section, we will abstract some of the properties that a binary relation might have, and use those properties to define classes of relations. In particular, we'll explain this section's title, *partial orders*.

10.6.1 The Properties of the Walk Relation in DAGs

To begin, let's talk about some features common to all digraphs. Since merging a walk from u to v with a walk from v to w gives a walk from u to w, both the walk and positive walk relations have a relational property called *transitivity*:

Definition 10.6.1. A binary relation R on a set A is *transitive* iff

$$(a \ R \ b \ \text{AND} \ b \ R \ c) \ \text{IMPLIES} \ a \ R \ c$$

for every $a, b, c \in A$.

So we have

Lemma 10.6.2. *For any digraph G the walk relations G^+ and G^* are transitive.*

Since there is a length zero walk from any vertex to itself, the walk relation has another relational property called *reflexivity*:

Definition 10.6.3. A binary relation R on a set A is *reflexive* iff $a \mathrel{R} a$ for all $a \in A$.

Now we have

Lemma 10.6.4. *For any digraph G, the walk relation G^* is reflexive.*

We know that a digraph is a DAG iff it has no positive length closed walks. Since any vertex on a closed walk can serve as the beginning and end of the walk, saying a graph is a DAG is the same as saying that there is no positive length path from any vertex back to itself. This means that the positive walk relation of D^+ of a DAG has a relational property called *irreflexivity*.

Definition 10.6.5. A binary relation R on a set A is *irreflexive* iff

$$\text{NOT}(a \mathrel{R} a)$$

for all $a \in A$.

So we have

Lemma 10.6.6. *R is a DAG iff R^+ is irreflexive.*

10.6.2   Strict Partial Orders

Here is where we begin to define interesting classes of relations:

Definition 10.6.7. A relation that is transitive and irreflexive is called a *strict partial order.*

A simple connection between strict partial orders and DAGs now follows from Lemma 10.6.6:

Theorem 10.6.8. *A relation R is a strict partial order iff R is the positive walk relation of a DAG.*

Strict partial orders come up in many situations which on the face of it have nothing to do with digraphs. For example, the less-than order $<$ on numbers is a strict partial order:

- if $x < y$ and $y < z$ then $x < z$, so less-than is transitive, and

- $\text{NOT}(x < x)$, so less-than is irreflexive.

The proper containment relation $\subset$ is also a partial order:

- if $A \subset B$ and $B \subset C$ then $A \subset C$, so containment is transitive, and

- $\text{NOT}(A \subset A)$, so proper containment is irreflexive.

If there are two vertices that are reachable from each other, then there is a positive length closed walk that starts at one vertex, goes to the other, and then comes back. So DAGs are digraphs in which no two vertices are mutually reachable. This corresponds to a relational property called *asymmetry*.

Definition 10.6.9. A binary relation R on a set A is *asymmetric* iff

$$a \; R \; b \;\;\; \text{IMPLIES} \;\;\; \text{NOT}(b \; R \; a)$$

for all $a, b \in A$.

So we can also characterize DAGs in terms of asymmetry:

Corollary 10.6.10. *A digraph D is a DAG iff D^+ is asymmetric.*

Corollary 10.6.10 and Theorem 10.6.8 combine to give

Corollary 10.6.11. *A binary relation R on a set A is a strict partial order iff it is transitive and asymmetric.*[9]

A strict partial order may be the positive walk relation of different DAGs. This raises the question of finding a DAG with the *smallest* number of edges that determines a given strict partial order. For *finite* strict partial orders, the smallest such DAG turns out to be unique and easy to find (see Problem 10.30).

10.6.3 Weak Partial Orders

The less-than-or-equal relation $\leq$ is at least as familiar as the less-than strict partial order, and the ordinary containment relation $\subseteq$ is even more common than the proper containment relation. These are examples of *weak partial orders*, which are just strict partial orders with the additional condition that every element is related to itself. To state this precisely, we have to relax the asymmetry property so it does not apply when a vertex is compared to itself; this relaxed property is called *antisymmetry*:

---

[9] Some texts use this corollary to define strict partial orders.

Definition 10.6.12. A binary relation R on a set A, is *antisymmetric* iff, for all $a \neq b \in A$,

$$a \, R \, b \text{ IMPLIES NOT}(b \, R \, a)$$

Now we can give an axiomatic definition of weak partial orders that parallels the definition of strict partial orders.

Definition 10.6.13. A binary relation on a set is a *weak partial order* iff it is transitive, reflexive, and antisymmetric.

The following lemma gives another characterization of weak partial orders that follows directly from this definition.

Lemma 10.6.14. *A relation R on a set A is a weak partial order iff there is a strict partial order S on A such that*

$$a \, R \, b \quad \text{iff} \quad (a \, S \, b \text{ OR } a = b),$$

for all $a, b \in A$.

Since a length zero walk goes from a vertex to itself, this lemma combined with Theorem 10.6.8 yields:

Corollary 10.6.15. *A relation is a weak partial order iff it is the walk relation of a DAG.*

For weak partial orders in general, we often write an ordering-style symbol like $\preceq$ or $\sqsubseteq$ instead of a letter symbol like R.[10] Likewise, we generally use $\prec$ or $\sqsubset$ to indicate a strict partial order.

Two more examples of partial orders are worth mentioning:

Example 10.6.16. Let A be some family of sets and define $a \, R \, b$ iff $a \supset b$. Then R is a strict partial order.

Example 10.6.17. The divisibility relation is a weak partial order on the nonnegative integers.

For practice with the definitions, you can check that two more examples are vacuously partial orders on a set D: the identity relation Id_D is a weak partial order, and the *empty relation*—the relation with no arrows—is a strict partial order.

Note that some authors define "partial orders" to be what we call weak partial orders. However, we'll use the phrase "partial order" to mean a relation that may be either a weak or strict partial order.

---

[10] General relations are usually denoted by a letter like R instead of a cryptic squiggly symbol, so $\preceq$ is kind of like the musical performer/composer Prince, who redefined the spelling of his name to be his own squiggly symbol. A few years ago he gave up and went back to the spelling "Prince."

10.7   Representing Partial Orders by Set Containment

Axioms can be a great way to abstract and reason about important properties of objects, but it helps to have a clear picture of the things that satisfy the axioms. DAGs provide one way to picture partial orders, but it also can help to picture them in terms of other familiar mathematical objects. In this section, we'll show that every partial order can be pictured as a collection of sets related by containment. That is, every partial order has the "same shape" as such a collection. The technical word for "same shape" is "isomorphic."

Definition 10.7.1. A binary relation R on a set A is *isomorphic* to a relation S on a set B iff there is a relation-preserving bijection from A to B; that is, there is a bijection $f : A \to B$ such that for all $a, a' \in A$,

$$a \ R \ a' \quad \text{iff} \quad f(a) \ S \ f(a').$$

To picture a partial order $\preceq$ on a set A as a collection of sets, we simply represent each element A by the set of elements that are $\preceq$ to that element, that is,

$$a \longleftrightarrow \{b \in A \mid b \preceq a\}.$$

For example, if $\preceq$ is the divisibility relation on the set of integers $\{1, 3, 4, 6, 8, 12\}$, then we represent each of these integers by the set of integers in A that divides it. So

$$
\begin{aligned}
1 &\longleftrightarrow \{1\} \\
3 &\longleftrightarrow \{1, 3\} \\
4 &\longleftrightarrow \{1, 4\} \\
6 &\longleftrightarrow \{1, 3, 6\} \\
8 &\longleftrightarrow \{1, 4, 8\} \\
12 &\longleftrightarrow \{1, 3, 4, 6, 12\}
\end{aligned}
$$

So, the fact that $3 \mid 12$ corresponds to the fact that $\{1, 3\} \subseteq \{1, 3, 4, 6, 12\}$.

In this way we have completely captured the weak partial order $\preceq$ by the subset relation on the corresponding sets. Formally, we have

Lemma 10.7.2. *Let $\preceq$ be a weak partial order on a set A. Then $\preceq$ is isomorphic to the subset relation $\subseteq$ on the collection of inverse images under the $\preceq$ relation of elements $a \in A$.*

We leave the proof to Problem 10.36. Essentially the same construction shows that strict partial orders can be represented by sets under the proper subset relation, $\subset$ (Problem 10.37). To summarize:

Theorem 10.7.3. *Every weak partial order $\preceq$ is isomorphic to the subset relation $\subseteq$ on a collection of sets.*

Every strict partial order $\prec$ is isomorphic to the proper subset relation $\subset$ on a collection of sets.

10.8   Linear Orders

The familiar order relations on numbers have an important additional property: given two different numbers, one will be bigger than the other. Partial orders with this property are said to be *linear orders*. You can think of a linear order as one where all the elements are lined up so that everyone knows exactly who is ahead and who is behind them in the line.[11]

Definition 10.8.1. Let R be a binary relation on a set A and let a, b be elements of A. Then a and b are *comparable* with respect to R iff [$a \ R \ b$ OR $b \ R \ a$]. A partial order for which every two different elements are comparable is called a *linear order*.

So $<$ and $\leq$ are linear orders on $\mathbb{R}$. On the other hand, the subset relation is *not* linear, since, for example, any two different finite sets of the same size will be incomparable under $\subseteq$. The prerequisite relation on Course 6 required subjects is also not linear because, for example, neither 8.01 nor 6.042 is a prerequisite of the other.

10.9   Product Orders

Taking the product of two relations is a useful way to construct new relations from old ones.

---

[11] Linear orders are often called "total" orders, but this terminology conflicts with the definition of "total relation," and it regularly confuses students.

Being a linear order is a much stronger condition than being a partial order that is a total relation. For example, any weak partial order is a total relation but generally won't be linear.

Definition 10.9.1. The product $R_1 \times R_2$ of relations R_1 and R_2 is defined to be the relation with

$$\text{domain}(R_1 \times R_2) \quad ::= \quad \text{domain}(R_1) \times \text{domain}(R_2),$$
$$\text{codomain}(R_1 \times R_2) \quad ::= \quad \text{codomain}(R_1) \times \text{codomain}(R_2),$$
$$(a_1, a_2)\,(R_1 \times R_2)\,(b_1, b_2) \quad \text{iff} \quad [a_1\, R_1\, b_1 \text{ and } a_2\, R_2\, b_2].$$

It follows directly from the definitions that products preserve the properties of transitivity, reflexivity, irreflexivity, and antisymmetry (see Problem 10.50). If R_1 and R_2 both have one of these properties, then so does $R_1 \times R_2$. This implies that if R_1 and R_2 are both partial orders, then so is $R_1 \times R_2$.

Example 10.9.2. Define a relation Y on age-height pairs of being younger *and* shorter. This is the relation on the set of pairs (y, h) where y is a nonnegative integer ≤ 2400 that we interpret as an age in months, and h is a nonnegative integer ≤ 120 describing height in inches. We define Y by the rule

$$(y_1, h_1)\, Y\, (y_2, h_2) \quad \text{iff} \quad y_1 \leq y_2 \text{ AND } h_1 \leq h_2.$$

That is, Y is the product of the $\leq$-relation on ages and the $\leq$-relation on heights.

Since both ages and heights are ordered numerically, the age-height relation Y is a partial order. Now suppose we have a class of 101 students. Then we can apply Dilworth's lemma 10.5.12 to conclude that there is a chain of 11 students—that is, 11 students who get taller as they get older–or an antichain of 11 students—that is, 11 students who get taller as they get younger, which makes for an amusing in-class demo.

On the other hand, the property of being a linear order is not preserved. For example, the age-height relation Y is the product of two linear orders, but it is not linear: the age 240 months, height 68 inches pair, (240,68), and the pair (228,72) are incomparable under Y.

10.10   Equivalence Relations

Definition 10.10.1. A relation is an *equivalence relation* if it is reflexive, symmetric, and transitive.

Congruence modulo n is an important example of an equivalence relation:

- It is reflexive because $x \equiv x \pmod{n}$.

- It is symmetric because $x \equiv y \pmod{n}$ implies $y \equiv x \pmod{n}$.

- It is transitive because $x \equiv y \pmod{n}$ and $y \equiv z \pmod{n}$ imply that $x \equiv z \pmod{n}$.

There is an even more well-known example of an equivalence relation: equality itself.

Any total function defines an equivalence relation on its domain:

Definition 10.10.2. If $f : A \to B$ is a total function, define a relation $\equiv_f$ by the rule:

$$a \equiv_f a' \text{ IFF } f(a) = f(a').$$

From its definition, $\equiv_f$ is reflexive, symmetric and transitive because these are properties of equality. That is, $\equiv_f$ is an equivalence relation. This observation gives another way to see that congruence modulo n is an equivalence relation: the Remainder Lemma 9.6.1 implies that congruence modulo n is the same as $\equiv_r$ where $r(a)$ is the remainder of a divided by n.

In fact, a relation is an equivalence relation iff it equals $\equiv_f$ for some total function f (see Problem 10.56). So equivalence relations could have been defined using Definition 10.10.2.

10.10.1   Equivalence Classes

Equivalence relations are closely related to partitions because the images of elements under an equivalence relation are the blocks of a partition.

Definition 10.10.3. Given an equivalence relation $R : A \to A$, the *equivalence class* $[a]_R$ of an element $a \in A$ is the set of all elements of A related to a by R. Namely,

$$[a]_R ::= \{x \in A \mid a \ R \ x\}.$$

In other words, $[a]_R$ is the image $R(a)$.

For example, suppose that $A = \mathbb{Z}$ and $a \ R \ b$ means that $a \equiv b \pmod{5}$. Then

$$[7]_R = \{\ldots, -3, 2, 7, 12, 22, \ldots\}.$$

Notice that 7, 12, 17, etc., all have the same equivalence class; that is, $[7]_R = [12]_R = [17]_R = \cdots$.

There is an exact correspondence between equivalence relations on A and partitions of A. Namely, given any partition of a set, being in the same block is obviously an equivalence relation. On the other hand we have:

Theorem 10.10.4. *The equivalence classes of an equivalence relation on a set A are the blocks of a partition of A.*

We'll leave the proof of Theorem 10.10.4 as a basic exercise in axiomatic reasoning (see Problem 10.55), but let's look at an example. The congruent-mod-5 relation partitions the integers into five equivalence classes:

$$\{\ldots, -5, 0, 5, 10, 15, 20, \ldots\}$$
$$\{\ldots, -4, 1, 6, 11, 16, 21, \ldots\}$$
$$\{\ldots, -3, 2, 7, 12, 17, 22, \ldots\}$$
$$\{\ldots, -2, 3, 8, 13, 18, 23, \ldots\}$$
$$\{\ldots, -1, 4, 9, 14, 19, 24, \ldots\}$$

In these terms, $x \equiv y \pmod 5$ is equivalent to the assertion that x and y are both in the same block of this partition. For example, $6 \equiv 16 \pmod 5$, because they're both in the second block, but $2 \not\equiv 9 \pmod 5$ because 2 is in the third block while 9 is in the last block.

In social terms, if "likes" were an equivalence relation, then everyone would be partitioned into cliques of friends who all like each other and no one else.

10.11 Summary of Relational Properties

A relation $R : A \rightarrow A$ is the same as a digraph with vertices A.

Reflexivity R is *reflexive* when

$$\forall x \in A. \ x \ R \ x.$$

Every vertex in R has a self-loop.

Irreflexivity R is *irreflexive* when

$$\text{NOT}[\exists x \in A. \ x \ R \ x].$$

There are no self-loops in R.

Symmetry R is *symmetric* when

$$\forall x, y \in A. \ x \ R \ y \ \text{IMPLIES} \ y \ R \ x.$$

If there is an edge from x to y in R, then there is an edge back from y to x as well.

Asymmetry R is *asymmetric* when

$$\forall x, y \in A. \; x \, R \, y \;\; \text{IMPLIES NOT}(y \, R \, x).$$

There is at most one directed edge between any two vertices in R, and there are no self-loops.

Antisymmetry R is *antisymmetric* when

$$\forall x \neq y \in A. \; x \, R \, y \;\; \text{IMPLIES NOT}(y \, R \, x).$$

Equivalently,

$$\forall x, y \in A. \; (x \, R \, y \;\text{AND}\; y \, R \, x) \;\; \text{IMPLIES} \;\; x = y.$$

There is at most one directed edge between any two distinct vertices, but there may be self-loops.

Transitivity R is *transitive* when

$$\forall x, y, z \in A. \; (x \, R \, y \;\text{AND}\; y \, R \, z) \;\; \text{IMPLIES} \; x \, R \, z.$$

If there is a positive length path from u to v, then there is an edge from u to v.

Linear R is *linear* when

$$\forall x \neq y \in A. \; (x \, R \, y \;\; \text{OR} \;\; y \, R \, x)$$

Given any two vertices in R, there is an edge in one direction or the other between them.

Strict Partial Order R is a *strict partial order* iff R is transitive and irreflexive iff R is transitive and asymmetric iff it is the positive length walk relation of a DAG.

Weak Partial Order R is a *weak partial order* iff R is transitive and anti-symmetric and reflexive iff R is the walk relation of a DAG.

Equivalence Relation R is an *equivalence relation* iff R is reflexive, symmetric and transitive iff R equals the *in-the-same-block*-relation for some partition of domain(R).

Problems for Section 10.1

Practice Problems

Problem 10.1.
Let S be a nonempty set of size $n \in \mathbb{Z}^+$, and let $f : S \to S$ be total function. Let D_f be the digraph with vertices S whose edges are $\{\langle s \to f(s) \rangle \mid s \in S\}$.

(a) What are the possible values of the out-degrees of vertices of D_f?

(b) What are the possible values of the in-degrees of the vertices?

(c) Suppose f is a surjection. Now what are the possible values of the in-degrees of the vertices?

Exam Problems

Problem 10.2.
The proof of the Handshaking Lemma 10.1.2 invoked the "obvious" fact that in any finite digraph, the sum of the in-degrees of the vertices equals the number of arrows in the graph. That is,

Claim. *For any finite digraph G*

$$\sum_{v \in V(G)} \mathrm{indeg}(v) = |\mathrm{graph}(G)|, \tag{10.10}$$

But this Claim might not be obvious to everyone. So prove it by induction on the number $|\mathrm{graph}(G)|$ of arrows.

Problems for Section 10.2

Practice Problems

Problem 10.3.
Lemma 10.2.5 states that dist $(u, v) \le$ dist $(u, x) +$ dist (x, v). It also states that equality holds iff x is on a shortest path from u to v.

(a) Prove the "iff" statement from left to right.

(b) Prove the "iff" from right to left.

Class Problems

Problem 10.4. (a) Give an example of a digraph that has a closed walk including two vertices but has no cycle including those vertices.

(b) Prove Lemma 10.2.6:

Lemma. *The shortest positive length closed walk through a vertex is a cycle.*

Problem 10.5.

A 3-bit string is a string made up of 3 characters, each a 0 or a 1. Suppose you'd like to write out, in one string, all eight of the 3-bit strings in any convenient order. For example, if you wrote out the 3-bit strings in the usual order starting with 000 001 010..., you could concatenate them together to get a length $3 \cdot 8 = 24$ string that started 000001010....

But you can get a shorter string containing all eight 3-bit strings by starting with 00010.... Now 000 is present as bits 1 through 3, and 001 is present as bits 2 through 4, and 010 is present as bits 3 through 5, ...

(a) Say a string is *3-good* if it contains every 3-bit string as 3 consecutive bits somewhere in it. Find a 3-good string of length 10, and explain why this is the minimum length for any string that is 3-good.

(b) Explain how any walk that includes every edge in the graph shown in Figure 10.10 determines a string that is 3-good. Find the walk in this graph that determines your 3-good string from part (a).

(c) Explain why a walk in the graph of Figure 10.10 that includes every every edge *exactly once* provides a minimum-length 3-good string.[12]

(d) Generalize the 2-bit graph to a k-bit digraph B_k for $k \geq 2$, where $V(B_k) ::= \{0, 1\}^k$, and any walk through B_k that contains every edge exactly once determines a minimum length $(k + 1)$-good bit-string.[13]

What is this minimum length?

Define the transitions of B_k. Verify that the in-degree of each vertex is the same as its out-degree and that there is a positive path from any vertex to any other vertex (including itself) of length at most k.

---

[12]The 3-good strings explained here generalize to n-good strings for $n \geq 3$. They were studied by the great Dutch mathematician/logician Nicolaas de Bruijn, and are known as *de Bruijn sequences*. de Bruijn died in February, 2012 at the age of 94.

[13]Problem 10.7 explains why such "Eulerian" paths exist.

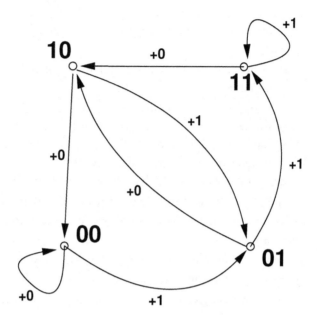

Figure 10.10   The 2-bit graph.

Homework Problems

Problem 10.6. (a) Give an example of a digraph in which a vertex v is on a positive even-length closed walk, but *no* vertex is on an even-length cycle.

(b) Give an example of a digraph in which a vertex v is on an odd-length closed walk but not on an odd-length cycle.

(c) Prove that every odd-length closed walk contains a vertex that is on an odd-length cycle.

Problem 10.7.

An *Euler tour*[14] of a graph is a closed walk that includes every edge exactly once. Such walks are named after the famous 17th century mathematician Leonhard Euler. (Same Euler as for the constant $e \approx 2.718$ and the totient function ϕ—he did a lot of stuff.)

So how do you tell in general whether a graph has an Euler tour? At first glance this may seem like a daunting problem (the similar sounding problem of finding a cycle that touches every vertex exactly once is one of those million dollar NP-

---

[14]In some other texts, this is called an *Euler circuit*.

complete problems known as the *Hamiltonian Cycle Problem*)—but it turns out to be easy.

(a) Show that if a graph has an Euler tour, then the in-degree of each vertex equals its out-degree.

A digraph is *weakly connected* if there is a "path" between any two vertices that may follow edges backwards or forwards.[15] In the remaining parts, we'll work out the converse. Suppose a graph is weakly connected, and the in-degree of every vertex equals its out-degree. We will show that the graph has an Euler tour.

A *trail* is a walk in which each edge occurs *at most* once.

(b) Suppose that a trail in a weakly connected graph does not include every edge. Explain why there must be an edge not on the trail that starts or ends at a vertex on the trail.

In the remaining parts, assume the graph is weakly connected, and the in-degree of every vertex equals its out-degree. Let **w** be the *longest* trail in the graph.

(c) Show that if **w** is closed, then it must be an Euler tour.

Hint: part (b)

(d) Explain why all the edges starting at the end of **w** must be on **w**.

(e) Show that if **w** was not closed, then the in-degree of the end would be bigger than its out-degree.

Hint: part (d)

(f) Conclude that if the in-degree of every vertex equals its out-degree in a finite, weakly connected digraph, then the digraph has an Euler tour.

Problems for Section 10.3

Homework Problems

Problem 10.8.

The *weight of a walk* in a weighted graph is the sum of the weights of the successive

---

[15]More precisely, a graph G is weakly connected iff there is a path from any vertex to any other vertex in the graph H with

$$V(H) = V(G), \text{ and}$$
$$E(H) = E(G) \cup \{\langle v \to u \rangle \mid \langle u \to v \rangle \in E(G)\}.$$

In other words $H = G \cup G^{-1}$.

edges in the walk. The *minimum weight matrix* for length k walks in an n-vertex graph G is the $n \times n$ matrix W such that for $u, v \in V(G)$,

$$W_{uv} ::= \begin{cases} w & \text{if } w \text{ is the minimum weight among length } k \text{ walks from } u \text{ to } v, \\ \infty & \text{if there is no length } k \text{ walk from } u \text{ to } v. \end{cases}$$

The min+ product of two $n \times n$ matrices W and M with entries in $\mathbb{R} \cup \{\infty\}$ is the $n \times n$ matrix $W \underset{min+}{\cdot} M$ whose ij entry is

$$(W \underset{min+}{\cdot} V)_{ij} ::= \min\{W_{ik} + V_{kj} \mid 1 \leq k \leq n\}.$$

Prove the following theorem.

Theorem. *If W is the minimum weight matrix for length k walks in a weighted graph G, and V is the minimum weight matrix for length m walks, then $W \underset{min+}{\cdot} V$ is the minimum weight matrix for length $k + m$ walks.*

Problems for Section 10.4

Practice Problems

Problem 10.9.
Let

$$A ::= \{1, 2, 3\}$$
$$B ::= \{4, 5, 6\}$$
$$R ::= \{(1, 4), (1, 5), (2, 5), (3, 6)\}$$
$$S ::= \{(4, 5), (4, 6), (5, 4)\}.$$

Note that R is a relation from A to B and S is a relation from B to B.
   List the pairs in each of the relations below.
(a) $S \circ R$.

(b) $S \circ S$.

(c) $S^{-1} \circ R$.

Problem 10.10.

In a round-robin tournament, every two distinct players play against each other just once. For a round-robin tournament with no tied games, a record of who beat whom can be described with a *tournament digraph*, where the vertices correspond to players and there is an edge $\langle x \to y \rangle$ iff x beat y in their game.

A *ranking* is a path that includes all the players. So in a ranking, each player won the game against the next lowest ranked player, but may very well have lost their games against much lower ranked players—whoever does the ranking may have a lot of room to play favorites.

(a) Give an example of a tournament digraph with more than one ranking.

(b) Prove that if a tournament digraph is a DAG, then it has at most one ranking.

(c) Prove that every finite tournament digraph has a ranking.

Optional

(d) Prove that the greater-than relation $>$ on the rational numbers $\mathbb{Q}$ is a DAG and a tournament graph that has no ranking.

Homework Problems

Problem 10.11.

Let R be a binary relation on a set A. Regarding R as a digraph, let $W^{(n)}$ denote the length-n walk relation in the digraph R, that is,

$$a \; W^{(n)} \; b ::= \text{there is a length } n \text{ walk from } a \text{ to } b \text{ in } R.$$

(a) Prove that

$$W^{(n)} \circ W^{(m)} = W^{(m+n)} \tag{10.11}$$

for all $m, n \in \mathbb{N}$, where $\circ$ denotes relational composition.

(b) Let R^n be the composition of R with itself n times for $n \geq 0$. So $R^0 ::= \mathrm{Id}_A$, and $R^{n+1} ::= R \circ R^n$.

Conclude that

$$R^n = W^{(n)} \tag{10.12}$$

for all $n \in \mathbb{N}$.

(c) Conclude that

$$R^+ = \bigcup_{i=1}^{|A|} R^i$$

where R^+ is the positive length walk relation determined by R on the set A.

Problem 10.12.

We can represent a relation S between two sets $A = \{a_1, \ldots, a_n\}$ and $B = \{b_1, \ldots, b_m\}$ as an $n \times m$ matrix M_S of zeroes and ones, with the elements of M_S defined by the rule

$$M_S(i, j) = 1 \quad \text{IFF} \quad a_i \, S \, b_j.$$

If we represent relations as matrices this way, then we can compute the composition of two relations R and S by a "boolean" matrix multiplication $\otimes$ of their matrices. Boolean matrix multiplication is the same as matrix multiplication except that addition is replaced by OR, multiplication is replaced by AND, and 0 and 1 are used as the Boolean values **False** and **True**. Namely, suppose $R : B \to C$ is a binary relation with $C = \{c_1, \ldots, c_p\}$. So M_R is an $m \times p$ matrix. Then $M_S \otimes M_R$ is an $n \times p$ matrix defined by the rule:

$$[M_S \otimes M_R](i, j) ::= \text{OR}_{k=1}^{m}[M_S(i, k) \text{ AND } M_R(k, j)]. \tag{10.13}$$

Prove that the matrix representation $M_{R \circ S}$ of $R \circ S$ equals $M_S \otimes M_R$ (note the reversal of R and S).

Problem 10.13.

Suppose that there are n chickens in a farmyard. Chickens are rather aggressive birds that tend to establish dominance in relationships by pecking; hence the term "pecking order." In particular, for each pair of distinct chickens, either the first pecks the second or the second pecks the first, but not both. We say that chicken u *virtually pecks* chicken v if either:

- Chicken u directly pecks chicken v, or

- Chicken u pecks some other chicken w who in turn pecks chicken v.

A chicken that virtually pecks every other chicken is called a *king chicken*.

We can model this situation with a *chicken digraph* whose vertices are chickens with an edge from chicken u to chicken v precisely when u pecks v. In the graph in Figure 10.11, three of the four chickens are kings. Chicken c is not a king in this example since it does not peck chicken b and it does not peck any chicken that pecks chicken b. Chicken a *is* a king since it pecks chicken d, who in turn pecks chickens b and c.

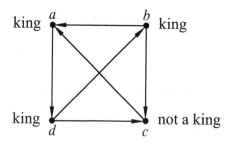

Figure 10.11   A 4-chicken tournament in which chickens a, b and d are kings.

In general, a *tournament digraph* is a digraph with exactly one edge between each pair of distinct vertices.

(a) Define a 10-chicken tournament graph with a king chicken that has outdegree 1.

(b) Describe a 5-chicken tournament graph in which every player is a king.

(c) Prove

Theorem (King Chicken Theorem). *Any chicken with maximum outdegree in a tournament is a king.*

The King Chicken Theorem means that if the player with the most victories is defeated by another player x, then at least he/she defeats some third player that defeats x. In this sense, the player with the most victories has some sort of bragging rights over every other player. Unfortunately, as Figure 10.11 illustrates, there can be many other players with such bragging rights, even some with fewer victories.

Problems for Section 10.5

Practice Problems

Problem 10.14.
What is the size of the longest chain that is guaranteed to exist in any partially ordered set of n elements? What about the largest antichain?

Problem 10.15.
Let $\{A, ..., H\}$ be a set of tasks that we must complete. The following DAG de-

scribes which tasks must be done before others, where there is an arrow from S to T iff S must be done before T.

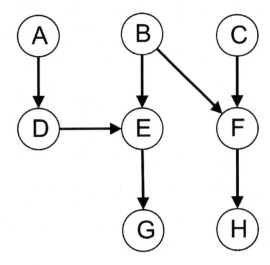

(a) Write the longest chain.

(b) Write the longest antichain.

(c) If we allow parallel scheduling, and each task takes 1 minute to complete, what is the minimum amount of time needed to complete all tasks?

Problem 10.16.
Describe a sequence consisting of the integers from 1 to 10,000 in some order so that there is no increasing or decreasing subsequence of size 101.

Problem 10.17.
What is the smallest number of partially ordered tasks for which there can be more than one minimum time schedule, if there are unlimited number of processors? Explain your answer.

Problem 10.18.
The following DAG describes the prerequisites among tasks $\{1, \ldots, 9\}$.

(a) If each task takes unit time to complete, what is the minimum parallel time to complete all the tasks? Briefly explain.

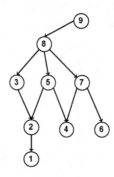

(b) What is the minimum parallel time if no more than two tasks can be completed in parallel? Briefly explain.

Problem 10.19.

The following DAG describes the prerequisites among tasks $\{1, \ldots, 9\}$.

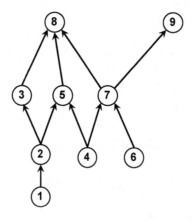

(a) If each task takes unit time to complete, what is the minimum parallel time to complete all the tasks? Briefly explain.

(b) What is the minimum parallel time if no more than two tasks can be completed in parallel? Briefly explain.

Class Problems

Problem 10.20.

The table below lists some prerequisite information for some subjects in the MIT Computer Science program (in 2006). This defines an indirect prerequisite relation that is a DAG with these subjects as vertices.

$$18.01 \rightarrow 6.042 \qquad\qquad 18.01 \rightarrow 18.02$$
$$18.01 \rightarrow 18.03 \qquad\qquad 6.046 \rightarrow 6.840$$
$$8.01 \rightarrow 8.02 \qquad\qquad 6.001 \rightarrow 6.034$$
$$6.042 \rightarrow 6.046 \qquad\qquad 18.03, 8.02 \rightarrow 6.002$$
$$6.001, 6.002 \rightarrow 6.003 \qquad\qquad 6.001, 6.002 \rightarrow 6.004$$
$$6.004 \rightarrow 6.033 \qquad\qquad 6.033 \rightarrow 6.857$$

(a) Explain why exactly six terms are required to finish all these subjects, if you can take as many subjects as you want per term. Using a *greedy* subject selection strategy, you should take as many subjects as possible each term. Exhibit your complete class schedule each term using a greedy strategy.

(b) In the second term of the greedy schedule, you took five subjects including 18.03. Identify a set of five subjects not including 18.03 such that it would be possible to take them in any one term (using some nongreedy schedule). Can you figure out how many such sets there are?

(c) Exhibit a schedule for taking all the courses—but only one per term.

(d) Suppose that you want to take all of the subjects, but can handle only two per term. Exactly how many terms are required to graduate? Explain why.

(e) What if you could take three subjects per term?

Problem 10.21.

A pair of Math for Computer Science Teaching Assistants, Lisa and Annie, have decided to devote some of their spare time this term to establishing dominion over the entire galaxy. Recognizing this as an ambitious project, they worked out the following table of tasks on the back of Annie's copy of the lecture notes.

1. **Devise a logo** and cool imperial theme music - 8 days.

2. **Build a fleet** of Hyperwarp Stardestroyers out of eating paraphernalia swiped from Lobdell - 18 days.

3. **Seize control** of the United Nations - 9 days, after task #1.

4. **Get shots** for Lisa's cat, Tailspin - 11 days, after task #1.

5. **Open a Starbucks chain** for the army to get their caffeine - 10 days, after task #3.

6. **Train an army** of elite interstellar warriors by dragging people to see *The Phantom Menace* dozens of times - 4 days, after tasks #3, #4, and #5.

7. **Launch the fleet** of Stardestroyers, crush all sentient alien species, and establish a Galactic Empire - 6 days, after tasks #2 and #6.

8. **Defeat Microsoft** - 8 days, after tasks #2 and #6.

We picture this information in Figure 10.12 below by drawing a point for each task, and labelling it with the name and weight of the task. An edge between two points indicates that the task for the higher point must be completed before beginning the task for the lower one.

(a) Give some valid order in which the tasks might be completed.

Lisa and Annie want to complete all these tasks in the shortest possible time. However, they have agreed on some constraining work rules.

- Only one person can be assigned to a particular task; they cannot work together on a single task.

- Once a person is assigned to a task, that person must work exclusively on the assignment until it is completed. So, for example, Lisa cannot work on building a fleet for a few days, run to get shots for Tailspin, and then return to building the fleet.

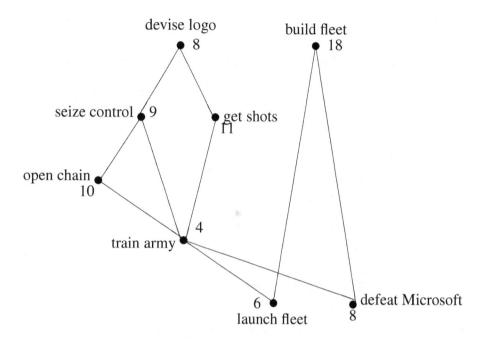

Figure 10.12 Graph representing the task precedence constraints.

(b) Lisa and Annie want to know how long conquering the galaxy will take. Annie suggests dividing the total number of days of work by the number of workers, which is two. What lower bound on the time to conquer the galaxy does this give, and why might the actual time required be greater?

(c) Lisa proposes a different method for determining the duration of their project. She suggests looking at the duration of the *critical path*, the most time-consuming sequence of tasks such that each depends on the one before. What lower bound does this give, and why might it also be too low?

(d) What is the minimum number of days that Lisa and Annie need to conquer the galaxy? No proof is required.

Problem 10.22.
Answer the following questions about the powerset $\mathrm{pow}(\{1, 2, 3, 4\})$ partially ordered by the strict subset relation $\subset$.

(a) Give an example of a maximum length chain.

(b) Give an example of an antchain of size 6.

(c) Describe an example of a topological sort of pow($\{1, 2, 3, 4\}$).

(d) Suppose the partial order describes scheduling constraints on 16 tasks. That is, if

$$A \subset B \subseteq \{1, 2, 3, 4\},$$

then A has to be completed before B starts.[16] What is the minimum number of processors needed to complete all the tasks in minimum parallel time?

Prove it.

(e) What is the length of a minimum time **3**-processor schedule?

Prove it.

Homework Problems

Problem 10.23.

The following operations can be applied to any digraph, G:

1. Delete an edge that is in a cycle.

2. Delete edge $\langle u \to v \rangle$ if there is a path from vertex u to vertex v that does not include $\langle u \to v \rangle$.

3. Add edge $\langle u \to v \rangle$ if there is no path in either direction between vertex u and vertex v.

The procedure of repeating these operations until none of them are applicable can be modeled as a state machine. The start state is G, and the states are all possible digraphs with the same vertices as G.

(a) Let G be the graph with vertices $\{1, 2, 3, 4\}$ and edges

$$\{\langle 1 \to 2 \rangle, \langle 2 \to 3 \rangle, \langle 3 \to 4 \rangle, \langle 3 \to 2 \rangle, \langle 1 \to 4 \rangle\}$$

What are the possible final states reachable from G?

A *line graph* is a graph whose edges are all on one path. All the final graphs in part (a) are line graphs.

(b) Prove that if the procedure terminates with a digraph H then H is a line graph with the same vertices as G.

Hint: Show that if H is *not* a line graph, then some operation must be applicable.

---

[16] As usual, we assume each task requires one time unit to complete.

(c) Prove that being a DAG is a preserved invariant of the procedure.

(d) Prove that if G is a DAG and the procedure terminates, then the walk relation of the final line graph is a topological sort of G.

Hint: Verify that the predicate

$$P(u, v) ::= \text{there is a directed path from } u \text{ to } v$$

is a preserved invariant of the procedure, for any two vertices u, v of a DAG.

(e) Prove that if G is finite, then the procedure terminates.

Hint: Let s be the number of cycles, e be the number of edges, and p be the number of pairs of vertices with a directed path (in either direction) between them. Note that $p \le n^2$ where n is the number of vertices of G. Find coefficients a, b, c such that $as + bp + e + c$ is nonnegative integer valued and decreases at each transition.

Problem 10.24.
Let $\prec$ be a strict partial order on a set A and let

$$A_k ::= \{a \mid \text{depth}(a) = k\}$$

where $k \in \mathbb{N}$.

(a) Prove that $A_0, A_1, \ldots$ is a parallel schedule for $\prec$ according to Definition 10.5.7.

(b) Prove that A_k is an antichain.

Problem 10.25.
We want to schedule n tasks with prerequisite constraints among the tasks defined by a DAG.

(a) Explain why any schedule that requires only p processors must take time at least $\lceil n/p \rceil$.

(b) Let $D_{n,t}$ be the DAG with n elements that consists of a chain of $t - 1$ elements, with the bottom element in the chain being a prerequisite of all the remaining elements as in the following figure:

What is the minimum time schedule for $D_{n,t}$? Explain why it is unique. How many processors does it require?

(c) Write a simple formula $M(n, t, p)$ for the minimum time of a p-processor schedule to complete $D_{n,t}$.

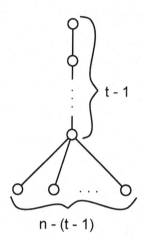

(d) Show that *every* partial order with n vertices and maximum chain size t has a p-processor schedule that runs in time $M(n, t, p)$.

Hint: Use induction on t.

Problems for Section 10.6

Practice Problems

Problem 10.26.
In this DAG (Figure 10.13) for the divisibility relation on $\{1, \ldots, 12\}$, there is an upward path from a to b iff $a \mid b$. If 24 was added as a vertex, what is the minimum number of edges that must be added to the DAG to represent divisibility on $\{1, \ldots, 12, 24\}$? What are those edges?

Problem 10.27. (a) Prove that every strict partial order is a DAG.

(b) Give an example of a DAG that is not a strict partial order.

(c) Prove that the positive walk relation of a DAG a strict partial order.

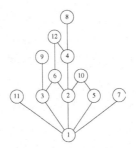

Figure 10.13

Class Problems

Problem 10.28. (a) What are the maxim*al* and minim*al* elements, if any, of the power set $\text{pow}(\{1, \ldots, n\})$, where n is a positive integer, under the empty relation?

(b) What are the maxim*al* and minim*al* elements, if any, of the set $\mathbb{N}$ of all non-negative integers under divisibility? Is there a minim*um* or maxim*um* element?

(c) What are the minimal and maximal elements, if any, of the set of integers greater than 1 under divisibility?

(d) Describe a partially ordered set that has no minimal or maximal elements.

(e) Describe a partially ordered set that has a *unique minimal* element, but no minimum element. *Hint:* It will have to be infinite.

Problem 10.29.
The proper subset relation $\subset$ defines a strict partial order on the subsets of $[1..6]$, that is, on $\text{pow}([1..6])$.

(a) What is the size of a maximal chain in this partial order? Describe one.

(b) Describe the largest antichain you can find in this partial order.

(c) What are the maximal and minimal elements? Are they maximum and minimum?

(d) Answer the previous part for the $\subset$ partial order on the set $\text{pow}\,[1..6] - \emptyset$.

Problem 10.30.
If a and b are distinct nodes of a digraph, then a is said to *cover* b if there is an

edge from a to b and every path from a to b includes this edge. If a covers b, the edge from a to b is called a *covering edge*.

(a) What are the covering edges in the DAG in Figure 10.14?

(b) Let covering (D) be the subgraph of D consisting of only the covering edges. Suppose D is a finite DAG. Explain why covering (D) has the same positive walk relation as D.

Hint: Consider *longest* paths between a pair of vertices.

(c) Show that if two *DAG*'s have the same positive walk relation, then they have the same set of covering edges.

(d) Conclude that covering (D) is the *unique* DAG with the smallest number of edges among all digraphs with the same positive walk relation as D.

The following examples show that the above results don't work in general for digraphs with cycles.

(e) Describe two graphs with vertices $\{1, 2\}$ which have the same set of covering edges, but not the same positive walk relation (*Hint:* Self-loops.)

(f)   (i) The *complete digraph* without self-loops on vertices $1, 2, 3$ has directed edges in each direction between every two distinct vertices. What are its covering edges?

   (ii) What are the covering edges of the graph with vertices $1, 2, 3$ and edges $\langle 1 \rightarrow 2 \rangle$, $\langle 2 \rightarrow 3 \rangle$, $\langle 3 \rightarrow 1 \rangle$?

   (iii) What about their positive walk relations?

Problems for Section 10.6

Exam Problems

Problem 10.31.
Prove that for any nonempty set D, there is a unique binary relation on D that is both asymmetric and symmetric.

Problem 10.32.
Let D be a set of size $n > 0$. Shown that there are exactly 2^n binary relations on D that are both symmetric and antisymmetric.

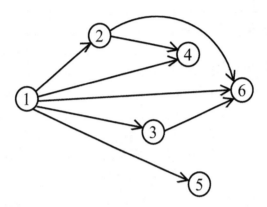

Figure 10.14   DAG with edges not needed in paths

Homework Problems

Problem 10.33.
Prove that if R is a transitive binary relation on a set A then $R = R^+$.

Class Problems

Problem 10.34.
Let R be a binary relation on a set D. Each of the following equalities and containments expresses the fact that R has one of the basic relational properties: reflexive, irreflexive, symmetric, asymmetric, antisymmetric, transitive. Identify which property is expressed by each of these formulas and explain your reasoning.

(a) $R \cap \mathrm{Id}_D = \emptyset$

(b) $R \subseteq R^{-1}$

(c) $R = R^{-1}$

(d) $\mathrm{Id}_D \subseteq R$

(e) $R \circ R \subseteq R$

(f) $R \cap R^{-1} = \emptyset$

(g) $R \cap R^{-1} \subseteq \mathrm{Id}_D$

Problems for Section 10.7

Class Problems

Problem 10.35.

Direct Prerequisites	Subject
18.01	6.042
18.01	18.02
18.01	18.03
8.01	8.02
8.01	6.01
6.042	6.046
18.02, 18.03, 8.02, 6.01	6.02
6.01, 6.042	6.006
6.01	6.034
6.02	6.004

(a) For the above table of MIT subject prerequisites, draw a diagram showing the subject numbers with a line going down to every subject from each of its (direct) prerequisites.

(b) Give an example of a collection of sets partially ordered by the proper subset relation $\subset$ that is isomorphic to ("same shape as") the prerequisite relation among MIT subjects from part (a).

(c) Explain why the empty relation is a strict partial order and describe a collection of sets partially ordered by the proper subset relation that is isomorphic to the empty relation on five elements—that is, the relation under which none of the five elements is related to anything.

(d) Describe a *simple* collection of sets partially ordered by the proper subset relation that is isomorphic to the "properly contains" relation $\supset$ on pow $\{1, 2, 3, 4\}$.

Problem 10.36.
This problem asks for a proof of Lemma 10.7.2 showing that every weak partial order can be represented by (is isomorphic to) a collection of sets partially ordered under set inclusion ($\subseteq$). Namely,

Lemma. *Let $\preceq$ be a weak partial order on a set A. For any element $a \in A$, let*

$$L(a) ::= \{b \in A \mid b \preceq a\},$$
$$\mathcal{L} ::= \{L(a) \mid a \in A\}.$$

Then the function $L : A \to \mathcal{L}$ is an isomorphism from the $\preceq$ relation on A, to the subset relation on $\mathcal{L}$.

(a) Prove that the function $L : A \to \mathcal{L}$ is a bijection.

(b) Complete the proof by showing that

$$a \preceq b \quad \text{iff} \quad L(a) \subseteq L(b) \tag{10.14}$$

for all $a, b \in A$.

Homework Problems

Problem 10.37.
Every partial order is isomorphic to a collection of sets under the subset relation (see Section 10.7). In particular, if R is a *strict* partial order on a set A and $a \in A$, define

$$L(a) ::= \{a\} \cup \{x \in A \mid x \, R \, a\}. \tag{10.15}$$

Then

$$a \, R \, b \quad \text{iff} \quad L(a) \subset L(b) \tag{10.16}$$

holds for all $a, b \in A$.

(a) Carefully prove statement (10.16), starting from the definitions of strict partial order and the strict subset relation $\subset$.

(b) Prove that if $L(a) = L(b)$ then $a = b$.

(c) Give an example showing that the conclusion of part (b) would not hold if the definition of $L(a)$ in equation (10.15) had omitted the expression "$\{a\}\cup$."

Problems for Section 10.8

Practice Problems

Problem 10.38.
For each of the binary relations below, state whether it is a strict partial order, a weak partial order, or neither. If it is not a partial order, indicate which of the axioms for partial order it violates.

(a) The superset relation, $\supseteq$ on the power set pow $\{1, 2, 3, 4, 5\}$.

(b) The relation between any two nonnegative integers a, b given by $a \equiv b$ (mod 8).

(c) The relation between propositional formulas G, H given by G IMPLIES H is valid.

(d) The relation 'beats' on Rock, Paper and Scissor (for those who don't know the game "Rock, Paper, Scissors:" Rock beats Scissors, Scissors beats Paper and Paper beats Rock).

(e) The empty relation on the set of real numbers.

(f) The identity relation on the set of integers.

Problem 10.39. (a) Verify that the divisibility relation on the set of nonnegative integers is a weak partial order.

(b) What about the divisibility relation on the set of integers?

Problem 10.40.
Prove directly from the definitions (without appealing to DAG properties) that if a binary relation R on a set A is transitive and irreflexive, then it is asymmetric.

Class Problems

Problem 10.41.
Show that the set of nonnegative integers partially ordered under the divides relation...

(a) ...has a minimum element.

(b) ...has a maximum element.

(c) ...has an infinite chain.

(d) ...has an infinite antichain.

(e) What are the minimal elements of divisibility on the integers greater than 1? What are the maximal elements?

Problem 10.42.

How many binary relations are there on the set $\{0, 1\}$?

How many are there that are transitive?, . . . asymmetric?, . . . reflexive?, . . . irreflexive?, . . . strict partial orders?, . . . weak partial orders?

Hint: There are easier ways to find these numbers than listing all the relations and checking which properties each one has.

Problem 10.43.

Prove that if R is a partial order, then so is R^{-1}.

Problem 10.44. (a) Indicate which of the following relations below are equivalence relations, (**Eq**), strict partial orders (**SPO**), weak partial orders (**WPO**). For the partial orders, also indicate whether it is *linear* (**Lin**).

If a relation is none of the above, indicate whether it is *transitive* (**Tr**), *symmetric* (**Sym**), or *asymmetric* (**Asym**).

   (i) The relation $a = b + 1$ between integers a, b,

  (ii) The superset relation $\supseteq$ on the power set of the integers.

 (iii) The empty relation on the set of rationals.

  (iv) The divides relation on the nonegative integers $\mathbb{N}$.

   (v) The divides relation on all the integers $\mathbb{Z}$.

  (vi) The divides relation on the positive powers of 4.

 (vii) The relatively prime relation on the nonnegative integers.

(viii) The relation "has the same prime factors" on the integers.

(b) A set of functions $f, g : D \to \mathbb{R}$ can be partially ordered by the $\leq$ relation, where

$$[f \leq g] ::= \forall d \in D.\ f(d) \leq g(d).$$

Let L be the set of functions $f : \mathbb{R} \to \mathbb{R}$ of the form

$$f(x) = ax + b$$

for constants $a, b \in \mathbb{R}$.

Describe an infinite chain and an infinite anti-chain in L.

Problem 10.45.

In an *n*-player *round-robin tournament*, every pair of distinct players compete in a single game. Assume that every game has a winner—there are no ties. The results of such a tournament can then be represented with a *tournament digraph* where the vertices correspond to players and there is an edge $\langle x \to y \rangle$ iff x beat y in their game.

(a) Explain why a tournament digraph cannot have cycles of length one or two.

(b) Is the "beats" relation for a tournament graph always/sometimes/never:

- asymmetric?
- reflexive?
- irreflexive?
- transitive?

Explain.

(c) Show that a tournament graph is a linear order iff there are no cycles of length three.

Homework Problems

Problem 10.46.

Let R and S be transitive binary relations on the same set A. Which of the following new relations must also be transitive? For each part, justify your answer with a brief argument if the new relation is transitive and a counterexample if it is not.

(a) R^{-1}

(b) $R \cap S$

(c) $R \circ R$

(d) $R \circ S$

Exam Problems

Problem 10.47.

Suppose the precedence constraints on a set of 32 unit time tasks was isomorphic to the powerset, $\text{pow}(\{1, 2, 3, 4, 5\})$ under the strict subset relation $\subset$.

For example, the task corresponding to the set $\{2, 4\}$ must be completed before the task corresponding to the set $\{1, 2, 4\}$ because $\{2, 4\} \subset \{1, 2, 4\}$; the task corresponding to the empty set must be scheduled first because $\emptyset \subset S$ for every nonempty set $S \subseteq \{1, 2, 3, 4, 5\}$.

(a) What is the minimum parallel time to complete these tasks?

(b) Describe a maximum size antichain in this partial order.

(c) Briefly explain why the minimum number of processors required to complete these tasks in minimum parallel time is equal to the size of the maximum antichain.

Problem 10.48.
Let R be a weak partial order on a set A. Suppose C is a finite chain.[17]

(a) Prove that C has a maximum element. *Hint:* Induction on the size of C.

(b) Conclude that there is a unique sequence of all the elements of C that is strictly increasing.

Hint: Induction on the size of C, using part (a).

Problems for Section 10.9

Practice Problems

Problem 10.49.
Verify that if *either* of R_1 or R_2 is irreflexive, then so is $R_1 \times R_2$.

Class Problems

Problem 10.50.
Let R_1, R_2 be binary relations on the same set A. A relational property is preserved under product, if $R_1 \times R_2$ has the property whenever both R_1 and R_2 have the property.

(a) Verify that each of the following properties are preserved under product.

1. reflexivity,

2. antisymmetry,

3. transitivity.

---

[17] A set C is a *chain* when it is nonempty, and all elements $c, d \in C$ are comparable. Elements c and d are *comparable* iff [$c \ R \ d$ OR $d \ R \ c$].

(b) Verify that if R_1 and R_2 are partial orders and at least one of them is strict, then $R_1 \times R_2$ is a strict partial order.

Problem 10.51.

A partial order on a set A is *well founded* when every non-empty subset of A has a *minimal* element. For example, the less-than relation on a well ordered set of real numbers (see 2.4) is a linear order that is well founded.

Prove that if R and S are well founded partial orders, then so is their product $R \times S$.

Homework Problems

Problem 10.52.

Let S be a sequence of n different numbers. A *subsequence* of S is a sequence that can be obtained by deleting elements of S.

For example, if S is

$$(6, 4, 7, 9, 1, 2, 5, 3, 8),$$

then 647 and 7253 are both subsequences of S (for readability, we have dropped the parentheses and commas in sequences, so 647 abbreviates $(6, 4, 7)$, for example).

An *increasing subsequence* of S is a subsequence of whose successive elements get larger. For example, 1238 is an increasing subsequence of S. Decreasing subsequences are defined similarly; 641 is a decreasing subsequence of S.

(a) List all the maximum-length increasing subsequences of S, and all the maximum-length decreasing subsequences.

Now let A be the *set* of numbers in S. (So A is the integers $[1..9]$ for the example above.) There are two straightforward linear orders for A. The first is numerical order where A is ordered by the $<$ relation. The second is to order the elements by which comes first in S; call this order $<_S$. So for the example above, we would have

$$6 <_S 4 <_S 7 <_S 9 <_S 1 <_S 2 <_S 5 <_S 3 <_S 8$$

Let $\prec$ be the product relation of the linear orders $<_s$ and $<$. That is, $\prec$ is defined by the rule

$$a \prec a' \quad ::= \quad a < a' \text{ AND } a <_S a'.$$

So $\prec$ is a partial order on A (Section 10.9).

(b) Draw a diagram of the partial order $\prec$ on A. What are the maximal and minimal elements?

(c) Explain the connection between increasing and decreasing subsequences of S, and chains and anti-chains under $\prec$.

(d) Prove that every sequence S of length n has an increasing subsequence of length greater than $\sqrt{n}$ or a decreasing subsequence of length at least $\sqrt{n}$.

Problems for Section 10.10

Practice Problems

Problem 10.53.
For each of the following relations, decide whether it is reflexive, whether it is symmetric, whether it is transitive, and whether it is an equivalence relation.

(a) $\{(a, b) \mid a$ and b are the same age$\}$

(b) $\{(a, b) \mid a$ and b have the same parents$\}$

(c) $\{(a, b) \mid a$ and b speak a common language$\}$

Problem 10.54.
For each of the binary relations below, state whether it is a strict partial order, a weak partial order, an equivalence relation, or none of these. If it is a partial order, state whether it is a linear order. If it is none, indicate which of the axioms for partial-order and equivalence relations it violates.

(a) The superset relation $\supseteq$ on the power set pow $\{1, 2, 3, 4, 5\}$.

(b) The relation between any two nonnegative integers a and b such that $a \equiv b$ (mod 8).

(c) The relation between propositional formulas G and H such that $[G$ IMPLIES $H]$ is valid.

(d) The relation between propositional formulas G and H such that $[G$ IFF $H]$ is valid.

(e) The relation 'beats' on Rock, Paper, and Scissors (for those who don't know the game Rock, Paper, Scissors, Rock beats Scissors, Scissors beats Paper, and Paper beats Rock).

(f) The empty relation on the set of real numbers.

(g) The identity relation on the set of integers.

(h) The divisibility relation on the integers $\mathbb{Z}$.

Class Problems

Problem 10.55.
Prove Theorem 10.10.4: The equivalence classes of an equivalence relation form a partition of the domain.

   Namely, let R be an equivalence relation on a set A and define the equivalence class of an element $a \in A$ to be

$$[a]_R ::= \{b \in A \mid a \: R \: b\}.$$

That is, $[a]_R = R(a)$.

(a) Prove that every block is nonempty and every element of A is in some block.

(b) Prove that if $[a]_R \cap [b]_R \neq \emptyset$, then $a \: R \: b$. Conclude that the sets $[a]_R$ for $a \in A$ are a partition of A.

(c) Prove that $a \: R \: b$ iff $[a]_R = [b]_R$.

Problem 10.56.
For any total function $f : A \to B$ define a relation $\equiv_f$ by the rule:

$$a \equiv_f a' \quad \text{iff} \quad f(a) = f(a'). \tag{10.17}$$

(a) Sketch a proof that $\equiv_f$ is an equivalence relation on A.

(b) Prove that every equivalence relation R on a set A is equal to $\equiv_f$ for the function $f : A \to \mathrm{pow}(A)$ defined as

$$f(a) ::= \{a' \in A \mid a \: R \: a'\}.$$

That is, $f(a) = R(a)$.

Problem 10.57.
Let R be a binary relation on a set D. Each of the following formulas expresses the fact that R has a familiar relational property such as reflexivity, asymmetry, transitivity. Predicate formulas have roman numerals i.,ii.,..., and relational formulas (equalities and containments) are labelled with letters (a),(b),....

Next to each of the relational formulas, write the roman numerals of all the predicate formulas equivalent to it. It is not necessary to name the property expressed, but you can get partial credit if you do. For example, part (a) gets the label "i." It expresses *irreflexivity*.

    i. $\forall d.$ NOT$(d\ R\ d)$

    ii. $\forall d.$ $d\ R\ d$

    iii. $\forall c, d.$ $c\ R\ d$ IFF $d\ R\ c$

    iv. $\forall c, d.$ $c\ R\ d$ IMPLIES $d\ R\ c$

    v. $\forall c, d.$ $c\ R\ d$ IMPLIES NOT$(d\ R\ c)$

    vi. $\forall c \neq d.$ $c\ R\ d$ IMPLIES NOT$(d\ R\ c)$

    vii. $\forall c \neq d.$ $c\ R\ d$ IFF NOT$(d\ R\ c)$

    viii. $\forall b, c, d.$ $(b\ R\ c$ AND $c\ R\ d)$ IMPLIES $b\ R\ d$

    ix. $\forall b, d.$ $[\exists c.\ (b\ R\ c$ AND $c\ R\ d)]$ IMPLIES $b\ R\ d$

    x. $\forall b, d.$ $b\ R\ d$ IMPLIES $[\exists c.\ (b\ R\ c$ AND $c\ R\ d)]$

(a) $R \cap \mathrm{Id}_D = \emptyset$ ____i.____

(b) $R \subseteq R^{-1}$

(c) $R = R^{-1}$

(d) $\mathrm{Id}_D \subseteq R$

(e) $R \circ R \subseteq R$

(f) $R \subseteq R \circ R$

(g) $R \cap R^{-1} \subseteq \mathrm{Id}_D$

(h) $\overline{R} \subseteq R^{-1}$

(i) $\overline{R} \cap \mathrm{Id}_R = R^{-1} \cap \mathrm{Id}_R$

(j) $R \cap R^{-1} = \emptyset$

Homework Problems

Problem 10.58.

Let R_1 and R_2 be two equivalence relations on a set A. Prove or give a counterexample to the claims that the following are also equivalence relations:

(a) $R_1 \cap R_2$.

(b) $R_1 \cup R_2$.

Problem 10.59.

Prove that for any nonempty set D, there is a unique binary relation on D that is both a weak partial order and also an equivalence relation.

Exam Problems

Problem 10.60.

Let A be a nonempty set.

(a) Describe a single relation on A that is *both* an equivalence relation and a weak partial order on A.

(b) Prove that the relation of part (a) is the only relation on A with these properties.

11   Communication Networks

Modeling communication networks is an important application of digraphs in computer science. In this such models, vertices represent computers, processors, and switches; edges will represent wires, fiber, or other transmission lines through which data flows. For some communication networks, like the internet, the corresponding graph is enormous and largely chaotic. Highly structured networks, by contrast, find application in telephone switching systems and the communication hardware inside parallel computers. In this chapter, we'll look at some of the nicest and most commonly used structured networks.

11.1   Routing

The kinds of communication networks we consider aim to transmit packets of data between computers, processors, telephones, or other devices. The term *packet* refers to some roughly fixed-size quantity of data—256 bytes or 4096 bytes or whatever.

11.1.1   Complete Binary Tree

Let's start with a *complete binary tree*. Figure 11.1 is an example with 4 inputs and 4 outputs.

In this diagram, and many that follow, the squares represent *terminals*—sources and destinations for packets of data. The circles represent *switches*, which direct packets through the network. A switch receives packets on incoming edges and relays them forward along the outgoing edges. Thus, you can imagine a data packet hopping through the network from an input terminal, through a sequence of switches joined by directed edges, to an output terminal.

In a tree there is a unique path between every pair of vertices, so there is only one way to route a packet of data from an input terminal to an output. For example, the route of a packet traveling from input 1 to output 3 is shown in bold.

11.1.2   Routing Problems

Communication networks are supposed to get packets from inputs to outputs, with each packet entering the network at its own input switch and arriving at its own output switch. We're going to consider several different communication network

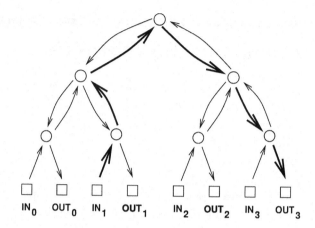

Figure 11.1   Binary Tree net with 4 inputs and outputs

designs, where each network has N inputs and N outputs; for convenience, we'll assume N is a power of two.

Which input is supposed to go where is specified by a permutation of $[0..N-1]$. So a permutation π defines a *routing problem*: get a packet that starts at input i to output $\pi(i)$. A *routing* that *solves* a routing problem π is a set P of paths from each input to its specified output. That is, P is a set of paths P_i where P_i goes from input i to output $\pi(i)$ for $i \in [0..N-1]$.

11.2   Routing Measures

11.2.1   Network Diameter

The delay between the time that a packets arrives at an input and arrives at its designated output is a critical issue in communication networks. Generally, this delay is proportional to the length of the path a packet follows. Assuming it takes one time unit to travel across a wire, the delay of a packet will be the number of wires it crosses going from input to output.

Packets are usually routed from input to output by the shortest path possible. With a shortest-path routing, the worst-case delay is the distance between the input and output that are farthest apart. This is called the *diameter* of the network. In other words, the diameter of a network[1] is the maximum length of any shortest

---

[1] The usual definition of *diameter* for a general *graph* (simple or directed) is the largest distance between *any* two vertices, but in the context of a communication network we're only interested in the

path between an input and an output. For example, in the complete binary tree above, the distance from input 1 to output 3 is six. No input and output are farther apart than this, so the diameter of this tree is also six.

More broadly, the diameter of a complete binary tree with N inputs and outputs is $2\log N + 2$. This is quite good, because the logarithm function grows very slowly. We could connect up $2^{10} = 1024$ inputs and outputs using a complete binary tree and the worst input-output delay for any packet would be $2\log(2^{10}) + 2 = 22$.

Switch Size

One way to reduce the diameter of a network is to use larger switches. For example, in the complete binary tree, most of the switches have three incoming edges and three outgoing edges, which makes them 3×3 switches. If we had 4×4 switches, then we could construct a complete *ternary* tree with an even smaller diameter. In principle, we could even connect up all the inputs and outputs via a single monster $N \times N$ switch.

Of course this isn't very productive. Using an $N \times N$ switch would just conceal the original network design problem inside this abstract switch. Eventually, we'll have to design the internals of the monster switch using simpler components, and then we're right back where we started. So, the challenge in designing a communication network is figuring out how to get the functionality of an $N \times N$ switch using fixed size, elementary devices, like 3×3 switches.

11.2.2 Switch Count

Another goal in designing a communication network is to use as few switches as possible. In a complete binary tree, there is one "root" switch at the top, and the number of switches doubles at successive rows, so the number of switches in an N-input complete binary tree is $1 + 2 + 4 + 8 + \cdots + N$. So the total number of switches is $2N - 1$ by the formula for geometric sums (Problem 5.4). This is nearly the best possible with 3×3 switches.

11.2.3 Network Latency

We'll sometimes be choosing routings through a network that optimize some quantity besides delay. For example, in the next section we'll be trying to minimize packet congestion. When we're not minimizing delay, shortest routings are not always the best, and in general, the delay of a packet will depend on how it is routed. For any routing, the most delayed packet will be the one that follows the longest path in the routing. The length of the longest path in a routing is called its *latency*.

---

distance between inputs and outputs, not between arbitrary pairs of vertices.

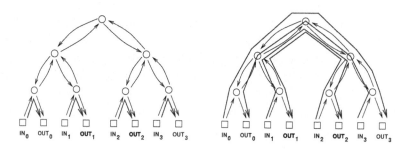

Figure 11.2   Two Routings in the Binary Tree Net

The latency of a *network* depends on what's being optimized. It is measured by assuming that optimal routings are always chosen in getting inputs to their specified outputs. That is, for each routing problem π, we choose an optimal routing that solves π. Then *network latency* is defined to be the largest routing latency among these optimal routings. Network latency will equal network diameter if routings are always chosen to optimize delay, but it may be significantly larger if routings are chosen to optimize something else.

For the networks we consider below, paths from input to output are uniquely determined (in the case of the tree) or all paths are the same length, so network latency will always equal network diameter.

11.2.4   Congestion

The complete binary tree has a fatal drawback: the root switch is a bottleneck. At best, this switch must handle right and vice-versa. Passing all these packets through a single switch could take a long time. At worst, if this switch fails, the network is broken into two equal-sized pieces.

It's true that if the routing problem is given by the identity permutation, $\mathrm{Id}(i) ::= i$, then there is an easy routing P that solves the problem: let P_i be the path from input i up through one switch and back down to output i. On the other hand, if the problem was given by $\pi(i) ::= (N-1) - i$, then in *any* solution Q for π, each path Q_i beginning at input i must eventually loop all the way up through the root switch and then travel back down to output $(N-1) - i$. These two situations are illustrated in Figure 11.2. We can distinguish between a "good" set of paths and a "bad" set based on congestion. The *congestion* of a routing P is equal to the largest number of paths in P that pass through a single switch. For example, the congestion of the routing on the left is 1, since at most 1 path passes through each switch. However, the congestion of the routing on the right is 4, since 4 paths pass through the root switch (and the two switches directly below the root). Generally, lower congestion is better since packets can be delayed at an overloaded switch.

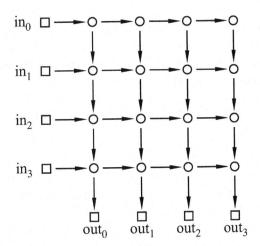

Figure 11.3   Two-dimensional Array with $N = 4$.

By extending the notion of congestion to networks, we can also distinguish between "good" and "bad" networks with respect to bottleneck problems. For each routing problem π for the network, we assume a routing is chosen that optimizes congestion, that is, that has the minimum congestion among all routings that solve π. Then the largest congestion that will ever be suffered by a switch will be the maximum congestion among these optimal routings. This "maximin" congestion is called the *congestion of the network.*

So for the complete binary tree, the worst permutation would be $\pi(i) ::= (N - 1) - i$. Then in every possible solution for π, *every* packet would have to follow a path passing through the root switch. Thus, the max congestion of the complete binary tree is N—which is horrible!

Let's tally the results of our analysis so far:

network	diameter	switch size	# switches	congestion
complete binary tree	$2 \log N + 2$	3×3	$2N - 1$	N

11.3   Network Designs

11.3.1   2-D Array

Communication networks can also be designed as *2-dimensional arrays* or *grids*. A 2-D array with four inputs and outputs is shown in Figure 11.3.

The diameter in this example is 8, which is the number of edges between input 0 and output 3. More generally, the diameter of an array with N inputs and outputs is $2N$, which is much worse than the diameter of $2 \log N + 2$ in the complete binary tree. But we get something in exchange: replacing a complete binary tree with an array almost eliminates congestion.

Theorem 11.3.1. *The congestion of an N-input array is 2.*

Proof. First, we show that the congestion is at most 2. Let π be any permutation. Define a solution P for π to be the set of paths, P_i, where P_i goes to the right from input i to column $\pi(i)$ and then goes down to output $\pi(i)$. Thus, the switch in row i and column j transmits at most two packets: the packet originating at input i and the packet destined for output j.

Next, we show that the congestion is at least 2. This follows because in any routing problem π, where $\pi(0) = 0$ and $\pi(N-1) = N-1$, two packets must pass through the lower left switch. ∎

As with the tree, the network latency when minimizing congestion is the same as the diameter. That's because all the paths between a given input and output are the same length.

Now we can record the characteristics of the 2-D array.

network	diameter	switch size	# switches	congestion
complete binary tree	$2 \log N + 2$	3×3	$2N - 1$	N
2-D array	$2N$	2×2	N^2	2

The crucial entry here is the number of switches, which is N^2. This is a major defect of the 2-D array; a network of size $N = 1000$ would require a *million* 2×2 switches! Still, for applications where N is small, the simplicity and low congestion of the array make it an attractive choice.

11.3.2 Butterfly

The Holy Grail of switching networks would combine the best properties of the complete binary tree (low diameter, few switches) and of the array (low congestion). The *butterfly* is a widely-used compromise between the two.

A good way to understand butterfly networks is as a recursive data type. The recursive definition works better if we define just the switches and their connections, omitting the terminals. So we recursively define F_n to be the switches and connections of the butterfly net with $N ::= 2^n$ input and output switches.

The base case is F_1 with 2 input switches and 2 output switches connected as in Figure 11.4.

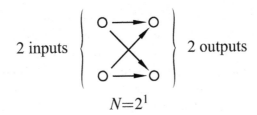

Figure 11.4 F_1, the Butterfly Net with $N = 2^1$.

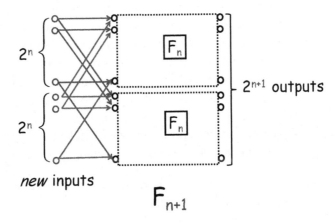

Figure 11.5 Butterfly Net F_{n+1} with 2^{n+1} inputs from two F_n's.

In the constructor step, we construct F_{n+1} out of two F_n nets connected to a new set of 2^{n+1} input switches, as shown in as in Figure 11.5. That is, the ith and $2^n + i$th new input switches are each connected to the same two switches, the ith input switches of each of two F_n components for $i = 1, \ldots, 2^n$. The output switches of F_{n+1} are simply the output switches of each of the F_n copies.

So F_{n+1} is laid out in columns of height 2^{n+1} by adding one more column of switches to the columns in F_n. Since the construction starts with two columns when $n = 1$, the F_{n+1} switches are arrayed in $n + 1$ columns. The total number of switches is the height of the columns times the number $2^{n+1}(n + 1)$ of columns. Remembering that $n = \log N$, we conclude that the Butterfly Net with N inputs has $N(\log N + 1)$ switches.

Since every path in F_{n+1} from an input switch to an output is length-$n+1$ the diameter of the Butterfly net with 2^{n+1} inputs is this length plus two because of the two edges connecting to the terminals (square boxes)—one edge from input terminal to input switch (circle) and one from output switch to output terminal.

There is an easy recursive procedure to route a packet through the Butterfly Net. In the base case, there is only one way to route a packet from one of the two inputs to one of the two outputs. Now suppose we want to route a packet from an input switch to an output switch in F_{n+1}. If the output switch is in the "top" copy of F_n, then the first step in the route must be from the input switch to the unique switch it is connected to in the top copy; the rest of the route is determined by recursively routing the rest of the way in the top copy of F_n. Likewise, if the output switch is in the "bottom" copy of F_n, then the first step in the route must be to the switch in the bottom copy, and the rest of the route is determined by recursively routing in the bottom copy of F_n. In fact, this argument shows that the routing is *unique*: there is exactly one path in the Butterfly Net from each input to each output, which implies that the network latency when minimizing congestion is the same as the diameter.

The congestion of the butterfly network is about $\sqrt{N}$. More precisely, the congestion is $\sqrt{N}$ if N is an even power of 2 and $\sqrt{N/2}$ if N is an odd power of 2. A simple proof of this appears in Problem 11.8.

Let's add the butterfly data to our comparison table:

network	diameter	switch size	# switches	congestion
complete binary tree	$2\log N + 2$	3×3	$2N - 1$	N
2-D array	$2N$	2×2	N^2	2
butterfly	$\log N + 2$	2×2	$N(\log(N) + 1)$	$\sqrt{N}$ or $\sqrt{N/2}$

The butterfly has lower congestion than the complete binary tree. It also uses fewer switches and has lower diameter than the array. However, the butterfly does not capture the best qualities of each network, but rather is a compromise somewhere between the two. Our quest for the Holy Grail of routing networks goes on.

11.3.3   Beneš Network

In the 1960's, a researcher at Bell Labs named Václav E. Beneš had a remarkable idea. He obtained a marvelous communication network with congestion 1 by placing *two* butterflies back-to-back. This amounts to recursively growing *Beneš nets* by adding both inputs and outputs at each stage. Now we recursively define B_n to be the switches and connections (without the terminals) of the Beneš net with $N ::= 2^n$ input and output switches.

The base case B_1 with 2 input switches and 2 output switches is exactly the same as F_1 in Figure 11.4.

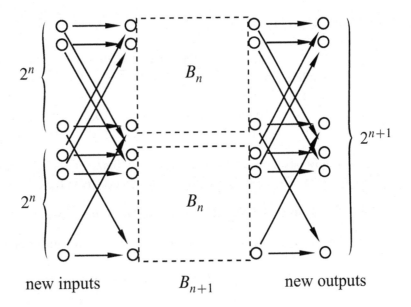

Figure 11.6 Beneš Net B_{n+1} with 2^{n+1} inputs from two B_n's.

In the constructor step, we construct B_{n+1} out of two B_n nets connected to a new set of 2^{n+1} input switches *and also* a new set of 2^{n+1} output switches. This is illustrated in Figure 11.6.

The ith and $2^n + i$th new input switches are each connected to the same two switches: the ith input switches of each of two B_n components for $i = 1, \ldots, 2^n$, exactly as in the Butterfly net. In addition, the ith and $2^n + i$th new *output* switches are connected to the same two switches, namely, to the ith output switches of each of two B_n components.

Now, B_{n+1} is laid out in columns of height 2^{n+1} by adding two more columns of switches to the columns in B_n. So, the B_{n+1} switches are arrayed in $2(n + 1)$ columns. The total number of switches is the number of columns times the height $2(n + 1)2^{n+1}$ of the columns.

All paths in B_{n+1} from an input switch to an output are length $2(n + 1) - 1$, and the diameter of the Beneš net with 2^{n+1} inputs is this length plus two because of the two edges connecting to the terminals.

So Beneš has doubled the number of switches and the diameter, but by doing so he has completely eliminated congestion problems! The proof of this fact relies on a clever induction argument that we'll come to in a moment. Let's first see how the

Beneš network stacks up:

network	diameter	switch size	# switches	congestion
complete binary tree	$2\log N + 2$	3×3	$2N - 1$	N
2-D array	$2N$	2×2	N^2	2
butterfly	$\log N + 2$	2×2	$N(\log(N) + 1)$	$\sqrt{N}$ or $\sqrt{N/2}$
Beneš	$2\log N + 1$	2×2	$2N \log N$	1

The Beneš network has small size and diameter, and it completely eliminates congestion. The Holy Grail of routing networks is in hand!

Theorem 11.3.2. *The congestion of the N-input Beneš network is 1.*

Proof. By induction on n where $N = 2^n$. So the induction hypothesis is

$$P(n) ::= \text{the congestion of } B_n \text{ is } 1.$$

Base case ($n = 1$): $B_1 = F_1$ is shown in Figure 11.4. The unique routings in F_1 have congestion 1.

Inductive step: We assume that the congestion of an $N = 2^n$-input Beneš network is 1 and prove that the congestion of a $2N$-input Beneš network is also 1.

    Digression. Time out! Let's work through an example, develop some intuition, and then complete the proof. In the Beneš network shown in Figure 11.7 with $N = 8$ inputs and outputs, the two 4-input/output subnetworks are in dashed boxes.

    By the inductive assumption, the subnetworks can each route an arbitrary permutation with congestion 1. So if we can guide packets safely through just the first and last levels, then we can rely on induction for the rest! Let's see how this works in an example. Consider the following permutation routing problem:

$$\pi(0) = 1 \qquad\qquad \pi(4) = 3$$
$$\pi(1) = 5 \qquad\qquad \pi(5) = 6$$
$$\pi(2) = 4 \qquad\qquad \pi(6) = 0$$
$$\pi(3) = 7 \qquad\qquad \pi(7) = 2$$

    We can route each packet to its destination through either the upper subnetwork or the lower subnetwork. However, the choice for one packet may constrain the choice for another. For example, we cannot route both packet 0 *and* packet 4 through the same network, since that would cause two packets to collide at a single switch, resulting in congestion. Rather, one packet must go through the upper network and the other through the lower network. Similarly, packets 1 and 5, 2 and

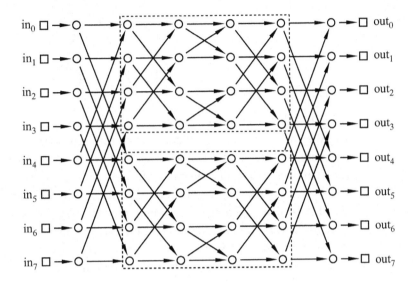

Figure 11.7 Beneš net B_3.

6, and 3 and 7 must be routed through different networks. Let's record these constraints in a graph. The vertices are the 8 packets. If two packets must pass through different networks, then there is an edge between them. Thus, our constraint graph looks like this:

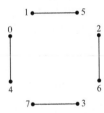

Notice that at most one edge is incident to each vertex.

The output side of the network imposes some further constraints. For example, the packet destined for output 0 (which is packet 6) and the packet destined for output 4 (which is packet 2) cannot both pass through the same network; that would require both packets to arrive from the same switch. Similarly, the packets destined for outputs 1 and 5, 2 and 6, and 3 and 7 must also pass through different switches. We can record these additional constraints in our graph with gray edges:

Notice that at most one new edge is incident to each vertex. The two lines drawn between vertices 2 and 6 reflect the two different reasons why these packets must be routed through different networks. However, we intend this to be a simple graph; the two lines still signify a single edge.

Now here's the key insight: suppose that we could color each vertex either red or blue so that adjacent vertices are colored differently. Then all constraints are satisfied if we send the red packets through the upper network and the blue packets through the lower network. Such a *2-coloring of the graph corresponds to a solution to the routing problem*. The only remaining question is whether the constraint graph is 2-colorable, which is easy to verify:

Lemma 11.3.3. *Prove that if the edges of a graph can be grouped into two sets such that every vertex has at most 1 edge from each set incident to it, then the graph is 2-colorable.*

Proof. It is not hard to show that a graph is 2-colorable iff every cycle in it has even length (see Theorem 12.8.3). We'll take this for granted here.

So all we have to do is show that every cycle has even length. Since the two sets of edges may overlap, let's call an edge that is in both sets a *doubled edge*.

There are two cases:

Case 1: [The cycle contains a doubled edge.] No other edge can be incident to either of the endpoints of a doubled edge, since that endpoint would then be incident to two edges from the same set. So a cycle traversing a doubled edge has nowhere to go but back and forth along the edge an even number of times.

Case 2: [No edge on the cycle is doubled.] Since each vertex is incident to at most one edge from each set, any path with no doubled edges must traverse successive edges that alternate from one set to the other. In particular, a cycle must traverse a path of alternating edges that begins and ends with edges from different sets. This means the cycle has to be of even length. ∎

For example, here is a 2-coloring of the constraint graph:

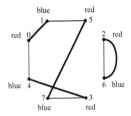

The solution to this graph-coloring problem provides a start on the packet routing problem:

We can complete the routing in the two smaller Beneš networks by induction! Back to the proof. **End of Digression.**

Let π be an arbitrary permutation of $[0..N - 1]$. Let G be the graph whose vertices are packet numbers $0, 1, \ldots, N - 1$ and whose edges come from the union of these two sets:

$$E_1 ::= \{\langle u\text{---}v \rangle \mid |u - v| = N/2\}, \text{ and}$$
$$E_2 ::= \{\langle u\text{---}w \rangle \mid |\pi(u) - \pi(w)| = N/2\}.$$

Now any vertex u is incident to at most two edges: a unique edge $\langle u\text{---}v \rangle \in E_1$ and a unique edge $\langle u\text{---}w \rangle \in E_2$. So according to Lemma 11.3.3, there is a 2-coloring for the vertices of G. Now route packets of one color through the upper subnetwork and packets of the other color through the lower subnetwork. Since for each edge in E_1, one vertex goes to the upper subnetwork and the other to the lower subnetwork, there will not be any conflicts in the first level. Since for each edge in E_2, one vertex comes from the upper subnetwork and the other from the lower subnetwork, there will not be any conflicts in the last level. We can complete the routing within each subnetwork by the induction hypothesis $P(n)$. ∎

Problems for Section 11.2

Exam Problems

Problem 11.1.
Consider the following communication network:

(a) What is the max congestion?

(b) Give an input/output permutation π_0 that forces maximum congestion.

(c) Give an input/output permutation π_1 that allows *minimum* congestion.

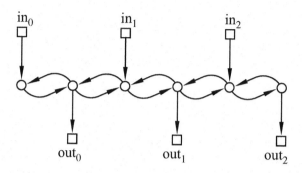

(d) What is the latency for the permutation π_1? (If you could not find π_1, just choose a permutation and find its latency.)

Problems for Section 11.3

Class Problems

Problem 11.2.

The Beneš network has a max congestion of one—every permutation can be routed in such a way that a single packet passes through each switch. Let's work through an example. A diagram of the Beneš network B_3 of size $N = 8$ appears in Figure 11.7. The two subnetworks of size $N = 4$ are marked. We'll refer to these as the *upper* and *lower* subnetworks.

(a) Now consider the following permutation routing problem:

$$\pi(0) = 3 \qquad\qquad \pi(4) = 2$$
$$\pi(1) = 1 \qquad\qquad \pi(5) = 0$$
$$\pi(2) = 6 \qquad\qquad \pi(6) = 7$$
$$\pi(3) = 5 \qquad\qquad \pi(7) = 4$$

Each packet must be routed through either the upper subnetwork or the lower subnetwork. Construct a graph with vertices numbered by integers 0 to 7 and draw a *dashed* edge between each pair of packets that cannot go through the same subnetwork because a collision would occur in the second column of switches.

(b) Add a *solid* edge in your graph between each pair of packets that cannot go through the same subnetwork because a collision would occur in the next-to-last column of switches.

(c) Assign colors red and blue to the vertices of your graph so that vertices that are adjacent by either a dashed or a solid edge get different colors. Why must this be possible, regardless of the permutation π?

(d) Suppose that red vertices correspond to packets routed through the upper subnetwork and blue vertices correspond to packets routed through the lower subnetwork. Referring to the Beneš network shown in Figure 11.6, indicate the first and last edge traversed by each packet.

(e) All that remains is to route packets through the upper and lower subnetworks. One way to do this is by applying the procedure described above recursively on each subnetwork. However, since the remaining problems are small, see if you can complete all the paths on your own.

Problem 11.3.

A *multiple binary-tree network* has N inputs and N outputs, where N is a power of 2. Each input is connected to the root of a binary tree with $N/2$ leaves and with edges pointing away from the root. Likewise, each output is connected to the root of a binary tree with $N/2$ leaves and with edges pointing toward the root.

Two edges point from each leaf of an input tree, and each of these edges points to a leaf of an output tree. The matching of leaf edges is arranged so that for every input and output tree, there is an edge from a leaf of the input tree to a leaf of the output tree, and every output tree leaf has exactly two edges pointing to it.

(a) Draw such a multiple binary-tree net for $N = 4$.

(b) Fill in the table, and explain your entries.

# switches	switch size	diameter	max congestion

Problem 11.4.

The n-input *2-D array* network was shown to have congestion 2. An n-input *2-layer array* consisting of two n-input 2-D Arrays connected as pictured below for $n = 4$.

In general, an n-input 2-layer array has two layers of switches, with each layer connected like an n-input 2-D array. There is also an edge from each switch in the first layer to the corresponding switch in the second layer. The inputs of the 2-layer

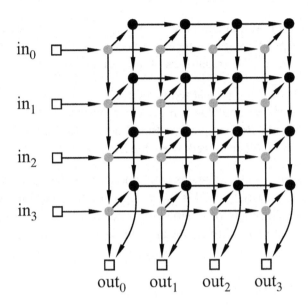

array enter the left side of the first layer, and the n outputs leave from the bottom row of either layer.

(a) For any given input-output permutation, there is a way to route packets that achieves congestion 1. Describe how to route the packets in this way.

(b) What is the latency of a routing designed to minimize latency?

(c) Explain why the congestion of any minimum latency (CML) routing of packets through this network is greater than the network's congestion.

Problem 11.5.
A *5-path* communication network is shown below. From this, it's easy to see what an n-path network would be. Fill in the table of properties below, and be prepared to justify your answers.

network	# switches	switch size	diameter	max congestion
5-path				
n-path				

Problem 11.6.

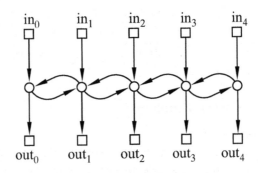

Figure 11.8 5-Path

Tired of being a TA, Megumi has decided to become famous by coming up with a new, better communication network design. Her network has the following specifications: every input node will be sent to a butterfly network, a Beneš network and a 2-d array network. At the end, the outputs of all three networks will converge on the new output.

In the Megumi-net a minimum latency routing does not have minimum congestion. The *latency for min-congestion (LMC)* of a net is the best bound on latency achievable using routings that minimize congestion. Likewise, the *congestion for min-latency (CML)* is the best bound on congestion achievable using routings that minimize latency.

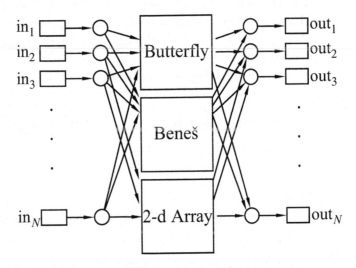

Fill in the following chart for Megumi's new net and explain your answers.

network	diameter	# switches	congestion	LMC	CML
Megumi's net					

Homework Problems

Problem 11.7.

Louis Reasoner figures that, wonderful as the Beneš network may be, the butterfly network has a few advantages, namely: fewer switches, smaller diameter, and an easy way to route packets through it. So Louis designs an N-input/output network he modestly calls a *Reasoner-net* with the aim of combining the best features of both the butterfly and Beneš nets:

> The ith input switch in a Reasoner-net connects to two switches, a_i and b_i, and likewise, the jth output switch has two switches, y_j and z_j, connected to it. Then the Reasoner-net has an N-input Beneš network connected using the a_i switches as input switches and the y_j switches as its output switches. The Reasoner-net also has an N-input butterfly net connected using the b_i switches as inputs and; the z_j switches as outputs.

In the Reasoner-net a minimum latency routing does not have minimum congestion. The *latency for min-congestion* (*LMC*) of a net is the best bound on latency achievable using routings that minimize congestion. Likewise, the *congestion for min-latency* (*CML*) is the best bound on congestion achievable using routings that minimize latency.

Fill in the following chart for the Reasoner-net and briefly explain your answers.

diameter	switch size(s)	# switches	congestion	LMC	CML

Problem 11.8.

Show that the congestion of the butterfly net, F_n, is exactly $\sqrt{N}$ when n is even.
  Hint:

- There is a unique path from each input to each output, so the congestion is the maximum number of messages passing through a vertex for any routing problem.

- If v is a vertex in column i of the butterfly network, there is a path from exactly 2^i input vertices to v and a path from v to exactly 2^{n-i} output vertices.

- At which column of the butterfly network must the congestion be worst? What is the congestion of the topmost switch in that column of the network?

12   Simple Graphs

Simple graphs model relationships that are *symmetric*, meaning that the relationship is mutual. Examples of such mutual relationships are being married, speaking the same language, not speaking the same language, occurring during overlapping time intervals, or being connected by a conducting wire. They come up in all sorts of applications, including scheduling, constraint satisfaction, computer graphics, and communications, but we'll start with an application designed to get your attention: we are going to make a professional inquiry into sexual behavior. Specifically, we'll look at some data about who, on average, has more opposite-gender partners: men or women.

Sexual demographics have been the subject of many studies. In one of the largest, researchers from the University of Chicago interviewed a random sample of 2500 people over several years to try to get an answer to this question. Their study, published in 1994 and entitled *The Social Organization of Sexuality*, found that men have on average 74% more opposite-gender partners than women.

Other studies have found that the disparity is even larger. In particular, ABC News claimed that the average man has 20 partners over his lifetime, and the average woman has 6, for a percentage disparity of 233%. The ABC News study, aired on Primetime Live in 2004, purported to be one of the most scientific ever done, with only a 2.5% margin of error. It was called "American Sex Survey: A peek between the sheets"—raising some questions about the seriousness of their reporting.

Yet again in August, 2007, the New York Times reported on a study by the National Center for Health Statistics of the U.S. government showing that men had seven partners while women had four. So, whose numbers do you think are more accurate: the University of Chicago, ABC News, or the National Center?

Don't answer—this is a trick question designed to trip you up. Using a little graph theory, we'll explain why none of these findings can be anywhere near the truth.

12.1   Vertex Adjacency and Degrees

Simple graphs are defined in almost the same way as digraphs, except that edges are *undirected*—they connect two vertices without pointing in either direction between the vertices. So instead of a directed edge $\langle v \to w \rangle$ which starts at vertex v and ends at vertex w, a simple graph only has an undirected edge $\langle v{-}w \rangle$ that connects v and w.

Definition 12.1.1. A *simple graph* G consists of a nonempty set, $V(G)$, called the *vertices* of G, and a set $E(G)$ called the *edges* of G. An element of $V(G)$ is called a *vertex*. A vertex is also called a *node*; the words "vertex" and "node" are used interchangeably. An element of $E(G)$ is an *undirected edge* or simply an "edge." An undirected edge has two vertices $u \neq v$ called its *endpoints*. Such an edge can be represented by the two element set $\{u, v\}$. The notation $\langle u{-}v \rangle$ denotes this edge.

Both $\langle u{-}v \rangle$ and $\langle v{-}u \rangle$ define the same undirected edge, whose endpoints are u and v.

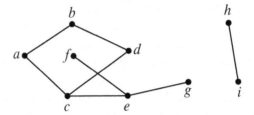

Figure 12.1   An example of a graph with 9 nodes and 8 edges.

For example, let H be the graph pictured in Figure 12.1. The vertices of H correspond to the nine dots in Figure 12.1, that is,

$$V(H) = \{a, b, c, d, e, f, g, h, i\}.$$

The edges correspond to the eight lines, that is,

$$E(H) = \{ \langle a{-}b \rangle, \langle a{-}c \rangle, \langle b{-}d \rangle, \langle c{-}d \rangle, \langle c{-}e \rangle, \langle e{-}f \rangle, \langle e{-}g \rangle, \langle h{-}i \rangle \}.$$

Mathematically, that's all there is to the graph H.

Definition 12.1.2. Two vertices in a simple graph are said to be *adjacent* iff they are the endpoints of the same edge, and an edge is said to be *incident* to each of its endpoints. The number of edges incident to a vertex v is called the *degree* of the vertex and is denoted by $\deg(v)$. Equivalently, the degree of a vertex is the number of vertices adjacent to it.

For example, for the graph H of Figure 12.1, vertex a is adjacent to vertex b, and b is adjacent to d. The edge $\langle a{-}c \rangle$ is incident to its endpoints a and c. Vertex h has degree 1, d has degree 2, and $\deg(e) = 3$. It is possible for a vertex to have degree 0, in which case it is not adjacent to any other vertices. A simple graph G does not need to have any edges at all. $|E(G)|$ could be zero, implying that the degree of every vertex would also be zero. But a simple graph must have at least one vertex—$|V(G)|$ is required to be at least one.

An edge whose endpoints are the same is called a *self-loop*. Self-loops aren't allowed in simple graphs.[1] In a more general class of graphs called *multigraphs*, there can be more than one edge with the same two endpoints, but this doesn't happen in simple graphs, because every edge is uniquely determined by its two endpoints. Sometimes graphs with no vertices, with self-loops, or with more than one edge between the same two vertices are convenient to have, but we don't need them, and sticking with simple graphs is simpler.

For the rest of this chapter we'll use "graphs" as an abbreviation for "simple graphs."

A synonym for "vertices" is "*nodes*," and we'll use these words interchangeably. Simple graphs are sometimes called *networks*, edges are sometimes called *arcs*. We mention this as a "heads up" in case you look at other graph theory literature; we won't use these words.

12.2 Sexual Demographics in America

Let's model the question of heterosexual partners in graph theoretic terms. To do this, we'll let G be the graph whose vertices V are all the people in America. Then we split V into two separate subsets: M which contains all the males, and F which contains all the females.[2] We'll put an edge between a male and a female iff they have been sexual partners. This graph is pictured in Figure 12.2 with males on the left and females on the right.

Actually, this is a pretty hard graph to figure out, let alone draw. The graph is *enormous*: the US population is about 300 million, so $|V| \approx 300M$. Of these, approximately 50.8% are female and 49.2% are male, so $|M| \approx 147.6M$, and $|F| \approx 152.4M$. And we don't even have trustworthy estimates of how many edges there are, let alone exactly which couples are adjacent. But it turns out that we don't need to know any of this—we just need to figure out the relationship between the average number of partners per male and partners per female. To do this, we note that every edge has exactly one endpoint at an M vertex (remember, we're only considering male-female relationships); so the sum of the degrees of the M

---

[1] You might try to represent a self-loop going between a vertex v and itself as $\{v, v\}$, but this equals $\{v\}$. It wouldn't be an edge, which is defined to be a set of *two* vertices.

[2] For simplicity, we'll ignore the possibility of someone being *both* a man and a woman, or neither.

M   F

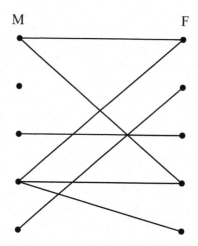

Figure 12.2   The sex partners graph.

vertices equals the number of edges. For the same reason, the sum of the degrees of the F vertices equals the number of edges. So these sums are equal:

$$\sum_{x \in M} \deg(x) = \sum_{y \in F} \deg(y).$$

Now suppose we divide both sides of this equation by the product of the sizes of the two sets, $|M| \cdot |F|$:

$$\left(\frac{\sum_{x \in M} \deg(x)}{|M|} \right) \cdot \frac{1}{|F|} = \left(\frac{\sum_{y \in F} \deg(y)}{|F|} \right) \cdot \frac{1}{|M|}$$

The terms above in parentheses are the *average degree of an M vertex* and the *average degree of an F* vertex. So we know:

$$\text{Avg. deg in } M = \frac{|F|}{|M|} \cdot \text{Avg. deg in } F \qquad (12.1)$$

In other words, we've proved that the average number of female partners of males in the population compared to the average number of males per female is *determined solely by the relative number of males and females in the population.*

Now the Census Bureau reports that there are slightly more females than males in America; in particular $|F|/|M|$ is about 1.035. So we know that males have on average 3.5% more opposite-gender partners than females, and that this tells us nothing about any sex's promiscuity or selectivity. Rather, it just has to do with the relative number of males and females. Collectively, males and females have the same number of opposite gender partners, since it takes one of each set for every partnership, but there are fewer males, so they have a higher ratio. This means that the University of Chicago, ABC, and the Federal government studies are way off. After a huge effort, they gave a totally wrong answer.

There's no definite explanation for why such surveys are consistently wrong. One hypothesis is that males exaggerate their number of partners—or maybe females downplay theirs—but these explanations are speculative. Interestingly, the principal author of the National Center for Health Statistics study reported that she knew the results had to be wrong, but that was the data collected, and her job was to report it.

The same underlying issue has led to serious misinterpretations of other survey data. For example, a couple of years ago, the Boston Globe ran a story on a survey of the study habits of students on Boston area campuses. Their survey showed that on average, minority students tended to study with non-minority students more than the other way around. They went on at great length to explain why this "remarkable phenomenon" might be true. But it's not remarkable at all. Using our graph theory formulation, we can see that all it says is that there are fewer students in a minority than students not in that minority, which is, of course, what "minority" means.

12.2.1 Handshaking Lemma

The previous argument hinged on the connection between a sum of degrees and the number of edges. There is a simple connection between these in any graph:

Lemma 12.2.1. *The sum of the degrees of the vertices in a graph equals twice the number of edges.*

Proof. Every edge contributes two to the sum of the degrees, one for each of its endpoints. ∎

We refer to Lemma 12.2.1 as the *Handshaking Lemma*: if we total up the number of people each person at a party shakes hands with, the total will be twice the number of handshakes that occurred.

12.3 Some Common Graphs

Some graphs come up so frequently that they have names. A *complete graph K_n* has n vertices and an edge between every two vertices, for a total of $n(n-1)/2$ edges. For example, K_5 is shown in Figure 12.3.

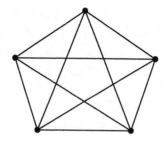

Figure 12.3 K_5: the complete graph on 5 nodes.

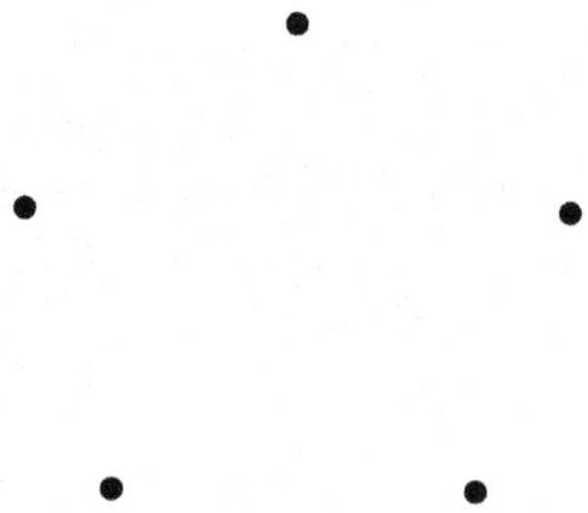

Figure 12.4   An empty graph with 5 nodes.

The *empty graph* has no edges at all. For example, the empty graph with 5 nodes is shown in Figure 12.4.

An n-node graph containing $n-1$ edges in sequence is known as a *line graph* L_n. More formally, L_n has

$$V(L_n) = \{v_1, v_2, \ldots, v_n\}$$

and

$$E(L_n) = \{\, \langle v_1{-}v_2 \rangle, \langle v_2{-}v_3 \rangle, \ldots, \langle v_{n-1}{-}v_n \rangle \,\}$$

For example, L_5 is pictured in Figure 12.5.

There is also a one-way infinite line graph L_∞ which can be defined by letting the nonnegative integers $\mathbb{N}$ be the vertices with edges $\langle k{-}(k+1) \rangle$ for all $k \in \mathbb{N}$.

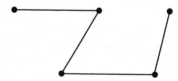

Figure 12.5 L_5: a 5-node line graph.

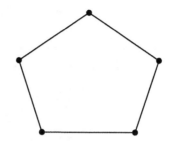

Figure 12.6 C_5: a 5-node cycle graph.

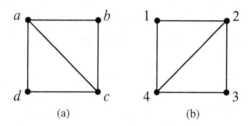

Figure 12.7 Two Isomorphic graphs.

If we add the edge $\langle v_n\!-\!v_1 \rangle$ to the line graph L_n, we get a graph called a *length-n cycle C_n*. Figure 12.6 shows a picture of length-5 cycle.

12.4 Isomorphism

Two graphs that look different might actually be the same in a formal sense. For example, the two graphs in Figure 12.7 are both 4-vertex, 5-edge graphs and you get graph (b) by a 90° clockwise rotation of graph (a).

Strictly speaking, these graphs are different mathematical objects, but this difference doesn't reflect the fact that the two graphs can be described by the same picture—except for the labels on the vertices. This idea of having the same picture "up to relabeling" can be captured neatly by adapting Definition 10.7.1 of isomorphism of digraphs to handle simple graphs. An isomorphism between two graphs is an edge-preserving bijection between their sets of vertices:

Definition 12.4.1. An isomorphism between graphs G and H is a bijection $f : V(G) \to V(H)$ such that

$$\langle u\!-\!v \rangle \in E(G) \quad \text{iff} \quad \langle f(u)\!-\!f(v) \rangle \in E(H)$$

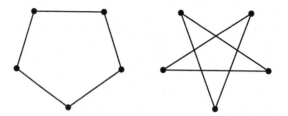

Figure 12.8   Isomorphic C_5 graphs.

for all $u, v \in V(G)$. Two graphs are isomorphic when there is an isomorphism between them.

Here is an isomorphism f between the two graphs in Figure 12.7:

$$f(a) ::= 2 \qquad f(b) ::= 3$$
$$f(c) ::= 4 \qquad f(d) ::= 1.$$

You can check that there is an edge between two vertices in the graph on the left if and only if there is an edge between the two corresponding vertices in the graph on the right.

Two isomorphic graphs may be drawn very differently. For example, Figure 12.8 shows two different ways of drawing C_5.

Notice that if f is an isomorphism between G and H, then f^{-1} is an isomorphism between H and G. Isomorphism is also transitive because the composition of isomorphisms is an isomorphism. In fact, isomorphism is an equivalence relation.

Isomorphism preserves the connection properties of a graph, abstracting out what the vertices are called, what they are made out of, or where they appear in a drawing of the graph. More precisely, a property of a graph is said to be *preserved under isomorphism* if whenever G has that property, every graph isomorphic to G also has that property. For example, since an isomorphism is a bijection between sets of vertices, isomorphic graphs must have the same number of vertices. What's more, if f is a graph isomorphism that maps a vertex v of one graph to the vertex $f(v)$ of an isomorphic graph, then by definition of isomorphism, every vertex adjacent to v in the first graph will be mapped by f to a vertex adjacent to $f(v)$ in the isomorphic graph. Thus, v and $f(v)$ will have the same degree. If one graph has a vertex of degree 4 and another does not, then they can't be isomorphic. In fact, they can't be isomorphic if the number of degree 4 vertices in each of the graphs is not the same.

Looking for preserved properties can make it easy to determine that two graphs are not isomorphic, or to guide the search for an isomorphism when there is one.

It's generally easy in practice to decide whether two graphs are isomorphic. How-ever, no one has yet found a procedure for determining whether two graphs are isomorphic that is *guaranteed* to run in polynomial time on all pairs of graphs.[3]

Having such a procedure would be useful. For example, it would make it easy to search for a particular molecule in a database given the molecular bonds. On the other hand, knowing there is no such efficient procedure would also be valu-able: secure protocols for encryption and remote authentication can be built on the hypothesis that graph isomorphism is computationally exhausting.

The definitions of bijection and isomorphism apply to infinite graphs as well as finite graphs, as do most of the results in the rest of this chapter. But graph theory focuses mostly on finite graphs, and we will too. *In the rest of this chapter we'll assume graphs are finite.*

We've actually been taking isomorphism for granted ever since we wrote "K_n has n vertices..." at the beginning of Section 12.3.

Graph theory is all about properties preserved by isomorphism.

12.5 Bipartite Graphs & Matchings

There were two kinds of vertices in the "Sex in America" graph, males and females, and edges only went between the two kinds. Graphs like this come up so frequently that they have earned a special name: *bipartite graphs.*

Definition 12.5.1. A *bipartite graph* is a graph whose vertices can be divided into two sets, $L(G)$ and $R(G)$, such that every edge has one endpoint in $L(G)$ and the other endpoint in $R(G)$.

So every bipartite graph looks something like the graph in Figure 12.2.

12.5.1 The Bipartite Matching Problem

The bipartite matching problem is related to the sex-in-America problem that we just studied; only now, the goal is to get everyone happily married. As you might imagine, this is not possible for a variety of reasons, not the least of which is the fact that there are more women in America than men. So, it is simply not possible to marry every woman to a man so that every man is married at most once.

But what about getting a mate for every man so that every woman is married at most once? Is it possible to do this so that each man is paired with a woman that

---

[3] A procedure runs in *polynomial time* when it needs an amount of time of at most $p(n)$, where n is the total number of vertices and $p()$ is a fixed polynomial.

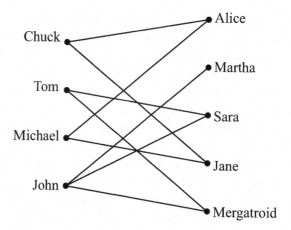

Figure 12.9   A graph where an edge between a man and woman denotes that the man likes the woman.

he likes? The answer, of course, depends on the bipartite graph that represents who likes who, but the good news is that it is possible to find natural properties of the who-likes-who graph that completely determine the answer to this question.

In general, suppose that we have a set of men and an equal-sized or larger set of women, and there is a graph with an edge between a man and a woman if the man likes the woman. In this scenario, the "likes" relationship need not be symmetric, since for the time being, we will only worry about finding a mate for each man that he likes.[4]   Later, we will consider the "likes" relationship from the female perspective as well. For example, we might obtain the graph in Figure 12.9.

A *matching* is defined to be an assignment of a woman to each man so that different men are assigned to different women, and a man is always assigned a woman that he likes. For example, one possible matching for the men is shown in Figure 12.10.

12.5.2   The Matching Condition

A famous result known as Hall's Matching Theorem gives necessary and sufficient conditions for the existence of a matching in a bipartite graph. It turns out to be a remarkably useful mathematical tool.

We'll state and prove Hall's Theorem using man-likes-woman terminology. Define *the set of women liked by a given set of men* to consist of all women liked by

---

[4]By the way, we do not mean to imply that marriage should or should not be heterosexual. Nor do we mean to imply that men should get their choice instead of women. It's just that there are fewer men than women in America, making it impossible to match up all the women with different men.

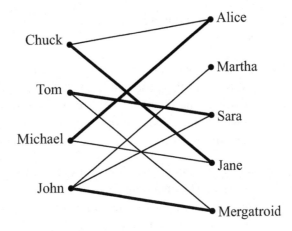

Figure 12.10   One possible matching for the men is shown with bold edges. For example, John is matched with Mergatroid.

at least one of those men. For example, the set of women liked by Tom and John in Figure 12.9 consists of Martha, Sara, and Mergatroid. For us to have any chance at all of matching up the men, the following *matching condition* must hold:

The Matching Condition: every subset of men likes at least as large a set of women.

For example, we cannot find a matching if some set of 4 men like only 3 women. Hall's Theorem says that this necessary condition is actually sufficient; if the matching condition holds, then a matching exists.

Theorem 12.5.2. *A matching for a set M of men with a set W of women can be found if and only if the matching condition holds.*

Proof. First, let's suppose that a matching exists and show that the matching condition holds. For any subset of men, each man likes at least the woman he is matched with and a woman is matched with at most one man. Therefore, every subset of men likes at least as large a set of women. Thus, the matching condition holds.

Next, let's suppose that the matching condition holds and show that a matching exists. We use strong induction on $|M|$, the number of men, on the predicate:

$$P(m) ::= \text{ if the matching condition holds for a set, } M,$$
$$\text{of } m \text{ men, then there is a matching for } M.$$

Base case ($|M| = 1$): If $|M| = 1$, then the matching condition implies that the lone man likes at least one woman, and so a matching exists.

Inductive Step: Suppose that $|M| = m + 1 \geq 2$. To find a matching for M, there are two cases.

Case 1: Every nonempty subset of at most m men likes a *strictly larger* set of women. In this case, we have some latitude: we pair an arbitrary man with a woman he likes and send them both away. This leaves m men and one fewer women, and the matching condition will still hold. So the induction hypothesis $P(m)$ implies we can match the remaining m men.

Case 2: Some nonempty subset X of at most m men likes an *equal-size* set Y of women. The matching condition must hold within X, so the strong induction hypothesis implies we can match the men in X with the women in Y. This leaves the problem of matching the set $M - X$ of men to the set $W - Y$ of women.

But the problem of matching $M - X$ against $W - Y$ also satisfies the Matching condition, because any subset of men in $M - X$ who liked fewer women in $W - Y$ would imply there was a set of men who liked fewer women in the whole set W. Namely, if a subset $M_0 \subseteq M - X$ liked only a strictly smaller subset of women $W_0 \subseteq W - Y$, then the set $M_0 \cup X$ of men would like only women in the strictly smaller set $W_0 \cup Y$. So again the strong induction hypothesis implies we can match the men in $M - X$ with the women in $W - Y$, which completes a matching for M.

So in both cases, there is a matching for the men, which completes the proof of the Inductive step. The theorem follows by induction. ∎

The proof of Theorem 12.5.2 gives an algorithm for finding a matching in a bipartite graph, albeit not a very efficient one. However, efficient algorithms for finding a matching in a bipartite graph do exist. Thus, if a problem can be reduced to finding a matching, instances of the problem can be solved in a reasonably efficient way.

A Formal Statement

Let's restate Theorem 12.5.2 in abstract terms so that you'll not always be condemned to saying, "Now this group of men likes at least as many women..."

Definition 12.5.3. A *matching* in a graph G is a set M of edges of G such that no vertex is an endpoint of more than one edge in M. A matching is said to *cover* a set S of vertices iff each vertex in S is an endpoint of an edge of the matching. A matching is said to be *perfect* if it covers $V(G)$. In any graph G the set $N(S)$ of *neighbors* of some set S of vertices is the image of S under the edge-relation, that is,

$$N(S) ::= \{\, r \mid \langle s\text{—}r \rangle \in E(G) \text{ for some } s \in S \,\}.$$

S is called a *bottleneck* if

$$|S| > |N(S)|.$$

Theorem 12.5.4 (Hall's Theorem). *Let G be a bipartite graph. There is a matching in G that covers $L(G)$ iff no subset of $L(G)$ is a bottleneck.*

An Easy Matching Condition

The bipartite matching condition requires that *every* subset of men has a certain property. In general, verifying that every subset has some property, even if it's easy to check any particular subset for the property, quickly becomes overwhelming because the number of subsets of even relatively small sets is enormous—over a billion subsets for a set of size 30. However, there is a simple property of vertex degrees in a bipartite graph that guarantees the existence of a matching. Call a bipartite graph *degree-constrained* if vertex degrees on the left are at least as large as those on the right. More precisely,

Definition 12.5.5. A bipartite graph G is *degree-constrained* when $\deg(l) \geq \deg(r)$ for every $l \in L(G)$ and $r \in R(G)$.

For example, the graph in Figure 12.9 is degree-constrained since every node on the left is adjacent to at least two nodes on the right while every node on the right is adjacent to at most two nodes on the left.

Theorem 12.5.6. *If G is a degree-constrained bipartite graph, then there is a matching that covers $L(G)$.*

Proof. We will show that G satisfies Hall's condition, namely, if S is an arbitrary subset of $L(G)$, then

$$|N(S)| \geq |S|. \tag{12.2}$$

Since G is degree-constrained, there is a $d > 0$ such that $\deg(l) \geq d \geq \deg(r)$ for every $l \in L$ and $r \in R$. Since every edge with an endpoint in S has its other endpoint in $N(S)$ by definition, and every node in $N(S)$ is incident to at most d edges, we know that

$$d|N(S)| \geq \#\text{edges with an endpoint in } S.$$

Also, since every node in S is the endpoint of at least d edges,

$$\#\text{edges incident to a vertex in } S \geq d|S|.$$

It follows that $d\,|\,N(S)| \geq d\,|S|$. Cancelling d completes the derivation of equation (12.2). ∎

Regular graphs are a large class of degree-constrained graphs that often arise in practice. Hence, we can use Theorem 12.5.6 to prove that every regular bipartite graph has a perfect matching. This turns out to be a surprisingly useful result in computer science.

Definition 12.5.7. A graph is said to be *regular* if every node has the same degree.

Theorem 12.5.8. *Every regular bipartite graph has a perfect matching.*

Proof. Let G be a regular bipartite graph. Since regular graphs are degree-constrained, we know by Theorem 12.5.6 that there must be a matching in G that covers $L(G)$. Such a matching is only possible when $|L(G)| \leq |R(G)|$. But G is also degree-constrained if the roles of $L(G)$ and $R(G)$ are switched, which implies that $|R(G)| \leq |L(G)|$ also. That is, $L(G)$ and $R(G)$ are the same size, and any matching covering $L(G)$ will also cover $R(G)$. So every node in G is an endpoint of an edge in the matching, and thus G has a perfect matching. ∎

12.6 Coloring

In Section 12.2, we used edges to indicate an affinity between a pair of nodes. But there are lots of situations in which edges will correspond to *conflicts* between nodes. Exam scheduling is a typical example.

12.6.1 An Exam Scheduling Problem

Each term, the MIT Schedules Office must assign a time slot for each final exam. This is not easy, because some students are taking several classes with finals, and (even at MIT) a student can take only one test during a particular time slot. The Schedules Office wants to avoid all conflicts. Of course, you can make such a schedule by having every exam in a different slot, but then you would need hundreds of slots for the hundreds of courses, and the exam period would run all year! So, the Schedules Office would also like to keep exam period short.

The Schedules Office's problem is easy to describe as a graph. There will be a vertex for each course with a final exam, and two vertices will be adjacent exactly when some student is taking both courses. For example, suppose we need to schedule exams for 6.041, 6.042, 6.002, 6.003 and 6.170. The scheduling graph might appear as in Figure 12.11.

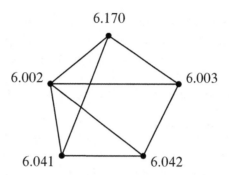

Figure 12.11 A scheduling graph for five exams. Exams connected by an edge cannot be given at the same time.

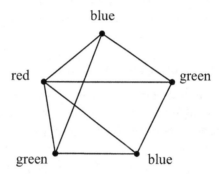

Figure 12.12 A 3-coloring of the exam graph from Figure 12.11.

6.002 and 6.042 cannot have an exam at the same time since there are students in both courses, so there is an edge between their nodes. On the other hand, 6.042 and 6.170 can have an exam at the same time if they're taught at the same time (which they sometimes are), since no student can be enrolled in both (that is, no student *should* be enrolled in both when they have a timing conflict).

We next identify each time slot with a color. For example, Monday morning is red, Monday afternoon is blue, Tuesday morning is green, etc. Assigning an exam to a time slot is then equivalent to coloring the corresponding vertex. The main constraint is that *adjacent vertices must get different colors*—otherwise, some student has two exams at the same time. Furthermore, in order to keep the exam period short, we should try to color all the vertices using as *few different colors as possible*. As shown in Figure 12.12, three colors suffice for our example.

The coloring in Figure 12.12 corresponds to giving one final on Monday morning (red), two Monday afternoon (blue), and two Tuesday morning (green). Can we use fewer than three colors? No! We can't use only two colors since there is a triangle in the graph, and three vertices in a triangle must all have different colors.

This is an example of a *graph coloring* problem: given a graph G, assign colors to each node such that adjacent nodes have different colors. A color assignment with this property is called a *valid coloring* of the graph—a "*coloring*," for short. A graph G is *k-colorable* if it has a coloring that uses at most k colors.

Definition 12.6.1. The minimum value of k for which a graph G has a valid coloring is called its *chromatic number*, $\chi(G)$.

So G is k-colorable iff $\chi(G) \leq k$.

In general, trying to figure out if you can color a graph with a fixed number of colors can take a long time. It's a classic example of a problem for which no fast algorithms are known. In fact, it is easy to check if a coloring works, but it seems really hard to find it. (If you figure out how, then you can get a \$1 million Clay prize.)

12.6.2   Some Coloring Bounds

There are some simple properties of graphs that give useful bounds on colorability.

The simplest property is being a cycle: an even-length closed cycle is 2-colorable. Cycles in simple graphs by convention have positive length and so are not 1-colorable. So

$$\chi(C_{\text{even}}) = 2.$$

On the other hand, an odd-length cycle requires 3 colors, that is,

$$\chi(C_{\text{odd}}) = 3. \tag{12.3}$$

You should take a moment to think about why this equality holds.

Another simple example is a complete graph K_n:

$$\chi(K_n) = n$$

since no two vertices can have the same color.

Being bipartite is another property closely related to colorability. If a graph is bipartite, then you can color it with 2 colors using one color for the nodes on the "left" and a second color for the nodes on the "right." Conversely, graphs with chromatic number 2 are all bipartite with all the vertices of one color on the "left" and those with the other color on the right. Since only graphs with no edges—the *empty graphs*—have chromatic number 1, we have:

Lemma 12.6.2. *A graph G with at least one edge is bipartite iff $\chi(G) = 2$.*

The chromatic number of a graph can also be shown to be small if the vertex degrees of the graph are small. In particular, if we have an upper bound on the degrees of all the vertices in a graph, then we can easily find a coloring with only one more color than the degree bound.

Theorem 12.6.3. *A graph with maximum degree at most k is $(k + 1)$-colorable.*

Since k is the only nonnegative integer valued variable mentioned in the theorem, you might be tempted to try to prove this theorem using induction on k. Unfortunately, this approach leads to disaster—we don't know of any reasonable way to do this and expect it would ruin your week if you tried it on a problem set. When you encounter such a disaster using induction on graphs, it is usually best to change what you are inducting on. In graphs, typical good choices for the induction parameter are n, the number of nodes, or e, the number of edges.

Proof of Theorem 12.6.3. We use induction on the number of vertices in the graph, which we denote by n. Let $P(n)$ be the proposition that an n-vertex graph with maximum degree at most k is $(k + 1)$-colorable.

Base case ($n = 1$): A 1-vertex graph has maximum degree 0 and is 1-colorable, so $P(1)$ is true.

Inductive step: Now assume that $P(n)$ is true, and let G be an $(n+1)$-vertex graph with maximum degree at most k. Remove a vertex v (and all edges incident to it), leaving an n-vertex subgraph H. The maximum degree of H is at most k, and so H is $(k + 1)$-colorable by our assumption $P(n)$. Now add back vertex v. We can assign v a color (from the set of $k + 1$ colors) that is different from all its adjacent vertices, since there are at most k vertices adjacent to v and so at least one of the $k + 1$ colors is still available. Therefore, G is $(k + 1)$-colorable. This completes the inductive step, and the theorem follows by induction. ∎

Sometimes $k + 1$ colors is the best you can do. For example, $\chi(K_n) = n$ and every node in K_n has degree $k = n - 1$ and so this is an example where Theorem 12.6.3 gives the best possible bound. By a similar argument, we can show that Theorem 12.6.3 gives the best possible bound for *any* graph with degree bounded by k that has K_{k+1} as a subgraph.

But sometimes $k + 1$ colors is far from the best that you can do. For example, the n-node *star graph* shown in Figure 12.13 has maximum degree $n - 1$ but can be colored using just 2 colors.

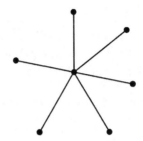

Figure 12.13   A 7-node star graph.

12.6.3   Why coloring?

One reason coloring problems frequently arise in practice is because scheduling conflicts are so common. For example, at the internet company Akamai, cofounded by Tom Leighton, a new version of software is deployed over each of its servers (200,000 servers in 2016) every few days. It would take more than twenty years to update all these the servers one at a time, so the deployment must be carried out for many servers simultaneouly. On the other hand, certain pairs of servers with common critical functions cannot be updated simultaneouly, since a server needs to be taken offline while being updated.

This problem gets solved by making a 200,000-node conflict graph and coloring it with with a dozen or so colors—so only a dozen or so waves of installs are needed!

Another example comes from the need to assign frequencies to radio stations. If two stations have an overlap in their broadcast area, they can't be given the same frequency. Frequencies are precious and expensive, it is important to minimize the number handed out. This amounts to finding the minimum coloring for a graph whose vertices are the stations and whose edges connect stations with overlapping areas.

Coloring also comes up in allocating registers for program variables. While a variable is in use, its value needs to be saved in a register. Registers can be reused for different variables, but two variables need different registers if they are referenced during overlapping intervals of program execution. So register allocation is the coloring problem for a graph whose vertices are the variables: vertices are adjacent if their intervals overlap, and the colors are registers. Once again, the goal is to minimize the number of colors needed to color the graph.

Finally, there's the famous map coloring problem stated in Proposition 1.1.4. The question is how many colors are needed to color a map so that adjacent territories get different colors? This is the same as the number of colors needed to color a graph that can be drawn in the plane without edges crossing. A proof that four colors are enough for *planar* graphs was acclaimed when it was discovered about forty years ago. Implicit in that proof was a 4-coloring procedure that takes time proportional to the number of vertices in the graph (countries in the map).

Surprisingly, it's another of those million dollar prize questions to find an efficient procedure to tell if any particular planar graph really *needs* four colors, or if three will actually do the job. A proof that testing 3-colorability of graphs is as hard as the million dollar SAT problem is given in Problem 12.29; this turns out to be true even for planar graphs. (It is easy to tell if a graph is 2-colorable, as explained in Section 12.8.2.) In Chapter 13, we'll develop enough planar graph theory to present an easy proof that all planar graphs are 5-colorable.

12.7 Simple Walks

12.7.1 Walks, Paths, Cycles in Simple Graphs

Walks and paths in simple graphs are esentially the same as in digraphs. We just modify the digraph definitions using undirected edges instead of directed ones. For example, the formal definition of a walk in a simple graph is a virtually the same as the Definition 10.2.1 of a walk in a digraph:

Definition 12.7.1. A *walk in a simple graph G* is an alternating sequence of vertices and edges that begins with a vertex, ends with a vertex, and such that for every edge $\langle u\text{---}v \rangle$ in the walk, one of the endpoints u, v is the element just before the edge, and the other endpoint is the next element after the edge. The *length of a walk* is the total number of occurrences of edges in it.

So a walk **v** is a sequence of the form

$$\mathbf{v} ::= v_0 \ \langle v_0\text{---}v_1 \rangle \ v_1 \ \langle v_1\text{---}v_2 \rangle \ v_2 \ \ldots \ \langle v_{k-1}\text{---}v_k \rangle \ v_k$$

where $\langle v_i\text{---}v_{i+1} \rangle \in E(G)$ for $i \in [0..k)$. The walk is said to *start* at v_0, to *end* at v_k, and the *length*, $|\mathbf{v}|$, of the walk is k. The walk is a *path* iff all the v_i's are different, that is, if $i \neq j$, then $v_i \neq v_j$.

A walk that begins and ends at the same vertex is a *closed walk*. A single vertex counts as a length zero closed walk as well as a length zero path.

A *cycle* can be represented by a closed walk of length three or more whose vertices are distinct except for the beginning and end vertices.

Note that in contrast to digraphs, we don't count length two closed walks as cycles in simple graphs. That's because a walk going back and forth on the same

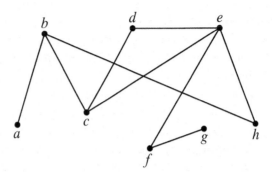

Figure 12.14   *A graph with 3 cycles: bhecb, cdec, bcdehb.*

edge is always possible in a simple graph, and it has no importance. Also, there are no closed walks of length one, since simple graphs don't have self loops.

As in digraphs, the length of a walk is *one less* than the number of occurrences of vertices in it. For example, the graph in Figure 12.14 has a length 6 path through the seven successive vertices $abcdefg$. This is the longest path in the graph. The graph in Figure 12.14 also has three cycles through successive vertices $bhecb$, $cdec$ and $bcdehb$.

12.7.2   Cycles as Subgraphs

We don't want think of a cycle as having a beginning or an end, so *any* of the paths that go around it can represent the cycle. For example, in the graph in Figure 12.14, the cycle starting at b and going through vertices $bcdehb$ can also be described as starting at d and going through $dehbcd$. Furthermore, cycles in simple graphs don't have a direction: $dcbhed$ describes the same cycle as though it started and ended at d but went in the opposite direction.

A precise way to explain which closed walks represent the same cycle is to define cycle as a subgraph. Specifically, we could define a cycle in G to be a *subgraph* of G that looks like a length-n cycle for $n \geq 3$.

Definition 12.7.2. A graph G is said to be a *subgraph* of a graph H if $V(G) \subseteq V(H)$ and $E(G) \subseteq E(H)$.

For example, the one-edge graph G where

$$V(G) = \{g, h, i\} \quad \text{and} \quad E(G) = \{\langle h\!-\!i \rangle\}$$

is a subgraph of the graph H in Figure 12.1. On the other hand, any graph containing an edge $\langle g\!-\!h \rangle$ will not be a subgraph of H because this edge is not in $E(H)$. Another example is an empty graph on n nodes, which will be a subgraph of an L_n with the same set of nodes; similarly, L_n is a subgraph of C_n, and C_n is a subgraph of K_n.

Definition 12.7.3. For $n \geq 3$, let C_n be the graph with vertices $1, \ldots, n$ and edges

$$\langle 1\text{---}2 \rangle, \ \langle 2\text{---}3 \rangle, \ \ldots, \ \langle (n-1)\text{---}n \rangle, \ \langle n\text{---}1 \rangle.$$

A *cycle of a graph* G is a subgraph of G that is isomorphic to C_n for some $n \geq 3$.

This definition formally captures the idea that cycles don't have direction or beginnings or ends.

12.8   Connectivity

Definition 12.8.1. *Two vertices are connected* in a graph when there is a path that begins at one and ends at the other. By convention, every vertex is connected to itself by a path of length zero. A *graph is connected* when every pair of vertices are connected.

12.8.1   Connected Components

Being connected is usually a good property for a graph to have. For example, it could mean that it is possible to get from any node to any other node, or that it is possible to communicate between any pair of nodes, depending on the application.

But not all graphs are connected. For example, the graph where nodes represent cities and edges represent highways might be connected for North American cities, but would surely not be connected if you also included cities in Australia. The same is true for communication networks like the internet—in order to be protected from viruses that spread on the internet, some government networks are completely isolated from the internet.

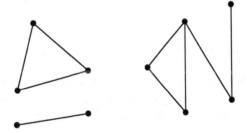

Figure 12.15   One graph with 3 connected components.

Another example is shown in Figure 12.15, which looks like a picture of three graphs, but is intended to be a picture of *one* graph. This graph consists of three pieces. Each piece is a subgraph that by itself is connected, but there are no paths between vertices in different pieces. These connected pieces of a graph are called its *connected components*.

Definition 12.8.2. A *connected component* of a graph is a subgraph consisting of some vertex and every node and edge that is connected to that vertex.

So, a graph is connected iff it has exactly one connected component. At the other extreme, the empty graph on n vertices has n connected components, each consisting of a single vertex.

12.8.2   Odd Cycles and 2-Colorability

We have already seen that determining the chromatic number of a graph is a challenging problem. There is one special case where this problem is very easy, namely, when the graph is 2-colorable.

Theorem 12.8.3. *The following graph properties are equivalent:*

1. The graph contains an odd length cycle.

2. The graph is not 2-colorable.

3. The graph contains an odd length closed walk.

In other words, if a graph has any one of the three properties above, then it has all of the properties.

We will show the following implications among these properties:

$$1. \text{ IMPLIES } 2. \text{ IMPLIES } 3. \text{ IMPLIES } 1.$$

So each of these properties implies the other two, which means they all are equivalent.

1 IMPLIES 2 *Proof.* This follows from equation 12.3.   ∎

2 IMPLIES 3   If we prove this implication for connected graphs, then it will hold for an arbitrary graph because it will hold for each connected component. So we can assume that G is connected.

Proof. Pick an arbitrary vertex r of G. Since G is connected, for every node $u \in V(G)$, there will be a walk $\mathbf{w}_u$ starting at u and ending at r. Assign colors to vertices of G as follows:

$$\text{color}(u) = \begin{cases} \text{black}, & \text{if } |\mathbf{w}_u| \text{ is even}, \\ \text{white}, & \text{otherwise}. \end{cases}$$

Now since G is not colorable, this can't be a valid coloring. So there must be an edge between two nodes u and v with the same color. But in that case

$$\mathbf{w}_u \widehat{\ }\, \text{reverse}(\mathbf{w}_v) \widehat{\ }\, \langle v\!-\!u \rangle$$

is a closed walk starting and ending at u, and its length is

$$|\mathbf{w}_u| + |\mathbf{w}_v| + 1$$

which is odd. ∎

3 IMPLIES 1 *Proof.* Since there is an odd length closed walk, the WOP implies there is an odd length closed walk $\mathbf{w}$ of minimum length. We claim $\mathbf{w}$ must be a cycle. To show this, assume to the contrary that $\mathbf{w}$ is not a cycle, so there is a repeat vertex occurrence besides the start and end. There are then two cases to consider depending on whether the additional repeat is different from, or the same as, the start vertex.

In the first case, the start vertex has an extra occurrence. That is,

$$\mathbf{w} = \mathbf{f}\,\widehat{x}\,\mathbf{r}$$

for some positive length walks $\mathbf{f}$ and $\mathbf{r}$ that begin and end at x. Since

$$|\mathbf{w}| = |\mathbf{f}| + |\mathbf{r}|$$

is odd, exactly one of $\mathbf{f}$ and $\mathbf{r}$ must have odd length, and that one will be an odd length closed walk shorter than $\mathbf{w}$, a contradiction.

In the second case,

$$\mathbf{w} = \mathbf{f}\,\widehat{y}\,\mathbf{g}\,\widehat{y}\,\mathbf{r}$$

where $\mathbf{f}$ is a walk from x to y for some $y \neq x$, and $\mathbf{r}$ is a walk from y to x, and $|\mathbf{g}| > 0$. Now $\mathbf{g}$ cannot have odd length or it would be an odd-length closed walk shorter than $\mathbf{w}$. So $\mathbf{g}$ has even length. That implies that $\mathbf{f}\,\widehat{y}\,\mathbf{r}$ must be an odd-length closed walk shorter than $\mathbf{w}$, again a contradiction.

This completes the proof of Theorem 12.8.3. ∎

Theorem 12.8.3 turns out to be useful, since bipartite graphs come up fairly often in practice.[5]

12.8.3   *k*-connected Graphs

If we think of a graph as modeling cables in a telephone network, or oil pipelines, or electrical power lines, then we not only want connectivity, but we want connectivity that survives component failure. So more generally, we want to define how strongly two vertices are connected. One measure of connection strength is how many links must fail before connectedness fails. In particular, two vertices are *k-edge connected* when it takes at least *k* "edge-failures" to disconnect them. More precisely:

Definition 12.8.4. Two vertices in a graph are *k-edge connected* when they remain connected in every subgraph obtained by deleting up to *k* − 1 edges. A graph is *k*-edge connected when it has more than one vertex, and every pair of distinct vertices in the graph are *k*-edge connected.

From now on we'll drop the "edge" modifier and just say "*k*-connected."[6]

Notice that according to Definition 12.8.4, if a graph is *k*-connected, it is also *j*-connected for $j \leq k$. This convenient convention implies that two vertices are connected according to definition 12.8.1 iff they are 1-connected according to Definition 12.8.4.

For example, in the graph in figure 12.14, vertices *c* and *e* are 3-connected, *b* and *e* are 2-connected, *g* and *e* are 1 connected, and no vertices are 4-connected. The graph as a whole is only 1-connected. A complete graph K_n is $(n − 1)$-connected. Every cycle is 2-connected.

The idea of a *cut edge* is a useful way to explain 2-connectivity.

Definition 12.8.5. If two vertices are connected in a graph *G*, but not connected when an edge *e* is removed, then *e* is called a *cut edge* of *G*.

So a graph with more than one vertex is 2-connected iff it is connected and has no cut edges. The following Lemma is another immediate consequence of the definition:

Lemma 12.8.6. *An edge is a cut edge iff it is not on a cycle.*

---

[5]One example concerning routing networks already came up in Lemma 11.3.3. Corollary 13.5.4 reveals the importance of another example in planar graph theory.

[6]There is a corresponding definition of *k*-vertex connectedness based on deleting vertices rather than edges. Graph theory texts usually use "*k*-connected" as shorthand for "*k*-vertex connected." But edge-connectedness will be enough for us.

More generally, if two vertices are connected by k edge-disjoint paths—that is, no edge occurs in two paths—then they must be k-connected, since at least one edge will have to be removed from each of the paths before they could disconnect. A fundamental fact, whose ingenious proof we omit, is Menger's theorem which confirms that the converse is also true: if two vertices are k-connected, then there are k edge-disjoint paths connecting them. It takes some ingenuity to prove this just for the case $k = 2$.

12.8.4 The Minimum Number of Edges in a Connected Graph

The following theorem says that a graph with few edges must have many connected components.

Theorem 12.8.7. *Every graph G has at least $|V(G)| - |E(G)|$ connected components.*

Of course for Theorem 12.8.7 to be of any use, there must be fewer edges than vertices.

Proof. We use induction on the number k of edges. Let $P(k)$ be the proposition that

> every graph G with k edges has at least $|V(G)| - k$ connected components.

Base case ($k = 0$): In a graph with 0 edges, each vertex is itself a connected component, and so there are exactly $|V(G)| = |V(G)| - 0$ connected components. So $P(0)$ holds.

Inductive step:

Let G_e be the graph that results from removing an edge, $e \in E(G)$. So G_e has k edges, and by the induction hypothesis $P(k)$, we may assume that G_e has at least $(|V(G)| - k)$ connected components. Now add back the edge e to obtain the original graph G. If the endpoints of e were in the same connected component of G_e, then G has the same sets of connected vertices as G_e, so G has at least $(|V(G)| - k) > (|V(G)| - (k + 1))$ components. Alternatively, if the endpoints of e were in different connected components of G_e, then these two components are merged into one component in G, while all other components remain unchanged, so that G has one fewer connected component than G_e. That is, G has at least $(|V(G)| - k) - 1 = (|V(G)| - (k + 1))$ connected components. So in either case, G has at least $|V(G)| - (k + 1)$ components, as claimed.

This completes the inductive step and hence the entire proof by induction. ∎

Figure 12.16   A 6-node forest consisting of 2 component trees.

Corollary 12.8.8. *Every connected graph with n vertices has at least n − 1 edges.*

A couple of points about the proof of Theorem 12.8.7 are worth noticing. First, we used induction on the number of edges in the graph. This is very common in proofs involving graphs, as is induction on the number of vertices. When you're presented with a graph problem, these two approaches should be among the first you consider.

The second point is more subtle. Notice that in the inductive step, we took an arbitrary $(k+1)$-edge graph, threw out an edge so that we could apply the induction assumption, and then put the edge back. You'll see this shrink-down, grow-back process very often in the inductive steps of proofs related to graphs. This might seem like needless effort: why not start with an k-edge graph and add one more to get an $(k + 1)$-edge graph? That would work fine in this case, but opens the door to a nasty logical error called *buildup error*, illustrated in Problem 12.40.

12.9   Forests & Trees

We've already made good use of digraphs without cycles, but *simple* graphs without cycles are arguably the most important graphs in computer science.

12.9.1   Leaves, Parents & Children

Definition 12.9.1. An acyclic graph is called a *forest*. A connected acyclic graph is called a *tree*.

The graph shown in Figure 12.16 is a forest. Each of its connected components is by definition a tree.

One of the first things you will notice about trees is that they tend to have a lot of nodes with degree one. Such nodes are called *leaves*.

Definition 12.9.2. A degree 1 node in a forest is called a *leaf.*

The forest in Figure 12.16 has 4 leaves. The tree in Figure 12.17 has 5 leaves.

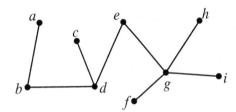

Figure 12.17   A 9-node tree with 5 leaves.

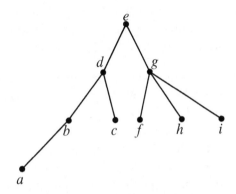

Figure 12.18   The tree from Figure 12.17 redrawn with node e as the root and the other nodes arranged in levels.

Trees are a fundamental data structure in computer science. For example, information is often stored in tree-like data structures, and the execution of many recursive programs can be modeled as the traversal of a tree. In such cases, it is often useful to arrange the nodes in levels, where the node at the top level is identified as the *root* and where every edge joins a *parent* to a *child* one level below. Figure 12.18 shows the tree of Figure 12.17 redrawn in this way. Node d is a child of node e and the parent of nodes b and c.

12.9.2   Properties

Trees have many unique properties. We have listed some of them in the following theorem.

Theorem 12.9.3. *Every tree has the following properties:*

1. *Every connected subgraph is a tree.*

2. *There is a unique path between every pair of vertices.*

3. *Adding an edge between nonadjacent nodes in a tree creates a graph with a cycle.*

4. *Removing any edge disconnects the graph. That is, every edge is a cut edge.*

5. *If the tree has at least two vertices, then it has at least two leaves.*

6. *The number of vertices in a tree is one larger than the number of edges.*

Proof.   1. A cycle in a subgraph is also a cycle in the whole graph, so any subgraph of an acyclic graph must also be acyclic. If the subgraph is also connected, then by definition, it is a tree.

2. Since a tree is connected, there is at least one path between every pair of vertices. Suppose for the purposes of contradiction, that there are two different paths between some pair of vertices. Then there are two distinct paths $\mathbf{p} \neq \mathbf{q}$ between the same two vertices with minimum total length $|\mathbf{p}| + |\mathbf{q}|$. If these paths shared a vertex w other than at the start and end of the paths, then the parts of $\mathbf{p}$ and $\mathbf{q}$ from start to w, or the parts of $\mathbf{p}$ and $\mathbf{q}$ from w to the end, must be distinct paths between the same vertices with total length less than $|\mathbf{p}| + |\mathbf{q}|$, contradicting the minimality of this sum. Therefore, $\mathbf{p}$ and $\mathbf{q}$ have no vertices in common besides their endpoints, and so $\mathbf{p} \,\hat{}\, \text{reverse}(\mathbf{q})$ is a cycle.

3. An additional edge $\langle u\!-\!v \rangle$ together with the unique path between u and v forms a cycle.

4. Suppose that we remove edge $\langle u\!-\!v \rangle$. Since the tree contained a unique path between u and v, that path must have been $\langle u\!-\!v \rangle$. Therefore, when that edge is removed, no path remains, and so the graph is not connected.

5. Since the tree has at least two vertices, the longest path in the tree will have different endpoints u and v. We claim u is a leaf. This follows because, by definition of endpoint, u is incident to at most one edge on the path. Also, if u was incident to an edge not on the path, then the path could be lengthened by adding that edge, contradicting the fact that the path was as long as possible. It follows that u is incident only to a single edge, that is u is a leaf. The same hold for v.

6. We use induction on the proposition

$$P(n) ::= \text{there are } n - 1 \text{ edges in any } n\text{-vertex tree.}$$

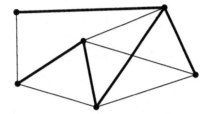

Figure 12.19 A graph where the edges of a spanning tree have been thickened.

Base case ($n = 1$): $P(1)$ is true since a tree with 1 node has 0 edges and $1 - 1 = 0$.

Inductive step: Now suppose that $P(n)$ is true and consider an $(n+1)$-vertex tree T. Let v be a leaf of the tree. You can verify that deleting a vertex of degree 1 (and its incident edge) from any connected graph leaves a connected subgraph. So by Theorem 12.9.3.1, deleting v and its incident edge gives a smaller tree, and this smaller tree has $n - 1$ edges by induction. If we re-attach the vertex v and its incident edge, we find that T has $n = (n + 1) - 1$ edges. Hence, $P(n + 1)$ is true, and the induction proof is complete. ∎

Various subsets of properties in Theorem 12.9.3 provide alternative characterizations of trees. For example,

Lemma 12.9.4. *A graph G is a tree iff G is a forest and* $|V(G)| = |E(G)| + 1$.

The proof is an easy consequence of Theorem 12.9.3.6 (Problem 12.47).

12.9.3 Spanning Trees

Trees are everywhere. In fact, every connected graph contains a subgraph that is a tree with the same vertices as the graph. This is called a *spanning tree* for the graph. For example, Figure 12.19 is a connected graph with a spanning tree highlighted.

Definition 12.9.5. Define a *spanning subgraph* of a graph G to be a subgraph containing all the vertices of G.

Theorem 12.9.6. *Every connected graph contains a spanning tree.*

Proof. Suppose G is a connected graph, so the graph G itself is a connected, spanning subgraph. So by WOP, G must have a minimum-edge connected, spanning subgraph T. We claim T is a spanning tree. Since T is a connected, spanning subgraph by definition, all we have to show is that T is acyclic.

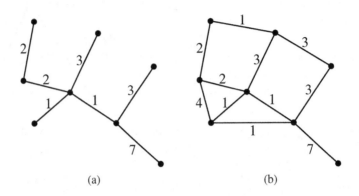

(a)   (b)

Figure 12.20   A spanning tree (a) with weight 19 for a graph (b).

But suppose to the contrary that T contained a cycle C. By Lemma 12.8.6, an edge e of C will not be a cut edge, so removing it would leave a connected, spanning subgraph that was smaller than T, contradicting the minimality to T. ∎

12.9.4   Minimum Weight Spanning Trees

Spanning trees are interesting because they connect all the nodes of a graph using the smallest possible number of edges. For example the spanning tree for the 6-node graph shown in Figure 12.19 has 5 edges.

In many applications, there are numerical costs or weights associated with the edges of the graph. For example, suppose the nodes of a graph represent buildings and edges represent connections between them. The cost of a connection may vary a lot from one pair of buildings or towns to another. Another example is where the nodes represent cities and the weight of an edge is the distance between them: the weight of the Los Angeles/New York City edge is much higher than the weight of the NYC/Boston edge. The *weight of a graph* is simply defined to be the sum of the weights of its edges. For example, the weight of the spanning tree shown in Figure 12.20 is 19.

Definition 12.9.7. A *minimum weight spanning tree* (MST) of an edge-weighted graph G is a spanning tree of G with the smallest possible sum of edge weights.

Is the spanning tree shown in Figure 12.20(a) an MST of the weighted graph shown in Figure 12.20(b)? It actually isn't, since the tree shown in Figure 12.21 is also a spanning tree of the graph shown in Figure 12.20(b), and this spanning tree has weight 17.

What about the tree shown in Figure 12.21? It seems to be an MST, but how do we prove it? In general, how do we find an MST for a connected graph G? We

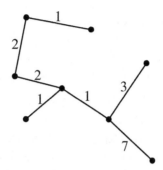

Figure 12.21   An MST with weight 17 for the graph in Figure 12.20(b).

could try enumerating all subtrees of G, but that approach would be hopeless for large graphs.

There actually are many good ways to find MST's based on a property of some subgraphs of G called *pre-MST*'s.

Definition 12.9.8. A *pre-MST* for a graph G is a spanning subgraph of G that is also a subgraph of some MST of G.

So a pre-MST will necessarily be a forest.

For example, the empty graph with the same vertices as G is guaranteed to be a pre-MST of G, and so is any actual MST of G.

If e is an edge of G and S is a spanning subgraph, we'll write $S + e$ for the spanning subgraph with edges $E(S) \cup \{e\}$.

Definition 12.9.9. If F is a pre-MST and e is a new edge, that is $e \in E(G) - E(F)$, then e *extends* F when $F + e$ is also a pre-MST.

So being a pre-MST is contrived to be an invariant under addition of extending edges, by the definition of extension.

The standard methods for finding MST's all start with the empty spanning forest and build up to an MST by adding one extending edge after another. Since the empty spanning forest is a pre-MST, and being a pre-MST is, by definition, invariant under extensions, every forest built in this way will be a pre-MST. But no spanning tree can be a subgraph of a different spanning tree. So when the pre-MST finally grows enough to become a tree, it will be an MST. By Lemma 12.9.4, this happens after exactly $|V(G)| - 1$ edge extensions.

So the problem of finding MST's reduces to the question of how to tell if an edge is an extending edge. Here's how:

Definition 12.9.10. Let F be a pre-MST, and color the vertices in each connected component of F either all black or all white. At least one component of each color is required. Call this a *solid coloring* of F. A *gray edge* of a solid coloring is an edge of G with different colored endpoints.

Any path in G from a white vertex to a black vertex obviously must include a gray edge, so for any solid coloring, there is guaranteed to be at least one gray edge. In fact, there will have to be at least as many gray edges as there are components with the same color. Here's the punchline:

Lemma 12.9.11. *An edge extends a pre-MST F if it is a minimum weight gray edge in some solid coloring of F.*

So to extend a pre-MST, choose any solid coloring, find the gray edges, and among them choose one with minimum weight. Each of these steps is easy to do, so it is easy to keep extending and arrive at an MST. For example, here are three known algorithms that are explained by Lemma 12.9.11:

Algorithm 1. *[Prim] Grow a tree one edge at a time by adding a minimum weight edge among the edges that have exactly one endpoint in the tree.*

This is the algorithm that comes from coloring the growing tree white and all the vertices not in the tree black. Then the gray edges are the ones with exactly one endpoint in the tree.

Algorithm 2. *[Kruskal] Grow a forest one edge at a time by adding a minimum weight edge among the edges with endpoints in different connected components.*

An edge does not create a cycle iff it connects different components. The edge chosen by Kruskal's algorithm will be the minimum weight gray edge when the components it connects are assigned different colors.

For example, in the weighted graph we have been considering, we might run Algorithm 1 as follows. Start by choosing one of the weight 1 edges, since this is the smallest weight in the graph. Suppose we chose the weight 1 edge on the bottom of the triangle of weight 1 edges in our graph. This edge is incident to the same vertex as two weight 1 edges, a weight 4 edge, a weight 7 edge, and a weight 3 edge. We would then choose the incident edge of minimum weight. In this case, one of the two weight 1 edges. At this point, we cannot choose the third weight 1 edge: it won't be gray because its endpoints are both in the tree, and so are both colored white. But we can continue by choosing a weight 2 edge. We might end up with the spanning tree shown in Figure 12.22, which has weight 17, the smallest we've seen so far.

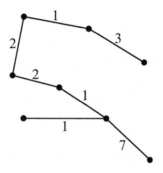

Figure 12.22 A spanning tree found by Algorithm 1.

Now suppose we instead ran Algorithm 2 on our graph. We might again choose the weight 1 edge on the bottom of the triangle of weight 1 edges in our graph. Now, instead of choosing one of the weight 1 edges it touches, we might choose the weight 1 edge on the top of the graph. This edge still has minimum weight, and will be gray if we simply color its endpoints differently, so Algorithm 2 can choose it. We would then choose one of the remaining weight 1 edges. Note that neither causes us to form a cycle. Continuing the algorithm, we could end up with the same spanning tree in Figure 12.22, though this will depend on the tie breaking rules used to choose among gray edges with the same minimum weight. For example, if the weight of every edge in G is one, then all spanning trees are MST's with weight $|V(G)| - 1$, and both of these algorithms can arrive at each of these spanning trees by suitable tie-breaking.

The coloring that explains Algorithm 1 also justifies a more flexible algorithm which has Algorithm 1 as a special case:

Algorithm 3. *Grow a forest one edge at a time by picking any component and adding a minimum weight edge among the edges leaving that component.*

This algorithm allows components that are not too close to grow in parallel and independently, which is great for "distributed" computation where separate processors share the work with limited communication between processors.[7]

These are examples of greedy approaches to optimization. Sometimes greediness works and sometimes it doesn't. The good news is that it does work to find the MST. Therefore, we can be sure that the MST for our example graph has weight 17, since it was produced by Algorithm 2. Furthermore we have a fast algorithm for finding a minimum weight spanning tree for any graph.

---

[7]The idea of growing trees seems first to have been developed in by Borůvka (1926), ref TBA. Efficient MST algorithms running in parallel time $O(\log |V|)$ are described in Karger, Klein, and Tarjan (1995), ref TBA.

Ok, to wrap up this story, all that's left is the proof that minimal gray edges are extending edges. This might sound like a chore, but it just uses the same reasoning we used to be sure there would be a gray edge when you need it.

Proof. (of Lemma 12.9.11)

Let F be a pre-MST that is a subgraph of some MST M of G, and suppose e is a minimum weight gray edge under some solid coloring of F. We want to show that $F + e$ is also a pre-MST.

If e happens to be an edge of M, then $F + e$ remains a subgraph of M, and so is a pre-MST.

The other case is when e is not an edge of M. In that case, $M + e$ will be a connected, spanning subgraph. Also M has a path **p** between the different colored endpoints of e, so $M + e$ has a cycle consisting of e together with **p**. Now **p** has both a black endpoint and a white one, so it must contain some gray edge $g \neq e$. The trick is to remove g from $M + e$ to obtain a subgraph $M + e - g$. Since gray edges by definition are not edges of F, the graph $M + e - g$ contains $F + e$. We claim that $M + e - g$ is an MST, which proves the claim that e extends F.

To prove this claim, note that $M + e$ is a connected, spanning subgraph, and g is on a cycle of $M + e$, so by Lemma 12.8.6, removing g won't disconnect anything. Therefore, $M + e - g$ is still a connected, spanning subgraph. Moreover, $M + e - g$ has the same number of edges as M, so Lemma 12.9.4 implies that it must be a spanning tree. Finally, since e is minimum weight among gray edges,

$$w(M + e - g) = w(M) + w(e) - w(g) \leq w(M).$$

This means that $M + e - g$ is a spanning tree whose weight is at most that of an MST, which implies that $M + e - g$ is also an MST. ∎

Another interesting fact falls out of the proof of Lemma 12.9.11:

Corollary 12.9.12. *If all edges in a weighted graph have distinct weights, then the graph has a unique MST.*

The proof of Corollary 12.9.12 is left to Problem 12.63.

12.10   References

[8], [13], [22], [25], [27]

Problems for Section 12.2

Practice Problems

Problem 12.1.
The average degree of the vertices in an n-vertex graph is twice the average number of edges of per vertex. Explain why.

Problem 12.2.
Among *connected* simple graphs whose sum of vertex degrees is 20:

(a) what is the largest possible number of vertices?

(b) what is the smallest possible number of vertices?

Class Problems

Problem 12.3. (a) Prove that in every simple graph, there are an even number of vertices of odd degree.

(b) Conclude that at a party where some people shake hands, the number of people who shake hands an odd number of times is an even number.

(c) Call a sequence of people at the party a *handshake sequence* if each person in the sequence has shaken hands with the next person, if any, in the sequence.

Suppose George was at the party and has shaken hands with an odd number of people. Explain why, starting with George, there must be a handshake sequence ending with a different person who has shaken an odd number of hands.

Exam Problems

Problem 12.4.
A researcher analyzing data on heterosexual sexual behavior in a group of m males and f females found that within the group, the male average number of female partners was 10% larger that the female average number of male partners.

(a) Comment on the following claim. "Since we're assuming that each encounter involves one man and one woman, the average numbers should be the same, so the males must be exaggerating."

(b) For what constant c is $m = c \cdot f$?

(c) The data shows that approximately 20% of the females were virgins, while only 5% of the males were. The researcher wonders how excluding virgins from the population would change the averages. If he knew graph theory, the researcher would realize that the nonvirgin male average number of partners will be $x(f/m)$ times the nonvirgin female average number of partners. What is x?

(d) For purposes of further research, it would be helpful to pair each female in the group with a unique male in the group. Explain why this is not possible.

Problems for Section 12.4

Practice Problems

Problem 12.5.
Which of the items below are simple-graph properties preserved under isomorphism?

(a) There is a cycle that includes all the vertices.

(b) The vertices are numbered 1 through 7.

(c) The vertices can be numbered 1 through 7.

(d) There are two degree 8 vertices.

(e) Two edges are of equal length.

(f) No matter which edge is removed, there is a path between any two vertices.

(g) There are two cycles that do not share any vertices.

(h) The vertices are sets.

(i) The graph can be drawn in a way that all the edges have the same length.

(j) No two edges cross.

(k) The OR of two properties that are preserved under isomorphism.

(l) The negation of a property that is preserved under isomorphism.

Class Problems

Problem 12.6.

For each of the following pairs of simple graphs, either define an isomorphism between them, or prove that there is none. (We write ab as shorthand for $\langle a\text{—}b\rangle$.)

(a)

$$G_1 \text{ with } V_1 = \{1, 2, 3, 4, 5, 6\}, \ E_1 = \{12, 23, 34, 14, 15, 35, 45\}$$
$$G_2 \text{ with } V_2 = \{1, 2, 3, 4, 5, 6\}, \ E_2 = \{12, 23, 34, 45, 51, 24, 25\}$$

(b)

$$G_3 \text{ with } V_3 = \{1, 2, 3, 4, 5, 6\}, \ E_3 = \{12, 23, 34, 14, 45, 56, 26\}$$
$$G_4 \text{ with } V_4 = \{a, b, c, d, e, f\}, \ E_4 = \{ab, bc, cd, de, ae, ef, cf\}$$

Problem 12.7.

List all the isomorphisms between the two graphs given in Figure 12.23. Explain why there are no others.

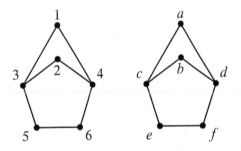

Figure 12.23 Graphs with several isomorphisms

Homework Problems

Problem 12.8.

Determine which among the four graphs pictured in Figure 12.24 are isomorphic. For each pair of isomorphic graphs, describe an isomorphism between them. For each pair of graphs that are not isomorphic, give a property that is preserved under isomorphism such that one graph has the property, but the other does not. For at least one of the properties you choose, *prove* that it is indeed preserved under isomorphism (you only need prove one of them).

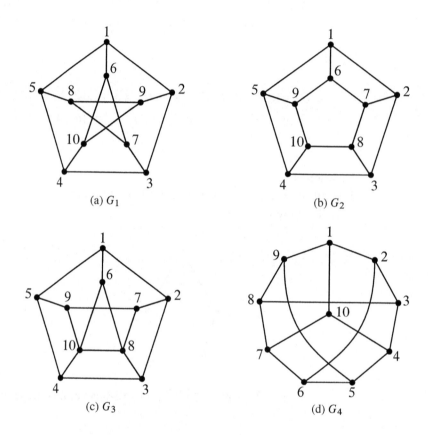

(a) G_1

(b) G_2

(c) G_3

(d) G_4

Figure 12.24   Which graphs are isomorphic?

Problem 12.9. (a) For any vertex v in a graph, let $N(v)$ be the set of *neighbors* of v, namely, the vertices adjacent to v:

$$N(v) ::= \{u \mid \langle u\text{—}v \rangle \text{ is an edge of the graph}\}.$$

Suppose f is an isomorphism from graph G to graph H. Prove that $f(N(v)) = N(f(v))$.

Your proof should follow by simple reasoning using the definitions of isomorphism and neighbors—no pictures or handwaving.

Hint: Prove by a chain of iff's that

$$h \in N(f(v)) \quad \text{iff} \quad h \in f(N(v))$$

for every $h \in V_H$. Use the fact that $h = f(u)$ for some $u \in V_G$.

(b) Conclude that if G and H are isomorphic graphs, then for each $k \in \mathbb{N}$, they have the same number of degree k vertices.

Problem 12.10.

Let's say that a graph has "two ends" if it has exactly two vertices of degree 1 and all its other vertices have degree 2. For example, here is one such graph:

(a) A *line graph* is a graph whose vertices can be listed in a sequence with edges between consecutive vertices only. So the two-ended graph above is also a line graph of length 4.

Prove that the following theorem is false by drawing a counterexample.
False Theorem. *Every two-ended graph is a line graph.*

(b) Point out the first erroneous statement in the following bogus proof of the false theorem and describe the error.

Bogus proof. We use induction. The induction hypothesis is that every two-ended graph with n edges is a line graph.

Base case ($n = 1$): The only two-ended graph with a single edge consists of two vertices joined by an edge:

Sure enough, this is a line graph.

Inductive case: We assume that the induction hypothesis holds for some $n \geq 1$ and prove that it holds for $n + 1$. Let G_n be any two-ended graph with n edges. By the induction assumption, G_n is a line graph. Now suppose that we create a two-ended graph G_{n+1} by adding one more edge to G_n. This can be done in only one way: the new edge must join one of the two endpoints of G_n to a new vertex; otherwise, G_{n+1} would not be two-ended.

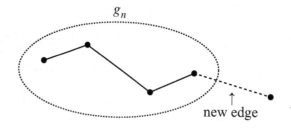

Clearly, G_{n+1} is also a line graph. Therefore, the induction hypothesis holds for all graphs with $n + 1$ edges, which completes the proof by induction.

∎

Problems for Section 12.5

Practice Problems

Problem 12.11.
Let B be a bipartite graph with vertex sets $L(B), R(B)$. Explain why the sum of the degrees of the vertices in $L(B)$ equals the sum of the degrees of the vertices in $R(B)$.

Class Problems

Problem 12.12.
A certain Institute of Technology has a lot of student clubs; these are loosely overseen by the Student Association. Each eligible club would like to delegate one of its members to appeal to the Dean for funding, but the Dean will not allow a student to be the delegate of more than one club. Fortunately, the Association VP took Math for Computer Science and recognizes a matching problem when she sees one.

(a) Explain how to model the delegate selection problem as a bipartite matching problem. (This is a *modeling problem*; we aren't looking for a description of an algorithm to solve the problem.)

(b) The VP's records show that no student is a member of more than 9 clubs. The VP also knows that to be eligible for support from the Dean's office, a club must have at least 13 members. That's enough for her to guarantee there is a proper delegate selection. Explain. (If only the VP had taken an *Algorithms* class, she could even have found a delegate selection without much effort.)

Problem 12.13.

A simple graph is called *regular* when every vertex has the same degree. Call a graph *balanced* when it is regular and is also a bipartite graph with the same number of left and right vertices.

Prove that if G is a balanced graph, then the edges of G can be partitioned into blocks such that each block is a perfect matching.

For example, if G is a balanced graph with $2k$ vertices each of degree j, then the edges of G can be partitioned into j blocks, where each block consists of k edges, each of which is a perfect matching.

Exam Problems

Problem 12.14.

Overworked and over-caffeinated, the Teaching Assistant's (TA's) decide to oust the lecturer and teach their own recitations. They will run a recitation session at 4 different times in the same room. There are exactly 20 chairs to which a student can be assigned in each recitation. Each student has provided the TA's with a list of the recitation sessions her schedule allows and each student's schedule conflicts with at most two sessions. The TA's must assign each student to a chair during recitation at a time she can attend, if such an assignment is possible.

(a) Describe how to model this situation as a matching problem. Be sure to specify what the vertices/edges should be and briefly describe how a matching would determine seat assignments for each student in a recitation that does not conflict with his schedule. (This is a *modeling problem*; we aren't looking for a description of an algorithm to solve the problem.)

(b) Suppose there are 41 students. Given the information provided above, is a matching guaranteed? Briefly explain.

Problem 12.15.

Because of the incredible popularity of his class *Math for Computer Science*, TA Mike decides to give up on regular office hours. Instead, he arranges for each student to join some study groups. Each group must choose a representative to talk to the staff, but there is a staff rule that a student can only represent one group. The problem is to find a representative from each group while obeying the staff rule.

(a) Explain how to model the delegate selection problem as a bipartite matching problem. (This is a *modeling problem*; we aren't looking for a description of an algorithm to solve the problem.)

(b) The staff's records show that each student is a member of at most 4 groups, and all the groups have 4 or more members. Is that enough to guarantee there is a proper delegate selection? Explain.

Problem 12.16.

Let $\widehat{R}$ be the "implies" binary relation on propositional formulas defined by the rule that

$$F \ \widehat{R} \ G \quad \text{iff} \quad [(F \text{ IMPLIES } G) \text{ is a valid formula}]. \qquad (12.4)$$

For example, $(P \text{ AND } Q) \ \widehat{R} \ P$, because the formula $(P \text{ AND } Q)$ IMPLIES P is valid. Also, it is not true that $(P \text{ OR } Q) \ \widehat{R} \ P$ since $(P \text{ OR } Q)$ IMPLIES P is not valid.

(a) Let A and B be the sets of formulas listed below. Explain why $\widehat{R}$ is not a weak partial order on the set $A \cup B$.

(b) Fill in the $\widehat{R}$ arrows from A to B.

A	arrows	B

Q

P XOR Q

$\overline{P}$ OR $\overline{Q}$

P AND Q

$\overline{P}$ OR $\overline{Q}$ OR $(\overline{P}$ AND $\overline{Q})$

NOT$(P$ AND $Q)$

P

(c) The diagram in part (b) defines a bipartite graph G with $L(G) = A$, $R(G) = B$ and an edge between F and G iff $F \; \widehat{R} \; G$. Exhibit a subset S of A such that both S and $A - S$ are nonempty, and the set $N(S)$ of neighbors of S is the same size as S, that is, $|N(S)| = |S|$.

(d) Let G be an arbitrary, finite, bipartite graph. For any subset $S \subseteq L(G)$, let $\overline{S} ::= L(G) - S$, and likewise for any $M \subseteq R(G)$, let $\overline{M} ::= R(G) - M$. Suppose S is a subset of $L(G)$ such that $|N(S)| = |S|$, and both S and $\overline{S}$ are nonempty. **Circle the formula** that correctly completes the following statement:

There is a matching from $L(G)$ to $R(G)$ if and only if there is both a matching from S to its neighbors, $N(S)$, and also a matching from $\overline{S}$ to

$$N(\overline{S}) \qquad \overline{N(S)} \qquad N^{-1}(N(S)) \qquad N^{-1}(N(\overline{S})) \qquad N(\overline{S})-\overline{N(S)} \qquad N(S)-N(\overline{S})$$

Hint: The proof of Hall's Bottleneck Theorem.

Problem 12.17. (a) Show that there is no matching for the bipartite graph G in Figure 12.25 that covers $L(G)$.

(b) The bipartite graph H in Figure 12.26 has an easily verified property that implies it has a matching that covers $L(H)$. What is the property?

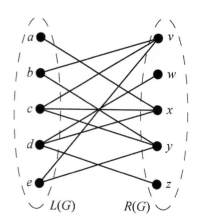

Figure 12.25   Bipartite graph G.

Homework Problems

Problem 12.18.

A *Latin square* is $n \times n$ array whose entries are the number $1, \ldots, n$. These entries satisfy two constraints: every row contains all n integers in some order, and also every column contains all n integers in some order. Latin squares come up frequently in the design of scientific experiments for reasons illustrated by a little story in a footnote[8]

---

[8] At Guinness brewery in the eary 1900's, W. S. Gosset (a chemist) and E. S. Beavan (a "maltster") were trying to improve the barley used to make the brew. The brewery used different varieties of barley according to price and availability, and their agricultural consultants suggested a different fertilizer mix and best planting month for each variety.

Somewhat sceptical about paying high prices for customized fertilizer, Gosset and Beavan planned a season long test of the influence of fertilizer and planting month on barley yields. For as many months as there were varieties of barley, they would plant one sample of each variety using a different one of the fertilizers. So every month, they would have all the barley varieties planted and all the fertilizers used, which would give them a way to judge the overall quality of that planting month. But they also wanted to judge the fertilizers, so they wanted each fertilizer to be used on each variety during the course of the season. Now they had a little mathematical problem, which we can abstract as follows.

Suppose there are n barley varieties and an equal number of recommended fertilizers. Form an $n \times n$ array with a column for each fertilizer and a row for each planting month. We want to fill in the entries of this array with the integers $1, \ldots, n$ numbering the barley varieties, so that every row contains all n integers in some order (so every month each variety is planted and each fertilizer is used), and also every column contains all n integers (so each fertilizer is used on all the varieties over the course of the growing season).

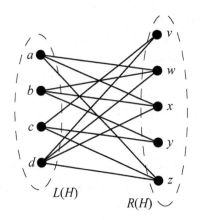

Figure 12.26   Bipartite Graph H.

For example, here is a 4×4 Latin square:

1	2	3	4
3	4	2	1
2	1	4	3
4	3	1	2

(a) Here are three rows of what could be part of a 5×5 Latin square:

2	4	5	3	1
4	1	3	2	5
3	2	1	5	4

Fill in the last two rows to extend this "Latin rectangle" to a complete Latin square.

(b) Show that filling in the next row of an $n \times n$ Latin rectangle is equivalent to finding a matching in some $2n$-vertex bipartite graph.

(c) Prove that a matching must exist in this bipartite graph and, consequently, a Latin rectangle can always be extended to a Latin square.

Problem 12.19.

Take a regular deck of 52 cards. Each card has a suit and a value. The suit is one of four possibilities: heart, diamond, club, spade. The value is one of 13 possibilities, $A, 2, 3, \ldots, 10, J, Q, K$. There is exactly one card for each of the 4×13 possible combinations of suit and value.

Ask your friend to lay the cards out into a grid with 4 rows and 13 columns. They can fill the cards in any way they'd like. In this problem you will show that you can always pick out 13 cards, one from each column of the grid, so that you wind up with cards of all 13 possible values.

(a) Explain how to model this trick as a bipartite matching problem between the 13 column vertices and the 13 value vertices. Is the graph necessarily degree-constrained?

(b) Show that any n columns must contain at least n different values and prove that a matching must exist.

Problem 12.20.

Scholars through the ages have identified *twenty* fundamental human virtues: honesty, generosity, loyalty, prudence, completing the weekly course reading-response, etc. At the beginning of the term, every student in Math for Computer Science possessed exactly *eight* of these virtues. Furthermore, every student was unique; that is, no two students possessed exactly the same set of virtues. The Math for Computer Science course staff must select *one* additional virtue to impart to each student by the end of the term. Prove that there is a way to select an additional virtue for each student so that every student is unique at the end of the term as well.

Suggestion: Use Hall's theorem. Try various interpretations for the vertices on the left and right sides of your bipartite graph.

Problems for Section 12.6

Class Problems

Problem 12.21.
Let G be the graph below.[9] Carefully explain why $\chi(G) = 4$.

---

[9]From [30], Exercise 13.3.1

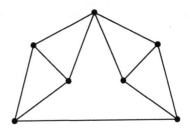

Problem 12.22.

A portion of a computer program consists of a sequence of calculations where the results are stored in variables, like this:

$$
\begin{aligned}
\text{Inputs:} \quad & a, b \\
\text{Step 1.} \quad c &= a + b \\
2. \quad d &= a * c \\
3. \quad e &= c + 3 \\
4. \quad f &= c - e \\
5. \quad g &= a + f \\
6. \quad h &= f + 1 \\
\text{Outputs:} \quad & d, g, h
\end{aligned}
$$

A computer can perform such calculations most quickly if the value of each variable is stored in a *register*, a chunk of very fast memory inside the microprocessor. Programming language compilers face the problem of assigning each variable in a program to a register. Computers usually have few registers, however, so they must be used wisely and reused often. This is called the *register allocation* problem.

In the example above, variables a and b must be assigned different registers, because they hold distinct input values. Furthermore, c and d must be assigned different registers; if they used the same one, then the value of c would be overwritten in the second step and we'd get the wrong answer in the third step. On the other hand, variables b and d may use the same register; after the first step, we no longer need b and can overwrite the register that holds its value. Also, f and h may use the same register; once $f + 1$ is evaluated in the last step, the register holding the value of f can be overwritten.

(a) Recast the register allocation problem as a question about graph coloring. What do the vertices correspond to? Under what conditions should there be an edge between two vertices? Construct the graph corresponding to the example above.

(b) Color your graph using as few colors as you can. Call the computer's registers $R1$, $R2$ etc. Describe the assignment of variables to registers implied by your coloring. How many registers do you need?

(c) Suppose that a variable is assigned a value more than once, as in the code snippet below:

$$\cdots$$
$$t = r + s$$
$$u = t * 3$$
$$t = m - k$$
$$v = t + u$$
$$\cdots$$

How might you cope with this complication?

Problem 12.23.

Suppose an n-vertex bipartite graph has exactly k connected components, each of which has two or more vertices. How many ways are there color it using a given set of two colors?

Homework Problems

Problem 12.24.

6.042 is often taught using recitations. Suppose it happened that 8 recitations were needed, with two or three staff members running each recitation. The assignment of staff to recitation sections, using their secret codenames, is as follows:

- R1: Maverick, Goose, Iceman

- R2: Maverick, Stinger, Viper

- R3: Goose, Merlin

- R4: Slider, Stinger, Cougar

- R5: Slider, Jester, Viper

- R6: Jester, Merlin

- R7: Jester, Stinger

- R8: Goose, Merlin, Viper

Two recitations can not be held in the same 90-minute time slot if some staff member is assigned to both recitations. The problem is to determine the minimum number of time slots required to complete all the recitations.

(a) Recast this problem as a question about coloring the vertices of a particular graph. Draw the graph and explain what the vertices, edges, and colors represent.

(b) Show a coloring of this graph using the fewest possible colors. What schedule of recitations does this imply?

Problem 12.25.

This problem generalizes the result proved Theorem 12.6.3 that any graph with maximum degree at most w is $(w + 1)$-colorable.

A simple graph G is said to have *width* w iff its vertices can be arranged in a sequence such that each vertex is adjacent to at most w vertices that precede it in the sequence. If the degree of every vertex is at most w, then the graph obviously has width at most w—just list the vertices in any order.

(a) Prove that every graph with width at most w is $(w + 1)$-colorable.

(b) Describe a 2-colorable graph with minimum width n.

(c) Prove that the average degree of a graph of width w is at most $2w$.

(d) Describe an example of a graph with 100 vertices, width 3, but *average* degree more than 5.

Problem 12.26.

A sequence of vertices of a graph has *width* w iff each vertex is adjacent to at most w vertices that precede it in the sequence. A simple graph G has width w if there is a width-w sequence of all its vertices.

(a) Explain why the width of a graph must be at least the minimum degree of its vertices.

(b) Prove that if a finite graph has width w, then there is a width-w sequence of all its vertices that ends with a minimum degree vertex.

(c) Describe a simple algorithm to find the minimum width of a graph.

Problem 12.27.

Let G be a simple graph whose vertex degrees are all $\leq k$. Prove by induction on number of vertices that if every connected component of G has a vertex of degree strictly less than k, then G is k-colorable.

Problem 12.28.

A basic example of a simple graph with chromatic number n is the complete graph on n vertices, that is $\chi(K_n) = n$. This implies that any graph with K_n as a subgraph must have chromatic number at least n. It's a common misconception to think that, conversely, graphs with high chromatic number must contain a large complete subgraph. In this problem we exhibit a simple example countering this misconception, namely a graph with chromatic number four that contains no *triangle*—length three cycle—and hence no subgraph isomorphic to K_n for $n \geq 3$. Namely, let G be the 11-vertex graph of Figure 12.27. The reader can verify that G is triangle-free.

Figure 12.27   Graph G with no triangles and $\chi(G) = 4$.

(a) Show that G is 4-colorable.

(b) Prove that G can't be colored with 3 colors.

Problem 12.29.

This problem will show that 3-coloring a graph is just as difficult as finding a satisfying truth assignment for a propositional formula. The graphs considered will all be taken to have three designated *color-vertices* connected in a triangle to force them to have different colors in any coloring of the graph. The colors assigned to the color-vertices will be called T, F and N.

Suppose f is an n-argument truth function. That is,

$$f : \{T, F\}^n \to \{T, F\}.$$

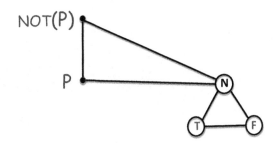

[h]

Figure 12.28   A 3-color NOT-gate

A graph G is called a *3-color-f-gate* iff G has n designated *input vertices* and a designated *output vertex*, such that

- G can be 3-colored *only* if its input vertices are colored with T's and F's.

- For every sequence $b_1, b_2, \ldots, b_n \in \{T, F\}$, there is a 3-coloring of G in which the input vertices $v_1, v_2, \ldots, v_n \in V(G)$ have the colors $b_1, b_2, \ldots, b_n \in \{T, F\}$.

- In any 3-coloring of G where the input vertices $v_1, v_2, \ldots, v_n \in V(G)$ have colors $b_1, b_2, \ldots, b_n \in \{T, F\}$, the output vertex has color $f(b_1, b_2, \ldots, b_n)$.

For example, a 3-color-NOT-gate consists simply of two adjacent vertices. One vertex is designated to be the input vertex P and the other is designated to be the output vertex. Both vertices have to be constrained so they can only be colored with T's or F's in any proper 3-coloring. This constraint can be imposed by making them adjacent to the color-vertex N, as shown in Figure 12.28.

   (a) Verify that the graph in Figure 12.29 is a 3-color-OR-gate. (The dotted lines indicate edges to color-vertex N; these edges constrain the P, Q and P OR Q vertices to be colored T or F in any proper 3-coloring.)

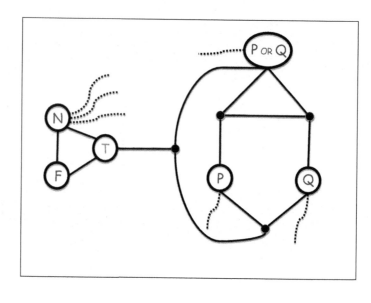

[h]

Figure 12.29   A 3-color OR-gate

(b) Let E be an n-variable propositional formula, and suppose E defines a truth function $f : \{T, F\}^n \to \{T, F\}$. Explain a simple way to construct a graph that is a 3-color-f-gate.

(c) Explain why an efficient procedure for determining if a graph was 3-colorable would lead to an efficient procedure to solve the satisfiability problem, SAT.

Problem 12.30.

The 3-coloring problem for planar graphs turns out to be no easier than the 3-coloring problem for arbitrary graphs. This claim follows very simply from the existence of a "3-color cross-over gadget." Such a gadget is a planar graph whose outer face is a cycle with four designated vertices u, v, w, x occurring in clockwise order such that

1. Any assignment of colors to vertices u and v can be completed into a 3-coloring of the gadget.

2. In every 3-coloring of the gadget, the colors of u and w are the same, and the colors of v and x are the also same.

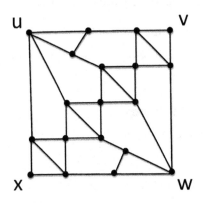

[h]

Figure 12.30   A 3-color cross-over gadget.

Figure 12.30 shows such a 3-color cross-over gadget.[10]

So to find a 3-coloring for *any* simple graph, simply draw it in the plane with edges crossing as needed, and then replace each occurrence of an edge crossing by a copy of the gadget as shown in Figure 12.31. This yields a planar graph which has a 3-coloring iff the original graph had one.

 (a) Prove that the graph in Figure 12.30 satisfies condition (1) by exhibiting the claimed 3-colorings.

---

[10]This gadget and reduction of 3-colorability to planar 3-colorability are due to Larry Stockmeyer [43].

[h]

Figure 12.31   Replacing an edge-crossing with a planar gadget.

Hint: Only two colorings are needed, one where u and v are the same color and another where they are not the same color.

(b) Prove that the graph in Figure 12.30 satisfies condition (2).

Hint: The colorings for part (a) are almost completely forced by the coloring of u and v.

Exam Problems

Problem 12.31.

False Claim. *Let G be a graph whose vertex degrees are all $\leq k$. If G has a vertex of degree strictly less than k, then G is k-colorable.*

(a) Give a counterexample to the False Claim when $k = 2$.

(b) Underline the exact sentence or part of a sentence that is the first unjustified step in the following bogus proof of the False Claim.

> *Bogus proof.* Proof by induction on the number n of vertices:
> The induction hypothesis $P(n)$ is:
>
> > Let G be an n-vertex graph whose vertex degrees are all $\leq k$. If G also has a vertex of degree strictly less than k, then G is k-colorable.
>
> **Base case:** ($n = 1$) G has one vertex, the degree of which is 0. Since G is 1-colorable, $P(1)$ holds.
>
> **Inductive step:** We may assume $P(n)$. To prove $P(n + 1)$, let G_{n+1} be a graph with $n + 1$ vertices whose vertex degrees are all k or less. Also, suppose G_{n+1} has a vertex v of degree strictly less than k. Now we only need to prove that G_{n+1} is k-colorable.
>
> To do this, first remove the vertex v to produce a graph G_n with n vertices. Let u be a vertex that is adjacent to v in G_{n+1}. Removing v reduces the degree of u by 1. So in G_n, vertex u has degree strictly less than k. Since no edges were added, the vertex degrees of G_n remain $\leq k$. So G_n satisfies the conditions of the induction hypothesis $P(n)$, and so we conclude that G_n is k-colorable.
>
> Now a k-coloring of G_n gives a coloring of all the vertices of G_{n+1}, except for v. Since v has degree less than k, there will be fewer than k colors assigned to the nodes adjacent to v. So among the k possible colors, there will be a

color not used to color these adjacent nodes, and this color can be assigned to v to form a k-coloring of G_{n+1}.

■

(c) With a slightly strengthened condition, the preceding proof of the False Claim could be revised into a sound proof of the following Claim:

Claim. *Let G be a graph whose vertex degrees are all $\leq k$.*
*If ⟨**statement inserted from below**⟩ has a vertex of degree strictly less than k, then G is k-colorable.*

Indicate each of the statements below that could be inserted to make the proof correct.

- G is connected and
- G has no vertex of degree zero and
- G does not contain a complete graph on k vertices and
- every connected component of G
- some connected component of G

Problem 12.32.
In the graph shown in Figure 12.32, the vertices connected in the triangle on the left are called *color-vertices*; since they form a triangle, they are forced to have different colors in any coloring of the graph. The colors assigned to the color-vertices will be called **T**, **F** and **N**. The dotted lines indicate edges to the color-vertex **N**.

(a) Explain why for any assignment of *different* truth-colors to P and Q, there is a unique 3-coloring of the graph.

(b) Prove that in any 3-coloring of the whole graph, the vertex labeled P XOR Q is colored with the XOR of the colors of vertices P and Q.

Problems for Section 12.7

Exam Problems

Problem 12.33.
Since you can go back and forth on an edge in a simple graph, every vertex is on

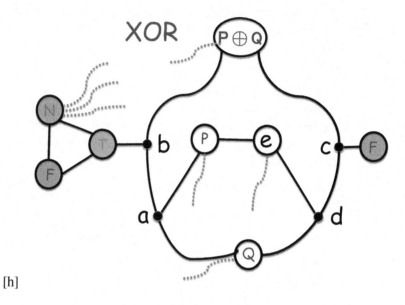

Figure 12.32   A 3-color XOR-gate

an even length closed walk. So even length closed walks don't tell you much about even length cycles. The situation with odd-length closed walks is more interesting.

(a) Give an example of a simple graph in which every vertex is on a unique odd-length cycle and a unique even-length cycle.

Hint: Four vertices.

(b) Give an example of a simple graph in which every vertex is on a unique odd-length cycle and no vertex is on an even-length cycle.

(c) Prove that in a digraph, a smallest size odd-length closed walk must be a cycle. Note that there will always be lots of even-length closed walks that are shorter than the smallest odd-length one.

Hint: Let **e** be an odd-length closed walk of minimum size, and suppose it begins and ends at vertex a. If it is not a cycle, then it must include a repeated vertex $b \neq a$. That is, **e** starts with a walk **f** from a to b, followed by a walk **g** from b to b, followed by a walk **h** from b to a.[11]

---

[11]In the notation of the text

$$\mathbf{e} = a\,\mathbf{f}\,\widehat{b}\,\mathbf{g}\,\widehat{b}\,\mathbf{h}\,a.$$

Homework Problems

Problem 12.34. (a) Give an example of a simple graph that has two vertices $u \neq v$ and two distinct paths between u and v, but neither u nor v is on a cycle.

(b) Prove that if there are different paths between two vertices in a simple graph, then the graph has a cycle.

Problem 12.35.

The entire field of graph theory began when Euler asked whether there was a walk through his home city of Königsberg in which all seven of its famous bridges were each crossed exactly once. Abstractly, we can represent the parts of the city separated by rivers as vertices and the bridges as edges between the vertices. Then Euler's question asks whether there is a closed walk through the graph that includes every edge in a graph exactly once. In his honor, such a walk is called an *Euler tour*.

So how do you tell in general whether a graph has an Euler tour? At first glance this may seem like a daunting problem. The similar sounding problem of finding a cycle that touches every vertex exactly once is one of those Millenium Prize NP-complete problems known as the *Hamiltonian Cycle Problem*). But it turns out to be easy to characterize which graphs have Euler tours.

Theorem. *A connected graph has an Euler tour if and only if every vertex has even degree.*

(a) Show that if a graph has an Euler tour, then the degree of each of its vertices is even.

In the remaining parts, we'll work out the converse: if the degree of every vertex of a connected finite graph is even, then it has an Euler tour. To do this, let's define an Euler *walk* to be a walk that includes each edge *at most* once.

(b) Suppose that an Euler walk in a connected graph does not include every edge. Explain why there must be an unincluded edge that is incident to a vertex on the walk.

In the remaining parts, let **w** be the *longest* Euler walk in some finite, connected graph.

(c) Show that if **w** is a closed walk, then it must be an Euler tour.

Hint: part (b)

(d) Explain why all the edges incident to the end of **w** must already be in **w**.

(e) Show that if the end of **w** was not equal to the start of **w**, then the degree of the end would be odd.

Hint: part (d)

(f) Conclude that if every vertex of a finite, connected graph has even degree, then it has an Euler tour.

Problems for Section 12.8

Class Problems

Problem 12.36.
A simple graph G is *2-removable* iff it contains two vertices $v \neq w$ such that $G - v$ is connected, and $G - w$ is also connected. Prove that every connected graph with at least two vertices is 2-removable.
   Hint: Consider a maximum length path.

Problem 12.37.
The n-dimensional *hypercube* H_n is a graph whose vertices are the binary strings of length n. Two vertices are adjacent if and only if they differ in exactly 1 bit. For example, in H_3, vertices `111` and `011` are adjacent because they differ only in the first bit, while vertices `101` and `011` are not adjacent because they differ at both the first and second bits.

(a) Prove that it is impossible to find two spanning trees of H_3 that do not share some edge.

(b) Verify that for any two vertices $x \neq y$ of H_3, there are 3 paths from x to y in H_3, such that, besides x and y, no two of those paths have a vertex in common.

(c) Conclude that the connectivity of H_3 is 3.

(d) Try extending your reasoning to H_4. (In fact, the connectivity of H_n is n for all $n \geq 1$. A proof appears in the problem solution.)

Problem 12.38.
A set M of vertices of a graph is a *maximal connected* set if every pair of vertices

in the set are connected, and any set of vertices properly containing M will contain two vertices that are not connected.

(a) What are the maximal connected subsets of the following (unconnected) graph?

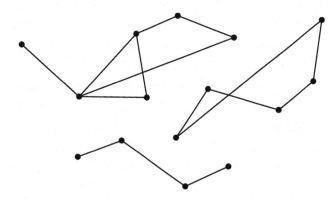

(b) Explain the connection between maximal connected sets and connected components. Prove it.

Problem 12.39. (a) Prove that K_n is $(n-1)$-edge connected for $n > 1$.

Let M_n be a graph defined as follows: begin by taking n graphs with non-overlapping sets of vertices, where each of the n graphs is $(n-1)$-edge connected (they could be disjoint copies of K_n, for example). These will be subgraphs of M_n. Then pick n vertices, one from each subgraph, and add enough edges between pairs of picked vertices that the subgraph of the n picked vertices is also $(n-1)$-edge connected.

(b) Draw a picture of $M_3(\ldots M_4)$.

(c) Explain why M_n is $(n-1)$-edge connected.

Problem 12.40.

False Claim. *If every vertex in a graph has positive degree, then the graph is connected.*

(a) Prove that this Claim is indeed false by providing a counterexample.

(b) Since the Claim is false, there must be a logical mistake in the following bogus proof. Pinpoint the *first* logical mistake (unjustified step) in the proof.

Bogus proof. We prove the Claim above by induction. Let $P(n)$ be the proposition that if every vertex in an n-vertex graph has positive degree, then the graph is connected.

Base cases: ($n \leq 2$). In a graph with 1 vertex, that vertex cannot have positive degree, so $P(1)$ holds vacuously.

$P(2)$ holds because there is only one graph with two vertices of positive degree, namely, the graph with an edge between the vertices, and this graph is connected.

Inductive step: We must show that $P(n)$ implies $P(n+1)$ for all $n \geq 2$. Consider an n-vertex graph in which every vertex has positive degree. By the assumption $P(n)$, this graph is connected; that is, there is a path between every pair of vertices. Now we add one more vertex x to obtain an $(n+1)$-vertex graph:

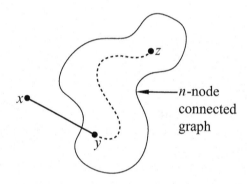

All that remains is to check that there is a path from x to every other vertex z. Since x has positive degree, there is an edge from x to some other vertex y. Thus, we can obtain a path from x to z by going from x to y and then following the path from y to z. This proves $P(n+1)$.

By the principle of induction, $P(n)$ is true for all $n \geq 0$, which proves the Claim.

■

Homework Problems

Problem 12.41.

An edge is said to *leave* a set of vertices if one end of the edge is in the set and the other end is not.

(a) An n-node graph is said to be *mangled* if there is an edge leaving every set of $\lfloor n/2 \rfloor$ or fewer vertices. Prove the following:

Claim. *Every mangled graph is connected.*

An n-node graph is said to be *tangled* if there is an edge leaving every set of $\lceil n/3 \rceil$ or fewer vertices.

(b) Draw a tangled graph that is not connected.

(c) Find the error in the bogus proof of the following
False Claim. *Every tangled graph is connected.*

Bogus proof. The proof is by strong induction on the number of vertices in the graph. Let $P(n)$ be the proposition that if an n-node graph is tangled, then it is connected. In the base case, $P(1)$ is true because the graph consisting of a single node is trivially connected.

For the inductive case, assume $n \geq 1$ and $P(1), \ldots, P(n)$ hold. We must prove $P(n + 1)$, namely, that if an $(n + 1)$-node graph is tangled, then it is connected.

So let G be a tangled, $(n + 1)$-node graph. Choose $\lceil n/3 \rceil$ of the vertices and let G_1 be the tangled subgraph of G with these vertices and G_2 be the tangled subgraph with the rest of the vertices. Note that since $n \geq 1$, the graph G has a least two vertices, and so both G_1 and G_2 contain at least one vertex. Since G_1 and G_2 are tangled, we may assume by strong induction that both are connected. Also, since G is tangled, there is an edge leaving the vertices of G_1 which necessarily connects to a vertex of G_2. This means there is a path between any two vertices of G: a path within one subgraph if both vertices are in the same subgraph, and a path traversing the connecting edge if the vertices are in separate subgraphs. Therefore, the entire graph G is connected. This completes the proof of the inductive case, and the Claim follows by strong induction.

∎

Problem 12.42.
In the cycle C_{2n} of length $2n$, we'll call two vertices *opposite* if they are on opposite sides of the cycle, that is that are distance n apart in C_{2n}. Let G be the graph formed from C_{2n} by adding an edge, which we'll call a *crossing edge*, between each pair of opposite vertices. So G has n crossing edges.

(a) Give a simple description of the shortest path between any two vertices of G.

Hint: Argue that a shortest path between two vertices in G uses at most one crossing edge.

(b) What is the *diameter* of G, that is, the largest distance between two vertices?

(c) Prove that the graph is not 4-connected.

(d) Prove that the graph is 3-connected.

Exam Problems

Problem 12.43.

We apply the following operation to a **simple graph** G: pick two vertices $u \neq v$ such that either

1. there is an edge of G between u and v, and there is also a path from u to v which does *not* include this edge; in this case, delete the edge $\langle u\text{---}v \rangle$.

2. there is no path from u to v; in this case, add the edge $\langle u\text{---}v \rangle$.

Keep repeating these operations until it is no longer possible to find two vertices $u \neq v$ to which an operation applies.

Assume the vertices of G are the integers $1, 2, \ldots, n$ for some $n \geq 2$. This procedure can be modelled as a state machine whose states are all possible simple graphs with vertices $1, 2, \ldots, n$. G is the start state, and the final states are the graphs on which no operation is possible.

(a) Let G be the graph with vertices $\{1, 2, 3, 4\}$ and edges

$$\{\{1, 2\}, \{3, 4\}\}$$

How many possible final states are reachable from start state G?   1in

(b) On the line next to each of the derived state variables below, indicate the *strongest* property from the list below that the variable is guaranteed to satisfy, no matter what the starting graph G is. The properties are:

> *constant   increasing   decreasing*
> *nonincreasing   nondecreasing   none of these*

For any state, let e be the number of edges in it, and let c be the number of **connected components** it has. Since e may increase or decrease in a transition, it does not have any of the first four properties. The derived variables are:

0) e *none of these*

i) c

ii) $c + e$

iii) $2c + e$

iv) $c + \frac{e}{e+1}$

(c) Explain why, starting from any state G, the procedure terminates. If your explanation depends on answers you gave to part (b), you must justify those answers.

(d) Prove that any final state must be an **unordered tree** on the set of vertices, that is, a spanning tree.

Problem 12.44.

If a simple graph has e edges, v vertices, and k connected components, then it has at least $e - v + k$ cycles.

Prove this by induction on the number of edges e.

Problems for Section 12.9

Practice Problems

Problem 12.45. (a) Prove that the average degree of a tree is less than 2.

(b) Suppose every vertex in a graph has degree at least k. Explain why the graph has a path of length k.

Hint: Consider a longest path.

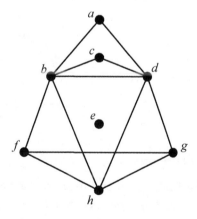

Figure 12.33 The graph G.

Problem 12.46. (a) How many spanning trees are there for the graph G in Figure 12.33?

(b) For $G - e$, the graph G with vertex e deleted, describe two spanning trees that have no edges in common.

(c) For $G - e$ with edge $\langle a\!-\!d \rangle$ deleted, explain why there cannot be two edge-disjoint spanning trees.

Hint: : Count vertices and edges.

Problem 12.47.
Prove that if G is a forest and

$$|V(G)| = |E(G)| + 1, \tag{12.5}$$

then G is a tree.

Problem 12.48.
Let H_3 be the graph shown in Figure 12.34. Explain why it is impossible to find two spanning trees of H_3 that have no edges in common.

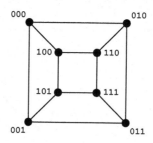

Figure 12.34 H_3 .

Exam Problems

Problem 12.49. (a) Let T be a tree and e a new edge between two vertices of T. Explain why $T + e$ must contain a cycle.

(b) Conclude that $T + e$ must have another spanning tree besides T.

Problem 12.50.
The *diameter* of a connected graph is the largest distance between any two vertices.

(a) What is the largest possible diameter in any connected graph with n vertices? Describe a graph with this maximum diameter.

(b) What is the smallest possible diameter of an n-vertex tree for $n > 2$? Describe an n-vertex tree with this minimum diameter.

Problem 12.51.

(a) Indicate all the properties below that are preserved under graph isomorphism.

- There is a cycle that includes all the vertices.
- Two edges are of equal length.
- The graph remains connected if any two edges are removed.
- There exists an edge that is an edge of every spanning tree.
- The negation of a property that is preserved under isomorphism.

(b) For the following statements about **finite trees**, indicate whether they are **true** or **false**, and *provide counterexamples* for those that are **false**.

- Any connected subgraph is a tree.   **true**   **false**
- Adding an edge between two nonadjacent vertices creates a cycle.   **true**
  false
- The number of vertices is one less than twice the number of leaves.   **true**
  false
- The number of vertices is one less than the number of edges. **true**   **false**
- For every finite graph (not necessarily a tree), there is one (a finite tree) that
  spans it.   **true**   **false**

Problem 12.52.

Circle true or false for the following statements about finite simple graphs G.

(a) G has a spanning tree.   **true**   **false**

(b) $\|V(G)\| = O(\|E(G)\|)$ for connected G.	**true**	**false**
(c) $\chi(G) \leq \max\{\deg(v) \mid v \in V(G)\}.$[12]	**true**	**false**
(d) $\|V(G)\| = O(\chi(G))$.	**true**	**false**

Problem 12.53.

A simple graph G is said to have *width* 1 iff there is a way to list all its vertices so that each vertex is adjacent to at most one vertex that appears earlier in the list. All the graphs mentioned below are assumed to be finite.

(a) Prove that every graph with width one is a forest.

Hint: By induction, removing the last vertex.

(b) Prove that every finite tree has width one. Conclude that a graph is a forest iff it has width one.

Problem 12.54.

Prove by induction that, using a fixed set of $n > 1$ colors, there are exactly $n \cdot (n - 1)^{m-1}$ different colorings of any tree with m vertices.

Problem 12.55.

Let G be a connected weighted simple graph and let v be a vertex of G. Suppose $e ::= \langle v\!-\!w \rangle$ is an edge of G that is strictly smaller than the weight of every other edge incident to v. Let T be a minimum weight spanning tree of G. Prove that e is an edge of T. *Hint:* By contradiction.

Problem 12.56.

Let G be a connected simple graph, T be a spanning tree of G, and e be an edge of G.

(a) Prove that if e is *not* on a cycle in G, then e is an edge of T.

(b) Prove that if e *is* on a cycle in G, and e is in T, then there is an edge $f \neq e$ such that $T - e + f$ is also a spanning tree.

---

[12] $\chi(G)$ is the chromatic number of G.

(c) Suppose G is edge-weighted, the weight of e is larger than the weights of all the other edges, e is on a cycle in G, and e is an edge of T. Conclude that T is *not* a minimum weight spanning tree of G.

Class Problems

Problem 12.57.

Procedure *Mark* starts with a connected, simple graph with all edges unmarked and then marks some edges. At any point in the procedure a path that includes only marked edges is called a *fully marked* path, and an edge that has no fully marked path between its endpoints is called *eligible*.

Procedure *Mark* simply keeps marking eligible edges, and terminates when there are none.

Prove that *Mark* terminates, and that when it does, the set of marked edges forms a spanning tree of the original graph.

Problem 12.58.

A procedure for connecting up a (possibly disconnected) simple graph and creating a spanning tree can be modelled as a state machine whose states are finite simple graphs. A state is *final* when no further transitions are possible. The transitions are determined by the following rules:

Procedure create-spanning-tree

1. If there is an edge $\langle u\!-\!v \rangle$ on a cycle, then delete $\langle u\!-\!v \rangle$.

2. If vertices u and v are not connected, then add the edge $\langle u\!-\!v \rangle$.

(a) Draw all the possible final states reachable starting with the graph with vertices $\{1, 2, 3, 4\}$ and edges

$$\{ \langle 1\!-\!2 \rangle , \langle 3\!-\!4 \rangle \}.$$

(b) Prove that if the machine reaches a final state, then the final state will be a tree on the vertices of the agraph on which it started.

(c) For any graph G', let e be the number of edges in G', c be the number of connected components it has, and s be the number of cycles. For each of the quantities below, indicate the *strongest* of the properties that it is guaranteed to satisfy, no matter what the starting graph is.

The choices for properties are: *constant, strictly increasing, strictly decreasing, weakly increasing, weakly decreasing, none of these.*

(i) e

(ii) c

(iii) s

(iv) $e - s$

(v) $c + e$

(vi) $3c + 2e$

(vii) $c + s$

(d) Prove that one of the quantities from part (c) strictly decreases at each transition. Conclude that for every starting state, the machine will reach a final state.

Problem 12.59.

Let G be a weighted graph and suppose there is a unique edge $e \in E(G)$ with smallest weight, that is, $w(e) < w(f)$ for all edges $f \in E(G) - \{e\}$. Prove that any minimum weight spanning tree (MST) of G must include e.

Problem 12.60.

Let G be the 4×4 grid with vertical and horizontal edges between neighboring vertices and edge weights as shown in Figure 12.35.

In this problem you will practice some of the ways to build minimum weight spanning trees. For each part, list the edge weights in the order in which the edges with those weights were chosen by the given rules.

(a) Construct a minimum weight spanning tree (MST) for G by initially selecting the minimum weight edge, and then successively selecting the minimum weight edge that does not create a cycle with the previously selected edges. Stop when the selected edges form a spanning tree of G. (This is Kruskal's MST algorithm.)

For any step in Kruskal's procedure, describe a black-white coloring of the graph components so that the edge Kruskal chooses is the minimum weight "gray edge" according to Lemma 12.9.11.

(b) Grow an MST for G by starting with the tree consisting of the single vertex u and then successively adding the minimum weight edge with exactly one endpoint in the tree. Stop when the tree spans G. (This is Prim's MST algorithm.)

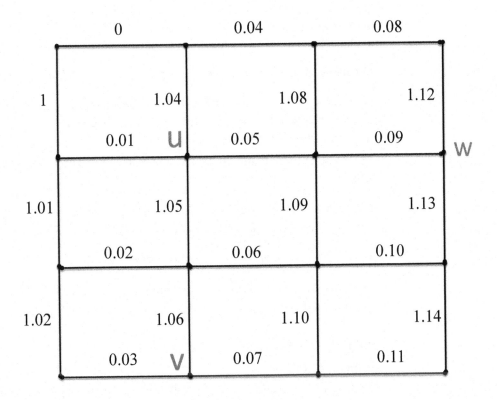

Figure 12.35   The 4x4 array graph G

For any step in Prim's procedure, describe a black-white coloring of the graph components so that the edge Prim chooses is the minimum weight "gray edge" according to Lemma 12.9.11.

(c) The 6.042 "parallel" MST algorithm can grow an MST for G by starting with the upper left corner vertex along with the vertices labelled v and w. Regard each of the three vertices as one-vertex trees. Successively add, for each tree in parallel, the minimum weight edge among the edges with exactly one endpoint in the tree. Stop working on a tree when it is within distance two of another tree. Continue until there are no more eligible trees—that is, each tree is within distance two of some other tree—then go back to applying the general gray-edge method until the parallel trees merge to form a spanning tree of G.

(d) Verify that you got the same MST each time. Problem 12.63 explains why there is a unique MST for any finite, connected, weighted graph where no two edges have the same weight.

Problem 12.61.

In this problem you will prove:

Theorem. *A graph G is 2-colorable iff it contains no odd length closed walk.*

As usual with "iff" assertions, the proof splits into two proofs: part (a) asks you to prove that the left side of the "iff" implies the right side. The other problem parts prove that the right side implies the left.

(a) Assume the left side and prove the right side. Three to five sentences should suffice.

(b) Now assume the right side. As a first step toward proving the left side, explain why we can focus on a single connected component H within G.

(c) As a second step, explain how to 2-color any tree.

(d) Choose any 2-coloring of a spanning tree T of H. Prove that H is 2-colorable by showing that any edge *not* in T must also connect different-colored vertices.

Homework Problems

Problem 12.62.

Suppose $D = (d_1, d_2, \ldots, d_n)$ is a list of the vertex degrees of some n-vertex tree T for $n \geq 2$. That is, we assume the vertices of T are numbered, and $d_i > 0$ is the degree of the ith vertex of T.

(a) Explain why

$$\sum_{i=1}^{n} d_i = 2(n-1). \tag{12.6}$$

(b) Prove conversely that if D is a sequence of positive integers satisfying equation (12.6), then D is a list of the degrees of the vertices of some n-vertex tree. *Hint:* Induction.

(c) Assume that D satisfies equation (12.6). Show that it is possible to partition D into two sets S_1, S_2 such that the sum of the elements in each set is the same. *Hint:* Trees are bipartite.

Problem 12.63.

Prove Corollary 12.9.12: If all edges in a finite weighted graph have distinct weights, then the graph has a *unique* MST.

Hint: Suppose M and N were different MST's of the same graph. Let e be the smallest edge in one and not the other, say $e \in M - N$, and observe that $N + e$ must have a cycle.

13 Planar Graphs

13.1 Drawing Graphs in the Plane

Suppose there are three dog houses and three human houses, as shown in Figure 13.1. Can you find a route from each dog house to each human house such that no route crosses any other route?

A similar question comes up about a little-known animal called a *quadrapus* that looks like an octopus with four stretchy arms instead of eight. If five quadrapi are resting on the sea floor, as shown in Figure 13.2, can each quadrapus simultaneously shake hands with every other in such a way that no arms cross?

Both these puzzles can be understood as asking about drawing graphs in the plane. Replacing dogs and houses by nodes, the dog house puzzle can be rephrased as asking whether there is a planar drawing of the graph with six nodes and edges between each of the first three nodes and each of the second three nodes. This graph is called the *complete bipartite graph* $K_{3,3}$ and is shown in Figure 13.3.(a). The quadrapi puzzle asks whether there is a planar drawing of the complete graph K_5 shown in Figure 13.3.(b).

In each case, the answer is, "No—but almost!" In fact, if you remove an edge from either of these graphs, then the resulting graph *can* be redrawn in the plane so that no edges cross, as shown in Figure 13.4.

Planar drawings have applications in circuit layout and are helpful in displaying graphical data such as program flow charts, organizational charts and scheduling conflicts. For these applications, the goal is to draw the graph in the plane with as few edge crossings as possible. (See the box on the following page for one such example.)

13.2 Definitions of Planar Graphs

We took the idea of a planar drawing for granted in the previous section, but if we're going to *prove* things about planar graphs, we better have precise definitions.

Definition 13.2.1. A *drawing* of a graph assigns to each node a distinct point in the plane and assigns to each edge a smooth curve in the plane whose endpoints correspond to the nodes incident to the edge. The drawing is *planar* if none of the

Figure 13.1   Three dog houses and and three human houses. Is there a route from each dog house to each human house so that no pair of routes cross each other?

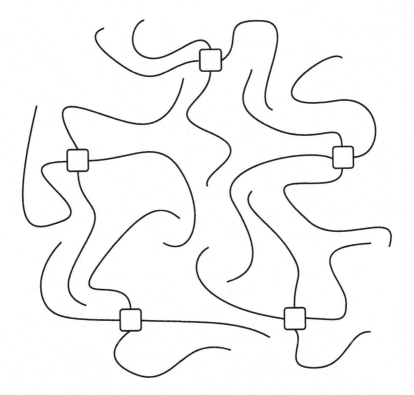

Figure 13.2   Five quadrapi (4-armed creatures).

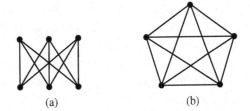

Figure 13.3 $K_{3,3}$ (a) and K_5 (b). Can you redraw these graphs so that no pairs of edges cross?

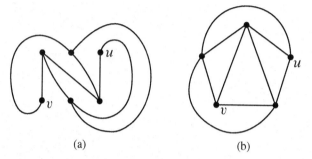

Figure 13.4   Planar drawings of (a) $K_{3,3}$ without $\langle u\!-\!v\rangle$, and (b) K_5 without $\langle u\!-\!v\rangle$.

Steve Wozniak and a Planar Circuit Design

When wires are arranged on a surface, like a circuit board or microchip, crossings require troublesome three-dimensional structures. When Steve Wozniak designed the disk drive for the early Apple II computer, he struggled mightily to achieve a nearly planar design according to the following excerpt from `apple2history.org` which in turn quotes *Fire in the Valley* by Freiberger and Swaine:

> For two weeks, he worked late each night to make a satisfactory design. When he was finished, he found that if he moved a connector he could cut down on feedthroughs, making the board more reliable. To make that move, however, he had to start over in his design. This time it only took twenty hours. He then saw another feedthrough that could be eliminated, and again started over on his design. "The final design was generally recognized by computer engineers as brilliant and was by engineering aesthetics beautiful. Woz later said, 'It's something you can only do if you're the engineer and the PC board layout person yourself. That was an artistic layout. The board has virtually no feedthroughs.'

curves cross themselves or other curves, namely, the only points that appear more than once on any of the curves are the node points. A graph is *planar* when it has a planar drawing.

Definition 13.2.1 is precise but depends on further concepts: "smooth planar curves" and "points appearing more than once" on them. We haven't defined these concepts—we just showed the simple picture in Figure 13.4 and hoped you would get the idea.

Pictures can be a great way to get a new idea across, but it is generally not a good idea to use a picture to replace precise mathematics. Relying solely on pictures can sometimes lead to disaster—or to bogus proofs, anyway. There is a long history of bogus proofs about planar graphs based on misleading pictures.

The bad news is that to prove things about planar graphs using the planar drawings of Definition 13.2.1, we'd have to take a chapter-long excursion into continuous mathematics just to develop the needed concepts from plane geometry and point-set topology. The good news is that there is another way to define planar graphs that uses only discrete mathematics. In particular, we can define planar graphs as a recursive data type. In order to understand how it works, we first need to understand the concept of a *face* in a planar drawing.

13.2.1 Faces

The curves in a planar drawing divide up the plane into connected regions called the *continuous faces*[1] of the drawing. For example, the drawing in Figure 13.5 has four continuous faces. Face IV, which extends off to infinity in all directions, is called the *outside face*.

The vertices along the boundary of each continuous face in Figure 13.5 form a cycle. For example, labeling the vertices as in Figure 13.6, the cycles for each of the face boundaries can be described by the vertex sequences

$$abca \qquad abda \qquad bcdb \qquad acda. \qquad (13.1)$$

These four cycles correspond nicely to the four continuous faces in Figure 13.6— so nicely, in fact, that we can identify each of the faces in Figure 13.6 by its cycle. For example, the cycle *abca* identifies face III. The cycles in list 13.1 are called the *discrete faces* of the graph in Figure 13.6. We use the term "discrete" since cycles in a graph are a discrete data type—as opposed to a region in the plane, which is a continuous data type.

---

[1]Most texts drop the adjective *continuous* from the definition of a face as a connected region. We need the adjective to distinguish continuous faces from the *discrete* faces we're about to define.

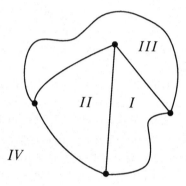

Figure 13.5   A planar drawing with four continuous faces.

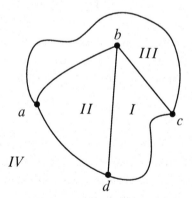

Figure 13.6   The drawing with labeled vertices.

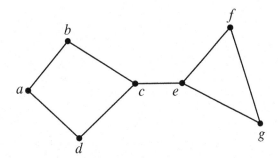

Figure 13.7   A planar drawing with a *bridge*.

Unfortunately, continuous faces in planar drawings are not always bounded by cycles in the graph—things can get a little more complicated. For example, the planar drawing in Figure 13.7 has what we will call a *bridge*, namely, a cut edge $\langle c\text{—}e \rangle$. The sequence of vertices along the boundary of the outer region of the drawing is

$$abcefgecda.$$

This sequence defines a closed walk, but does not define a cycle since the walk has two occurrences of the bridge $\langle c\text{—}e \rangle$ and each of its endpoints.

The planar drawing in Figure 13.8 illustrates another complication. This drawing has what we will call a *dongle*, namely, the nodes v, x, y and w, and the edges incident to them. The sequence of vertices along the boundary of the inner region is

$$rstvxyxvwvtur.$$

This sequence defines a closed walk, but once again does not define a cycle because it has two occurrences of *every* edge of the dongle—once "coming" and once "going."

It turns out that bridges and dongles are the only complications, at least for connected graphs. In particular, every continuous face in a planar drawing corresponds to a closed walk in the graph. These closed walks will be called the *discrete faces* of the drawing, and we'll define them next.

13.2.2   A Recursive Definition for Planar Embeddings

The association between the continuous faces of a planar drawing and closed walks provides the discrete data type we can use instead of continuous drawings. We'll define a *planar embedding* of *connected* graph to be the set of closed walks that are its face boundaries. Since all we care about in a graph are the connections between

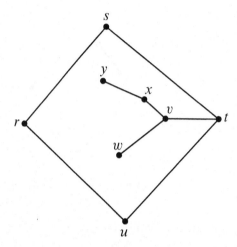

Figure 13.8   A planar drawing with a *dongle*.

vertices—not what a drawing of the graph actually looks like—planar embeddings are exactly what we need.

The question is how to define planar embeddings without appealing to continuous drawings. There is a simple way to do this based on the idea that any continuous drawing can drawn step by step:

- either draw a new point somewhere in the plane to represent a vertex,

- or draw a curve between two vertex points that have already been laid down, making sure the new curve doesn't cross any of the previously drawn curves.

A new curve won't cross any other curves precisely when it stays within one of the continuous faces. Alternatively, a new curve won't have to cross any other curves if it can go between the outer faces of two different drawings. So to be sure it's ok to draw a new curve, we just need to check that its endpoints are on the boundary of the same face, or that its endpoints are on the outer faces of different drawings. Of course drawing the new curve changes the faces slightly, so the face boundaries will have to be updated once the new curve is drawn. This is the idea behind the following recursive definition.

Definition 13.2.2. A *planar embedding* of a *connected* graph consists of a nonempty set of closed walks of the graph called the *discrete faces* of the embedding. Planar embeddings are defined recursively as follows:

Base case: If G is a graph consisting of a single vertex v then a planar embedding of G has one discrete face, namely, the length zero closed walk v.

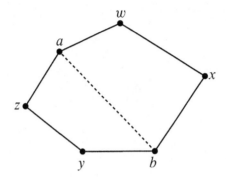

Figure 13.9 The "split a face" case: $awxbyza$ splits into $awxba$ and $abyza$.

Constructor case (split a face): Suppose G is a connected graph with a planar embedding, and suppose a and b are distinct, nonadjacent vertices of G that occur in some discrete face γ of the planar embedding. That is, γ is a closed walk of the form

$$\gamma = \alpha \,\widehat{}\, \beta$$

where α is a walk from a to b and β is a walk from b to a. Then the graph obtained by adding the edge $\langle a\!-\!b \rangle$ to the edges of G has a planar embedding with the same discrete faces as G, except that face γ is replaced by the two discrete faces[2]

$$\alpha \,\widehat{}\, \langle b\!-\!a \rangle \quad \text{and} \quad \langle a\!-\!b \rangle \,\widehat{}\, \beta \tag{13.2}$$

as illustrated in Figure 13.9.[3]

Constructor case (add a bridge): Suppose G and H are connected graphs with planar embeddings and disjoint sets of vertices. Let γ be a discrete face of the embedding of G and suppose that γ begins and ends at vertex a.

Similarly, let δ be a discrete face of the embedding of H that begins and ends at vertex b.

---

[2] There is a minor exception to this definition of embedding in the special case when G is a line graph beginning with a and ending with b. In this case the cycles into which γ splits are actually the same. That's because adding edge $\langle a\!-\!b \rangle$ creates a cycle that divides the plane into "inner" and "outer" continuous faces that are both bordered by this cycle. In order to maintain the correspondence between continuous faces and discrete faces in this case, we define the two discrete faces of the embedding to be two "copies" of this same cycle.

[3] Formally, merge is an operation on walks, not a walk and an edge, so in (13.2), we should have used a walk $(a \ \langle a\!-\!b \rangle \ b)$ instead of an edge $\langle a\!-\!b \rangle$ and written

$$\alpha \,\widehat{}\, (b \ \langle b\!-\!a \rangle \ a) \quad \text{and} \quad (a \ \langle a\!-\!b \rangle \ b) \,\widehat{}\, \beta$$

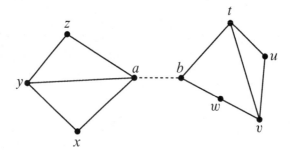

Figure 13.10   The "add a bridge" case.

Then the graph obtained by connecting G and H with a new edge $\langle a\!-\!b\rangle$ has a planar embedding whose discrete faces are the union of the discrete faces of G and H, except that faces γ and δ are replaced by one new face

$$\gamma \,\widehat{} \,\langle a\!-\!b\rangle \,\widehat{} \,\delta \,\widehat{} \,\langle b\!-\!a\rangle .$$

This is illustrated in Figure 13.10, where the vertex sequences of the faces of G and H are:

$$G : \{axyza,\ axya,\ ayza\} \qquad H : \{btuvwb,\ btvwb,\ tuvt\},$$

and after adding the bridge $\langle a\!-\!b\rangle$, there is a single connected graph whose faces have the vertex sequences

$$\{axyzabtuvwba,\ axya,\ ayza,\ btvwb,\ tuvt\}.$$

A bridge is simply a cut edge, but in the context of planar embeddings, the bridges are precisely the edges that occur *twice on the same discrete face*—as opposed to once on each of two faces. Dongles are trees made of bridges; we only use dongles in illustrations, so there's no need to define them more precisely.

13.2.3   Does It Work?

Yes! In general, a graph is planar because it has a planar drawing according to Definition 13.2.1 if and only if each of its connected components has a planar embedding as specified in Definition 13.2.2. Of course we can't prove this without an excursion into exactly the kind of continuous math that we're trying to avoid. But now that the recursive definition of planar graphs is in place, we won't ever need to fall back on the continuous stuff. That's the good news.

The bad news is that Definition 13.2.2 is a lot more technical than the intuitively simple notion of a drawing whose edges don't cross. In many cases it's easier to

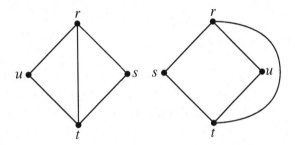

Figure 13.11   Two illustrations of the same embedding.

stick to the idea of planar drawings and give proofs in those terms. For example, erasing edges from a planar drawing will surely leave a planar drawing. On the other hand, it's not so obvious, though of course it is true, that you can delete an edge from a planar embedding and still get a planar embedding (see Problem 13.9).

In the hands of experts, and perhaps in your hands too with a little more experience, proofs about planar graphs by appeal to drawings can be convincing and reliable. But given the long history of mistakes in such proofs, it's safer to work from the precise definition of planar embedding. More generally, it's also important to see how the abstract properties of curved drawings in the plane can be modelled successfully using a discrete data type.

13.2.4   Where Did the Outer Face Go?

Every planar drawing has an immediately-recognizable outer face —it's the one that goes to infinity in all directions. But where is the outer face in a planar embedding?

There isn't one! That's because there really isn't any need to distinguish one face from another. In fact, a planar embedding could be drawn with any given face on the outside. An intuitive explanation of this is to think of drawing the embedding on a *sphere* instead of the plane. Then any face can be made the outside face by "puncturing" that face of the sphere, stretching the puncture hole to a circle around the rest of the faces, and flattening the circular drawing onto the plane.

So pictures that show different "outside" boundaries may actually be illustrations of the same planar embedding. For example, the two embeddings shown in Figure 13.11 are really the same—check it: they have the same boundary cycles.

This is what justifies the "add bridge" case in Definition 13.2.2: whatever face is chosen in the embeddings of each of the disjoint planar graphs, we can draw a bridge between them without needing to cross any other edges in the drawing, because we can assume the bridge connects two "outer" faces.

13.3   Euler's Formula

The value of the recursive definition is that it provides a powerful technique for proving properties of planar graphs, namely, structural induction. For example, we will now use Definition 13.2.2 and structural induction to establish one of the most basic properties of a connected planar graph, namely, that the number of vertices and edges completely determines the number of faces in every possible planar embedding of the graph.

Theorem 13.3.1 (Euler's Formula). *If a connected graph has a planar embedding, then*

$$v - e + f = 2$$

where v is the number of vertices, e is the number of edges and f is the number of faces.

For example, in Figure 13.5, $v = 4$, $e = 6$ and $f = 4$. Sure enough, $4 - 6 + 4 = 2$, as Euler's Formula claims.

Proof. The proof is by structural induction on the definition of planar embeddings. Let $P(\mathcal{E})$ be the proposition that $v - e + f = 2$ for an embedding $\mathcal{E}$.

Base case ($\mathcal{E}$ is the one-vertex planar embedding): By definition, $v = 1$, $e = 0$ and $f = 1$, and $1 - 0 + 1 = 2$, so $P(\mathcal{E})$ indeed holds.

Constructor case (split a face): Suppose G is a connected graph with a planar embedding, and suppose a and b are distinct, nonadjacent vertices of G that appear on some discrete face $\gamma = a \ldots b \cdots a$ of the planar embedding.

Then the graph obtained by adding the edge $\langle a\!-\!b\rangle$ to the edges of G has a planar embedding with one more face and one more edge than G. So the quantity $v - e + f$ will remain the same for both graphs, and since by structural induction this quantity is 2 for G's embedding, it's also 2 for the embedding of G with the added edge. So P holds for the constructed embedding.

Constructor case (add bridge): Suppose G and H are connected graphs with planar embeddings and disjoint sets of vertices. Then connecting these two graphs with a bridge merges the two bridged faces into a single face, and leaves all other faces unchanged. So the bridge operation yields a planar embedding of a connected graph with $v_G + v_H$ vertices, $e_G + e_H + 1$ edges, and $f_G + f_H - 1$ faces. Since

$$
\begin{aligned}
(v_G + v_H) &- (e_G + e_H + 1) + (f_G + f_H - 1) \\
&= (v_G - e_G + f_G) + (v_H - e_H + f_H) - 2 \\
&= (2) + (2) - 2 \quad \text{(by structural induction hypothesis)} \\
&= 2,
\end{aligned}
$$

$v - e + f$ remains equal to 2 for the constructed embedding. That is, $P(\mathcal{E})$ also holds in this case.

This completes the proof of the constructor cases, and the theorem follows by structural induction. ∎

13.4 Bounding the Number of Edges in a Planar Graph

Like Euler's formula, the following lemmas follow by structural induction directly from Definition 13.2.2.

Lemma 13.4.1. *In a planar embedding of a connected graph, each edge occurs once in each of two different faces, or occurs exactly twice in one face.*

Lemma 13.4.2. *In a planar embedding of a connected graph with at least three vertices, each face is of length at least three.*

Combining Lemmas 13.4.1 and 13.4.2 with Euler's Formula, we can now prove that planar graphs have a limited number of edges:

Theorem 13.4.3. *Suppose a connected planar graph has $v \geq 3$ vertices and e edges. Then*

$$e \leq 3v - 6. \tag{13.3}$$

Proof. By definition, a connected graph is planar iff it has a planar embedding. So suppose a connected graph with v vertices and e edges has a planar embedding with f faces. By Lemma 13.4.1, every edge has exactly two occurrences in the face boundaries. So the sum of the lengths of the face boundaries is exactly $2e$. Also by Lemma 13.4.2, when $v \geq 3$, each face boundary is of length at least three, so this sum is at least $3f$. This implies that

$$3f \leq 2e. \tag{13.4}$$

But $f = e - v + 2$ by Euler's formula, and substituting into (13.4) gives

$$3(e - v + 2) \leq 2e$$
$$e - 3v + 6 \leq 0$$
$$e \leq 3v - 6 \qquad\qquad \blacksquare$$

13.5   Returning to K_5 and $K_{3,3}$

Finally we have a simple way to answer the quadrapi question at the beginning of this chapter: the five quadrapi can't all shake hands without crossing. The reason is that we know the quadrupi question is the same as asking whether a complete graph K_5 is planar, and Theorem 13.4.3 has the immediate:

Corollary 13.5.1. *K_5 is not planar.*

Proof. K_5 is connected and has 5 vertices and 10 edges. But since $10 > 3 \cdot 5 - 6$, K_5 does not satisfy the inequality (13.3) that holds in all planar graphs. $\blacksquare$

We can also use Euler's Formula to show that $K_{3,3}$ is not planar. The proof is similar to that of Theorem 13.3 except that we use the additional fact that $K_{3,3}$ is a bipartite graph.

Lemma 13.5.2. *In a planar embedding of a connected bipartite graph with at least 3 vertices, each face has length at least 4.*

Proof. By Lemma 13.4.2, every face of a planar embedding of the graph has length at least 3. But by Lemma 12.6.2 and Theorem 12.8.3.3, a bipartite graph can't have odd length closed walks. Since the faces of a planar embedding are closed walks, there can't be any faces of length 3 in a bipartite embedding. So every face must have length at least 4. $\blacksquare$

Theorem 13.5.3. *Suppose a connected bipartite graph with $v \geq 3$ vertices and e edges is planar. Then*

$$e \leq 2v - 4. \qquad\qquad (13.5)$$

Proof. Lemma 13.5.2 implies that all the faces of an embedding of the graph have length at least 4. Now arguing as in the proof of Theorem 13.4.3, we find that the sum of the lengths of the face boundaries is exactly $2e$ and at least $4f$. Hence,

$$4f \leq 2e \qquad\qquad (13.6)$$

for any embedding of a planar bipartite graph. By Euler's theorem, $f = 2 - v + e$. Substituting $2 - v + e$ for f in (13.6), we have

$$4(2 - v + e) \le 2e,$$

which simplies to (13.5). ∎

Corollary 13.5.4. $K_{3,3}$ *is not planar.*

Proof. $K_{3,3}$ is connected, bipartite and has 6 vertices and 9 edges. But since $9 > 2 \cdot 6 - 4$, $K_{3,3}$ does not satisfy the inequality (13.3) that holds in all bipartite planar graphs. ∎

13.6   Coloring Planar Graphs

We've covered a lot of ground with planar graphs, but not nearly enough to prove the famous 4-color theorem. But we can get awfully close. Indeed, we have done almost enough work to prove that every planar graph can be colored using only 5 colors.

There are two familiar facts about planarity that we will need.

Lemma 13.6.1. *Any subgraph of a planar graph is planar.*

Lemma 13.6.2. *Merging two adjacent vertices of a planar graph leaves another planar graph.*

Merging two adjacent vertices, n_1 and n_2 of a graph means deleting the two vertices and then replacing them by a new "merged" vertex m adjacent to all the vertices that were adjacent to either of n_1 or n_2, as illustrated in Figure 13.12.

Many authors take Lemmas 13.6.1 and 13.6.2 for granted for continuous drawings of planar graphs described by Definition 13.2.1. With the recursive Definition 13.2.2 both Lemmas can actually be proved using structural induction (see Problem 13.9).

We need only one more lemma:

Lemma 13.6.3. *Every planar graph has a vertex of degree at most five.*

Proof. Assuming to the contrary that every vertex of some planar graph had degree at least 6, then the sum of the vertex degrees is at least $6v$. But the sum of the vertex degrees equals $2e$ by the Handshake Lemma 12.2.1, so we have $e \ge 3v$ contradicting the fact that $e \le 3v - 6 < 3v$ by Theorem 13.4.3. ∎

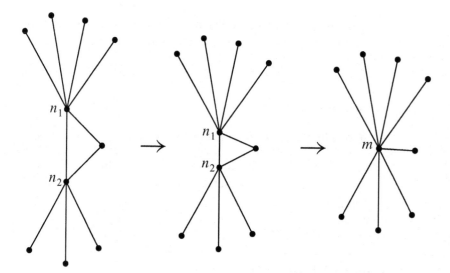

Figure 13.12   Merging adjacent vertices n_1 and n_2 into new vertex m.

Theorem 13.6.4. *Every planar graph is five-colorable.*

Proof. The proof will be by strong induction on the number v of vertices, with induction hypothesis:

> Every planar graph with v vertices is five-colorable.

Base cases ($v \leq 5$): immediate.

Inductive case: Suppose G is a planar graph with $v + 1$ vertices. We will describe a five-coloring of G.

First, choose a vertex g of G with degree at most 5; Lemma 13.6.3 guarantees there will be such a vertex.

Case 1: ($\deg(g) < 5$): Deleting g from G leaves a graph H that is planar by Lemma 13.6.1, and since H has v vertices, it is five-colorable by induction hypothesis. Now define a five coloring of G as follows: use the five-coloring of H for all the vertices besides g, and assign one of the five colors to g that is not the same as the color assigned to any of its neighbors. Since there are fewer than 5 neighbors, there will always be such a color available for g.

Case 2: ($\deg(g) = 5$): If the five neighbors of g in G were all adjacent to each other, then these five vertices would form a nonplanar subgraph isomorphic to K_5, contradicting Lemma 13.6.1 (since K_5 is not planar). So there must be two neighbors, n_1 and n_2, of g that are not adjacent. Now merge n_1 and g into a new vertex, m. In this new graph, n_2 is adjacent to m, and the graph is planar by Lemma 13.6.2. So we can then merge m and n_2 into a another new vertex m', resulting in a new graph G' which by Lemma 13.6.2 is also planar. Since G' has $v - 1$ vertices, it is five-colorable by the induction hypothesis.

Now define a five coloring of G as follows: use the five-coloring of G' for all the vertices besides g, n_1 and n_2. Next assign the color of m' in G' to be the color of the neighbors n_1 and n_2. Since n_1 and n_2 are not adjacent in G, this defines a proper five-coloring of G except for vertex g. But since these two neighbors of g have the same color, the neighbors of g have been colored using fewer than five colors altogether. So complete the five-coloring of G by assigning one of the five colors to g that is not the same as any of the colors assigned to its neighbors.

∎

13.7 Classifying Polyhedra

The Pythagoreans had two great mathematical secrets, the irrationality of $\sqrt{2}$ and a geometric construct that we're about to rediscover!

A *polyhedron* is a convex, three-dimensional region bounded by a finite number of polygonal faces. If the faces are identical regular polygons and an equal number of polygons meet at each corner, then the polyhedron is *regular*. Three examples of regular polyhedra are shown in Figure 13.13: the tetrahedron, the cube, and the octahedron.

We can determine how many more regular polyhedra there are by thinking about planarity. Suppose we took *any* polyhedron and placed a sphere inside it. Then we could project the polyhedron face boundaries onto the sphere, which would give an image that was a planar graph embedded on the sphere, with the images of the corners of the polyhedron corresponding to vertices of the graph. We've already observed that embeddings on a sphere are the same as embeddings on the plane, so Euler's formula for planar graphs can help guide our search for regular polyhedra.

For example, planar embeddings of the three polyhedra in Figure 13.1 are shown in Figure 13.14.

Let m be the number of faces that meet at each corner of a polyhedron, and let n be the number of edges on each face. In the corresponding planar graph, there are m edges incident to each of the v vertices. By the Handshake Lemma 12.2.1, we

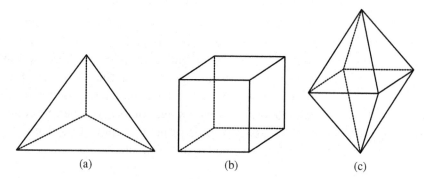

Figure 13.13   The tetrahedron (a), cube (b), and octahedron (c).

v

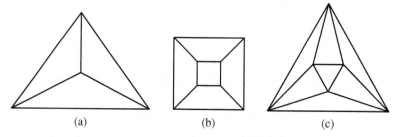

Figure 13.14   Planar embeddings of the tetrahedron (a), cube (b), and octahedron (c).

n	m	v	e	f	polyhedron
3	3	4	6	4	tetrahedron
4	3	8	12	6	cube
3	4	6	12	8	octahedron
3	5	12	30	20	icosahedron
5	3	20	30	12	dodecahedron

Figure 13.15   The only possible regular polyhedra.

know:

$$mv = 2e.$$

Also, each face is bounded by n edges. Since each edge is on the boundary of two faces, we have:

$$nf = 2e$$

Solving for v and f in these equations and then substituting into Euler's formula gives:

$$\frac{2e}{m} - e + \frac{2e}{n} = 2$$

which simplifies to

$$\frac{1}{m} + \frac{1}{n} = \frac{1}{e} + \frac{1}{2} \tag{13.7}$$

Equation 13.7 places strong restrictions on the structure of a polyhedron. Every nondegenerate polygon has at least 3 sides, so $n \geq 3$. And at least 3 polygons must meet to form a corner, so $m \geq 3$. On the other hand, if either n or m were 6 or more, then the left side of the equation could be at most $1/3 + 1/6 = 1/2$, which is less than the right side. Checking the finitely-many cases that remain turns up only five solutions, as shown in Figure 13.15. For each valid combination of n and m, we can compute the associated number of vertices v, edges e, and faces f. And polyhedra with these properties do actually exist. The largest polyhedron, the dodecahedron, was the other great mathematical secret of the Pythagorean sect.

The 5 polyhedra in Figure 13.15 are the only possible regular polyhedra. So if you want to put more than 20 geocentric satellites in orbit so that they *uniformly* blanket the globe—tough luck!

13.8   Another Characterization for Planar Graphs

We did not pick K_5 and $K_{3,3}$ as examples because of their application to dog houses or quadrapi shaking hands. We really picked them because they provide another, famous, discrete characterizarion of planar graphs:

Theorem 13.8.1 (Kuratowski). *A graph is not planar if and only if it contains K_5 or $K_{3,3}$ as a minor.*

Definition 13.8.2. A *minor* of a graph G is a graph that can be obtained by repeatedly[4] deleting vertices, deleting edges, and merging *adjacent* vertices of G.

For example, Figure 13.16 illustrates why C_3 is a minor of the graph in Figure 13.16(a). In fact C_3 is a minor of a connected graph G if and only if G is not a tree.

The known proofs of Kuratowski's Theorem 13.8.1 are a little too long to include in an introductory text, so we won't give one.

Problems for Section 13.2

Practice Problems

Problem 13.1.
What are the discrete faces of the following two graphs?

Write each cycle as a sequence of letters without spaces, starting with the alphabetically earliest letter in the clockwise direction, for example "adbfa." Separate the sequences with spaces.

(a)

(b)

---

[4]The three operations can each be performed any number of times in any order.

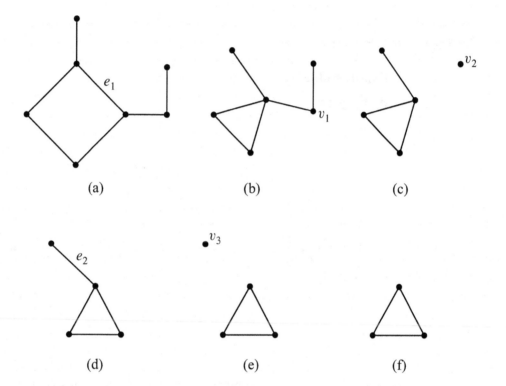

Figure 13.16 One method by which the graph in (a) can be reduced to C_3 (f), thereby showing that C_3 is a minor of the graph. The steps are: merging the nodes incident to e_1 (b), deleting v_1 and all edges incident to it (c), deleting v_2 (d), deleting e_2, and deleting v_3 (f).

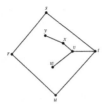

Problems for Section 13.8

Exam Problems

Problem 13.2.

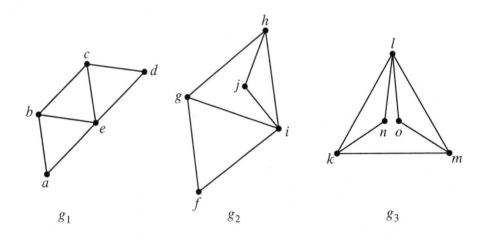

G_1 G_2 G_3

(a) Describe an isomorphism between graphs G_1 and G_2, and another isomorphism between G_2 and G_3.

(b) Why does part (a) imply that there is an isomorphism between graphs G_1 and G_3?

Let G and H be planar graphs. An embedding E_G of G is isomorphic to an embedding E_H of H iff there is an isomorphism from G to H that also maps each face of E_G to a face of E_H.

(c) One of the embeddings pictured above is not isomorphic to either of the others. Which one? Briefly explain why.

(d) Explain why all embeddings of two isomorphic planar graphs must have the same number of faces.

Problem 13.3. **(a)** Give an example of a planar graph with two planar embeddings, where the first embedding has a face whose length is not equal to the length of any face in the secoind embedding. Draw the two embeddings to demonstrate this.

(b) Define the length of a planar embedding $\mathcal{E}$ to be the sum of the lengths of the faces of $\mathcal{E}$. Prove that all embeddings of the same planar graph have the same length.

Problem 13.4.

Definition 13.2.2 of planar graph embeddings applied only to connected planar graphs. The definition can be extended to planar graphs that are not necessarily connected by adding the following additional constructor case to the definition:

- **Constructor Case:** (collect disjoint graphs) Suppose $\mathcal{E}_1$ and $\mathcal{E}_2$ are planar embeddings with no vertices in common. Then $\mathcal{E}_1 \cup \mathcal{E}_2$ is a planar embedding.

Euler's Planar Graph Theorem now generalizes to unconnected graphs as follows: if a planar embedding $\mathcal{E}$ has v vertices, e edges, f faces and c connected components, then

$$v - e + f - 2c = 0. \tag{13.8}$$

This can be proved by structural induction on the definition of planar embedding.

(a) State and prove the base case of the structural induction.

(b) Let v_i, e_i, f_i, and c_i be the number of vertices, edges, faces, and connected components in embedding $\mathcal{E}_i$ and let v, e, f, c be the numbers for the embedding from the (collect disjoint graphs) constructor case. Express v, e, f, c in terms of v_i, e_i, f_i, c_i.

(c) Prove the (collect disjoint graphs) case of the structural induction.

Problem 13.5. **(a)** A simple graph has 8 vertices and 24 edges. What is the average degree per vertex?

(b) A connected planar simple graph has 5 more edges than it has vertices. How many faces does it have?

(c) A connected simple graph has one more vertex than it has edges. Explain why it is a planar graph.

(d) How many faces does a planar graph from part c have?

(e) How many distinct isomorphisms are there between the graph given in Figure 13.17 and itself? (Include the identity isomorphism.)

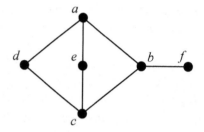

Figure 13.17

Class Problems

X

Problem 13.6.

Figure 13.18 shows four different pictures of planar graphs.

(a) For each picture, describe its discrete faces (closed walks that define the region borders).

(b) Which of the pictured graphs are isomorphic? Which pictures represent the same planar embedding?—that is, they have the same discrete faces.

(c) Describe a way to construct the embedding in Figure 4 according to the recursive Definition 13.2.2 of planar embedding. For each application of a constructor rule, be sure to indicate the faces (cycles) to which the rule was applied and the cycles which result from the application.

Problem 13.7.

Prove the following assertions by structural induction on the definition of planar embedding.

(a) In a planar embedding of a graph, each edge occurs exactly twice in the faces of the embedding.

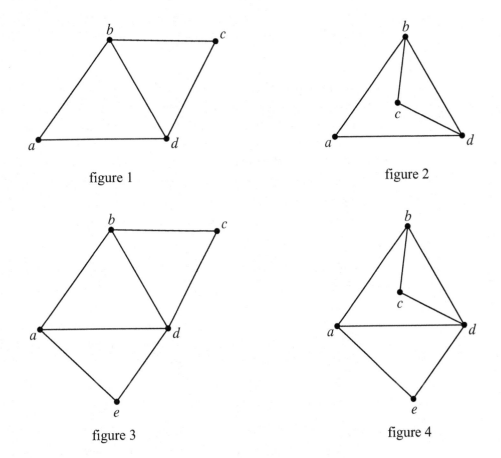

figure 1

figure 2

figure 3

figure 4

Figure 13.18

(b) In a planar embedding of a connected graph with at least three vertices, each face is of length at least three.

Homework Problems

Problem 13.8.
A simple graph is *triangle-free* when it has no cycle of length three.

(a) Prove for any connected triangle-free planar graph with $v > 2$ vertices and e edges,

$$e \leq 2v - 4. \tag{13.9}$$

(b) Show that any connected triangle-free planar graph has at least one vertex of degree three or less.

(c) Prove that any connected triangle-free planar graph is 4-colorable.

Problem 13.9. (a) Prove

Lemma (Switch Edges). *Suppose that, starting from some embeddings of planar graphs with disjoint sets of vertices, it is possible by two successive applications of constructor operations to add edges e and then f to obtain a planar embedding F. Then starting from the same embeddings, it is also possible to obtain F by adding f and then e with two successive applications of constructor operations.*

Hint: There are four cases to analyze, depending on which two constructor operations are applied to add e and then f. Structural induction is not needed.

(b) Prove

Corollary (Permute Edges). *Suppose that, starting from some embeddings of planar graphs with disjoint sets of vertices, it is possible to add a sequence of edges $e_0, e_1, \ldots, e_n$ by successive applications of constructor operations to obtain a planar embedding F. Then starting from the same embeddings, it is also possible to obtain F by applications of constructor operations that successively add any permutation[5] of the edges $e_0, e_1, \ldots, e_n$.*

Hint: By induction on the number of switches of adjacent elements needed to convert the sequence $0,1,\ldots,n$ into a permutation $\pi(0), \pi(1), \ldots, \pi(n)$.

(c) Prove

Corollary (Delete Edge). *Deleting an edge from a planar graph leaves a planar graph.*

(d) Conclude that any subgraph of a planar graph is planar.

---

[5]If $\pi : \{0, 1, \ldots, n\} \to \{0, 1, \ldots, n\}$ is a bijection, then the sequence $e_{\pi(0)}, e_{\pi(1)}, \ldots, e_{\pi(n)}$ is called a *permutation* of the sequence $e_0, e_1, \ldots, e_n$.

III Counting

Introduction

Counting seems easy enough: 1, 2, 3, 4, etc. This direct approach works well for counting simple things—like your toes—and may be the only approach for extremely complicated things with no identifiable structure. However, subtler methods can help you count many things in the vast middle ground, such as:

- The number of different ways to select a dozen doughnuts when there are five varieties available.

- The number of 16-bit numbers with exactly 4 ones.

Perhaps surprisingly, but certainly not coincidentally, these two numbers are the same: 1820.

Counting is useful in computer science for several reasons:

- Determining the time and storage required to solve a computational problem—a central objective in computer science—often comes down to solving a counting problem.

- Password and encryption security counts on having a very large set of possible passwords and encryption keys.

- Counting is the basis of probability theory, which plays a central role in all sciences, including computer science.

We begin our study of counting in Chapter 14 with a collection of rules and methods for finding closed-form expressions for commonly-occurring sums and products such as $\sum_{i=0}^{n} x^i$ and $\prod_{i=1}^{n} i$. We also introduce asymptotic notations such as $\sim$, O and Θ that are commonly used in computer science to express how a quantity such as the running time of a program grows with the size of the input.

Chapter 15 describes the most basic rules for determining the cardinality of a set. These rules are actually theorems, but our focus here will be less on their proofs than on teaching their use in simple counting as a practical skill, like integration.

But counting can be tricky, and people make counting mistakes all the time, so a crucial part of counting skill is being able to verify a counting argument. Sometimes this can be done simply by finding an alternative way to count and then comparing answers—they better agree. But most elementary counting arguments reduce to finding a bijection between objects to be counted and easy-to-count sequences. The chapter shows how explicitly defining these bijections—and verifying that they are bijections—is another useful way to verify counting arguments. The material in Chapter 15 is simple yet powerful, and it provides a great tool set for use in your future career.

Finally, Chapter 16 introduces generating functions which allow many counting problems to be solved by simple algebraic formula simplification.

14 Sums and Asymptotics

Sums and products arise regularly in the analysis of algorithms, financial applications, physical problems, and probabilistic systems. For example, according to Theorem 2.2.1,

$$1 + 2 + 3 + \cdots + n = \frac{n(n+1)}{2}. \qquad (14.1)$$

Of course, the left-hand sum could be expressed concisely as a subscripted summation

$$\sum_{i=1}^{n} i$$

but the right-hand expression $n(n+1)/2$ is not only concise but also easier to evaluate. Furthermore, it more clearly reveals properties such as the growth rate of the sum. Expressions like $n(n+1)/2$ that do not make use of subscripted summations or products—or those handy but sometimes troublesome sequences of three dots—are called *closed forms*.

Another example is the closed form for a *geometric sum*

$$1 + x + x^2 + x^3 + \cdots + x^n = \frac{1 - x^{n+1}}{1 - x} \qquad (14.2)$$

given in Problem 5.4. The sum as described on the left-hand side of (14.2) involves n additions and $1 + 2 + \cdots + (n-1) = (n-1)n/2$ multiplications, but its closed form on the right-hand side can be evaluated using fast exponentiation with at most $2 \log n$ multiplications, a division, and a couple of subtractions. Also, the closed form makes the growth and limiting behavior of the sum much more apparent.

Equations (14.1) and (14.2) were easy to verify by induction, but, as is often the case, the proofs by induction gave no hint about how these formulas were found in the first place. Finding them is part math and part art, which we'll start examining in this chapter.

Our first motivating example will be the value of a financial instrument known as an annuity. This value will be a large and nasty-looking sum. We will then describe several methods for finding closed forms for several sorts of sums, including those for annuities. In some cases, a closed form for a sum may not exist, and so we will provide a general method for finding closed forms for good upper and lower bounds on the sum.

The methods we develop for sums will also work for products, since any product can be converted into a sum by taking its logarithm. For instance, later in the chapter we will use this approach to find a good closed-form approximation to the *factorial function*

$$n! ::= 1 \cdot 2 \cdot 3 \cdots n.$$

We conclude the chapter with a discussion of asymptotic notation, especially "Big Oh" notation. Asymptotic notation is often used to bound the error terms when there is no exact closed form expression for a sum or product. It also provides a convenient way to express the growth rate or order of magnitude of a sum or product.

14.1   The Value of an Annuity

Would you prefer a million dollars today or $50,000 a year for the rest of your life? On the one hand, instant gratification is nice. On the other hand, the *total dollars* received at $50K per year is much larger if you live long enough.

Formally, this is a question about the value of an annuity. An *annuity* is a financial instrument that pays out a fixed amount of money at the beginning of every year for some specified number of years. In particular, an *n*-year, *m*-payment annuity pays *m* dollars at the start of each year for *n* years. In some cases, *n* is finite, but not always. Examples include lottery payouts, student loans, and home mortgages. There are even firms on Wall Street that specialize in trading annuities.[1]

A key question is, "What is an annuity worth?" For example, lotteries often pay out jackpots over many years. Intuitively, $50,000 a year for 20 years ought to be worth less than a million dollars right now. If you had all the cash right away, you could invest it and begin collecting interest. But what if the choice were between $50,000 a year for 20 years and a *half* million dollars today? Suddenly, it's not clear which option is better.

14.1.1   The Future Value of Money

In order to answer such questions, we need to know what a dollar paid out in the future is worth today. To model this, let's assume that money can be invested at a fixed annual interest rate *p*. We'll assume an 8% rate[2] for the rest of the discussion, so $p = 0.08$.

---

[1] Such trading ultimately led to the subprime mortgage disaster in 2008–2009. We'll talk more about that in a later chapter.

[2] U.S. interest rates have dropped steadily for several years, and ordinary bank deposits now earn around 1.0%. But just a few years ago the rate was 8%; this rate makes some of our examples a little more dramatic. The rate has been as high as 17% in the past thirty years.

Here is why the interest rate p matters. Ten dollars invested today at interest rate p will become $(1 + p) \cdot 10 = 10.80$ dollars in a year, $(1 + p)^2 \cdot 10 \approx 11.66$ dollars in two years, and so forth. Looked at another way, ten dollars paid out a year from now is only really worth $1/(1 + p) \cdot 10 \approx 9.26$ dollars today, because if we had the $9.26 today, we could invest it and would have $10.00 in a year anyway. Therefore, p determines the value of money paid out in the future.

So for an n-year, m-payment annuity, the first payment of m dollars is truly worth m dollars. But the second payment a year later is worth only $m/(1 + p)$ dollars. Similarly, the third payment is worth $m/(1 + p)^2$, and the n-th payment is worth only $m/(1 + p)^{n-1}$. The total value V of the annuity is equal to the sum of the payment values. This gives:

$$
\begin{aligned}
V &= \sum_{i=1}^{n} \frac{m}{(1 + p)^{i-1}} \\
&= m \cdot \sum_{j=0}^{n-1} \left(\frac{1}{1 + p} \right)^{j} \qquad \text{(substitute } j = i - 1\text{)} \\
&= m \cdot \sum_{j=0}^{n-1} x^{j} \qquad\qquad \text{(substitute } x = 1/(1 + p)\text{).} \qquad (14.3)
\end{aligned}
$$

The goal of the preceding substitutions was to get the summation into the form of a simple geometric sum. This leads us to an explanation of a way you could have discovered the closed form (14.2) in the first place using the *Perturbation Method*.

14.1.2   The Perturbation Method

Given a sum that has a nice structure, it is often useful to "perturb" the sum so that we can somehow combine the sum with the perturbation to get something much simpler. For example, suppose

$$
S = 1 + x + x^2 + \cdots + x^n.
$$

An example of a perturbation would be

$$
xS = x + x^2 + \cdots + x^{n+1}.
$$

The difference between S and xS is not so great, and so if we were to subtract xS from S, there would be massive cancellation:

$$
\begin{aligned}
S &= 1 + x + x^2 + x^3 + \cdots + x^n \\
-xS &= \quad\; - x - x^2 - x^3 - \cdots - x^n - x^{n+1}.
\end{aligned}
$$

The result of the subtraction is

$$S - xS = 1 - x^{n+1}.$$

Solving for S gives the desired closed-form expression in equation 14.2, namely,

$$S = \frac{1 - x^{n+1}}{1 - x}.$$

We'll see more examples of this method when we introduce *generating functions* in Chapter 16.

14.1.3   A Closed Form for the Annuity Value

Using equation 14.2, we can derive a simple formula for V, the value of an annuity that pays m dollars at the start of each year for n years.

$$V = m\left(\frac{1 - x^n}{1 - x}\right) \qquad \text{(by equations 14.3 and 14.2)} \qquad (14.4)$$

$$= m\left(\frac{1 + p - (1/(1 + p))^{n-1}}{p}\right) \qquad \text{(substituting } x = 1/(1 + p)). \qquad (14.5)$$

Equation 14.5 is much easier to use than a summation with dozens of terms. For example, what is the real value of a winning lottery ticket that pays \$50,000 per year for 20 years? Plugging in $m = \$50,000$, $n = 20$ and $p = 0.08$ gives $V \approx \$530,180$. So because payments are deferred, the million dollar lottery is really only worth about a half million dollars! This is a good trick for the lottery advertisers.

14.1.4   Infinite Geometric Series

We began this chapter by asking whether you would prefer a million dollars today or \$50,000 a year for the rest of your life. Of course, this depends on how long you live, so optimistically assume that the second option is to receive \$50,000 a year *forever*. This sounds like infinite money! But we can compute the value of an annuity with an infinite number of payments by taking the limit of our geometric sum in equation 14.2 as n tends to infinity.

Theorem 14.1.1. *If $|x| < 1$, then*

$$\sum_{i=0}^{\infty} x^i = \frac{1}{1 - x}.$$

Proof.

$$\sum_{i=0}^{\infty} x^i ::= \lim_{n \to \infty} \sum_{i=0}^{n} x^i$$

$$= \lim_{n \to \infty} \frac{1 - x^{n+1}}{1 - x} \qquad \text{(by equation 14.2)}$$

$$= \frac{1}{1 - x}.$$

The final line follows from the fact that $\lim_{n \to \infty} x^{n+1} = 0$ when $|x| < 1$. ■

In our annuity problem $x = 1/(1 + p) < 1$, so Theorem 14.1.1 applies, and we get

$$V = m \cdot \sum_{j=0}^{\infty} x^j \qquad \text{(by equation 14.3)}$$

$$= m \cdot \frac{1}{1 - x} \qquad \text{(by Theorem 14.1.1)}$$

$$= m \cdot \frac{1 + p}{p} \qquad (x = 1/(1 + p)).$$

Plugging in $m = \$50{,}000$ and $p = 0.08$, we see that the value V is only $\$675{,}000$. It seems amazing that a million dollars today is worth much more than $\$50{,}000$ paid every year for eternity! But on closer inspection, if we had a million dollars today in the bank earning 8% interest, we could take out and spend $\$80{,}000$ a year, *forever*. So as it turns out, this answer really isn't so amazing after all.

14.1.5 Examples

Equation 14.2 and Theorem 14.1.1 are incredibly useful in computer science.

Here are some other common sums that can be put into closed form using equation 14.2 and Theorem 14.1.1:

$$1 + 1/2 + 1/4 + \cdots = \sum_{i=0}^{\infty} \left(\frac{1}{2}\right)^i = \frac{1}{1 - (1/2)} = 2 \tag{14.6}$$

$$0.99999\cdots = 0.9 \sum_{i=0}^{\infty} \left(\frac{1}{10}\right)^i = 0.9 \left(\frac{1}{1 - 1/10}\right) = 0.9 \left(\frac{10}{9}\right) = 1 \tag{14.7}$$

$$1 - 1/2 + 1/4 - \cdots = \sum_{i=0}^{\infty} \left(\frac{-1}{2}\right)^i = \frac{1}{1 - (-1/2)} = \frac{2}{3} \tag{14.8}$$

$$1 + 2 + 4 + \cdots + 2^{n-1} = \sum_{i=0}^{n-1} 2^i = \frac{1 - 2^n}{1 - 2} = 2^n - 1 \tag{14.9}$$

$$1 + 3 + 9 + \cdots + 3^{n-1} = \sum_{i=0}^{n-1} 3^i = \frac{1 - 3^n}{1 - 3} = \frac{3^n - 1}{2} \tag{14.10}$$

If the terms in a geometric sum grow smaller, as in equation 14.6, then the sum is said to be *geometrically decreasing*. If the terms in a geometric sum grow progressively larger, as in equations 14.9 and 14.10, then the sum is said to be *geometrically increasing*. In either case, the sum is usually approximately equal to the term in the sum with the greatest absolute value. For example, in equations 14.6 and 14.8, the largest term is equal to 1 and the sums are 2 and 2/3, both relatively close to 1. In equation 14.9, the sum is about twice the largest term. In equation 14.10, the largest term is 3^{n-1} and the sum is $(3^n - 1)/2$, which is only about a factor of 1.5 greater. You can see why this rule of thumb works by looking carefully at equation 14.2 and Theorem 14.1.1.

14.1.6   Variations of Geometric Sums

We now know all about geometric sums—if you have one, life is easy. But in practice one often encounters sums that cannot be transformed by simple variable substitutions to the form $\sum x^i$.

A non-obvious but useful way to obtain new summation formulas from old ones is by differentiating or integrating with respect to x. As an example, consider the following sum:

$$\sum_{i=1}^{n-1} i x^i = x + 2x^2 + 3x^3 + \cdots + (n-1)x^{n-1}$$

This is not a geometric sum. The ratio between successive terms is not fixed, and so our formula for the sum of a geometric sum cannot be directly applied. But differentiating equation 14.2 leads to:

$$\frac{d}{dx}\left(\sum_{i=0}^{n-1} x^i\right) = \frac{d}{dx}\left(\frac{1-x^n}{1-x}\right). \tag{14.11}$$

The left-hand side of equation 14.11 is simply

$$\sum_{i=0}^{n-1} \frac{d}{dx}(x^i) = \sum_{i=0}^{n-1} i x^{i-1}.$$

The right-hand side of equation 14.11 is

$$\frac{-nx^{n-1}(1-x) - (-1)(1-x^n)}{(1-x)^2} = \frac{-nx^{n-1} + nx^n + 1 - x^n}{(1-x)^2}$$

$$= \frac{1 - nx^{n-1} + (n-1)x^n}{(1-x)^2}.$$

Hence, equation 14.11 means that

$$\sum_{i=0}^{n-1} i x^{i-1} = \frac{1 - nx^{n-1} + (n-1)x^n}{(1-x)^2}.$$

Incidentally, Problem 14.2 shows how the perturbation method could also be applied to derive this formula.

Often, differentiating or integrating messes up the exponent of x in every term. In this case, we now have a formula for a sum of the form $\sum i x^{i-1}$, but we want a formula for the series $\sum i x^i$. The solution is simple: multiply by x. This gives:

$$\sum_{i=1}^{n-1} i x^i = \frac{x - nx^n + (n-1)x^{n+1}}{(1-x)^2} \tag{14.12}$$

and we have the desired closed-form expression for our sum. It seems a little complicated, but it's easier to work with than the sum.

Notice that if $|x| < 1$, then this series converges to a finite value even if there are infinitely many terms. Taking the limit of equation 14.12 as n tends to infinity gives the following theorem:

Theorem 14.1.2. *If $|x| < 1$, then*

$$\sum_{i=1}^{\infty} i x^i = \frac{x}{(1-x)^2}. \tag{14.13}$$

As a consequence, suppose that there is an annuity that pays im dollars at the end of each year i, forever. For example, if $m = \$50,000$, then the payouts are \$50,000 and then \$100,000 and then \$150,000 and so on. It is hard to believe that the value of this annuity is finite! But we can use Theorem 14.1.2 to compute the value:

$$
\begin{aligned}
V &= \sum_{i=1}^{\infty} \frac{im}{(1+p)^i} \\
&= m \cdot \frac{1/(1+p)}{(1 - \frac{1}{1+p})^2} \\
&= m \cdot \frac{1+p}{p^2}.
\end{aligned}
$$

The second line follows by an application of Theorem 14.1.2. The third line is obtained by multiplying the numerator and denominator by $(1+p)^2$.

For example, if $m = \$50,000$, and $p = 0.08$ as usual, then the value of the annuity is $V = \$8,437,500$. Even though the payments increase every year, the increase is only additive with time; by contrast, dollars paid out in the future decrease in value exponentially with time. The geometric decrease swamps out the additive increase. Payments in the distant future are almost worthless, so the value of the annuity is finite.

The important thing to remember is the trick of taking the derivative (or integral) of a summation formula. Of course, this technique requires one to compute nasty derivatives correctly, but this is at least theoretically possible!

14.2   Sums of Powers

In Chapter 5, we verified the formula (14.1), but the source of this formula is still a mystery. Sure, we can prove that it's true by using well ordering or induction, but where did the expression on the right come from in the first place? Even more inexplicable is the closed form expression for the sum of consecutive squares:

$$
\sum_{i=1}^{n} i^2 = \frac{(2n+1)(n+1)n}{6}. \tag{14.14}
$$

It turns out that there is a way to derive these expressions, but before we explain it, we thought it would be fun—OK, our definition of "fun" may be different than yours—to show you how Gauss is supposed to have proved equation 14.1 when he was a young boy.

Gauss's idea is related to the perturbation method we used in Section 14.1.2. Let

$$S = \sum_{i=1}^{n} i.$$

Then we can write the sum in two orders:

$$S = 1 + \quad 2 \quad + \ldots + (n-1) + n,$$
$$S = n + (n-1) + \ldots + \quad 2 \quad + 1.$$

Adding these two equations gives

$$2S = (n+1) + (n+1) + \cdots + (n+1) + (n+1)$$
$$= n(n+1).$$

Hence,

$$S = \frac{n(n+1)}{2}.$$

Not bad for a young child—Gauss showed some potential. . . .

Unfortunately, the same trick does not work for summing consecutive squares. However, we can observe that the result might be a third-degree polynomial in n, since the sum contains n terms that average out to a value that grows quadratically in n. So we might guess that

$$\sum_{i=1}^{n} i^2 = an^3 + bn^2 + cn + d.$$

If our guess is correct, then we can determine the parameters a, b, c and d by plugging in a few values for n. Each such value gives a linear equation in a, b, c and d. If we plug in enough values, we may get a linear system with a unique solution. Applying this method to our example gives:

$$
\begin{aligned}
n = 0 \quad &\text{implies} \quad 0 = d \\
n = 1 \quad &\text{implies} \quad 1 = a + b + c + d \\
n = 2 \quad &\text{implies} \quad 5 = 8a + 4b + 2c + d \\
n = 3 \quad &\text{implies} \quad 14 = 27a + 9b + 3c + d.
\end{aligned}
$$

Solving this system gives the solution $a = 1/3$, $b = 1/2$, $c = 1/6$, $d = 0$. Therefore, *if* our initial guess at the form of the solution was correct, then the summation is equal to $n^3/3 + n^2/2 + n/6$, which matches equation 14.14.

The point is that if the desired formula turns out to be a polynomial, then once you get an estimate of the *degree* of the polynomial, all the coefficients of the polynomial can be found automatically.

Be careful! This method lets you discover formulas, but it doesn't guarantee they are right! After obtaining a formula by this method, it's important to go back and *prove* it by induction or some other method. If the initial guess at the solution was not of the right form, then the resulting formula will be completely wrong! A later chapter will describe a method based on generating functions that does not require any guessing at all.

14.3   Approximating Sums

Unfortunately, it is not always possible to find a closed-form expression for a sum. For example, no closed form is known for

$$S = \sum_{i=1}^{n} \sqrt{i}.$$

In such cases, we need to resort to approximations for S if we want to have a closed form. The good news is that there is a general method to find closed-form upper and lower bounds that works well for many sums. Even better, the method is simple and easy to remember. It works by replacing the sum by an integral and then adding either the first or last term in the sum.

Definition 14.3.1. A function $f : \mathbb{R}^+ \to \mathbb{R}^+$ is *strictly increasing* when

$$x < y \text{ IMPLIES } f(x) < f(y),$$

and it is *weakly increasing*[3] when

$$x < y \text{ IMPLIES } f(x) \le f(y).$$

Similarly, f is *strictly decreasing* when

$$x < y \text{ IMPLIES } f(x) > f(y),$$

and it is *weakly decreasing*[4] when

$$x < y \text{ IMPLIES } f(x) \ge f(y).$$

---

[3]Weakly increasing functions are usually called *nondecreasing* functions. We will avoid this terminology to prevent confusion between being a nondecreasing function and the much weaker property of *not* being a decreasing function.

[4]Weakly decreasing functions are usually called *nonincreasing*.

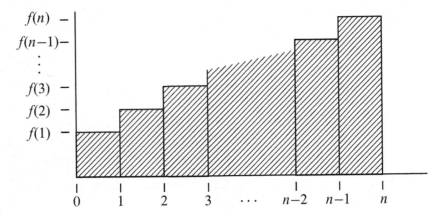

Figure 14.1 The area of the ith rectangle is $f(i)$. The shaded region has area $\sum_{i=1}^{n} f(i)$.

For example, 2^x and $\sqrt{x}$ are strictly increasing functions, while $\max\{x, 2\}$ and $\lceil x \rceil$ are weakly increasing functions. The functions $1/x$ and 2^{-x} are strictly decreasing, while $\min\{1/x, 1/2\}$ and $\lfloor 1/x \rfloor$ are weakly decreasing.

Theorem 14.3.2. *Let* $f : \mathbb{R}^+ \to \mathbb{R}^+$ *be a weakly increasing function. Define*

$$S ::= \sum_{i=1}^{n} f(i) \tag{14.15}$$

and

$$I ::= \int_{1}^{n} f(x)\,dx.$$

Then

$$I + f(1) \leq S \leq I + f(n). \tag{14.16}$$

Similarly, if f *is weakly decreasing, then*

$$I + f(n) \leq S \leq I + f(1).$$

Proof. Suppose $f : \mathbb{R}^+ \to \mathbb{R}^+$ is weakly increasing. The value of the sum S in (14.15) is the sum of the areas of n unit-width rectangles of heights $f(1), f(2), \ldots, f(n)$. This area of these rectangles is shown shaded in Figure 14.1.

The value of

$$I = \int_{1}^{n} f(x)\,dx$$

is the shaded area under the curve of $f(x)$ from 1 to n shown in Figure 14.2.

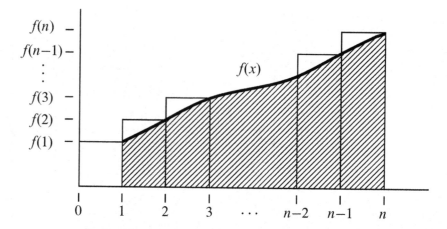

Figure 14.2   The shaded area under the curve of $f(x)$ from 1 to n (shown in bold) is $I = \int_1^n f(x)\,dx$.

Comparing the shaded regions in Figures 14.1 and 14.2 shows that S is at least I plus the area of the leftmost rectangle. Hence,

$$S \geq I + f(1) \tag{14.17}$$

This is the lower bound for S given in (14.16).

To derive the upper bound for S given in (14.16), we shift the curve of $f(x)$ from 1 to n one unit to the left as shown in Figure 14.3.

Comparing the shaded regions in Figures 14.1 and 14.3 shows that S is at most I plus the area of the rightmost rectangle. That is,

$$S \leq I + f(n),$$

which is the upper bound for S given in (14.16).

The very similar argument for the weakly decreasing case is left to Problem 14.10.
■

Theorem 14.3.2 provides good bounds for most sums. At worst, the bounds will be off by the largest term in the sum. For example, we can use Theorem 14.3.2 to bound the sum

$$S = \sum_{i=1}^{n} \sqrt{i}$$

as follows.

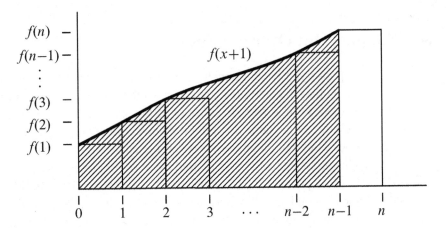

Figure 14.3 This curve is the same as the curve in Figure 14.2 shifted left by 1.

We begin by computing

$$I = \int_1^n \sqrt{x}\, dx$$

$$= \frac{x^{3/2}}{3/2}\bigg|_1^n$$

$$= \frac{2}{3}(n^{3/2} - 1).$$

We then apply Theorem 14.3.2 to conclude that

$$\frac{2}{3}(n^{3/2} - 1) + 1 \;\leq\; S \;\leq\; \frac{2}{3}(n^{3/2} - 1) + \sqrt{n}$$

and thus that

$$\frac{2}{3}n^{3/2} + \frac{1}{3} \;\leq\; S \;\leq\; \frac{2}{3}n^{3/2} + \sqrt{n} - \frac{2}{3}.$$

In other words, the sum is very close to $\frac{2}{3}n^{3/2}$. We'll define several ways that one thing can be "very close to" something else at the end of this chapter.

As a first application of Theorem 14.3.2, we explain in the next section how it helps in resolving a classic paradox in structural engineering.

14.4   Hanging Out Over the Edge

Suppose you have a bunch of books and you want to stack them up, one on top of another in some off-center way, so the top book sticks out past books below it without falling over. If you moved the stack to the edge of a table, how far past the edge of the table do you think you could get the top book to go? Could the top book stick out completely beyond the edge of table? You're not supposed to use glue or any other support to hold the stack in place.

Most people's first response to the Book Stacking Problem—sometimes also their second and third responses—is "No, the top book will never get completely past the edge of the table." But in fact, you can get the top book to stick out as far as you want: one booklength, two booklengths, any number of booklengths!

14.4.1   Formalizing the Problem

We'll approach this problem recursively. How far past the end of the table can we get one book to stick out? It won't tip as long as its center of mass is over the table, so we can get it to stick out half its length, as shown in Figure 14.4.

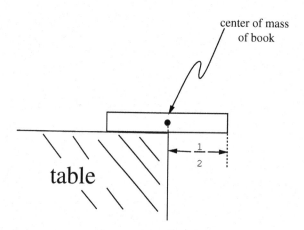

Figure 14.4   One book can overhang half a book length.

Now suppose we have a stack of books that will not tip over if the bottom book rests on the table—call that a *stable stack*. Let's define the *overhang* of a stable stack to be the horizontal distance from the center of mass of the stack to the furthest edge of the top book. So the overhang is purely a property of the stack, regardless of its placement on the table. If we place the center of mass of the stable stack at the edge of the table as in Figure 14.5, the overhang is how far we can get the top

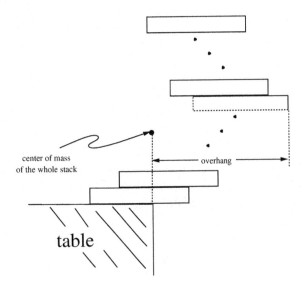

Figure 14.5 Overhanging the edge of the table.

book in the stack to stick out past the edge.

In general, a stack of n books will be stable if and only if the center of mass of the top i books sits over the $(i + 1)$st book for $i = 1, 2, \ldots, n - 1$.

So we want a formula for the maximum possible overhang B_n achievable with a stable stack of n books.

We've already observed that the overhang of one book is 1/2 a book length. That is,

$$B_1 = \frac{1}{2}.$$

Now suppose we have a stable stack of $n + 1$ books with maximum overhang. If the overhang of the n books on top of the bottom book was not maximum, we could get a book to stick out further by replacing the top stack with a stack of n books with larger overhang. So the maximum overhang B_{n+1} of a stack of $n + 1$ books is obtained by placing a maximum overhang stable stack of n books on top of the bottom book. And we get the biggest overhang for the stack of $n + 1$ books by placing the center of mass of the n books right over the edge of the bottom book as in Figure 14.6.

So we know where to place the $n + 1$st book to get maximum overhang. In fact, the reasoning above actually shows that this way of stacking $n + 1$ books is the *unique* way to build a stable stack where the top book extends as far as possible. All we have to do is calculate what this extension is.

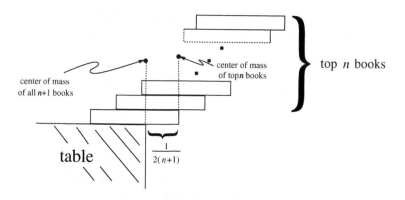

Figure 14.6   Additional overhang with $n + 1$ books.

The simplest way to do that is to let the center of mass of the top n books be the origin. That way the horizontal coordinate of the center of mass of the whole stack of $n + 1$ books will equal the increase in the overhang. But now the center of mass of the bottom book has horizontal coordinate $1/2$, so the horizontal coordinate of center of mass of the whole stack of $n + 1$ books is

$$\frac{0 \cdot n + (1/2) \cdot 1}{n + 1} = \frac{1}{2(n + 1)}.$$

In other words,

$$B_{n+1} = B_n + \frac{1}{2(n + 1)}, \tag{14.18}$$

as shown in Figure 14.6.

Expanding equation (14.18), we have

$$
\begin{aligned}
B_{n+1} &= B_{n-1} + \frac{1}{2n} + \frac{1}{2(n + 1)} \\
&= B_1 + \frac{1}{2 \cdot 2} + \cdots + \frac{1}{2n} + \frac{1}{2(n + 1)} \\
&= \frac{1}{2} \sum_{i=1}^{n+1} \frac{1}{i}.
\end{aligned}
\tag{14.19}
$$

So our next task is to examine the behavior of B_n as n grows.

14.4.2 Harmonic Numbers

Definition 14.4.1. The *n*th *harmonic number* H_n is

$$H_n ::= \sum_{i=1}^{n} \frac{1}{i}.$$

So (14.19) means that

$$B_n = \frac{H_n}{2}.$$

The first few harmonic numbers are easy to compute. For example, $H_4 = 1 + \frac{1}{2} + \frac{1}{3} + \frac{1}{4} = \frac{25}{12} > 2$. The fact that H_4 is greater than 2 has special significance: it implies that the total extension of a 4-book stack is greater than one full book! This is the situation shown in Figure 14.7.

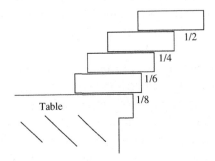

Figure 14.7   Stack of four books with maximum overhang.

There is good news and bad news about harmonic numbers. The bad news is that there is no known closed-form expression for the harmonic numbers. The good news is that we can use Theorem 14.3.2 to get close upper and lower bounds on H_n. In particular, since

$$\int_{1}^{n} \frac{1}{x}\,dx = \ln(x) \Big|_{1}^{n} = \ln(n),$$

Theorem 14.3.2 means that

$$\ln(n) + \frac{1}{n} \leq H_n \leq \ln(n) + 1. \tag{14.20}$$

In other words, the *n*th harmonic number is very close to $\ln(n)$.

Because the harmonic numbers frequently arise in practice, mathematicians have worked hard to get even better approximations for them. In fact, it is now known that

$$H_n = \ln(n) + \gamma + \frac{1}{2n} + \frac{1}{12n^2} + \frac{\epsilon(n)}{120n^4} \tag{14.21}$$

Here γ is a value $0.577215664\ldots$ called *Euler's constant*, and $\epsilon(n)$ is between 0 and 1 for all n. We will not prove this formula.

We are now finally done with our analysis of the book stacking problem. Plugging the value of H_n into (14.19), we find that the maximum overhang for n books is very close to $1/2\ln(n)$. Since $\ln(n)$ grows to infinity as n increases, this means that if we are given enough books we can get a book to hang out arbitrarily far over the edge of the table. Of course, the number of books we need will grow as an exponential function of the overhang; it will take 227 books just to achieve an overhang of 3, never mind an overhang of 100.

Extending Further Past the End of the Table

The overhang we analyzed above was the furthest out the *top* book could extend past the table. This leaves open the question of if there is some better way to build a stable stack where some book other than the top stuck out furthest. For example, Figure 14.8 shows a stable stack of two books where the bottom book extends further out than the top book. Moreover, the bottom book extends 3/4 of a book length past the end of the table, which is the same as the maximum overhang for the top book in a two book stack.

Since the two book arrangement in Figure 14.8(a) ties the maximum overhang stack in Figure 14.8(b), we could take the unique stable stack of n books where the top book extends furthest, and switch the top two books to look like Figure 14.8(a). This would give a stable stack of n books where the second from the top book extends the same maximum overhang distance. So for $n > 1$, there are at least two ways of building a stable stack of n books which both extend the maximum overhang distance—one way where the top book is furthest out, and another way where the second from the top book is furthest out.

It turns out that there is no way to beat these two ways of making stable stacks. In fact, it's not too hard to show that these are the *only* two ways to get a stable stack of books that achieves maximum overhang.

But there is more to the story. All our reasoning above was about stacks in which *one* book rests on another. It turns out that by building structures in which more than one book rests on top of another book—think of an inverted pyramid—it is possible to get a stack of n books to extend proportional to $\sqrt[3]{n}$—much more than $\ln n$—book lengths without falling over. See [14], *Maximum Overhang*.

14.4.3   Asymptotic Equality

For cases like equation 14.21 where we understand the growth of a function like H_n up to some (unimportant) error terms, we use a special notation, $\sim$, to denote the leading term of the function. For example, we say that $H_n \sim \ln(n)$ to indicate that

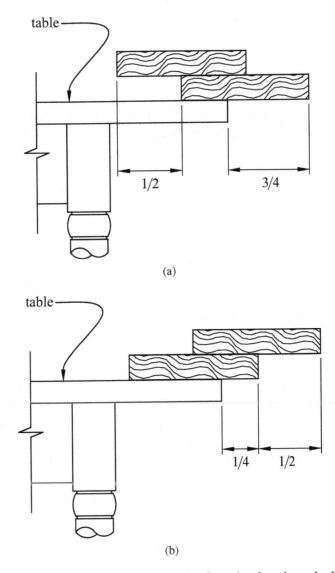

(a)

(b)

Figure 14.8 Figure (a) shows a stable stack of two books where the bottom book extends the same amount past the end of the table as the maximum overhang two-book stack shown in Figure (b).

the leading term of H_n is $\ln(n)$. More precisely:

Definition 14.4.2. For functions $f, g : \mathbb{R} \to \mathbb{R}$, we say f is *asymptotically equal to g*, in symbols,

$$f(x) \sim g(x)$$

iff

$$\lim_{x \to \infty} f(x)/g(x) = 1.$$

Although it is tempting to write $H_n \sim \ln(n) + \gamma$ to indicate the two leading terms, this is not really right. According to Definition 14.4.2, $H_n \sim \ln(n) + c$ where c is *any constant*. The correct way to indicate that γ is the second-largest term is $H_n - \ln(n) \sim \gamma$.

The reason that the $\sim$ notation is useful is that often we do not care about lower order terms. For example, if $n = 100$, then we can compute $H(n)$ to great precision using only the two leading terms:

$$|H_n - \ln(n) - \gamma| \leq \left| \frac{1}{200} - \frac{1}{120000} + \frac{1}{120 \cdot 100^4} \right| < \frac{1}{200}.$$

We will spend a lot more time talking about asymptotic notation at the end of the chapter. But for now, let's get back to using sums.

14.5   Products

We've covered several techniques for finding closed forms for sums but no methods for dealing with products. Fortunately, we do not need to develop an entirely new set of tools when we encounter a product such as

$$n! ::= \prod_{i=1}^{n} i. \tag{14.22}$$

That's because we can convert any product into a sum by taking a logarithm. For example, if

$$P = \prod_{i=1}^{n} f(i),$$

then

$$\ln(P) = \sum_{i=1}^{n} \ln(f(i)).$$

We can then apply our summing tools to find a closed form (or approximate closed form) for $\ln(P)$ and then exponentiate at the end to undo the logarithm.

For example, let's see how this works for the factorial function $n!$. We start by taking the logarithm:

$$\begin{aligned} \ln(n!) &= \ln(1 \cdot 2 \cdot 3 \cdots (n-1) \cdot n) \\ &= \ln(1) + \ln(2) + \ln(3) + \cdots + \ln(n-1) + \ln(n) \\ &= \sum_{i=1}^{n} \ln(i). \end{aligned}$$

Unfortunately, no closed form for this sum is known. However, we can apply Theorem 14.3.2 to find good closed-form bounds on the sum. To do this, we first compute

$$\begin{aligned} \int_{1}^{n} \ln(x)\,dx &= x\ln(x) - x \Big|_{1}^{n} \\ &= n\ln(n) - n + 1. \end{aligned}$$

Plugging into Theorem 14.3.2, this means that

$$n\ln(n) - n + 1 \;\leq\; \sum_{i=1}^{n} \ln(i) \;\leq\; n\ln(n) - n + 1 + \ln(n).$$

Exponentiating then gives

$$\frac{n^n}{e^{n-1}} \;\leq\; n! \;\leq\; \frac{n^{n+1}}{e^{n-1}}. \tag{14.23}$$

This means that $n!$ is within a factor of n of n^n/e^{n-1}.

14.5.1 Stirling's Formula

The most commonly used product in discrete mathematics is probably $n!$, and mathematicians have workedto find tight closed-form bounds on its value. The most useful bounds are given in Theorem 14.5.1.

Theorem 14.5.1 (*Stirling's Formula*). *For all $n \geq 1$,*

$$n! = \sqrt{2\pi n} \left(\frac{n}{e}\right)^n e^{\epsilon(n)}$$

where

$$\frac{1}{12n+1} \leq \epsilon(n) \leq \frac{1}{12n}.$$

Theorem 14.5.1 can be proved by induction (with some pain), and there are lots of proofs using elementary calculus, but we won't go into them.

There are several important things to notice about Stirling's Formula. First, $\epsilon(n)$ is always positive. This means that

$$n! > \sqrt{2\pi n}\left(\frac{n}{e}\right)^n \tag{14.24}$$

for all $n \in \mathbb{N}^+$.

Second, $\epsilon(n)$ tends to zero as n gets large. This means that

$$n! \sim \sqrt{2\pi n}\left(\frac{n}{e}\right)^n \tag{14.25}$$

which is impressive. After all, who would expect both π and e to show up in a closed-form expression that is asymptotically equal to $n!$?

Third, $\epsilon(n)$ is small even for small values of n. This means that Stirling's Formula provides good approximations for $n!$ for most all values of n. For example, if we use

$$\sqrt{2\pi n}\left(\frac{n}{e}\right)^n$$

as the approximation for $n!$, as many people do, we are guaranteed to be within a factor of

$$e^{\epsilon(n)} \le e^{\frac{1}{12n}}$$

of the correct value. For $n \ge 10$, this means we will be within 1% of the correct value. For $n \ge 100$, the error will be less than 0.1%.

If we need an even closer approximation for $n!$, then we could use either

$$\sqrt{2\pi n}\left(\frac{n}{e}\right)^n e^{1/12n}$$

or

$$\sqrt{2\pi n}\left(\frac{n}{e}\right)^n e^{1/(12n+1)}$$

depending on whether we want an upper, or a lower, bound. By Theorem 14.5.1, we know that both bounds will be within a factor of

$$e^{\frac{1}{12n}-\frac{1}{12n+1}} = e^{\frac{1}{144n^2+12n}}$$

of the correct value. For $n \ge 10$, this means that either bound will be within 0.01% of the correct value. For $n \ge 100$, the error will be less than 0.0001%.

For quick future reference, these facts are summarized in Corollary 14.5.2 and Table 14.1.

Approximation	$n \geq 1$	$n \geq 10$	$n \geq 100$	$n \geq 1000$
$\sqrt{2\pi n}\left(\frac{n}{e}\right)^n$	$< 10\%$	$< 1\%$	$< 0.1\%$	$< 0.01\%$
$\sqrt{2\pi n}\left(\frac{n}{e}\right)^n e^{1/12n}$	$< 1\%$	$< 0.01\%$	$< 0.0001\%$	$< 0.000001\%$

Table 14.1 Error bounds on common approximations for $n!$ from Theorem 14.5.1. For example, if $n \geq 100$, then $\sqrt{2\pi n}\left(\frac{n}{e}\right)^n$ approximates $n!$ to within 0.1%.

Corollary 14.5.2.

$$n! < \sqrt{2\pi n}\left(\frac{n}{e}\right)^n \cdot \begin{cases} 1.09 & \text{for } n \geq 1, \\ 1.009 & \text{for } n \geq 10, \\ 1.0009 & \text{for } n \geq 100. \end{cases}$$

14.6 Double Trouble

Sometimes we have to evaluate sums of sums, otherwise known as *double summations*. This sounds hairy, and sometimes it is. But usually, it is straightforward—you just evaluate the inner sum, replace it with a closed form, and then evaluate the outer sum (which no longer has a summation inside it). For example,[5]

$$\sum_{n=0}^{\infty} \left(y^n \sum_{i=0}^{n} x^i \right) = \sum_{n=0}^{\infty} \left(y^n \frac{1 - x^{n+1}}{1 - x} \right) \qquad \text{equation 14.2}$$

$$= \left(\frac{1}{1-x} \right) \sum_{n=0}^{\infty} y^n - \left(\frac{1}{1-x} \right) \sum_{n=0}^{\infty} y^n x^{n+1}$$

$$= \frac{1}{(1-x)(1-y)} - \left(\frac{x}{1-x} \right) \sum_{n=0}^{\infty} (xy)^n \qquad \text{Theorem 14.1.1}$$

$$= \frac{1}{(1-x)(1-y)} - \frac{x}{(1-x)(1-xy)} \qquad \text{Theorem 14.1.1}$$

$$= \frac{(1-xy) - x(1-y)}{(1-x)(1-y)(1-xy)}$$

$$= \frac{1-x}{(1-x)(1-y)(1-xy)}$$

$$= \frac{1}{(1-y)(1-xy)}.$$

When there's no obvious closed form for the inner sum, a special trick that is often useful is to try *exchanging the order of summation*. For example, suppose we want to compute the sum of the first n harmonic numbers

$$\sum_{k=1}^{n} H_k = \sum_{k=1}^{n} \sum_{j=1}^{k} \frac{1}{j} \qquad (14.26)$$

For intuition about this sum, we can apply Theorem 14.3.2 to equation 14.20 to conclude that the sum is close to

$$\int_{1}^{n} \ln(x)\, dx = x \ln(x) - x \Big|_{1}^{n} = n \ln(n) - n + 1.$$

Now let's look for an exact answer. If we think about the pairs (k, j) over which

---

[5]OK, so maybe this one is a little hairy, but it is also fairly straightforward. Wait till you see the next one!

we are summing, they form a triangle:

		j						
		1	2	3	4	5	...	n
k	1	1						
	2	1	1/2					
	3	1	1/2	1/3				
	4	1	1/2	1/3	1/4			
		...						
	n	1	1/2		...			$1/n$

The summation in equation 14.26 is summing each row and then adding the row sums. Instead, we can sum the columns and then add the column sums. Inspecting the table we see that this double sum can be written as

$$\sum_{k=1}^{n} H_k = \sum_{k=1}^{n} \sum_{j=1}^{k} \frac{1}{j}$$

$$= \sum_{j=1}^{n} \sum_{k=j}^{n} \frac{1}{j}$$

$$= \sum_{j=1}^{n} \frac{1}{j} \sum_{k=j}^{n} 1$$

$$= \sum_{j=1}^{n} \frac{1}{j} (n - j + 1)$$

$$= \sum_{j=1}^{n} \frac{n+1}{j} - \sum_{j=1}^{n} \frac{j}{j}$$

$$= (n+1) \sum_{j=1}^{n} \frac{1}{j} - \sum_{j=1}^{n} 1$$

$$= (n+1) H_n - n. \tag{14.27}$$

14.7   Asymptotic Notation

Asymptotic notation is a shorthand used to give a quick measure of the behavior of a function $f(n)$ as n grows large. For example, the asymptotic notation $\sim$ of Definition 14.4.2 is a binary relation indicating that two functions grow at the *same* rate. There is also a binary relation "little oh" indicating that one function grows at a significantly *slower* rate than another and "Big Oh" indicating that one function grows not much more rapidly than another.

14.7.1   Little O

Definition 14.7.1. For functions $f, g : \mathbb{R} \to \mathbb{R}$, with g nonnegative, we say f is *asymptotically smaller* than g, in symbols,

$$f(x) = o(g(x)),$$

iff

$$\lim_{x \to \infty} f(x)/g(x) = 0.$$

For example, $1000x^{1.9} = o(x^2)$ because $1000x^{1.9}/x^2 = 1000/x^{0.1}$ and since $x^{0.1}$ goes to infinity with x and 1000 is constant, we have $\lim_{x \to \infty} 1000x^{1.9}/x^2 = 0$. This argument generalizes directly to yield

Lemma 14.7.2. $x^a = o(x^b)$ *for all nonnegative constants* $a < b$.

Using the familiar fact that $\log x < x$ for all $x > 1$, we can prove

Lemma 14.7.3. $\log x = o(x^\epsilon)$ *for all* $\epsilon > 0$.

Proof. Choose $\epsilon > \delta > 0$ and let $x = z^\delta$ in the inequality $\log x < x$. This implies

$$\log z < z^\delta/\delta = o(z^\epsilon) \qquad \text{by Lemma 14.7.2.} \tag{14.28}$$

■

Corollary 14.7.4. $x^b = o(a^x)$ *for any* $a, b \in \mathbb{R}$ *with* $a > 1$.

Lemma 14.7.3 and Corollary 14.7.4 can also be proved using l'Hôpital's Rule or the Maclaurin Series for $\log x$ and e^x. Proofs can be found in most calculus texts.

14.7.2   Big O

"Big Oh" is the most frequently used asymptotic notation. It is used to give an upper bound on the growth of a function, such as the running time of an algorithm. There is a standard definition of Big Oh given below in 14.7.9, but we'll begin with an alternative definition that makes apparent several basic properties of Big Oh.

Definition 14.7.5. Given functions $f, g : \mathbb{R} \to \mathbb{R}$ with g nonnegative, we say that

$$f = O(g)$$

iff

$$\limsup_{x \to \infty} |f(x)| / g(x) < \infty.$$

Here we're using the technical notion of *limit superior*[6] instead of just limit. But because limits and lim sup's are the same when limits exist, this formulation makes it easy to check basic properties of Big Oh. We'll take the following Lemma for granted.

Lemma 14.7.6. *If a function $f : \mathbb{R} \to \mathbb{R}$ has a finite or infinite limit as its argument approaches infinity, then its limit and limit superior are the same.*

Now Definition 14.7.5 immediately implies:

Lemma 14.7.7. *If $f = o(g)$ or $f \sim g$, then $f = O(g)$.*

Proof. $\lim f/g = 0$ or $\lim f/g = 1$ implies $\lim f/g < \infty$, so by Lemma 14.7.6, $\limsup f/g < \infty$. ∎

Note that the converse of Lemma 14.7.7 is not true. For example, $2x = O(x)$, but $2x \nsim x$ and $2x \neq o(x)$.

We also have:

Lemma 14.7.8. *If $f = o(g)$, then it is not true that $g = O(f)$.*

Proof.

$$\lim_{x \to \infty} \frac{g(x)}{f(x)} = \frac{1}{\lim_{x \to \infty} f(x)/g(x)} = \frac{1}{0} = \infty,$$

so by Lemma 14.7.6, $g \neq O(f)$. ∎

---

[6]The precise definition of lim sup is

$$\limsup_{x \to \infty} h(x) ::= \lim_{x \to \infty} \mathrm{lub}_{y \geq x} h(y),$$

where "lub" abbreviates "least upper bound."

We need lim sup's in Definition 14.7.5 to cover cases when limits don't exist. For example, if $f(x)/g(x)$ oscillates between 3 and 5 as x grows, then $\lim_{x\to\infty} f(x)/g(x)$ does not exist, but $f = O(g)$ because $\limsup_{x\to\infty} f(x)/g(x) = 5$.

An equivalent, more usual formulation of big O does not mention lim sup's:

Definition 14.7.9. Given functions $f, g : \mathbb{R} \to \mathbb{R}$ with g nonnegative, we say

$$f = O(g)$$

iff there exists a constant $c \geq 0$ and an x_0 such that for all $x \geq x_0$, $|f(x)| \leq cg(x)$.

This definition is rather complicated, but the idea is simple: $f(x) = O(g(x))$ means $f(x)$ is less than or equal to $g(x)$, except that we're willing to ignore a constant factor, namely c and to allow exceptions for small x, namely, $x < x_0$. So in the case that $f(x)/g(x)$ oscillates between 3 and 5, $f = O(g)$ according to Definition 14.7.9 because $f \leq 5g$.

Proposition 14.7.10. $100x^2 = O(x^2)$.

Proof. Choose $c = 100$ and $x_0 = 1$. Then the proposition holds, since for all $x \geq 1$, $\left|100x^2\right| \leq 100x^2$. ∎

Proposition 14.7.11. $x^2 + 100x + 10 = O(x^2)$.

Proof. $(x^2+100x+10)/x^2 = 1+100/x+10/x^2$ and so its limit as x approaches infinity is $1+0+0 = 1$. So in fact, $x^2+100x+10 \sim x^2$, and therefore $x^2+100x+10 = O(x^2)$. Indeed, it's conversely true that $x^2 = O(x^2 + 100x + 10)$. ∎

Proposition 14.7.11 generalizes to an arbitrary polynomial:

Proposition 14.7.12. $a_k x^k + a_{k-1} x^{k-1} + \cdots + a_1 x + a_0 = O(x^k)$.

We'll omit the routine proof.

Big O notation is especially useful when describing the running time of an algorithm. For example, the usual algorithm for multiplying $n \times n$ matrices uses a number of operations proportional to n^3 in the worst case. This fact can be expressed concisely by saying that the running time is $O(n^3)$. So this asymptotic notation allows the speed of the algorithm to be discussed without reference to constant factors or lower-order terms that might be machine specific. It turns out that there is another matrix multiplication procedure that uses $O(n^{2.55})$ operations. The fact that this procedure is asymptotically faster indicates that it involves new ideas that go beyond a simply more efficient implementation of the $O(n^3)$ method.

Of course the asymptotically faster procedure will also definitely be much more efficient on large enough matrices, but being asymptotically faster does not mean that it is a better choice. The $O(n^{2.55})$-operation multiplication procedure is almost never used in practice because it only becomes more efficient than the usual $O(n^3)$ procedure on matrices of impractical size.[7]

14.7.3 Theta

Sometimes we want to specify that a running time $T(n)$ is precisely quadratic up to constant factors (both upper bound *and* lower bound). We could do this by saying that $T(n) = O(n^2)$ and $n^2 = O(T(n))$, but rather than say both, mathematicians have devised yet another symbol Θ to do the job.

Definition 14.7.13.

$$f = \Theta(g) \quad \text{iff} \quad f = O(g) \text{ and } g = O(f).$$

The statement $f = \Theta(g)$ can be paraphrased intuitively as "f and g are equal to within a constant factor."

The Theta notation allows us to highlight growth rates and suppress distracting factors and low-order terms. For example, if the running time of an algorithm is

$$T(n) = 10n^3 - 20n^2 + 1,$$

then we can more simply write

$$T(n) = \Theta(n^3).$$

In this case, we would say that *T is of order* n^3 or that $T(n)$ *grows cubically*, which is often the main thing we really want to know. Another such example is

$$\pi^2 3^{x-7} + \frac{(2.7x^{113} + x^9 - 86)^4}{\sqrt{x}} - 1.08^{3x} = \Theta(3^x).$$

Just knowing that the running time of an algorithm is $\Theta(n^3)$, for example, is useful, because if n doubles we can predict that the running time will *by and large*[8] increase by a factor of at most 8 for large n. In this way, Theta notation preserves information about the scalability of an algorithm or system. Scalability is, of course, a big issue in the design of algorithms and systems.

---

[7]It is even conceivable that there is an $O(n^2)$ matrix multiplication procedure, but none is known.

[8]Since $\Theta(n^3)$ only implies that the running time $T(n)$ is between cn^3 and dn^3 for constants $0 < c < d$, the time $T(2n)$ could regularly exceed $T(n)$ by a factor as large as $8d/c$. The factor is sure to be close to 8 for all large n only if $T(n) \sim n^3$.

14.7.4   Pitfalls with Asymptotic Notation

There is a long list of ways to make mistakes with asymptotic notation. This section presents some of the ways that big O notation can lead to trouble. With minimal effort, you can cause just as much chaos with the other symbols.

The Exponential Fiasco

Sometimes relationships involving big O are not so obvious. For example, one might guess that $4^x = O(2^x)$ since 4 is only a constant factor larger than 2. This reasoning is incorrect, however; 4^x actually grows as the square of 2^x.

Constant Confusion

Every constant is $O(1)$. For example, $17 = O(1)$. This is true because if we let $f(x) = 17$ and $g(x) = 1$, then there exists a $c > 0$ and an x_0 such that $|f(x)| \leq cg(x)$. In particular, we could choose $c = 17$ and $x_0 = 1$, since $|17| \leq 17 \cdot 1$ for all $x \geq 1$. We can construct a false theorem that exploits this fact.

False Theorem 14.7.14.

$$\sum_{i=1}^{n} i = O(n)$$

Bogus proof. Define $f(n) = \sum_{i=1}^{n} i = 1 + 2 + 3 + \cdots + n$. Since we have shown that every constant i is $O(1)$, $f(n) = O(1) + O(1) + \cdots + O(1) = O(n)$.   ∎

Of course in reality $\sum_{i=1}^{n} i = n(n+1)/2 \neq O(n)$.

The error stems from confusion over what is meant in the statement $i = O(1)$. For any *constant* $i \in \mathbb{N}$ it is true that $i = O(1)$. More precisely, if f is any constant function, then $f = O(1)$. But in this False Theorem, i is not constant—it ranges over a set of values $0, 1, \ldots, n$ that depends on n.

And anyway, we should not be adding $O(1)$'s as though they were numbers. We never even defined what $O(g)$ means by itself; it should only be used in the context "$f = O(g)$" to describe a relation between functions f and g.

Equality Blunder

The notation $f = O(g)$ is too firmly entrenched to avoid, but the use of "=" is regrettable. For example, if $f = O(g)$, it seems quite reasonable to write $O(g) = f$. But doing so might tempt us to the following blunder: because $2n = O(n)$, we can say $O(n) = 2n$. But $n = O(n)$, so we conclude that $n = O(n) = 2n$, and therefore $n = 2n$. To avoid such nonsense, we will never write "$O(f) = g$."

Similarly, you will often see statements like

$$H_n = \ln(n) + \gamma + O\left(\frac{1}{n}\right)$$

or

$$n! = (1 + o(1))\sqrt{2\pi n}\left(\frac{n}{e}\right)^n$$

In such cases, the true meaning is

$$H_n = \ln(n) + \gamma + f(n)$$

for some $f(n)$ where $f(n) = O(1/n)$, and

$$n! = (1 + g(n))\sqrt{2\pi n}\left(\frac{n}{e}\right)^n$$

where $g(n) = o(1)$. These last transgressions are OK as long as you (and your reader) know what you mean.

Operator Application Blunder

It's tempting to assume that familiar operations preserve asymptotic relations, but it ain't necessarily so. For example, $f \sim g$ in general does not even imply that $3^f = \Theta(3^g)$. On the other hand, some operations preserve and even strengthen asymptotic relations, for example,

$$f = \Theta(g) \quad \text{IMPLIES} \quad \ln f \sim \ln g.$$

See Problem 14.25.

14.7.5   Omega (Optional)

Sometimes people incorrectly use Big Oh in the context of a lower bound. For example, they might say, "The running time $T(n)$ is at least $O(n^2)$." This is another blunder! Big Oh can only be used for *upper* bounds. The proper way to express the lower bound would be

$$n^2 = O(T(n)).$$

The lower bound can also be described with another special notation "big Omega."

Definition 14.7.15. Given functions $f, g : \mathbb{R} \to \mathbb{R}$ with f nonnegative, define

$$f = \Omega(g)$$

to mean

$$g = O(f).$$

For example, $x^2 = \Omega(x)$, $2^x = \Omega(x^2)$ and $x/100 = \Omega(100x + \sqrt{x})$.

So if the running time of your algorithm on inputs of size n is $T(n)$, and you want to say it is at least quadratic, say

$$T(n) = \Omega(n^2).$$

There is a similar "little omega" notation for lower bounds corresponding to little o:

Definition 14.7.16. For functions $f, g : \mathbb{R} \to \mathbb{R}$ with f nonnegative, define

$$f = \omega(g)$$

to mean

$$g = o(f).$$

For example, $x^{1.5} = \omega(x)$ and $\sqrt{x} = \omega(\ln^2(x))$.

The little omega symbol is not as widely used as the other asymptotic symbols we defined.

Problems for Section 14.1

Class Problems

Problem 14.1.
We begin with two large glasses. The first glass contains a pint of water, and the second contains a pint of wine. We pour 1/3 of a pint from the first glass into the second, stir up the wine/water mixture in the second glass, and then pour 1/3 of a pint of the mix back into the first glass and repeat this pouring back-and-forth process a total of n times.

 (a) Describe a closed-form formula for the amount of wine in the first glass after n back-and-forth pourings.

 (b) What is the limit of the amount of wine in each glass as n approaches infinity?

Problem 14.2.

You've seen this neat trick for evaluating a geometric sum:

$$S = 1 + z + z^2 + \ldots + z^n$$
$$zS = z + z^2 + \ldots + z^n + z^{n+1}$$
$$S - zS = 1 - z^{n+1}$$
$$S = \frac{1 - z^{n+1}}{1 - z} \quad \text{(where } z \neq 1\text{)}$$

Use the same approach to find a closed-form expression for this sum:

$$T = 1z + 2z^2 + 3z^3 + \ldots + nz^n$$

Problem 14.3.
Sammy the Shark is a financial service provider who offers loans on the following terms.

- Sammy loans a client m dollars in the morning. This puts the client m dollars in debt to Sammy.

- Each evening, Sammy first charges a service fee which increases the client's debt by f dollars, and then Sammy charges interest, which multiplies the debt by a factor of p. For example, Sammy might charge a "modest" ten cent service fee and 1% interest rate per day, and then f would be 0.1 and p would be 1.01.

(a) What is the client's debt at the end of the first day?

(b) What is the client's debt at the end of the second day?

(c) Write a formula for the client's debt after d days and find an equivalent closed form.

(d) If you borrowed $10 from Sammy for a year, how much would you owe him?

Homework Problems

Problem 14.4.
Is a Harvard degree really worth more than an MIT degree? Let us say that a person with a Harvard degree starts with $40,000 and gets a $20,000 raise every year after graduation, whereas a person with an MIT degree starts with $30,000, but gets a 20% raise every year. Assume inflation is a fixed 8% every year. That is, $1.08 a year from now is worth $1.00 today.

(a) How much is a Harvard degree worth today if the holder will work for n years following graduation?

(b) How much is an MIT degree worth in this case?

(c) If you plan to retire after twenty years, which degree would be worth more?

Problem 14.5.
Suppose you deposit $100 into your MIT Credit Union account today, $99 in one month from now, $98 in two months from now, and so on. Given that the interest rate is constantly 0.3% per month, how long will it take to save $5,000?

Problems for Section 14.2

Class Problems

Problem 14.6.
Find a closed form for each of the following sums:
(a)

$$\sum_{i=1}^{n} \left(\frac{1}{i + 2012} - \frac{1}{i + 2013} \right).$$

(b) Assuming the following sum equals a polynomial in n, find the polynomial. Then verify by induction that the sum equals the polynomial you find.

$$\sum_{i=1}^{n} i^3$$

Problems for Section 14.3

Practice Problems

Problem 14.7.
Let

$$S ::= \sum_{n=1}^{5} \sqrt{3n}.$$

Using the Integral Method of Section 14.3, we can find integers a, b, c, d and a real number e such that

$$\int_a^b x^e \, dx \leq S \leq \int_c^d x^e \, dx$$

What are appropriate values for $a, \ldots, e$?

Class Problems

Problem 14.8.
Let $f : \mathbb{R} \to \mathbb{R}$ be a continuous, weakly increasing function. Say that f *grows slowly* when

$$f(n) = o\left(\int_1^n f(x) \, dx\right).$$

(a) Prove that the function $f_a(n) ::= n^a$ grows slowly for any $a > 0$.

(b) Prove that the function e^n does not grow slowly.

(c) Prove that if f grows slowly, then

$$\int_1^n f(x) \, dx \sim \sum_{i=1}^n f(i).$$

Exam Problems

Problem 14.9.
Assume n is an integer larger than 1. Circle all the correct inequalities below.

Explanations are not required, but partial credit for wrong answers will not be given without them. *Hint:* You may find the graphs in Figure 14.9 helpful.

- $\displaystyle\sum_{i=1}^n \ln(i+1) \leq \ln 2 + \int_1^n \ln(x+1) dx$

- $\displaystyle\sum_{i=1}^n \ln(i+1) \leq \int_0^n \ln(x+2) dx$

- $\displaystyle\sum_{i=1}^n \frac{1}{i} \geq \int_0^n \frac{1}{x+1} dx$

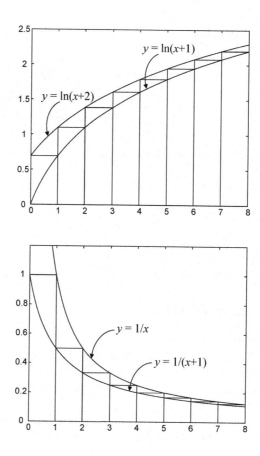

Figure 14.9   Integral bounds for two sums

Homework Problems

Problem 14.10.
Let $f : \mathbb{R}^+ \to \mathbb{R}^+$ be a weakly decreasing function. Define

$$S ::= \sum_{i=1}^{n} f(i)$$

and

$$I ::= \int_{1}^{n} f(x)\, dx.$$

Prove that

$$I + f(n) \leq S \leq I + f(1).$$

(Proof by very clear picture is OK.)

Problem 14.11.
Use integration to find upper and lower bounds that differ by at most 0.1 for the following sum. (You may need to add the first few terms explicitly and then use integrals to bound the sum of the remaining terms.)

$$\sum_{i=1}^{\infty} \frac{1}{(2i+1)^2}$$

Problems for Section 14.4

Class Problems

Problem 14.12.
An explorer is trying to reach the Holy Grail, which she believes is located in a desert shrine d days walk from the nearest oasis. In the desert heat, the explorer must drink continuously. She can carry at most 1 gallon of water, which is enough for 1 day. However, she is free to make multiple trips carrying up to a gallon each time to create water caches out in the desert.

For example, if the shrine were $2/3$ of a day's walk into the desert, then she could recover the Holy Grail after two days using the following strategy. She leaves the oasis with 1 gallon of water, travels $1/3$ day into the desert, caches $1/3$ gallon, and then walks back to the oasis—arriving just as her water supply runs out. Then she picks up another gallon of water at the oasis, walks $1/3$ day into the desert, tops off her water supply by taking the 1/3 gallon in her cache, walks the remaining 1/3 day to the shrine, grabs the Holy Grail, and then walks for 2/3 of a day back to the oasis—again arriving with no water to spare.

But what if the shrine were located farther away?

(a) What is the most distant point that the explorer can reach and then return to the oasis, with no water precached in the desert, if she takes a total of only 1 gallon from the oasis?

(b) What is the most distant point the explorer can reach and still return to the oasis if she takes a total of only 2 gallons from the oasis? No proof is required; just do the best you can.

(c) The explorer will travel using a recursive strategy to go far into the desert and back, drawing a total of n gallons of water from the oasis. Her strategy is to build up a cache of $n - 1$ gallons, plus enough to get home, a certain fraction of a day's distance into the desert. On the last delivery to the cache, instead of returning home, she proceeds recursively with her $n - 1$ gallon strategy to go farther into the desert and return to the cache. At this point, the cache has just enough water left to get her home.

Prove that with n gallons of water, this strategy will get her $H_n/2$ days into the desert and back, where H_n is the nth Harmonic number:

$$H_n ::= \frac{1}{1} + \frac{1}{2} + \frac{1}{3} + \cdots + \frac{1}{n}.$$

Conclude that she can reach the shrine, however far it is from the oasis.

(d) Suppose that the shrine is $d = 10$ days walk into the desert. Use the asymptotic approximation $H_n \sim \ln n$ to show that it will take more than a million years for the explorer to recover the Holy Grail.

Problem 14.13.
There is a number a such that $\sum_{i=1}^{\infty} i^p$ converges iff $p < a$. What is the value of a?

Hint: Find a value for a you think that works, then apply the integral bound.

Homework Problems

Problem 14.14.
There is a bug on the edge of a 1-meter rug. The bug wants to cross to the other side of the rug. It crawls at 1 cm per second. However, at the end of each second,

a malicious first-grader named Mildred Anderson *stretches* the rug by 1 meter. Assume that her action is instantaneous and the rug stretches uniformly. Thus, here's what happens in the first few seconds:

- The bug walks 1 cm in the first second, so 99 cm remain ahead.

- Mildred stretches the rug by 1 meter, which doubles its length. So now there are 2 cm behind the bug and 198 cm ahead.

- The bug walks another 1 cm in the next second, leaving 3 cm behind and 197 cm ahead.

- Then Mildred strikes, stretching the rug from 2 meters to 3 meters. So there are now $3 \cdot (3/2) = 4.5$ cm behind the bug and $197 \cdot (3/2) = 295.5$ cm ahead.

- The bug walks another 1 cm in the third second, and so on.

Your job is to determine this poor bug's fate.

(a) During second i, what *fraction* of the rug does the bug cross?

(b) Over the first n seconds, what fraction of the rug does the bug cross altogether? Express your answer in terms of the Harmonic number H_n.

(c) The known universe is thought to be about $3 \cdot 10^{10}$ light years in diameter. How many universe diameters must the bug travel to get to the end of the rug? (This distance is NOT the inflated distance caused by the stretching but only the actual walking done by the bug).

Exam Problems

Problem 14.15.
Show that

$$\sum_{i=1}^{\infty} i^p$$

converges to a finite value iff $p < -1$.

Problems for Section 14.7

Practice Problems

Problem 14.16.

Find the least nonnegative integer n such that $f(x)$ is $O(x^n)$ when f is defined by each of the expressions below.

(a) $2x^3 + (\log x)x^2$

(b) $2x^2 + (\log x)x^3$

(c) $(1.1)^x$

(d) $(0.1)^x$

(e) $(x^4 + x^2 + 1)/(x^3 + 1)$

(f) $(x^4 + 5\log x)/(x^4 + 1)$

(g) $2^{(3\log_2 x^2)}$

Problem 14.17.

Let $f(n) = n^3$. For each function $g(n)$ in the table below, indicate which of the indicated asymptotic relations hold.

$g(n)$	$f = O(g)$	$f = o(g)$	$g = O(f)$	$g = o(f)$
$6 - 5n - 4n^2 + 3n^3$				
$n^3 \log n$				
$(\sin(\pi n/2) + 2)n^3$				
$n^{\sin(\pi n/2)+2}$				
$\log n!$				
$e^{0.2n} - 100n^3$				

Problem 14.18.

Circle each of the true statements below.

Explanations are not required, but partial credit for wrong answers will not be given without them.

- $n^2 \sim n^2 + n$

- $3^n = O\left(2^n\right)$

- $n^{\sin(n\pi/2)+1} = o\left(n^2\right)$

- $n = \Theta\left(\dfrac{3n^3}{(n+1)(n-1)}\right)$

Problem 14.19.
Show that
$$\ln(n^2!) = \Theta(n^2 \ln n)$$

Hint: Stirling's formula for $(n^2)!$.

Problem 14.20.
The quantity
$$\frac{(2n)!}{2^{2n}(n!)^2} \tag{14.29}$$

will come up later in the course (it is the probability that in 2^{2n} flips of a fair coin, exactly n will be Heads). Show that it is asymptotically equal to $\dfrac{1}{\sqrt{\pi n}}$.

Problem 14.21.
Suppose let f and g be real-valued functions.

 (a) Give an example of f, g such that

$$\limsup fg < \limsup f \cdot \limsup g,$$

and all the lim sup's are finite.

 (b) Give an example of f, g such that

$$\limsup fg > \limsup f \cdot \limsup g.$$

and all the lim sup's are finite.

Homework Problems

Problem 14.22. (a) Prove that $\log x < x$ for all $x > 1$ (requires elementary calculus).

(b) Prove that the relation R on functions such that $f \mathrel{R} g$ iff $g = o(f)$ is a strict partial order.

(c) Prove that $f \sim g$ iff $f = g + h$ for some function $h = o(g)$.

Problem 14.23.
Indicate which of the following holds for each pair of functions $(f(n), g(n))$ in the table below. Assume $k \geq 1$, $\epsilon > 0$, and $c > 1$ are constants. Pick the four table entries you consider to be the most challenging or interesting and justify your answers to these.

$f(n)$	$g(n)$	$f = O(g)$	$f = o(g)$	$g = O(f)$	$g = o(f)$	$f = \Theta(g)$	$f \sim g$
2^n	$2^{n/2}$						
$\sqrt{n}$	$n^{\sin(n\pi/2)}$						
$\log(n!)$	$\log(n^n)$						
n^k	c^n						
$\log^k n$	n^ϵ						

Problem 14.24.
Arrange the following functions in a sequence $f_1, f_2, \dots f_{24}$ so that $f_i = O(f_{i+1})$. Additionally, if $f_i = \Theta(f_{i+1})$, indicate that too:

1. $n \log n$

2. $2^{100} n$

3. n^{-1}

4. $n^{-1/2}$

5. $(\log n)/n$

6. $\binom{n}{64}$

7. $n!$

8. $2^{2^{100}}$

9. 2^{2^n}

10. 2^n

11. 3^n

12. $n2^n$

13. 2^{n+1}

14. $2n$

15. $3n$

16. $\log(n!)$

17. $\log_2 n$

18. $\log_{10} n$

19. $2.1^{\sqrt{n}}$

20. 2^{2n}

21. 4^n

22. n^{64}

23. n^{65}

24. n^n

Problem 14.25.
Let f, g be nonnegative real-valued functions such that $\lim_{x\to\infty} f(x) = \infty$ and $f \sim g$.

(a) Give an example of f, g such that $\text{NOT}(2^f \sim 2^g)$.

(b) Prove that $\log f \sim \log g$.

(c) Use Stirling's formula to prove that in fact

$$\log(n!) \sim n \log n$$

Problem 14.26.

Determine which of these choices

$$\Theta(n), \quad \Theta(n^2 \log n), \quad \Theta(n^2), \quad \Theta(1), \quad \Theta(2^n), \quad \Theta(2^{n \ln n}), \quad \text{none of these}$$

describes each function's asymptotic behavior. Full proofs are not required, but briefly explain your answers.

(a)
$$n + \ln n + (\ln n)^2$$

(b)
$$\frac{n^2 + 2n - 3}{n^2 - 7}$$

(c)
$$\sum_{i=0}^{n} 2^{2i+1}$$

(d)
$$\ln(n^2!)$$

(e)
$$\sum_{k=1}^{n} k \left(1 - \frac{1}{2^k}\right)$$

Problem 14.27. (a) Either prove or disprove each of the following statements.

- $n! = O((n+1)!)$
- $(n+1)! = O(n!)$
- $n! = \Theta((n+1)!)$
- $n! = o((n+1)!)$
- $(n+1)! = o(n!)$

(b) Show that $\left(\frac{n}{3}\right)^{n+e} = o(n!)$.

Problem 14.28.

Prove that

$$\sum_{k=1}^{n} k^6 = \Theta(n^7).$$

Class Problems

Problem 14.29.
Give an elementary proof (without appealing to Stirling's formula) that $\log(n!) = \Theta(n \log n)$.

Problem 14.30.
Suppose $f, g : \mathbb{N}^+ \to \mathbb{N}^+$ and $f \sim g$.

(a) Prove that $2f \sim 2g$.

(b) Prove that $f^2 \sim g^2$.

(c) Give examples of f and g such that $2^f \not\sim 2^g$.

Problem 14.31.
Recall that for functions f, g on $\mathbb{N}$, $f = O(g)$ iff

$$\exists c \in \mathbb{N}\, \exists n_0 \in \mathbb{N}\, \forall n \geq n_0 \quad c \cdot g(n) \geq |f(n)|. \tag{14.30}$$

For each pair of functions below, determine whether $f = O(g)$ and whether $g = O(f)$. In cases where one function is O() of the other, indicate the *smallest nonnegative integer c* and for that smallest c, the *smallest corresponding nonnegative integer n_0* ensuring that condition (14.30) applies.

(a) $f(n) = n^2, g(n) = 3n$.

$f = O(g)$	YES	NO	If YES, $c = \underline{\quad\quad}$, $n_0 = \underline{\quad\quad}$
$g = O(f)$	YES	NO	If YES, $c = \underline{\quad\quad}$, $n_0 = \underline{\quad\quad}$

(b) $f(n) = (3n - 7)/(n + 4), g(n) = 4$

$f = O(g)$	YES	NO	If YES, $c = \underline{\quad\quad}$, $n_0 = \underline{\quad\quad}$
$g = O(f)$	YES	NO	If YES, $c = \underline{\quad\quad}$, $n_0 = \underline{\quad\quad}$

(c) $f(n) = 1 + (n \sin(n\pi/2))^2, g(n) = 3n$

$f = O(g)$	YES	NO	If yes, $c = \underline{\quad\quad}$ $n_0 = \underline{\quad\quad}$
$g = O(f)$	YES	NO	If yes, $c = \underline{\quad\quad}$ $n_0 = \underline{\quad\quad}$

Problem 14.32.

False Claim.

$$2^n = O(1). \tag{14.31}$$

Explain why the claim is false. Then identify and explain the mistake in the following bogus proof.

Bogus proof. The proof is by induction on n where the induction hypothesis $P(n)$ is the assertion (14.31).

base case: $P(0)$ holds trivially.

inductive step: We may assume $P(n)$, so there is a constant $c > 0$ such that $2^n \leq c \cdot 1$. Therefore,

$$2^{n+1} = 2 \cdot 2^n \leq (2c) \cdot 1,$$

which implies that $2^{n+1} = O(1)$. That is, $P(n+1)$ holds, which completes the proof of the inductive step.

We conclude by induction that $2^n = O(1)$ for all n. That is, the exponential function is bounded by a constant.

■

Problem 14.33. **(a)** Prove that the relation R on functions such that $f \, R \, g$ iff $f = o(g)$ is a strict partial order.

(b) Describe two functions f, g that are incomparable under big Oh:

$$f \neq O(g) \text{ AND } g \neq O(f).$$

Conclude that R is not a linear order. How about three such functions?

Exam Problems

Problem 14.34.
Give an example of a pair of strictly increasing total functions, $f : \mathbb{N}^+ \to \mathbb{N}^+$ and $g : \mathbb{N}^+ \to \mathbb{N}^+$, that satisfy $f \sim g$ but **not** $3^f = O(3^g)$.

Problem 14.35.
Let f, g be real-valued functions such that $f = \Theta(g)$ and $\lim_{x \to \infty} f(x) = \infty$. Prove that

$$\ln f \sim \ln g.$$

Problem 14.36. (a) Show that

$$(an)^{b/n} \sim 1.$$

where a, b are positive constants and $\sim$ denotes asymptotic equality. *Hint: $an = a2^{\log_2 n}$.*

(b) You may assume that if $f(n) \geq 1$ and $g(n) \geq 1$ for all n, then $f \sim g \longrightarrow f^{\frac{1}{n}} \sim g^{\frac{1}{n}}$. Show that

$$\sqrt[n]{n!} = \Theta(n).$$

Problem 14.37.

(a) Define a function $f(n)$ such that $f = \Theta(n^2)$ and $\text{NOT}(f \sim n^2)$.

$$f(n) =$$

(b) Define a function $g(n)$ such that $g = O(n^2)$, $g \neq \Theta(n^2)$, $g \neq o(n^2)$, and $n = O(g)$.

$$g(n) =$$

Problem 14.38. (a) Show that

$$(an)^{b/n} \sim 1.$$

where a, b are positive constants and $\sim$ denotes asymptotic equality. *Hint: $an = a2^{\log_2 n}$.*

(b) Show that

$$\sqrt[n]{n!} = \Theta(n).$$

Problem 14.39.

(a) Indicate which of the following asymptotic relations below on the set of nonnegative real-valued functions are equivalence relations (**E**), strict partial orders (**S**), weak partial orders (**W**), or *none* of the above (**N**).

- $f \sim g$, the "asymptotically equal" relation.
- $f = o(g)$, the "little Oh" relation.
- $f = O(g)$, the "big Oh" relation.
- $f = \Theta(g)$, the "Theta" relation.
- $f = O(g)$ AND NOT$(g = O(f))$.

(b) Indicate the implications among the assertions in part (a). For example,

$$f = o(g) \text{ IMPLIES } f = O(g).$$

Problem 14.40.

Recall that if f and g are nonnegative real-valued functions on $\mathbb{Z}^+$, then $f = O(g)$ iff there exist $c, n_0 \in \mathbb{Z}^+$ such that

$$\forall n \geq n_0. \ f(n) \leq cg(n).$$

For each pair of functions f and g below, indicate the **smallest** $c \in \mathbb{Z}^+$, and for that smallest c, the **smallest corresponding** $n_0 \in \mathbb{Z}^+$, that would establish $f = O(g)$ by the definition given above. If there is no such c, write ∞.

(a) $f(n) = \frac{1}{2}\ln n^2, g(n) = n.$ $c = \underline{\hspace{1cm}}, n_0 = \underline{\hspace{1cm}}$

(b) $f(n) = n, g(n) = n\ln n.$ $c = \underline{\hspace{1cm}}, n_0 = \underline{\hspace{1cm}}$

(c) $f(n) = 2^n, g(n) = n^4\ln n$ $c = \underline{\hspace{1cm}}, n_0 = \underline{\hspace{1cm}}$

(d) $f(n) = 3\sin\left(\dfrac{\pi(n-1)}{100}\right) + 2, g(n) = 0.2.$ $c = \underline{\hspace{1cm}}, n_0 = \underline{\hspace{1cm}}$

Problem 14.41.

Let f, g be positive real-valued functions on finite, *connected*, simple graphs. We will extend the $O()$ notation to such graph functions as follows: $f = O(g)$ iff there is a constant $c > 0$ such that

$$f(G) \leq c \cdot g(G) \text{ for all connected simple graphs } G \text{ with more than one vertex.}$$

For each of the following assertions, state whether it is **True** or **False** and briefly explain your answer. You are **not** expected to offer a careful proof or detailed counterexample.

Reminder: $V(G)$ is the set of vertices and $E(G)$ is the set of edges of G, and G is connected.

(a) $|V(G)| = O(|E(G)|)$.

(b) $|E(G)| = O(|V(G)|)$.

(c) $|V(G)| = O(\chi(G))$, where $\chi(G)$ is the chromatic number of G.

(d) $\chi(G) = O(|V(G)|)$.

15 Cardinality Rules

15.1 Counting One Thing by Counting Another

How do you count the number of people in a crowded room? You could count heads, since for each person there is exactly one head. Alternatively, you could count ears and divide by two. Of course, you might have to adjust the calculation if someone lost an ear in a pirate raid or someone was born with three ears. The point here is that you can often *count one thing by counting another*, though some fudging may be required. This is a central theme of counting, from the easiest problems to the hardest. In fact, we've already seen this technique used in Theorem 4.5.5, where the number of subsets of an n-element set was proved to be the same as the number of length-n bit-strings, by describing a bijection between the subsets and the bit-strings.

The most direct way to count one thing by counting another is to find a bijection between them, since if there is a bijection between two sets, then the sets have the same size. This important fact is commonly known as the *Bijection Rule*. We've already seen it as the Mapping Rules bijective case (4.7).

15.1.1 The Bijection Rule

The Bijection Rule acts as a magnifier of counting ability; if you figure out the size of one set, then you can immediately determine the sizes of many other sets via bijections. For example, let's look at the two sets mentioned at the beginning of Part III:

A = all ways to select a dozen donuts when five varieties are available

B = all 16-bit sequences with exactly 4 ones

An example of an element of set A is:

$$\underbrace{0\,0}_{\text{chocolate}} \quad \underbrace{}_{\text{lemon-filled}} \quad \underbrace{0\,0\,0\,0\,0\,0}_{\text{sugar}} \quad \underbrace{0\,0}_{\text{glazed}} \quad \underbrace{0\,0}_{\text{plain}}$$

Here, we've depicted each donut with a 0 and left a gap between the different varieties. Thus, the selection above contains two chocolate donuts, no lemon-filled, six sugar, two glazed, and two plain. Now let's put a 1 into each of the four gaps:

$$\underbrace{0\,0}_{\text{chocolate}} \quad 1 \quad \underbrace{}_{\text{lemon-filled}} \quad 1 \quad \underbrace{0\,0\,0\,0\,0\,0}_{\text{sugar}} \quad 1 \quad \underbrace{0\,0}_{\text{glazed}} \quad 1 \quad \underbrace{0\,0}_{\text{plain}}$$

and close up the gaps:

$$0011000000100100\,.$$

We've just formed a 16-bit number with exactly 4 ones—an element of B!

This example suggests a bijection from set A to set B: map a dozen donuts consisting of:

$$c \text{ chocolate, } l \text{ lemon-filled, } s \text{ sugar, } g \text{ glazed, and } p \text{ plain}$$

to the sequence:

$$\underbrace{0\ldots0}_{c} \quad 1 \quad \underbrace{0\ldots0}_{l} \quad 1 \quad \underbrace{0\ldots0}_{s} \quad 1 \quad \underbrace{0\ldots0}_{g} \quad 1 \quad \underbrace{0\ldots0}_{p}$$

The resulting sequence always has 16 bits and exactly 4 ones, and thus is an element of B. Moreover, the mapping is a bijection: every such bit sequence comes from exactly one order of a dozen donuts. Therefore, $|A| = |B|$ by the Bijection Rule. More generally,

Lemma 15.1.1. *The number of ways to select n donuts when k flavors are available is the same as the number of binary sequences with exactly n zeroes and k − 1 ones.*

This example demonstrates the power of the bijection rule. We managed to prove that two very different sets are actually the same size—even though we don't know exactly how big either one is. But as soon as we figure out the size of one set, we'll immediately know the size of the other.

This particular bijection might seem frighteningly ingenious if you've not seen it before. But you'll use essentially this same argument over and over, and soon you'll consider it routine.

15.2   Counting Sequences

The Bijection Rule lets us count one thing by counting another. This suggests a general strategy: get really good at counting just a few things, then use bijections to count everything else! This is the strategy we'll follow. In particular, we'll get really good at counting *sequences*. When we want to determine the size of some other set T, we'll find a bijection from T to a set of sequences S. Then we'll use our super-ninja sequence-counting skills to determine $|S|$, which immediately gives us $|T|$. We'll need to hone this idea somewhat as we go along, but that's pretty much it!

15.2.1 The Product Rule

The *Product Rule* gives the size of a product of sets. Recall that if $P_1, P_2, \ldots, P_n$ are sets, then

$$P_1 \times P_2 \times \cdots \times P_n$$

is the set of all sequences whose first term is drawn from P_1, second term is drawn from P_2 and so forth.

Rule 15.2.1 (Product Rule). *If $P_1, P_2, \ldots P_n$ are finite sets, then:*

$$|P_1 \times P_2 \times \cdots \times P_n| = |P_1| \cdot |P_2| \cdots |P_n|$$

For example, suppose a *daily diet* consists of a breakfast selected from set B, a lunch from set L, and a dinner from set D where:

$$B = \{\text{pancakes, bacon and eggs, bagel, Doritos}\}$$
$$L = \{\text{burger and fries, garden salad, Doritos}\}$$
$$D = \{\text{macaroni, pizza, frozen burrito, pasta, Doritos}\}$$

Then $B \times L \times D$ is the set of all possible daily diets. Here are some sample elements:

$$(\text{pancakes, burger and fries, pizza})$$
$$(\text{bacon and eggs, garden salad, pasta})$$
$$(\text{Doritos, Doritos, frozen burrito})$$

The Product Rule tells us how many different daily diets are possible:

$$
\begin{aligned}
|B \times L \times D| &= |B| \cdot |L| \cdot |D| \\
&= 4 \cdot 3 \cdot 5 \\
&= 60.
\end{aligned}
$$

15.2.2 Subsets of an *n*-element Set

The fact that there are 2^n subsets of an n-element set was proved in Theorem 4.5.5 by setting up a bijection between the subsets and the length-n bit-strings. So the original problem about subsets was tranformed into a question about sequences—*exactly according to plan*! Now we can fill in the missing explanation of why there are 2^n length-n bit-strings: we can write the set of all n-bit sequences as a product of sets:

$$\{0, 1\}^n ::= \underbrace{\{0, 1\} \times \{0, 1\} \times \cdots \times \{0, 1\}}_{n \text{ terms}}.$$

Then Product Rule gives the answer:

$$|\{0, 1\}^n| = |\{0, 1\}|^n = 2^n.$$

15.2.3   The Sum Rule

Bart allocates his little sister Lisa a quota of 20 crabby days, 40 irritable days, and 60 generally surly days. On how many days can Lisa be out-of-sorts one way or another? Let set C be her crabby days, I be her irritable days, and S be the generally surly. In these terms, the answer to the question is $|C \cup I \cup S|$. Now assuming that she is permitted at most one bad quality each day, the size of this union of sets is given by the *Sum Rule*:

Rule 15.2.2 (Sum Rule). *If $A_1, A_2, \ldots, A_n$ are disjoint sets, then:*

$$|A_1 \cup A_2 \cup \ldots \cup A_n| = |A_1| + |A_2| + \ldots + |A_n|$$

Thus, according to Bart's budget, Lisa can be out-of-sorts for:

$$\begin{aligned} |C \cup I \cup S| &= |C| + |I| + |S| \\ &= 20 + 40 + 60 \\ &= 120 \text{ days} \end{aligned}$$

Notice that the Sum Rule holds only for a union of *disjoint* sets. Finding the size of a union of overlapping sets is a more complicated problem that we'll take up in Section 15.9.

15.2.4   Counting Passwords

Few counting problems can be solved with a single rule. More often, a solution is a flurry of sums, products, bijections, and other methods.

For solving problems involving passwords, telephone numbers, and license plates, the sum and product rules are useful together. For example, on a certain computer system, a valid password is a sequence of between six and eight symbols. The first symbol must be a letter (which can be lowercase or uppercase), and the remaining symbols must be either letters or digits. How many different passwords are possible?

Let's define two sets, corresponding to valid symbols in the first and subsequent positions in the password.

$$\begin{aligned} F &= \{a, b, \ldots, z, A, B, \ldots, Z\} \\ S &= \{a, b, \ldots, z, A, B, \ldots, Z, 0, 1, \ldots, 9\} \end{aligned}$$

In these terms, the set of all possible passwords is:[1]

$$(F \times S^5) \cup (F \times S^6) \cup (F \times S^7)$$

---

[1] The notation S^5 means $S \times S \times S \times S \times S$.

Thus, the length-six passwords are in the set $F \times S^5$, the length-seven passwords are in $F \times S^6$, and the length-eight passwords are in $F \times S^7$. Since these sets are disjoint, we can apply the Sum Rule and count the total number of possible passwords as follows:

$$
\begin{aligned}
|(F \times S^5) &\cup (F \times S^6) \cup (F \times S^7)| \\
&= |F \times S^5| + |F \times S^6| + |F \times S^7| \qquad \text{Sum Rule} \\
&= |F| \cdot |S|^5 + |F| \cdot |S|^6 + |F| \cdot |S|^7 \qquad \text{Product Rule} \\
&= 52 \cdot 62^5 + 52 \cdot 62^6 + 52 \cdot 62^7 \\
&\approx 1.8 \cdot 10^{14} \text{ different passwords.}
\end{aligned}
$$

15.3 The Generalized Product Rule

In how many ways can, say, a Nobel prize, a Japan prize, and a Pulitzer prize be awarded to n people? This is easy to answer using our strategy of translating the problem about awards into a problem about sequences. Let P be the set of n people taking the course. Then there is a bijection from ways of awarding the three prizes to the set $P^3 ::= P \times P \times P$. In particular, the assignment:

"Barack wins a Nobel, George wins a Japan, and Bill wins a Pulitzer prize"

maps to the sequence (Barack, George, Bill). By the Product Rule, we have $|P^3| = |P|^3 = n^3$, so there are n^3 ways to award the prizes to a class of n people. Notice that P^3 includes triples like (Barack, Bill, Barack) where one person wins more than one prize.

But what if the three prizes must be awarded to *different* students? As before, we could map the assignment to the triple (Bill, George, Barack) $\in P^3$. But this function is *no longer a bijection*. For example, no valid assignment maps to the triple (Barack, Bill, Barack) because now we're not allowing Barack to receive two prizes. However, there *is* a bijection from prize assignments to the set:

$$
S = \{(x, y, z) \in P^3 \mid x, y \text{ and } z \text{ are different people}\}
$$

This reduces the original problem to a problem of counting sequences. Unfortunately, the Product Rule does not apply directly to counting sequences of this type because the entries depend on one another; in particular, they must all be different. However, a slightly sharper tool does the trick.

Prizes for *truly exceptional* Coursework

Given everyone's hard work on this material, the instructors considered awarding some prizes for truly exceptional coursework. Here are three possible prize categories:

Best Administrative Critique   We asserted that the quiz was closed-book. On the cover page, one strong candidate for this award wrote, "There is no book."

Awkward Question Award   "Okay, the left sock, right sock, and pants are in an antichain, but how—even with assistance—could I put on all three at once?"

Best Collaboration Statement   Inspired by a student who wrote "I worked alone" on Quiz 1.

Rule 15.3.1 (Generalized Product Rule). *Let S be a set of length-k sequences. If there are:*

- *n_1 possible first entries,*

- *n_2 possible second entries for each first entry,*
  $\vdots$

- *n_k possible kth entries for each sequence of first $k - 1$ entries,*

then:

$$|S| = n_1 \cdot n_2 \cdot n_3 \cdots n_k$$

In the awards example, S consists of sequences (x, y, z). There are n ways to choose x, the recipient of prize #1. For each of these, there are $n - 1$ ways to choose y, the recipient of prize #2, since everyone except for person x is eligible. For each combination of x and y, there are $n - 2$ ways to choose z, the recipient of prize #3, because everyone except for x and y is eligible. Thus, according to the Generalized Product Rule, there are

$$|S| = n \cdot (n - 1) \cdot (n - 2)$$

ways to award the 3 prizes to different people.

15.3.1 Defective Dollar Bills

A dollar bill is *defective* if some digit appears more than once in the 8-digit serial number. If you check your wallet, you'll be sad to discover that defective bills are all-too-common. In fact, how common are *nondefective* bills? Assuming that the digit portions of serial numbers all occur equally often, we could answer this question by computing

$$\text{fraction of nondefective bills} = \frac{|\{\text{serial \#'s with all digits different}\}|}{|\{\text{serial numbers}\}|}. \quad (15.1)$$

Let's first consider the denominator. Here there are no restrictions; there are 10 possible first digits, 10 possible second digits, 10 third digits, and so on. Thus, the total number of 8-digit serial numbers is 10^8 by the Product Rule.

Next, let's turn to the numerator. Now we're not permitted to use any digit twice. So there are still 10 possible first digits, but only 9 possible second digits, 8 possible third digits, and so forth. Thus, by the Generalized Product Rule, there are

$$10 \cdot 9 \cdot 8 \cdot 7 \cdot 6 \cdot 5 \cdot 4 \cdot 3 = \frac{10!}{2} = 1,814,400$$

serial numbers with all digits different. Plugging these results into Equation 15.1, we find:

$$\text{fraction of nondefective bills} = \frac{1,814,400}{100,000,000} = 1.8144\%$$

15.3.2 A Chess Problem

In how many different ways can we place a pawn (P), a knight (N), and a bishop (B) on a chessboard so that no two pieces share a row or a column? A valid configuration is shown in Figure 15.1(a), and an invalid configuration is shown in Figure 15.1(b).

First, we map this problem about chess pieces to a question about sequences. There is a bijection from configurations to sequences

$$(r_P, c_P, r_N, c_N, r_B, c_B)$$

where r_P, r_N and r_B are distinct rows and c_P, c_N and c_B are distinct columns. In particular, r_P is the pawn's row c_P is the pawn's column r_N is the knight's row, etc. Now we can count the number of such sequences using the Generalized Product Rule:

- r_P is one of 8 rows

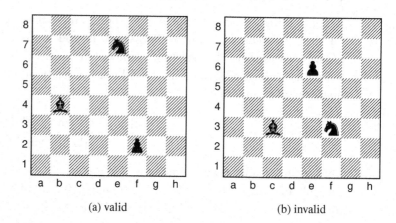

Figure 15.1   Two ways of placing a pawn ($\triangle$), a knight ($\knight$), and a bishop ($\bishop$) on a chessboard. The configuration shown in (b) is invalid because the bishop and the knight are in the same row.

- c_P is one of 8 columns
- r_N is one of 7 rows (any one but r_P)
- c_N is one of 7 columns (any one but c_P)
- r_B is one of 6 rows (any one but r_P or r_N)
- c_B is one of 6 columns (any one but c_P or c_N)

Thus, the total number of configurations is $(8 \cdot 7 \cdot 6)^2$.

15.3.3   Permutations

A *permutation* of a set S is a sequence that contains every element of S exactly once. For example, here are all the permutations of the set $\{a, b, c\}$:

$$(a, b, c) \quad (a, c, b) \quad (b, a, c)$$
$$(b, c, a) \quad (c, a, b) \quad (c, b, a)$$

How many permutations of an n-element set are there? Well, there are n choices for the first element. For each of these, there are $n - 1$ remaining choices for the second element. For every combination of the first two elements, there are $n - 2$ ways to choose the third element, and so forth. Thus, there are a total of

$$n \cdot (n - 1) \cdot (n - 2) \cdots 3 \cdot 2 \cdot 1 = n!$$

permutations of an n-element set. In particular, this formula says that there are

$3! = 6$ permutations of the 3-element set $\{a, b, c\}$, which is the number we found above.

Permutations will come up again in this course approximately 1.6 bazillion times. In fact, permutations are the reason why factorial comes up so often and why we taught you Stirling's approximation:

$$n! \sim \sqrt{2\pi n} \left(\frac{n}{e}\right)^n .$$

15.4 The Division Rule

Counting ears and dividing by two is a silly way to count the number of people in a room, but this approach is representative of a powerful counting principle.

A *k-to-1 function* maps exactly k elements of the domain to every element of the codomain. For example, the function mapping each ear to its owner is 2-to-1. Similarly, the function mapping each finger to its owner is 10-to-1, and the function mapping each finger and toe to its owner is 20-to-1. The general rule is:

Rule 15.4.1 (Division Rule). *If $f : A \to B$ is k-to-1, then $|A| = k \cdot |B|$.*

For example, suppose A is the set of ears in the room and B is the set of people. There is a 2-to-1 mapping from ears to people, so by the Division Rule, $|A| = 2 \cdot |B|$. Equivalently, $|B| = |A|/2$, expressing what we knew all along: the number of people is half the number of ears. Unlikely as it may seem, many counting problems are made much easier by initially counting every item multiple times and then correcting the answer using the Division Rule. Let's look at some examples.

15.4.1 Another Chess Problem

In how many different ways can you place two identical rooks on a chessboard so that they do not share a row or column? A valid configuration is shown in Figure 15.2(a), and an invalid configuration is shown in Figure 15.2(b).

Let A be the set of all sequences

$$(r_1, c_1, r_2, c_2)$$

where r_1 and r_2 are distinct rows and c_1 and c_2 are distinct columns. Let B be the set of all valid rook configurations. There is a natural function f from set A to set B; in particular, f maps the sequence (r_1, c_1, r_2, c_2) to a configuration with one rook in row r_1, column c_1 and the other rook in row r_2, column c_2.

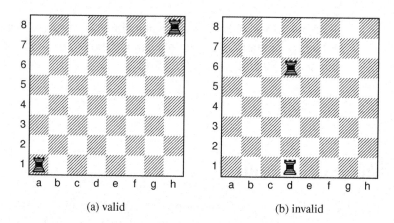

Figure 15.2   Two ways to place 2 rooks (♜) on a chessboard. The configuration in (b) is invalid because the rooks are in the same column.

But now there's a snag. Consider the sequences:

$$(1, a, 8, h) \qquad \text{and} \qquad (8, h, 1, a)$$

The first sequence maps to a configuration with a rook in the lower-left corner and a rook in the upper-right corner. The second sequence maps to a configuration with a rook in the upper-right corner and a rook in the lower-left corner. The problem is that those are two different ways of describing the *same* configuration! In fact, this arrangement is shown in Figure 15.2(a).

More generally, the function f maps exactly two sequences to *every* board configuration; f is a 2-to-1 function. Thus, by the quotient rule, $|A| = 2 \cdot |B|$. Rearranging terms gives:

$$|B| = \frac{|A|}{2} = \frac{(8 \cdot 7)^2}{2}.$$

On the second line, we've computed the size of A using the General Product Rule just as in the earlier chess problem.

15.4.2   Knights of the Round Table

In how many ways can King Arthur arrange to seat his n different knights at his round table? A seating defines who sits where. Two seatings are considered to be the same *arrangement* if each knight sits between the same two knights in both seatings. An equivalent way to say this is that two seatings yield the same arrangement when they yield the same sequence of knights starting at knight number 1 and going clockwise around the table. For example, the following two seatings determine the same arrangement:

A seating is determined by the sequence of knights going clockwise around the table starting at the top seat. So seatings correspond to permutations of the knights, and there are $n!$ of them. For example,

$$(k_2, k_4, k_1, k_3) \quad \longrightarrow \quad$$

Two seatings determine the same arrangement if they are the same when the table is rotated so knight 1 is at the top seat. For example with $n = 4$, there are 4 different sequences that correspond to the seating arrangement:

$$
\begin{aligned}
&(k_2, k_4, k_1, k_3)\\
&(k_4, k_1, k_3, k_2)\\
&(k_1, k_3, k_2, k_4)\\
&(k_3, k_2, k_4, k_1)
\end{aligned}
\quad \longrightarrow \quad
$$

This mapping from seating to arrangments is actually an n-to-1 function, since all n cyclic shifts of the sequence of knights in the seating map to the same arrangement. Therefore, by the division rule, the number of circular seating arrangements is:

$$\frac{\#\,\text{seatings}}{n} = \frac{n!}{n} = (n-1)!\,.$$

15.5   Counting Subsets

How many k-element subsets of an n-element set are there? This question arises all the time in various guises:

- In how many ways can I select 5 books from my collection of 100 to bring on vacation?

- How many different 13-card bridge hands can be dealt from a 52-card deck?

- In how many ways can I select 5 toppings for my pizza if there are 14 available toppings?

This number comes up so often that there is a special notation for it:

$$\binom{n}{k} ::= \text{ the number of } k\text{-element subsets of an } n\text{-element set.}$$

The expression $\binom{n}{k}$ is read "n choose k." Now we can immediately express the answers to all three questions above:

- I can select 5 books from 100 in $\binom{100}{5}$ ways.

- There are $\binom{52}{13}$ different bridge hands.

- There are $\binom{14}{5}$ different 5-topping pizzas, if 14 toppings are available.

15.5.1   The Subset Rule

We can derive a simple formula for the n choose k number using the Division Rule. We do this by mapping any permutation of an n-element set $\{a_1, \ldots, a_n\}$ into a k-element subset simply by taking the first k elements of the permutation. That is, the permutation $a_1 a_2 \ldots a_n$ will map to the set $\{a_1, a_2, \ldots, a_k\}$.

Notice that any other permutation with the same first k elements $a_1, \ldots, a_k$ *in any order* and the same remaining elements $n - k$ elements *in any order* will also map to this set. What's more, a permutation can only map to $\{a_1, a_2, \ldots, a_k\}$ if its first k elements are the elements $a_1, \ldots, a_k$ in some order. Since there are $k!$ possible permutations of the first k elements and $(n - k)!$ permutations of the remaining elements, we conclude from the Product Rule that exactly $k!(n - k)!$ permutations of the n-element set map to the particular subset S. In other words, the mapping from permutations to k-element subsets is $k!(n - k)!$-to-1.

But we know there are $n!$ permutations of an n-element set, so by the Division Rule, we conclude that

$$n! = k!(n-k)!\binom{n}{k}$$

which proves:

Rule 15.5.1 (Subset Rule). *The number of k-element subsets of an n-element set is*

$$\binom{n}{k} = \frac{n!}{k!\,(n-k)!}.$$

Notice that this works even for 0-element subsets: $n!/0!n! = 1$. Here we use the fact that $0!$ is a *product* of 0 terms, which by convention[2] equals 1.

15.5.2 Bit Sequences

How many n-bit sequences contain exactly k ones? We've already seen the straight-forward bijection between subsets of an n-element set and n-bit sequences. For example, here is a 3-element subset of $\{x_1, x_2, \ldots, x_8\}$ and the associated 8-bit sequence:

$$\begin{array}{ccccccccc} \{ & x_1, & & & x_4, & x_5 & & & \} \\ (& 1, & 0, & 0, & 1, & 1, & 0, & 0, & 0 \ ) \end{array}$$

Notice that this sequence has exactly 3 ones, each corresponding to an element of the 3-element subset. More generally, the n-bit sequences corresponding to a k-element subset will have exactly k ones. So by the Bijection Rule,

Corollary 15.5.2. *The number of n-bit sequences with exactly k ones is* $\binom{n}{k}$.

Also, the bijection between selections of flavored donuts and bit sequences of Lemma 15.1.1 now implies,

Corollary 15.5.3. *The number of ways to select n donuts when k flavors are available is*

$$\binom{n+(k-1)}{n}.$$

---

[2]We don't use it here, but a *sum* of zero terms equals 0.

15.6 Sequences with Repetitions

15.6.1 Sequences of Subsets

Choosing a k-element subset of an n-element set is the same as splitting the set into a pair of subsets: the first subset of size k and the second subset consisting of the remaining $n - k$ elements. So, the Subset Rule can be understood as a rule for counting the number of such splits into pairs of subsets.

We can generalize this to a way to count splits into more than two subsets. Let A be an n-element set and $k_1, k_2, \ldots, k_m$ be nonnegative integers whose sum is n. A $(k_1, k_2, \ldots, k_m)$-*split of* A is a sequence

$$(A_1, A_2, \ldots, A_m)$$

where the A_i are disjoint subsets of A and $|A_i| = k_i$ for $i = 1, \ldots, m$.

To count the number of splits we take the same approach as for the Subset Rule. Namely, we map any permutation $a_1 a_2 \ldots a_n$ of an n-element set A into a $(k_1, k_2, \ldots, k_m)$-split by letting the 1st subset in the split be the first k_1 elements of the permutation, the 2nd subset of the split be the next k_2 elements, $\ldots$, and the mth subset of the split be the final k_m elements of the permutation. This map is a $k_1! \, k_2! \, \cdots \, k_m!$-to-1 function from the $n!$ permutations to the $(k_1, k_2, \ldots, k_m)$-splits of A, so from the Division Rule we conclude the *Subset Split Rule*:

Definition 15.6.1. For $n, k_1, \ldots, k_m \in \mathbb{N}$, such that $k_1 + k_2 + \cdots + k_m = n$, define the *multinomial coefficient*

$$\binom{n}{k_1, k_2, \ldots, k_m} ::= \frac{n!}{k_1! \, k_2! \ldots k_m!}.$$

Rule 15.6.2 (Subset Split Rule). *The number of* $(k_1, k_2, \ldots, k_m)$-*splits of an n-element set is*

$$\binom{n}{k_1, \ldots, k_m}.$$

15.6.2 The Bookkeeper Rule

We can also generalize our count of n-bit sequences with k ones to counting sequences of n letters over an alphabet with more than two letters. For example, how many sequences can be formed by permuting the letters in the 10-letter word BOOKKEEPER?

Notice that there are 1 B, 2 O's, 2 K's, 3 E's, 1 P, and 1 R in BOOKKEEPER. This leads to a straightforward bijection between permutations of BOOKKEEPER and (1,2,2,3,1,1)-splits of $\{1, 2, \ldots, 10\}$. Namely, map a permutation to the sequence of sets of positions where each of the different letters occur.

For example, in the permutation BOOKKEEPER itself, the B is in the 1st position, the O's occur in the 2nd and 3rd positions, K's in 4th and 5th, the E's in the 6th, 7th and 9th, P in the 8th, and R is in the 10th position. So BOOKKEEPER maps to

$$(\{1\}, \{2, 3\}, \{4, 5\}, \{6, 7, 9\}, \{8\}, \{10\}).$$

From this bijection and the Subset Split Rule, we conclude that the number of ways to rearrange the letters in the word BOOKKEEPER is:

$$\frac{\overbrace{10!}^{\text{total letters}}}{\underbrace{1!}_{\text{B's}}\ \underbrace{2!}_{\text{O's}}\ \underbrace{2!}_{\text{K's}}\ \underbrace{3!}_{\text{E's}}\ \underbrace{1!}_{\text{P's}}\ \underbrace{1!}_{\text{R's}}}$$

This example generalizes directly to an exceptionally useful counting principle which we will call the

Rule 15.6.3 (Bookkeeper Rule). *Let $l_1, \ldots, l_m$ be distinct elements. The number of sequences with k_1 occurrences of l_1, and k_2 occurrences of l_2, ..., and k_m occurrences of l_m is*

$$\binom{k_1 + k_2 + \cdots + k_m}{k_1, \ldots, k_m}.$$

For example, suppose you are planning a 20-mile walk, which should include 5 northward miles, 5 eastward miles, 5 southward miles, and 5 westward miles. How many different walks are possible?

There is a bijection between such walks and sequences with 5 N's, 5 E's, 5 S's, and 5 W's. By the Bookkeeper Rule, the number of such sequences is:

$$\frac{20!}{(5!)^4}.$$

A Word about Words

Someday you might refer to the Subset Split Rule or the Bookkeeper Rule in front of a roomful of colleagues and discover that they're all staring back at you blankly. This is not because they're dumb, but rather because we made up the name "Bookkeeper Rule." However, the rule is excellent and the name is apt, so we suggest that you play through: "You know? The Bookkeeper Rule? Don't you guys know *anything?*"

The Bookkeeper Rule is sometimes called the "formula for permutations with indistinguishable objects." The size k subsets of an n-element set are sometimes called *k-combinations*. Other similar-sounding descriptions are "combinations with repetition, permutations with repetition, r-permutations, permutations with indistinguishable objects," and so on. However, the counting rules we've taught you are sufficient to solve all these sorts of problems without knowing this jargon, so we won't burden you with it.

15.6.3   The Binomial Theorem

Counting gives insight into one of the basic theorems of algebra. A *binomial* is a sum of two terms, such as $a + b$. Now consider its fourth power $(a + b)^4$.

By repeatedly using distributivity of products over sums to multiply out this 4th power expression completely, we get

$$
\begin{aligned}
(a + b)^4 = \quad & aaaa \; + \; aaab \; + \; aaba \; + \; aabb \\
+ \; & abaa \; + \; abab \; + \; abba \; + \; abbb \\
+ \; & baaa \; + \; baab \; + \; baba \; + \; babb \\
+ \; & bbaa \; + \; bbab \; + \; bbba \; + \; bbbb
\end{aligned}
$$

Notice that there is one term for every sequence of a's and b's. So there are 2^4 terms, and the number of terms with k copies of b and $n - k$ copies of a is:

$$
\frac{n!}{k! \, (n - k)!} = \binom{n}{k}
$$

by the Bookkeeper Rule. Hence, the coefficient of $a^{n-k}b^k$ is $\binom{n}{k}$. So for $n = 4$, this means:

$$
(a + b)^4 = \binom{4}{0} \cdot a^4 b^0 + \binom{4}{1} \cdot a^3 b^1 + \binom{4}{2} \cdot a^2 b^2 + \binom{4}{3} \cdot a^1 b^3 + \binom{4}{4} \cdot a^0 b^4
$$

In general, this reasoning gives the Binomial Theorem:

Theorem 15.6.4 (*Binomial Theorem*). *For all $n \in \mathbb{N}$ and $a, b \in \mathbb{R}$:*

$$
(a + b)^n = \sum_{k=0}^{n} \binom{n}{k} a^{n-k} b^k
$$

The Binomial Theorem explains why the n choose k number is called a *binomial coefficient*.

This reasoning about binomials extends nicely to *multinomials*, which are sums of two or more terms. For example, suppose we wanted the coefficient of

$$bo^2k^2e^3pr$$

in the expansion of $(b + o + k + e + p + r)^{10}$. Each term in this expansion is a product of 10 variables where each variable is one of b, o, k, e, p or r. Now, the coefficient of $bo^2k^2e^3pr$ is the number of those terms with exactly 1 b, 2 o's, 2 k's, 3 e's, 1 p and 1 r. And the number of such terms is precisely the number of rearrangements of the word BOOKKEEPER:

$$\binom{10}{1, 2, 2, 3, 1, 1} = \frac{10!}{1!\, 2!\, 2!\, 3!\, 1!\, 1!}.$$

This reasoning extends to a general theorem:

Theorem 15.6.5 (Multinomial Theorem). *For all $n \in \mathbb{N}$,*

$$(z_1 + z_2 + \cdots + z_m)^n = \sum_{\substack{k_1, \ldots, k_m \in \mathbb{N} \\ k_1 + \cdots + k_m = n}} \binom{n}{k_1, k_2, \ldots, k_m} z_1^{k_1} z_2^{k_2} \cdots z_m^{k_m}.$$

But you'll be better off remembering the reasoning behind the Multinomial Theorem rather than this cumbersome formal statement.

15.7 Counting Practice: Poker Hands

Five-Card Draw is a card game in which each player is initially dealt a *hand* consisting of 5 cards from a deck of 52 cards.[3] The number of different hands in

---

[3]There are 52 cards in a standard deck. Each card has a *suit* and a *rank*. There are four suits:

♠ (spades)   ♡ (hearts)   ♣ (clubs)   ♢ (diamonds)

And there are 13 ranks, listed here from lowest to highest:

$$\overset{\text{Ace}}{A}, 2, 3, 4, 5, 6, 7, 8, 9, \overset{\text{Jack}}{J}, \overset{\text{Queen}}{Q}, \overset{\text{King}}{K}.$$

Thus, for example, $8\heartsuit$ is the 8 of hearts and $A\spadesuit$ is the ace of spades.

Five-Card Draw is the number of 5-element subsets of a 52-element set, which is

$$\binom{52}{5} = 2,598,960.$$

Let's get some counting practice by working out the number of hands with various special properties.

15.7.1   Hands with a Four-of-a-Kind

A *Four-of-a-Kind* is a set of four cards with the same rank. How many different hands contain a Four-of-a-Kind? Here are a couple examples:

$$\{8\spadesuit,\ 8\diamondsuit,\ Q\heartsuit,\ 8\heartsuit,\ 8\clubsuit\}$$
$$\{A\clubsuit,\ 2\clubsuit,\ 2\heartsuit,\ 2\diamondsuit,\ 2\spadesuit\}$$

As usual, the first step is to map this question to a sequence-counting problem. A hand with a Four-of-a-Kind is completely described by a sequence specifying:

1. The rank of the four cards.

2. The rank of the extra card.

3. The suit of the extra card.

Thus, there is a bijection between hands with a Four-of-a-Kind and sequences consisting of two distinct ranks followed by a suit. For example, the three hands above are associated with the following sequences:

$$(8, Q, \heartsuit) \leftrightarrow \{\,8\spadesuit,\ 8\diamondsuit,\ 8\heartsuit,\ 8\clubsuit,\ Q\heartsuit\}$$
$$(2, A, \clubsuit) \leftrightarrow \{2\clubsuit,\ 2\heartsuit,\ 2\diamondsuit,\ 2\spadesuit,\ A\clubsuit\}$$

Now we need only count the sequences. There are 13 ways to choose the first rank, 12 ways to choose the second rank, and 4 ways to choose the suit. Thus, by the Generalized Product Rule, there are $13 \cdot 12 \cdot 4 = 624$ hands with a Four-of-a-Kind. This means that only 1 hand in about 4165 has a Four-of-a-Kind. Not surprisingly, Four-of-a-Kind is considered to be a very good poker hand!

15.7.2 Hands with a Full House

A *Full House* is a hand with three cards of one rank and two cards of another rank. Here are some examples:

$$\{2\spadesuit, 2\clubsuit, 2\diamondsuit, J\clubsuit, J\diamondsuit\}$$
$$\{5\diamondsuit, 5\clubsuit, 5\heartsuit, 7\heartsuit, 7\clubsuit\}$$

Again, we shift to a problem about sequences. There is a bijection between Full Houses and sequences specifying:

1. The rank of the triple, which can be chosen in 13 ways.

2. The suits of the triple, which can be selected in $\binom{4}{3}$ ways.

3. The rank of the pair, which can be chosen in 12 ways.

4. The suits of the pair, which can be selected in $\binom{4}{2}$ ways.

The example hands correspond to sequences as shown below:

$$(2, \{\spadesuit, \clubsuit, \diamondsuit\}, J, \{\clubsuit, \diamondsuit\}) \leftrightarrow \{2\spadesuit, 2\clubsuit, 2\diamondsuit, J\clubsuit, J\diamondsuit\}$$
$$(5, \{\diamondsuit, \clubsuit, \heartsuit\}, 7, \{\heartsuit, \clubsuit\}) \leftrightarrow \{5\diamondsuit, 5\clubsuit, 5\heartsuit, 7\heartsuit, 7\clubsuit\}$$

By the Generalized Product Rule, the number of Full Houses is:

$$13 \cdot \binom{4}{3} \cdot 12 \cdot \binom{4}{2}.$$

We're on a roll—but we're about to hit a speed bump.

15.7.3 Hands with Two Pairs

How many hands have *Two Pairs*; that is, two cards of one rank, two cards of another rank, and one card of a third rank? Here are examples:

$$\{3\diamondsuit, 3\spadesuit, Q\diamondsuit, Q\heartsuit, A\clubsuit\}$$
$$\{9\heartsuit, 9\diamondsuit, 5\heartsuit, 5\clubsuit, K\spadesuit\}$$

Each hand with Two Pairs is described by a sequence consisting of:

1. The rank of the first pair, which can be chosen in 13 ways.

2. The suits of the first pair, which can be selected $\binom{4}{2}$ ways.

3. The rank of the second pair, which can be chosen in 12 ways.

4. The suits of the second pair, which can be selected in $\binom{4}{2}$ ways.

5. The rank of the extra card, which can be chosen in 11 ways.

6. The suit of the extra card, which can be selected in $\binom{4}{1} = 4$ ways.

Thus, it might appear that the number of hands with Two Pairs is:

$$13 \cdot \binom{4}{2} \cdot 12 \cdot \binom{4}{2} \cdot 11 \cdot 4.$$

Wrong answer! The problem is that there is *not* a bijection from such sequences to hands with Two Pairs. This is actually a 2-to-1 mapping. For example, here are the pairs of sequences that map to the hands given above:

$$(3, \{\diamondsuit, \spadesuit\}, Q, \{\diamondsuit, \heartsuit\}, A, \clubsuit) \searrow$$
$$ \{3\diamondsuit, 3\spadesuit, Q\diamondsuit, Q\heartsuit, A\clubsuit\}$$
$$(Q, \{\diamondsuit, \heartsuit\}, 3, \{\diamondsuit, \spadesuit\}, A, \clubsuit) \nearrow$$

$$(9, \{\heartsuit, \diamondsuit\}, 5, \{\heartsuit, \clubsuit\}, K, \spadesuit) \searrow$$
$$ \{9\heartsuit, 9\diamondsuit, 5\heartsuit, 5\clubsuit, K\spadesuit\}$$
$$(5, \{\heartsuit, \clubsuit\}, 9, \{\heartsuit, \diamondsuit\}, K, \spadesuit) \nearrow$$

The problem is that nothing distinguishes the first pair from the second. A pair of 5's and a pair of 9's is the same as a pair of 9's and a pair of 5's. We avoided this difficulty in counting Full Houses because, for example, a pair of 6's and a triple of kings is different from a pair of kings and a triple of 6's.

We ran into precisely this difficulty last time, when we went from counting arrangements of *different* pieces on a chessboard to counting arrangements of two *identical* rooks. The solution then was to apply the Division Rule, and we can do the same here. In this case, the Division rule says there are twice as many sequences as hands, so the number of hands with Two Pairs is actually:

$$\frac{13 \cdot \binom{4}{2} \cdot 12 \cdot \binom{4}{2} \cdot 11 \cdot 4}{2}.$$

Another Approach

The preceding example was disturbing! One could easily overlook the fact that the mapping was 2-to-1 on an exam, fail the course, and turn to a life of crime. You can make the world a safer place in two ways:

1. Whenever you use a mapping $f : A \to B$ to translate one counting problem to another, check that the same number of elements in A are mapped to each element in B. If k elements of A map to each of element of B, then apply the Division Rule using the constant k.

2. As an extra check, try solving the same problem in a different way. Multiple approaches are often available—and all had better give the same answer! (Sometimes different approaches give answers that *look* different, but turn out to be the same after some algebra.)

We already used the first method; let's try the second. There is a bijection between hands with two pairs and sequences that specify:

1. The ranks of the two pairs, which can be chosen in $\binom{13}{2}$ ways.

2. The suits of the lower-rank pair, which can be selected in $\binom{4}{2}$ ways.

3. The suits of the higher-rank pair, which can be selected in $\binom{4}{2}$ ways.

4. The rank of the extra card, which can be chosen in 11 ways.

5. The suit of the extra card, which can be selected in $\binom{4}{1} = 4$ ways.

For example, the following sequences and hands correspond:

$$(\{3, Q\}, \{\diamondsuit, \spadesuit\}, \{\diamondsuit, \heartsuit\}, A, \clubsuit) \leftrightarrow \{3\diamondsuit, 3\spadesuit, Q\diamondsuit, Q\heartsuit, A\clubsuit\}$$
$$(\{9, 5\}, \{\heartsuit, \clubsuit\}, \{\heartsuit, \diamondsuit\}, K, \spadesuit) \leftrightarrow \{9\heartsuit, 9\diamondsuit, 5\heartsuit, 5\clubsuit, K\spadesuit\}$$

Thus, the number of hands with two pairs is:

$$\binom{13}{2} \cdot \binom{4}{2} \cdot \binom{4}{2} \cdot 11 \cdot 4.$$

This is the same answer we got before, though in a slightly different form.

15.7.4 Hands with Every Suit

How many hands contain at least one card from every suit? Here is an example of such a hand:

$$\{7\diamondsuit, K\clubsuit, 3\diamondsuit, A\heartsuit, 2\spadesuit\}$$

Each such hand is described by a sequence that specifies:

1. The ranks of the diamond, the club, the heart, and the spade, which can be selected in $13 \cdot 13 \cdot 13 \cdot 13 = 13^4$ ways.

2. The suit of the extra card, which can be selected in 4 ways.

3. The rank of the extra card, which can be selected in 12 ways.

For example, the hand above is described by the sequence:

$$(7, K, A, 2, \diamondsuit, 3) \leftrightarrow \{7\diamondsuit, K\clubsuit, A\heartsuit, 2\spadesuit, 3\diamondsuit\}.$$

Are there other sequences that correspond to the same hand? There is one more! We could equally well regard either the $3\diamondsuit$ or the $7\diamondsuit$ as the extra card, so this is actually a 2-to-1 mapping. Here are the two sequences corresponding to the example hand:

$$(7, K, A, 2, \diamondsuit, 3) \searrow$$
$$\{7\diamondsuit, K\clubsuit, A\heartsuit, 2\spadesuit, 3\diamondsuit\}$$
$$(3, K, A, 2, \diamondsuit, 7) \nearrow$$

Therefore, the number of hands with every suit is:

$$\frac{13^4 \cdot 4 \cdot 12}{2}.$$

15.8   The Pigeonhole Principle

Here is an old puzzle:

A drawer in a dark room contains red socks, green socks, and blue socks. How many socks must you withdraw to be sure that you have a matching pair?

For example, picking out three socks is not enough; you might end up with one red, one green, and one blue. The solution relies on the

---

Pigeonhole Principle

If there are more pigeons than holes they occupy, then at least two pigeons must be in the same hole.

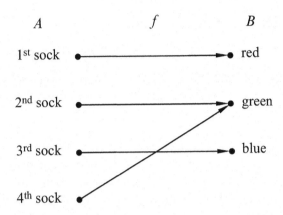

Figure 15.3 One possible mapping of four socks to three colors.

What pigeons have to do with selecting footwear under poor lighting conditions may not be immediately obvious, but if we let socks be pigeons and the colors be three pigeonholes, then as soon as you pick four socks, there are bound to be two in the same hole, that is, with the same color. So four socks are enough to ensure a matched pair. For example, one possible mapping of four socks to three colors is shown in Figure 15.3.

A rigorous statement of the Principle goes this way:

Rule 15.8.1 (Pigeonhole Principle). *If* $|A| > |B|$*, then for every total function* $f : A \rightarrow B$*, there exist two different elements of A that are mapped by f to the same element of B.*

Stating the Principle this way may be less intuitive, but it should now sound familiar: it is simply the contrapositive of the Mapping Rules injective case (4.6). Here, the pigeons form set A, the pigeonholes are the set B, and f describes which hole each pigeon occupies.

Mathematicians have come up with many ingenious applications for the pigeonhole principle. If there were a cookbook procedure for generating such arguments, we'd give it to you. Unfortunately, there isn't one. One helpful tip, though: when you try to solve a problem with the pigeonhole principle, the key is to clearly identify three things:

1. The set A (the pigeons).

2. The set B (the pigeonholes).

3. The function f (the rule for assigning pigeons to pigeonholes).

15.8.1   Hairs on Heads

There are a number of generalizations of the pigeonhole principle. For example:

Rule 15.8.2 (Generalized Pigeonhole Principle). *If* $|A| > k \cdot |B|$*, then every total function* $f : A \to B$ *maps at least* $k+1$ *different elements of* A *to the same element of* B*.*

For example, if you pick two people at random, surely they are extremely unlikely to have *exactly* the same number of hairs on their heads. However, in the remarkable city of Boston, Massachusetts, there is a group of *three* people who have exactly the same number of hairs! Of course, there are many completely bald people in Boston, and they all have zero hairs. But we're talking about non-bald people; say a person is non-bald if they have at least ten thousand hairs on their head.

Boston has about 500,000 non-bald people, and the number of hairs on a person's head is at most 200,000. Let A be the set of non-bald people in Boston, let $B = \{10,000, 10,001, \ldots, 200,000\}$, and let f map a person to the number of hairs on his or her head. Since $|A| > 2|B|$, the Generalized Pigeonhole Principle implies that at least three people have exactly the same number of hairs. We don't know who they are, but we know they exist!

15.8.2   Subsets with the Same Sum

For your reading pleasure, we have displayed ninety 25-digit numbers in Figure 15.4. Are there two different subsets of these 25-digit numbers that have the same sum? For example, maybe the sum of the last ten numbers in the first column is equal to the sum of the first eleven numbers in the second column?

Finding two subsets with the same sum may seem like a silly puzzle, but solving these sorts of problems turns out to be useful in diverse applications such as finding good ways to fit packages into shipping containers and decoding secret messages.

It turns out that it is hard to find different subsets with the same sum, which is why this problem arises in cryptography. But it is easy to prove that two such subsets *exist*. That's where the Pigeonhole Principle comes in.

Let A be the collection of all subsets of the 90 numbers in the list. Now the sum of any subset of numbers is at most $90 \cdot 10^{25}$, since there are only 90 numbers and every 25-digit number is less than 10^{25}. So let B be the set of integers $\{0, 1, \ldots, 90 \cdot 10^{25}\}$, and let f map each subset of numbers (in A) to its sum (in B).

We proved that an n-element set has 2^n different subsets in Section 15.2. Therefore:

$$|A| = 2^{90} \geq 1.237 \times 10^{27}$$

0020480135385502964448038	3171004832173501394113017
5763257331083479647409398	8247331000042995311646021
0489445991866915676240992	3208234421597368647019265
5800949123548989122628663	8496243997123475922766310
1082662032430379651370981	3437254656355157864869113
6042900801199280218026001	8518399140676002660747477
1178480894769706178994993	3574883393058653923711365
6116171789137737896701405	8543691283470191452333763
1253127351683239693851327	3644909946040480189969149
6144868973001582369723512	8675309258374137092461352
1301505129234077811069011	3790044132737084094417246
6247314593851169234746152	8694321112363996867296665
1311567111143866433882194	3870332127437971355322815
6814428944266874963488274	8772321203608477245851154
1470029452721203587686214	4080505804577801451363100
6870852945543886849147881	8791422161722582546341091
1578271047286257499433886	4167283461025702348124920
6914955508120950093732397	9062628024592126283973285
1638243921852176243192354	4235996831123777788211249
6949632451365987152423541	9137845566925526349897794
1763580219131985963102365	4670939445749439042111220
7128211143613619828415650	9153762966803189291934419
1826227795601842231029694	4815379351865384279613427
7173920083651862307925394	9270880194077636406984249
1843971862675102037201420	4837052948212922604442190
7215654874211755676220587	9324301480722103490379204
2396951193722134526177237	5106389423855018550671530
7256932847164391040233050	9436090832146695147140581
2781394568268599801096354	5142368192004769218069910
7332822657075235431620317	9475308159734538249013238
2796605196713610405408019	5181234096130144084041856
7426441829541573444964139	9492376623917486974923202
2931016394761975263190347	5198267398125617994391348
7632198126531809327186321	9511972558779880288252979
2933458058294405155197296	5317592940316231219758372
7712154432211912882310511	9602413424619187112552264
3075514410490975920315348	5384358126771794128356947
7858918664240262356610010	9631217114906129219461111
8149436716871371161932035	3157693105325111284321993
3111474985252793452860017	5439211712248901995423441
7898156786763212963178679	9908189853102753335981319
3145621587936120118438701	5610379826092838192760458
8147591017037573337848616	9913237476341764299813987
3148901255628881103198549	5632317555465228677676044
5692168374637019617423712	8176063831682536571306791

Figure 15.4   Ninety 25-digit numbers. Can you find two different subsets of these numbers that have the same sum?

On the other hand:

$$|B| = 90 \cdot 10^{25} + 1 \le 0.901 \times 10^{27}.$$

Both quantities are enormous, but $|A|$ is a bit greater than $|B|$. This means that f maps at least two elements of A to the same element of B. In other words, by the Pigeonhole Principle, two different subsets must have the same sum!

Notice that this proof gives no indication *which* two sets of numbers have the same sum. This frustrating variety of argument is called a *nonconstructive proof*.

The $100 prize for two same-sum subsets

To see if it was possible to actually *find* two different subsets of the ninety 25-digit numbers with the same sum, we offered a $100 prize to the first student who did it. We didn't expect to have to pay off this bet, but we underestimated the ingenuity and initiative of the students. One computer science major wrote a program that cleverly searched only among a reasonably small set of "plausible" sets, sorted them by their sums, and actually found a couple with the same sum. He won the prize. A few days later, a math major figured out how to reformulate the sum problem as a "lattice basis reduction" problem; then he found a software package implementing an efficient basis reduction procedure, and using it, he very quickly found lots of pairs of subsets with the same sum. He didn't win the prize, but he got a standing ovation from the class—staff included.

The $500 Prize for Sets with Distinct Subset Sums

How can we construct a set of n positive integers such that all its subsets have *distinct* sums? One way is to use powers of two:

$$\{1, 2, 4, 8, 16\}$$

This approach is so natural that one suspects all other such sets must involve larger numbers. (For example, we could safely replace 16 by 17, but not by 15.) Remarkably, there are examples involving *smaller* numbers. Here is one:

$$\{6, 9, 11, 12, 13\}$$

One of the top mathematicians of the Twentieth Century, Paul Erdős, conjectured in 1931 that there are no such sets involving *significantly* smaller numbers. More precisely, he conjectured that the largest number in such a set must be greater than $c2^n$ for some constant $c > 0$. He offered $500 to anyone who could prove or disprove his conjecture, but the problem remains unsolved.

15.8.3 A Magic Trick

A Magician sends an Assistant into the audience with a deck of 52 cards while the Magician looks away.

Five audience members each select one card from the deck. The Assistant then gathers up the five cards and holds up four of them so the Magician can see them. The Magician concentrates for a short time and then correctly names the secret, fifth card!

Since we don't really believe the Magician can read minds, we know the Assistant has somehow communicated the secret card to the Magician. Real Magicians and Assistants are not to be trusted, so we expect that the Assistant would secretly signal the Magician with coded phrases or body language, but for this trick they don't have to cheat. In fact, the Magician and Assistant could be kept out of sight of each other while some audience member holds up the 4 cards designated by the Assistant for the Magician to see.

Of course, without cheating, there is still an obvious way the Assistant can communicate to the Magician: he can choose any of the $4! = 24$ permutations of the 4 cards as the order in which to hold up the cards. However, this alone won't quite work: there are 48 cards remaining in the deck, so the Assistant doesn't have enough choices of orders to indicate exactly what the secret card is (though he could narrow it down to two cards).

15.8.4 The Secret

The method the Assistant can use to communicate the fifth card exactly is a nice application of what we know about counting and matching.

The Assistant has a second legitimate way to communicate: he can choose *which of the five cards to keep hidden*. Of course, it's not clear how the Magician could determine which of these five possibilities the Assistant selected by looking at the four visible cards, but there is a way, as we'll now explain.

The problem facing the Magician and Assistant is actually a bipartite matching problem. Each vertex on the left will correspond to the information available to the Assistant, namely, a *set* of 5 cards. So the set X of left-hand vertices will have $\binom{52}{5}$ elements.

Each vertex on the right will correspond to the information available to the Magician, namely, a *sequence* of 4 distinct cards. So the set Y of right-hand vertices will have $52 \cdot 51 \cdot 50 \cdot 49$ elements. When the audience selects a set of 5 cards, then the Assistant must reveal a sequence of 4 cards from that hand. This constraint is represented by having an edge between a set of 5 cards on the left and a sequence of 4 cards on the right precisely when every card in the sequence is also in the set. This specifies the bipartite graph. Some edges are shown in the diagram in

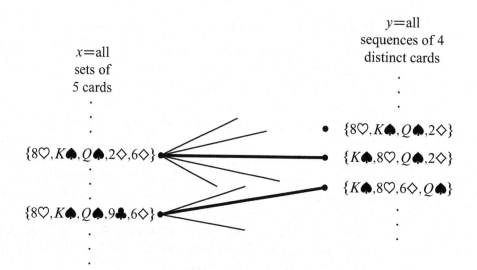

Figure 15.5 The bipartite graph where the nodes on the left correspond to *sets* of 5 cards and the nodes on the right correspond to *sequences* of 4 cards. There is an edge between a set and a sequence whenever all the cards in the sequence are contained in the set.

Figure 15.5.

For example,

$$\{8\heartsuit, K\spadesuit, Q\spadesuit, 2\diamondsuit, 6\diamondsuit\} \tag{15.2}$$

is an element of X on the left. If the audience selects this set of 5 cards, then there are many different 4-card sequences on the right in set Y that the Assistant could choose to reveal, including $(8\heartsuit, K\spadesuit, Q\spadesuit, 2\diamondsuit)$, $(K\spadesuit, 8\heartsuit, Q\spadesuit, 2\diamondsuit)$ and $(K\spadesuit, 8\heartsuit, 6\diamondsuit, Q\spadesuit)$.

What the Magician and his Assistant need to perform the trick is a *matching* for the X vertices. If they agree in advance on some matching, then when the audience selects a set of 5 cards, the Assistant reveals the matching sequence of 4 cards. The Magician uses the matching to find the audience's chosen set of 5 cards, and so he can name the one not already revealed.

For example, suppose the Assistant and Magician agree on a matching containing the two bold edges in Figure 15.5. If the audience selects the set

$$\{8\heartsuit, K\spadesuit, Q\spadesuit, 9\clubsuit, 6\diamondsuit\}, \tag{15.3}$$

then the Assistant reveals the corresponding sequence

$$(K\spadesuit, 8\heartsuit, 6\diamondsuit, Q\spadesuit). \tag{15.4}$$

Using the matching, the Magician sees that the hand (15.3) is matched to the sequence (15.4), so he can name the one card in the corresponding set not already revealed, namely, the 9♣. Notice that the fact that the sets are *matched*, that is, that different sets are paired with *distinct* sequences, is essential. For example, if the audience picked the previous hand (15.2), it would be possible for the Assistant to reveal the same sequence (15.4), but he better not do that; if he did, then the Magician would have no way to tell if the remaining card was the 9♣ or the 2◇.

So how can we be sure the needed matching can be found? The answer is that each vertex on the left has degree $5 \cdot 4! = 120$, since there are five ways to select the card kept secret and there are 4! permutations of the remaining 4 cards. In addition, each vertex on the right has degree 48, since there are 48 possibilities for the fifth card. So this graph is *degree-constrained* according to Definition 12.5.5, and so has a matching by Theorem 12.5.6.

In fact, this reasoning shows that the Magician could still pull off the trick if 120 cards were left instead of 48, that is, the trick would work with a deck as large as 124 different cards—without any magic!

15.8.5 The Real Secret

But wait a minute! It's all very well in principle to have the Magician and his Assistant agree on a matching, but how are they supposed to remember a matching with $\binom{52}{5} = 2,598,960$ edges? For the trick to work in practice, there has to be a way to match hands and card sequences mentally and on the fly.

We'll describe one approach. As a running example, suppose that the audience selects:

$$10\heartsuit \quad 9\diamondsuit \quad 3\heartsuit \quad Q\spadesuit \quad J\diamondsuit.$$

- The Assistant picks out two cards of the same suit. In the example, the assistant might choose the 3♡ and 10♡. This is always possible because of the Pigeonhole Principle—there are five cards and 4 suits so two cards must be in the same suit.

- The Assistant locates the ranks of these two cards on the cycle shown in Figure 15.6. For any two distinct ranks on this cycle, one is always between 1 and 6 hops clockwise from the other. For example, the 3♡ is 6 hops clockwise from the 10♡.

- The more counterclockwise of these two cards is revealed first, and the other becomes the secret card. Thus, in our example, the 10♡ would be revealed, and the 3♡ would be the secret card. Therefore:

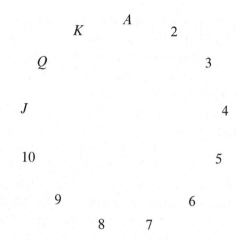

Figure 15.6   The 13 card ranks arranged in cyclic order.

- The suit of the secret card is the same as the suit of the first card revealed.

- The rank of the secret card is between 1 and 6 hops clockwise from the rank of the first card revealed.

• All that remains is to communicate a number between 1 and 6. The Magician and Assistant agree beforehand on an ordering of all the cards in the deck from smallest to largest such as:

$$A\clubsuit \ A\diamondsuit \ A\heartsuit \ A\spadesuit \ 2\clubsuit \ 2\diamondsuit \ 2\heartsuit \ 2\spadesuit \ \ldots \ K\heartsuit \ K\spadesuit$$

The order in which the last three cards are revealed communicates the number according to the following scheme:

(small,	medium,	large)	= 1
(small,	large,	medium)	= 2
(medium,	small,	large)	= 3
(medium,	large,	small)	= 4
(large,	small,	medium)	= 5
(large,	medium,	small)	= 6

In the example, the Assistant wants to send 6 and so reveals the remaining three cards in large, medium, small order. Here is the complete sequence that the Magician sees:

$$10\heartsuit \quad Q\spadesuit \quad J\diamondsuit \quad 9\diamondsuit$$

- The Magician starts with the first card $10\heartsuit$ and hops 6 ranks clockwise to reach $3\heartsuit$, which is the secret card!

So that's how the trick can work with a standard deck of 52 cards. On the other hand, Hall's Theorem implies that the Magician and Assistant can *in principle* perform the trick with a deck of up to 124 cards. It turns out that there is a method which they could actually learn to use with a reasonable amount of practice for a 124-card deck, but we won't explain it here.[4]

15.8.6 The Same Trick with Four Cards?

Suppose that the audience selects only *four* cards and the Assistant reveals a sequence of *three* to the Magician. Can the Magician determine the fourth card?

Let X be all the sets of four cards that the audience might select, and let Y be all the sequences of three cards that the Assistant might reveal. Now, on one hand, we have

$$|X| = \binom{52}{4} = 270,725$$

by the Subset Rule. On the other hand, we have

$$|Y| = 52 \cdot 51 \cdot 50 = 132,600$$

by the Generalized Product Rule. Thus, by the Pigeonhole Principle, the Assistant must reveal the *same* sequence of three cards for at least

$$\left\lceil \frac{270,725}{132,600} \right\rceil = 3$$

different four-card hands. This is bad news for the Magician: if he sees that sequence of three, then there are at least three possibilities for the fourth card which he cannot distinguish. So there is no legitimate way for the Assistant to communicate exactly what the fourth card is!

15.9 Inclusion-Exclusion

How big is a union of sets? For example, suppose there are 60 math majors, 200 EECS majors, and 40 physics majors. How many students are there in these three

---

[4]See *The Best Card Trick* by Michael Kleber for more information.

departments? Let M be the set of math majors, E be the set of EECS majors, and P be the set of physics majors. In these terms, we're asking for $|M \cup E \cup P|$.

The Sum Rule says that if M, E and P are disjoint, then the sum of their sizes is

$$|M \cup E \cup P| = |M| + |E| + |P|.$$

However, the sets M, E and P might *not* be disjoint. For example, there might be a student majoring in both math and physics. Such a student would be counted twice on the right side of this equation, once as an element of M and once as an element of P. Worse, there might be a triple-major[5] counted *three* times on the right side!

Our most-complicated counting rule determines the size of a union of sets that are not necessarily disjoint. Before we state the rule, let's build some intuition by considering some easier special cases: unions of just two or three sets.

15.9.1   Union of Two Sets

For two sets, S_1 and S_2, the *Inclusion-Exclusion Rule* is that the size of their union is:

$$|S_1 \cup S_2| = |S_1| + |S_2| - |S_1 \cap S_2| \tag{15.5}$$

Intuitively, each element of S_1 is accounted for in the first term, and each element of S_2 is accounted for in the second term. Elements in *both* S_1 and S_2 are counted *twice*—once in the first term and once in the second. This double-counting is corrected by the final term.

15.9.2   Union of Three Sets

So how many students are there in the math, EECS, and physics departments? In other words, what is $|M \cup E \cup P|$ if:

$$|M| = 60$$
$$|E| = 200$$
$$|P| = 40.$$

The size of a union of three sets is given by a more complicated Inclusion-Exclusion formula:

$$\begin{aligned}
|S_1 \cup S_2 \cup S_3| = {} & |S_1| + |S_2| + |S_3| \\
& - |S_1 \cap S_2| - |S_1 \cap S_3| - |S_2 \cap S_3| \\
& + |S_1 \cap S_2 \cap S_3|.
\end{aligned}$$

---

[5]...though not at MIT anymore.

Remarkably, the expression on the right accounts for each element in the union of S_1, S_2 and S_3 exactly once. For example, suppose that x is an element of all three sets. Then x is counted three times (by the $|S_1|$, $|S_2|$ and $|S_3|$ terms), subtracted off three times (by the $|S_1 \cap S_2|$, $|S_1 \cap S_3|$ and $|S_2 \cap S_3|$ terms), and then counted once more (by the $|S_1 \cap S_2 \cap S_3|$ term). The net effect is that x is counted just once.

If x is in two sets (say, S_1 and S_2), then x is counted twice (by the $|S_1|$ and $|S_2|$ terms) and subtracted once (by the $|S_1 \cap S_2|$ term). In this case, x does not contribute to any of the other terms, since $x \notin S_3$.

So we can't answer the original question without knowing the sizes of the various intersections. Let's suppose that there are:

4	math - EECS double majors
3	math - physics double majors
11	EECS - physics double majors
2	triple majors

Then $|M \cap E| = 4+2$, $|M \cap P| = 3+2$, $|E \cap P| = 11+2$, and $|M \cap E \cap P| = 2$. Plugging all this into the formula gives:

$$\begin{aligned} |M \cup E \cup P| &= |M| + |E| + |P| - |M \cap E| - |M \cap P| - |E \cap P| \\ &\quad + |M \cap E \cap P| \\ &= 60 + 200 + 40 - 6 - 5 - 13 + 2 \\ &= 278 \end{aligned}$$

15.9.3 Sequences with 42, 04, or 60

In how many permutations of the set $\{0, 1, 2, \ldots, 9\}$ do either 4 and 2, 0 and 4, or 6 and 0 appear consecutively? For example, none of these pairs appears in:

$$(7, 2, 9, 5, 4, 1, 3, 8, 0, 6).$$

The 06 at the end doesn't count; we need 60. On the other hand, both 04 and 60 appear consecutively in this permutation:

$$(7, 2, 5, \underline{6}, \underline{0}, \underline{4}, 3, 8, 1, 9).$$

Let P_{42} be the set of all permutations in which 42 appears. Define P_{60} and P_{04} similarly. Thus, for example, the permutation above is contained in both P_{60} and P_{04}, but not P_{42}. In these terms, we're looking for the size of the set $P_{42} \cup P_{04} \cup P_{60}$.

First, we must determine the sizes of the individual sets, such as P_{60}. We can use a trick: group the 6 and 0 together as a single symbol. Then there is an immediate bijection between permutations of $\{0, 1, 2, \ldots 9\}$ containing 6 and 0 consecutively and permutations of:

$$\{60, 1, 2, 3, 4, 5, 7, 8, 9\}.$$

For example, the following two sequences correspond:

$$(7, 2, 5, \underline{6}, \underline{0}, 4, 3, 8, 1, 9) \quad \longleftrightarrow \quad (7, 2, 5, \underline{60}, 4, 3, 8, 1, 9).$$

There are 9! permutations of the set containing 60, so $|P_{60}| = 9!$ by the Bijection Rule. Similarly, $|P_{04}| = |P_{42}| = 9!$ as well.

Next, we must determine the sizes of the two-way intersections, such as $P_{42} \cap P_{60}$. Using the grouping trick again, there is a bijection with permutations of the set:

$$\{42, 60, 1, 3, 5, 7, 8, 9\}.$$

Thus, $|P_{42} \cap P_{60}| = 8!$. Similarly, $|P_{60} \cap P_{04}| = 8!$ by a bijection with the set:

$$\{604, 1, 2, 3, 5, 7, 8, 9\}.$$

And $|P_{42} \cap P_{04}| = 8!$ as well by a similar argument. Finally, note that $|P_{60} \cap P_{04} \cap P_{42}| = 7!$ by a bijection with the set:

$$\{6042, 1, 3, 5, 7, 8, 9\}.$$

Plugging all this into the formula gives:

$$|P_{42} \cup P_{04} \cup P_{60}| = 9! + 9! + 9! - 8! - 8! - 8! + 7!.$$

15.9.4   Union of *n* Sets

The size of a union of n sets is given by the following rule.

Rule 15.9.1 (Inclusion-Exclusion).

$$|S_1 \cup S_2 \cup \cdots \cup S_n| =$$

	the sum of the sizes of the individual sets
minus	*the sizes of all two-way intersections*
plus	*the sizes of all three-way intersections*
minus	*the sizes of all four-way intersections*
plus	*the sizes of all five-way intersections, etc.*

The formulas for unions of two and three sets are special cases of this general rule.

This way of expressing Inclusion-Exclusion is easy to understand and nearly as precise as expressing it in mathematical symbols, but we'll need the symbolic version below, so let's work on deciphering it now.

We already have a concise notation for the sum of sizes of the individual sets, namely,

$$\sum_{i=1}^{n} |S_i|.$$

A "two-way intersection" is a set of the form $S_i \cap S_j$ for $i \neq j$. We regard $S_j \cap S_i$ as the same two-way intersection as $S_i \cap S_j$, so we can assume that $i < j$. Now we can express the sum of the sizes of the two-way intersections as

$$\sum_{1 \leq i < j \leq n} |S_i \cap S_j|.$$

Similarly, the sum of the sizes of the three-way intersections is

$$\sum_{1 \leq i < j < k \leq n} |S_i \cap S_j \cap S_k|.$$

These sums have alternating signs in the Inclusion-Exclusion formula, with the sum of the k-way intersections getting the sign $(-1)^{k-1}$. This finally leads to a symbolic version of the rule:

Rule (Inclusion-Exclusion).

$$\left| \bigcup_{i=1}^{n} S_i \right| = \sum_{i=1}^{n} |S_i|$$

$$- \sum_{1 \leq i < j \leq n} |S_i \cap S_j|$$

$$+ \sum_{1 \leq i < j < k \leq n} |S_i \cap S_j \cap S_k| + \cdots$$

$$+ (-1)^{n-1} \left| \bigcap_{i=1}^{n} S_i \right|.$$

While it's often handy express the rule in this way as a sum of sums, it is not necessary to group the terms by how many sets are in the intersections. So another way to state the rule is:

Rule (Inclusion-Exclusion-II).

$$\left| \bigcup_{i=1}^{n} S_i \right| = \sum_{\emptyset \neq I \subseteq \{1,\ldots,n\}} (-1)^{|I|+1} \left| \bigcap_{i \in I} S_i \right| \tag{15.6}$$

A proof of these rules using just highschool algebra is given in Problem 15.58.

15.9.5 Computing Euler's Function

We can also use Inclusion-Exclusion to derive the explicit formula for Euler's function claimed in Corollary 9.10.11: if the prime factorization of n is $p_1^{e_1} \cdots p_m^{e_m}$ for distinct primes p_i, then

$$\phi(n) = n \prod_{i=1}^{m} \left(1 - \frac{1}{p_i} \right). \tag{15.7}$$

To begin, let S be the set of integers in $[0..n)$ that are *not* relatively prime to n. So $\phi(n) = n - |S|$. Next, let C_a be the set of integers in $[0..n)$ that are divisible by a:

$$C_a ::= \{k \in [0..n) \mid a \mid k\}.$$

So the integers in S are precisely the integers in $[0..n)$ that are divisible by at least one of the p_i's. Namely,

$$S = \bigcup_{i=1}^{m} C_{p_i}. \tag{15.8}$$

We'll be able to find the size of this union using Inclusion-Exclusion because the intersections of the C_{p_i}'s are easy to count. For example, $C_p \cap C_q \cap C_r$ is the set of integers in $[0..n)$ that are divisible by each of p, q and r. But since the p, q, r are distinct primes, being divisible by each of them is the same as being divisible by their product. Now if k is a positive divisor of n, then there are exactly n/k multiples of k in $[0..n)$. So exactly n/pqr of the integers in $[0..n)$ are divisible by all three primes p, q, r. In other words,

$$|C_p \cap C_q \cap C_r| = \frac{n}{pqr}.$$

This reasoning extends to arbitrary intersections of C_p's, namely,

$$\left| \bigcap_{j \in I} C_{p_j} \right| = \frac{n}{\prod_{j \in I} p_j}, \tag{15.9}$$

for any nonempty set $I \subseteq [1..m]$. This lets us calculate:

$$|S| = \left| \bigcup_{i=1}^{m} C_{p_i} \right| \qquad \text{(by (15.8))}$$

$$= \sum_{\emptyset \neq I \subseteq [1..m]} (-1)^{|I|+1} \left| \bigcap_{i \in I} C_{p_i} \right| \qquad \text{(by Inclusion-Exclusion (15.6))}$$

$$= \sum_{\emptyset \neq I \subseteq [1..m]} (-1)^{|I|+1} \frac{n}{\prod_{j \in I} p_j} \qquad \text{(by (15.9))}$$

$$= -n \sum_{\emptyset \neq I \subseteq [1..m]} \frac{1}{\prod_{j \in I} (-p_j)}$$

$$= -n \left(\prod_{i=1}^{m} \left(1 - \frac{1}{p_i} \right) \right) + n,$$

so

$$\phi(n) = n - |S| = n \prod_{i=1}^{m} \left(1 - \frac{1}{p_i} \right),$$

which proves (15.7).

Yikes! That was pretty hairy. Are you getting tired of all that nasty algebra? If so, then good news is on the way. In the next section, we will show you how to prove some heavy-duty formulas without using any algebra at all. Just a few words and you are done. No kidding.

15.10   Combinatorial Proofs

Suppose you have n different T-shirts, but only want to keep k. You could equally well select the k shirts you want to keep or select the complementary set of $n - k$ shirts you want to throw out. Thus, the number of ways to select k shirts from among n must be equal to the number of ways to select $n - k$ shirts from among n. Therefore:

$$\binom{n}{k} = \binom{n}{n-k}.$$

This is easy to prove algebraically, since both sides are equal to:

$$\frac{n!}{k! \, (n-k)!}.$$

But we didn't really have to resort to algebra; we just used counting principles. Hmmm....

15.10.1   Pascal's Triangle Identity

Bob, famed Math for Computer Science Teaching Assistant, has decided to try out for the US Olympic boxing team. After all, he's watched all of the *Rocky* movies and spent hours in front of a mirror sneering, "Yo, you wanna piece a' *me*?!" Bob figures that n people (including himself) are competing for spots on the team and only k will be selected. As part of maneuvering for a spot on the team, he needs to work out how many different teams are possible. There are two cases to consider:

- Bob *is* selected for the team, and his $k - 1$ teammates are selected from among the other $n - 1$ competitors. The number of different teams that can be formed in this way is:

$$\binom{n - 1}{k - 1}.$$

- Bob is *not* selected for the team, and all k team members are selected from among the other $n - 1$ competitors. The number of teams that can be formed this way is:

$$\binom{n - 1}{k}.$$

All teams of the first type contain Bob, and no team of the second type does; therefore, the two sets of teams are disjoint. Thus, by the Sum Rule, the total number of possible Olympic boxing teams is:

$$\binom{n - 1}{k - 1} + \binom{n - 1}{k}.$$

Ted, equally-famed Teaching Assistant, thinks Bob isn't so tough and so he might as well also try out. He reasons that n people (including himself) are trying out for k spots. Thus, the number of ways to select the team is simply:

$$\binom{n}{k}.$$

Ted and Bob each correctly counted the number of possible boxing teams. Thus, their answers must be equal. So we know:

Lemma 15.10.1 (Pascal's *Triangle Identity*).

$$\binom{n}{k} = \binom{n-1}{k-1} + \binom{n-1}{k}. \qquad (15.10)$$

We proved *Pascal's Triangle Identity without any algebra!* Instead, we relied purely on counting techniques.

15.10.2 Giving a Combinatorial Proof

A *combinatorial proof* is an argument that establishes an algebraic fact by relying on counting principles. Many such proofs follow the same basic outline:

1. Define a set S.

2. Show that $|S| = n$ by counting one way.

3. Show that $|S| = m$ by counting another way.

4. Conclude that $n = m$.

In the preceding example, S was the set of all possible Olympic boxing teams. Bob computed

$$|S| = \binom{n-1}{k-1} + \binom{n-1}{k}$$

by counting one way, and Ted computed

$$|S| = \binom{n}{k}$$

by counting another way. Equating these two expressions gave Pascal's Identity.

Checking a Combinatorial Proof

Combinatorial proofs are based on counting the same thing in different ways. This is fine when you've become practiced at different counting methods, but when in doubt, you can fall back on bijections and sequence counting to check such proofs.

For example, let's take a closer look at the combinatorial proof of Pascal's Identity (15.10). In this case, the set S of things to be counted is the collection of all size-k subsets of integers in the interval $[1..n]$.

Now we've already counted S one way, via the Bookkeeper Rule, and found $|S| = \binom{n}{k}$. The other "way" corresponds to defining a bijection between S and the disjoint union of two sets A and B where,

$$A ::= \{(1, X) \mid X \subseteq [2, n] \text{ AND } |X| = k - 1\}$$
$$B ::= \{(0, Y) \mid Y \subseteq [2, n] \text{ AND } |Y| = k\}.$$

Clearly A and B are disjoint since the pairs in the two sets have different first coordinates, so $|A \cup B| = |A| + |B|$. Also,

$$|A| = \# \text{ specified sets } X = \binom{n-1}{k-1},$$

$$|B| = \# \text{ specified sets } Y = \binom{n-1}{k}.$$

Now finding a bijection $f : (A \cup B) \to S$ will prove the identity (15.10). In particular, we can define

$$f(c) ::= \begin{cases} X \cup \{1\} & \text{if } c = (1, X), \\ Y & \text{if } c = (0, Y). \end{cases}$$

It should be obvious that f is a bijection.

15.10.3   A Colorful Combinatorial Proof

The set that gets counted in a combinatorial proof in different ways is usually defined in terms of simple sequences or sets rather than an elaborate story about Teaching Assistants. Here is another colorful example of a combinatorial argument.

Theorem 15.10.2.

$$\sum_{r=0}^{n} \binom{n}{r}\binom{2n}{n-r} = \binom{3n}{n}$$

Proof. We give a combinatorial proof. Let S be all n-card hands that can be dealt from a deck containing n different red cards and $2n$ different black cards. First, note that every $3n$-element set has

$$|S| = \binom{3n}{n}$$

n-element subsets.

From another perspective, the number of hands with exactly r red cards is

$$\binom{n}{r}\binom{2n}{n-r}$$

since there are $\binom{n}{r}$ ways to choose the r red cards and $\binom{2n}{n-r}$ ways to choose the $n - r$ black cards. Since the number of red cards can be anywhere from 0 to n, the total number of n-card hands is:

$$|S| = \sum_{r=0}^{n}\binom{n}{r}\binom{2n}{n-r}.$$

Equating these two expressions for $|S|$ proves the theorem. ∎

Finding a Combinatorial Proof

Combinatorial proofs are almost magical. Theorem 15.10.2 looks pretty scary, but we proved it without any algebraic manipulations at all. The key to constructing a combinatorial proof is choosing the set S properly, which can be tricky. Generally, the simpler side of the equation should provide some guidance. For example, the right side of Theorem 15.10.2 is $\binom{3n}{n}$, which suggests that it will be helpful to choose S to be all n-element subsets of some $3n$-element set.

15.11   References

[5], [15]

Problems for Section 15.2

Practice Problems

Problem 15.1.
Alice is thinking of a number between 1 and 1000.

What is the least number of yes/no questions you could ask her and be guaranteed to discover what it is? (Alice always answers truthfully.)

(a)

Problem 15.2.
In how many different ways is it possible to answer the next chapter's practice problems if:

- the first problem has four *true/false* questions,

- the second problem requires choosing one of four alternatives, and

- the answer to the third problem is an integer ≥ 15 and ≤ 20?

Problem 15.3.
How many total functions are there from set A to set B if $|A| = 3$ and $|B| = 7$?

Problem 15.4.
Let X be the six element set $\{x_1, x_2, x_3, x_4, x_5, x_6\}$.

(a) How many subsets of X contain x_1?

(b) How many subsets of X contain x_2 and x_3 but do not contain x_6?

Class Problems

Problem 15.5.
A license plate consists of either:

- 3 letters followed by 3 digits (standard plate)

- 5 letters (vanity plate)

- 2 characters—letters or numbers (big shot plate)

Let L be the set of all possible license plates.

(a) Express L in terms of

$$\mathcal{A} = \{A, B, C, \ldots, Z\}$$
$$\mathcal{D} = \{0, 1, 2, \ldots, 9\}$$

using unions ($\cup$) and set products ($\times$).

(b) Compute $|L|$, the number of different license plates, using the sum and product rules.

Problem 15.6. (a) How many of the billion numbers in the range from 1 to 10^9 contain the digit 1? (*Hint:* How many don't?)

(b) There are 20 books arranged in a row on a shelf. Describe a bijection between ways of choosing 6 of these books so that no two adjacent books are selected and 15-bit strings with exactly 6 ones.

Problem 15.7.

(a) Let $\mathcal{S}_{n,k}$ be the possible nonnegative integer solutions to the inequality

$$x_1 + x_2 + \cdots + x_k \leq n. \tag{15.11}$$

That is

$$\mathcal{S}_{n,k} ::= \{(x_1, x_2, \ldots, x_k) \in \mathbb{N}^k \mid (15.11) \text{ is true}\}.$$

Describe a bijection between $\mathcal{S}_{n,k}$ and the set of binary strings with n zeroes and k ones.

(b) Let $\mathcal{L}_{n,k}$ be the length k weakly increasing sequences of nonnegative integers $\leq n$. That is

$$\mathcal{L}_{n,k} ::= \{(y_1, y_2, \ldots, y_k) \in \mathbb{N}^k \mid y_1 \leq y_2 \leq \cdots \leq y_k \leq n\}.$$

Describe a bijection between $\mathcal{L}_{n,k}$ and $\mathcal{S}_{n,k}$.

Problem 15.8.

An *n*-vertex *numbered tree* is a tree whose vertex set is $\{1, 2, \ldots, n\}$ for some $n > 2$. We define the *code* of the numbered tree to be a sequence of $n - 2$ integers from 1 to n obtained by the following recursive process:[6]

> If there are more than two vertices left, write down the *father* of the largest leaf, delete this *leaf*, and continue this process on the resulting smaller tree. If there are only two vertices left, then stop—the code is complete.

For example, the codes of a couple of numbered trees are shown in the Figure 15.7.

---

[6]The necessarily unique node adjacent to a leaf is called its *father*.

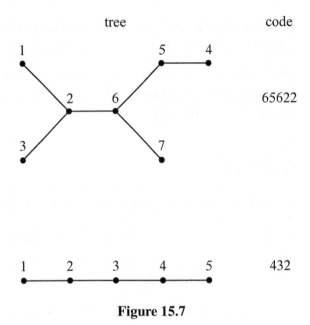

Figure 15.7

(a) Describe a procedure for reconstructing a numbered tree from its code.

(b) Conclude there is a bijection between the n-vertex numbered trees and $\{1, \ldots, n\}^{n-2}$, and state how many n-vertex numbered trees there are.

Problem 15.9.

Let X and Y be finite sets.

(a) How many binary relations from X to Y are there?

(b) Define a bijection between the set $[X \to Y]$ of all total functions from X to Y and the set $Y^{|X|}$. (Recall Y^n is the Cartesian product of Y with itself n times.) Based on that, what is $|[X \to Y]|$?

(c) Using the previous part, how many *functions*, not necessarily total, are there from X to Y? How does the fraction of functions vs. total functions grow as the size of X grows? Is it $O(1)$, $O(|X|)$, $O(2^{|X|})$, \ldots?

(d) Show a bijection between the powerset $\mathrm{pow}(X)$ and the set $[X \to \{0, 1\}]$ of 0-1-valued total functions on X.

(e) Let X be a set of size n and B_X be the set of all bijections from X to X.

Describe a bijection from B_X to the set of permutations of X.[7] This implies that there are how may bijections from X to X?

Problems for Section 15.4

Class Problems

Problem 15.10.
Use induction to prove that there are 2^n subsets of an n-element set (Theorem 4.5.5).

Homework Problems

Problem 15.11.
Fermat's Little Theorem 9.10.8[8] asserts that

$$a^p \equiv a \pmod{p} \tag{15.12}$$

for all primes p and nonnegative integers a. This is immediate for $a = 0, 1$ so we assume that $a \geq 2$.

This problem offers a proof of (15.12) by counting strings over a fixed alphabet with a characters.

(a) How many length-k strings are there over an a-character alphabet? How many of these are strings use more than one character?

Let z be a length-k string. The *length-n rotation* of z is the string yx, where $z = xy$ and the length $|x|$ of x is remainder(n, k).

(b) Verify that if u is a length-n rotation of z, and v is a length-m rotation of u, then v is a length-$(n + m)$ rotation of z.

(c) Let $\approx$ be the "is a rotation of" relation on strings. That is,

$$v \approx z \quad \text{IFF} \quad v \text{ is a length-}n \text{ rotation of } z$$

for some $n \in \mathbb{N}$. Prove that $\approx$ is an equivalence relation.

---

[7] A sequence in which all the elements of a set X appear exactly once is called a *permutation* of X (see Section 15.3.3).

[8] This Theorem is usually stated as

$$a^{p-1} \equiv 1 \pmod{p},$$

for all primes p and integers a not divisible by p. This follows immediately from (15.12) by canceling a.

(d) Prove that if $xy = yx$ then x and y each consist of repetitions of some string u. That is, if $xy = yx$, then $x, y \in u^*$ for some string u.

Hint: By induction on the length $|xy|$ of xy.

(e) Conclude that if p is prime and z is a length-p string containing at least two different characters, then z is equivalent under $\approx$ to exactly p strings (counting itself).

(f) Conclude from parts (a) and (e) that $p \mid (a^p - a)$, which proves Fermat's Little Theorem (15.12).

Problems for Section 15.5

Practice Problems

Problem 15.12.
Eight students—Anna, Brian, Caine,...—are to be seated around a circular table in a circular room. Two seatings are regarded as defining the same *arrangement* if each student has the same student on his or her right in both seatings: it does not matter which way they face. We'll be interested in counting how many arrangements there are of these 8 students, given some restrictions.

(a) As a start, how many different arrangements of these 8 students around the table are there without any restrictions?

(b) How many arrangements of these 8 students are there with Anna sitting next to Brian?

(c) How many arrangements are there with if Brian sitting next to both Anna AND Caine?

(d) How many arrangements are there with Brian sitting next to Anna *OR* Caine?

Problem 15.13.
How many different ways are there to select three dozen colored roses if red, yellow, pink, white, purple and orange roses are available?

Problem 15.14.

Suppose n books are lined up on a shelf. The number of selections of m of the books so that selected books are separated by at least three unselected books is the same as the number of *all* length k binary strings with exactly m ones.

(a) What is the value of k?

(b) Describe a bijection between between the set of all length k binary strings with exactly m ones and such book selections.

Problem 15.15.

Six women and nine men are on the faculty of a school's EECS department. The individuals are distinguishable. How many ways are there to select a committee of 5 members if at least 1 woman must be on the committee?

Class Problems

Problem 15.16.

Your class tutorial has 12 students, who are supposed to break up into 4 groups of 3 students each. Your Teaching Assistant (TA) has observed that the students waste too much time trying to form balanced groups, so he decided to pre-assign students to groups and email the group assignments to his students.

(a) Your TA has a list of the 12 students in front of him, so he divides the list into consecutive groups of 3. For example, if the list is ABCDEFGHIJKL, the TA would define a sequence of four groups to be $(\{A, B, C\}, \{D, E, F\}, \{G, H, I\}, \{J, K, L\})$. This way of forming groups defines a mapping from a list of twelve students to a sequence of four groups. This is a k-to-1 mapping for what k?

(b) A group assignment specifies which students are in the same group, but not any order in which the groups should be listed. If we map a sequence of 4 groups,

$$(\{A, B, C\}, \{D, E, F\}, \{G, H, I\}, \{J, K, L\}),$$

into a group assignment

$$\{\{A, B, C\}, \{D, E, F\}, \{G, H, I\}, \{J, K, L\}\},$$

this mapping is j-to-1 for what j?

(c) How many group assignments are possible?

(d) In how many ways can $3n$ students be broken up into n groups of 3?

Problem 15.17.

A pizza house is having a promotional sale. Their commercial reads:

> We offer 9 different toppings for your pizza! Buy 3 large pizzas at
> the regular price, and you can get each one with as many different
> toppings as you wish, absolutely free. That's $22,369,621$ different
> ways to choose your pizzas!

The ad writer was a former Harvard student who had evaluated the formula $(2^9)^3/3!$
on his calculator and gotten close to $22,369,621$. Unfortunately, $(2^9)^3/3!$ can't be
an integer, so clearly something is wrong. What mistaken reasoning might have
led the ad writer to this formula? Explain how to fix the mistake and get a correct
formula.

Problem 15.18.

Answer the following quesions using the Generalized Product Rule.

(a) Next week, I'm going to get really fit! On day 1, I'll exercise for 5 minutes.
On each subsequent day, I'll exercise 0, 1, 2, or 3 minutes more than the previous
day. For example, the number of minutes that I exercise on the seven days of next
week might be 5, 6, 9, 9, 9, 11, 12. How many such sequences are possible?

(b) An *r-permutation* of a set is a sequence of r distinct elements of that set. For
example, here are all the 2-permutations of $\{a, b, c, d\}$:

$$(a,b) \quad (a,c) \quad (a,d)$$
$$(b,a) \quad (b,c) \quad (b,d)$$
$$(c,a) \quad (c,b) \quad (c,d)$$
$$(d,a) \quad (d,b) \quad (d,c)$$

How many r-permutations of an n-element set are there? Express your answer
using factorial notation.

(c) How many $n \times n$ matrices are there with *distinct* entries drawn from $\{1, \ldots, p\}$,
where $p \geq n^2$?

Problem 15.19. (a) There are 30 books arranged in a row on a shelf. In how many
ways can eight of these books be selected so that there are at least two unselected
books between any two selected books?

(b) How many nonnegative integer solutions are there for the following equality?

$$x_1 + x_2 + \cdots + x_m = k. \tag{15.13}$$

(c) How many nonnegative integer solutions are there for the following inequality?

$$x_1 + x_2 + \cdots + x_m \leq k. \tag{15.14}$$

(d) How many length m weakly increasing sequences of nonnegative integers $\leq k$ are there?

Homework Problems

Problem 15.20.
This problem is about binary relations on the set of integers in the interval $[1..n]$ and digraphs whose vertex set is $[1..n]$.

(a) How many digraphs are there?

(b) How many simple graphs are there?

(c) How many asymmetric binary relations are there?

(d) How many linear strict partial orders are there?

Problem 15.21.
Answer the following questions with a number or a simple formula involving factorials and binomial coefficients. Briefly explain your answers.

(a) How many ways are there to order the 26 letters of the alphabet so that no two of the vowels a, e, i, o, u appear consecutively and the last letter in the ordering is not a vowel?

Hint: Every vowel appears to the left of a consonant.

(b) How many ways are there to order the 26 letters of the alphabet so that there are *at least two* consonants immediately following each vowel?

(c) In how many different ways can $2n$ students be paired up?

(d) Two n-digit sequences of digits $0,1,\ldots,9$ are said to be of the *same type* if the digits of one are a permutation of the digits of the other. For $n = 8$, for example, the sequences 03088929 and 00238899 are the same type. How many types of n-digit sequences are there?

Problem 15.22.

In a standard 52-card deck, each card has one of thirteen *rank*s in the set R and one of four *suit*s in the set S where

$$R ::= \{A, 2, \ldots, 10, J, Q, K\},$$
$$S ::= \{\clubsuit, \diamondsuit, \heartsuit, \spadesuit\}.$$

A 5-card *hand* is a set of five distinct cards from the deck.

For each part describe a bijection between a set that can easily be counted using the Product and Sum Rules of Ch. 15.1, and the set of hands matching the specification. *Give bijections, not numerical answers.*

For instance, consider the set of 5-card hands containing all 4 suits. Each such hand must have 2 cards of one suit. We can describe a bijection between such hands and the set $S \times R_2 \times R^3$ where R_2 is the set of two-element subsets of R. Namely, an element

$$(s, \{r_1, r_2\}, (r_3, r_4, r_5)) \in S \times R_2 \times R^3$$

indicates

1. the repeated suit $s \in S$,

2. the set $\{r_1, r_2\} \in R_2$ of ranks of the cards of suit s and

3. the ranks (r_3, r_4, r_5) of the remaining three cards, listed in increasing suit order where

$$\clubsuit \prec \diamondsuit \prec \heartsuit \prec \spadesuit.$$

For example,

$$(\clubsuit, \{10, A\}, (J, J, 2)) \longleftrightarrow \{A\clubsuit, 10\clubsuit, J\diamondsuit, J\heartsuit, 2\spadesuit\}.$$

(a) A single pair of the same rank (no 3-of-a-kind, 4-of-a-kind, or second pair).

(b) Three or more aces.

Problem 15.23.

Suppose you have seven dice—each a different color of the rainbow; otherwise the dice are standard, with faces numbered 1 to 6. A *roll* is a sequence specifying a value for each die in rainbow (ROYGBIV) order. For example, one roll is $(3, 1, 6, 1, 4, 5, 2)$ indicating that the red die showed a 3, the orange die showed 1, the yellow 6,....

For the problems below, describe a bijection between the specified set of rolls and another set that is easily counted using the Product, Generalized Product, and similar rules. Then write a simple arithmetic formula, possibly involving factorials and binomial coefficients, for the size of the set of rolls. You do not need to prove that the correspondence between sets you describe is a bijection, and you do not need to simplify the expression you come up with.

For example, let A be the set of rolls where 4 dice come up showing the same number, and the other 3 dice also come up the same, but with a different number. Let R be the set of seven rainbow colors and $S ::= [1, 6]$ be the set of dice values.

Define $B ::= P_{S,2} \times R_3$, where $P_{S,2}$ is the set of 2-permutations of S and R_3 is the set of size-3 subsets of R. Then define a bijection from A to B by mapping a roll in A to the sequence in B whose first element is a pair consisting of the number that came up three times followed by the number that came up four times, and whose second element is the set of colors of the three matching dice.

For example, the roll

$$(4, 4, 2, 2, 4, 2, 4) \in A$$

maps to

$$((2, 4), \{\text{yellow,green,indigo}\}) \in B.$$

Now by the Bijection rule $|A| = |B|$, and by the Generalized Product and Subset rules,

$$|B| = 6 \cdot 5 \cdot \binom{7}{3}.$$

(a) For how many rolls do *exactly* two dice have the value 6 and the remaining five dice all have different values? Remember to describe a bijection and write a simple arithmetic formula.

Example: $(6, 2, 6, 1, 3, 4, 5)$ is a roll of this type, but $(1, 1, 2, 6, 3, 4, 5)$ and $(6, 6, 1, 2, 4, 3, 4)$ are not.

(b) For how many rolls do two dice have the same value and the remaining five dice all have different values? Remember to describe a bijection and write a simple arithmetic formula.

Example: $(4, 2, 4, 1, 3, 6, 5)$ is a roll of this type, but $(1, 1, 2, 6, 1, 4, 5)$ and $(6, 6, 1, 2, 4, 3, 4)$ are not.

(c) For how many rolls do two dice have one value, two different dice have a second value, and the remaining three dice a third value? Remember to describe a bijection and write a simple arithmetic formula.

Example: $(6, 1, 2, 1, 2, 6, 6)$ is a roll of this type, but $(4, 4, 4, 4, 1, 3, 5)$ and $(5, 5, 5, 6, 6, 1, 2)$ are not.

Problem 15.24 (Counting trees).

What is the number T_n of different trees that can be formed from a set of n distinct vertices?[9] Cayley's formula gives the answer

$$T_n = n^{n-2}.$$

One way to derive this appears in Problem 15.8. This and three additional derivations are given by Aigner & Ziegler (1998), who comment that "the most beautiful of them all" is a counting argument due to Jim Pitman that we now describe.

Pitman's derivation counts in two different ways the number of different sequences of edges that can be added to an empty graph on n vertices to form a rooted tree. One way to form such a sequence is to start with one of the T_n possible unrooted trees, choose one of its n vertices as root, and choose one of the $(n-1)!$ possible sequences in which to add its $n-1$ edges. Therefore, the total number of sequences that can be formed in this way is

$$T_n n(n-1)! = T_n n!.$$

Another way to count these edge sequences is to start with the empty graph and build up a spanning forest of rooted trees by adding edges in sequence. When $n - k$ edges have been added, the graph with these edges will be a spanning forest consisting of k rooted trees. To add the next edge, we choose any vertex to be the root of a new tree. Then we add an edge between this new root and the root of any one of the $k - 1$ subtrees that did not include the chosen vertex. So the next edge can be chosen in $n(k-1)$ ways to form a new spanning forest consisting of $k - 1$ rooted trees.

Therefore, if one multiplies together the number of choices from the first step, the second step, etc., the total number of choices is

$$\prod_{k=2}^{n} n(k-1) = n^{n-1}(n-1)! = n^{n-2}n!.$$

Equating these two formulas for the number of edge sequences, we get $T_n n! = n^{n-2}n!$, and cancelling $n!$ we arrive at Cayley's formula

$$T_n = n^{n-2}.$$

---

[9]From Double counting, wikipedia, Aug. 30, 2014. **See also** Prüfer Sequences

Generalize Pitman's derivation to count the number of spanning forests consisting of k rooted trees on n vertices.

Exam Problems

Problem 15.25.
Suppose that two identical 52-card decks are mixed together. Write a simple formula for the number of distinct permutations of the 104 cards.

Problems for Section 15.6

Class Problems

Problem 15.26.
The Tao of BOOKKEEPER: we seek enlightenment through contemplation of the word $BOOKKEEPER$.

 (a) In how many ways can you arrange the letters in the word $POKE$?

 (b) In how many ways can you arrange the letters in the word BO_1O_2K? Observe that we have subscripted the O's to make them distinct symbols.

 (c) Suppose we map arrangements of the letters in BO_1O_2K to arrangements of the letters in $BOOK$ by erasing the subscripts. Indicate with arrows how the arrangements on the left are mapped to the arrangements on the right.

$$O_2BO_1K$$
$$KO_2BO_1$$
$$O_1BO_2K$$
$$KO_1BO_2$$
$$BO_1O_2K$$
$$BO_2O_1K$$
$$\cdots$$

$$BOOK$$
$$OBOK$$
$$KOBO$$
$$\cdots$$

(d) What kind of mapping is this, young grasshopper?

(e) In light of the Division Rule, how many arrangements are there of $BOOK$?

 (f) Very good, young master! How many arrangements are there of the letters in $KE_1E_2PE_3R$?

(g) Suppose we map each arrangement of $KE_1E_2PE_3R$ to an arrangement of $KEEPER$ by erasing subscripts. List all the different arrangements of $KE_1E_2PE_3R$ that are mapped to $REPEEK$ in this way.

(h) What kind of mapping is this?

(i) So how many arrangements are there of the letters in $KEEPER$?

Now you are ready to face the BOOKKEEPER!

(j) How many arrangements of $BO_1O_2K_1K_2E_1E_2PE_3R$ are there?

(k) How many arrangements of $BOOK_1K_2E_1E_2PE_3R$ are there?

(l) How many arrangements of $BOOKKE_1E_2PE_3R$ are there?

(m) How many arrangements of $BOOKKEEPER$ are there?

Remember well what you have learned: subscripts on, subscripts off.
This is the Tao of Bookkeeper.

(n) How many arrangements of $VOODOODOLL$ are there?

(o) How many length 52 sequences of digits contain exactly 17 two's, 23 fives, and 12 nines?

Problems for Section 15.6

Practice Problems

Problem 15.27.
How many different permutations are there of the sequence of letters in "MISSIS-SIPPI"?

Class Problems

Problem 15.28.
Find the coefficients of

(a) x^5 in $(1+x)^{11}$

(b) x^8y^9 in $(3x+2y)^{17}$

(c) a^6b^6 in $(a^2+b^3)^5$

Problem 15.29.

Let p be a **prime number**.

(a) Explain why the multinomial coefficient

$$\binom{p}{k_1, k_2, \ldots, k_n}$$

is divisible by p if all the k_i's are nonnegative integers less than p.

(b) Conclude from part (a) that

$$(x_1 + x_2 + \cdots + x_n)^p \equiv x_1^p + x_2^p + \cdots + x_n^p \quad (\text{mod } p). \qquad (15.15)$$

(Do not prove this using Fermat's "little" Theorem. The point of this problem is to offer an independent proof of Fermat's theorem.)

(c) Explain how (15.15) immediately proves Fermat's Little Theorem 9.10.8:

$$n^{p-1} \equiv 1 \quad (\text{mod } p)$$

when n is not a multiple of p.

Homework Problems

Problem 15.30.

The *degree sequence* of a simple graph is the weakly decreasing sequence of degrees of its vertices. For example, the degree sequence for the 5-vertex numbered tree pictured in the Figure 15.7 in Problem 15.8 is $(2, 2, 2, 1, 1)$ and for the 7-vertex tree it is $(3, 3, 2, 1, 1, 1, 1)$.

We're interested in counting how many numbered trees there are with a given degree sequence. We'll do this using the bijection defined in Problem 15.8 between n-vertex numbered trees and length $n - 2$ code words whose characters are integers between 1 and n.

The *occurrence number* for a character in a word is the number of times that the character occurs in the word. For example, in the word 65622, the occurrence number for 6 is two, and the occurrence number for 5 is one. The *occurrence sequence* of a word is the weakly decreasing sequence of occurrence numbers of characters in the word. The occurrence sequence for this word is $(2, 2, 1)$ because it has two occurrences of each of the characters 6 and 2, and one occurrence of 5.

(a) There is a simple relationship between the degree sequence of an n-vertex numbered tree and the occurrence sequence of its code. Describe this relationship and explain why it holds. Conclude that counting n-vertex numbered trees with a given degree sequence is the same as counting the number of length $n - 2$ code words with a given occurrence sequence.

Hint: How many times does a vertex of degree d occur in the code?

For simplicity, let's focus on counting 9-vertex numbered trees with a given degree sequence. By part (a), this is the same as counting the number of length 7 code words with a given occurrence sequence.

Any length 7 code word has a *pattern*, which is another length 7 word over the alphabet a, b, c, d, e, f, g that has the same occurrence sequence.

(b) How many length 7 patterns are there with three occurrences of a, two occurrences of b, and one occurrence of c and d?

(c) How many ways are there to assign occurrence numbers to integers $1, 2, \ldots, 9$ so that a code word with those occurrence numbers would have the occurrence sequence $3, 2, 1, 1, 0, 0, 0, 0, 0$?

In general, to find the pattern of a code word, list its characters in decreasing order by *number of occurrences*, and list characters with the same number of occurrences in decreasing order. Then replace successive characters in the list by successive letters a, b, c, d, e, f, g. The code word 2468751, for example, has the pattern fecabdg, which is obtained by replacing its characters 8, 7, 6, 5, 4, 2, 1 by a, b, c, d, e, f, g, respectively. The code word 2449249 has pattern caabcab, which is obtained by replacing its characters 4, 9, 2 by a, b, c, respectively.

(d) What length 7 code word has three occurrences of 7, two occurrences of 8, one occurrence each of 2 and 9, and pattern abacbad?

(e) Explain why the number of 9-vertex numbered trees with degree sequence $(4, 3, 2, 2, 1, 1, 1, 1, 1)$ is the product of the answers to parts (b) and (c).

Problem 15.31.
Let G be a simple graph with 6 vertices and an edge between every pair of vertices (that is, G is a *complete* graph). A length-3 cycle in G is called a *triangle*.

A set of two edges that share a vertex is called an *incident pair* (i.p.); the shared vertex is called the *center* of the i.p. That is, an i.p. is a set,

$$\{\langle u\text{—}v\rangle, \langle v\text{—}w\rangle\},$$

where u, v and w are distinct vertices, and its center is v.

(a) How many triangles are there?

(b) How many incident pairs are there?

Now suppose that every edge in G is colored either red or blue. A triangle or i.p. is called *multicolored* when its edges are not all the same color.

(c) Map the i.p.

$$\{\langle u\text{---}v\rangle, \langle v\text{---}w\rangle\}$$

to the triangle

$$\{\langle u\text{---}v\rangle, \langle v\text{---}w\rangle, \langle u\text{---}w\rangle\}.$$

Notice that multicolored i.p.'s map to multicolored triangles. Explain why this mapping is 2-to-1 on these multicolored objects.

(d) Show that at most six multicolored i.p.'s can have the same center. Conclude that there are at most 36 possible multicolored i.p.'s.

Hint: A vertex incident to r red edges and b blue edges is the center of $r \cdot b$ different multicolored i.p.'s.

(e) If two people are not friends, they are called *strangers*. If every pair of people in a group are friends, or if every pair are strangers, the group is called *uniform*.

Explain why parts (a), (c), and (d) imply that

Every set of six people includes *two* uniform three-person groups.

Exam Problems

Problem 15.32.
There is a robot that steps between integer positions in 3-dimensional space. Each step of the robot increments one coordinate and leaves the other two unchanged.

(a) How many paths can the robot follow going from the origin $(0, 0, 0)$ to $(3, 4, 5)$?

(b) How many paths can the robot follow going from the origin (i, j, k) to (m, n, p)?

Problems for Section 15.7

Practice Problems

Problem 15.33.
Indicate how many 5-card hands there are of each of the following kinds.

(a) A **Sequence** is a hand consisting of five consecutive cards of any suit, such as

$$5\heartsuit - 6\heartsuit - 7\spadesuit - 8\diamondsuit - 9\clubsuit.$$

Note that an ace may either be high (as in 10-J-Q-K-A), or low (as in A-2-3-4-5), but can't go "around the corner" (that is, Q-K-A-2-3 is *not* a sequence).

How many different **Sequence** hands are possible?

(b) A **Matching Suit** is a hand consisting of cards that are all of the same suit in any order.

How many different **Matching Suit** hands are possible?

(c) A **Straight Flush** is a hand that is both a *Sequence* and a *Matching Suit*.

How many different **Straight Flush** hands are possible?

(d) A **Straight** is a hand that is a *Sequence* but not a *Matching Suit*.

How many possible **Straights** are there?

(e) A **Flush** is a hand that is a *Matching Suit* but not a *Sequence*.

How many possible **Flushes** are there?

Class Problems

Problem 15.34.
Here are the solutions to the next 7 short answer questions, in no particular order. Indicate the solutions for the questions and briefly explain your answers.

$$1.\ \ \frac{n!}{(n-m)!} \qquad 2.\ \ \binom{n+m}{m} \qquad\quad 3.\ \ (n-m)! \quad 4.\ \ m^n$$

$$5.\ \ \binom{n-1+m}{m} \quad 6.\ \ \binom{n-1+m}{n} \quad 7.\ \ 2^{mn} \qquad 8.\ \ n^m$$

(a) How many length m words can be formed from an n-letter alphabet, if no letter is used more than once?

(b) How many length m words can be formed from an n-letter alphabet, if letters can be reused?

(c) How many binary relations are there from set A to set B when $|A| = m$ and $|B| = n$?

(d) How many total injective functions are there from set A to set B, where $|A| = m$ and $|B| = n \geq m$?

(e) How many ways are there to place a total of m distinguishable balls into n distinguishable urns, with some urns possibly empty or with several balls?

(f) How many ways are there to place a total of m indistinguishable balls into n distinguishable urns, with some urns possibly empty or with several balls?

(g) How many ways are there to put a total of m distinguishable balls into n distinguishable urns with at most one ball in each urn?

Exam Problems

Problem 15.35. (a) How many solutions over the *positive* integers are there to the inequality:

$$x_1 + x_2 + \ldots + x_{10} \leq 100$$

(b) In how many ways can Mr. and Mrs. Grumperson distribute 13 identical pieces of coal to their three children for Christmas so that each child gets at least one piece?

Problem 15.36.
Answer the following questions about **finite simple graphs**. You may answer with formulas involving exponents, binomial coefficents, and factorials.

(a) How many edges are there in the *complete graph* K_{41}?

(b) How many edges are there in a spanning tree of K_{41}?

(c) What is the chromatic number $\chi(K_{41})$?

(d) What is the chromatic number $\chi(C_{41})$, of the cycle of length 41?

(e) Let H be the graph in Figure 15.8. How many distinct isomorphisms are there from H to H?

Figure 15.8   The graph H.

(f) A graph G is created by adding a single edge to a tree with 41 vertices. How many cycles does G have?

(g) What is the smallest number of leaves possible in a tree with 41 vertices?

(h) What is the largest number of leaves possible in a tree with 41 vertices?

(i) How many length-10 paths are there in K_{41}?

(j) Let s be the number of length-10 paths in K_{41}—that is, s is the correct answer to part (i).
In terms of s, how many length-11 *cycles* are in K_{41}?

Hint: For vertices a, b, c, d, e, the sequences $abcde, bcdea$ and $edcba$ all describe the same length-5 cycle, for example.

Problems for Section 15.8

Practice Problems

Problem 15.37.
Below is a list of properties that a group of people might possess.

For each property, either give the minimum number of people that must be in a group to ensure that the property holds, or else indicate that the property need not hold even for arbitrarily large groups of people.

(Assume that every year has exactly 365 days; ignore leap years.)

(a) At least 2 people were born on the same day of the year (ignore year of birth).

(b) At least 2 people were born on January 1.

(c) At least 3 people were born on the same day of the week.

(d) At least 4 people were born in the same month.

(e) At least 2 people were born exactly one week apart.

Class Problems

Problem 15.38.
Solve the following problems using the pigeonhole principle. For each problem, try to identify the *pigeons*, the *pigeonholes*, and a *rule* assigning each pigeon to a pigeonhole.

(a) In a certain Institute of Technology, every ID number starts with a 9. Suppose that each of the 75 students in a class sums the nine digits of their ID number. Explain why two people must arrive at the same sum.

(b) In every set of 100 integers, there exist two whose difference is a multiple of 37.

(c) For any five points inside a unit square (not on the boundary), there are two points at distance *less than* $1/\sqrt{2}$.

(d) Show that if $n + 1$ numbers are selected from $\{1, 2, 3, \ldots, 2n\}$, two must be consecutive, that is, equal to k and $k + 1$ for some k.

Problem 15.39. (a) Prove that every positive integer divides a number such as 70, 700, 7770, 77000, whose decimal representation consists of one or more 7's followed by one or more 0's.

Hint: $7, 77, 777, 7777, \ldots$

(b) Conclude that if a positive number is not divisible by 2 or 5, then it divides a number whose decimal representation is all 7's.

Problem 15.40.
The aim of this problem is to prove that there exist a natural number n such that 3^n has at least 2013 consecutive zeros in its decimal expansion.

(a) Prove that there exist a nonnegative integer n such that

$$3^n \equiv 1 \bmod 10^{2014}.$$

Hint: Use pigeonhole principle or Euler's theorem.

(b) Conclude that there exist a natural number n such that 3^n has at least 2013 consecutive zeros.

Problem 15.41. (a) Show that the Magician could not pull off the trick with a deck larger than 124 cards.

Hint: Compare the number of 5-card hands in an n-card deck with the number of 4-card sequences.

(b) Show that, in principle, the Magician could pull off the Card Trick with a deck of 124 cards.

Hint: Hall's Theorem and degree-constrained (12.5.5) graphs.

Problem 15.42.
The Magician can determine the 5th card in a poker hand when his Assisant reveals the other 4 cards. Describe a similar method for determining 2 hidden cards in a hand of 9 cards when your Assisant reveals the other 7 cards.

Problem 15.43.
Suppose $2n + 1$ numbers are selected from $\{1, 2, 3, \ldots, 4n\}$. Using the Pigeonhole Principle, show that there must be two selected numbers whose difference is 2. Clearly indicate what are the pigeons, holes, and rules for assigning a pigeon to a hole.

Problem 15.44.
Let

$$k_1, k_2, \ldots, k_{101}$$

be a sequence of 101 integers. A sequence

$$k_{m+1}, k_{m+2}, \ldots, k_n$$

where $0 \le m < n \le 101$ is called a *subsequence*. Prove that there is a subsequence whose elements sum to a number divisible by 100.

Homework Problems

Problem 15.45. (a) Show that any odd integer x in the range $10^9 < x < 2 \cdot 10^9$ containing all ten digits $0, 1, \ldots, 9$ must have consecutive even digits. *Hint:* What can you conclude about the parities of the first and last digit?

(b) Show that there are 2 vertices of equal degree in any finite undirected graph with $n \ge 2$ vertices. *Hint:* Cases conditioned upon the existence of a degree zero vertex.

Problem 15.46.
Suppose $n + 1$ numbers are selected from $\{1, 2, 3, \ldots, 2n\}$. Using the Pigeonhole

Principle, show that there must be two selected numbers whose quotient is a power of two. Clearly indicate what are the pigeons, holes, and rules for assigning a pigeon to a hole.

Hint: Factor each number into the product of an odd number and a power of 2.

Problem 15.47. (a) Let R be an 82×4 rectangular matrix each of whose entries are colored red, white or blue. Explain why at least two of the 82 rows in R must have identical color patterns.

 (b) Conclude that R contains four points with the same color that form the corners of a rectangle.

 (c) Now show that the conclusion from part (b) holds even when R has only 19 rows.

Hint: How many ways are there to pick two positions in a row of length four and color them the same?

Problem 15.48.

Section 15.8.6 explained why it is not possible to perform a four-card variant of the hidden-card magic trick with one card hidden. But the Magician and her Assistant are determined to find a way to make a trick like this work. They decide to change the rules slightly: instead of the Assistant lining up the three unhidden cards for the Magician to see, he will line up all four cards with one card face down and the other three visible. We'll call this the *face-down four-card trick*.

 For example, suppose the audience members had selected the cards $9\heartsuit$, $10\diamondsuit$, $A\clubsuit$, $5\clubsuit$. Then the Assistant could choose to arrange the 4 cards in any order so long as one is face down and the others are visible. Two possibilities are:

$A\clubsuit$	?	$10\diamondsuit$	$5\clubsuit$
?	$5\clubsuit$	$9\heartsuit$	$10\diamondsuit$

 (a) Explain how to model this face-down four-card trick as a matching problem, and show that there must be a bipartite matching which theoretically will allow the Magician and Assistant to perform the trick.

(b) There is actually a simple way to perform the face-down four-card trick.[10]

Case 1. *there are two cards with the same suit*: Say there are two ♠ cards. The Assistant proceeds as in the original card trick: he puts one of the ♠ cards *face up as the first card*. He will place the second ♠ card *face down*. He then uses a permutation of the face down card and the remaining two face up cards to code the offset of the face down card from the first card.

Case 2. *all four cards have different suits*: Assign numbers $0, 1, 2, 3$ to the four suits in some agreed upon way. The Assistant computes s the sum modulo 4 of the ranks of the four cards, and chooses the card with suit s to be placed *face down as the first card*. He then uses a permutation of the remaining three face-up cards to code the rank of the face down card.

Explain how in Case 2. the Magician can determine the face down card from the cards the Assistant shows her.

(c) Explain how any method for performing the face-down four-card trick can be adapted to perform the regular (5-card hand, show 4 cards) with a 52-card deck consisting of the usual 52 cards along with a 53rd card called the *joker*.

Problem 15.49.

Suppose $2n + 1$ numbers are selected from $\{1, 2, 3, \ldots, 4n\}$. Using the Pigeonhole Principle, show that for any positive integer j that divides $2n$, there must be two selected numbers whose difference is j. Clearly indicate what are the pigeons, holes, and rules for assigning a pigeon to a hole.

Problem 15.50.

Let's start by marking a point on a circle of length one. Next, mark the point that is distance $\sqrt{2}$ clockwise around the circle. So you wrap around once and actually mark the point at distance $\sqrt{2} - 1$ clockwise from the start. Now repeat with the newly marked point as the starting point. In other words, the marked points are those at clockwise distances

$$0, \sqrt{2}, 2\sqrt{2}, 3\sqrt{2}, \ldots, n\sqrt{2}, \ldots,$$

from the start.

---

[10]This elegant method was devised in Fall '09 by student Katie E Everett.

We will use a pigeonhole argument to prove that marked points are *dense* on the circle: for any point p on the circle, and any $\epsilon > 0$, there is a marked point within distance ϵ of p.

(a) Prove that no point gets marked twice. That is, the points at clockwise distance $k\sqrt{2}$ and $m\sqrt{2}$ are the same iff $k = m$.

(b) Prove that among the first $n > 1$ marked points, there have to be two that are at most distance $1/n$ from each other.

(c) Prove that every point on the circle is within $1/n$ of a marked point. This implies the claim that the marked points are dense on the circle.

Exam Problems

Problem 15.51.
A standard 52 card deck has 13 cards of each suit. Use the Pigeonhole Principle to determine the smallest k such that every set of k cards from the deck contains five cards of the same suit (called a *flush*). Clearly indicate what are the pigeons, holes, and rules for assigning a pigeon to a hole.

Problem 15.52.
Use the Pigeonhole Principle to determine the smallest nonnegative integer n such that every set of n integers is guaranteed to contain three integers that are congruent mod 211. Clearly indicate what are the pigeons, holes, and rules for assigning a pigeon to a hole, and give the value of n.

Problems for Section 15.9

Practice Problems

Problem 15.53.
Let A_1, A_2, A_3 be sets with $|A_1| = 100$, $|A_2| = 1,000$, and $|A_3| = 10,000$.
Determine $|A_1 \cup A_2 \cup A_3|$ in each of the following cases:

(a) $A_1 \subset A_2 \subset A_3$.

(b) The sets are pairwise disjoint.

(c) For any two of the sets, there is exactly one element in both.

(d) There are two elements common to each pair of sets and one element in all three sets.

Problem 15.54.
The working days in the next year can be numbered 1, 2, 3, ..., 300. I'd like to avoid as many as possible.

- On even-numbered days, I'll say I'm sick.

- On days that are a multiple of 3, I'll say I was stuck in traffic.

- On days that are a multiple of 5, I'll refuse to come out from under the blankets.

In total, how many work days will I *avoid* in the coming year?

    ein

Problem 15.55.
Twenty people work at CantorCorp, a small, unsuccessful start-up. A single six-person committee is to be formed. (It will be charged with the sole task of working to prove the Continuum Hypothesis.) Employees appointed to serve on the committee join as equals—they do not get assigned distinct roles or ranks.

(a) Let D denote the set of all possible committees. Find $|D|$.

(b) Two of the workers, Aleph and Beth, will be unhappy if they are to serve together.

Let P denote the set of all possible committees on which Aleph and Beth would serve together. Find $|P|$.

(c) Beth will also be unhappy if she has to serve with **both** Ferdinand and Georg.

Let Q denote the set of all possible committees on which Beth, Ferdinand, and Georg would all serve together. Find $|Q|$.

(d) Find $|P \cap Q|$.

(e) Let S denote the set of all possible committees on which there is at least one unhappy employee. Express S in terms of P and Q **only**.

(f) Find $|S|$.

(g) If we want to form a committee with no unhappy employees, how many choices do we have to choose from?

(h) Suddenly, we realize that it would be better to have two six-person committees instead of one. (One committee would work on proving the Continuum Hypothesis, while the other would work to disprove it!) Each employee can serve on at most one committee. How many ways are there to form such a pair of committees, if employee happiness is **not** taken into consideration?

Class Problems

Problem 15.56.
To ensure password security, a company requires their employees to choose a password. A length 10 word containing each of the characters:

> a, d, e, f, i, l, o, p, r, s,

is called a *cword*. A password can be a cword which does not contain any of the subwords "fails", "failed", or "drop."

For example, the following two words are passwords: adefiloprs, srpolifeda,
but the following three cwords are not: a**drop**eflis, **failedrops**, **dropefails**.

(a) How many cwords contain the subword "drop"?

(b) How many cwords contain both "drop" and "fails"?

(c) Use the Inclusion-Exclusion Principle to find a simple arithmetic formula involving factorials for the number of passwords.

Problem 15.57.
We want to count step-by-step paths between points in the plane with integer coordinates. Only two kinds of step are allowed: a right-step which increments the x coordinate, and an up-step which increments the y coordinate.

(a) How many paths are there from $(0, 0)$ to $(20, 30)$?

(b) How many paths are there from $(0, 0)$ to $(20, 30)$ that go through the point $(10, 10)$?

(c) How many paths are there from $(0, 0)$ to $(20, 30)$ that do *not* go through either of the points $(10, 10)$ and $(15, 20)$?

Hint: Let P be the set of paths from $(0, 0)$ to $(20, 30)$, N_1 be the paths in P that go through $(10, 10)$ and N_2 be the paths in P that go through $(15, 20)$.

Problem 15.58.

Let's develop a proof of the Inclusion-Exclusion formula using high school algebra.

 (a) Most high school students will get freaked by the following formula, even though they actually know the rule it expresses. How would you explain it to them?

$$\prod_{i=1}^{n} (1 - x_i) = \sum_{I \subseteq \{1,\ldots,n\}} (-1)^{|I|} \prod_{j \in I} x_j. \tag{15.16}$$

Hint: Show them an example.

Now to start proving (15.16), let M_S be the *membership* function for any set S:

$$M_S(x) = \begin{cases} 1 & \text{if } x \in S, \\ 0 & \text{if } x \notin S. \end{cases}$$

Let $S_1, \ldots, S_n$ be a sequence of finite sets, and abbreviate M_{S_i} as M_i. Let the domain of discourse D be the union of the S_i's. That is, we let

$$D ::= \bigcup_{i=1}^{n} S_i,$$

and take complements with respect to D, that is,

$$\overline{T} ::= D - T,$$

for $T \subseteq D$.

 (b) Verify that for $T \subseteq D$ and $I \subseteq \{1, \ldots n\}$,

$$M_{\overline{T}} = 1 - M_T, \tag{15.17}$$

$$M_{(\bigcap_{i \in I} S_i)} = \prod_{i \in I} M_i, \tag{15.18}$$

$$M_{(\bigcup_{i \in I} S_i)} = 1 - \prod_{i \in I} (1 - M_i). \tag{15.19}$$

(Note that (15.18) holds when I is empty because, by convention, an empty product equals 1, and an empty intersection equals the domain of discourse D.)

 (c) Use (15.16) and (15.19) to prove

$$M_D = \sum_{\emptyset \neq I \subseteq \{1,\ldots,n\}} (-1)^{|I|+1} \prod_{j \in I} M_j. \tag{15.20}$$

(d) Prove that

$$|T| = \sum_{u \in D} M_T(u). \tag{15.21}$$

(e) Now use the previous parts to prove

$$|D| = \sum_{\emptyset \neq I \subseteq \{1,\ldots,n\}} (-1)^{|I|+1} \left| \bigcap_{i \in I} S_i \right| \tag{15.22}$$

(f) Finally, explain why (15.22) immediately implies the usual form of the Inclusion-Exclusion Principle:

$$|D| = \sum_{i=1}^{n} (-1)^{i+1} \sum_{\substack{I \subseteq \{1,\ldots,n\} \\ |I|=i}} \left| \bigcap_{j \in I} S_j \right|. \tag{15.23}$$

Homework Problems

Problem 15.59.

A *derangement* is a permutation $(x_1, x_2, \ldots, x_n)$ of the set $\{1, 2, \ldots, n\}$ such that $x_i \neq i$ for all i. For example, $(2, 3, 4, 5, 1)$ is a derangement, but $(2, 1, 3, 5, 4)$ is not because 3 appears in the third position. The objective of this problem is to count derangements.

It turns out to be easier to start by counting the permutations that are *not* derangements. Let S_i be the set of all permutations $(x_1, x_2, \ldots, x_n)$ that are not derangements because $x_i = i$. So the set of non-derangements is

$$\bigcup_{i=1}^{n} S_i.$$

(a) What is $|S_i|$?

(b) What is $\left| S_i \cap S_j \right|$ where $i \neq j$?

(c) What is $\left| S_{i_1} \cap S_{i_2} \cap \cdots \cap S_{i_k} \right|$ where $i_1, i_2, \ldots, i_k$ are all distinct?

(d) Use the inclusion-exclusion formula to express the number of non-derangements in terms of sizes of possible intersections of the sets $S_1, \ldots, S_n$.

(e) How many terms in the expression in part (d) have the form

$$\left| S_{i_1} \cap S_{i_2} \cap \cdots \cap S_{i_k} \right|?$$

(f) Combine your answers to the preceding parts to prove the number of non-derangements is:

$$n!\left(\frac{1}{1!} - \frac{1}{2!} + \frac{1}{3!} - \cdots \pm \frac{1}{n!}\right).$$

Conclude that the number of derangements is

$$n!\left(1 - \frac{1}{1!} + \frac{1}{2!} - \frac{1}{3!} + \cdots \pm \frac{1}{n!}\right).$$

(g) As n goes to infinity, the number of derangements approaches a constant fraction of all permutations. What is that constant? *Hint:*

$$e^x = 1 + x + \frac{x^2}{2!} + \frac{x^3}{3!} + \cdots$$

Problem 15.60.

How many of the numbers $2, \ldots, n$ are prime? The Inclusion-Exclusion Principle offers a useful way to calculate the answer when n is large. Actually, we will use Inclusion-Exclusion to count the number of *composite* (nonprime) integers from 2 to n. Subtracting this from $n - 1$ gives the number of primes.

Let C_n be the set of composites from 2 to n, and let A_m be the set of numbers in the range $m + 1, \ldots, n$ that are divisible by m. Notice that by definition, $A_m = \emptyset$ for $m \geq n$. So

$$C_n = \bigcup_{i=2}^{n-1} A_i. \tag{15.24}$$

(a) Verify that if $m \mid k$, then $A_m \supseteq A_k$.

(b) Explain why the right-hand side of (15.24) equals

$$\bigcup_{\text{primes } p \leq \sqrt{n}} A_p. \tag{15.25}$$

(c) Explain why $|A_m| = \lfloor n/m \rfloor - 1$ for $m \geq 2$.

(d) Consider any two relatively prime numbers $p, q \leq n$. What is the one number in $(A_p \cap A_q) - A_{p \cdot q}$?

(e) Let $\mathcal{P}$ be a finite set of at least two primes. Give a simple formula for

$$\left|\bigcap_{p \in \mathcal{P}} A_p\right|.$$

(f) Use the Inclusion-Exclusion principle to obtain a formula for $|C_{150}|$ in terms the sizes of intersections among the sets $A_2, A_3, A_5, A_7, A_{11}$. (Omit the intersections that are empty; for example, any intersection of more than three of these sets must be empty.)

(g) Use this formula to find the number of primes up to 150.

Exam Problems

Problem 15.61.

We want to count the number of length-n binary strings in which the substring 011 occurs in various places. For example, the length-14 string

$$00100110011101,$$

has 011 in the 4th position and the 8th position. (Note that by convention, a length-n string starts with position zero and ends with position $n - 1$.) Assume $n \geq 7$.

(a) Let r be the number of length-n binary strings in which 011 occurs starting at the 4th position. Write a formula for r in terms of n.

(b) Let A_i be the set of length-n binary strings in which 011 occurs starting at the ith position. (A_i is empty for $i > n - 3$.) If $i \neq j$, the intersection $A_i \cap A_j$ is either empty or of size s. Write a formula for s in terms of n.

(c) Let t be the number of pairs (i, j) such that $A_i \cap A_j$ is nonempty, where $0 \leq i < j$. Write a binomial coefficient for t in terms of n.

(d) How many length 9 binary strings are there that contain the substring 011? You should express your answer as an integer or as a simple expression which may include the above constants r, s and t for $n = 9$.

Hint: Inclusion-exclusion for $\left| \bigcup_0^8 A_i \right|$.

Problem 15.62.

There are 10 students $A, B, \ldots, J$ who will be lined up left to right according to the some rules below.

Rule I: Student A must not be rightmost.

Rule II: Student B must be adjacent to C (directly to the left or right of C).

Rule III: Student D is always second.

You may answer the following questions with a numerical formula that may involve factorials.

(a) How many possible lineups are there that satisfy all three of these rules?

(b) How many possible lineups are there that satisfy at least one of these rules?

Problem 15.63.

A robot on a point in the 3-D integer lattice can move a unit distance in one positive direction at a time. That is, from position (x, y, z), it can move to either $(x + 1, y, z)$, $(x, y + 1, z)$ or $(x, y, z + 1)$. For any two points P and Q in space, let $n(P, Q)$ denote the number of distinct paths the spacecraft can follow to go from P to Q.

Let

$$A = (0, 10, 20),\ B = (30, 50, 70),\ C = (80, 90, 100),\ D = (200, 300, 400).$$

(a) Express $n(A, B)$ as a **single multinomial coefficient**.

Answer the following questions with arithmetic expressions involving terms $n(P, Q)$ for $P, Q \in \{A, B, C, D\}$. Do not use numbers.

(b) How many paths from A to C go through B?

(c) How many paths from B to D do *not* go through C?

(d) How many paths from A to D go through **neither B nor C**?

Problem 15.64.

In a standard 52-card deck (13 ranks and 4 suits), a hand is a 5-card subset of the set of 52 cards. Express the answer to each part as a formula using factorial, binomial, or multinomial notation.

(a) Let H be the set of all hands. What is $|H|$?

(b) Let H_{NP} be the set of all hands that include no pairs; that is, no two cards in the hand have the same rank. What is $|H_{NP}|$?

(c) Let H_S be the set of all hands that are straights, that is, the ranks of the five cards are consecutive. The order of the ranks is $(A, 2, 3, 4, 5, 6, 7, 8, 9, 10, J, Q, K, A)$; note that A appears twice.
What is $|H_S|$?

(d) Let H_F be the set of all hands that are flushes, that is, the suits of the five cards are identical. What is $|H_F|$?

(e) Let H_{SF} be the set of all straight flush hands, that is, the hand is both a straight and a flush. What is $|H_{SF}|$?

(f) Let H_{HC} be the set of all high-card hands; that is, hands that do not include pairs, are not straights, and are not flushes. Write a formula for $|H_{HC}|$ in terms of $|H_{NP}|, |H_S|, |H_F|, |H_{SF}|$.

Problems for Section 15.10

Practice Problems

Problem 15.65.
Prove the following identity by algebraic manipulation and by giving a combinatorial argument:

$$\binom{n}{r}\binom{r}{k} = \binom{n}{k}\binom{n-k}{r-k}$$

Problem 15.66.
Give a combinatorial proof for this identity:

$$\sum_{\substack{i+j+k=n \\ i,j,k \geq 0}} \binom{n}{i, j, k} = 3^n$$

Class Problems

Problem 15.67.
According to the Multinomial theorem, $(w + x + y + z)^n$ can be expressed as a

sum of terms of the form

$$\binom{n}{r_1, r_2, r_3, r_4} w^{r_1} x^{r_2} y^{r_3} z^{r_4}.$$

(a) How many terms are there in the sum?

(b) The sum of these multinomial coefficients has an easily expressed value. What is it?

$$\sum_{\substack{r_1+r_2+r_3+r_4=n, \\ r_i \in \mathbb{N}}} \binom{n}{r_1,\ r_2,\ r_3,\ r_4} =? \tag{15.26}$$

Hint: How many terms are there when $(w + x + y + z)^n$ is expressed as a sum of monomials in w, x, y, z *before* terms with like powers of these variables are collected together under a single coefficient?

Problem 15.68.

(a) Give a combinatorial proof of the following identity by letting S be the set of all length-n sequences of letters a, b and a single c and counting $|S|$ is two different ways.

$$n2^{n-1} = \sum_{k=1}^{n} k \binom{n}{k} \tag{15.27}$$

(b) Now prove (15.27) algebraically by applying the Binomial Theorem to $(1 + x)^n$ and taking derivatives.

Problem 15.69.

What do the following expressions equal? Give both algebraic and combinatorial proofs for your answers.

(a)

$$\sum_{i=0}^{n} \binom{n}{i}$$

(b)

$$\sum_{i=0}^{n} \binom{n}{i}(-1)^i$$

Hint: Consider the bit strings with an even number of ones and an odd number of ones.

Problem 15.70.

When an integer k occurs as the kth element of a sequence, we'll say it is "in place" in the sequence. For example, in the sequence

$$12453678$$

precisely the integers $1, 2, 6, 7$ and 8 occur in place. We're going to classify the sequences of distinct integers from 1 to n, that is the permutations of $[1..n]$, according to which integers do not occur "in place." Then we'll use this classification to prove the combinatorial identity[11]

$$n! = 1 + \sum_{k=1}^{n} (k-1) \cdot (k-1)! \, . \tag{15.28}$$

If π is a permutation of $[1..n]$, let mnp (π) be the *maximum* integer in $[1..n]$ that does not occur in place in π. For example, for $n = 8$,

$$\text{mnp} \, (12345687) = 8,$$
$$\text{mnp} \, (21345678) = 2,$$
$$\text{mnp} \, (23145678) = 3.$$

(a) For how many permutations of $[1..n]$ is every element in place?

(b) How many permutations π of $[1..n]$ have mnp $(\pi) = 1$?

(c) How many permutations of $[1..n]$ have mnp $(\pi) = k$?

(d) Conclude the equation (15.28).

---

[11] This problem is based on "Use of everywhere divergent generating function," mathoverflow, response 8,147 by Aaron Meyerowitz, Nov. 12, 2010.

Problem 15.71.

Each day, an MIT student selects a breakfast from among b possibilities, lunch from among l possibilities, and dinner from among d possibilities. In each case one of the possibilities is Doritos. However, a legitimate daily menu may include Doritos for at most one meal. Give a combinatorial (not algebraic) proof based on the number of legitimate daily menus that

$$bld - [(b-1) + (l-1) + (d-1) + 1]$$
$$= b(l-1)(d-1) + (b-1)l(d-1) + (b-1)(l-1)d$$
$$-3(b-1)(l-1)(d-1) + (b-1)(l-1)(d-1)$$

Hint: Let M_b be the number of menus where, if Doritos appear at all, they only appear at *b*reakfast; likewise, for M_l, M_d.

Homework Problems

Problem 15.72. (a) Find a combinatorial (*not* algebraic) proof that

$$\sum_{i=0}^{n} \binom{n}{i} = 2^n.$$

(b) Below is a combinatorial proof of an equation. What is the equation?

Proof. Stinky Peterson owns n newts, t toads, and s slugs. Conveniently, he lives in a dorm with $n + t + s$ other students. (The students are distinguishable, but creatures of the same variety are not distinguishable.) Stinky wants to put one creature in each neighbor's bed. Let W be the set of all ways in which this can be done.

On one hand, he could first determine who gets the slugs. Then, he could decide who among his remaining neighbors has earned a toad. Therefore, $|W|$ is equal to the expression on the left.

On the other hand, Stinky could first decide which people deserve newts and slugs and then, from among those, determine who truly merits a newt. This shows that $|W|$ is equal to the expression on the right.

Since both expressions are equal to $|W|$, they must be equal to each other.   ∎

(Combinatorial proofs are real proofs. They are not only rigorous, but also convey an intuitive understanding that a purely algebraic argument might not reveal. However, combinatorial proofs are usually less colorful than this one.)

Problem 15.73.

Give a combinatorial proof for this identity:

$$\sum_{i=0}^{n} \binom{k+i}{k} = \binom{k+n+1}{k+1}$$

Hint: Let S_i be the set of binary sequences with exactly n zeroes, $k+1$ ones, and a total of exactly i occurrences of zeroes appearing before the rightmost occurrence of a one.

Problem 15.74.

According to the Multinomial Theorem 15.6.5, $(x_1 + x_2 + \cdots + x_k)^n$ can be expressed as a sum of terms of the form

$$\binom{n}{r_1, r_2, \ldots, r_k} x_1^{r_1} x_2^{r_2} \ldots x_k^{r_k}.$$

(a) How many terms are there in the sum?

(b) The sum of these multinomial coefficients has an easily expressed value:

$$\sum_{\substack{r_1+r_2+\cdots+r_k=n, \\ r_i \in \mathbb{N}}} \binom{n}{r_1, r_2, \ldots, r_k} = k^n \qquad (15.29)$$

Give a combinatorial proof of this identity.

Hint: How many terms are there when $(x_1 + x_2 + \cdots + x_k)^n$ is expressed as a sum of monomials in x_i *before* terms with like powers of these variables are collected together under a single coefficient?

Problem 15.75.

You want to choose a team of m people for your startup company from a pool of n applicants, and from these m people you want to choose k to be the team managers. You took a Math for Computer Science subject, so you know you can do this in

$$\binom{n}{m}\binom{m}{k}$$

ways. But your CFO, who went to Harvard Business School, comes up with the formula

$$\binom{n}{k}\binom{n-k}{m-k}.$$

Before doing the reasonable thing—dump on your CFO or Harvard Business School—you decide to check his answer against yours.

(a) Give a *combinatorial proof* that your CFO's formula agrees with yours.

(b) Verify this combinatorial proof by giving an *algebraic* proof of this same fact.

Exam Problems

Problem 15.76.
Each day, an MIT student selects a breakfast from among b possibilities, lunch from among l possibilities, and dinner from among d possibilities. In each case one of the possibilities is Doritos. However, a legitimate daily menu may include Doritos for at most one meal. Give a combinatorial (not algebraic) proof based on the number of legitimate daily menus that

$$bld - [(b-1) + (l-1) + (d-1) + 1]$$
$$= (l-1)(d-1) + (b-1)(d-1) + (b-1)(l-1) + (b-1)(l-1)(d-1).$$

Problem 15.77.
Give a combinatorial proof of

$$1 \cdot 2 + 2 \cdot 3 + 3 \cdot 4 + \cdots + (n-1) \cdot n = 2\binom{n+1}{3}$$

Hint: Classify sets of three numbers from the integer interval $[0..n]$ by their maximum element.

16 Generating Functions

Generating Functions are one of the most surprising and useful inventions in Discrete Mathematics. Roughly speaking, generating functions transform problems about *sequences* into problems about *algebra*. This is great because we've got piles of algebraic rules. Thanks to generating functions, we can reduce problems about sequences to checking properties of algebraic expressions. This will allow us to use generating functions to solve all sorts of counting problems.

Several flavors of generating functions such as *ordinary*, *exponential*, and *Dirichlet* come up regularly in combinatorial mathematics. In addition, *Z-transforms*, which are closely related to ordinary generating functions, are important in control theory and signal processing. But ordinary generating functions are enough to illustrate the power of the idea, so we'll stick to them. So from now on *generating function* will mean the ordinary kind, and we will offer a taste of this large subject by showing how generating functions can be used to solve certain kinds of counting problems and how they can be used to find simple formulas for *linear-recursive* functions.

16.1 Infinite Series

Informally, a generating function $F(x)$ is an infinite series

$$F(x) = f_0 + f_1 x + f_2 x^2 + f_3 x^3 + \cdots . \qquad (16.1)$$

We use the notation $[x^n]F(x)$ for the coefficient of x^n in the generating function $F(x)$. That is, $[x^n]F(x) ::= f_n$.

We can analyze the behavior of any sequence of numbers $f_0, f_1 \ldots f_n \ldots$ by regarding the elements of the sequence as successive coefficients of a generating function. It turns out that properties of complicated sequences that arise from counting, recursive definition, and programming problems are easy to explain by treating them as generating functions.

Generating functions can produce noteworthy insights even when the sequence of coefficients is trivial. For example, let $G(x)$ be the generating function for the infinite sequence of ones $1, 1, \ldots$, namely, the geometric series.

$$G(x) ::= 1 + x + x^2 + \cdots + x^n + \cdots . \qquad (16.2)$$

We'll use typical generating function reasoning to derive a simple formula for $G(x)$. The approach is actually an easy version of the perturbation method of Section 14.1.2. Specifically,

$$
\begin{aligned}
G(x) &= 1 + x + x^2 + x^3 + \cdots + x^n + \cdots \\
-xG(x) &= - x - x^2 - x^3 - \cdots - x^n - \cdots \\
\hline
G(x) - xG(x) &= 1.
\end{aligned}
$$

Solving for $G(x)$ gives

$$\frac{1}{1-x} = G(x) ::= \sum_{n=0}^{\infty} x^n. \tag{16.3}$$

In other words,

$$[x^n]\left(\frac{1}{1-x}\right) = 1$$

Continuing with this approach yields a nice formula for

$$N(x) ::= 1 + 2x + 3x^2 + \cdots + (n+1)x^n + \cdots . \tag{16.4}$$

Specifically,

$$
\begin{aligned}
N(x) &= 1 + 2x + 3x^2 + 4x^3 + \cdots + (n+1)x^n + \cdots \\
-xN(x) &= - x - 2x^2 - 3x^3 - \cdots - nx^n - \cdots \\
\hline
N(x) - xN(x) &= 1 + x + x^2 + x^3 + \cdots + x^n + \cdots \\
&= G(x).
\end{aligned}
$$

Solving for $N(x)$ gives

$$\frac{1}{(1-x)^2} = \frac{G(x)}{1-x} = N(x) ::= \sum_{n=0}^{\infty} (n+1)x^n. \tag{16.5}$$

On other words,

$$[x^n]\left(\frac{1}{(1-x)^2}\right) = n+1.$$

16.1.1   Never Mind Convergence

Equations (16.3) and (16.5) hold numerically only when $|x| < 1$, because both generating function series diverge when $|x| \geq 1$. But in the context of generating functions, we regard infinite series as formal algebraic objects. Equations such as (16.3) and (16.5) define symbolic identities that hold for purely algebraic reasons. In fact, good use can be made of generating functions determined by infinite series that don't converge *anywhere* (besides $x = 0$). We'll explain this further in Section 16.5 at the end of this chapter, but for now, take it on faith that you don't need to worry about convergence.

16.2   Counting with Generating Functions

Generating functions are particularly useful for representing and counting the number of ways to select n things. For example, suppose there are two flavors of donuts, chocolate and plain. Let d_n be the number of ways to select n chocolate or plain flavored donuts. $d_n = n + 1$, because there are $n + 1$ such donut selections—all chocolate, 1 plain and $n - 1$ chocolate, 2 plain and $n - 2$ chocolate,..., all plain. We define a generating function $D(x)$ for counting these donut selections by letting the coefficient of x^n be d_n. This gives us equation (16.5)

$$D(x) = \frac{1}{(1 - x)^2}. \tag{16.6}$$

16.2.1   Apples and Bananas too

More generally, suppose we have two kinds of things—say, apples and bananas—and some constraints on how many of each may be selected. Say there are a_n ways to select n apples and b_n ways to select n bananas. The generating function for counting apples would be

$$A(x) ::= \sum_{n=0}^{\infty} a_n x^n,$$

and for bananas would be

$$B(x) ::= \sum_{n=0}^{\infty} b_n x^n.$$

Now suppose apples come in baskets of 6, so there is no way to select 1 to 5 apples, one way to select 6 apples, no way to select 7, etc. In other words,

$$a_n = \begin{cases} 1 & \text{if } n \text{ is a multiple of 6,} \\ 0 & \text{otherwise.} \end{cases}$$

In this case we would have

$$\begin{aligned} A(x) &= 1 + x^6 + x^{12} + \cdots + x^{6n} + \cdots \\ &= 1 + y + y^2 + \cdots + y^n + \cdots \qquad \text{where } y = x^6, \\ &= \frac{1}{1 - y} = \frac{1}{1 - x^6}. \end{aligned}$$

Let's also suppose there are two kinds of bananas—red and yellow. Now, $b_n = n + 1$ by the same reasoning used to count selections of n chocolate and plain donuts, and by (16.6) we have

$$B(x) = \frac{1}{(1-x)^2}.$$

So how many ways are there to select a mix of n apples and bananas? First, we decide how many apples to select. This can be any number k from 0 to n. We can then select these apples in a_k ways, by definition. This leaves $n - k$ bananas to be selected, which by definition can be done in b_{n-k} ways. So the total number of ways to select k apples and $n - k$ bananas is $a_k b_{n-k}$. This means that the total number of ways to select some size n mix of apples and bananas is

$$a_0 b_n + a_1 b_{n-1} + a_2 b_{n-2} + \cdots + a_n b_0. \tag{16.7}$$

16.2.2   Products of Generating Functions

Now here's the cool connection between counting and generating functions: expression (16.7) is equal to the coefficient of x^n in the product $A(x)B(x)$.

In other words, we're claiming that

Rule (Product).

$$[x^n](A(x) \cdot B(x)) = a_0 b_n + a_1 b_{n-1} + a_2 b_{n-2} + \cdots + a_n b_0. \tag{16.8}$$

To explain the generating function Product Rule, we can think about evaluating the product $A(x) \cdot B(x)$ by using a table to identify all the cross-terms from the product of the sums:

	$b_0 x^0$	$b_1 x^1$	$b_2 x^2$	$b_3 x^3$	$\ldots$
$a_0 x^0$	$a_0 b_0 x^0$	$a_0 b_1 x^1$	$a_0 b_2 x^2$	$a_0 b_3 x^3$	$\ldots$
$a_1 x^1$	$a_1 b_0 x^1$	$a_1 b_1 x^2$	$a_1 b_2 x^3$	$\ldots$	
$a_2 x^2$	$a_2 b_0 x^2$	$a_2 b_1 x^3$	$\ldots$		
$a_3 x^3$	$a_3 b_0 x^3$	$\ldots$			
$\vdots$	$\ldots$				

In this layout, all the terms involving the same power of x lie on a 45-degree sloped diagonal. So, the index-n diagonal contains all the x^n-terms, and the coefficient of

x^n in the product $A(x) \cdot B(x)$ is the sum of all the coefficients of the terms on this diagonal, namely, (16.7). The sequence of coefficients of the product $A(x) \cdot B(x)$ is called the *convolution* of the sequences $(a_0, a_1, a_2, \dots)$ and $(b_0, b_1, b_2, \dots)$. In addition to their algebraic role, convolutions of sequences play a prominent role in signal processing and control theory.

This Product Rule provides the algebraic justification for the fact that a geometric series equals $1/(1 - x)$ regardless of convergence. Specifically, the constant 1 describes the generating function

$$1 = 1 + 0x + 0x^2 + \cdots + 0x^n + \cdots.$$

Likewise, the expression $1 - x$ describes the generating function

$$1 - x = 1 + (-1)x + 0x^2 + \cdots + 0x^n + \cdots.$$

So for the series $G(x)$ whose coefficients are all equal to 1, the Product Rule implies in a purely formal way that

$$(1 - x) \cdot G(x) = 1 + 0x + 0x^2 + \cdots + 0x^n + \cdots = 1.$$

In other words, under the Product Rule, the geometric series $G(x)$ is the multiplicative inverse $1/(1 - x)$ of $1 - x$.

Similar reasoning justifies multiplying a generating function by a constant term by term. That is, a special case of the Product Rule is the

Rule (Constant Factor). *For any constant c and generating function $F(x)$*

$$[x^n](c \cdot F(x)) = c \cdot [x^n]F(x). \tag{16.9}$$

16.2.3 The Convolution Rule

We can summarize the discussion above with the

Rule (Convolution). *Let $A(x)$ be the generating function for selecting items from a set $\mathcal{A}$, and let $B(x)$ be the generating function for selecting items from a set $\mathcal{B}$ disjoint from $\mathcal{A}$. The generating function for selecting items from the union $\mathcal{A} \cup \mathcal{B}$ is the product $A(x) \cdot B(x)$.*

The Rule depends on a precise definition of what "selecting items from the union $\mathcal{A} \cup \mathcal{B}$" means. Informally, the idea is that the restrictions on the selection of items from sets $\mathcal{A}$ and $\mathcal{B}$ carry over to selecting items from $\mathcal{A} \cup \mathcal{B}$.[1]

---

[1] Formally, the Convolution Rule applies when there is a bijection between n-element selections from $\mathcal{A} \cup \mathcal{B}$ and ordered pairs of selections from the sets $\mathcal{A}$ and $\mathcal{B}$ containing a total of n elements. We think the informal statement is clear enough.

16.2.4   Counting Donuts with the Convolution Rule

We can use the Convolution Rule to derive in another way the generating function $D(x)$ for the number of ways to select chocolate and plain donuts given in (16.6). To begin, there is only one way to select exactly n chocolate donuts. That means every coefficient of the generating function for selecting n chocolate donuts equals one. So the generating function for chocolate donut selections is $1/(1-x)$; likewise for the generating function for selecting only plain donuts. Now by the Convolution Rule, the generating function for the number of ways to select n donuts when both chocolate and plain flavors are available is

$$D(x) = \frac{1}{1-x} \cdot \frac{1}{1-x} = \frac{1}{(1-x)^2}.$$

So we have derived (16.6) without appeal to (16.5).

Our application of the Convolution Rule for two flavors carries right over to the general case of k flavors; the generating function for selections of donuts when k flavors are available is $1/(1-x)^k$. We already derived the formula for the number of ways to select a n donuts when k flavors are available, namely, $\binom{n+(k-1)}{n}$ from Corollary 15.5.3. So we have

$$[x^n]\left(\frac{1}{(1-x)^k}\right) = \binom{n+(k-1)}{n}. \tag{16.10}$$

Extracting Coefficients from Maclaurin's Theorem

We've used a donut-counting argument to derive the coefficients of $1/(1-x)^k$, but it's instructive to derive this coefficient algebraically, which we can do using Maclaurin's Theorem:

Theorem 16.2.1 (Maclaurin's Theorem).

$$f(x) = f(0) + f'(0)x + \frac{f''(0)}{2!}x^2 + \frac{f'''(0)}{3!}x^3 + \cdots + \frac{f^{(n)}(0)}{n!}x^n + \cdots.$$

This theorem says that the nth coefficient of $1/(1-x)^k$ is equal to its nth derivative evaluated at 0 and divided by $n!$. Computing the nth derivative turns out not to be very difficult

$$\frac{d^n}{d^n x}\frac{1}{(1-x)^k} = k(k+1)\cdots(k+n-1)(1-x)^{-(k+n)}$$

(see Problem 16.5), so

$$[x^n] \left(\frac{1}{(1-x)^k} \right) = \left(\frac{d^n}{d^n x} \frac{1}{(1-x)^k} \right) (0) \frac{1}{n!}$$

$$= \frac{k(k+1) \cdots (k+n-1)(1-0)^{-(k+n)}}{n!}$$

$$= \binom{n + (k-1)}{n}.$$

In other words, instead of using the donut-counting formula (16.10) to find the coefficients of x^n, we could have used this algebraic argument and the Convolution Rule to derive the donut-counting formula.

16.2.5   The Binomial Theorem from the Convolution Rule

The Convolution Rule also provides a new perspective on the Binomial Theorem 15.6.4. Here's how: first, work with the single-element set $\{a_1\}$. The generating function for the number of ways to select n different elements from this set is simply $1 + x$: we have 1 way to select zero elements, 1 way to select the one element, and 0 ways to select more than one element. Similarly, the number of ways to select n elements from any single-element set $\{a_i\}$ has the same generating function $1 + x$. Now by the Convolution Rule, the generating function for choosing a subset of n elements from the set $\{a_1, a_2, \ldots, a_m\}$ is the product $(1+x)^m$ of the generating functions for selecting from each of the m one-element sets. Since we know that the number of ways to select n elements from a set of size m is $\binom{m}{n}$, we conclude that that

$$[x^n](1+x)^m = \binom{m}{n},$$

which is a restatement of the Binomial Theorem 15.6.4. Thus, we have proved the Binomial Theorem without having to analyze the expansion of the expression $(1 + x)^m$ into a sum of products.

These examples of counting donuts and deriving the binomial coefficients illustrate where generating functions get their power:

> Generating functions can allow counting problems to be solved by algebraic manipulation, and conversely, they can allow algebraic identities to be derived by counting techniques.

16.2.6   An Absurd Counting Problem

So far everything we've done with generating functions we could have done another way. But here is an absurd counting problem—really over the top! In how many ways can we fill a bag with n fruits subject to the following constraints?

- The number of apples must be even.

- The number of bananas must be a multiple of 5.

- There can be at most four oranges.

- There can be at most one pear.

For example, there are 7 ways to form a bag with 6 fruits:

Apples	6	4	4	2	2	0	0
Bananas	0	0	0	0	0	5	5
Oranges	0	2	1	4	3	1	0
Pears	0	0	1	0	1	0	1

These constraints are so complicated that getting a nice answer may seem impossible. But let's see what generating functions reveal.

First, we'll construct a generating function for choosing apples. We can choose a set of 0 apples in one way, a set of 1 apple in zero ways (since the number of apples must be even), a set of 2 apples in one way, a set of 3 apples in zero ways, and so forth. So, we have:

$$A(x) = 1 + x^2 + x^4 + x^6 + \cdots = \frac{1}{1-x^2}$$

Similarly, the generating function for choosing bananas is:

$$B(x) = 1 + x^5 + x^{10} + x^{15} + \cdots = \frac{1}{1-x^5}$$

Now, we can choose a set of 0 oranges in one way, a set of 1 orange in one way, and so on. However, we cannot choose more than four oranges, so we have the generating function:

$$O(x) = 1 + x + x^2 + x^3 + x^4 = \frac{1-x^5}{1-x}.$$

Here the right-hand expression is simply the formula (14.2) for a finite geometric sum. Finally, we can choose only zero or one pear, so we have:

$$P(x) = 1 + x$$

The Convolution Rule says that the generating function for choosing from among all four kinds of fruit is:

$$A(x)B(x)O(x)P(x) = \frac{1}{1-x^2}\frac{1}{1-x^5}\frac{1-x^5}{1-x}(1+x)$$

$$= \frac{1}{(1-x)^2}$$

$$= 1 + 2x + 3x^2 + 4x^3 + \cdots$$

Almost everything cancels! We're left with $1/(1-x)^2$, which we found a power series for earlier: the coefficient of x^n is simply $n+1$. Thus, the number of ways to form a bag of n fruits is just $n+1$. This is consistent with the example we worked out, since there were 7 different fruit bags containing 6 fruits. *Amazing!*

This example was contrived to seem complicated at first sight so we could highlight the power of counting with generating functions. But the simple suggests that there ought to be an elementary derivation without resort to generating functions, and indeed there is (Problem 16.8).

16.3 Partial Fractions

We got a simple solution to the seemingly impossible counting problem of Section 16.2.6 because its generating function simplified to the expression $1/(1-x)^2$, whose power series coefficients we already knew. This problem was set up so the answer would work out neatly, but other problems are not so neat. To solve more general problems using generating functions, we need ways to find power series coefficients for generating functions given as formulas. Maclaurin's Theorem 16.2.1 is a very general method for finding coefficients, but it only applies when formulas for repeated derivatives can be found, which isn't often. However, there is an automatic way to find the power series coefficients for any formula that is a quotient of polynomials, namely, the method of partial fractions from elementary calculus.

The partial fraction method is based on the fact that quotients of polynomials can be expressed as sums of terms whose power series coefficients have nice formulas. For example when the denominator polynomial has distinct nonzero roots, the method rests on

Lemma 16.3.1. *Let $p(x)$ be a polynomial of degree less than n and let $\alpha_1, \ldots, \alpha_n$ be distinct, nonzero numbers. Then there are constants $c_1, \ldots, c_n$ such that*

$$\frac{p(x)}{(1-\alpha_1 x)(1-\alpha_2 x)\cdots(1-\alpha_n x)} = \frac{c_1}{1-\alpha_1 x} + \frac{c_2}{1-\alpha_2 x} + \cdots + \frac{c_n}{1-\alpha_n x}.$$

Let's illustrate the use of Lemma 16.3.1 by finding the power series coefficients for the function

$$R(x) ::= \frac{x}{1 - x - x^2}.$$

We can use the quadratic formula to find the roots r_1, r_2 of the denominator $1 - x - x^2$.

$$r_1 = \frac{-1 - \sqrt{5}}{2}, r_2 = \frac{-1 + \sqrt{5}}{2}.$$

So

$$1 - x - x^2 = (x - r_1)(x - r_2) = r_1 r_2 (1 - x/r_1)(1 - x/r_2).$$

With a little algebra, we find that

$$R(x) = \frac{x}{(1 - \alpha_1 x)(1 - \alpha_2 x)}$$

where

$$\alpha_1 = \frac{1 + \sqrt{5}}{2}$$

$$\alpha_2 = \frac{1 - \sqrt{5}}{2}.$$

Next we find c_1 and c_2 which satisfy:

$$\frac{x}{(1 - \alpha_1 x)(1 - \alpha_2 x)} = \frac{c_1}{1 - \alpha_1 x} + \frac{c_2}{1 - \alpha_2 x} \qquad (16.11)$$

In general, we can do this by plugging in a couple of values for x to generate two linear equations in c_1 and c_2 and then solve the equations for c_1 and c_2. A simpler approach in this case comes from multiplying both sides of (16.11) by the left-hand denominator to get

$$x = c_1(1 - \alpha_2 x) + c_2(1 - \alpha_1 x).$$

Now letting $x = 1/\alpha_2$ we obtain

$$c_2 = \frac{1/\alpha_2}{1 - \alpha_1/\alpha_2} = \frac{1}{\alpha_2 - \alpha_1} = -\frac{1}{\sqrt{5}},$$

and similarly, letting $x = 1/\alpha_1$ we obtain

$$c_1 = \frac{1}{\sqrt{5}}.$$

Plugging these values for c_1, c_2 into equation (16.11) finally gives the partial fraction expansion

$$R(x) = \frac{x}{1 - x - x^2} = \frac{1}{\sqrt{5}}\left(\frac{1}{1 - \alpha_1 x} - \frac{1}{1 - \alpha_2 x}\right)$$

Each term in the partial fractions expansion has a simple power series given by the geometric sum formula:

$$\frac{1}{1 - \alpha_1 x} = 1 + \alpha_1 x + \alpha_1^2 x^2 + \cdots$$

$$\frac{1}{1 - \alpha_2 x} = 1 + \alpha_2 x + \alpha_2^2 x^2 + \cdots$$

Substituting in these series gives a power series for the generating function:

$$R(x) = \frac{1}{\sqrt{5}}\left((1 + \alpha_1 x + \alpha_1^2 x^2 + \cdots) - (1 + \alpha_2 x + \alpha_2^2 x^2 + \cdots)\right),$$

so

$$[x^n]R(x) = \frac{\alpha_1^n - \alpha_2^n}{\sqrt{5}}$$

$$= \frac{1}{\sqrt{5}}\left(\left(\frac{1 + \sqrt{5}}{2}\right)^n - \left(\frac{1 - \sqrt{5}}{2}\right)^n\right) \qquad (16.12)$$

16.3.1 Partial Fractions with Repeated Roots

Lemma 16.3.1 generalizes to the case when the denominator polynomial has a repeated nonzero root with multiplicity m by expanding the quotient into a sum a terms of the form

$$\frac{c}{(1 - \alpha x)^k}$$

where α is the reciprocal of the root and $k \leq m$. A formula for the coefficients of such a term follows from the donut formula (16.10).

$$[x^n]\left(\frac{c}{(1 - \alpha x)^k}\right) = c\alpha^n \binom{n + (k - 1)}{n}. \qquad (16.13)$$

When $\alpha = 1$, this follows from the donut formula (16.10) and termwise multiplication by the constant c. The case for arbitrary α follows by substituting αx for x in the power series; this changes x^n into $(\alpha x)^n$ and so has the effect of multiplying the coefficient of x^n by α^n.[2]

---

[2]In other words,

$$[x^n]F(\alpha x) = \alpha^n \cdot [x^n]F(x).$$

16.4   Solving Linear Recurrences

16.4.1   A Generating Function for the Fibonacci Numbers

The Fibonacci numbers $f_0, f_1, \ldots, f_n, \ldots$ are defined recursively as follows:

$$f_0 ::= 0$$
$$f_1 ::= 1$$
$$f_n = ::= f_{n-1} + f_{n-2} \qquad \text{(for } n \geq 2\text{)}.$$

Generating functions will now allow us to derive an astonishing closed formula for f_n.

Let $F(x)$ be the generating function for the sequence of Fibonacci numbers, that is,

$$F(x) ::= f_0 + f_1 x + f_2 x^2 + \cdots f_n x^n + \cdots.$$

Reasoning as we did at the start of this chapter to derive the formula for a geometric series, we have

$$
\begin{array}{rcccccccl}
F(x) & = & f_0 & + & f_1 x & + & f_2 x^2 & + \cdots + & f_n x^n + \cdots. \\
-x F(x) & = & & - & f_0 x & - & f_1 x^2 & - \cdots - & f_{n-1} x^n + \cdots. \\
-x^2 F(x) & = & & & & - & f_0 x^2 & - \cdots - & f_{n-2} x^n + \cdots. \\
\hline
F(x)(1 - x - x^2) & = & f_0 & + & (f_1 - f_0)x & + & 0x^2 & + \cdots + & 0x^n + \cdots. \\
& = & 0 & + & 1x & + & 0x^2 & = \quad x,
\end{array}
$$

so

$$F(x) = \frac{x}{1 - x - x^2}.$$

But $F(x)$ is the same as the function we used to illustrate the partial fraction method for finding coefficients in Section 16.3. So by equation (16.12), we arrive at what is called *Binet's formula*:

$$f_n = \frac{1}{\sqrt{5}} \left(\left(\frac{1 + \sqrt{5}}{2} \right)^n - \left(\frac{1 - \sqrt{5}}{2} \right)^n \right) \qquad (16.14)$$

Binet's formula for Fibonacci numbers is astonishing and maybe scary. It's not even obvious that the expression on the right-hand side (16.14) is an integer. But the formula is very useful. For example, it provides—via the repeated squaring method—a much more efficient way to compute Fibonacci numbers than crunching through the recurrence. It also make explicit the exponential growth of these numbers.

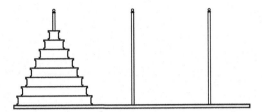

Figure 16.1 The initial configuration of the disks in the Towers of Hanoi problem.

16.4.2 The Towers of Hanoi

According to legend, there is a temple in Hanoi with three posts and 64 gold disks of different sizes. Each disk has a hole through the center so that it fits on a post. In the misty past, all the disks were on the first post, with the largest on the bottom and the smallest on top, as shown in Figure 16.1.

Monks in the temple have labored through the years since to move all the disks to one of the other two posts according to the following rules:

- The only permitted action is removing the top disk from one post and dropping it onto another post.

- A larger disk can never lie above a smaller disk on any post.

So, for example, picking up the whole stack of disks at once and dropping them on another post is illegal. That's good, because the legend says that when the monks complete the puzzle, the world will end!

To clarify the problem, suppose there were only 3 gold disks instead of 64. Then the puzzle could be solved in 7 steps as shown in Figure 16.2.

The questions we must answer are, "Given sufficient time, can the monks succeed?" If so, "How long until the world ends?" And, most importantly, "Will this happen before the final exam?"

A Recursive Solution

The Towers of Hanoi problem can be solved recursively. As we describe the procedure, we'll also analyze the minimum number t_n of steps required to solve the n-disk problem. For example, some experimentation shows that $t_1 = 1$ and $t_2 = 3$. The procedure illustrated above uses 7 steps, which shows that t_3 is at most 7.

The recursive solution has three stages, which are described below and illustrated in Figure 16.3. For clarity, the largest disk is shaded in the figures.

Stage 1. Move the top $n-1$ disks from the first post to the second using the solution for $n - 1$ disks. This can be done in t_{n-1} steps.

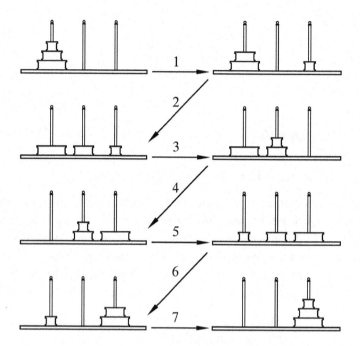

Figure 16.2   The 7-step solution to the Towers of Hanoi problem when there are $n = 3$ disks.

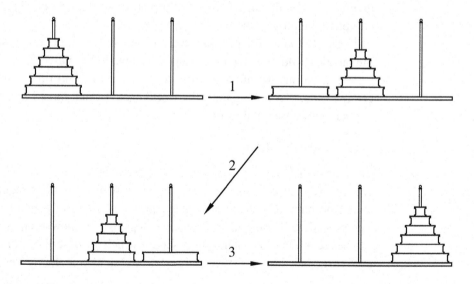

Figure 16.3   A recursive solution to the Towers of Hanoi problem.

Stage 2. Move the largest disk from the first post to the third post. This takes just 1 step.

Stage 3. Move the $n-1$ disks from the second post to the third post, again using the solution for $n-1$ disks. This can also be done in t_{n-1} steps.

This algorithm shows that t_n, the minimum number of steps required to move n disks to a different post, is at most $t_{n-1} + 1 + t_{n-1} = 2t_{n-1} + 1$. We can use this fact to upper bound the number of operations required to move towers of various heights:

$$t_3 \le 2 \cdot t_2 + 1 = 7$$
$$t_4 \le 2 \cdot t_3 + 1 \le 15$$

Continuing in this way, we could eventually compute an upper bound on t_{64}, the number of steps required to move 64 disks. So this algorithm answers our first question: given sufficient time, the monks can finish their task and end the world. This is a shame. After all that effort, they'd probably want to smack a few high-fives and go out for burgers and ice cream, but nope—world's over.

Finding a Recurrence

We cannot yet compute the exact number of steps that the monks need to move the 64 disks, only an upper bound. Perhaps, having pondered the problem since the beginning of time, the monks have devised a better algorithm.

Lucky for us, there is no better algorithm. Here's why: at some step, the monks must move the largest disk from the first post to a different post. For this to happen, the $n-1$ smaller disks must all be stacked out of the way on the only remaining post. Arranging the $n-1$ smaller disks this way requires at least t_{n-1} moves. After the largest disk is moved, at least another t_{n-1} moves are required to pile the $n-1$ smaller disks on top.

This argument shows that the number of steps required is at least $2t_{n-1} + 1$. Since we gave an algorithm using exactly that number of steps, we can now write an expression for t_n, the number of moves required to complete the Towers of Hanoi problem with n disks:

$$t_0 = 0$$
$$t_n = 2t_{n-1} + 1 \qquad \text{(for } n \ge 1\text{).}$$

Solving the Recurrence

We can now find a formula for t_n using generating functions. Let $T(x)$ be the generating function for the t_n's, that is,

$$T(x) ::= t_0 + t_1 x + t_2 x^2 + \cdots t_n x^n + \cdots .$$

Reasoning as we did for the Fibonacci recurrence, we have

$$
\begin{array}{rcrcrcrcr}
T(x) & = & t_0 & + & t_1 x & + & \cdots & + & t_n x^n + \cdots \\
-2xT(x) & = & & - & 2t_0 x & - & \cdots & - & 2t_{n-1} x^n + \cdots \\
-1/(1-x) & = & -1 & - & 1x & - & \cdots & - & 1x^n + \cdots \\
\hline
T(x)(1-2x) - 1/(1-x) & = & t_0 - 1 & + & 0x & + & \cdots & + & 0x^n + \cdots \\
& = & -1, & & & & & &
\end{array}
$$

so

$$
T(x)(1-2x) = \frac{1}{1-x} - 1 = \frac{x}{1-x},
$$

and

$$
T(x) = \frac{x}{(1-2x)(1-x)}.
$$

Using partial fractions,

$$
\frac{x}{(1-2x)(1-x)} = \frac{c_1}{1-2x} + \frac{c_2}{1-x}
$$

for some constants c_1, c_2. Now multiplying both sides by the left hand denominator gives

$$
x = c_1(1-x) + c_2(1-2x).
$$

Substituting $1/2$ for x yields $c_1 = 1$ and substituting 1 for x yields $c_2 = -1$, which gives

$$
T(x) = \frac{1}{1-2x} - \frac{1}{1-x}.
$$

Finally we can read off the simple formula for the numbers of steps needed to move a stack of n disks:

$$
t_n = [x^n] T(x) = [x^n]\left(\frac{1}{1-2x}\right) - [x^n]\left(\frac{1}{1-x}\right) = 2^n - 1.
$$

16.4.3   Solving General Linear Recurrences

An equation of the form

$$
f(n) = c_1 f(n-1) + c_2 f(n-2) + \cdots + c_d f(n-d) + h(n) \qquad (16.15)
$$

for constants $c_i \in \mathbb{C}$ is called a *degree d linear recurrence* with inhomogeneous term $h(n)$.

The methods above can be used to solve linear recurrences with a large class of inhomogeneous terms. In particular, when the inhomogeneous term itself has a generating function that can be expressed as a quotient of polynomials, the approach used above to derive generating functions for the Fibonacci and Tower of Hanoi examples carries over to yield a quotient of polynomials that defines the generating function $f(0) + f(1)x + f(2)x^2 + \cdots$. Then partial fractions can be used to find a formula for $f(n)$ that is a linear combination of terms of the form $n^k \alpha^n$ where k is a nonnegative integer $\leq d$ and α is the reciprocal of a root of the denominator polynomial. For example, see Problems 16.14, 16.15, 16.18, and 16.19.

16.5 Formal Power Series

16.5.1 Divergent Generating Functions

Let $F(x)$ be the generating function for $n!$, that is,

$$F(x) ::= 1 + 1x + 2x^2 + \cdots + n!x^n + \cdots .$$

Because $x^n = o(n!)$ for all $x \neq 0$, this generating function converges only at $x = 0$.[3]

Next, let $H(x)$ be the generating function for $n \cdot n!$, that is,

$$H(x) ::= 0 + 1x + 4x^2 + \cdots + n \cdot n! x^n + \cdots .$$

Again, $H(x)$ converges only for $x = 0$, so $H(x)$ and $F(x)$ describe the same, trivial, partial function on the reals.

On the other hand, $F(x)$ and $H(x)$ have different coefficients for all powers of x greater than 1, and we can usefully distinguish them as formal, symbolic objects.

To illustrate this, note than by subtracting 1 from $F(x)$ and then dividing each of the remaining terms by x, we get a series where the coefficient if x^n is $(n + 1)!$. That is

$$[x^n] \left(\frac{F(x) - 1}{x} \right) = (n + 1)! . \tag{16.16}$$

Now a little further formal reasoning about $F(x)$ and $H(x)$ will allow us to deduce the following identity for $n!$:[4]

$$n! = 1 + \sum_{i=1}^{n} (i - 1) \cdot (i - 1)! \tag{16.17}$$

---

[3] This section is based on an example from "Use of everywhere divergent generating function," math**overflow**, response 8,147 by Aaron Meyerowitz, Nov. 12, 2010.

[4] A combinatorial proof of (16.17) is given in Problem 15.70

To prove this identity, note that from (16.16), we have

$$[x^n]H(x) ::= n \cdot n! = (n+1)! - n! = [x^n]\left(\frac{F(x)-1}{x}\right) - [x^n]F(x).$$

In other words,

$$H(x) = \frac{F(x)-1}{x} - F(x), \tag{16.18}$$

Solving (16.18) for $F(x)$, we get

$$F(x) = \frac{xH(x)+1}{1-x}. \tag{16.19}$$

But $[x^n](xH(x)+1)$ is $(n-1) \cdot (n-1)!$ for $n \geq 1$ and is 1 for $n = 0$, so by the convolution formula,

$$[x^n]\left(\frac{xH(x)+1}{1-x}\right) = 1 + \sum_{i=1}^{n}(i-1) \cdot (i-1)!.$$

The identity (16.17) now follows immediately from (16.19).

16.5.2   The Ring of Power Series

So why don't we have to worry about series whose radius of convergence is zero, and how do we justify the kind of manipulation in the previous section to derive the formula (16.19)? The answer comes from thinking abstractly about infinite sequences of numbers and operations that can be performed on them.

For example, one basic operation combining two infinite sequences is adding them coordinatewise. That is, if we let

$$G ::= (g_0, g_1, g_2, \dots),$$
$$H ::= (h_0, h_1, h_2, \dots),$$

then we can define the sequence sum $\oplus$ by the rule:

$$G \oplus H ::= (g_0 + h_0, g_1 + h_1, \dots, g_n + h_n, \dots).$$

Another basic operation is sequence multiplication $\otimes$ defined by the convolution rule (*not* coordinatewise):

$$G \otimes H ::= \left(g_0 + h_0, g_0h_1 + g_1h_0, \dots, \sum_{i=0}^{n}g_ih_{n-i}, \dots\right).$$

These operations on infinite sequences have lots of nice properties. For example, it's easy to check that sequence addition and multiplication are commutative:

$$G \oplus H = H \oplus G,$$
$$G \otimes H = H \otimes G.$$

If we let

$$Z ::= (0, 0, 0, \dots),$$
$$I ::= (1, 0, 0, \dots, 0, \dots),$$

then it's equally easy to check that Z acts like a zero for sequences and I acts like the number one:

$$Z \oplus G = G,$$
$$Z \otimes G = Z, \tag{16.20}$$
$$I \otimes G = G.$$

Now if we define

$$-G ::= (-g_0, -g_1, -g_2, \dots)$$

then

$$G \oplus (-G) = Z.$$

In fact, the operations $\oplus$ and $\otimes$ satisfy all the *commutative ring* axioms described in Section 9.7.1. The set of infinite sequences of numbers together with these operations is called the ring of *formal power series* over these numbers.[5]

A sequence H is the *reciprocal* of a sequence G when

$$G \otimes H = I.$$

A reciprocal of G is also called a *multiplicative inverse* or simply an "inverse" of G. The ring axioms imply that if there is a reciprocal, it is unique (see Problem 9.32), so the suggestive notation $1/G$ can be used unambiguously to denote this reciprocal, if it exists. For example, letting

$$J ::= (1, -1, 0, 0, \dots, 0, \dots)$$
$$K ::= (1, 1, 1, 1, \dots, 1, \dots),$$

the definition of $\otimes$ implies that $J \otimes K = I$, and so $K = 1/J$ and $J = 1/K$.

---

[5]The elements in the sequences may be the real numbers, complex numbers, or, more generally, may be the elements from any given commutative ring.

In the ring of formal power series, equation (16.20) implies that the zero sequence Z has no inverse, so $1/Z$ is undefined—just as the expression $1/0$ is undefined over the real numbers or the ring $\mathbb{Z}_n$ of Section 9.7.1. It's not hard to verify that a series has an inverse iff its initial element is nonzero (see Problem 16.25).

Now we can explain the proper way to understand a generating function definition

$$G(x) ::= \sum_{n=0}^{\infty} g_n x^n.$$

It simply means that $G(x)$ really refers to its infinite sequence of coefficients $(g_0, g_1, \ldots)$ in the ring of formal power series. The simple expression x can be understood as referring to the sequence

$$X ::= (0, 1, 0, 0, \ldots, 0, \ldots).$$

Likewise, $1 - x$ abbreviates the sequence J above, and the familiar equation

$$\frac{1}{1-x} = 1 + x + x^2 + x^3 + \cdots \tag{16.21}$$

can be understood as a way of restating the assertion that K is $1/J$. In other words, the powers of the variable x just serve as a place holders—and as reminders of the definition of convolution. The equation (16.21) has nothing to do with the values of x or the convergence of the series. Rather, it is stating a property that holds in the ring of formal power series. The reasoning about the divergent series in the previous section is completely justified as properties of formal power series.

16.6   References

[47], [23], [9] [18]

Problems for Section 16.1

Practice Problems

Problem 16.1.
The notation $[x^n] F(x)$ refers to the coefficient of x^n in the generating function

$F(x)$. Indicate all the expressions below that equal $[x^n]4xG(x)$ (most of them do).

$4[x^n]xG(x)$ $\qquad\qquad$ $4x[x^n]G(x)$ $\qquad\qquad$ $[x^{n-1}]4G(x)$

$([x^n]4x) \cdot [x^n]G(x)$ $\qquad$ $([x]4x) \cdot [x^n]xG(x)$ $\qquad$ $[x^{n+1}]4x^2G(x)$

Problem 16.2.
What is the coefficient of x^n in the generating function

$$\frac{1+x}{(1-x)^2} \quad ?$$

Problems for Section 16.2

Practice Problems

Problem 16.3.
You would like to buy a bouquet of flowers. You find an online service that will make bouquets of **lilies**, **roses** and **tulips**, subject to the following constraints:

- there must be at most 1 lily,

- there must be an odd number of tulips,

- there must be at least two roses.

Example: A bouquet of no lilies, 3 tulips, and 5 roses satisfies the constraints.

Express $B(x)$, the generating function for the number of ways to select a bouquet of n flowers, as a quotient of polynomials (or products of polynomials). You do not need to simplify this expression.

Problem 16.4.
Write a formula for the generating function whose successive coefficients are given by the sequence:

(a) $0, 0, 1, 1, 1, \ldots$

(b) $1, 1, 0, 0, 0, \ldots$

(c) 1, 0, 1, 0, 1, 0, 1,...

(d) 1, 4, 6, 4, 1, 0, 0, 0,...

(e) 1, 2, 3, 4, 5,...

(f) 1, 4, 9, 16, 25,...

(g) 1, 1, 1/2, 1/6, 1/24, 1/120,...

Class Problems

Problem 16.5.
Let $A(x) = \sum_{n=0}^{\infty} a_n x^n$. Then it's easy to check that

$$a_n = \frac{A^{(n)}(0)}{n!},$$

where $A^{(n)}$ is the nth derivative of A. Use this fact (which you may assume) instead of the Convolution Counting Principle 16.2.3, to prove that

$$\frac{1}{(1-x)^k} = \sum_{n=0}^{\infty} \binom{n+k-1}{k-1} x^n.$$

So if we didn't already know the Bookkeeper Rule from Section 15.6, we could have proved it from this calculation and the Convolution Rule for generating functions.

Problem 16.6. (a) Let

$$S(x) ::= \frac{x^2 + x}{(1-x)^3}.$$

What is the coefficient of x^n in the generating function series for $S(x)$?

(b) Explain why $S(x)/(1-x)$ is the generating function for the sums of squares. That is, the coefficient of x^n in the series for $S(x)/(1-x)$ is $\sum_{k=1}^{n} k^2$.

(c) Use the previous parts to prove that

$$\sum_{k=1}^{n} k^2 = \frac{n(n+1)(2n+1)}{6}.$$

Homework Problems

Problem 16.7.
We will use generating functions to determine how many ways there are to use pennies, nickels, dimes, quarters, and half-dollars to give n cents change.

(a) Write the generating function $P(x)$ for for the number of ways to use only pennies to make n cents.

(b) Write the generating function $N(x)$ for the number of ways to use only nickels to make n cents.

(c) Write the generating function for the number of ways to use only nickels and pennies to change n cents.

(d) Write the generating function for the number of ways to use pennies, nickels, dimes, quarters, and half-dollars to give n cents change.

(e) Explain how to use this function to find out how many ways are there to change 50 cents; you do *not* have to provide the answer or actually carry out the process.

Problem 16.8.
The answer derived by generating functions for the "absurd" counting problem in Section 16.2.6 is not impossibly complicated at all. Describe a direct simple counting argument to derive this answer without using generating functions.

Problems for Section 16.3

Class Problems

Problem 16.9.
We are interested in generating functions for the number of different ways to compose a bag of n donuts subject to various restrictions. For each of the restrictions in parts (a)-(e) below, find a closed form for the corresponding generating function.

(a) All the donuts are chocolate and there are at least 3.

(b) All the donuts are glazed and there are at most 2.

(c) All the donuts are coconut and there are exactly 2 or there are none.

(d) All the donuts are plain and their number is a multiple of 4.

(e) The donuts must be chocolate, glazed, coconut, or plain with the numbers of each flavor subject to the constraints above.

(f) Now find a closed form for the number of ways to select n donuts subject to the above constraints.

Homework Problems

Problem 16.10.

Miss McGillicuddy never goes outside without a collection of pets. In particular:

- She brings a positive number of songbirds, which always come in pairs.

- She may or may not bring her alligator, Freddy.

- She brings at least 2 cats.

- She brings two or more chihuahuas and labradors leashed together in a line.

Let P_n denote the number of different collections of n pets that can accompany her, where we regard chihuahuas and labradors leashed in different orders as different collections.

For example, $P_6 = 4$ since there are 4 possible collections of 6 pets:

- 2 songbirds, 2 cats, 2 chihuahuas leashed in line

- 2 songbirds, 2 cats, 2 labradors leashed in line

- 2 songbirds, 2 cats, a labrador leashed behind a chihuahua

- 2 songbirds, 2 cats, a chihuahua leashed behind a labrador

(a) Let
$$P(x) ::= P_0 + P_1 x + P_2 x^2 + P_3 x^3 + \cdots$$

be the generating function for the number of Miss McGillicuddy's pet collections. Verify that
$$P(x) = \frac{4x^6}{(1-x)^2(1-2x)}.$$

(b) Find a closed form expression for P_n.

Exam Problems

Problem 16.11.

T-Pain is planning an epic boat trip and he needs to decide what to bring with him.

- He must bring some burgers, but they only come in packs of 6.

- He and his two friends can't decide whether they want to dress formally or casually. He'll either bring 0 pairs of flip flops or 3 pairs.

- He doesn't have very much room in his suitcase for towels, so he can bring at most 2.

- In order for the boat trip to be truly epic, he has to bring at least 1 nautical-themed pashmina afghan.

(a) Let $B(x)$ be the generating function for the number of ways to bring n burgers, $F(x)$ for the number of ways to bring n pairs of flip flops, $T(x)$ for towels, and $A(x)$ for Afghans. Write simple formulas for each of these.

(b) Let g_n be the the number of different ways for T-Pain to bring n items (burgers, pairs of flip flops, towels, and/or afghans) on his boat trip. Let $G(x)$ be the generating function $\sum_{n=0}^{\infty} g_n x^n$. Verify that

$$G(x) = \frac{x^7}{(1-x)^2}.$$

(c) Find a simple formula for g_n.

Problem 16.12.

Every day in the life of Dangerous Dan is a potential disaster:

- Dan may or may not spill his breakfast cereal on his computer keyboard.

- Dan may or may not fall down the front steps on his way out the door.

- Dan stubs his toe zero or more times.

- Dan blurts something foolish an even number of times.

Let T_n be the number of different combinations of n mishaps Dan can suffer in one day. For example, $T_3 = 7$, because there are seven possible combinations of three mishaps:

spills	0	1	0	1	1	0	0
falls	0	0	1	1	0	1	0
stubs	3	2	2	1	0	0	1
blurts	0	0	0	0	2	2	2

(a) Express the generating function

$$T(x) ::= T_0 + T_1 x + T_2 x^2 + \cdots$$

as a quotient of polynomials.

(b) Put integers in the boxes that make this equation true:

$$g(x) = \frac{\boxed{}}{1 - x} + \frac{\boxed{}}{(1 - x)^2}$$

(c) Write a closed-form expression for T_n:

Problems for Section 16.4

Practice Problems

Problem 16.13.
Let $b, c, a_0, a_1, a_2, \ldots$ be real numbers such that

$$a_n = b(a_{n-1}) + c$$

for $n \geq 1$.
   Let $G(x)$ be the generating function for this sequence.

(a) Express the coefficient of x^n for $n \geq 1$ in the series expansion of $bxG(x)$ in terms of b and a_i for suitable i.

(b) What is the coefficient of x^n for $n \geq 1$ in the series expansion of $cx/(1-x)$?

(c) Use the previous results to Exhibit a very simple expression for $G(x) - bxG(x) - cx/(1-x)$.

(d) Using the method of partial fractions, we can find real numbers d and e such that

$$G(x) = d/L(x) + e/M(x).$$

What are $L(x)$ and $M(x)$?

Class Problems

Problem 16.14.
The famous mathematician, Fibonacci, has decided to start a rabbit farm to fill up his time while he's not making new sequences to torment future college students. Fibonacci starts his farm on month zero (being a mathematician), and at the start of month one he receives his first pair of rabbits. Each pair of rabbits takes a month to mature, and after that breeds to produce one new pair of rabbits each month. Fibonacci decides that in order never to run out of rabbits or money, every time a batch of new rabbits is born, he'll sell a number of newborn pairs equal to the total number of pairs he had three months earlier. Fibonacci is convinced that this way he'll never run out of stock.

(a) Define the number r_n of pairs of rabbits Fibonacci has in month n, using a recurrence relation. That is, define r_n in terms of various r_i where $i < n$.

(b) Let $R(x)$ be the generating function for rabbit pairs,

$$R(x) ::= r_0 + r_1 x + r_2 x^2 + \cdots$$

Express $R(x)$ as a quotient of polynomials.

(c) Find a partial fraction decomposition of the generating function $R(x)$.

(d) Finally, use the partial fraction decomposition to come up with a closed form expression for the number of pairs of rabbits Fibonacci has on his farm on month n.

Problem 16.15.
Less well-known than the Towers of Hanoi—but no less fascinating—are the Towers of Sheboygan. As in Hanoi, the puzzle in Sheboygan involves 3 posts and n

rings of different sizes. The rings are placed on post #1 in order of size with the smallest ring on top and largest on bottom.

The objective is to transfer all n rings to post #2 via a sequence of moves. As in the Hanoi version, a move consists of removing the top ring from one post and dropping it onto another post with the restriction that a larger ring can never lie above a smaller ring. But unlike Hanoi, a local ordinance requires that **a ring can only be moved from post #1 to post #2, from post #2 to post #3, or from post #3 to post #1.** Thus, for example, moving a ring directly from post #1 to post #3 is not permitted.

(a) One procedure that solves the Sheboygan puzzle is defined recursively: to move an initial stack of n rings to the next post, move the top stack of $n-1$ rings to the furthest post by moving it to the next post two times, then move the big, nth ring to the next post, and finally move the top stack another two times to land on top of the big ring. Let s_n be the number of moves that this procedure uses. Write a simple linear recurrence for s_n.

(b) Let $S(x)$ be the generating function for the sequence $\langle s_0, s_1, s_2, \dots \rangle$. Carefully show that

$$S(x) = \frac{x}{(1-x)(1-4x)}.$$

(c) Give a simple formula for s_n.

(d) A better (indeed optimal, but we won't prove this) procedure to solve the Towers of Sheboygan puzzle can be defined in terms of two mutually recursive procedures, procedure $P_1(n)$ for moving a stack of n rings 1 pole forward, and $P_2(n)$ for moving a stack of n rings 2 poles forward. This is trivial for $n = 0$. For $n > 0$, define:

$P_1(n)$: Apply $P_2(n-1)$ to move the top $n-1$ rings two poles forward to the third pole. Then move the remaining big ring once to land on the second pole. Then apply $P_2(n-1)$ again to move the stack of $n-1$ rings two poles forward from the third pole to land on top of the big ring.

$P_2(n)$: Apply $P_2(n-1)$ to move the top $n-1$ rings two poles forward to land on the third pole. Then move the remaining big ring to the second pole. Then apply $P_1(n-1)$ to move the stack of $n-1$ rings one pole forward to land on the first pole. Now move the big ring 1 pole forward again to land on the third pole. Finally, apply $P_2(n-1)$ again to move the stack of $n-1$ rings two poles forward to land on the big ring.

Let t_n be the number of moves needed to solve the Sheboygan puzzle using procedure $P_1(n)$. Show that

$$t_n = 2t_{n-1} + 2t_{n-2} + 3, \qquad\qquad (16.22)$$

for $n > 1$.

Hint: Let u_n be the number of moves used by procedure $P_2(n)$. Express each of t_n and u_n as linear combinations of t_{n-1} and u_{n-1} and solve for t_n.

(e) Derive values a, b, c, α, β such that

$$t_n = a\alpha^n + b\beta^n + c.$$

Conclude that $t_n = o(s_n)$.

Homework Problems

Problem 16.16.

Taking derivatives of generating functions is another useful operation. This is done termwise, that is, if

$$F(x) = f_0 + f_1 x + f_2 x^2 + f_3 x^3 + \cdots,$$

then

$$F'(x) ::= f_1 + 2f_2 x + 3f_3 x^2 + \cdots.$$

For example,

$$\frac{1}{(1-x)^2} = \left(\frac{1}{(1-x)}\right)' = 1 + 2x + 3x^2 + \cdots$$

so

$$H(x) ::= \frac{x}{(1-x)^2} = 0 + 1x + 2x^2 + 3x^3 + \cdots$$

is the generating function for the sequence of nonnegative integers. Therefore

$$\frac{1+x}{(1-x)^3} = H'(x) = 1 + 2^2 x + 3^2 x^2 + 4^2 x^3 + \cdots,$$

so

$$\frac{x^2 + x}{(1-x)^3} = xH'(x) = 0 + 1x + 2^2 x^2 + 3^2 x^3 + \cdots + n^2 x^n + \cdots$$

is the generating function for the nonnegative integer squares.

(a) Prove that for all $k \in \mathbb{N}$, the generating function for the nonnegative integer kth powers is a quotient of polynomials in x. That is, for all $k \in \mathbb{N}$ there are polynomials $R_k(x)$ and $S_k(x)$ such that

$$[x^n]\left(\frac{R_k(x)}{S_k(x)}\right) = n^k. \tag{16.23}$$

Hint: Observe that the derivative of a quotient of polynomials is also a quotient of polynomials. It is not necessary work out explicit formulas for R_k and S_k to prove this part.

(b) Conclude that if $f(n)$ is a function on the nonnegative integers defined recursively in the form

$$f(n) = af(n-1) + bf(n-2) + cf(n-3) + p(n)\alpha^n$$

where the $a, b, c, \alpha \in \mathbb{C}$ and p is a polynomial with complex coefficients, then the generating function for the sequence $f(0), f(1), f(2), \ldots$ will be a quotient of polynomials in x, and hence there is a closed form expression for $f(n)$.

Hint: Consider

$$\frac{R_k(\alpha x)}{S_k(\alpha x)}$$

Problem 16.17.
Generating functions provide an interesting way to count the number of strings of matched brackets. To do this, we'll use a description of these strings as the set GoodCount of strings of brackets with a good count.[6]

Namely, one precise way to determine if a string is matched is to start with 0 and read the string from left to right, adding 1 to the count for each left bracket and subtracting 1 from the count for each right bracket. For example, here are the counts for the two strings above

$$
\begin{array}{cccccccccccc}
[&] &] & [& [& [& [& [&] &] &] &] \\
0 & 1 & 0 & -1 & 0 & 1 & 2 & 3 & 4 & 3 & 2 & 1 & 0
\end{array}
$$

$$
\begin{array}{ccccccccccc}
[& [& & [&] &] & [&] &] & [&] \\
0 & 1 & 2 & & 3 & 2 & 1 & 2 & 1 & 0 & 1 & 0
\end{array}
$$

---

[6]Problem 7.20 also examines these strings.

A string has a *good count* if its running count never goes negative and ends with 0. So the second string above has a good count, but the first one does not because its count went negative at the third step.

Definition. Let

$$\text{GoodCount} ::= \{s \in \{], [\}^* \mid s \text{ has a good count}\}.$$

The matched strings can now be characterized precisely as this set of strings with good counts.

Let c_n be the number of strings in GoodCount with exactly n left brackets, and let $C(x)$ be the generating function for these numbers:

$$C(x) ::= c_0 + c_1 x + c_2 x^2 + \cdots.$$

(a) The *wrap* of a string s is the string, $[s]$, that starts with a left bracket followed by the characters of s, and then ends with a right bracket. Explain why the generating function for the wraps of strings with a good count is $xC(x)$.

Hint: The wrap of a string with good count also has a good count that starts and ends with 0 and remains *positive* everywhere else.

(b) Explain why, for every string s with a good count, there is a unique sequence of strings $s_1, \ldots, s_k$ that are wraps of strings with good counts and $s = s_1 \cdots s_k$. For example, the string $r ::= [[]][][[][]] \in \text{GoodCount}$ equals $s_1 s_2 s_3$ where $s_1 ::= [[]], s_2 ::= [], s_3 ::= [[][]]$, and this is the only way to express r as a sequence of wraps of strings with good counts.

(c) Conclude that

$$C = 1 + xC + (xC)^2 + \cdots + (xC)^n + \cdots, \tag{i}$$

so

$$C = \frac{1}{1 - xC}, \tag{ii}$$

and hence

$$C = \frac{1 \pm \sqrt{1 - 4x}}{2x}. \tag{iii}$$

Let $D(x) ::= 2xC(x)$. Expressing D as a power series

$$D(x) = d_0 + d_1 x + d_2 x^2 + \cdots,$$

we have

$$c_n = \frac{d_{n+1}}{2}. \tag{iv}$$

(d) Use (iii), (iv), and the value of c_0 to conclude that

$$D(x) = 1 - \sqrt{1 - 4x}.$$

(e) Prove that
$$d_n = \frac{(2n - 3) \cdot (2n - 5) \cdots 5 \cdot 3 \cdot 1 \cdot 2^n}{n!}.$$

Hint: $d_n = D^{(n)}(0)/n!$

(f) Conclude that

$$c_n = \frac{1}{n + 1}\binom{2n}{n}.$$

Exam Problems

Problem 16.18.
Define the sequence $r_0, r_1, r_2, \ldots$ recursively by the rule that $r_0 ::= 1$ and

$$r_n ::= 7r_{n-1} + (n + 1) \qquad \text{for } n > 0.$$

Let $R(x) ::= \sum_0^\infty r_n x^n$ be the generating function of this sequence. Express $R(x)$ as a quotient of polynomials or products of polynomials. You do *not* have to find a closed form for r_n.

Problem 16.19.
Alyssa Hacker sends out a video that spreads like wildfire over the UToob network. On the day of the release—call it *day zero*—and the day following—call it *day one*—the video doesn't receive any hits. However, starting with day two, the number of hits r_n can be expressed as seven times the number of hits on the previous day, four times the number of hits the day before that, and the number of days that has passed since the release of the video plus one. So, for example on day 2, there will be $7 \times 0 + 4 \times 0 + 3 = 3$ hits.

(a) Give a linear a recurrence for r_n.

(b) Express the generating function $R(x) ::= \sum_0^\infty r_n x^n$ as a quotient of polynomials or products of polynomials. You do *not* have to find a closed form for r_n.

Problem 16.20.
Consider the following sequence of predicates:

$$
\begin{aligned}
Q_1(x_1) &::= x_1 \\
Q_2(x_1, x_2) &::= x_1 \text{ IMPLIES } x_2 \\
Q_3(x_1, x_2, x_3) &::= (x_1 \text{ IMPLIES } x_2) \text{ IMPLIES } x_3 \\
Q_4(x_1, x_2, x_3, x_4) &::= ((x_1 \text{ IMPLIES } x_2) \text{ IMPLIES } x_3) \text{ IMPLIES } x_4 \\
Q_5(x_1, x_2, x_3, x_4, x_5) &::= (((x_1 \text{ IMPLIES } x_2) \text{ IMPLIES } x_3) \text{ IMPLIES } x_4) \text{ IMPLIES } x_5 \\
&\vdots
\end{aligned}
$$

Let T_n be the number of different true/false settings of the variables $x_1, x_2, \ldots, x_n$ for which $Q_n(x_1, x_2, \ldots, x_n)$ is true. For example, $T_2 = 3$ since $Q_2(x_1, x_2)$ is true for 3 different settings of the variables x_1 and x_2:

x_1	x_2	$Q_2(x_1, x_2)$
T	T	T
T	F	F
F	T	T
F	F	T

We let $T_0 = 1$ by convention.

(a) Express T_{n+1} in terms of T_n and n, assuming $n \geq 0$.

(b) Use a generating function to prove that

$$
T_n = \frac{2^{n+1} + (-1)^n}{3}
$$

for $n \geq 1$.

Problem 16.21.
Define the *Triple Fibonacci* numbers $T_0, T_1, \ldots$ recursively by the rules

$$
\begin{aligned}
T_0 = T_1 &::= 3, \\
T_n &::= T_{n-1} + T_{n-2} \qquad \text{(for } n \geq 2\text{).} \qquad (16.24)
\end{aligned}
$$

(a) Prove that all Triple Fibonacci numbers are divisible by 3.

(b) Prove that the GCD of every pair of consecutive Triple Fibonacci numbers is 3.

(c) Express the generating function $T(x)$ for the Triple Fibonacci as a quotient of polynomials. (You do *not* have to find a formula for $[x^n]T(x)$.)

Problem 16.22.

Define the *Double Fibonacci* numbers $D_0, D_1, \ldots$ recursively by the rules

$$D_0 = D_1 ::= 1,$$
$$D_n ::= 2D_{n-1} + D_{n-2} \qquad \text{(for } n \geq 2\text{).} \qquad (16.25)$$

(a) Prove that all Double Fibonacci numbers are odd.

(b) Prove that every two consecutive Double Fibonacci numbers are relatively prime.

(c) Express the generating function $D(x)$ for the Double Fibonacci as a quotient of polynomials. (You do *not* have to find a formula for $[x^n]D(x)$.)

Problems for Section 16.5

Practice Problems

Problem 16.23.

In the context of formal series, a number r may be used to indicate the sequence

$$(r, 0, 0, \ldots, 0, \ldots).$$

For example the number 1 may be used to indicate the identity series I and 0 may indicate the zero series Z. Whether "r" means the number or the sequence is supposed to be clear from context.

Verify that in the ring of formal power series,

$$r \otimes (g_0, g_1, g_2, \ldots) = (rg_0, rg_1, rg_2, \ldots).$$

In particular,

$$-(g_0, g_1, g_2, \ldots) = -1 \otimes (g_0, g_1, g_2, \ldots).$$

Problem 16.24.

Define the formal power series

$$X ::= (0, 1, 0, 0, \ldots, 0, \ldots).$$

(a) Explain why X has no reciprocal.

Hint: What can you say about $x \cdot (g_0 + g_1 x + g_2 x^2 + \cdots)$?

(b) Use the definition of power series multiplication $\otimes$ to prove carefully that

$$X \otimes (g_0, g_1, g_2, \dots) = (0, g_0, g_1, g_2, \dots).$$

(c) Recursively define X^n for $n \in \mathbb{N}$ by

$$X^0 ::= I ::= (1, 0, 0, \dots, 0, \dots),$$
$$X^{n+1} ::= X \otimes X^n.$$

Verify that the monomial x^n refers to the same power series as X^n.

Class Problems

Problem 16.25.
Show that a sequence $G ::= (g_0, g_1, \dots)$ has a multiplicative inverse in the ring of formal power series iff $g_0 \neq 0$.

IV Probability

Introduction

Probability is one of the most important disciplines in all of the sciences. It is also one of the least well understood.

Probability is especially important in computer science—it arises in virtually every branch of the field. In algorithm design and game theory, for example, algorithms and strategies that make random choices at certain steps frequently outperform deterministic algorithms and strategies. In information theory and signal processing, an understanding of randomness is critical for filtering out noise and compressing data. In cryptography and digital rights management, probability is crucial for achieving security. The list of examples is long.

Given the impact that probability has on computer science, it seems strange that probability should be so misunderstood by so many. The trouble is that "common-sense" intuition is demonstrably unreliable when it comes to problems involving random events. As a consequence, many students develop a fear of probability. We've witnessed many graduate oral exams where a student will solve the most horrendous calculation, only to then be tripped up by the simplest probability question. Even some faculty will start squirming if you ask them a question that starts "What is the probability that...?"

Our goal in the remaining chapters is to equip you with the tools that will enable you to solve basic problems involving probability easily and confidently.

Chapter 17 introduces the basic definitions and an elementary 4-step process that can be used to determine the probability that a specified event occurs. We illustrate the method on two famous problems where your intuition will probably fail you. The key concepts of conditional probability and independence are introduced, along with examples of their use, and regrettable misuse, in practice: the probability you have a disease given that a diagnostic test says you do, and the probability that a suspect is guilty given that his blood type matches the blood found at the scene of the crime.

Random variables provide a more quantitative way to measure random events, and we study them in Chapter 19. For example, instead of determining the probability that it will rain, we may want to determine *how much* or *how long* it is likely to rain. The fundamental concept of the *expected value* of a random variable is introduced and some of its key properties are developed.

Chapter 20 examines the probability that a random variable deviates significantly from its expected value. Probability of deviation provides the theoretical basis for estimation by sampling which is fundamental in science, engineering, and human affairs. It is also especially important in engineering practice, where things are generally fine if they are going as expected, and you would like to be assured that the probability of an unexpected event is very low.

A final chapter applies the previous probabilistic tools to solve problems involving more complex random processes. You will see why you will probably never get very far ahead at the casino and how two Stanford graduate students became billionaires by combining graph theory and probability theory to design a better search engine for the web.

17   Events and Probability Spaces

17.1   Let's Make a Deal

In the September 9, 1990 issue of *Parade* magazine, columnist Marilyn vos Savant responded to this letter:

> *Suppose you're on a game show, and you're given the choice of three doors. Behind one door is a car, behind the others, goats. You pick a door, say number 1, and the host, who knows what's behind the doors, opens another door, say number 3, which has a goat. He says to you, "Do you want to pick door number 2?" Is it to your advantage to switch your choice of doors?*

Craig. F. Whitaker
Columbia, MD

The letter describes a situation like one faced by contestants in the 1970's game show *Let's Make a Deal*, hosted by Monty Hall and Carol Merrill. Marilyn replied that the contestant should indeed switch. She explained that if the car was behind either of the two unpicked doors—which is twice as likely as the the car being behind the picked door—the contestant wins by switching. But she soon received a torrent of letters, many from mathematicians, telling her that she was wrong. The problem became known as the *Monty Hall Problem* and it generated thousands of hours of heated debate.

This incident highlights a fact about probability: the subject uncovers lots of examples where ordinary intuition leads to completely wrong conclusions. So until you've studied probabilities enough to have refined your intuition, a way to avoid errors is to fall back on a rigorous, systematic approach such as the Four Step Method that we will describe shortly. First, let's make sure we really understand the setup for this problem. This is always a good thing to do when you are dealing with probability.

17.1.1   Clarifying the Problem

Craig's original letter to Marilyn vos Savant is a bit vague, so we must make some assumptions in order to have any hope of modeling the game formally. For example, we will assume that:

1. The car is equally likely to be hidden behind each of the three doors.

2. The player is equally likely to pick each of the three doors, regardless of the car's location.

3. After the player picks a door, the host *must* open a different door with a goat behind it and offer the player the choice of staying with the original door or switching.

4. If the host has a choice of which door to open, then he is equally likely to select each of them.

In making these assumptions, we're reading a lot into Craig Whitaker's letter. There are other plausible interpretations that lead to different answers. But let's accept these assumptions for now and address the question, "What is the probability that a player who switches wins the car?"

17.2   The Four Step Method

Every probability problem involves some sort of randomized experiment, process, or game. And each such problem involves two distinct challenges:

1. How do we model the situation mathematically?

2. How do we solve the resulting mathematical problem?

In this section, we introduce a four step approach to questions of the form, "What is the probability that...?" In this approach, we build a probabilistic model step by step, formalizing the original question in terms of that model. Remarkably, this structured approach provides simple solutions to many famously confusing problems. For example, as you'll see, the four step method cuts through the confusion surrounding the Monty Hall problem like a Ginsu knife.

17.2.1   Step 1: Find the Sample Space

Our first objective is to identify all the possible outcomes of the experiment. A typical experiment involves several randomly-determined quantities. For example, the Monty Hall game involves three such quantities:

1. The door concealing the car.

2. The door initially chosen by the player.

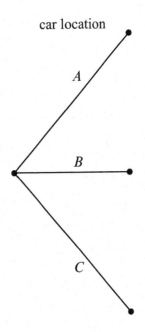

Figure 17.1 The first level in a tree diagram for the Monty Hall Problem. The branches correspond to the door behind which the car is located.

    3. The door that the host opens to reveal a goat.

Every possible combination of these randomly-determined quantities is called an *outcome*. The set of all possible outcomes is called the *sample space* for the experiment.

A *tree diagram* is a graphical tool that can help us work through the four step approach when the number of outcomes is not too large or the problem is nicely structured. In particular, we can use a tree diagram to help understand the sample space of an experiment. The first randomly-determined quantity in our experiment is the door concealing the prize. We represent this as a tree with three branches, as shown in Figure 17.1. In this diagram, the doors are called *A*, *B* and *C* instead of 1, 2, and 3, because we'll be adding a lot of other numbers to the picture later.

For each possible location of the prize, the player could initially choose any of the three doors. We represent this in a second layer added to the tree. Then a third layer represents the possibilities of the final step when the host opens a door to reveal a goat, as shown in Figure 17.2.

Notice that the third layer reflects the fact that the host has either one choice or two, depending on the position of the car and the door initially selected by the player. For example, if the prize is behind door A and the player picks door B, then

car location   player's   door
                      initial   revealed
                      guess

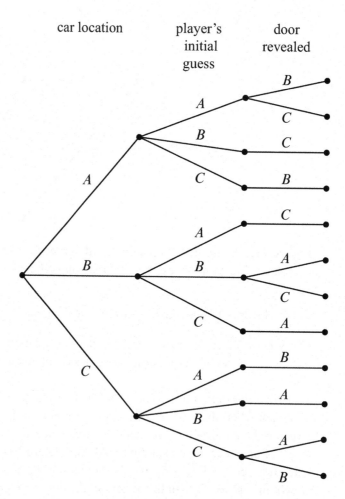

Figure 17.2   The full tree diagram for the Monty Hall Problem. The second level indicates the door initially chosen by the player. The third level indicates the door revealed by Monty Hall.

the host must open door C. However, if the prize is behind door A and the player picks door A, then the host could open either door B or door C.

Now let's relate this picture to the terms we introduced earlier: the leaves of the tree represent *outcomes* of the experiment, and the set of all leaves represents the *sample space*. Thus, for this experiment, the sample space consists of 12 outcomes. For reference, we've labeled each outcome in Figure 17.3 with a triple of doors indicating:

(door concealing prize, door initially chosen, door opened to reveal a goat).

In these terms, the sample space is the set

$$S = \left\{ \begin{array}{l} (A, A, B), (A, A, C), (A, B, C), (A, C, B), (B, A, C), (B, B, A), \\ (B, B, C), (B, C, A), (C, A, B), (C, B, A), (C, C, A), (C, C, B) \end{array} \right\}$$

The tree diagram has a broader interpretation as well: we can regard the whole experiment as following a path from the root to a leaf, where the branch taken at each stage is "randomly" determined. Keep this interpretation in mind; we'll use it again later.

17.2.2 Step 2: Define Events of Interest

Our objective is to answer questions of the form "What is the probability that . . . ?", where, for example, the missing phrase might be "the player wins by switching," "the player initially picked the door concealing the prize," or "the prize is behind door C."

A set of outcomes is called an *event*. Each of the preceding phrases characterizes an event. For example, the event [prize is behind door C] refers to the set:

$$\{(C, A, B), (C, B, A), (C, C, A), (C, C, B)\},$$

and the event [prize is behind the door first picked by the player] is:

$$\{(A, A, B), (A, A, C), (B, B, A), (B, B, C), (C, C, A), (C, C, B)\}.$$

Here we're using square brackets around a property of outcomes as a notation for the event whose outcomes are the ones that satisfy the property.

What we're really after is the event [player wins by switching]:

$$\{(A, B, C), (A, C, B), (B, A, C), (B, C, A), (C, A, B), (C, B, A)\}. \qquad (17.1)$$

The outcomes in this event are marked with checks in Figure 17.4.

Notice that exactly half of the outcomes are checked, meaning that the player wins by switching in half of all outcomes. You might be tempted to conclude that a player who switches wins with probability $1/2$. *This is wrong*. The reason is that these outcomes are not all equally likely, as we'll see shortly.

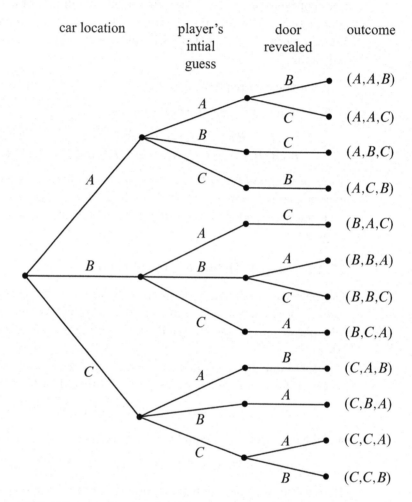

Figure 17.3   The tree diagram for the Monty Hall Problem with the outcomes labeled for each path from root to leaf. For example, outcome (A, A, B) corresponds to the car being behind door A, the player initially choosing door A, and Monty Hall revealing the goat behind door B.

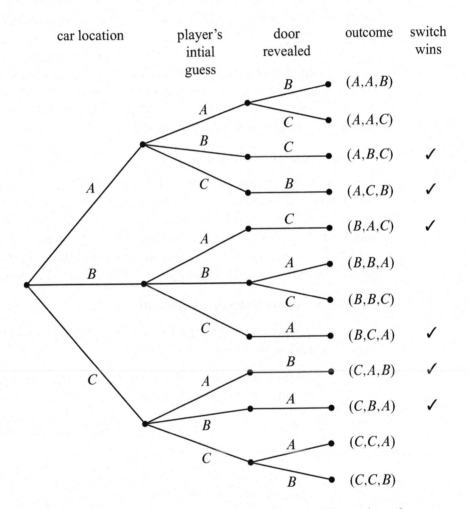

Figure 17.4   The tree diagram for the Monty Hall Problem, where the outcomes where the player wins by switching are denoted with a check mark.

17.2.3   Step 3: Determine Outcome Probabilities

So far we've enumerated all the possible outcomes of the experiment. Now we must start assessing the likelihood of those outcomes. In particular, the goal of this step is to assign each outcome a probability, indicating the fraction of the time this outcome is expected to occur. The sum of all the outcome probabilities must equal one, reflecting the fact that there always must be an outcome.

Ultimately, outcome probabilities are determined by the phenomenon we're modeling and thus are not quantities that we can derive mathematically. However, mathematics can help us compute the probability of every outcome *based on fewer and more elementary modeling decisions*. In particular, we'll break the task of determining outcome probabilities into two stages.

Step 3a: Assign Edge Probabilities

First, we record a probability on each *edge* of the tree diagram. These edge-probabilities are determined by the assumptions we made at the outset: that the prize is equally likely to be behind each door, that the player is equally likely to pick each door, and that the host is equally likely to reveal each goat, if he has a choice. Notice that when the host has no choice regarding which door to open, the single branch is assigned probability 1. For example, see Figure 17.5.

Step 3b: Compute Outcome Probabilities

Our next job is to convert edge probabilities into outcome probabilities. This is a purely mechanical process:

> calculate the probability of an outcome by multiplying the edge-probabilities on the path from the root to that outcome.

For example, the probability of the topmost outcome in Figure 17.5, (A, A, B), is

$$\frac{1}{3} \cdot \frac{1}{3} \cdot \frac{1}{2} = \frac{1}{18}. \tag{17.2}$$

We'll examine the official justification for this rule in Section 18.4, but here's an easy, intuitive justification: as the steps in an experiment progress randomly along a path from the root of the tree to a leaf, the probabilities on the edges indicate how likely the path is to proceed along each branch. For example, a path starting at the root in our example is equally likely to go down each of the three top-level branches.

How likely is such a path to arrive at the topmost outcome (A, A, B)? Well, there is a 1-in-3 chance that a path would follow the A-branch at the top level, a 1-in-3 chance it would continue along the A-branch at the second level, and 1-in-2 chance it would follow the B-branch at the third level. Thus, there is half of a one third of a one third chance, of arriving at the (A, A, B) leaf. That is, the chance is $1/3 \cdot 1/3 \cdot 1/2 = 1/18$—the same product (in reverse order) we arrived at in (17.2).

We have illustrated all of the outcome probabilities in Figure 17.5.

Specifying the probability of each outcome amounts to defining a function that maps each outcome to a probability. This function is usually called $\Pr[\cdot]$. In these terms, we've just determined that:

$$\Pr[(A, A, B)] = \frac{1}{18},$$
$$\Pr[(A, A, C)] = \frac{1}{18},$$
$$\Pr[(A, B, C)] = \frac{1}{9},$$

etc.

17.2.4 Step 4: Compute Event Probabilities

We now have a probability for each *outcome*, but we want to determine the probability of an *event*. The probability of an event E is denoted by $\Pr[E]$, and it is the sum of the probabilities of the outcomes in E. For example, the probability of the [switching wins] event (17.1) is

$$
\begin{aligned}
&\Pr[\text{switching wins}] \\
&= \Pr[(A, B, C)] + \Pr[(A, C, B)] + \Pr[(B, A, C)] + \\
&\quad \Pr[(B, C, A)] + \Pr[(C, A, B)] + \Pr[(C, B, A)] \\
&= \frac{1}{9} + \frac{1}{9} + \frac{1}{9} + \frac{1}{9} + \frac{1}{9} + \frac{1}{9} \\
&= \frac{2}{3}.
\end{aligned}
$$

It seems Marilyn's answer is correct! A player who switches doors wins the car with probability $2/3$. In contrast, a player who stays with his or her original door wins with probability $1/3$, since staying wins if and only if switching loses.

We're done with the problem! We didn't need any appeals to intuition or ingenious analogies. In fact, no mathematics more difficult than adding and multiplying fractions was required. The only hard part was resisting the temptation to leap to an "intuitively obvious" answer.

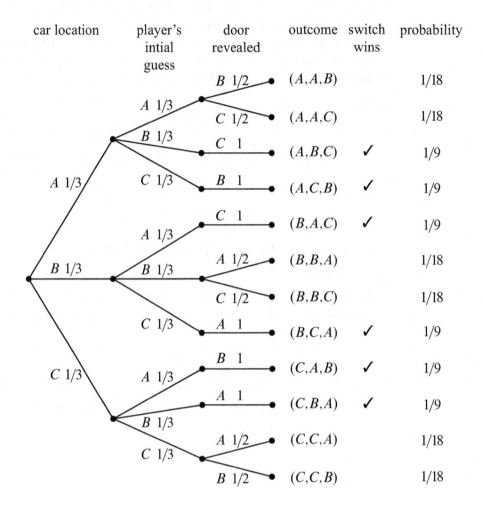

car location	player's initial guess	door revealed	outcome	switch wins	probability
		B 1/2	(A,A,B)		1/18
	A 1/3	C 1/2	(A,A,C)		1/18
	B 1/3	C 1	(A,B,C)	✓	1/9
A 1/3	C 1/3	B 1	(A,C,B)	✓	1/9
	A 1/3	C 1	(B,A,C)	✓	1/9
B 1/3	B 1/3	A 1/2	(B,B,A)		1/18
		C 1/2	(B,B,C)		1/18
	C 1/3	A 1	(B,C,A)	✓	1/9
	A 1/3	B 1	(C,A,B)	✓	1/9
C 1/3	B 1/3	A 1	(C,B,A)	✓	1/9
	C 1/3	A 1/2	(C,C,A)		1/18
		B 1/2	(C,C,B)		1/18

Figure 17.5   The tree diagram for the Monty Hall Problem where edge weights denote the probability of that branch being taken given that we are at the parent of that branch. For example, if the car is behind door A, then there is a 1/3 chance that the player's initial selection is door B. The rightmost column shows the outcome probabilities for the Monty Hall Problem. Each outcome probability is simply the product of the probabilities on the path from the root to the outcome leaf.

17.2.5 An Alternative Interpretation of the Monty Hall Problem

Was Marilyn really right? Our analysis indicates that she was. But a more accurate conclusion is that her answer is correct *provided we accept her interpretation of the question*. There is an equally plausible interpretation in which Marilyn's answer is wrong. Notice that Craig Whitaker's original letter does not say that the host is *required* to reveal a goat and offer the player the option to switch, merely that he *did* these things. In fact, on the *Let's Make a Deal* show, Monty Hall sometimes simply opened the door that the contestant picked initially. Therefore, if he wanted to, Monty could give the option of switching only to contestants who picked the correct door initially. In this case, switching never works!

17.3   Strange Dice

The four-step method is surprisingly powerful. Let's get some more practice with it. Imagine, if you will, the following scenario.

It's a typical Saturday night. You're at your favorite pub, contemplating the true meaning of infinite cardinalities, when a burly-looking biker plops down on the stool next to you. Just as you are about to get your mind around $\text{pow}(\text{pow}(\mathbb{R}))$, biker dude slaps three strange-looking dice on the bar and challenges you to a $100 wager. His rules are simple. Each player selects one die and rolls it once. The player with the lower value pays the other player $100.

Naturally, you are skeptical, especially after you see that these are not ordinary dice. Each die has the usual six sides, but opposite sides have the same number on them, and the numbers on the dice are different, as shown in Figure 17.6.

Biker dude notices your hesitation, so he sweetens his offer: he will pay you $105 if you roll the higher number, but you only need pay him $100 if he rolls higher, *and* he will let you pick a die first, after which he will pick one of the other two. The sweetened deal sounds persuasive since it gives you a chance to pick what you think is the best die, so you decide you will play. But which of the dice should you choose? Die B is appealing because it has a 9, which is a sure winner if it comes up. Then again, die A has two fairly large numbers, and die C has an 8 and no really small values.

In the end, you choose die B because it has a 9, and then biker dude selects die A. Let's see what the probability is that you will win. (Of course, you probably should have done this before picking die B in the first place.) Not surprisingly, we will use the four-step method to compute this probability.

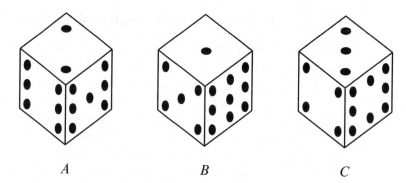

Figure 17.6   The strange dice. The number of pips on each concealed face is the same as the number on the opposite face. For example, when you roll die *A*, the probabilities of getting a 2, 6, or 7 are each 1/3.

17.3.1   Die *A* versus Die *B*

Step 1: Find the sample space.

The tree diagram for this scenario is shown in Figure 17.7. In particular, the sample space for this experiment are the nine pairs of values that might be rolled with Die *A* and Die *B*:

For this experiment, the sample space is a set of nine outcomes:

$$\mathcal{S} = \{\,(2,1),\ (2,5),\ (2,9),\ (6,1),\ (6,5),\ (6,9),\ (7,1),\ (7,5),\ (7,9)\,\}.$$

Step 2: Define events of interest.

We are interested in the event that the number on die *A* is greater than the number on die *B*. This event is a set of five outcomes:

$$\{\,(2,1),\ (6,1),\ (6,5),\ (7,1),\ (7,5)\,\}.$$

These outcomes are marked *A* in the tree diagram in Figure 17.7.

Step 3: Determine outcome probabilities.

To find outcome probabilities, we first assign probabilities to edges in the tree diagram. Each number on each die comes up with probability 1/3, regardless of the value of the other die. Therefore, we assign all edges probability 1/3. The probability of an outcome is the product of the probabilities on the corresponding root-to-leaf path, which means that every outcome has probability 1/9. These probabilities are recorded on the right side of the tree diagram in Figure 17.7.

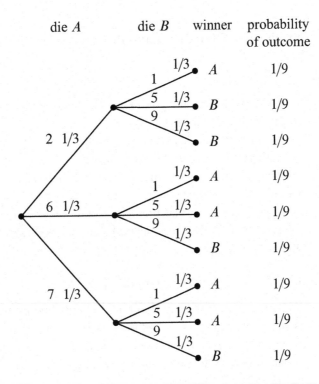

Figure 17.7 The tree diagram for one roll of die A versus die B. Die A wins with probability 5/9.

Step 4: Compute event probabilities.
The probability of an event is the sum of the probabilities of the outcomes in that event. In this case, all the outcome probabilities are the same, so we say that the sample space is *uniform*. Computing event probabilities for uniform sample spaces is particularly easy since you just have to compute the number of outcomes in the event. In particular, for any event E in a uniform sample space S,

$$\Pr[E] = \frac{|E|}{|S|}. \tag{17.3}$$

In this case, E is the event that die A beats die B, so $|E| = 5$, $|S| = 9$, and

$$\Pr[E] = 5/9.$$

This is bad news for you. Die A beats die B more than half the time and, not surprisingly, you just lost \$100.

Biker dude consoles you on your "bad luck" and, given that he's a sensitive guy beneath all that leather, he offers to go double or nothing.[1] Given that your wallet only has \$25 in it, this sounds like a good plan. Plus, you figure that choosing die A will give *you* the advantage.

So you choose A, and then biker dude chooses C. Can you guess who is more likely to win? (Hint: it is generally not a good idea to gamble with someone you don't know in a bar, especially when you are gambling with strange dice.)

17.3.2   Die A versus Die C

We can construct the tree diagram and outcome probabilities as before. The result is shown in Figure 17.8, and there is bad news again. Die C will beat die A with probability 5/9, and you lose once again.

You now owe the biker dude \$200 and he asks for his money. You reply that you need to go to the bathroom.

17.3.3   Die B versus Die C

Being a sensitive guy, biker dude nods understandingly and offers yet another wager. This time, he'll let you have die C. He'll even let you raise the wager to \$200 so you can win your money back.

This is too good a deal to pass up. You know that die C is likely to beat die A and that die A is likely to beat die B, and so die C is *surely* the best. Whether biker

---

[1] *Double or nothing* is slang for doing another wager after you have lost the first. If you lose again, you will owe biker dude *double* what you owed him before. If you win, you will owe him *nothing*; in fact, since he should pay you \$210 if he loses, you would come out \$10 ahead.

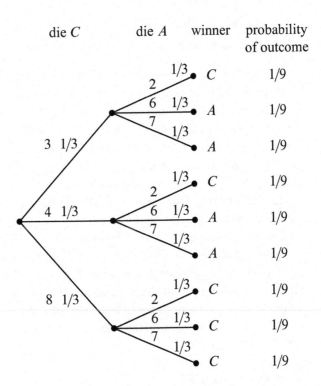

Figure 17.8   The tree diagram for one roll of die C versus die A. Die C wins with probability $5/9$.

dude picks A or B, the odds would be in your favor this time. Biker dude must really be a nice guy.

So you pick C, and then biker dude picks B. Wait—how come you haven't caught on yet and worked out the tree diagram before you took this bet? If you do it now, you'll see by the same reasoning as before that B beats C with probability $5/9$. But surely there is a mistake! How is it possible that

C beats A with probability $5/9$,

A beats B with probability $5/9$,

B beats C with probability $5/9$?

The problem is not with the math, but with your intuition. Since A will beat B more often than not, and B will beat C more often than not, it *seems* like A ought to beat C more often than not, that is, the "beats more often" relation ought to be *transitive*. But this intuitive idea is simply false: whatever die you pick, biker dude can pick one of the others and be likely to win. So picking first is actually a disadvantage, and as a result, you now owe biker dude $400.

Just when you think matters can't get worse, biker dude offers you one final wager for $1,000. This time, instead of rolling each die once, you will each roll your die twice, and your score is the sum of your rolls, and he will even let you pick your die second, that is, after he picks his. Biker dude chooses die B. Now you know that die A will beat die B with probability $5/9$ on one roll, so, jumping at this chance to get ahead, you agree to play, and you pick die A. After all, you figure that since a roll of die A beats a roll of die B more often that not, two rolls of die A are even more likely to beat two rolls of die B, right?

Wrong! (Did we mention that playing strange gambling games with strangers in a bar is a bad idea?)

17.3.4   Rolling Twice

If each player rolls twice, the tree diagram will have four levels and $3^4 = 81$ outcomes. This means that it will take a while to write down the entire tree diagram. But it's easy to write down the first two levels as in Figure 17.9(a) and then notice that the remaining two levels consist of nine identical copies of the tree in Figure 17.9(b).

The probability of each outcome is $(1/3)^4 = 1/81$ and so, once again, we have a uniform probability space. By equation (17.3), this means that the probability that A wins is the number of outcomes where A beats B divided by 81.

To compute the number of outcomes where A beats B, we observe that the two rolls of die A result in nine equally likely outcomes in a sample space $\mathcal{S}_A$ in which

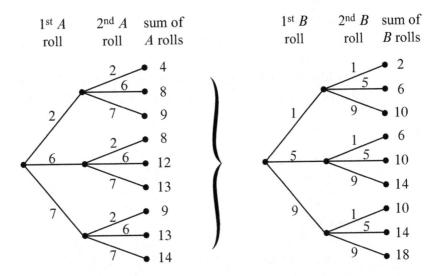

1st A roll	2nd A roll	sum of A rolls		1st B roll	2nd B roll	sum of B rolls

Figure 17.9 Parts of the tree diagram for die B versus die A where each die is rolled twice. The first two levels are shown in (a). The last two levels consist of nine copies of the tree in (b).

the two-roll sums take the values

$$(4, 8, 8, 9, 9, 12, 13, 13, 14).$$

Likewise, two rolls of die B result in nine equally likely outcomes in a sample space $\mathcal{S}_B$ in which the two-roll sums take the values

$$(2, 6, 6, 10, 10, 10, 14, 14, 18).$$

We can treat the outcome of rolling both dice twice as a pair $(x, y) \in \mathcal{S}_A \times \mathcal{S}_B$, where A wins iff the sum of the two A-rolls of outcome x is larger the sum of the two B-rolls of outcome y. If the A-sum is 4, there is only one y with a smaller B-sum, namely, when the B-sum is 2. If the A-sum is 8, there are three y's with a smaller B-sum, namely, when the B-sum is 2 or 6. Continuing the count in this way, the number of pairs (x, y) for which the A-sum is larger than the B-sum is

$$1 + 3 + 3 + 3 + 3 + 6 + 6 + 6 + 6 = 37.$$

A similar count shows that there are 42 pairs for which B-sum is larger than the A-sum, and there are two pairs where the sums are equal, namely, when they both equal 14. This means that A *loses* to B with probability $42/81 > 1/2$ and ties with probability $2/81$. Die A wins with probability only $37/81$.

How can it be that A is more likely than B to win with one roll, but B is more likely to win with two rolls? Well, why not? The only reason we'd think otherwise is our unreliable, untrained intuition. (Even the authors were surprised when they first learned about this, but at least they didn't lose $1400 to biker dude.) In fact, the die strength reverses no matter which two die we picked. So for one roll,

$$A \succ B \succ C \succ A,$$

but for two rolls,

$$A \prec B \prec C \prec A,$$

where we have used the symbols $\succ$ and $\prec$ to denote which die is more likely to result in the larger value.

The weird behavior of the three strange dice above generalizes in a remarkable way: there are arbitrarily large sets of dice which will beat each other in any desired pattern according to how many times the dice are rolled.[2]

17.4   The Birthday Principle

There are 95 students in a class. What is the probability that some birthday is shared by two people? Comparing 95 students to the 365 possible birthdays, you might guess the probability lies somewhere around $1/4$—but you'd be wrong: the probability that there will be two people in the class with matching birthdays is actually more than 0.9999.

To work this out, we'll assume that the probability that a randomly chosen student has a given birthday is $1/d$. We'll also assume that a class is composed of n randomly and independently selected students. Of course $d = 365$ and $n = 95$ in this case, but we're interested in working things out in general. These randomness assumptions are not really true, since more babies are born at certain times of year, and students' class selections are typically not independent of each other, but simplifying in this way gives us a start on analyzing the problem. More importantly, these assumptions are justifiable in important computer science applications of birthday matching. For example, birthday matching is a good model for collisions between items randomly inserted into a hash table. So we won't worry about things like spring procreation preferences that make January birthdays more common, or about twins' preferences to take classes together (or not).

---

[2] TBA - Reference Ron Graham paper.

17.4.1 Exact Formula for Match Probability

There are d^n sequences of n birthdays, and under our assumptions, these are equally likely. There are $d(d-1)(d-2)\cdots(d-(n-1))$ length n sequences of distinct birthdays. That means the probability that everyone has a different birthday is:

$$\frac{d(d-1)(d-2)\cdots(d-(n-1))}{d^n}$$

$$= \frac{d}{d} \cdot \frac{d-1}{d} \cdot \frac{d-2}{d} \cdots \frac{d-(n-1)}{d} \qquad (17.4)$$

$$= \left(1-\frac{0}{d}\right)\left(1-\frac{1}{d}\right)\left(1-\frac{2}{d}\right)\cdots\left(1-\frac{n-1}{d}\right) \qquad (17.5)$$

Now we simplify (17.5) using the fact that $1 - x < e^{-x}$ for all $x > 0$. This follows by truncating the Taylor series $e^{-x} = 1 - x + x^2/2! - x^3/3! + \cdots$. The approximation $e^{-x} \approx 1 - x$ is pretty accurate when x is small.

$$\left(1-\frac{0}{d}\right)\left(1-\frac{1}{d}\right)\left(1-\frac{2}{d}\right)\cdots\left(1-\frac{n-1}{d}\right)$$

$$< e^0 \cdot e^{-1/d} \cdot e^{-2/d} \cdots e^{-(n-1)/d} \qquad (17.6)$$

$$= e^{-\left(\sum_{i=1}^{n-1} i/d\right)}$$

$$= e^{-(n(n-1)/2d)}. \qquad (17.7)$$

For $n = 95$ and $d = 365$, the value of (17.7) is less than $1/200,000$, which means the probability of having some pair of matching birthdays actually is more than $1 - 1/200,000 > 0.99999$. So it would be pretty astonishing if there were no pair of students in the class with matching birthdays.

For $d \leq n^2/2$, the probability of no match turns out to be asymptotically equal to the upper bound (17.7). For $d = n^2/2$ in particular, the probability of no match is asymptotically equal to $1/e$. This leads to a rule of thumb which is useful in many contexts in computer science:

The Birthday Principle

If there are d days in a year and $\sqrt{2d}$ people in a room, then the probability that two share a birthday is about $1 - 1/e \approx 0.632$.

For example, the Birthday Principle says that if you have $\sqrt{2 \cdot 365} \approx 27$ people in a room, then the probability that two share a birthday is about 0.632. The actual probability is about 0.626, so the approximation is quite good.

Among other applications, it implies that to use a hash function that maps n items into a hash table of size d, you can expect many collisions if n^2 is more than a small fraction of d. The Birthday Principle also famously comes into play as the basis of "birthday attacks" that crack certain cryptographic systems.

17.5   Set Theory and Probability

Let's abstract what we've just done into a general mathematical definition of sample spaces and probability.

17.5.1   Probability Spaces

Definition 17.5.1. A countable *sample space* S is a nonempty countable set.[3] An element $\omega \in S$ is called an *outcome*. A subset of S is called an *event*.

Definition 17.5.2. A *probability function* on a sample space S is a total function $\Pr : S \to \mathbb{R}$ such that

- $\Pr[\omega] \geq 0$ for all $\omega \in S$, and

- $\sum_{\omega \in S} \Pr[\omega] = 1$.

A sample space together with a probability function is called a *probability space*. For any event $E \subseteq S$, the *probability of E* is defined to be the sum of the probabilities of the outcomes in E:

$$\Pr[E] ::= \sum_{\omega \in E} \Pr[\omega].$$

In the previous examples there were only finitely many possible outcomes, but we'll quickly come to examples that have a countably infinite number of outcomes.

The study of probability is closely tied to set theory because any set can be a sample space and any subset can be an event. General probability theory deals with uncountable sets like the set of real numbers, but we won't need these, and sticking to countable sets lets us define the probability of events using sums instead of integrals. It also lets us avoid some distracting technical problems in set theory like the Banach-Tarski "paradox" mentioned in Chapter 8.

---

[3] Yes, sample spaces can be infinite. If you did not read Chapter 8, don't worry—*countable* just means that you can list the elements of the sample space as $\omega_0, \omega_1, \omega_2, \ldots$.

17.5.2   Probability Rules from Set Theory

Most of the rules and identities that we have developed for finite sets extend very naturally to probability.

An immediate consequence of the definition of event probability is that for *disjoint* events E and F,

$$\Pr[E \cup F] = \Pr[E] + \Pr[F].$$

This generalizes to a countable number of events:

Rule 17.5.3 (Sum Rule). *If $E_0, E_1, \ldots, E_n, \ldots$ are pairwise disjoint events, then*

$$\Pr\left[\bigcup_{n \in \mathbb{N}} E_n\right] = \sum_{n \in \mathbb{N}} \Pr[E_n].$$

The Sum Rule lets us analyze a complicated event by breaking it down into simpler cases. For example, if the probability that a randomly chosen MIT student is native to the United States is 60%, to Canada is 5%, and to Mexico is 5%, then the probability that a random MIT student is native to one of these three countries is 70%.

Another consequence of the Sum Rule is that $\Pr[A] + \Pr[\overline{A}] = 1$, which follows because $\Pr[\mathcal{S}] = 1$ and $\mathcal{S}$ is the union of the disjoint sets A and $\overline{A}$. This equation often comes up in the form:

$$\Pr[\overline{A}] = 1 - \Pr[A]. \qquad \text{(Complement Rule)}$$

Sometimes the easiest way to compute the probability of an event is to compute the probability of its complement and then apply this formula.

Some further basic facts about probability parallel facts about cardinalities of finite sets. In particular:

$$\begin{aligned}
\Pr[B - A] &= \Pr[B] - \Pr[A \cap B], & \text{(Difference Rule)} \\
\Pr[A \cup B] &= \Pr[A] + \Pr[B] - \Pr[A \cap B], & \text{(Inclusion-Exclusion)} \\
\Pr[A \cup B] &\leq \Pr[A] + \Pr[B], & \text{(Boole's Inequality)} \\
\text{If } A &\subseteq B, \text{ then } \Pr[A] \leq \Pr[B]. & \text{(Monotonicity Rule)}
\end{aligned}$$

The Difference Rule follows from the Sum Rule because B is the union of the disjoint sets $B - A$ and $A \cap B$. Inclusion-Exclusion then follows from the Sum and Difference Rules, because $A \cup B$ is the union of the disjoint sets A and $B - A$. Boole's inequality is an immediate consequence of Inclusion-Exclusion since probabilities are nonnegative. Monotonicity follows from the definition of event probability and the fact that outcome probabilities are nonnegative.

The two-event Inclusion-Exclusion equation above generalizes to any finite set of events in the same way as the corresponding Inclusion-Exclusion rule for n sets. Boole's inequality also generalizes to both finite and countably infinite sets of events:

Rule 17.5.4 (Union Bound).

$$\Pr[E_1 \cup \cdots \cup E_n \cup \cdots] \leq \Pr[E_1] + \cdots + \Pr[E_n] + \cdots . \qquad (17.8)$$

The Union Bound is useful in many calculations. For example, suppose that E_i is the event that the i-th critical component among n components in a spacecraft fails. Then $E_1 \cup \cdots \cup E_n$ is the event that *some* critical component fails. If $\sum_{i=1}^{n} \Pr[E_i]$ is small, then the Union Bound can provide a reassuringly small upper bound on this overall probability of critical failure.

17.5.3   Uniform Probability Spaces

Definition 17.5.5. A finite probability space S is said to be *uniform* if $\Pr[\omega]$ is the same for every outcome $\omega \in S$.

As we saw in the strange dice problem, uniform sample spaces are particularly easy to work with. That's because for any event $E \subseteq S$,

$$\Pr[E] = \frac{|E|}{|S|}. \qquad (17.9)$$

This means that once we know the cardinality of E and S, we can immediately obtain $\Pr[E]$. That's great news because we developed lots of tools for computing the cardinality of a set in Part III.

For example, suppose that you select five cards at random from a standard deck of 52 cards. What is the probability of having a full house? Normally, this question would take some effort to answer. But from the analysis in Section 15.7.2, we know that

$$|S| = \binom{52}{5}$$

and

$$|E| = 13 \cdot \binom{4}{3} \cdot 12 \cdot \binom{4}{2}$$

where E is the event that we have a full house. Since every five-card hand is equally

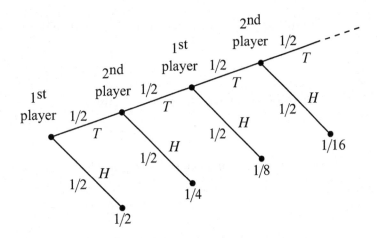

Figure 17.10 The tree diagram for the game where players take turns flipping a fair coin. The first player to flip heads wins.

likely, we can apply equation (17.9) to find that

$$\Pr[E] = \frac{13 \cdot 12 \cdot \binom{4}{3} \cdot \binom{4}{2}}{\binom{52}{5}}$$

$$= \frac{13 \cdot 12 \cdot 4 \cdot 6 \cdot 5 \cdot 4 \cdot 3 \cdot 2}{52 \cdot 51 \cdot 50 \cdot 49 \cdot 48} = \frac{18}{12495}$$

$$\approx \frac{1}{694}.$$

17.5.4 Infinite Probability Spaces

Infinite probability spaces are fairly common. For example, two players take turns flipping a fair coin. Whoever flips heads first is declared the winner. What is the probability that the first player wins? A tree diagram for this problem is shown in Figure 17.10.

The event that the first player wins contains an infinite number of outcomes, but we can still sum their probabilities:

$$\Pr[\text{first player wins}] = \frac{1}{2} + \frac{1}{8} + \frac{1}{32} + \frac{1}{128} + \cdots$$

$$= \frac{1}{2} \sum_{n=0}^{\infty} \left(\frac{1}{4}\right)^n$$

$$= \frac{1}{2} \left(\frac{1}{1 - 1/4}\right) = \frac{2}{3}.$$

Similarly, we can compute the probability that the second player wins:

$$\Pr[\text{second player wins}] = \frac{1}{4} + \frac{1}{16} + \frac{1}{64} + \frac{1}{256} + \cdots = \frac{1}{3}.$$

In this case, the sample space is the infinite set

$$\mathcal{S} ::= \{\, \text{T}^n\text{H} \mid n \in \mathbb{N} \,\},$$

where T^n stands for a length n string of T's. The probability function is

$$\Pr[\text{T}^n\text{H}] ::= \frac{1}{2^{n+1}}.$$

To verify that this is a probability space, we just have to check that all the probabilities are nonnegative and that they sum to 1. The given probabilities are all nonnegative, and applying the formula for the sum of a geometric series, we find that

$$\sum_{n \in \mathbb{N}} \Pr[\text{T}^n\text{H}] = \sum_{n \in \mathbb{N}} \frac{1}{2^{n+1}} = 1.$$

Notice that this model does not have an outcome corresponding to the possibility that both players keep flipping tails forever. (In the diagram, flipping forever corresponds to following the infinite path in the tree without ever reaching a leaf/outcome.) If leaving this possibility out of the model bothers you, you're welcome to fix it by adding another outcome ω_{forever} to indicate that that's what happened. Of course since the probabililies of the other outcomes already sum to 1, you have to define the probability of ω_{forever} to be 0. Now outcomes with probability zero will have no impact on our calculations, so there's no harm in adding it in if it makes you happier. On the other hand, in countable probability spaces it isn't necessary to have outcomes with probability zero, and we will generally ignore them.

17.6   References

[17], [24], [28], [31], [35], [36] [40], [39], [48]

Problems for Section 17.2

Practice Problems

Problem 17.1.

Let B be the number of heads that come up on $2n$ independent tosses of a fair coin.

(a) $\Pr[B = n]$ is asymptotically equal to one of the expressions given below. Explain which one.

1. $\dfrac{1}{\sqrt{2\pi n}}$

2. $\dfrac{2}{\sqrt{\pi n}}$

3. $\dfrac{1}{\sqrt{\pi n}}$

4. $\sqrt{\dfrac{2}{\pi n}}$

Exam Problems

Problem 17.2. (a) What's the probability that 0 doesn't appear among k digits chosen independently and uniformly at random?

(b) A box contains 90 good and 10 defective screws. What's the probability that if we pick 10 screws from the box, none will be defective?

(c) First one digit is chosen uniformly at random from $\{1, 2, 3, 4, 5\}$ and is removed from the set; then a second digit is chosen uniformly at random from the remaining digits. What is the probability that an odd digit is picked the second time?

(d) Suppose that you *randomly* permute the digits $1, 2, \cdots, n$, that is, you select a permutation uniformly at random. What is the probability the digit k ends up in the ith position after the permutation?

(e) A fair coin is flipped n times. What's the probability that all the heads occur at the end of the sequence? (If no heads occur, then "all the heads are at the end of the sequence" is vacuously true.)

Class Problems

Problem 17.3.

The New York Yankees and the Boston Red Sox are playing a two-out-of-three series. In other words, they play until one team has won two games. Then that team is declared the overall winner and the series ends. Assume that the Red Sox win each game with probability 3/5, regardless of the outcomes of previous games.

Answer the questions below using the four step method. You can use the same tree diagram for all three problems.

(a) What is the probability that a total of 3 games are played?

(b) What is the probability that the winner of the series loses the first game?

(c) What is the probability that the *correct* team wins the series?

Problem 17.4.

To determine which of two people gets a prize, a coin is flipped twice. If the flips are a Head and then a Tail, the first player wins. If the flips are a Tail and then a Head, the second player wins. However, if both coins land the same way, the flips don't count and the whole process starts over.

Assume that on each flip, a Head comes up with probability p, regardless of what happened on other flips. Use the four step method to find a simple formula for the probability that the first player wins. What is the probability that neither player wins?

Hint: The tree diagram and sample space are infinite, so you're not going to finish drawing the tree. Try drawing only enough to see a pattern. Summing all the winning outcome probabilities directly is cumbersome. However, a neat trick solves this problem—and many others. Let s be the sum of all winning outcome probabilities in the whole tree. Notice that *you can write the sum of all the winning probabilities in certain subtrees as a function of s*. Use this observation to write an equation in s and then solve.

Homework Problems

Problem 17.5.

Let's see what happens when *Let's Make a Deal* is played with **four** doors. A prize is hidden behind one of the four doors. Then the contestant picks a door. Next, the host opens an unpicked door that has no prize behind it. The contestant is allowed to stick with their original door or to switch to one of the two unopened, unpicked doors. The contestant wins if their final choice is the door hiding the prize.

Let's make the same assumptions as in the original problem:

1. The prize is equally likely to be behind each door.

2. The contestant is equally likely to pick each door initially, regardless of the prize's location.

3. The host is equally likely to reveal each door that does not conceal the prize and was not selected by the player.

Use The Four Step Method to find the following probabilities. The tree diagram may become awkwardly large, in which case just draw enough of it to make its structure clear.

(a) Contestant Stu, a sanitation engineer from Trenton, New Jersey, stays with his original door. What is the probability that Stu wins the prize?

(b) Contestant Zelda, an alien abduction researcher from Helena, Montana, switches to one of the remaining two doors with equal probability. What is the probability that Zelda wins the prize?

Now let's revise our assumptions about how contestants choose doors. Say the doors are labeled A, B, C, and D. Suppose that Carol always opens the *earliest* door possible (the door whose label is earliest in the alphabet) with the restriction that she can neither reveal the prize nor open the door that the player picked.

This gives contestant Mergatroid—an engineering student from Cambridge, MA— just a little more information about the location of the prize. Suppose that Mergatroid always switches to the earliest door, excluding his initial pick and the one Carol opened.

(c) What is the probability that Mergatroid wins the prize?

Problem 17.6.
There were n Immortal Warriors born into our world, but in the end there can be *only one*. The Immortals' original plan was to stalk the world for centuries, dueling one another with ancient swords in dramatic landscapes until only one survivor remained. However, after a thought-provoking discussion probability, they opt to give the following protocol a try:

(i) The Immortals forge a coin that comes up heads with probability p.

(ii) Each Immortal flips the coin once.

(iii) If *exactly one* Immortal flips heads, then they are declared The One. Otherwise, the protocol is declared a failure, and they all go back to hacking each other up with swords.

One of the Immortals (Kurgan from the Russian steppe) argues that as n grows large, the probability that this protocol succeeds must tend to zero. Another (McLeod from the Scottish highlands) argues that this need not be the case, provided p is chosen carefully.

(a) A natural sample space to use to model this problem is $\{H, T\}^n$ of length-n sequences of H and T's, where the successive H's and T's in an outcome correspond to the Head or Tail flipped on each one of the n successive flips. Explain how a tree diagram approach leads to assigning a probability to each outcome that depends only on p, n and the number h of H's in the outcome.

(b) What is the probability that the experiment succeeds as a function of p and n?

(c) How should p, the bias of the coin, be chosen in order to maximize the probability that the experiment succeeds?

(d) What is the probability of success if p is chosen in this way? What quantity does this approach when n, the number of Immortal Warriors, grows large?

Problem 17.7.
We play a game with a deck of 52 regular playing cards, of which 26 are red and 26 are black. I randomly shuffle the cards and place the deck face down on a table. You have the option of "taking" or "skipping" the top card. If you skip the top card, then that card is revealed and we continue playing with the remaining deck. If you take the top card, then the game ends; you win if the card you took was revealed to be black, and you lose if it was red. If we get to a point where there is only one card left in the deck, you must take it. Prove that you have no better strategy than to take the top card—which means your probability of winning is 1/2.

   Hint: Prove by induction the more general claim that for a randomly shuffled deck of n cards that are red or black—not necessarily with the same number of red cards and black cards—there is no better strategy than taking the top card.

Problems for Section 17.5

Class Problems

Problem 17.8.
Suppose there is a system, built by Caltech graduates, with n components. We know from past experience that any particular component will fail in a given year

with probability p. That is, letting F_i be the event that the ith component fails within one year, we have

$$\Pr[F_i] = p$$

for $1 \leq i \leq n$. The *system* will fail if *any one* of its components fails. What can we say about the probability that the system will fail within one year?

Let F be the event that the system fails within one year. Without any additional assumptions, we can't get an exact answer for $\Pr[F]$. However, we can give useful upper and lower bounds, namely,

$$p \leq \Pr[F] \leq np. \tag{17.10}$$

We may as well assume $p < 1/n$, since the upper bound is trivial otherwise. For example, if $n = 100$ and $p = 10^{-5}$, we conclude that there is at most one chance in 1000 of system failure within a year and at least one chance in 100,000.

Let's model this situation with the sample space $S ::= \text{pow}([1, n])$ whose outcomes are subsets of positive integers $\leq n$, where $s \in S$ corresponds to the indices of exactly those components that fail within one year. For example, $\{2, 5\}$ is the outcome that the second and fifth components failed within a year and none of the other components failed. So the outcome that the system did not fail corresponds to the empty set $\emptyset$.

(a) Show that the probability that the system fails could be as small as p by describing appropriate probabilities for the outcomes. Make sure to verify that the sum of your outcome probabilities is 1.

(b) Show that the probability that the system fails could actually be as large as np by describing appropriate probabilities for the outcomes. Make sure to verify that the sum of your outcome probabilities is 1.

(c) Prove inequality (17.10).

Problem 17.9.
Here are some handy rules for reasoning about probabilities that all follow directly from the Disjoint Sum Rule. Prove them.

$$\Pr[A - B] = \Pr[A] - \Pr[A \cap B] \qquad \text{(Difference Rule)}$$

$$\Pr[\overline{A}] = 1 - \Pr[A] \qquad \text{(Complement Rule)}$$

$$\Pr[A \cup B] = \Pr[A] + \Pr[B] - \Pr[A \cap B] \qquad \text{(Inclusion-Exclusion)}$$

$$\Pr[A \cup B] \le \Pr[A] + \Pr[B] \qquad \text{(2-event Union Bound)}$$

$$A \subseteq B \text{ IMPLIES } \Pr[A] \le \Pr[B] \qquad \text{(Monotonicity)}$$

Homework Problems

Problem 17.10.

Prove the following probabilistic inequality, referred to as the *Union Bound*.
Let $A_1, A_2, \ldots, A_n, \ldots$ be events. Then

$$\Pr\left[\bigcup_{n \in \mathbb{N}} A_n \right] \le \sum_{n \in \mathbb{N}} \Pr[A_n].$$

Hint: Replace the A_n's by pairwise disjoint events and use the Sum Rule.

Problem 17.11.

The results of a round robin tournament in which every two people play each other
and one of them wins can be modelled a *tournament digraph*—a digraph with exactly one edge between each pair of distinct vertices, but we'll continue to use the
language of players beating each other.

An n-player tournament is *k-neutral* for some $k \in [0, n)$, when, for every set of
k players, there is another player who beats them all. For example, being 1-neutral
is the same as not having a "best" player who beats everyone else.

This problem shows that for any fixed k, if n is large enough, there will be a
k-neutral tournament of n players. We will do this by reformulating the question in
terms of probabilities. In particular, for any fixed n, we assign probabilities to each
n-vertex tournament digraph by choosing a direction for the edge between any two
vertices, independently and with equal probability for each edge.

(a) For any set S of k players, let B_S be the event that no contestant beats everyone in S. Express $\Pr[B_S]$ in terms of n and k.

(b) Let Q_k be the event equal to the set of n-vertex tournament digraphs that are
not k-neutral. Prove that

$$\Pr[Q_k] \le \binom{n}{k} \alpha^{n-k},$$

where $\alpha ::= 1 - (1/2)^k$.

Hint: Let S range over the size-k subsets of players, so

$$Q_k = \bigcup_S B_S .$$

Use Boole's inequality.

(c) Conclude that if n is enough larger than k, then $\Pr[Q_k] < 1$.

(d) Explain why the previous result implies that for every integer k, there is a k-neutral tournament.

Homework Problems

Problem 17.12.
Suppose you repeatedly flip a fair coin until three consecutive flips match the pattern HHT or the pattern TTH occurs. What is the probability you will see HHT first? Define a suitable probability space that models the coin flipping and use it to explain your answer.

Hint: Symmetry between Heads and Tails.

18   Conditional Probability

18.1   Monty Hall Confusion

Remember how we said that the Monty Hall problem confused even professional mathematicians? Based on the work we did with tree diagrams, this may seem surprising—the conclusion we reached followed routinely and logically. How could this problem be so confusing to so many people?

Well, one flawed argument goes as follows: let's say the contestant picks door A. And suppose that Carol, Monty's assistant, opens door B and shows us a goat. Let's use the tree diagram 17.3 from Chapter 17 to capture this situation. There are exactly three outcomes where contestant chooses door A, and there is a goat behind door B:

$$(A, A, B), (A, A, C), (C, A, B). \tag{18.1}$$

These outcomes have respective probabilities 1/18, 1/18, 1/9.

Among those outcomes, switching doors wins only on the last outcome (C, A, B). The other two outcomes *together* have the *same* 1/9 probability as the last one So in this situation, the probability that we win by switching is the *same* as the probability that we lose. In other words, in this situation, switching isn't any better than sticking!

Something has gone wrong here, since we know that the actual probability of winning by switching in 2/3. The mistaken conclusion that sticking or switching are equally good strategies comes from a common blunder in reasoning about how probabilities change given some information about what happened. We have asked for the probability that one event, [win by switching], happens, *given* that another event, [pick A AND goat at B], happens. We use the notation

$$\Pr\big[[\text{win by switching}] \mid [\text{pick A AND goat at B}]\big]$$

for this probability which, by the reasoning above, equals 1/2.

18.1.1   Behind the Curtain

A "given" condition is essentially an instruction to focus on only some of the possible outcomes. Formally, we're defining a new sample space consisting only of some of the outcomes. In this particular example, we're given that the player chooses door A and that there is a goat behind B. Our new sample space therefore consists solely of the three outcomes listed in (18.1). In the opening of Section 18.1, we calculated the conditional probability of winning by switching given that one of these outcome happened, by weighing the 1/9 probability of the win-by-switching outcome (C, A, B) against the $1/18 + 1/18 + 1/9$ probability of the three outcomes in the new sample space.

$$\Pr\big[[\text{win by switching}] \mid [\text{pick A AND goat at B}]\big]$$
$$= \Pr\big[(C, A, B) \mid \{(C, A, B), (A, A, B), (A, A, C)\}\big] +$$
$$\frac{\Pr[(C, A, B)]}{\Pr[\{(C, A, B), (A, A, B), (A, A, C)\}]}$$
$$= \frac{1/9}{1/18 + 1/18 + 1/9} = \frac{1}{2}.$$

There is nothing wrong with this calculation. So how come it leads to an incorrect conclusion about whether to stick or switch? The answer is that this was the wrong thing to calculate, as we'll explain in the next section.

18.2   Definition and Notation

The expression $\Pr[X \mid Y]$ denotes the probability of event X, given that event Y happens. In the example above, event X is the event of winning on a switch, and event Y is the event that a goat is behind door B and the contestant chose door A. We calculated $\Pr[X \mid Y]$ using a formula which serves as the definition of conditional probability:

Definition 18.2.1. Let X and Y be events where Y has nonzero probability. Then

$$\Pr[X \mid Y] ::= \frac{\Pr[X \cap Y]}{\Pr[Y]}.$$

The conditional probability $\Pr[X \mid Y]$ is undefined when the probability of event Y is zero. To avoid cluttering up statements with uninteresting hypotheses that conditioning events like Y have nonzero probability, we will make an implicit assumption from now on that all such events have nonzero probability.

Pure probability is often counterintuitive, but conditional probability can be even worse. Conditioning can subtly alter probabilities and produce unexpected results in randomized algorithms and computer systems as well as in betting games. But Definition 18.2.1 is very simple and causes no trouble—provided it is properly applied.

18.2.1 What went wrong

So if everything in the opening Section 18.1 is mathematically sound, why does it seem to contradict the results that we established in Chapter 17? The problem is a common one: *we chose the wrong condition.* In our initial description of the scenario, we learned the location of the goat when Carol opened door B. But when we defined our condition as "the contestant opens A and the goat is behind B," we included the outcome (A, A, C) in which Carol opens door C! The correct conditional probability should have been "what are the odds of winning by switching given the contestant chooses door A and Carol opens door B." By choosing a condition that did not reflect everything known. we inadvertently included an extraneous outcome in our calculation. With the correct conditioning, we still win by switching 1/9 of the time, but the smaller set of known outcomes has smaller total probability:

$$\Pr[\{(A, A, B), (C, A, B)\}] = \frac{1}{18} + \frac{1}{9} = \frac{3}{18}.$$

The conditional probability would then be:

$$\Pr\Big[[\text{win by switching}] \mid [\text{pick A AND Carol opens B}]\Big]$$
$$= \Pr\Big[(C, A, B) \mid \{(C, A, B), (A, A, B)\}\Big] + \frac{\Pr[(C, A, B)]}{\Pr[\{(C, A, B), (A, A, B)\}]}$$
$$= \frac{1/9}{1/9 + 1/18} = \frac{2}{3},$$

which is exactly what we already deduced from the tree diagram 17.2 in Section 17.2.

The O. J. Simpson Trial

In an opinion article in the *New York Times*, Steven Strogatz points to the O. J. Simpson trial as an example of poor choice of conditions. O. J. Simpson was a retired football player who was accused, and later acquitted, of the murder of his wife, Nicole Brown Simpson. The trial was widely publicized and called the "trial of the century." Racial tensions, allegations of police misconduct, and new-at-the-time DNA evidence captured the public's attention. But Strogatz, citing mathematician and author I.J. Good, focuses on a less well-known aspect of the case: whether O. J.'s history of abuse towards his wife was admissible into evidence.

The prosecution argued that abuse is often a precursor to murder, pointing to statistics indicating that an abuser was as much as ten times more likely to commit murder than was a random individual. The defense, however, countered with statistics indicating that the odds of an abusive husband murdering his wife were "infinitesimal," roughly 1 in 2500. Based on those numbers, the actual relevance of a history of abuse to a murder case would appear limited at best. According to the defense, introducing that history would prejudice the jury against Simpson but would lack any probitive value, so the discussion should be barred.

In other words, both the defense and the prosecution were arguing conditional probability, specifically the likelihood that a woman will be murdered by her husband, given that her husband abuses her. But both defense and prosecution omitted a vital piece of data from their calculations: Nicole Brown Simpson *was* murdered. Strogatz points out that based on the defense's numbers and the crime statistics of the time, the probability that a woman was murdered by her abuser, given that she was abused *and* murdered, is around 80%.

Strogatz's article goes into more detail about the calculations behind that 80% figure. But the issue we want to illustrate is that conditional probability is used and misused all the time, and even experts under public scrutiny make mistakes.

18.3   The Four-Step Method for Conditional Probability

In a best-of-three tournament, the local C-league hockey team wins the first game with probability 1/2. In subsequent games, their probability of winning is determined by the outcome of the previous game. If the local team won the previous game, then they are invigorated by victory and win the current game with probability 2/3. If they lost the previous game, then they are demoralized by defeat and win the current game with probability only 1/3. What is the probability that the local team wins the tournament, given that they win the first game?

This is a question about a conditional probability. Let A be the event that the local team wins the tournament, and let B be the event that they win the first game. Our goal is then to determine the conditional probability $\Pr[A \mid B]$.

We can tackle conditional probability questions just like ordinary probability problems: using a tree diagram and the four step method. A complete tree diagram is shown in Figure 18.1.

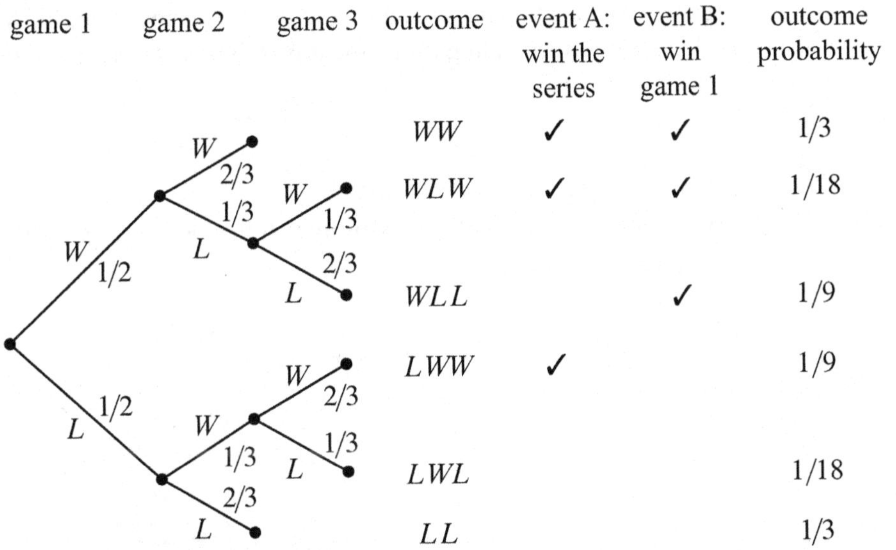

game 1	game 2	game 3	outcome	event A: win the series	event B: win game 1	outcome probability
			WW	✓	✓	1/3
			WLW	✓	✓	1/18
			WLL		✓	1/9
			LWW	✓		1/9
			LWL			1/18
			LL			1/3

Figure 18.1   The tree diagram for computing the probability that the local team wins two out of three games given that they won the first game.

Step 1: Find the Sample Space

Each internal vertex in the tree diagram has two children, one corresponding to a win for the local team (labeled W) and one corresponding to a loss (labeled L). The complete sample space is:

$$\mathcal{S} = \{WW, WLW, WLL, LWW, LWL, LL\}.$$

Step 2: Define Events of Interest

The event that the local team wins the whole tournament is:

$$T = \{WW, WLW, LWW\}.$$

And the event that the local team wins the first game is:

$$F = \{WW, WLW, WLL\}.$$

The outcomes in these events are indicated with check marks in the tree diagram in Figure 18.1.

Step 3: Determine Outcome Probabilities

Next, we must assign a probability to each outcome. We begin by labeling edges as specified in the problem statement. Specifically, the local team has a 1/2 chance of winning the first game, so the two edges leaving the root are each assigned probability 1/2. Other edges are labeled 1/3 or 2/3 based on the outcome of the preceding game. We then find the probability of each outcome by multiplying all probabilities along the corresponding root-to-leaf path. For example, the probability of outcome WLL is:

$$\frac{1}{2} \cdot \frac{1}{3} \cdot \frac{2}{3} = \frac{1}{9}.$$

Step 4: Compute Event Probabilities

We can now compute the probability that the local team wins the tournament, given that they win the first game:

$$\Pr\left[A \mid B\right] = \frac{\Pr[A \cap B]}{\Pr[B]}$$

$$= \frac{\Pr[\{WW, WLW\}]}{\Pr[\{WW, WLW, WLL\}]}$$

$$= \frac{1/3 + 1/18}{1/3 + 1/18 + 1/9}$$

$$= \frac{7}{9}.$$

We're done! If the local team wins the first game, then they win the whole tournament with probability 7/9.

18.4   Why Tree Diagrams Work

We've now settled into a routine of solving probability problems using tree diagrams. But we've left a big question unaddressed: mathematical justification behind those funny little pictures. Why do they work?

The answer involves conditional probabilities. In fact, the probabilities that we've been recording on the edges of tree diagrams *are* conditional probabilities. For example, consider the uppermost path in the tree diagram for the hockey team problem, which corresponds to the outcome WW. The first edge is labeled 1/2, which is the probability that the local team wins the first game. The second edge is labeled 2/3, which is the probability that the local team wins the second game, *given* that they won the first—a conditional probability! More generally, on each edge of a tree diagram, we record the probability that the experiment proceeds along that path, given that it reaches the parent vertex.

So we've been using conditional probabilities all along. For example, we concluded that:

$$\Pr[WW] = \frac{1}{2} \cdot \frac{2}{3} = \frac{1}{3}.$$

Why is this correct?

The answer goes back to Definition 18.2.1 of conditional probability which could be written in a form called the *Product Rule* for conditional probabilities:

Rule (Conditional Probability Product Rule: 2 Events).

$$\Pr[E_1 \cap E_2] = \Pr[E_1] \cdot \Pr\left[E_2 \mid E_1\right].$$

Multiplying edge probabilities in a tree diagram amounts to evaluating the right side of this equation. For example:

Pr[win first game ∩ win second game]

$$= \Pr[\text{win first game}] \cdot \Pr\left[\text{win second game} \mid \text{win first game}\right]$$

$$= \frac{1}{2} \cdot \frac{2}{3}.$$

So the Conditional Probability Product Rule is the formal justification for multiplying edge probabilities to get outcome probabilities.

To justify multiplying edge probabilities along a path of length three, we need a rule for three events:

Rule (Conditional Probability Product Rule: 3 Events).

$$\Pr[E_1 \cap E_2 \cap E_3] = \Pr[E_1] \cdot \Pr\left[E_2 \mid E_1\right] \cdot \Pr\left[E_3 \mid E_1 \cap E_2\right].$$

An *n*-event version of the Rule is given in Problem 18.1, but its form should be clear from the three event version.

18.4.1 Probability of Size-*k* Subsets

As a simple application of the product rule for conditional probabilities, we can use the rule to calculate the number of size-*k* subsets of the integers [1..*n*]. Of course we already know this number is $\binom{n}{k}$, but now the rule will give us a new derivation of the formula for $\binom{n}{k}$.

Let's pick some size-k subset $S \subseteq [1..n]$ as a target. Suppose we choose a size-k subset at random, with all subsets of $[1..n]$ equally likely to be chosen, and let p be the probability that our randomly chosen equals this target. That is, the probability of picking S is p, and since all sets are equally likely to be chosen, the number of size-k subsets equals $1/p$.

So what's p? Well, the probability that the *smallest* number in the random set is one of the k numbers in S is k/n. Then, *given* that the smallest number in the random set is in S, the probability that the *second* smallest number in the random set is one of the remaining $k-1$ elements in S is $(k-1)/(n-1)$. So by the product rule, the probability that the *two* smallest numbers in the random set are both in S is

$$\frac{k}{n} \cdot \frac{k-1}{n-1}.$$

Next, given that the two smallest numbers in the random set are in S, the probability that the third smallest number is one of the $k-2$ remaining elements in S is $(k-2)/(n-2)$. So by the product rule, the probability that the *three* smallest numbers in the random set are all in S is

$$\frac{k}{n} \cdot \frac{k-1}{n-1} \cdot \frac{k-2}{n-2}.$$

Continuing in this way, it follows that the probability that *all* k elements in the randomly chosen set are in S, that is, the probabilty that the randomly chosen set equals the target, is

$$
\begin{aligned}
p &= \frac{k}{n} \cdot \frac{k-1}{n-1} \cdot \frac{k-2}{n-2} \cdots \frac{k-(k-1)}{n-(k-1)} \\
&= \frac{k \cdot (k-1) \cdot (k-1) \cdots 1}{n \cdot (n-1) \cdot (n-2) \cdots (n-(k-1))} \\
&= \frac{k!}{n!/(n-k)!} \\
&= \frac{k!(n-k)!}{n!}.
\end{aligned}
$$

So we have again shown the number of size-k subsets of $[1..n]$, namely $1/p$, is

$$\frac{n!}{k!(n-k)!}.$$

18.4.2   Medical Testing

Breast cancer is a deadly disease that claims thousands of lives every year. Early detection and accurate diagnosis are high priorities, and routine mammograms are one of the first lines of defense. They're not very accurate as far as medical tests go, but they are correct between 90% and 95% of the time, which seems pretty good for a relatively inexpensive non-invasive test.[1] However, mammogram results are also an example of conditional probabilities having counterintuitive consequences. If the test was positive for breast cancer in you or a loved one, and the test is better than 90% accurate, you'd naturally expect that to mean there is better than 90% chance that the disease was present. But a mathematical analysis belies that naive intuitive expectation. Let's start by precisely defining how accurate a mammogram is:

- If you have the condition, there is a 10% chance that the test will say you do not have it. This is called a "false negative."

- If you do not have the condition, there is a 5% chance that the test will say you do. This is a "false positive."

18.4.3 Four Steps Again

Now suppose that we are testing middle-aged women with no family history of cancer. Among this cohort, incidence of breast cancer rounds up to about 1%.

Step 2: Define Events of Interest
Let A be the event that the person has breast cancer. Let B be the event that the test was positive. The outcomes in each event are marked in the tree diagram. We want to find $\Pr\left[A \mid B\right]$, the probability that a person has breast cancer, given that the test was positive.

Step 3: Find Outcome Probabilities
First, we assign probabilities to edges. These probabilities are drawn directly from the problem statement. By the Product Rule, the probability of an outcome is the product of the probabilities on the corresponding root-to-leaf path. All probabilities are shown in Figure 18.2.

Step 4: Compute Event Probabilities
From Definition 18.2.1, we have

$$\Pr\left[A \mid B\right] = \frac{\Pr[A \cap B]}{\Pr[B]} = \frac{0.009}{0.009 + 0.0495} \approx 15.4\%.$$

So, if the test is positive, then there is an 84.6% chance that the result is incorrect, even though the test is nearly 95% accurate! So this seemingly pretty accurate

---

[1] The statistics in this example are roughly based on actual medical data, but have been rounded or simplified for illustrative purposes.

Step 1: Find the Sample Space

The sample space is found with the tree diagram in Figure 18.2.

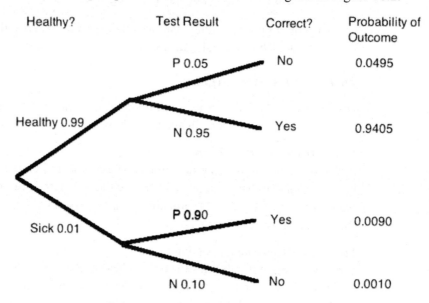

Healthy?	Test Result	Correct?	Probability of Outcome

Figure 18.2   The tree diagram for a breast cancer test.

test doesn't tell us much. To see why percent accuracy is no guarantee of value, notice that there is a simple way to make a test that is 99% accurate: always return a negative result! This test gives the right answer for all healthy people and the wrong answer only for the 1% that actually have cancer. This 99% accurate test tells us nothing; the "less accurate" mammogram is still a lot more useful.

18.4.4 Natural Frequencies

That there is only about a 15% chance that the patient actually has the condition when the test say so may seem surprising at first, but it makes sense with a little thought. There are two ways the patient could test positive: first, the patient could have the condition and the test could be correct; second, the patient could be healthy and the test incorrect. But almost everyone is healthy! The number of healthy individuals is so large that even the mere 5% with false positive results overwhelm the number of genuinely positive results from the truly ill.

Thinking like this in terms of these "natural frequencies" can be a useful tool for interpreting some of the strange seeming results coming from those formulas. For example, let's take a closer look at the mammogram example.

Imagine 10,000 women in our demographic. Based on the frequency of the disease, we'd expect 100 of them to have breast cancer. Of those, 90 would have a positve result. The remaining 9,900 woman are healthy, but 5% of them—500, give or take—will show a false positive on the mammogram. That gives us 90 real positives out of a little fewer than 600 positives. An 85% error rate isn't so surprising after all.

18.4.5 *A Posteriori* Probabilities

If you think about it much, the medical testing problem we just considered could start to trouble you. You may wonder if a statement like "If someone tested positive, then that person has the condition with probability 18%" makes sense, since a given person being tested either has the disease or they don't.

One way to understand such a statement is that it just means that 15% of the people who test positive will actually have the condition. Any particular person has it or they don't, but a *randomly selected* person among those who test positive will have the condition with probability 15%.

But what does this 15% probability tell you if you *personally* got a positive result? Should you be relieved that there is less than one chance in five that you have the disease? Should you worry that there is nearly one chance in five that you do have the disease? Should you start treatment just in case? Should you get more tests?

These are crucial practical questions, but it is important to understand that they are not *mathematical* questions. Rather, these are questions about statistical judgements and the philosophical meaning of probability. We'll say a bit more about this after looking at one more example of after-the-fact probabilities.

The Hockey Team in Reverse

Suppose that we turn the hockey question around: what is the probability that the local C-league hockey team won their first game, given that they won the series?

As we discussed earlier, some people find this question absurd. If the team has already won the tournament, then the first game is long since over. Who won the first game is a question of fact, not of probability. However, our mathematical theory of probability contains no notion of one event preceding another. There is no notion of time at all. Therefore, from a mathematical perspective, this is a perfectly valid question. And this is also a meaningful question from a practical perspective. Suppose that you're told that the local team won the series, but not told the results of individual games. Then, from your perspective, it makes perfect sense to wonder how likely it is that local team won the first game.

A conditional probability $\Pr\left[B \mid A\right]$ is called *a posteriori* if event B precedes event A in time. Here are some other examples of a posteriori probabilities:

- The probability it was cloudy this morning, given that it rained in the afternoon.

- The probability that I was initially dealt two queens in Texas No Limit Hold 'Em poker, given that I eventually got four-of-a-kind.

from ordinary probabilities; the distinction comes from our view of causality, which is a philosophical question rather than a mathematical one.

Let's return to the original problem. The probability that the local team won their first game, given that they won the series is $\Pr\left[B \mid A\right]$. We can compute this using the definition of conditional probability and the tree diagram in Figure 18.1:

$$\Pr\left[B \mid A\right] = \frac{\Pr[B \cap A]}{\Pr[A]} = \frac{1/3 + 1/18}{1/3 + 1/18 + 1/9} = \frac{7}{9}.$$

In general, such pairs of probabilities are related by Bayes' Rule:

Theorem 18.4.1 (Bayes' Rule).

$$\Pr\left[B \mid A\right] = \frac{\Pr\left[A \mid B\right] \cdot \Pr[B]}{\Pr[A]} \tag{18.2}$$

Proof. We have

$$\Pr\left[B \mid A\right] \cdot \Pr[A] = \Pr[A \cap B] = \Pr\left[A \mid B\right] \cdot \Pr[B]$$

by definition of conditional probability. Dividing by $\Pr[A]$ gives (18.2).   ∎

18.4.6   Philosphy of Probability

Let's try to assign a probability to the event

$$[2^{6972607} - 1 \text{ is a prime number}]$$

It's not obvious how to check whether such a large number is prime, so you might try an estimation based on the density of primes. The Prime Number Theorem implies that only about 1 in 5 million numbers in this range are prime, so you might say that the probability is about $2 \cdot 10^{-8}$. On the other hand, given that we chose this example to make some philosophical point, you might guess that we probably purposely chose an obscure looking prime number, and you might be willing to make an even money bet that the number is prime. In other words, you might think the probability is 1/2. Finally, we can take the position that assigning a probability to this statement is nonsense because there is no randomness involved; the number is either prime or it isn't. This is the view we take in this text.

An alternate view is the *Bayesian* approach, in which a probability is interpreted as a *degree of belief* in a proposition. A Bayesian would agree that the number above is either prime or composite, but they would be perfectly willing to assign a probability to each possibility. The Bayesian approach is very broad in its willingness to assign probabilities to any event, but the problem is that there is no single "right" probability for an event, since the probability depends on one's initial beliefs. On the other hand, if you have confidence in some set of initial beliefs, then Bayesianism provides a convincing framework for updating your beliefs as further information emerges.

As an aside, it is not clear whether Bayes himself was Bayesian in this sense. However, a Bayesian would be willing to talk about the probability that Bayes was Bayesian.

Another school of thought says that probabilities can only be meaningfully applied to *repeatable processes* like rolling dice or flipping coins. In this *frequentist* view, the probability of an event represents the fraction of trials in which the event occurred. So we can make sense of the *a posteriori* probabilities of the C-league hockey example of Section 18.4.5 by imagining that many hockey series were played, and the probability that the local team won their first game, given that they won the series, is simply the fraction of series where they won the first game among all the series they won.

Getting back to prime numbers, we mentioned in Section 9.5.1 that there is a probabilistic primality test. If a number N is composite, there is at least a 3/4 chance that the test will discover this. In the remaining 1/4 of the time, the test is inconclusive. But as long as the result is inconclusive, the test can be run independently again and again up to, say, 100 times. So if N actually is composite, then the probability that 000 repetitions of the probabilistic test do not discover this is at most:

$$\left(\frac{1}{4}\right)^{100}.$$

If the test remained inconclusive after 100 repetitions, it is still logically possible that N is composite, but betting that N is prime would be the best bet you'll ever get to make! If you're comfortable using probability to describe your personal belief about primality after such an experiment, you are being a Bayesian. A frequentist would not assign a probability to N's primality, but they would also be happy to bet on primality with tremendous confidence. We'll examine this issue again when we discuss polling and confidence levels in Section 18.9.

Despite the philosophical divide, the real world conclusions Bayesians and Frequentists reach from probabilities are pretty much the same, and even where their interpretations differ, they use the same theory of probability.

18.5   The Law of Total Probability

Breaking a probability calculation into cases simplifies many problems. The idea is to calculate the probability of an event A by splitting into two cases based on whether or not another event E occurs. That is, calculate the probability of $A \cap E$ and $A \cap \overline{E}$. By the Sum Rule, the sum of these probabilities equals $\Pr[A]$. Expressing the intersection probabilities as conditional probabilities yields:

Rule 18.5.1 (Law of Total Probability: single event).

$$\Pr[A] = \Pr\left[A \mid E\right] \cdot \Pr[E] + \Pr\left[A \mid \overline{E}\right] \cdot \Pr[\overline{E}].$$

For example, suppose we conduct the following experiment. First, we flip a fair coin. If heads comes up, then we roll one die and take the result. If tails comes up, then we roll two dice and take the sum of the two results. What is the probability that this process yields a 2? Let E be the event that the coin comes up heads, and let A be the event that we get a 2 overall. Assuming that the coin is fair, $\Pr[E] = \Pr[\overline{E}] = 1/2$. There are now two cases. If we flip heads, then we roll a 2 on a single die with probability $\Pr\left[A \mid E\right] = 1/6$. On the other hand, if we flip tails, then we get a sum of 2 on two dice with probability $\Pr\left[A \mid \overline{E}\right] = 1/36$. Therefore, the probability that the whole process yields a 2 is

$$\Pr[A] = \frac{1}{2} \cdot \frac{1}{6} + \frac{1}{2} \cdot \frac{1}{36} = \frac{7}{72}.$$

This rule extends to any set of disjoint events that make up the entire sample space. For example,

Rule (Law of Total Probability: 3-events). *If E_1, E_2 and E_3 are disjoint, and $\Pr[E_1 \cup E_2 \cup E_3] = 1$, then*

$$\Pr[A] = \Pr\left[A \mid E_1\right] \cdot \Pr[E_1] + \Pr\left[A \mid E_2\right] \cdot \Pr[E_2] + \Pr\left[A \mid E_3\right] \cdot \Pr[E_3].$$

This in turn leads to a three-event version of Bayes' Rule in which the probability of event E_1 given A is calculated from the "inverse" conditional probabilities of A given E_1, E_2, and E_3:

Rule (Bayes' Rule: 3-events).

$$\Pr\left[E_1 \mid A\right] = \frac{\Pr\left[A \mid E_1\right] \cdot \Pr[E_1]}{\Pr\left[A \mid E_1\right] \cdot \Pr[E_1] + \Pr\left[A \mid E_2\right] \cdot \Pr[E_2] + \Pr\left[A \mid E_3\right] \cdot \Pr[E_3]}$$

The generalization of these rules to n disjoint events is a routine exercise (Problems 18.3 and 18.4).

18.5.1 Conditioning on a Single Event

The probability rules that we derived in Section 17.5.2 extend to probabilities conditioned on the same event. For example, the Inclusion-Exclusion formula for two sets holds when all probabilities are conditioned on an event C:

$$\Pr\left[A \cup B \mid C\right] = \Pr\left[A \mid C\right] + \Pr\left[B \mid C\right] - \Pr\left[A \cap B \mid C\right].$$

This is easy to verify by plugging in the Definition 18.2.1 of conditional probability.[2]

It is important not to mix up events before and after the conditioning bar. For example, the following is *not* a valid identity:

False Claim.

$$\Pr\left[A \mid B \cup C\right] = \Pr\left[A \mid B\right] + \Pr\left[A \mid C\right] - \Pr\left[A \mid B \cap C\right]. \tag{18.3}$$

A simple counter-example is to let B and C be events over a uniform space with most of their outcomes in A, but not overlapping. This ensures that $\Pr\left[A \mid B\right]$ and $\Pr\left[A \mid C\right]$ are both close to 1. For example,

$$B ::= [0..9],$$
$$C ::= [10..18] \cup \{0\},$$
$$A ::= [1..18],$$

---

[2]Problem 18.13 explains why this and similar conditional identities follow on general principles from the corresponding unconditional identities.

so

$$\Pr[A \mid B] = \frac{9}{10} = \Pr[A \mid C].$$

Also, since 0 is the only outcome in $B \cap C$ and $0 \notin A$, we have

$$\Pr[A \mid B \cap C] = 0$$

So the right-hand side of (18.3) is 1.8, while the left-hand side is a probability which can be at most 1—actually, it is 18/19.

18.6   Simpson's Paradox

In 1973, a famous university was investigated for gender discrimination [6]. The investigation was prompted by evidence that, at first glance, appeared definitive: in 1973, 44% of male applicants to the school's graduate programs were accepted, but only 35% of female applicants were admitted.

However, this data turned out to be completely misleading. Analysis of the individual departments, showed not only that few showed significant evidence of bias, but also that among the few departments that *did* show statistical irregularities, most were slanted *in favor of women*. This suggests that if there was any sex discrimination, then it was against men!

Given the discrepancy in these findings, it feels like someone must be doing bad math—intentionally or otherwise. But the numbers are not actually inconsistent. In fact, this statistical hiccup is common enough to merit its own name: *Simpson's Paradox* occurs when multiple small groups of data all exhibit a similar trend, but that trend reverses when those groups are aggregated. To explain how this is possible, let's first clarify the problem by expressing both arguments in terms of conditional probabilities. For simplicity, suppose that there are only two departments EE and CS. Consider the experiment where we pick a random candidate. Define the following events:

- $A ::=$ the candidate is admitted to his or her program of choice,

- $F_{EE} ::=$ the candidate is a woman applying to the EE department,

- $F_{CS} ::=$ the candidate is a woman applying to the CS department,

- $M_{EE} ::=$ the candidate is a man applying to the EE department,

- $M_{CS} ::=$ the candidate is a man applying to the CS department.

CS	2 men admitted out of 5 candidates	40%
	50 women admitted out of 100 candidates	50%
EE	70 men admitted out of 100 candidates	70%
	4 women admitted out of 5 candidates	80%
Overall	72 men admitted, 105 candidates	$\approx 69\%$
	54 women admitted, 105 candidates	$\approx 51\%$

Table 18.1 A scenario in which men are overall more likely than women to be admitted to a school, despite being less likely to be admitted into any given program.

Assume that all candidates are either men or women, and that no candidate belongs to both departments. That is, the events F_{EE}, F_{CS}, M_{EE} and M_{CS} are all disjoint.

In these terms, the plaintiff's assertion—that a male candidate is more likely to be admitted to the university than a female—can be expressed by the following inequality:

$$\Pr\left[A \mid M_{EE} \cup M_{CS}\right] > \Pr\left[A \mid F_{EE} \cup F_{CS}\right].$$

The university's retort that *in any given department*, a male applicant is less likely to be admitted than a female can be expressed by a pair of inequalities:

$$\Pr\left[A \mid M_{EE}\right] < \Pr\left[A \mid F_{EE}\right] \quad \text{and}$$
$$\Pr\left[A \mid M_{CS}\right] < \Pr\left[A \mid F_{CS}\right].$$

We can explain how there could be such a discrepancy between university-wide and department-by-department admission statistics by supposing that the CS department is more selective than the EE department, but CS attracts a far larger number of woman applicants than EE.[3]. Table 18.1 shows some admission statistics for which the inequalities asserted by both the plaintiff and the university hold.

Initially, we and the plaintiffs both assumed that the overall admissions statistics for the university could only be explained by gender discrimination. The department by department statistics seems to belie the accusation of discrimination. But do they really?

Suppose we replaced "the candidate is a man/woman applying to the EE department," by "the candidate is a man/woman for whom an admissions decision was made during an odd-numbered day of the month," and likewise with CS and an even-numbered day of the month. Since we don't think the parity of a date is a

---

[3] At the actual university in the lawsuit, the "exclusive" departments more popular among women were those that did not require a mathematical foundation, such as English and education. Women's disproportionate choice of these careers reflects gender bias, but one which predates the university's involvement.

cause for the outcome of an admission decision, we would most likely dismiss the "coincidence" that on both odd and even dates, women are more frequently admitted. Instead we would judge, based on the overall data showing women less likely to be admitted, that gender bias against women *was* an issue in the university.

Bear in mind that it would be the *same numerical data* that we would be using to justify our different conclusions in the department-by-department case and the even-day-odd-day case. We interpreted the same numbers differently based on our implicit causal beliefs, specifically that departments matter and date parity does not. It is circular to claim that the data corroborated our beliefs that there is or is not discrimination. Rather, our interpretation of the data correlation depended on our beliefs about the causes of admission in the first place.[4] This example highlights a basic principle in statistics which people constantly ignore: *never assume that correlation implies causation*.

18.7   Independence

Suppose that we flip two fair coins simultaneously on opposite sides of a room. Intuitively, the way one coin lands does not affect the way the other coin lands. The mathematical concept that captures this intuition is called *independence*.

Definition 18.7.1. An event with probability 0 is defined to be independent of every event (including itself). If $\Pr[B] \neq 0$, then event A is independent of event B iff

$$\Pr\left[A \mid B\right] = \Pr[A]. \tag{18.4}$$

In other words, A and B are independent if knowing that B happens does not alter the probability that A happens, as is the case with flipping two coins on opposite sides of a room.

Potential Pitfall

Students sometimes get the idea that disjoint events are independent. The *opposite* is true: if $A \cap B = \emptyset$, then knowing that A happens means you know that B does not happen. Disjoint events are *never* independent—unless one of them has probability zero.

---

[4]These issues are thoughtfully examined in *Causality: Models, Reasoning and Inference*, Judea Pearl, Cambridge U. Press, 2001.

18.7.1 Alternative Formulation

Sometimes it is useful to express independence in an alternate form which follows immediately from Definition 18.7.1:

Theorem 18.7.2. *A is independent of B if and only if*

$$\Pr[A \cap B] = \Pr[A] \cdot \Pr[B]. \qquad (18.5)$$

Notice that Theorem 18.7.2 makes apparent the symmetry between A being independent of B and B being independent of A:

Corollary 18.7.3. *A is independent of B iff B is independent of A.*

18.7.2 Independence Is an Assumption

Generally, independence is something that you *assume* in modeling a phenomenon. For example, consider the experiment of flipping two fair coins. Let A be the event that the first coin comes up heads, and let B be the event that the second coin is heads. If we assume that A and B are independent, then the probability that both coins come up heads is:

$$\Pr[A \cap B] = \Pr[A] \cdot \Pr[B] = \frac{1}{2} \cdot \frac{1}{2} = \frac{1}{4}.$$

In this example, the assumption of independence is reasonable. The result of one coin toss should have negligible impact on the outcome of the other coin toss. And if we were to repeat the experiment many times, we would be likely to have $A \cap B$ about 1/4 of the time.

On the other hand, there are many examples of events where assuming independence isn't justified. For example, an hourly weather forecast for a clear day might list a 10% chance of rain every hour from noon to midnight, meaning each hour has a 90% chance of being dry. But that does *not* imply that the odds of a rainless day are a mere $0.9^{12} \approx 0.28$. In reality, if it doesn't rain as of 5pm, the odds are higher than 90% that it will stay dry at 6pm as well—and if it starts pouring at 5pm, the chances are much higher than 10% that it will still be rainy an hour later.

Deciding when to *assume* that events are independent is a tricky business. In practice, there are strong motivations to assume independence since many useful formulas (such as equation (18.5)) only hold if the events are independent. But you need to be careful: we'll describe several famous examples where (false) assumptions of independence led to trouble. This problem gets even trickier when there are more than two events in play.

18.8   Mutual Independence

We have defined what it means for two events to be independent. What if there are more than two events? For example, how can we say that the flips of n coins are all independent of one another? A set of events is said to be *mutually independent* if the probability of each event in the set is the same no matter which of the other events has occurred. This is equivalent to saying that for any selection of two or more of the events, the probability that all the selected events occur equals the product of the probabilities of the selected events.

For example, four events E_1, E_2, E_3, E_4 are mutually independent if and only if all of the following equations hold:

$$\Pr[E_1 \cap E_2] = \Pr[E_1] \cdot \Pr[E_2]$$
$$\Pr[E_1 \cap E_3] = \Pr[E_1] \cdot \Pr[E_3]$$
$$\Pr[E_1 \cap E_4] = \Pr[E_1] \cdot \Pr[E_4]$$
$$\Pr[E_2 \cap E_3] = \Pr[E_2] \cdot \Pr[E_3]$$
$$\Pr[E_2 \cap E_4] = \Pr[E_2] \cdot \Pr[E_4]$$
$$\Pr[E_3 \cap E_4] = \Pr[E_3] \cdot \Pr[E_4]$$
$$\Pr[E_1 \cap E_2 \cap E_3] = \Pr[E_1] \cdot \Pr[E_2] \cdot \Pr[E_3]$$
$$\Pr[E_1 \cap E_2 \cap E_4] = \Pr[E_1] \cdot \Pr[E_2] \cdot \Pr[E_4]$$
$$\Pr[E_1 \cap E_3 \cap E_4] = \Pr[E_1] \cdot \Pr[E_3] \cdot \Pr[E_4]$$
$$\Pr[E_2 \cap E_3 \cap E_4] = \Pr[E_2] \cdot \Pr[E_3] \cdot \Pr[E_4]$$
$$\Pr[E_1 \cap E_2 \cap E_3 \cap E_4] = \Pr[E_1] \cdot \Pr[E_2] \cdot \Pr[E_3] \cdot \Pr[E_4]$$

The generalization to mutual independence of n events should now be clear.

18.8.1   DNA Testing

Assumptions about independence are routinely made in practice. Frequently, such assumptions are quite reasonable. Sometimes, however, the reasonableness of an independence assumption is not so clear, and the consequences of a faulty assumption can be severe.

Let's return to the O. J. Simpson murder trial. The following expert testimony was given on May 15, 1995:

Mr. Clarke: When you make these estimations of frequency—and I believe you touched a little bit on a concept called independence?

Dr. Cotton: Yes, I did.

Mr. Clarke: And what is that again?

Dr. Cotton: It means whether or not you inherit one allele that you have is not— does not affect the second allele that you might get. That is, if you inherit a band at 5,000 base pairs, that doesn't mean you'll automatically or with some probability inherit one at 6,000. What you inherit from one parent is [independent of] what you inherit from the other.

Mr. Clarke: Why is that important?

Dr. Cotton: Mathematically that's important because if that were not the case, it would be improper to multiply the frequencies between the different genetic locations.

Mr. Clarke: How do you—well, first of all, are these markers independent that you've described in your testing in this case?

Presumably, this dialogue was as confusing to you as it was for the jury. Essentially, the jury was told that genetic markers in blood found at the crime scene matched Simpson's. Furthermore, they were told that the probability that the markers would be found in a randomly-selected person was at most 1 in 170 million. This astronomical figure was derived from statistics such as:

- 1 person in 100 has marker A.

- 1 person in 50 marker B.

- 1 person in 40 has marker C.

- 1 person in 5 has marker D.

- 1 person in 170 has marker E.

Then these numbers were multiplied to give the probability that a randomly-selected person would have all five markers:

$$\Pr[A \cap B \cap C \cap D \cap E] = \Pr[A] \cdot \Pr[B] \cdot \Pr[C] \cdot \Pr[D] \cdot \Pr[E]$$
$$= \frac{1}{100} \cdot \frac{1}{50} \cdot \frac{1}{40} \cdot \frac{1}{5} \cdot \frac{1}{170} = \frac{1}{170,000,000}.$$

The defense pointed out that this assumes that the markers appear mutually independently. Furthermore, all the statistics were based on just a few hundred blood samples.

After the trial, the jury was widely mocked for failing to "understand" the DNA evidence. If you were a juror, would *you* accept the 1 in 170 million calculation?

18.8.2   Pairwise Independence

The definition of mutual independence seems awfully complicated—there are so many selections of events to consider! Here's an example that illustrates the subtlety of independence when more than two events are involved. Suppose that we flip three fair, mutually-independent coins. Define the following events:

- A_1 is the event that coin 1 matches coin 2.

- A_2 is the event that coin 2 matches coin 3.

- A_3 is the event that coin 3 matches coin 1.

Are A_1, A_2, A_3 mutually independent?

The sample space for this experiment is:

$$\{HHH,\ HHT,\ HTH,\ HTT,\ THH,\ THT,\ TTH,\ TTT\}.$$

Every outcome has probability $(1/2)^3 = 1/8$ by our assumption that the coins are mutually independent.

To see if events A_1, A_2 and A_3 are mutually independent, we must check a sequence of equalities. It will be helpful first to compute the probability of each event A_i:

$$\Pr[A_1] = \Pr[HHH] + \Pr[HHT] + \Pr[TTH] + \Pr[TTT]$$
$$= \frac{1}{8} + \frac{1}{8} + \frac{1}{8} + \frac{1}{8} = \frac{1}{2}.$$

By symmetry, $\Pr[A_2] = \Pr[A_3] = 1/2$ as well. Now we can begin checking all the equalities required for mutual independence:

$$\Pr[A_1 \cap A_2] = \Pr[HHH] + \Pr[TTT] = \frac{1}{8} + \frac{1}{8} = \frac{1}{4} = \frac{1}{2} \cdot \frac{1}{2}$$
$$= \Pr[A_1]\Pr[A_2].$$

By symmetry, $\Pr[A_1 \cap A_3] = \Pr[A_1] \cdot \Pr[A_3]$ and $\Pr[A_2 \cap A_3] = \Pr[A_2] \cdot \Pr[A_3]$ must hold also. Finally, we must check one last condition:

$$\Pr[A_1 \cap A_2 \cap A_3] = \Pr[HHH] + \Pr[TTT] = \frac{1}{8} + \frac{1}{8} = \frac{1}{4}$$
$$\neq \frac{1}{8} = \Pr[A_1]\Pr[A_2]\Pr[A_3].$$

The three events A_1, A_2 and A_3 are not mutually independent even though any two of them are independent! This not-quite mutual independence seems weird at first, but it happens. It even generalizes:

Definition 18.8.1. A set A_1, A_2, ..., of events is *k-way independent* iff every set of k of these events is mutually independent. The set is *pairwise independent* iff it is 2-way independent.

So the events A_1, A_2, A_3 above are pairwise independent, but not mutually independent. Pairwise independence is a much weaker property than mutual independence.

For example, suppose that the prosecutors in the O. J. Simpson trial were wrong and markers A, B, C, D and E are only *pairwise* independently. Then the probability that a randomly-selected person has all five markers is no more than:

$$\Pr[A \cap B \cap C \cap D \cap E] \le \Pr[A \cap E] = \Pr[A] \cdot \Pr[E]$$
$$= \frac{1}{100} \cdot \frac{1}{170} = \frac{1}{17{,}000}.$$

The first line uses the fact that $A \cap B \cap C \cap D \cap E$ is a subset of $A \cap E$. (We picked out the A and E markers because they're the rarest.) We use pairwise independence on the second line. Now the probability of a random match is 1 in 17,000—a far cry from 1 in 170 million! And this is the strongest conclusion we can reach assuming only pairwise independence.

On the other hand, the 1 in 17,000 bound that we get by assuming pairwise independence is a lot better than the bound that we would have if there were no independence at all. For example, if the markers are dependent, then it is possible that

everyone with marker E has marker A,

everyone with marker A has marker B,

everyone with marker B has marker C, and

everyone with marker C has marker D.

In such a scenario, the probability of a match is

$$\Pr[E] = \frac{1}{170}.$$

So a stronger independence assumption leads to a smaller bound on the probability of a match. The trick is to figure out what independence assumption is reasonable. Assuming that the markers are *mutually* independent may well *not* be reasonable unless you have examined hundreds of millions of blood samples. Otherwise, how would you know that marker D does not show up more frequently whenever the other four markers are simultaneously present?

18.9   Probability versus Confidence

Let's look at some other problems like the breast cancer test of Section 18.4.2, but this time we'll use more extreme numbers to highlight some key issues.

18.9.1   Testing for Tuberculosis

Let's suppose we have a really terrific diagnostic test for tuberculosis (TB): if you have TB, the test is *guaranteed* to detect it, and if you don't have TB, then the test will report that correctly 99% of the time!

In other words, let "*TB*" be the event that a person has TB, "*pos*" be the event that the person tests positive for TB, so "$\overline{pos}$" is the event that they test negative. Now we can restate these guarantees in terms of conditional probabilities:

$$\Pr[pos \mid TB] = 1, \tag{18.6}$$

$$\Pr[\overline{pos} \mid \overline{TB}] = 0.99. \tag{18.7}$$

This means that the test produces the correct result at least 99% of the time, regardless of whether or not the person has TB. A careful statistician would assert:[5]

Lemma. *You can be 99% confident that the test result is correct.*

Corollary 18.9.1. *If you test positive, then*

> ***either*** *you have TB **or** something very unlikely (probability 1/100) happened.*

Lemma 18.9.1 and Corollary 18.9.1 may *seem* to be saying that

False Claim. *If you test positive, then the probability that you have TB is* 0.99.

But this would be a mistake.

To highlight the difference between confidence in the test diagnosis versus the probability of TB, let's think about what to do if you test positive. Corollary 18.9.1

---

[5]Confidence is usually used to describe the probability that a statistical estimations of some quantity is correct (Section 20.5). We are trying to simplify the discussion by using this one concept to illustrate standard approaches to both hypothesis testing and estimation.

In the context of hypothesis testing, statisticians would normally distinguish the "false positive" probability, in this case the probability 0.01 that a healthy person is incorrectly diagnosed as having TB, and call this the *significance* of the test. The "false negative" probability would be the probability that person with TB is incorrectly diagnosed as healthy; it is zero. The *power* of the test is one minus the false negative probability, so in this case the power is the highest possible, namely, one.

seems to suggest that it's worth betting with high odds that you have TB, because it makes sense to bet against something unlikely happening—like the test being wrong. But having TB actually turns out to be *a lot less likely* than the test being wrong. So the either-or of Corollary 18.9.1 is really an either-or between something happening that is extremely unlikely—having TB—and something that is only very unlikely—the diagnosis being wrong. You're better off betting against the extremely unlikely event, that is, it is better to bet the diagnosis is wrong.

So some knowledge of the probability of having TB is needed in order to figure out how seriously to take a positive diagnosis, even when the diagnosis is given with what seems like a high level of confidence. We can see exactly how the frequency of TB in a population influences the importance of a positive diagnosis by actually calculating the probability that someone who tests positive has TB. That is, we want to calculate $\Pr\left[TB \mid pos\right]$, which we do next.

18.9.2 Updating the Odds

Bayesian Updating

A standard way to convert the test probabilities into outcome probabilities is to use Bayes Theorem (18.2). It will be helpful to rephrase Bayes Theorem in terms of "odds" instead of probabilities.

If H is an event, we define the *odds* of H to be

$$\text{Odds}(H) ::= \frac{\Pr[H]}{\Pr[\overline{H}]} = \frac{\Pr[H]}{1 - \Pr[H]}.$$

For example, if H is the event of rolling a four using a fair, six-sided die, then

$$\Pr[\text{roll four}] = 1/6, \text{ so}$$
$$\text{Odds}(\text{roll four}) = \frac{1/6}{5/6} = \frac{1}{5}.$$

A gambler would say the odds of rolling a four were "one to five," or equivalently, "five to one *against*" rolling a four.

Odds are just another way to talk about probabilities. For example, saying the odds that a horse will win a race are "three to one" means that the horse will win with probability $1/4$. In general,

$$\Pr[H] = \frac{\text{Odds}(H)}{1 + \text{Odds}(H)}.$$

Now suppose an event E offers some evidence about H. We now want to find the conditional probability of H given E. We can just as well find the odds of H

given E,

$$
\begin{aligned}
\text{Odds}(H \mid E) &::= \frac{\Pr\left[H \mid E\right]}{\Pr\left[\overline{H} \mid E\right]} \\
&= \frac{\Pr\left[E \mid H\right]\Pr[H]/\Pr[E]}{\Pr\left[E \mid \overline{H}\right]\Pr[\overline{H}]/\Pr[E]} \qquad \text{(Bayes Theorem)} \\
&= \frac{\Pr\left[E \mid H\right]}{\Pr\left[E \mid \overline{H}\right]} \cdot \frac{\Pr[H]}{\Pr[\overline{H}]} \\
&= \text{Bayes-factor}(E, H) \cdot \text{Odds}(H),
\end{aligned}
$$

where

$$
\text{Bayes-factor}(E, H) ::= \frac{\Pr\left[E \mid H\right]}{\Pr\left[E \mid \overline{H}\right]}.
$$

So to update the odds of H given the evidence E, we just multiply by Bayes Factor:

Lemma 18.9.2.

$$
\text{Odds}(H \mid E) = \text{Bayes-factor}(E, H) \cdot \text{Odds}(H).
$$

Odds for the TB test

The probabilities of test outcomes given in (18.6) and (18.7) are exactly what we need to find Bayes factor for the TB test:

$$
\begin{aligned}
\text{Bayes-factor}(TB, pos) &= \frac{\Pr\left[pos \mid TB\right]}{\Pr\left[pos \mid \overline{TB}\right]} \\
&= \frac{1}{1 - \Pr\left[\overline{pos} \mid \overline{TB}\right]} \\
&= \frac{1}{1 - 0.99} = 100.
\end{aligned}
$$

So testing positive for TB increases the odds you have TB by a factor of 100, which means a positive test is significant evidence supporting a diagnosis of TB. That seems good to know. But Lemma 18.9.2 also makes it clear that when a random person tests positive, we still can't determine the odds they have TB unless we know what are the *odds of their having TB in the first place*, so let's examine that.

   In 2011, the United States Center for Disease Control got reports of 11,000 cases of TB in US. We can estimate that there were actually about 30,000 cases of TB that year, since it seems that only about one third of actual cases of TB get reported. The US population is a little over 300 million, which means

$$\Pr[TB] \approx \frac{30,000}{300,000,000} = \frac{1}{10,000}.$$

So the odds of TB are 1/9999. Therefore,

$$\text{Odds}(TB \mid pos) = 100 \cdot \frac{1}{9,999} \approx \frac{1}{100}.$$

In other words, even if someone tests positive for TB at the 99% confidence level, the odds remain about 100 to one *against* their having TB. The 99% confidence level is not nearly high enough to overcome the relatively tiny probability of having TB.

18.9.3 Facts that are Probably True

We have figured out that if a random person tests positive for TB, the probability they have TB is about 1/100. Now if you personally happened to test positive for TB, a competent doctor typically would tell you that the probability that you have TB has risen from 1/10,000 to 1/100. But has it? Not really.

Your doctor should have not have been talking in this way about your particular situation. He should just have stuck to the statement that for *randomly chosen* people, the positive test would be right only one percent of the time. But you are not a random person, and whether or not you have TB is a fact about reality. The truth about your having TB may be *unknown* to your doctor and you, but that does not mean it has some probability of being true. It is either true or false, we just don't know which.

In fact, if you were worried about a 1/100 probability of having this serious disease, you could use additional information about yourself to change this probability. For example, native born residents of the US are about half as likely to have TB as foreign born residents. So if you are native born, "your" probability of having TB halves. Conversely, TB is twenty-five times more frequent among native born Asian/Pacific Islanders than native born Caucasions. So your probability of TB would increase dramatically if your family was from an Asian/Pacific Island.

The point is that the probability of having TB that your doctor reports to you depends on the probability of TB for a random person whom the doctor thinks is *like you*. The doctor has made a judgment about you based, for example, on what personal factors he considers relevant to getting TB, or how serious he thinks the consequences of a mistaken diagnosis would be. These are important medical judgments, but they are not mathematical. Different doctors will make different judgments about who is like you, and they will report differing probabilities. There is no "true" model of who you are, and there is no true individual probability of your having TB.

18.9.4   Extreme events

The definition of a *fair* coin is one where the probability of flipping a Head is 1/2 and likewise for flipping a Tail. Now suppose you flip the coin one hundred times and get a Head every time. What do you think the odds are that the next flip will also be a Head?

The official answer is that, by definition of "fair coin," the probability of Heads on the next flip is still 1/2. But this reasoning completely contradicts what any sensible person would do, which is to bet heavily on the next flip being another Head.

How to make sense of this? To begin, let's recognize how absurd it is to wonder about what happens after one hundred heads, because the probability that a hundred flips of a fair coin will all come up Heads is unimaginably tiny. For example, the probability that just the *first fifty* out of the hundred fair flips come up Heads is 2^{-50}. We can try to make some sense of how small this number is with the observation that, using a reasonable estimation of the number of people worldwide who are killed by lightning in a given year, 2^{-50} is about equal to the probability that a random person would be struck by lightning during the time it takes to read this paragraph. Ain't gonna happen.

The negligible probability that one hundred flips of a fair coin will all be Heads simply undermines the credibility of the assumption that the coin is fair. Despite being told the coin is fair, we can't help but acknowledge at least some remote possibility that the coin being flipped was one that rarely produced heads. So let's assume that there are two coins, a fair one and a biased one that comes up Heads with probability 99/100. One of these coins is randomly chosen with the fair coin hugely favored: the biased coin will be chosen only with extremely small probability 2^{-50}. The chosen coin is then flipped one hundred times. Let E be the event of flipping one hundred heads and H be the event that the biased coin was chosen. Now

$$\text{Odds}(H) = \frac{2^{-50}}{1 - 2^{-50}} \approx 2^{-50},$$

$$\text{Bayes-factor}(E, H) = \frac{\Pr\left[E \mid H\right]}{\Pr\left[E \mid \overline{H}\right]} = \frac{(99/100)^{100}}{2^{-100}} > 0.36 \cdot 2^{100},$$

$$\text{Odds}(H \mid E) = \text{Bayes-factor}(E, H) \cdot \text{Odds}(H)$$

$$> 0.36 \cdot 2^{100} \cdot 2^{-50} = 0.36 \cdot 2^{50}.$$

This shows that after flipping one hundred heads, the odds that the biased coin was chosen are overwhelming, and so with high probability the next flip will be a Head. Thus, by assuming some tiny probability for the coin being heavily biased toward Heads, we can justify our intuition that after one hundred consecutive Heads, the next flip is very likely to be a Head.

Making an assumption about the probability that some unverified fact is true is known as the *Bayesian* approach to a hypthesis testing problem. By granting a tiny probability that the biased coin was being flipped, this Bayesian approach provided a reasonable justification for estimating that the odds of a Head on the next flip are ninety-nine to one in favor.

18.9.5   Confidence in the Next Flip

If we stick to confidence rather than probability, we don't need to make any Bayesian assumptions about the probability of a fair coin. We know that if one hundred Heads are flipped, then either the coin is biased, or something that virtually never happens (probability 2^{-100}) has occurred. That means we can assert that the coin is biased at the $1 - 2^{-100}$ confidence level. In short, when one hundred Heads are flipped, we can be essentially 100% confident that the coin is biased.

Problems for Section 18.4

Homework Problems

Problem 18.1.

The Conditional Probability Product Rule for n Events is

Rule.

$$\Pr[E_1 \cap E_2 \cap \ldots \cap E_n] = \Pr[E_1] \cdot \Pr\left[E_2 \mid E_1\right] \cdot \Pr\left[E_3 \mid E_1 \cap E_2\right] \cdots$$
$$\cdot \Pr\left[E_n \mid E_1 \cap E_2 \cap \ldots \cap E_{n-1}\right].$$

(a) Restate the Rule without using elipses ($\ldots$).

(b) Prove it by induction.

Problems for Section 18.5

Practice Problems

Problem 18.2.

Dirty Harry places two bullets in random chambers of the six-bullet cylinder of his revolver. He gives the cylinder a random spin and says "Feeling lucky?" as he holds the gun against your heart.

(a) What is the probability that you will get shot if he pulls the trigger?

(b) Suppose he pulls the trigger and you don't get shot. What is the probability that you will get shot if he pulls the trigger a second time?

(c) Suppose you noticed that he placed the two shells next to each other in the cylinder. How does this change the answers to the previous two questions?

Problem 18.3.

State and prove a version of the Law of Total Probability that applies to disjoint events $E_1, \ldots, E_n$ whose union is the whole sample space.

Problem 18.4.

State and prove a version of Bayes Rule that applies to disjoint events $E_1, \ldots, E_n$ whose union is the whole sample space. You may assume the n-event Law of Total Probability, Problem 18.3.

Class Problems

Problem 18.5.

There are two decks of cards. One is complete, but the other is missing the ace of spades. Suppose you pick one of the two decks with equal probability and then select a card from that deck uniformly at random. What is the probability that you picked the complete deck, given that you selected the eight of hearts? Use the four-step method and a tree diagram.

Problem 18.6.

Suppose you have three cards: A♡, A♠ and a jack. From these, you choose a random hand (that is, each card is equally likely to be chosen) of two cards, and let

n be the number of aces in your hand. You then randomly pick one of the cards in the hand and reveal it.

(a) Describe a simple probability space (that is, outcomes and their probabilities) for this scenario, and list the outcomes in each of the following events:

1. $[n \geq 1]$, (that is, your hand has an ace in it),
2. A♡ is in your hand,
3. the revealed card is an A♡,
4. the revealed card is an ace.

(b) Then calculate $\Pr\left[n = 2 \mid E\right]$ for E equal to each of the four events in part (a). Notice that most, but *not all*, of these probabilities are equal.

Now suppose you have a deck with d distinct cards, a different kinds of aces (including an A♡), you draw a random hand with h cards, and then reveal a random card from your hand.

(c) Prove that $\Pr[\text{A♡ is in your hand}] = h/d$.

(d) Prove that

$$\Pr\left[n = 2 \mid \text{A♡ is in your hand}\right] = \Pr[n = 2] \cdot \frac{2d}{ah}. \tag{18.8}$$

(e) Conclude that

$$\Pr\left[n = 2 \mid \text{the revealed card is an ace}\right] = \Pr\left[n = 2 \mid \text{A♡ is in your hand}\right].$$

Problem 18.7.
There are three prisoners in a maximum-security prison for fictional villains: the Evil Wizard Voldemort, the Dark Lord Sauron, and Little Bunny Foo-Foo. The parole board has declared that it will release two of the three, chosen uniformly at random, but has not yet released their names. Naturally, Sauron figures that he will be released to his home in Mordor, where the shadows lie, with probability $2/3$.

A guard offers to tell Sauron the name of one of the other prisoners who will be released (either Voldemort or Foo-Foo). If the guard has a choice of naming either Voldemort or Foo-Foo (because both are to be released), he names one of the two with equal probability.

Sauron knows the guard to be a truthful fellow. However, Sauron declines this offer. He reasons that knowing what the guards says will reduce his chances, so he is better off not knowing. For example, if the guard says, "Little Bunny Foo-Foo will be released", then his own probability of release will drop to $1/2$ because he will then know that either he or Voldemort will also be released, and these two events are equally likely.

Dark Lord Sauron has made a typical mistake when reasoning about conditional probability. Using a tree diagram and the four-step method, **explain his mistake**. What is the probability that Sauron is released given that the guard says Foo-Foo is released?

Hint: Define the events S, F and "F" as follows:

$$\text{"}F\text{"} = \text{Guard says Foo-Foo is released}$$
$$F = \text{Foo-Foo is released}$$
$$S = \text{Sauron is released}$$

Problem 18.8.
Every Skywalker serves either the *light side* or the *dark side*.

- The first Skywalker serves the dark side.

- For $n \geq 2$, the n-th Skywalker serves the same side as the $(n-1)$-st Skywalker with probability $1/4$, and the opposite side with probability $3/4$.

Let d_n be the probability that the n-th Skywalker serves the dark side.

(a) Express d_n with a recurrence equation and sufficient base cases.

(b) Derive a simple expression for the generating function $D(x) ::= \sum_1^\infty d_n x^n$.

(c) Give a simple closed formula for d_n.

Problem 18.9. (a) For the directed acyclic graph (DAG) G_0 in Figure 18.3, a minimum-edge DAG with the same walk relation can be obtained by removing some edges. List these edges (use notation $\langle u \rightarrow v \rangle$ for an edge from u to v):

(b) List the vertices in a maximal chain in G_0.

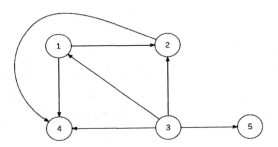

Figure 18.3   The DAG G_0

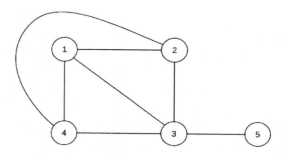

Figure 18.4   Simple graph G

Let G be the simple graph shown in Figure 18.4.

A directed graph $\overrightarrow{G}$ can be randomly constructed from G by assigning a direction to each edge independently with equal likelihood.

(c) What is the probability that $\overrightarrow{G} = G_0$?

Define the following events with respect to the random graph $\overrightarrow{G}$:

$T_1 ::=$ vertices $2, 3, 4$ are on a length three directed cycle,

$T_2 ::=$ vertices $1, 3, 4$ are on a length three directed cycle,

$T_3 ::=$ vertices $1, 2, 4$ are on a length three directed cycle,

$T_4 ::=$ vertices $1, 2, 3$ are on a length three directed cycle.

(d) What is

$$\Pr[T_1]?$$

$$\Pr[T_1 \cap T_2]?$$

$$\Pr[T_1 \cap T_2 \cap T_3]?$$

(e) $\overrightarrow{G}$ has the property that if it has a directed cycle, then it has a length three directed cycle. Use this fact to find the probability that $\overrightarrow{G}$ is a DAG.

Homework Problems

Problem 18.10.
There is a subject—naturally not *Math for Computer Science*—in which 10% of the assigned problems contain errors. If you ask a Teaching Assistant (TA) whether a problem has an error, then they will answer correctly 80% of the time, regardless of whether or not a problem has an error. If you ask a lecturer, he will identify whether or not there is an error with only 75% accuracy.

We formulate this as an experiment of choosing one problem randomly and asking a particular TA and Lecturer about it. Define the following events:

$$E ::= \text{[the problem has an error]},$$
$$T ::= \text{[the TA says the problem has an error]},$$
$$L ::= \text{[the lecturer says the problem has an error]}.$$

(a) Translate the description above into a precise set of equations involving conditional probabilities among the events E, T and L.

(b) Suppose you have doubts about a problem and ask a TA about it, and they tell you that the problem is correct. To double-check, you ask a lecturer, who says that the problem has an error. Assuming that the correctness of the lecturer's answer and the TA's answer are independent of each other, regardless of whether there is an error, what is the probability that there is an error in the problem?

(c) Is event T independent of event L (that is, $\Pr[T \mid L] = \Pr[T]$)? First, give an argument based on intuition, and then calculate both probabilities to verify your intuition.

Problem 18.11.

Suppose you repeatedly flip a fair coin until you see the sequence HTT or HHT. What is the probability you see the sequence HTT first?

Hint: Try to find the probability that HHT comes before HTT conditioning on whether you first toss an H or a T. The answer is not $1/2$.

Problem 18.12.

A 52-card deck is thoroughly shuffled and you are dealt a hand of 13 cards.

(a) If you have one ace, what is the probability that you have a second ace?

(b) If you have the ace of spades, what is the probability that you have a second ace? Remarkably, the answer is different from part (a).

Problem 18.13.

Suppose $\Pr[\cdot] : \mathcal{S} \to [0, 1]$ is a probability function on a sample space $\mathcal{S}$ and let B be an event such that $\Pr[B] > 0$. Define a function $\Pr_B[\cdot]$ on outcomes $\omega \in \mathcal{S}$ by the rule:

$$\Pr_B[\omega] ::= \begin{cases} \Pr[\omega]/\Pr[B] & \text{if } \omega \in B, \\ 0 & \text{if } \omega \notin B. \end{cases} \tag{18.9}$$

(a) Prove that $\Pr_B[\cdot]$ is also a probability function on $\mathcal{S}$ according to Definition 17.5.2.

(b) Prove that

$$\Pr_B[A] = \frac{\Pr[A \cap B]}{\Pr[B]}$$

for all $A \subseteq \mathcal{S}$.

(c) Explain why the Disjoint Sum Rule carries over for conditional probabilities, namely,

$$\Pr\left[C \cup D \mid B\right] = \Pr\left[C \mid B\right] + \Pr\left[D \mid B\right] \qquad (C, D \text{ disjoint}).$$

Give examples of several further such rules.

Problem 18.14.

Professor Meyer has a deck of 52 randomly shuffled playing cards, 26 red, 26 black. He proposes the following game: he will repeatedly draw a card off the top of the deck and turn it face up so that you can see it. At any point while there are still cards left in the deck, you may choose to stop, and he will turn over the next card. If the turned up card is black you win, and otherwise you lose. Either way, the game ends.

Suppose that after drawing off some top cards without stopping, the deck is left with r red cards and b black cards.

(a) Show that if you choose to stop at this point, the probability of winning is $b/(r+b)$.

(b) Prove if you choose *not* to stop at this point, the probability of winning is still $b/(r+b)$, regardless of your stopping strategy for the rest of the game.

Hint: Induction on $r + b$.

Exam Problems

Problem 18.15.
Sally Smart just graduated from high school. She was accepted to three reputable colleges.

- With probability 4/12, she attends Yale.

- With probability 5/12, she attends MIT.

- With probability 3/12, she attends Little Hoop Community College.

Sally is either happy or unhappy in college.

- If she attends Yale, she is happy with probability 4/12.

- If she attends MIT, she is happy with probability 7/12.

- If she attends Little Hoop, she is happy with probability 11/12.

(a) A tree diagram to help Sally project her chance at happiness is shown below. On the diagram, fill in the edge probabilities, and at each leaf write the probability of the corresponding outcome.

(b) What is the probability that Sally is happy in college?

(c) What is the probability that Sally attends Yale, given that she is happy in college?

(d) Show that the event that Sally attends Yale **is not** independent of the event that she is happy.

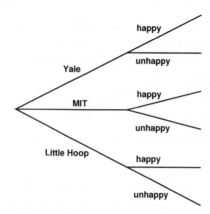

(e) Show that the event that Sally attends MIT **is** independent of the event that she is happy.

Problem 18.16.

Here's a variation of Monty Hall's game: the contestant still picks one of three doors, with a prize randomly placed behind one door and goats behind the other two. But now, instead of always opening a door to reveal a goat, Monty instructs Carol to *randomly* open one of the two doors that the contestant hasn't picked. This means she may reveal a goat, or she may reveal the prize. If she reveals the prize, then the entire game is *restarted*, that is, the prize is again randomly placed behind some door, the contestant again picks a door, and so on until Carol finally picks a door with a goat behind it. Then the contestant can choose to *stick* with his original choice of door or *switch* to the other unopened door. He wins if the prize is behind the door he finally chooses.

To analyze this setup, we define two events:

GP: The event that the contestant **g**uesses the door with the **p**rize behind it on his first guess.

OP: The event that the game is restarted at least once. Another way to describe this is as the event that the door Carol first **o**pens has a **p**rize behind it.

Give the values of the following probabilities:

(a) $\Pr[GP]$

(b) $\Pr\left[OP \mid \overline{GP}\right]$

(c) $\Pr[OP]$

(d) the probability that the game will continue forever

(e) When Carol finally picks the goat, the contestant has the choice of sticking or switching. Let's say that the contestant adopts the strategy of sticking. Let W be the event that the contestant wins with this strategy, and let $w ::= \Pr[W]$. Express the following conditional probabilities as simple closed forms in terms of w.

   i) $\Pr\big[W \mid GP\big]$

   ii) $\Pr\big[W \mid \overline{GP} \cap OP\big]$

   iii) $\Pr\big[W \mid \overline{GP} \cap \overline{OP}\big]$

(f) What is the value of $\Pr[W]$?

(g) For any final outcome where the contestant wins with a "stick" strategy, he would lose if he had used a "switch" strategy, and vice versa. In the original Monty Hall game, we concluded immediately that the probability that he would win with a "switch" strategy was $1 - \Pr[W]$. Why isn't this conclusion quite as obvious for this new, restartable game? Is this conclusion still sound? Briefly explain.

Problem 18.17.
There are two decks of cards, the red deck and the blue deck. They differ slightly in a way that makes drawing the eight of hearts slightly more likely from the red deck than from the blue deck.

One of the decks is randomly chosen and hidden in a box. You reach in the box and randomly pick a card that turns out to be the eight of hearts. You believe intuitively that this makes the red deck more likely to be in the box than the blue deck.

Your intuitive judgment about the red deck can be formalized and verified using some inequalities between probabilities and conditional probabilities involving the events

$$R ::= \textbf{R}\text{ed deck is in the box,}$$

$$B ::= \textbf{B}\text{lue deck is in the box,}$$

$$E ::= \textbf{E}\text{ight of hearts is picked from the deck in the box.}$$

(a) State an inequality between probabilities and/or conditional probabilities that formalizes the assertion, "picking the eight of hearts from the red deck is more likely than from the blue deck."

(b) State a similar inequality that formalizes the assertion "picking the eight of hearts from the deck in the box makes the red deck more likely to be in the box than the blue deck."

(c) Assuming the each deck is equally likely to be the one in the box, prove that the inequality of part (a) implies the inequality of part (b).

(d) Suppose you couldn't be sure that the red deck and blue deck were equally likely to be in the box. Could you still conclude that picking the eight of hearts from the deck in the box makes the red deck more likely to be in the box than the blue deck? Briefly explain.

Problem 18.18.
A flip of Coin 1 is x times as likely to come up Heads as a flip of Coin 2. A biased random choice of one of these coins will be made, where the probability of choosing Coin 1 is w times that of Coin 2.

(a) Restate the information above as equations between conditional probabilities involving the events

$$C1 ::= \text{Coin 1 was chosen},$$
$$C2 ::= \text{Coin 2 was chosen},$$
$$H ::= \text{the chosen coin came up Heads}.$$

(b) State an inequality involving conditional probabilities of the above events that formalizes the assertion "Given that the chosen coin came up Heads, the chosen coin is more likely to have been Coin 1 than Coin 2."

(c) Prove that, given that the chosen coin came up Heads, the chosen coin is more likely to have been Coin 1 than Coin 2 iff

$$wx > 1.$$

Problem 18.19.
There is an unpleasant, degenerative disease called Beaver Fever which causes people to tell math jokes unrelentingly in social settings, believing other people will think they're funny. Fortunately, Beaver Fever is rare, afflicting only about 1 in

1000 people. Doctor Meyer has a fairly reliable diagnostic test to determine who is going to suffer from this disease:

- If a person will suffer from Beaver Fever, the probability that Dr. Meyer diagnoses this is 0.99.

- If a person will not suffer from Beaver Fever, the probability that Dr. Meyer diagnoses this is 0.97.

Let B be the event that a randomly chosen person will suffer Beaver Fever, and Y be the event that Dr. Meyer's diagnosis is "Yes, this person will suffer from Beaver Fever," with $\overline{B}$ and $\overline{Y}$ being the complements of these events.

(a) The description above explicitly gives the values of the following quantities. What are their values?

$$\Pr[B] \qquad \Pr\left[Y \mid B\right] \qquad \Pr\left[\overline{Y} \mid \overline{B}\right]$$

(b) Write formulas for $\Pr[\overline{B}]$ and $\Pr\left[Y \mid \overline{B}\right]$ solely in terms of the explicitly given quantities in part (a)—literally use their expressions, not their numeric values.

(c) Write a formula for the probability that Dr. Meyer says a person will suffer from Beaver Fever solely in terms of $\Pr[B]$, $\Pr[\overline{B}]$, $\Pr\left[Y \mid B\right]$ and $\Pr\left[Y \mid \overline{B}\right]$.

(d) Write a formula solely in terms of the expressions given in part (a) for the probability that a person will suffer Beaver Fever given that Doctor Meyer says they will. Then calculate the numerical value of the formula.

Suppose there was a vaccine to prevent Beaver Fever, but the vaccine was expensive or slightly risky itself. If you were sure you were going to suffer from Beaver Fever, getting vaccinated would be worthwhile, but even if Dr. Meyer diagnosed you as a future sufferer of Beaver Fever, the probability you actually will suffer Beaver Fever remains low (about 1/32 by part (d)).

In this case, you might sensibly decide not to be vaccinated—after all, Beaver Fever is not *that* bad an affliction. So the diagnostic test serves no purpose in your case. You may as well not have bothered to get diagnosed. Even so, the test may be useful:

(e) Suppose Dr. Meyer had enough vaccine to treat 2% of the population. If he randomly chose people to vaccinate, he could expect to vaccinate only 2% of the people who needed it. But by testing everyone and only vaccinating those diagnosed as future sufferers, he can expect to vaccinate a much larger fraction people who were going to suffer from Beaver Fever. Estimate this fraction.

Problem 18.20.

Suppose that *Let's Make a Deal* is played according to slightly different rules and with a red goat and a blue goat. There are three doors, with a prize hidden behind one of them and the goats behind the others. No doors are opened until the contestant makes a final choice to stick or switch. The contestant is allowed to pick a door and ask a certain question that the host then answers honestly. The contestant may then stick with their chosen door, or switch to either of the other doors.

(a) If the contestant asks "is there is a goat behind one of the unchosen doors?" and the host answers "yes," is the contestant more likely to win the prize if they stick, switch, or does it not matter? Clearly identify the probability space of outcomes and their probabilities you use to model this situation. What is the contestant's probability of winning if he uses the best strategy?

(b) If the contestant asks "is the *red* goat behind one of the unchosen doors?" and the host answers "yes," is the contestant more likely to win the prize if they stick, switch, or does it not matter? Clearly identify the probability space of outcomes and their probabilities you use to model this situation. What is the contestant's probability of winning if he uses the best strategy?

Problem 18.21.

You are organizing a neighborhood census and instruct your census takers to knock on doors and note the sex of any child that answers the knock. Assume that there are two children in every household, that a random child is equally likely to be a girl or a boy, and that the two children in a household are equally likely to be the one that opens the door.

A sample space for this experiment has outcomes that are triples whose first element is either B or G for the sex of the elder child, whose second element is either B or G for the sex of the younger child, and whose third element is E or Y indicating whether the *e*lder child or *y*ounger child opened the door. For example, (B, G, Y) is the outcome that the elder child is a boy, the younger child is a girl, and the girl opened the door.

(a) Let O be the event that a girl opened the door, and let T be the event that the household has two girls. List the outcomes in O and T.

(b) What is the probability $\Pr\left[T \mid O\right]$, that both children are girls, given that a girl opened the door?

(c) What mistake is made in the following argument? (Note: merely stating the correct probability is not an explanation of the mistake.)

> If a girl opens the door, then we know that there is at least one girl in the household. The probability that there is at least one girl is
>
> $$1 - \Pr[\text{both children are boys}] = 1 - (1/2 \times 1/2) = 3/4.$$

So,

$$
\begin{aligned}
&\Pr\left[T \mid \text{there is at least one girl in the household}\right] \\
&= \frac{\Pr[T \cap \text{there is at least one girl in the household}]}{\Pr[\text{there is at least one girl in the household}]} \\
&= \frac{\Pr[T]}{\Pr[\text{there is at least one girl in the household}]} \\
&= (1/4)/(3/4) = 1/3.
\end{aligned}
$$

> Therefore, given that a girl opened the door, the probability that there are two girls in the household is 1/3.

Problem 18.22.

A guard is going to release exactly two of the three prisoners, Sauron, Voldemort, and Bunny Foo Foo, and he's equally likely to release any set of two prisoners.
(a) What is the probability that Voldemort will be released?

The guard will truthfully tell Voldemort the name of one of the prisoners to be released. We're interested in the following events:

V: Voldemort is released.

"F": The guard tells Voldemort that Foo Foo will be released.

"S": The guard tells Voldemort that Sauron will be released.

The guard has two rules for choosing whom he names:

- never say that Voldemort will be released,

- if both Foo Foo and Sauron are getting released, say "Foo Foo."

(b) What is $\Pr\left[V \mid \text{"}F\text{"}\right]$?

(c) What is $\Pr\left[V \mid \text{"}S\text{"}\right]$?

(d) Show how to use the Law of Total Probability to combine your answers to parts (b) and (c) to verify that the result matches the answer to part (a).

Problem 18.23.

We are interested in paths in the plane starting at $(0,0)$ that go one unit right or one unit up at each step. To model this, we use a state machine whose states are $\mathbb{N} \times \mathbb{N}$, whose start state is $(0,0)$, and whose transitions are

$$(x, y) \rightarrow (x + 1, y),$$
$$(x, y) \rightarrow (x, y + 1).$$

(a) How many length n paths are there starting from the origin?

(b) How many states are reachable in exactly n steps?

(c) How many states are reachable in at most n steps?

(d) If transitions occur independently at random, going right with probability p and up with probability $q ::= 1 - p$ at each step, what is the probability of reaching position (x, y)?

(e) What is the probability of reaching state (x, y) *given* that the path to (x, y) reached (m, n) before getting to (x, y)?

(f) Show that the probability that a path ending at (x, y) went through (m, n) is the same for all p.

Problems for Section 18.6

Practice Problems

Problem 18.24.
Define the events A, F_{EE}, F_{CS}, M_{EE}, and M_{CS} as in Section 18.6.

In these terms, the plaintiff in a discrimination suit against a university makes the argument that in both departments, the probability that a female is admitted is less than the probability for a male. That is,

$$\Pr\left[A \mid F_{EE}\right] < \Pr\left[A \mid M_{EE}\right] \quad \text{and} \qquad (18.10)$$

$$\Pr\left[A \mid F_{CS}\right] < \Pr\left[A \mid M_{CS}\right]. \qquad (18.11)$$

The university's defence attorneys retort that *overall*, a female applicant is *more* likely to be admitted than a male, namely, that

$$\Pr\left[A \mid F_{EE} \cup F_{CS}\right] > \Pr\left[A \mid M_{EE} \cup M_{CS}\right]. \qquad (18.12)$$

The judge then interrupts the trial and calls the plaintiff and defence attorneys to a conference in his office to resolve what he thinks are contradictory statements of facts about the admission data. The judge points out that:

$$
\begin{aligned}
&\Pr\left[A \mid F_{EE} \cup F_{CS}\right] \\
&= \Pr\left[A \mid F_{EE}\right] + \Pr\left[A \mid F_{CS}\right] \qquad \text{(because } F_{EE} \text{ and } F_{CS} \text{ are disjoint)} \\
&< \Pr\left[A \mid M_{EE}\right] + \Pr\left[A \mid M_{CS}\right] \qquad \text{(by (18.10) and (18.11))} \\
&= \Pr\left[A \mid M_{EE} \cup M_{CS}\right] \qquad \text{(because } M_{EE} \text{ and } M_{CS} \text{ are disjoint)}
\end{aligned}
$$

so

$$\Pr\left[A \mid F_{EE} \cup F_{CS}\right] < \Pr\left[A \mid M_{EE} \cup M_{CS}\right],$$

which directly contradicts the university's position (18.12)!

Of course the judge is mistaken; an example where the plaintiff and defence assertions are all true appears in Section 18.6. What is the mistake in the judge's proof?

Problems for Section 18.7

Practice Problems

Problem 18.25.
Outside of their hum-drum duties as Math for Computer Science Teaching Assis-

tants, Oscar is trying to learn to levitate using only intense concentration and Liz is trying to become the world champion flaming torch juggler. Suppose that Oscar's probability of success is $1/6$, Liz's chance of success is $1/4$, and these two events are independent.

(a) If at least one of them succeeds, what is the probability that Oscar learns to levitate?

(b) If at most one of them succeeds, what is the probability that Liz becomes the world flaming torch juggler champion?

(c) If exactly one of them succeeds, what is the probability that it is Oscar?

Problem 18.26.
What is the smallest size sample space in which there are two independent events, neither of which has probability zero or probability one? Explain.

Problem 18.27.
Give examples of event A, B, E such that

(a) A and B are independent, and are also conditionally independent given E, but are not conditionally independent given $\overline{E}$. That is,

$$\Pr[A \cap B] = \Pr[A]\Pr[B],$$
$$\Pr[A \cap B \mid E] = \Pr[A \mid E]\Pr[B \mid E],$$
$$\Pr[A \cap B \mid \overline{E}] \neq \Pr[A \mid \overline{E}]\Pr[B \mid \overline{E}].$$

Hint: Let $S = \{1, 2, 3, 4\}$.

(b) A and B are conditionally independent given E, or given $\overline{E}$, but are not independent. That is,

$$\Pr[A \cap B \mid E] = \Pr[A \mid E]\Pr[B \mid E],$$
$$\Pr[A \cap B \mid \overline{E}] = \Pr[A \mid \overline{E}]\Pr[B \mid \overline{E}],$$
$$\Pr[A \cap B] \neq \Pr[A]\Pr[B].$$

Hint: Let $S = \{1, 2, 3, 4, 5\}$.

An alternative example is

$$A ::= \{1\}$$
$$B ::= \{1, 2\}$$
$$E ::= \{3, 4, 5\}.$$

Class Problems

Problem 18.28.

Event E is *evidence in favor* of event H when $\Pr\left[H \mid E\right] > \Pr[H]$, and it is *evidence against* H when $\Pr\left[H \mid E\right] < \Pr[H]$.

(a) Give an example of events A, B, H such that A and B are independent, both are evidence for H, but $A \cup B$ is evidence against H.

Hint: Let $\mathcal{S} = [1..8]$

(b) Prove E is evidence in favor of H iff $\overline{E}$ is evidence against H.

Problem 18.29.

Let G be a simple graph with n vertices. Let "$A(u, v)$" mean that vertices u and v are adjacent, and let "$W(u, v)$" mean that there is a length-two walk between u and v.

(a) Explain why $W(u, u)$ holds iff $\exists v. \ A(u, v)$.

(b) Write a predicate-logic formula defining $W(u, v)$ in terms of the predicate $A(.,.)$ when $u \neq v$.

There are $e ::= \binom{n}{2}$ possible edges between the n vertices of G. Suppose the actual edges of $E(G)$ are chosen with randomly from this set of e possible edges. Each edge is chosen with probability p, and the choices are mutually independent.

(c) Write a simple formula in terms of p, e, and k for $\Pr[|E(G)| = k]$.

(d) Write a simple formula in terms of p and n for $\Pr[W(u, u)]$.

Let w, x, y and z be four distinct vertices.

Because edges are chosen mutually independently, events that depend on disjoint sets of edges will be mutually independent. For example, the events

$$A(w, y) \text{ AND } A(y, x)$$

and

$$A(w, z) \text{ AND } A(z, x)$$

are independent since $\langle w\text{---}y \rangle$, $\langle y\text{---}x \rangle$, $\langle w\text{---}z \rangle$, $\langle z\text{---}x \rangle$ are four distinct edges.

(e) Let

$$r ::= \Pr[\text{NOT}(W(w, x))], \tag{18.13}$$

where w and x are distinct vertices. Write a simple formula for r in terms of n and p.

Hint: Different length-two paths between x and y don't share any edges.

(f) Vertices x and y being on a three-cycle can be expressed simply as

$$A(x, y) \text{ AND } W(x, y).$$

Write a simple expression in terms of p and r for the probability that x and y lie on a three-cycle in G.

(g) Are $W(w, x)$ and $W(y, z)$ independent events? Briefly comment (proof not required).

Problems for Section 18.8

Practice Problems

Problem 18.30.
Suppose A, B and C are mutually independent events, what about $A \cap B$ and $B \cup C$?

Class Problems

Problem 18.31.
Suppose you flip three fair, mutually independent coins. Define the following events:

- Let A be the event that *the first* coin is heads.

- Let B be the event that *the second* coin is heads.

- Let C be the event that *the third* coin is heads.

- Let D be the event that *an even number of* coins are heads.

(a) Use the four step method to determine the probability space for this experiment and the probability of each of A, B, C, D.

(b) Show that these events are not mutually independent.

(c) Show that they are 3-way independent.

Problem 18.32.
Let A, B, C be events. For each of the following statements, prove it or give a counterexample.

(a) If A is independent of B, then A is also independent of $\overline{B}$.

(b) If A is independent of B, and A is independent of C, then A is independent of $B \cap C$.

Hint: Choose A, B, C pairwise but not 3-way independent.

(c) If A is independent of B, and A is independent of C, then A is independent of $B \cup C$.

Hint: Part (b).

(d) If A is independent of B, and A is independent of C, and A is independent of $B \cap C$, then A is independent of $B \cup C$.

Problem 18.33.
Let A, B, C, D be events. Describe counterexamples showing that the following claims are false.

(a)
False Claim. *If A and B are independent given C, and are also independent given D, then A and B are independent given $C \cup D$.*

(b)
False Claim. *If A and B are independent given C, and are also independent given D, then A and B are independent given $C \cap D$.*

Hint: Choose A, B, C, D 3-way but not 4-way independent.

so A and B are not independent given $C \cap D$.

Homework Problems

Problem 18.34.
Describe events A, B and C that:

- satisfy the "product rule," namely,

$$\Pr[A \cap B \cap C] = \Pr[A] \cdot \Pr[B] \cdot \Pr[C],$$

- no two out of the three events are independent.

Hint: Choose A, B, C events over the uniform probability space on $[1..6]$.

Exam Problems

Problem 18.35.
A classroom has sixteen desks in a 4×4 arrangement as shown below.

If two desks are next to each other, vertically or horizontally, they are called an *adjacent pair*. So there are three horizontally adjacent pairs in each row, for a total of twelve horizontally adjacent pairs. Likewise, there are twelve vertically adjacent pairs.

Boys and girls are assigned to desks mutually independently, with probability $p > 0$ of a desk being occupied by a boy and probability $q ::= 1 - p > 0$ of being occupied by a girl. An adjacent pair D of desks is said to have a *flirtation* when there is a boy at one desk and a girl at the other desk. Let F_D be the event that D has a flirtation.

(a) Different pairs D and E of adjacent desks are said to *overlap* when they share a desk. For example, the first and second pairs in each row overlap, and so do the second and third pairs, but the first and third pairs do not overlap. Prove that if D and E overlap, then F_D and F_E are independent events iff $p = q$.

(b) Find four pairs of desks D_1, D_2, D_3, D_4 and explain why $F_{D_1}, F_{D_2}, F_{D_3}, F_{D_4}$ are *not* mutually independent (even if $p = q = 1/2$).

Problems for Section 18.9

Problem 18.36.

An *International Journal of Pharmacological Testing* has a policy of publishing drug trial results only if the conclusion holds at the 95% confidence level. The editors and reviewers always carefully check that any results they publish came from a drug trial that genuinely deserved this level of confidence. They are also careful to check that trials whose results they publish have been conducted independently of each other.

The editors of the Journal reason that under this policy, their readership can be confident that at most 5% of the published studies will be mistaken. Later, the editors are embarrassed—and astonished—to learn that *every one* of the 20 drug trial results they published during the year was wrong. The editors thought that because the trials were conducted independently, the probability of publishing 20 wrong results was negligible, namely, $(1/20)^{20} < 10^{-25}$.

Write a brief explanation to these befuddled editors explaining what's wrong with their reasoning and how it could be that all 20 published studies were wrong.

Hint: xkcd comic: "significant" `xkcd.com/882/`

Practice Problems

Problem 18.37.

A somewhat reliable allergy test has the following properties:

- If you are allergic, there is a 10% chance that the test will say you are not.

- If you are not allergic, there is a 5% chance that the test will say you are.

(a) The test results are correct at what confidence level?

(b) What is the Bayes factor for being allergic when the test diagnoses a person as allergic?

(c) What can you conclude about the odds of a random person being allergic given that the test diagnoses them as allergic?

Suppose that your doctor tells you that because the test diagnosed you as allergic, and about 25% of people are allergic, the odds are six to one that you are allergic.

(d) How would your doctor calculate these odds of being allergic based on what's known about the allergy test?

(e) Another doctor reviews your test results and medical record and says your odds of being allergic are really much higher, namely thirty-six to one. Briefly explain how two conscientious doctors could disagree so much. Is there a way you could determine your actual odds of being allergic?

19   Random Variables

Thus far, we have focused on probabilities of events. For example, we computed the probability that you win the Monty Hall game or that you have a rare medical condition given that you tested positive. But, in many cases we would like to know more. For example, *how many* contestants must play the Monty Hall game until one of them finally wins? *How long* will this condition last? *How much* will I lose gambling with strange dice all night? To answer such questions, we need to work with random variables.

19.1   Random Variable Examples

Definition 19.1.1. A *random variable* R on a probability space is a total function whose domain is the sample space.

The codomain of R can be anything, but will usually be a subset of the real numbers. Notice that the name "random variable" is a misnomer; random variables are actually functions.

For example, suppose we toss three independent, unbiased coins. Let C be the number of heads that appear. Let $M = 1$ if the three coins come up all heads or all tails, and let $M = 0$ otherwise. Now every outcome of the three coin flips uniquely determines the values of C and M. For example, if we flip heads, tails, heads, then $C = 2$ and $M = 0$. If we flip tails, tails, tails, then $C = 0$ and $M = 1$. In effect, C counts the number of heads, and M indicates whether all the coins match.

Since each outcome uniquely determines C and M, we can regard them as functions mapping outcomes to numbers. For this experiment, the sample space is:

$$S = \{HHH, HHT, HTH, HTT, THH, THT, TTH, TTT\}.$$

Now C is a function that maps each outcome in the sample space to a number as follows:

$$
\begin{array}{llll}
C(HHH) & = & 3 & \quad C(THH) & = & 2 \\
C(HHT) & = & 2 & \quad C(THT) & = & 1 \\
C(HTH) & = & 2 & \quad C(TTH) & = & 1 \\
C(HTT) & = & 1 & \quad C(TTT) & = & 0.
\end{array}
$$

Similarly, M is a function mapping each outcome another way:

$$
\begin{array}{llll}
M(HHH) & = & 1 & \qquad M(THH) & = & 0 \\
M(HHT) & = & 0 & \qquad M(THT) & = & 0 \\
M(HTH) & = & 0 & \qquad M(TTH) & = & 0 \\
M(HTT) & = & 0 & \qquad M(TTT) & = & 1.
\end{array}
$$

So C and M are random variables.

19.1.1   Indicator Random Variables

An *indicator random variable* is a random variable that maps every outcome to either 0 or 1. Indicator random variables are also called *Bernoulli variables*. The random variable M is an example. If all three coins match, then $M = 1$; otherwise, $M = 0$.

Indicator random variables are closely related to events. In particular, an indicator random variable partitions the sample space into those outcomes mapped to 1 and those outcomes mapped to 0. For example, the indicator M partitions the sample space into two blocks as follows:

$$
\underbrace{HHH \quad TTT}_{M\,=\,1} \quad \underbrace{HHT \quad HTH \quad HTT \quad THH \quad THT \quad TTH}_{M\,=\,0}.
$$

In the same way, an event E partitions the sample space into those outcomes in E and those not in E. So E is naturally associated with an indicator random variable, I_E, where $I_E(\omega) = 1$ for outcomes $\omega \in E$ and $I_E(\omega) = 0$ for outcomes $\omega \notin E$. Thus, $M = I_E$ where E is the event that all three coins match.

19.1.2   Random Variables and Events

There is a strong relationship between events and more general random variables as well. A random variable that takes on several values partitions the sample space into several blocks. For example, C partitions the sample space as follows:

$$
\underbrace{TTT}_{C\,=\,0} \quad \underbrace{TTH \quad THT \quad HTT}_{C\,=\,1} \quad \underbrace{THH \quad HTH \quad HHT}_{C\,=\,2} \quad \underbrace{HHH}_{C\,=\,3}.
$$

Each block is a subset of the sample space and is therefore an event. So the assertion that $C = 2$ defines the event

$$
[C = 2] = \{THH, HTH, HHT\},
$$

and this event has probability

$$
\Pr[C = 2] = \Pr[THH] + \Pr[HTH] + \Pr[HHT] = \frac{1}{8} + \frac{1}{8} + \frac{1}{8} = 3/8.
$$

Likewise $[M = 1]$ is the event $\{TTT, HHH\}$ and has probability $1/4$.

More generally, any assertion about the values of random variables defines an event. For example, the assertion that $C \leq 1$ defines

$$[C \leq 1] = \{TTT, TTH, THT, HTT\},$$

and so $\Pr[C \leq 1] = 1/2$.

Another example is the assertion that $C \cdot M$ is an odd number. If you think about it for a minute, you'll realize that this is an obscure way of saying that all three coins came up heads, namely,

$$[C \cdot M \text{ is odd}] = \{HHH\}.$$

19.2 Independence

The notion of independence carries over from events to random variables as well. Random variables R_1 and R_2 are *independent* iff for all x_1, x_2, the two events

$$[R_1 = x_1] \quad \text{and} \quad [R_2 = x_2]$$

are independent.

For example, are C and M independent? Intuitively, the answer should be "no." The number of heads C completely determines whether all three coins match; that is, whether $M = 1$. But, to verify this intuition, we must find some $x_1, x_2 \in \mathbb{R}$ such that:

$$\Pr[C = x_1 \text{ AND } M = x_2] \neq \Pr[C = x_1] \cdot \Pr[M = x_2].$$

One appropriate choice of values is $x_1 = 2$ and $x_2 = 1$. In this case, we have:

$$\Pr[C = 2 \text{ AND } M = 1] = 0 \neq \frac{1}{4} \cdot \frac{3}{8} = \Pr[M = 1] \cdot \Pr[C = 2].$$

The first probability is zero because we never have exactly two heads ($C = 2$) when all three coins match ($M = 1$). The other two probabilities were computed earlier.

On the other hand, let H_1 be the indicator variable for the event that the first flip is a Head, so

$$[H_1 = 1] = \{HHH, HTH, HHT, HTT\}.$$

Then H_1 is independent of M, since

$$\Pr[M = 1] = 1/4 = \Pr\big[M = 1 \mid H_1 = 1\big] = \Pr\big[M = 1 \mid H_1 = 0\big]$$
$$\Pr[M = 0] = 3/4 = \Pr\big[M = 0 \mid H_1 = 1\big] = \Pr\big[M = 0 \mid H_1 = 0\big]$$

This example is an instance of:

Lemma 19.2.1. *Two events are independent iff their indicator variables are independent.*

The simple proof is left to Problem 19.1.

Intuitively, the independence of two random variables means that knowing some information about one variable doesn't provide any information about the other one. We can formalize what "some information" about a variable R is by defining it to be the value of some quantity that depends on R. This intuitive property of independence then simply means that functions of independent variables are also independent:

Lemma 19.2.2. *Let R and S be independent random variables, and f and g be functions such that* $\mathrm{domain}(f) = \mathrm{codomain}(R)$ *and* $\mathrm{domain}(g) = \mathrm{codomain}(S)$. *Then $f(R)$ and $g(S)$ are independent random variables.*

The proof is another simple exercise left to Problem 19.32.

As with events, the notion of independence generalizes to more than two random variables.

Definition 19.2.3. Random variables $R_1, R_2, \ldots, R_n$ are *mutually independent* iff for all $x_1, x_2, \ldots, x_n$, the n events

$$[R_1 = x_1], [R_2 = x_2], \ldots, [R_n = x_n]$$

are mutually independent. They are *k-way independent* iff every subset of k of them are mutually independent.

Lemmas 19.2.1 and 19.2.2 both extend straightforwardly to k-way independent variables.

19.3   Distribution Functions

A random variable maps outcomes to values. The probability density function, $\mathrm{PDF}_R(x)$, of a random variable R measures the probability that R takes the value

x, and the closely related cumulative distribution function $\mathrm{CDF}_R(x)$ measures the probability that $R \leq x$. Random variables that show up for different spaces of outcomes often wind up behaving in much the same way because they have the same probability of taking different values, that is, because they have the same pdf/cdf.

Definition 19.3.1. Let R be a random variable with codomain V. The *probability density function* of R is a function $\mathrm{PDF}_R : V \to [0, 1]$ defined by:

$$\mathrm{PDF}_R(x) ::= \begin{cases} \Pr[R = x] & \text{if } x \in \mathrm{range}(R), \\ 0 & \text{if } x \notin \mathrm{range}(R). \end{cases}$$

If the codomain is a subset of the real numbers, then the *cumulative distribution function* is the function $\mathrm{CDF}_R : \mathbb{R} \to [0, 1]$ defined by:

$$\mathrm{CDF}_R(x) ::= \Pr[R \leq x].$$

A consequence of this definition is that

$$\sum_{x \in \mathrm{range}(R)} \mathrm{PDF}_R(x) = 1.$$

This is because R has a value for each outcome, so summing the probabilities over all outcomes is the same as summing over the probabilities of each value in the range of R.

As an example, suppose that you roll two unbiased, independent, 6-sided dice. Let T be the random variable that equals the sum of the two rolls. This random variable takes on values in the set $V = \{2, 3, \ldots, 12\}$. A plot of the probability density function for T is shown in Figure 19.1. The lump in the middle indicates that sums close to 7 are the most likely. The total area of all the rectangles is 1 since the dice must take on exactly one of the sums in $V = \{2, 3, \ldots, 12\}$.

The cumulative distribution function for T is shown in Figure 19.2: The height of the ith bar in the cumulative distribution function is equal to the *sum* of the heights of the leftmost i bars in the probability density function. This follows from the definitions of pdf and cdf:

$$\mathrm{CDF}_R(x) = \Pr[R \leq x] = \sum_{y \leq x} \Pr[R = y] = \sum_{y \leq x} \mathrm{PDF}_R(y).$$

It also follows from the definition that

$$\lim_{x \to \infty} \mathrm{CDF}_R(x) = 1 \text{ and } \lim_{x \to -\infty} \mathrm{CDF}_R(x) = 0.$$

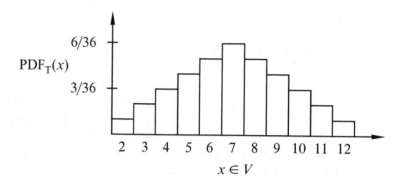

Figure 19.1   The probability density function for the sum of two 6-sided dice.

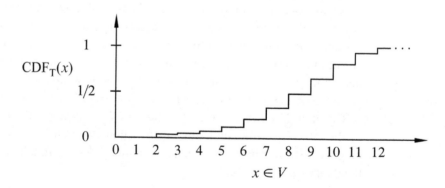

Figure 19.2   The cumulative distribution function for the sum of two 6-sided dice.

Both PDF_R and CDF_R capture the same information about R, so take your choice. The key point here is that neither the probability density function nor the cumulative distribution function involves the sample space of an experiment.

One of the really interesting things about density functions and distribution functions is that many random variables turn out to have the *same* pdf and cdf. In other words, even though R and S are different random variables on different probability spaces, it is often the case that

$$\mathrm{PDF}_R = \mathrm{PDF}_S.$$

In fact, some pdf's are so common that they are given special names. For example, the three most important distributions in computer science are the *Bernoulli distribution*, the *uniform distribution*, and the *binomial distribution*. We look more closely at these common distributions in the next several sections.

19.3.1   Bernoulli Distributions

A Bernoulli distribution is the distribution function for a Bernoulli variable. Specifically, the *Bernoulli distribution* has a probability density function of the form $f_p : \{0, 1\} \rightarrow [0, 1]$ where

$$f_p(0) = p, \quad \text{and}$$
$$f_p(1) = 1 - p,$$

for some $p \in [0, 1]$. The corresponding cumulative distribution function is $F_p : \mathbb{R} \rightarrow [0, 1]$ where

$$F_p(x) ::= \begin{cases} 0 & \text{if } x < 0 \\ p & \text{if } 0 \leq x < 1 \\ 1 & \text{if } 1 \leq x. \end{cases}$$

19.3.2   Uniform Distributions

A random variable that takes on each possible value in its codomain with the same probability is said to be *uniform*. If the codomain V has n elements, then the *uniform distribution* has a pdf of the form

$$f : V \rightarrow [0, 1]$$

where

$$f(v) = \frac{1}{n}$$

for all $v \in V$.

If the elements of V in increasing order are $a_1, a_2, \ldots, a_n$, then the cumulative distribution function would be $F : \mathbb{R} \to [0, 1]$ where

$$F(x) ::= \begin{cases} 0 & \text{if } x < a_1 \\ k/n & \text{if } a_k \le x < a_{k+1} \text{ for } 1 \le k < n \\ 1 & \text{if } a_n \le x. \end{cases}$$

Uniform distributions come up all the time. For example, the number rolled on a fair die is uniform on the set $\{1, 2, \ldots, 6\}$. An indicator variable is uniform when its pdf is $f_{1/2}$.

19.3.3   The Numbers Game

Enough definitions—let's play a game! We have two envelopes. Each contains an integer in the range $0, 1, \ldots, 100$, and the numbers are distinct. To win the game, you must determine which envelope contains the larger number. To give you a fighting chance, we'll let you peek at the number in one envelope selected at random. Can you devise a strategy that gives you a better than 50% chance of winning?

For example, you could just pick an envelope at random and guess that it contains the larger number. But this strategy wins only 50% of the time. Your challenge is to do better.

So you might try to be more clever. Suppose you peek in one envelope and see the number 12. Since 12 is a small number, you might guess that the number in the other envelope is larger. But perhaps we've been tricky and put small numbers in *both* envelopes. Then your guess might not be so good!

An important point here is that the numbers in the envelopes may *not* be random. We're picking the numbers and we're choosing them in a way that we think will defeat your guessing strategy. We'll only use randomization to choose the numbers if that serves our purpose: making you lose!

Intuition Behind the Winning Strategy

People are surprised when they first learn that there is a strategy that wins more than 50% of the time, regardless of what numbers we put in the envelopes.

Suppose that you somehow knew a number x that was in between the numbers in the envelopes. Now you peek in one envelope and see a number. If it is bigger than x, then you know you're peeking at the higher number. If it is smaller than x, then you're peeking at the lower number. In other words, if you know a number x between the numbers in the envelopes, then you are certain to win the game.

The only flaw with this brilliant strategy is that you do *not* know such an x. This sounds like a dead end, but there's a cool way to salvage things: try to *guess x*!

There is some probability that you guess correctly. In this case, you win 100% of the time. On the other hand, if you guess incorrectly, then you're no worse off than before; your chance of winning is still 50%. Combining these two cases, your overall chance of winning is better than 50%.

Many intuitive arguments about probability are wrong despite sounding persuasive. But this one goes the other way: it may not convince you, but it's actually correct. To justify this, we'll go over the argument in a more rigorous way—and while we're at it, work out the optimal way to play.

Analysis of the Winning Strategy

For generality, suppose that we can choose numbers from the integer interval $[0..n]$. Call the lower number L and the higher number H.

Your goal is to guess a number x between L and H. It's simplest if x does not equal L or H, so you should select x at random from among the half-integers:

$$\frac{1}{2}, \frac{3}{2}, \frac{5}{2}, \ldots, \frac{2n-1}{2}$$

But what probability distribution should you use?

The uniform distribution—selecting each of these half-integers with equal probability—turns out to be your best bet. An informal justification is that if we figured out that you were unlikely to pick some number—say $50\frac{1}{2}$—then we'd always put 50 and 51 in the envelopes. Then you'd be unlikely to pick an x between L and H and would have less chance of winning.

After you've selected the number x, you peek into an envelope and see some number T. If $T > x$, then you guess that you're looking at the larger number. If $T < x$, then you guess that the other number is larger.

All that remains is to determine the probability that this strategy succeeds. We can do this with the usual four step method and a tree diagram.

Step 1: Find the sample space.
You either choose x too low ($< L$), too high ($> H$), or just right ($L < x < H$). Then you either peek at the lower number ($T = L$) or the higher number ($T = H$). This gives a total of six possible outcomes, as show in Figure 19.3.

Step 2: Define events of interest.
The four outcomes in the event that you win are marked in the tree diagram.

Step 3: Assign outcome probabilities.
First, we assign edge probabilities. Your guess x is too low with probability L/n, too high with probability $(n - H)/n$, and just right with probability $(H - L)/n$. Next, you peek at either the lower or higher number with equal probability. Multiplying along root-to-leaf paths gives the outcome probabilities.

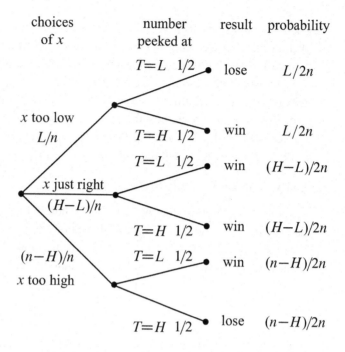

| choices of x | number peeked at | result | probability |

Figure 19.3   The tree diagram for the numbers game.

Step 4: Compute event probabilities.

The probability of the event that you win is the sum of the probabilities of the four outcomes in that event:

$$
\begin{aligned}
\Pr[\text{win}] &= \frac{L}{2n} + \frac{H-L}{2n} + \frac{H-L}{2n} + \frac{n-H}{2n} \\
&= \frac{1}{2} + \frac{H-L}{2n} \\
&\geq \frac{1}{2} + \frac{1}{2n}
\end{aligned}
$$

The final inequality relies on the fact that the higher number H is at least 1 greater than the lower number L since they are required to be distinct.

Sure enough, you win with this strategy more than half the time, regardless of the numbers in the envelopes! So with numbers chosen from the range $0, 1, \ldots, 100$, you win with probability at least $1/2 + 1/200 = 50.5\%$. If instead we agree to stick to numbers $0, \ldots, 10$, then your probability of winning rises to 55%. By Las Vegas standards, those are great odds.

Randomized Algorithms

The best strategy to win the numbers game is an example of a *randomized algorithm*—it uses random numbers to influence decisions. Protocols and algorithms that make use of random numbers are very important in computer science. There are many problems for which the best known solutions are based on a random number generator.

For example, the most commonly-used protocol for deciding when to send a broadcast on a shared bus or Ethernet is a randomized algorithm known as *exponential backoff*. One of the most commonly-used sorting algorithms used in practice, called *quicksort*, uses random numbers. You'll see many more examples if you take an algorithms course. In each case, randomness is used to improve the probability that the algorithm runs quickly or otherwise performs well.

19.3.4 Binomial Distributions

The third commonly-used distribution in computer science is the *binomial distribution*. The standard example of a random variable with a binomial distribution is the number of heads that come up in n independent flips of a coin. If the coin is fair, then the number of heads has an *unbiased binomial distribution*, specified by the pdf $f_n : [0..n] \to [0, 1]$:

$$f_n(k) ::= \binom{n}{k} 2^{-n}.$$

This is because there are $\binom{n}{k}$ sequences of n coin tosses with exactly k heads, and each such sequence has probability 2^{-n}.

A plot of $f_{20}(k)$ is shown in Figure 19.4. The most likely outcome is $k = 10$ heads, and the probability falls off rapidly for larger and smaller values of k. The falloff regions to the left and right of the main hump are called the *tails of the distribution*.

In many fields, including Computer Science, probability analyses come down to getting small bounds on the tails of the binomial distribution. In the context of a problem, this typically means that there is very small probability that something *bad* happens, which could be a server or communication link overloading or a randomized algorithm running for an exceptionally long time or producing the wrong result.

The tails do get small very fast. For example, the probability of flipping at most 25 heads in 100 tosses is less than 1 in 3,000,000. In fact, the tail of the distribution falls off so rapidly that the probability of flipping exactly 25 heads is nearly twice the probability of flipping exactly 24 heads *plus* the probability of flipping exactly

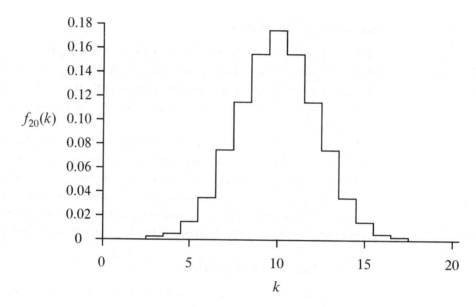

Figure 19.4   The pdf for the unbiased binomial distribution for $n = 20$, $f_{20}(k)$.

23 heads *plus* ... the probability of flipping no heads.

The General Binomial Distribution

If the coins are biased so that each coin is heads with probability p, then the number of heads has a *general binomial density function* specified by the pdf $f_{n,p} : [0..n] \rightarrow [0, 1]$ where

$$f_{n,p}(k) = \binom{n}{k} p^k (1 - p)^{n-k}. \tag{19.1}$$

for some $n \in \mathbb{N}^+$ and $p \in [0, 1]$. This is because there are $\binom{n}{k}$ sequences with k heads and $n - k$ tails, but now $p^k (1 - p)^{n-k}$ is the probability of each such sequence.

For example, the plot in Figure 19.5 shows the probability density function $f_{n,p}(k)$ corresponding to flipping $n = 20$ independent coins that are heads with probability $p = 0.75$. The graph shows that we are most likely to get $k = 15$ heads, as you might expect. Once again, the probability falls off quickly for larger and smaller values of k.

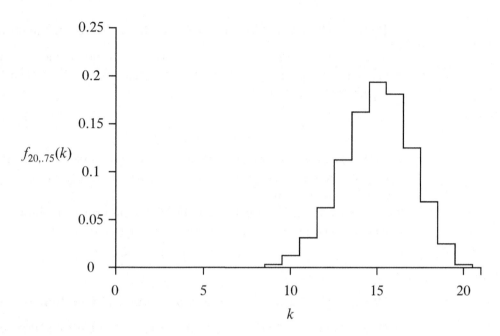

Figure 19.5 The pdf for the general binomial distribution $f_{n,p}(k)$ for $n = 20$ and $p = .75$.

19.4 Great Expectations

The *expectation* or *expected value* of a random variable is a single number that reveals a lot about the behavior of the variable. The expectation of a random variable is also known as its *mean* or *average*. For example, the first thing you typically want to know when you see your grade on an exam is the average score of the class. This average score turns out to be precisely the expectation of the random variable equal to the score of a random student.

More precisely, the expectation of a random variable is its "average" value when each value is weighted according to its probability. Formally, the expected value of a random variable is defined as follows:

Definition 19.4.1. If R is a random variable defined on a sample space S, then the expectation of R is

$$\text{Ex}[R] ::= \sum_{\omega \in S} R(\omega) \Pr[\omega]. \tag{19.2}$$

Let's work through some examples.

19.4.1   The Expected Value of a Uniform Random Variable

Rolling a 6-sided die provides an example of a uniform random variable. Let R be the value that comes up when you roll a fair 6-sided die. Then by (19.2), the expected value of R is

$$\text{Ex}[R] = 1 \cdot \frac{1}{6} + 2 \cdot \frac{1}{6} + 3 \cdot \frac{1}{6} + 4 \cdot \frac{1}{6} + 5 \cdot \frac{1}{6} + 6 \cdot \frac{1}{6} = \frac{7}{2}.$$

This calculation shows that the name "expected" value is a little misleading; the random variable might *never* actually take on that value. No one expects to roll a $3\frac{1}{2}$ on an ordinary die!

In general, if R_n is a random variable with a uniform distribution on $\{a_1, a_2, \ldots, a_n\}$, then the expectation of R_n is simply the average of the a_i's:

$$\text{Ex}[R_n] = \frac{a_1 + a_2 + \cdots + a_n}{n}.$$

19.4.2   The Expected Value of a Reciprocal Random Variable

Define a random variable S to be the reciprocal of the value that comes up when you roll a fair 6-sided die. That is, $S = 1/R$ where R is the value that you roll. Now,

$$\text{Ex}[S] = \text{Ex}\left[\frac{1}{R}\right] = \frac{1}{1} \cdot \frac{1}{6} + \frac{1}{2} \cdot \frac{1}{6} + \frac{1}{3} \cdot \frac{1}{6} + \frac{1}{4} \cdot \frac{1}{6} + \frac{1}{5} \cdot \frac{1}{6} + \frac{1}{6} \cdot \frac{1}{6} = \frac{49}{120}.$$

Notice that

$$\text{Ex}\left[1/R\right] \neq 1/\text{Ex}[R].$$

Assuming that these two quantities are equal is a common mistake.

19.4.3   The Expected Value of an Indicator Random Variable

The expected value of an indicator random variable for an event is just the probability of that event.

Lemma 19.4.2. *If I_A is the indicator random variable for event A, then*

$$\text{Ex}[I_A] = \text{Pr}[A].$$

Proof.

$$\text{Ex}[I_A] = 1 \cdot \text{Pr}[I_A = 1] + 0 \cdot \text{Pr}[I_A = 0] = \text{Pr}[I_A = 1]$$
$$= \text{Pr}[A]. \qquad \text{(def of } I_A\text{)}$$

For example, if A is the event that a coin with bias p comes up heads, then $\text{Ex}[I_A] = \text{Pr}[I_A = 1] = p$.

19.4.4 Alternate Definition of Expectation

There is another standard way to define expectation.

Theorem 19.4.3. *For any random variable R,*

$$\text{Ex}[R] = \sum_{x \in \text{range}(R)} x \cdot \Pr[R = x]. \tag{19.3}$$

The proof of Theorem 19.4.3, like many of the elementary proofs about expectation in this chapter, follows by regrouping of terms in equation (19.2):

Proof. Suppose R is defined on a sample space $\mathcal{S}$. Then,

$$
\begin{aligned}
\text{Ex}[R] &::= \sum_{\omega \in \mathcal{S}} R(\omega) \Pr[\omega] \\
&= \sum_{x \in \text{range}(R)} \sum_{\omega \in [R=x]} R(\omega) \Pr[\omega] \\
&= \sum_{x \in \text{range}(R)} \sum_{\omega \in [R=x]} x \Pr[\omega] && \text{(def of the event } [R = x]) \\
&= \sum_{x \in \text{range}(R)} x \left(\sum_{\omega \in [R=x]} \Pr[\omega] \right) && \text{(factoring } x \text{ from the inner sum)} \\
&= \sum_{x \in \text{range}(R)} x \cdot \Pr[R = x]. && \text{(def of } \Pr[R = x])
\end{aligned}
$$

The first equality follows because the events $[R = x]$ for $x \in \text{range}(R)$ partition the sample space $\mathcal{S}$, so summing over the outcomes in $[R = x]$ for $x \in \text{range}(R)$ is the same as summing over $\mathcal{S}$. ∎

In general, equation (19.3) is more useful than the defining equation (19.2) for calculating expected values. It also has the advantage that it does not depend on the sample space, but only on the density function of the random variable. On the other hand, summing over all outcomes as in equation (19.2) sometimes yields easier proofs about general properties of expectation.

19.4.5 Conditional Expectation

Just like event probabilities, expectations can be conditioned on some event. Given a random variable R, the expected value of R conditioned on an event A is the probability-weighted average value of R over outcomes in A. More formally:

Definition 19.4.4. The *conditional expectation* $\mathrm{Ex}[R \mid A]$ of a random variable R given event A is:

$$\mathrm{Ex}[R \mid A] ::= \sum_{r \in \mathrm{range}(R)} r \cdot \mathrm{Pr}\left[R = r \mid A\right]. \tag{19.4}$$

For example, we can compute the expected value of a roll of a fair die, given that the number rolled is at least 4. We do this by letting R be the outcome of a roll of the die. Then by equation (19.4),

$$\mathrm{Ex}[R \mid R \geq 4] = \sum_{i=1}^{6} i \cdot \mathrm{Pr}\left[R = i \mid R \geq 4\right] = 1 \cdot 0 + 2 \cdot 0 + 3 \cdot 0 + 4 \cdot \tfrac{1}{3} + 5 \cdot \tfrac{1}{3} + 6 \cdot \tfrac{1}{3} = 5.$$

Conditional expectation is useful in dividing complicated expectation calculations into simpler cases. We can find a desired expectation by calculating the conditional expectation in each simple case and averaging them, weighing each case by its probability.

For example, suppose that 49.6% of the people in the world are male and the rest female—which is more or less true. Also suppose the expected height of a randomly chosen male is $5'\ 11''$, while the expected height of a randomly chosen female is $5'\ 5.''$ What is the expected height of a randomly chosen person? We can calculate this by averaging the heights of men and women. Namely, let H be the height (in feet) of a randomly chosen person, and let M be the event that the person is male and F the event that the person is female. Then

$$\begin{aligned}
\mathrm{Ex}[H] &= \mathrm{Ex}[H \mid M]\,\mathrm{Pr}[M] + \mathrm{Ex}[H \mid F]\,\mathrm{Pr}[F] \\
&= (5 + 11/12) \cdot 0.496 + (5 + 5/12) \cdot (1 - 0.496) \\
&= 5.6646 \ldots .
\end{aligned}$$

which is a little less than 5' 8."

This method is justified by:

Theorem 19.4.5 (Law of Total Expectation). *Let R be a random variable on a sample space S, and suppose that $A_1, A_2, \ldots,$ is a partition of S. Then*

$$\mathrm{Ex}[R] = \sum_{i} \mathrm{Ex}[R \mid A_i]\,\mathrm{Pr}[A_i].$$

Proof.

$$\mathrm{Ex}[R] = \sum_{r \in \mathrm{range}(R)} r \cdot \Pr[R = r] \qquad \text{(by 19.3)}$$

$$= \sum_{r} r \cdot \sum_{i} \Pr\big[R = r \mid A_i\big] \Pr[A_i] \qquad \text{(Law of Total Probability)}$$

$$= \sum_{r} \sum_{i} r \cdot \Pr\big[R = r \mid A_i\big] \Pr[A_i] \qquad \text{(distribute constant } r\text{)}$$

$$= \sum_{i} \sum_{r} r \cdot \Pr\big[R = r \mid A_i\big] \Pr[A_i] \qquad \text{(exchange order of summation)}$$

$$= \sum_{i} \Pr[A_i] \sum_{r} r \cdot \Pr\big[R = r \mid A_i\big] \qquad \text{(factor constant } \Pr[A_i]\text{)}$$

$$= \sum_{i} \Pr[A_i] \, \mathrm{Ex}[R \mid A_i]. \qquad \text{(Def 19.4.4 of cond. expectation)}$$

■

19.4.6 Mean Time to Failure

A computer program crashes at the end of each hour of use with probability p, if it has not crashed already. What is the expected time until the program crashes? This will be easy to figure out using the Law of Total Expectation, Theorem 19.4.5. Specifically, we want to find $\mathrm{Ex}[C]$ where C is the number of hours until the first crash. We'll do this by conditioning on whether or not the crash occurs in the first hour.

So define A to be the event that the system fails on the first step and $\overline{A}$ to be the complementary event that the system does not fail on the first step. Then the mean time to failure $\mathrm{Ex}[C]$ is

$$\mathrm{Ex}[C] = \mathrm{Ex}[C \mid A] \Pr[A] + \mathrm{Ex}[C \mid \overline{A}] \Pr[\overline{A}]. \qquad (19.5)$$

Since A is the condition that the system crashes on the first step, we know that

$$\mathrm{Ex}[C \mid A] = 1. \qquad (19.6)$$

Since $\overline{A}$ is the condition that the system does *not* crash on the first step, conditioning on $\overline{A}$ is equivalent to taking a first step without failure and then starting over without conditioning. Hence,

$$\mathrm{Ex}[C \mid \overline{A}] = 1 + \mathrm{Ex}[C]. \qquad (19.7)$$

Plugging (19.6) and (19.7) into (19.5):

$$\mathrm{Ex}[C] = 1 \cdot p + (1 + \mathrm{Ex}[C])(1 - p)$$
$$= p + 1 - p + (1 - p)\,\mathrm{Ex}[C]$$
$$= 1 + (1 - p)\,\mathrm{Ex}[C].$$

Then, rearranging terms gives

$$1 = \mathrm{Ex}[C] - (1 - p)\,\mathrm{Ex}[C] = p\,\mathrm{Ex}[C],$$

and thus

$$\mathrm{Ex}[C] = 1/p.$$

The general principle here is well-worth remembering.

Mean Time to Failure

If a system independently fails at each time step with probability p, then the expected number of steps up to the first failure is $1/p$.

So, for example, if there is a 1% chance that the program crashes at the end of each hour, then the expected time until the program crashes is $1/0.01 = 100$ hours.

As a further example, suppose a couple insists on having children until they get a boy, then how many baby girls should they expect before their first boy? Assume for simplicity that there is a 50% chance that a child will be a boy and that the genders of siblings are mutually independent.

This is really a variant of the previous problem. The question, "How many hours until the program crashes?" is mathematically the same as the question, "How many children must the couple have until they get a boy?" In this case, a crash corresponds to having a boy, so we should set $p = 1/2$. By the preceding analysis, the couple should expect a baby boy after having $1/p = 2$ children. Since the last of these will be a boy, they should expect just one girl. So even in societies where couples pursue this commitment to boys, the expected population will divide evenly between boys and girls.

There is a simple intuitive argument that explains the mean time to failure formula (19.8). Suppose the system is restarted after each failure. This makes the mean time to failure the same as the mean time between successive repeated failures. Now if the probability of failure at a given step is p, then after n steps we expect to have pn failures. Now, by definition, the average number of steps between failures is equal to np/p, namely, $1/p$.

For the record, we'll state a formal version of this result. A random variable like C that counts steps to first failure is said to have a *geometric distribution* with parameter p.

Definition 19.4.6. A random variable C has a *geometric distribution* with parameter p iff $\text{codomain}(C) = \mathbb{Z}^+$ and

$$\Pr[C = i] = (1 - p)^{i-1} p.$$

Lemma 19.4.7. *If a random variable C has a geometric distribution with parameter p, then*

$$\text{Ex}[C] = \frac{1}{p}. \tag{19.8}$$

19.4.7 Expected Returns in Gambling Games

Some of the most interesting examples of expectation can be explained in terms of gambling games. For straightforward games where you win w dollars with probability p and you lose x dollars with probability $1 - p$, it is easy to compute your *expected return* or *winnings*. It is simply

$$pw - (1 - p)x \text{ dollars.}$$

For example, if you are flipping a fair coin and you win \$1 for heads and you lose \$1 for tails, then your expected winnings are

$$\frac{1}{2} \cdot 1 - \left(1 - \frac{1}{2}\right) \cdot 1 = 0.$$

In such cases, the game is said to be *fair* since your expected return is zero.

Splitting the Pot

We'll now look at a different game which is fair—but only on first analysis.

It's late on a Friday night in your neighborhood hangout when two new biker dudes, Eric and Nick, stroll over and propose a simple wager. Each player will put \$2 on the bar and secretly write "heads" or "tails" on their napkin. Then you will flip a fair coin. The \$6 on the bar will then be "split"—that is, be divided equally—among the players who correctly predicted the outcome of the coin toss. Pot splitting like this is a familiar feature in poker games, betting pools, and lotteries.

This sounds like a fair game, but after your regrettable encounter with strange dice (Section 17.3), you are definitely skeptical about gambling with bikers. So before agreeing to play, you go through the four-step method and write out the

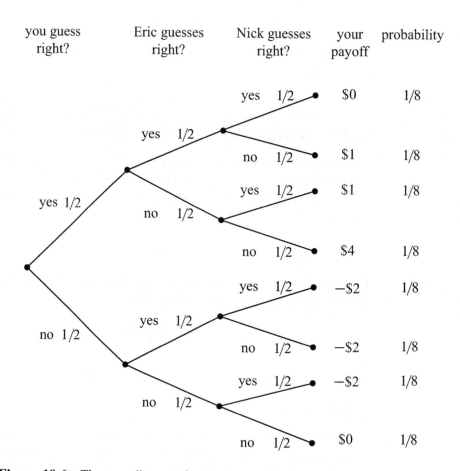

Figure 19.6   The tree diagram for the game where three players each wager $2 and then guess the outcome of a fair coin toss. The winners split the pot.

tree diagram to compute your expected return. The tree diagram is shown in Figure 19.6.

The "payoff" values in Figure 19.6 are computed by dividing the $6 pot[1] among those players who guessed correctly and then subtracting the $2 that you put into the pot at the beginning. For example, if all three players guessed correctly, then your payoff is $0, since you just get back your $2 wager. If you and Nick guess correctly and Eric guessed wrong, then your payoff is

$$\frac{6}{2} - 2 = 1.$$

In the case that everyone is wrong, you all agree to split the pot and so, again, your payoff is zero.

To compute your expected return, you use equation (19.3):

$$\begin{aligned}
\text{Ex[payoff]} = {} & 0 \cdot \frac{1}{8} + 1 \cdot \frac{1}{8} + 1 \cdot \frac{1}{8} + 4 \cdot \frac{1}{8} \\
& + (-2) \cdot \frac{1}{8} + (-2) \cdot \frac{1}{8} + (-2) \cdot \frac{1}{8} + 0 \cdot \frac{1}{8} \\
= {} & 0.
\end{aligned}$$

This confirms that the game is fair. So, for old time's sake, you break your solemn vow to never ever engage in strange gambling games.

The Impact of Collusion

Needless to say, things are not turning out well for you. The more times you play the game, the more money you seem to be losing. After 1000 wagers, you have lost over $500. As Nick and Eric are consoling you on your "bad luck," you do a back-of-the-envelope calculation and decide that the probability of losing $500 in 1000 fair $2 wagers is very, very small.

Now it is possible of course that you are very, very unlucky. But it is more likely that something fishy is going on. Somehow the tree diagram in Figure 19.6 is not a good model of the game.

The "something" that's fishy is the opportunity that Nick and Eric have to collude against you. The fact that the coin flip is fair certainly means that each of Nick and Eric can only guess the outcome of the coin toss with probability 1/2. But when you look back at the previous 1000 bets, you notice that Eric and Nick never made the same guess. In other words, Nick always guessed "tails" when Eric guessed "heads," and vice-versa. Modelling this fact now results in a slightly different tree diagram, as shown in Figure 19.7.

---

[1]The money invested in a wager is commonly referred to as the *pot*.

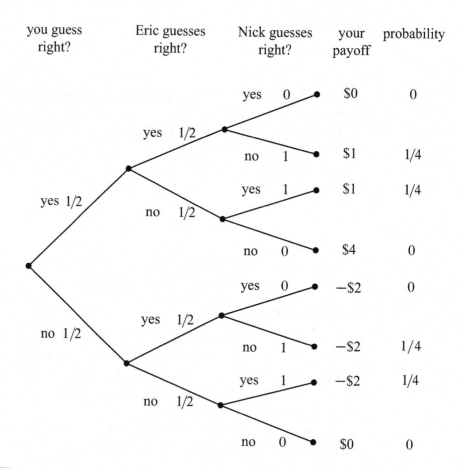

Figure 19.7   The revised tree diagram reflecting the scenario where Nick always guesses the opposite of Eric.

The payoffs for each outcome are the same in Figures 19.6 and 19.7, but the probabilities of the outcomes are different. For example, it is no longer possible for all three players to guess correctly, since Nick and Eric are always guessing differently. More importantly, the outcome where your payoff is $4 is also no longer possible. Since Nick and Eric are always guessing differently, one of them will always get a share of the pot. As you might imagine, this is not good for you!

When we use equation (19.3) to compute your expected return in the collusion scenario, we find that

$$\text{Ex[payoff]} = 0 \cdot 0 + 1 \cdot \frac{1}{4} + 1 \cdot \frac{1}{4} + 4 \cdot 0$$
$$+ (-2) \cdot 0 + (-2) \cdot \frac{1}{4} + (-2) \cdot \frac{1}{4} + 0 \cdot 0$$
$$= -\frac{1}{2}.$$

So watch out for these biker dudes! By colluding, Nick and Eric have made it so that you expect to lose $.50 every time you play. No wonder you lost $500 over the course of 1000 wagers.

How to Win the Lottery

Similar opportunities to collude arise in many betting games. For example, consider the typical weekly football betting pool, where each participant wagers $10 and the participants that pick the most games correctly split a large pot. The pool seems fair if you think of it as in Figure 19.6. But, in fact, if two or more players collude by guessing differently, they can get an "unfair" advantage at your expense!

In some cases, the collusion is inadvertent and you can profit from it. For example, many years ago, a former MIT Professor of Mathematics named Herman Chernoff figured out a way to make money by playing the state lottery. This was surprising since the state usually takes a large share of the wagers before paying the winners, and so the expected return from a lottery ticket is typically pretty poor. So how did Chernoff find a way to make money? It turned out to be easy!

In a typical state lottery,

- all players pay $1 to play and select 4 numbers from 1 to 36,
- the state draws 4 numbers from 1 to 36 uniformly at random,
- the states divides 1/2 of the money collected among the people who guessed correctly and spends the other half redecorating the governor's residence.

This is a lot like the game you played with Nick and Eric, except that there are more players and more choices. Chernoff discovered that a small set of numbers was selected by a large fraction of the population. Apparently many people think the same way; they pick the same numbers not on purpose as in the previous game with Nick and Eric, but based on the Red Sox winning average or today's date. The result is as though the players were intentionally colluding to lose. If any one of them guessed correctly, then they'd have to split the pot with many other players. By selecting numbers uniformly at random, Chernoff was unlikely to get one of these favored sequences. So if he won, he'd likely get the whole pot! By analyzing actual state lottery data, he determined that he could win an average of 7 cents on the dollar. In other words, his expected return was not −\$.50 as you might think, but +\$.07.[2] Inadvertent collusion often arises in betting pools and is a phenomenon that you can take advantage of.

19.5   Linearity of Expectation

Expected values obey a simple, very helpful rule called *Linearity of Expectation*. Its simplest form says that the expected value of a sum of random variables is the sum of the expected values of the variables.

Theorem 19.5.1. *For any random variables R_1 and R_2,*

$$\mathrm{Ex}[R_1 + R_2] = \mathrm{Ex}[R_1] + \mathrm{Ex}[R_2].$$

Proof. Let $T ::= R_1 + R_2$. The proof follows straightforwardly by rearranging terms in equation (19.2) in the definition of expectation:

$$
\begin{aligned}
\mathrm{Ex}[T] &::= \sum_{\omega \in \mathcal{S}} T(\omega) \cdot \mathrm{Pr}[\omega] \\
&= \sum_{\omega \in \mathcal{S}} (R_1(\omega) + R_2(\omega)) \cdot \mathrm{Pr}[\omega] && \text{(def of } T) \\
&= \sum_{\omega \in \mathcal{S}} R_1(\omega)\,\mathrm{Pr}[\omega] + \sum_{\omega \in \mathcal{S}} R_2(\omega)\,\mathrm{Pr}[\omega] && \text{(rearranging terms)} \\
&= \mathrm{Ex}[R_1] + \mathrm{Ex}[R_2]. && \text{(by (19.2))}
\end{aligned}
$$

∎

A small extension of this proof, which we leave to the reader, implies

---

[2]Most lotteries now offer randomized tickets to help smooth out the distribution of selected sequences.

Theorem 19.5.2. *For random variables R_1, R_2 and constants $a_1, a_2 \in \mathbb{R}$,*

$$\mathrm{Ex}[a_1 R_1 + a_2 R_2] = a_1 \,\mathrm{Ex}[R_1] + a_2 \,\mathrm{Ex}[R_2].$$

In other words, expectation is a linear function. A routine induction extends the result to more than two variables:

Corollary 19.5.3 (Linearity of Expectation). *For any random variables $R_1, \ldots, R_k$ and constants $a_1, \ldots, a_k \in \mathbb{R}$,*

$$\mathrm{Ex}\left[\sum_{i=1}^{k} a_i R_i\right] = \sum_{i=1}^{k} a_i \,\mathrm{Ex}[R_i].$$

The great thing about linearity of expectation is that *no independence is required*. This is really useful, because dealing with independence is a pain, and we often need to work with random variables that are not known to be independent.

As an example, let's compute the expected value of the sum of two fair dice.

19.5.1 Expected Value of Two Dice

What is the expected value of the sum of two fair dice?

Let the random variable R_1 be the number on the first die, and let R_2 be the number on the second die. We observed earlier that the expected value of one die is 3.5. We can find the expected value of the sum using linearity of expectation:

$$\mathrm{Ex}[R_1 + R_2] = \mathrm{Ex}[R_1] + \mathrm{Ex}[R_2] = 3.5 + 3.5 = 7.$$

Assuming that the dice were independent, we could use a tree diagram to prove that this expected sum is 7, but this would be a bother since there are 36 cases. And without assuming independence, it's not apparent how to apply the tree diagram approach at all. But notice that we did *not* have to assume that the two dice were independent. The expected sum of two dice is 7—even if they are controlled to act together in some way—as long as each individual controlled die remains fair.

19.5.2 Sums of Indicator Random Variables

Linearity of expectation is especially useful when you have a sum of indicator random variables. As an example, suppose there is a dinner party where n men check their hats. The hats are mixed up during dinner, so that afterward each man receives a random hat. In particular, each man gets his own hat with probability $1/n$. What is the expected number of men who get their own hat?

Letting G be the number of men that get their own hat, we want to find the expectation of G. But all we know about G is that the probability that a man gets his own hat back is $1/n$. There are many different probability distributions of hat permutations with this property, so we don't know enough about the distribution of G to calculate its expectation directly using equation (19.2) or (19.3). But linearity of expectation lets us sidestep this issue.

We'll use a standard, useful trick to apply linearity, namely, we'll express G as a sum of indicator variables. In particular, let G_i be an indicator for the event that the ith man gets his own hat. That is, $G_i = 1$ if the ith man gets his own hat, and $G_i = 0$ otherwise. The number of men that get their own hat is then the sum of these indicator random variables:

$$G = G_1 + G_2 + \cdots + G_n. \tag{19.9}$$

These indicator variables are *not* mutually independent. For example, if $n - 1$ men all get their own hats, then the last man is certain to receive his own hat. But again, we don't need to worry about this dependence, since linearity holds regardless.

Since G_i is an indicator random variable, we know from Lemma 19.4.2 that

$$\text{Ex}[G_i] = \text{Pr}[G_i = 1] = 1/n. \tag{19.10}$$

By Linearity of Expectation and equation (19.9), this means that

$$
\begin{aligned}
\text{Ex}[G] &= \text{Ex}[G_1 + G_2 + \cdots + G_n] \\
&= \text{Ex}[G_1] + \text{Ex}[G_2] + \cdots + \text{Ex}[G_n] \\
&= \overbrace{\frac{1}{n} + \frac{1}{n} + \cdots + \frac{1}{n}}^{n} \\
&= 1.
\end{aligned}
$$

So even though we don't know much about how hats are scrambled, we've figured out that on average, just one man gets his own hat back, regardless of the number of men with hats!

More generally, Linearity of Expectation provides a very good method for computing the expected number of events that will happen.

Theorem 19.5.4. *Given any collection of events $A_1, A_2, \ldots, A_n$, the expected number of events that will occur is*

$$\sum_{i=1}^{n} \text{Pr}[A_i].$$

For example, A_i could be the event that the ith man gets the right hat back. But in general, it could be any subset of the sample space, and we are asking for the expected number of events that will contain a random sample point.

Proof. Define R_i to be the indicator random variable for A_i, where $R_i(\omega) = 1$ if $w \in A_i$ and $R_i(\omega) = 0$ if $w \notin A_i$. Let $R = R_1 + R_2 + \cdots + R_n$. Then

$$\text{Ex}[R] = \sum_{i=1}^{n} \text{Ex}[R_i] \qquad \text{(by Linearity of Expectation)}$$

$$= \sum_{i=1}^{n} \Pr[R_i = 1] \qquad \text{(by Lemma 19.4.2)}$$

$$= \sum_{i=1}^{n} \Pr[A_i]. \qquad \text{(def of indicator variable)}$$

So whenever you are asked for the expected number of events that occur, all you have to do is sum the probabilities that each event occurs. Independence is not needed.

19.5.3 Expectation of a Binomial Distribution

Suppose that we independently flip n biased coins, each with probability p of coming up heads. What is the expected number of heads?

Let J be the random variable denoting the number of heads. Then J has a binomial distribution with parameters n, p, and

$$\Pr[J = k] = \binom{n}{k} p^k (1 - p)^{n-k}.$$

Applying equation (19.3), this means that

$$\text{Ex}[J] = \sum_{k=0}^{n} k \Pr[J = k] = \sum_{k=0}^{n} k \binom{n}{k} p^k (1 - p)^{n-k}. \qquad (19.11)$$

This sum looks a tad nasty, but linearity of expectation leads to an easy derivation of a simple closed form. We just express J as a sum of indicator random variables, which is easy. Namely, let J_i be the indicator random variable for the ith coin coming up heads, that is,

$$J_i ::= \begin{cases} 1 & \text{if the } i\text{th coin is heads} \\ 0 & \text{if the } i\text{th coin is tails.} \end{cases}$$

Then the number of heads is simply

$$J = J_1 + J_2 + \cdots + J_n.$$

By Theorem 19.5.4,

$$\text{Ex}[J] = \sum_{i=1}^{n} \text{Pr}[J_i] = pn. \tag{19.12}$$

That really was easy. If we flip n mutually independent coins, we expect to get pn heads. Hence the expected value of a binomial distribution with parameters n and p is simply pn.

But what if the coins are not mutually independent? It doesn't matter—the answer is still pn because Linearity of Expectation and Theorem 19.5.4 do not assume any independence.

If you are not yet convinced that Linearity of Expectation and Theorem 19.5.4 are powerful tools, consider this: without even trying, we have used them to prove a complicated looking identity, namely,

$$\sum_{k=0}^{n} k \binom{n}{k} p^k (1-p)^{n-k} = pn, \tag{19.13}$$

which follows by combining equations (19.11) and (19.12) (see also Exercise 19.28).

The next section has an even more convincing illustration of the power of linearity to solve a challenging problem.

19.5.4   The Coupon Collector Problem

Every time we purchase a kid's meal at Taco Bell, we are graciously presented with a miniature "Racin' Rocket" car together with a launching device which enables us to project our new vehicle across any tabletop or smooth floor at high velocity. Truly, our delight knows no bounds.

There are different colored Racin' Rocket cars. The color of car awarded to us by the kind server at the Taco Bell register appears to be selected uniformly and independently at random. What is the expected number of kid's meals that we must purchase in order to acquire at least one of each color of Racin' Rocket car?

The same mathematical question shows up in many guises: for example, what is the expected number of people you must poll in order to find at least one person with each possible birthday? The general question is commonly called the *coupon collector problem* after yet another interpretation.

A clever application of linearity of expectation leads to a simple solution to the coupon collector problem. Suppose there are five different colors of Racin' Rocket cars, and we receive this sequence:

    blue   green   green   red   blue   orange   blue   orange   gray.

Let's partition the sequence into 5 segments:

$$\underbrace{\text{blue}}_{X_0} \quad \underbrace{\text{green}}_{X_1} \quad \underbrace{\text{green} \quad \text{red}}_{X_2} \quad \underbrace{\text{blue} \quad \text{orange}}_{X_3} \quad \underbrace{\text{blue} \quad \text{orange} \quad \text{gray}}_{X_4}.$$

The rule is that a segment ends whenever we get a new kind of car. For example, the middle segment ends when we get a red car for the first time. In this way, we can break the problem of collecting every type of car into stages. Then we can analyze each stage individually and assemble the results using linearity of expectation.

In the general case there are n colors of Racin' Rockets that we're collecting. Let X_k be the length of the kth segment. The total number of kid's meals we must purchase to get all n Racin' Rockets is the sum of the lengths of all these segments:

$$T = X_0 + X_1 + \cdots + X_{n-1}.$$

Now let's focus our attention on X_k, the length of the kth segment. At the beginning of segment k, we have k different types of car, and the segment ends when we acquire a new type. When we own k types, each kid's meal contains a type that we already have with probability k/n. Therefore, each meal contains a new type of car with probability $1 - k/n = (n-k)/n$. Thus, the expected number of meals until we get a new kind of car is $n/(n-k)$ by the Mean Time to Failure rule. This means that

$$\text{Ex}[X_k] = \frac{n}{n-k}.$$

Linearity of expectation, together with this observation, solves the coupon collector problem:

$$\begin{aligned}
\text{Ex}[T] &= \text{Ex}[X_0 + X_1 + \cdots + X_{n-1}] \\
&= \text{Ex}[X_0] + \text{Ex}[X_1] + \cdots + \text{Ex}[X_{n-1}] \\
&= \frac{n}{n-0} + \frac{n}{n-1} + \cdots + \frac{n}{3} + \frac{n}{2} + \frac{n}{1} \\
&= n \left(\frac{1}{n} + \frac{1}{n-1} + \cdots + \frac{1}{3} + \frac{1}{2} + \frac{1}{1} \right) \\
&= n \left(\frac{1}{1} + \frac{1}{2} + \frac{1}{3} + \cdots + \frac{1}{n-1} + \frac{1}{n} \right) \\
&= n H_n \\
&\sim n \ln n.
\end{aligned} \tag{19.14}$$

Cool! It's those Harmonic Numbers again.

We can use equation (19.14) to answer some concrete questions. For example, the expected number of die rolls required to see every number from 1 to 6 is:

$$6H_6 = 14.7\ldots.$$

And the expected number of people you must poll to find at least one person with each possible birthday is:

$$365H_{365} = 2364.6\ldots.$$

19.5.5   Infinite Sums

Linearity of expectation also works for an infinite number of random variables provided that the variables satisfy an absolute convergence criterion.

Theorem 19.5.5 (Linearity of Expectation). *Let R_0, R_1, ..., be random variables such that*

$$\sum_{i=0}^{\infty} \mathrm{Ex}[\,|R_i|\,]$$

converges. Then

$$\mathrm{Ex}\left[\sum_{i=0}^{\infty} R_i\right] = \sum_{i=0}^{\infty} \mathrm{Ex}[R_i].$$

Proof. Let $T ::= \sum_{i=0}^{\infty} R_i$.

We leave it to the reader to verify that, under the given convergence hypothesis, all the sums in the following derivation are absolutely convergent, which justifies rearranging them as follows:

$$\sum_{i=0}^{\infty} \mathrm{Ex}[R_i] = \sum_{i=0}^{\infty} \sum_{s \in S} R_i(s) \cdot \mathrm{Pr}[s] \qquad\qquad \text{(Def. 19.4.1)}$$

$$= \sum_{s \in S} \sum_{i=0}^{\infty} R_i(s) \cdot \mathrm{Pr}[s] \qquad \text{(exchanging order of summation)}$$

$$= \sum_{s \in S} \left[\sum_{i=0}^{\infty} R_i(s)\right] \cdot \mathrm{Pr}[s] \qquad\qquad \text{(factoring out Pr[s])}$$

$$= \sum_{s \in S} T(s) \cdot \mathrm{Pr}[s] \qquad\qquad\qquad \text{(Def. of } T)$$

$$= \mathrm{Ex}[T] \qquad\qquad\qquad\qquad \text{(Def. 19.4.1)}$$

$$= \mathrm{Ex}\left[\sum_{i=0}^{\infty} R_i\right]. \qquad\qquad\qquad \text{(Def. of } T). \quad\blacksquare$$

19.5.6   A Gambling Paradox

One of the simplest casino bets is on "red" or "black" at the roulette table. In each play at roulette, a small ball is set spinning around a roulette wheel until it lands in a red, black, or green colored slot. The payoff for a bet on red or black matches the bet; for example, if you bet $10 on red and the ball lands in a red slot, you get back your original $10 bet plus another matching $10.

The casino gets its advantage from the green slots, which make the probability of both red and black each less than 1/2. In the US, a roulette wheel has 2 green slots among 18 black and 18 red slots, so the probability of red is $18/38 \approx 0.473$. In Europe, where roulette wheels have only 1 green slot, the odds for red are a little better—that is, $18/37 \approx 0.486$—but still less than even.

Of course you can't expect to win playing roulette, even if you had the good fortune to gamble against a *fair* roulette wheel. To prove this, note that with a fair wheel, you are equally likely win or lose each bet, so your expected win on any spin is zero. Therefore if you keep betting, your expected win is the sum of your expected wins on each bet: still zero.

Even so, gamblers regularly try to develop betting strategies to win at roulette despite the bad odds. A well known strategy of this kind is *bet doubling*, where you bet, say, $10 on red and keep doubling the bet until a red comes up. This means you stop playing if red comes up on the first spin, and you leave the casino with a $10 profit. If red does not come up, you bet $20 on the second spin. Now if the second spin comes up red, you get your $20 bet plus $20 back and again walk away with a net profit of $20 - 10 = \$10$. If red does not come up on the second spin, you next bet $40 and walk away with a net win of $40 - 20 - 10 = \$10$ if red comes up on on the third spin, and so on.

Since we've reasoned that you can't even win against a fair wheel, this strategy against an unfair wheel shouldn't work. But wait a minute! There is a 0.486 probability of red appearing on each spin of the wheel, so the mean time until a red occurs is less than three. What's more, red will come up *eventually* with probability one, and as soon as it does, you leave the casino $10 ahead. In other words, by bet doubling you are *certain* to win $10, and so your expectation is $10, not zero!

Something's wrong here.

19.5.7   Solution to the Paradox

The argument claiming the expectation is zero against a fair wheel is flawed by an implicit, invalid use of linearity of expectation for an infinite sum.

To explain this carefully, let B_n be the number of dollars you win on your nth bet, where B_n is defined to be zero if red comes up before the nth spin of the wheel.

Now the dollar amount you win in any gambling session is

$$\sum_{n=1}^{\infty} B_n,$$

and your expected win is

$$\mathrm{Ex}\left[\sum_{n=1}^{\infty} B_n\right]. \tag{19.15}$$

Moreover, since we're assuming the wheel is fair, it's true that $\mathrm{Ex}[B_n] = 0$, so

$$\sum_{n=1}^{\infty} \mathrm{Ex}[B_n] = \sum_{n=1}^{\infty} 0 = 0. \tag{19.16}$$

The flaw in the argument that you can't win is the implicit appeal to linearity of expectation to conclude that the expectation (19.15) equals the sum of expectations in (19.16). This is a case where linearity of expectation fails to hold—even though the expectation (19.15) is 10 and the sum (19.16) of expectations converges. The problem is that the expectation of the sum of the absolute values of the bets diverges, so the condition required for infinite linearity fails. In particular, under bet doubling your nth bet is $10 \cdot 2^{n-1}$ dollars while the probability that you will make an nth bet is 2^{-n}. So

$$\mathrm{Ex}[|B_n|] = 10 \cdot 2^{n-1} 2^{-n} = 20.$$

Therefore the sum

$$\sum_{n=1}^{\infty} \mathrm{Ex}[|B_n|] = 20 + 20 + 20 + \cdots$$

diverges rapidly.

So the presumption that you can't beat a fair game, and the argument we offered to support this presumption, are mistaken: by bet doubling, you can be sure to walk away a winner. Probability theory has led to an apparently absurd conclusion.

But probability theory shouldn't be rejected because it leads to this absurd conclusion. If you only had a finite amount of money to bet with—say enough money to make k bets before going bankrupt—then it would be correct to calculate your expection by summing $B_1 + B_2 + \cdots + B_k$, and your expectation would be zero for the fair wheel and negative against an unfair wheel. In other words, in order to follow the bet doubling strategy, you need to have an infinite bankroll. So it's absurd to assume you could actually follow a bet doubling strategy, and it's entirely reasonable that an absurd assumption leads to an absurd conclusion.

19.5.8 Expectations of Products

While the expectation of a sum is the sum of the expectations, the same is usually not true for products. For example, suppose that we roll a fair 6-sided die and denote the outcome with the random variable R. Does $\text{Ex}[R \cdot R] = \text{Ex}[R] \cdot \text{Ex}[R]$?

We know that $\text{Ex}[R] = 3\frac{1}{2}$ and thus $\text{Ex}[R]^2 = 12\frac{1}{4}$. Let's compute $\text{Ex}[R^2]$ to see if we get the same result.

$$\text{Ex}\left[R^2\right] = \sum_{\omega \in S} R^2(\omega) \Pr[w] = \sum_{i=1}^{6} i^2 \cdot \Pr[R_i = i]$$
$$= \frac{1^2}{6} + \frac{2^2}{6} + \frac{3^2}{6} + \frac{4^2}{6} + \frac{5^2}{6} + \frac{6^2}{6} = 15\ 1/6 \neq 12\ 1/4.$$

That is,

$$\text{Ex}[R \cdot R] \neq \text{Ex}[R] \cdot \text{Ex}[R].$$

So the expectation of a product is not always equal to the product of the expectations.

There is a special case when such a relationship *does* hold however; namely, when the random variables in the product are *independent*.

Theorem 19.5.6. *For any two* independent *random variables R_1, R_2,*

$$\text{Ex}[R_1 \cdot R_2] = \text{Ex}[R_1] \cdot \text{Ex}[R_2].$$

The proof follows by rearrangement of terms in the sum that defines $\text{Ex}[R_1 \cdot R_2]$. Details appear in Problem 19.26.

Theorem 19.5.6 extends routinely to a collection of mutually independent variables.

Corollary 19.5.7. *[Expectation of Independent Product]*
If random variables $R_1, R_2, \ldots, R_k$ are mutually independent, then

$$\text{Ex}\left[\prod_{i=1}^{k} R_i\right] = \prod_{i=1}^{k} \text{Ex}[R_i].$$

Problems for Section 19.2

Practice Problems

Problem 19.1.
Let I_A and I_B be the indicator variables for events A and B. Prove that I_A and I_B are independent iff A and B are independent.

Hint: Let $A^1 ::= A$ and $A^0 ::= \overline{A}$, so the event $[I_A = c]$ is the same as A^c for $c \in \{0, 1\}$; likewise for B^1, B^0.

Homework Problems

Problem 19.2.
Let R, S and T be random variables with the same codomain V.

(a) Suppose R is uniform—that is,

$$\Pr[R = b] = \frac{1}{|V|},$$

for all $b \in V$—and R is independent of S. Originally this text had the following argument:

> The probability that $R = S$ is the same as the probability that R takes whatever value S happens to have, therefore
> $$\Pr[R = S] = \frac{1}{|V|}. \tag{19.17}$$

Are you convinced by this argument? Write out a careful proof of (19.17).

Hint: The event $[R = S]$ is a disjoint union of events

$$[R = S] = \bigcup_{b \in V}[R = b \text{ AND } S = b].$$

(b) Let $S \times T$ be the random variable giving the values of S and T.[3] Now suppose R has a uniform distribution, and R is independent of $S \times T$. How about this argument?

> The probability that $R = S$ is the same as the probability that R equals the first coordinate of whatever value $S \times T$ happens to have, and this probability remains equal to $1/|V|$ by independence. Therefore the event $[R = S]$ is independent of $[S = T]$.

Write out a careful proof that $[R = S]$ is independent of $[S = T]$.

---

[3]That is, $S \times T : S \to V \times V$ where

$$(S \times T)(\omega) ::= (S(\omega), T(\omega))$$

for every outcome $\omega \in S$.

(c) Let $V = \{1, 2, 3\}$ and (R, S, T) take the following triples of values with equal probability,

$$(1, 1, 1), (2, 1, 1), (1, 2, 3), (2, 2, 3), (1, 3, 2), (2, 3, 2).$$

Verify that

1. R is independent of $S \times T$,

2. The event $[R = S]$ is not independent of $[S = T]$.

3. S and T have a uniform distribution.

Problem 19.3.
Let R, S and T be mutually independent indicator variables.

In general, the event that $S = T$ is not independent of $R = S$. We can explain this intuitively as follows: suppose for simplicity that S is uniform, that is, equally likely to be 0 or 1. This implies that S is equally likely as not to equal R, that is $\Pr[R = S] = 1/2$; likewise, $\Pr[S = T] = 1/2$.

Now suppose further that both R and T are more likely to equal 1 than to equal 0. This implies that $R = S$ makes it more likely than not that $S = 1$, and knowing that $S = 1$, makes it more likely than not that $S = T$. So knowing that $R = S$ makes it more likely than not that $S = T$, that is, $\Pr\left[S = T \mid R = S\right] > 1/2$.

Now prove rigorously (without any appeal to intuition) that the events $[R = S]$ and $[S = T]$ are independent iff either R is uniform[4], or T is uniform, or S is constant[5].

Problems for Section 19.3

Practice Problems

Problem 19.4.
Suppose R, S and T be mutually independent random variables on the same probability space with uniform distribution on the range $[1, 3]$.

Let $M = \max\{R, S, T\}$. Compute the values of the probability density function PDF_M of M.

[4]That is, $\Pr[R = 1] = 1/2$.
[5]That is, $\Pr[S = 1]$ is one or zero.

Class Problems

Guess the Bigger Number Game

Team 1:

- Write two different integers between 0 and 7 on separate pieces of paper.

- Put the papers face down on a table.

Team 2:

- Turn over one paper and look at the number on it.

- Either stick with this number or switch to the other (unseen) number.

Team 2 wins if it chooses the larger number; else, Team 1 wins.

Problem 19.5.

The analysis in Section 19.3.3 implies that Team 2 has a strategy that wins 4/7 of the time no matter how Team 1 plays. Can Team 2 do better? The answer is "no," because Team 1 has a strategy that guarantees that it wins at least 3/7 of the time, no matter how Team 2 plays. Describe such a strategy for Team 1 and explain why it works.

Problem 19.6.

Suppose you have a biased coin that has probability p of flipping heads. Let J be the number of heads in n independent coin flips. So J has the general binomial distribution:

$$\text{PDF}_J(k) = \binom{n}{k} p^k q^{n-k}$$

where $q ::= 1 - p$.

(a) Show that

$$\text{PDF}_J(k-1) < \text{PDF}_J(k) \qquad \text{for } k < np + p,$$
$$\text{PDF}_J(k-1) > \text{PDF}_J(k) \qquad \text{for } k > np + p.$$

(b) Conclude that the maximum value of PDF_J is asymptotically equal to

$$\frac{1}{\sqrt{2\pi npq}}.$$

Hint: For the asymptotic estimate, it's ok to assume that np is an integer, so by part (a), the maximum value is $PDF_J(np)$. Use Stirling's Formula.

Problem 19.7.
Let $R_1, R_2, \ldots, R_m$, be mutually independent random variables with uniform distribution on $[1, n]$. Let $M ::= \max\{R_i \mid i \in [1, m]\}$.

(a) Write a formula for $PDF_M(1)$.

(b) More generally, write a formula for $\Pr[M \leq k]$.

(c) For $k \in [1, n]$, write a formula for $PDF_M(k)$ in terms of expressions of the form "$\Pr[M \leq j]$" for $j \in [1, n]$.

Homework Problems

Problem 19.8.
A drunken sailor wanders along main street, which conveniently consists of the points along the x axis with integer coordinates. In each step, the sailor moves one unit left or right along the x axis. A particular *path* taken by the sailor can be described by a sequence of "left" and "right" steps. For example, $\langle$left,left,right$\rangle$ describes the walk that goes left twice then goes right.

We model this scenario with a random walk graph whose vertices are the integers and with edges going in each direction between consecutive integers. All edges are labelled $1/2$.

The sailor begins his random walk at the origin. This is described by an initial distribution which labels the origin with probability 1 and all other vertices with probability 0. After one step, the sailor is equally likely to be at location 1 or -1, so the distribution after one step gives label 1/2 to the vertices 1 and -1 and labels all other vertices with probability 0.

(a) Give the distributions after the 2nd, 3rd, and 4th step by filling in the table of probabilities below, where omitted entries are 0. For each row, write all the nonzero entries so they have the same denominator.

	location								
	-4	-3	-2	-1	0	1	2	3	4
initially					1				
after 1 step				1/2	0	1/2			
after 2 steps			?	?	?	?	?		
after 3 steps		?	?	?	?	?	?	?	
after 4 steps	?	?	?	?	?	?	?	?	?

(b)

1. What is the final location of a t-step path that moves right exactly i times?

2. How many different paths are there that end at that location?

3. What is the probability that the sailor ends at this location?

(c) Let L be the random variable giving the sailor's location after t steps, and let $B ::= (L+t)/2$. Use the answer to part (b) to show that B has an unbiased binomial density function.

(d) Again let L be the random variable giving the sailor's location after t steps, where t is even. Show that

$$\Pr[|L| < \frac{\sqrt{t}}{2}] < \frac{1}{2}.$$

So there is a better than even chance that the sailor ends up at least $\sqrt{t}/2$ steps from where he started.

Hint: Work in terms of B. Then you can use an estimate that bounds the binomial distribution. Alternatively, observe that the origin is the most likely final location and then use the asymptotic estimate

$$\Pr[L = 0] = \Pr[B = t/2] \sim \sqrt{\frac{2}{\pi t}}.$$

Problems for Section 19.4

Practice Problems

Problem 19.9.

Bruce Lee, on a movie that didn't go public, is practicing by breaking 5 boards with his fists. He is able to break a board with probability 0.8—he is practicing with his left fist, that's why it's not 1—and he breaks each board independently.

(a) What is the probability that Bruce breaks exactly 2 out of the 5 boards that are placed before him?

(b) What is the probability that Bruce breaks at most 3 out of the 5 boards that are placed before him?

(c) What is the expected number of boards Bruce will break?

Problem 19.10.
A news article reporting on the departure of a school official from California to Alabama dryly commented that this move would raise the average IQ in both states. Explain.

Class Problems

Problem 19.11.
Here's a dice game with maximum payoff k: make three independent rolls of a fair die, and if you roll a six

- no times, then you lose 1 dollar;

- exactly once, then you win 1 dollar;

- exactly twice, then you win 2 dollars;

- all three times, then you win k dollars.

For what value of k is this game fair?[6]

Problem 19.12. (a) Suppose we flip a fair coin and let N_{TT} be the number of flips until the first time two consecutive Tails appear. What is $Ex[N_{TT}]$?

Hint: Let D be the tree diagram for this process. Explain why D can be described by the tree in Figure 19.8. Use the **Law of Total Expectation** 19.4.5.

(b) Let N_{TH} be the number of flips until a Tail immediately followed by a Head comes up. What is $Ex[N_{TH}]$?

(c) Suppose we now play a game: flip a fair coin until either TT or TH occurs. You win if TT comes up first, and lose if TH comes up first. Since TT takes 50%

---

[6]This game is actually offered in casinos with $k = 3$, where it is called Carnival Dice.

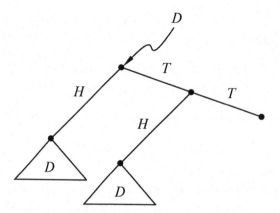

Figure 19.8   Sample space tree for coin toss until two consecutive tails.

longer on average to turn up, your opponent agrees that he has the advantage. So you tell him you're willing to play if you pay him \$5 when he wins, and he pays you with a mere 20% premium—that is \$6—when you win.

If you do this, you're sneakily taking advantage of your opponent's untrained intuition, since you've gotten him to agree to unfair odds. What is your expected profit per game?

Problem 19.13.

Let T be a positive integer valued random variable such that

$$\text{PDF}_T(n) = \frac{1}{an^2},$$

where

$$a ::= \sum_{n \in \mathbb{Z}^+} \frac{1}{n^2}.$$

(a) Prove that $\text{Ex}[T]$ is infinite.

(b) Prove that $\text{Ex}[\sqrt{T}]$ is finite.

Exam Problems

Problem 19.14.

A record of who beat whom in a round-robin tournament can be described with a *tournament digraph*, where the vertices correspond to players and there is an edge

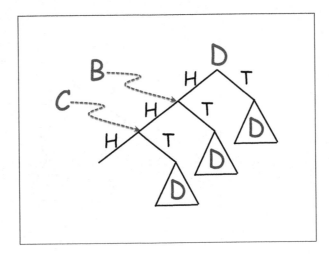

Figure 19.9   Outcome Tree for Flipping Until HHH

$\langle x \rightarrow y \rangle$ iff x beat y in their game. A *ranking* of the players is a path that includes all the players. A tournament digraph may in general have one or more rankings.[7]

Suppose we construct a random tournament digraph by letting each of the players in a match be equally likely to win and having results of all the matches be mutually independent. Find a formula for the expected number of rankings in a random 10-player tournament. Conclude that there is a 10-vertex tournament digraph with more than 7000 rankings.

This problem is an instance of the *probabilistic method*. It uses probability to prove the existence of an object without constructing it.

Problem 19.15.
A coin with probability p of flipping Heads and probability $q ::= 1 - p$ of flipping tails is repeatedly flipped until three consecutive Heads occur. The outcome tree D for this setup is illustrated in Figure 19.9.

Let $e(S)$ be the expected number of flips starting at the root of subtree S of D. So we're interested in finding $e(D)$.

Write a small system of equations involving $e(D), e(B)$, and $e(C)$ that could be solved to find $e(D)$. *You do **not** need to solve the equations.*

---

[7]It has a unique ranking iff it is a DAG, see Problem 10.10.

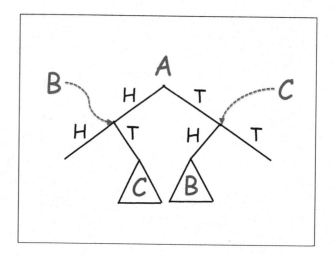

Figure 19.10   Outcome Tree for Flipping Until HH or TT

Problem 19.16.

A coin with probability p of flipping Heads and probability $q ::= 1 - p$ of flipping tails is repeatedly flipped until two consecutive flips match—that is, until HH or TT occurs. The outcome tree A for this setup is illustrated in Figure 19.10.

Let $e(T)$ be the expected number of flips starting at the root of subtree T of A. So we're interested in finding $e(A)$.

Write a small system of equations involving $e(A), e(B)$, and $e(C)$ that could be solved to find $e(A)$. *You do **not** need to solve the equations.*

Homework Problems

Problem 19.17.

We are given a random vector of n distinct numbers. We then determine the maximum of these numbers using the following procedure:

Pick the first number. Call it the *current maximum.* Go through the rest of the vector (in order) and each time we come across a number (call it x) that exceeds our current maximum, we update the current maximum with x.

What is the expected number of times we update the current maximum?

Hint: Let X_i be the indicator variable for the event that the ith element in the vector is larger than all the previous elements.

Problem 19.18 (Deviations from the mean).
Let B be a random variable with unbiased binomial distribution, nemely,

$$\Pr[B = k] = \binom{n}{k} 2^{-n}\ .$$

Assume n is even. Prove the following Lemma about the expected absolute deviation of B from its mean:

Lemma.

$$\text{Ex}[|B - \text{Ex}[B]|] = \binom{n}{\frac{n}{2}} \frac{n}{2^{n+1}}.$$

Problems for Section 19.5

Practice Problems

Problem 19.19.
MIT students sometimes delay doing laundry until they finish their problem sets. Assume all random values described below are mutually independent.

(a) A *busy* student must complete 3 problem sets before doing laundry. Each problem set requires 1 day with probability $2/3$ and 2 days with probability $1/3$. Let B be the number of days a busy student delays laundry. What is $\text{Ex}[B]$?

Example: If the first problem set requires 1 day and the second and third problem sets each require 2 days, then the student delays for $B = 5$ days.

(b) A *relaxed* student rolls a fair, 6-sided die in the morning. If he rolls a 1, then he does his laundry immediately (with zero days of delay). Otherwise, he delays for one day and repeats the experiment the following morning. Let R be the number of days a relaxed student delays laundry. What is $\text{Ex}[R]$?

Example: If the student rolls a 2 the first morning, a 5 the second morning, and a 1 the third morning, then he delays for $R = 2$ days.

(c) Before doing laundry, an *unlucky* student must recover from illness for a number of days equal to the product of the numbers rolled on two fair, 6-sided dice. Let U be the expected number of days an unlucky student delays laundry. What is $\text{Ex}[U]$?

Example: If the rolls are 5 and 3, then the student delays for $U = 15$ days.

(d) A student is *busy* with probability 1/2, *relaxed* with probability 1/3, and *unlucky* with probability 1/6. Let D be the number of days the student delays laundry. What is Ex[D]?

Problem 19.20.

Each Math for Computer Science final exam will be graded according to a rigorous procedure:

- With probability 4/7 the exam is graded by a *TA*, with probability 2/7 it is graded by a *lecturer*, and with probability 1/7, it is accidentally dropped behind the radiator and arbitrarily given a score of 84.

- TAs score an exam by scoring each problem individually and then taking the sum.

  - There are ten true/false questions worth 2 points each. For each, full credit is given with probability 3/4, and no credit is given with probability 1/4.

  - There are four questions worth 15 points each. For each, the score is determined by rolling two fair dice, summing the results, and adding 3.

  - The single 20 point question is awarded either 12 or 18 points with equal probability.

- Lecturers score an exam by rolling a fair die twice, multiplying the results, and then adding a "general impression" score.

  - With probability 4/10, the general impression score is 40.

  - With probability 3/10, the general impression score is 50.

  - With probability 3/10, the general impression score is 60.

Assume all random choices during the grading process are independent.

(a) What is the expected score on an exam graded by a TA?

(b) What is the expected score on an exam graded by a lecturer?

(c) What is the expected score on a Math for Computer Science final exam?

Class Problems

Problem 19.21.
A classroom has sixteen desks in a 4×4 arrangement as shown below.

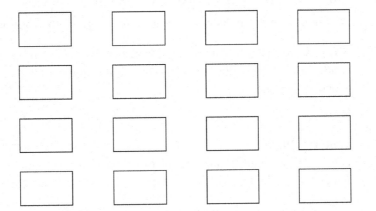

If there is a girl in front, behind, to the left, or to the right of a boy, then the two *flirt*. One student may be in multiple flirting couples; for example, a student in a corner of the classroom can flirt with up to two others, while a student in the center can flirt with as many as four others. Suppose that desks are occupied mutually independently by boys and girls with equal probability. What is the expected number of flirting couples? *Hint:* Linearity.

Problem 19.22.
Here are seven propositions:

$$
\begin{array}{ccccccc}
x_1 & \text{OR} & x_3 & \text{OR} & \overline{x_7} \\
\overline{x_5} & \text{OR} & x_6 & \text{OR} & x_7 \\
x_2 & \text{OR} & \overline{x_4} & \text{OR} & x_6 \\
\overline{x_4} & \text{OR} & x_5 & \text{OR} & \overline{x_7} \\
x_3 & \text{OR} & \overline{x_5} & \text{OR} & \overline{x_8} \\
x_9 & \text{OR} & \overline{x_8} & \text{OR} & x_2 \\
\overline{x_3} & \text{OR} & x_9 & \text{OR} & x_4
\end{array}
$$

Note that:

1. Each proposition is the disjunction (OR) of three terms of the form x_i or the form $\overline{x_i}$.

2. The variables in the three terms in each proposition are all different.

Suppose that we assign true/false values to the variables $x_1, \ldots, x_9$ independently and with equal probability.

(a) What is the expected number of true propositions?

Hint: Let T_i be an indicator for the event that the i-th proposition is true.

(b) Use your answer to prove that for *any* set of 7 propositions satisfying the conditions 1. and 2., there is an assignment to the variables that makes all 7 of the propositions true.

Problem 19.23.

A *literal* is a propositional variable or its negation. A k-*clause* is an OR of k literals, with no variable occurring more than once in the clause. For example,

$$P \text{ OR } \overline{Q} \text{ OR } \overline{R} \text{ OR } V,$$

is a 4-clause, but

$$\overline{V} \text{ OR } \overline{Q} \text{ OR } \overline{X} \text{ OR } V,$$

is not, since V appears twice.

Let S be a sequence of n distinct k-clauses involving v variables. The variables in different k-clauses may overlap or be completely different, so $k \leq v \leq nk$.

A random assignment of true/false values will be made independently to each of the v variables, with true and false assignments equally likely. Write formulas in n, k and v in answer to the first two parts below.

(a) What is the probability that the last k-clause in S is true under the random assignment?

(b) What is the expected number of true k-clauses in S?

(c) A set of propositions is *satisfiable* iff there is an assignment to the variables that makes all of the propositions true. Use your answer to part (b) to prove that if $n < 2^k$, then S is satisfiable.

Problem 19.24.

There are n students who are both taking Math for Computer Science (MCS) and Introduction to Signal Processing (SP) this term. To make it easier on themselves, the Professors in charge of these classes have decided to randomly permute their class lists and then assign students grades based on their rank in the permutation (just as many students have suspected). Assume the permutations are equally likely and independent of each other. What is the expected number of students that have in rank in SP that is higher by k than their rank in MCS?

Hint: Let X_r be the indicator variable for the rth ranked student in CS having a rank in SP of at least $r + k$.

Problem 19.25.

A man has a set of n keys, one of which fits the door to his apartment. He tries the keys randomly until he finds the key that fits. Let T be the number of times he tries keys until he finds the right key.

(a) Suppose each time he tries a key that does not fit the door, he simply puts it back. This means he might try the same ill-fitting key several times before he finds the right key. What is $\text{Ex}[T]$?

Hint: Mean time to failure.

Now suppose he throws away each ill-fitting key that he tries. That is, he chooses keys randomly from *among those he has not yet tried*. This way he is sure to find the right key within n tries.

(b) If he hasn't found the right key yet and there are m keys left, what is the probability that he will find the right key on the next try?

(c) Given that he did not find the right key on his first $k - 1$ tries, verify that the probability that he does not find it on the kth trial is given by

$$\Pr\left[T > k \mid T > k - 1\right] = \frac{n - k}{n - (k - 1)}.$$

(d) Prove that

$$\Pr[T > k] = \frac{n - k}{n}. \tag{19.18}$$

Hint: This can be argued directly, but if you don't see how, induction using part (c) will work.

(e) Conclude that in this case

$$\text{Ex}[T] = \frac{n + 1}{2}.$$

Problem 19.26.

Justify each line of the following proof that if R_1 and R_2 are *independent*, then

$$\text{Ex}[R_1 \cdot R_2] = \text{Ex}[R_1] \cdot \text{Ex}[R_2].$$

Proof.

$$\text{Ex}[R_1 \cdot R_2]$$
$$= \sum_{r \in \text{range}(R_1 \cdot R_2)} r \cdot \Pr[R_1 \cdot R_2 = r]$$
$$= \sum_{r_i \in \text{range}(R_i)} r_1 r_2 \cdot \Pr[R_1 = r_1 \text{ and } R_2 = r_2]$$
$$= \sum_{r_1 \in \text{range}(R_1)} \sum_{r_2 \in \text{range}(R_2)} r_1 r_2 \cdot \Pr[R_1 = r_1 \text{ and } R_2 = r_2]$$
$$= \sum_{r_1 \in \text{range}(R_1)} \sum_{r_2 \in \text{range}(R_2)} r_1 r_2 \cdot \Pr[R_1 = r_1] \cdot \Pr[R_2 = r_2]$$
$$= \sum_{r_1 \in \text{range}(R_1)} \left(r_1 \Pr[R_1 = r_1] \cdot \sum_{r_2 \in \text{range}(R_2)} r_2 \Pr[R_2 = r_2] \right)$$
$$= \sum_{r_1 \in \text{range}(R_1)} r_1 \Pr[R_1 = r_1] \cdot \text{Ex}[R_2]$$
$$= \text{Ex}[R_2] \cdot \sum_{r_1 \in \text{range}(R_1)} r_1 \Pr[R_1 = r_1]$$
$$= \text{Ex}[R_2] \cdot \text{Ex}[R_1].$$

■

Problem 19.27.

A gambler bets on the toss of a fair coin: if the toss is Heads, the gambler gets back the amount he bet along with an additional the amount equal to his bet. Otherwise he loses the amount bet. For example, the gambler bets $10 and wins, he gets back $20 for a net profit of $10. If he loses, he gets back nothing for a net profit of −$10—that is, a net loss of $10.

Gamblers often try to develop betting strategies to beat the odds is such a game. A well known strategy of this kind is *bet doubling*, namely, bet $10 on red, and keep doubling the bet until a red comes up. So if the gambler wins his first $10 bet, he stops playing and leaves with his $10 profit. If he loses the first bet, he bets

$20 on the second toss. Now if the second toss is Heads, he gets his $20 bet plus $20 back and again walks away with a net profit of $20 - 10 = \$10$. If he loses the second toss, he bets $40 on the third toss, and so on.

You would think that any such strategy will be doomed: in a fair game your expected win by definition is zero, so no strategy should have nonzero expectation. We can make this reasoning more precise as follows:

Let W_n be a random variable equal to the amount won in the nth coin toss. So with the bet doubling strategy starting with a $10 bet, $W_1 = \pm 10$ with equal probability. If the betting ends before the nth bet, define $W_n = 0$. So W_2 is zero with probability 1/2, is 10 with probability 1/4, and is -10 with probability 1/4. Now letting W be the amount won when the gambler stops betting, we have

$$ W = W_1 + W_2 + \cdots + W_n + \cdots . $$

Furthermore, since each toss is fair,

$$ \mathrm{Ex}[W_n] = 0 $$

for all $n > 0$. Now by linearity of expectation, we have

$$ \mathrm{Ex}[W] = \mathrm{Ex}[W_1] + \mathrm{Ex}[W_2] + \cdots + \mathrm{Ex}[W_n] + \cdots = 0 + 0 + \cdots + 0 + \cdots = 0, \tag{19.19} $$

confirming that with fair tosses, the expected win is zero.

But wait a minute!

(a) Explain why the gambler is certain to win eventually if he keeps betting.

(b) Prove that when the gambler finally wins a bet, his net profit is $10.

(c) Since the gambler's profit is always $10 when he wins, and he is certain to win, his expected profit is also $10. That is

$$ \mathrm{Ex}[W] = 10, $$

contradicting (19.19). So what's wrong with the reasoning that led to the false conclusion (19.19)?

Homework Problems

Problem 19.28.

Applying linearity of expectation to the binomial distribution $f_{n,p}$ immediately yielded the identity 19.13:

$$\mathrm{Ex}[f_{n,p}] ::= \sum_{k=0}^{n} k \binom{n}{k} p^k (1-p)^{n-k} = pn. \tag{$*$}$$

Though it might seem daunting to prove this equation without appeal to linearity, it is, after all, pretty similar to the binomial identity, and this connection leads to an immediate alternative algebraic derivation.

(a) Starting with the binomial identity for $(x+y)^n$, prove that

$$xn(x+y)^{n-1} = \sum_{k=0}^{n} k \binom{n}{k} x^k y^{n-k}. \tag{$**$}$$

(b) Now conclude equation ($*$).

Problem 19.29.

A coin will be flipped repeatedly until the sequence TTH (tail/tail/head) comes up. Successive flips are independent, and the coin has probability p of coming up heads. Let N_{TTH} be the number of coin flips until TTH first appears. What value of p minimizes $\mathrm{Ex}[N_{\mathrm{TTH}}]$?

Problem 19.30.

(A true story from World War Two.)

The army needs to test n soldiers for a disease. There is a blood test that accurately determines when a blood sample contains blood from a diseased soldier. The army presumes, based on experience, that the fraction of soldiers with the disease is approximately equal to some small number p.

Approach (1) is to test blood from each soldier individually; this requires n tests. Approach (2) is to randomly group the soldiers into g groups of k soldiers, where $n = gk$. For each group, blend the k blood samples of the people in the group, and test the blended sample. If the group-blend is free of the disease, we are done with that group after one test. If the group-blend tests positive for the disease, then someone in the group has the disease, and we to test all the people in the group for a total of $k + 1$ tests on that group.

Since the groups are chosen randomly, each soldier in the group has the disease with probability p, and it is safe to assume that whether one soldier has the disease is independent of whether the others do.

(a) What is the expected number of tests in Approach (2) as a function of the number of soldiers n, the disease fraction p, and the group size k?

(b) Show how to choose k so that the expected number of tests using Approach (2) is approximately $n\sqrt{p}$. *Hint:* Since p is small, you may assume that $(1-p)^k \approx 1$ and $\ln(1-p) \approx -p$.

(c) What fraction of the work does Approach (2) expect to save over Approach (1) in a million-strong army of whom approximately 1% are diseased?

(d) Can you come up with a better scheme by using multiple levels of grouping, that is, groups of groups?

Problem 19.31.
A wheel-of-fortune has the numbers from 1 to $2n$ arranged in a circle. The wheel has a spinner, and a spin randomly determines the two numbers at the opposite ends of the spinner. How would you arrange the numbers on the wheel to maximize the expected value of:

(a) the sum of the numbers chosen? What is this maximum?

(b) the product of the numbers chosen? What is this maximum?

Hint: For part (b), verify that the sum of the products of numbers oppposite each other is maximized when successive integers are on the opposite ends of the spinner, that is, 1 is opposite 2, 3 is opposite 4, 5 is opposite 6, ...

Problem 19.32.
Let R and S be independent random variables, and f and g be any functions such that $\mathrm{domain}(f) = \mathrm{codomain}(R)$ and $\mathrm{domain}(g) = \mathrm{codomain}(S)$. Prove that $f(R)$ and $g(S)$ are also independent random variables.

Hint: The event $[f(R) = a]$ is the disjoint union of all the events $[R = r]$ for r such that $f(r) = a$.

Problem 19.33.
Peeta bakes between 1 and $2n$ loaves of bread to sell every day. Each day he rolls

a fair, n-sided die to get a number from 1 to n, then flips a fair coin. If the coin is heads, he bakes m loaves of bread , where m is the number on the die that day, and if the coin is tails, he bakes $2m$ loaves.

(a) For any positive integer $k \leq 2n$, what is the probability that Peeta will make k loaves of bread on any given day? (Hint: you can express your solution by cases.)

(b) What is the expected number of loaves that Peeta would bake on any given day?

(c) Continuing this process, Peeta bakes bread every day for 30 days. What is the expected total number of loaves that Peeta would bake?

Exam Problems

Problem 19.34.
A box initially contains n balls, all colored black. A ball is drawn from the box at random.

- If the drawn ball is black, then a biased coin with probability, $p > 0$, of coming up heads is flipped. If the coin comes up heads, a white ball is put into the box; otherwise the black ball is returned to the box.

- If the drawn ball is white, then it is returned to the box.

This process is repeated until the box contains n white balls.

Let D be the number of balls drawn until the process ends with the box full of white balls. Prove that $\mathrm{Ex}[D] = nH_n/p$, where H_n is the nth Harmonic number.

Hint: Let D_i be the number of draws after the ith white ball until the draw when the $(i + 1)$st white ball is put into the box.

Problem 19.35.
A gambler bets \$10 on "red" at a roulette table (the odds of red are 18/38, slightly less than even) to win \$10. If he wins, he gets back twice the amount of his bet, and he quits. Otherwise, he doubles his previous bet and continues.

For example, if he loses his first two bets but wins his third bet, the total spent on his three bets is $10 + 20 + 40$ dollars, but he gets back $2 \cdot 40$ dollars after his win on the third bet, for a net profit of \$10.

(a) What is the expected number of bets the gambler makes before he wins?

(b) What is his probability of winning?

(c) What is his expected final profit (amount won minus amount lost)?

(d) You can beat a biased game by bet doubling, but bet doubling is not feasible because it requires an infinite bankroll. Verify this by proving that the expected size of the gambler's last bet is infinite.

Problem 19.36.
Six pairs of cards with ranks 1–6 are shuffled and laid out in a row, for example,

$$\boxed{1}\,\boxed{2}\,\boxed{3}\,\boxed{3}\,\boxed{4}\,\boxed{6}\,\boxed{1}\,\boxed{4}\,\boxed{5}\,\boxed{5}\,\boxed{2}\,\boxed{6}$$

In this case, there are two adjacent pairs with the same value, the two 3's and the two 5's. What is the expected number of adjacent pairs with the same value?

Problem 19.37.
There are six kinds of cards, three of each kind, for a total of eighteen cards. The cards are randonly shuffled and laid out in a row, for example,

$$\boxed{1}\,\boxed{2}\,\boxed{5}\,\boxed{5}\,\boxed{5}\,\boxed{1}\,\boxed{4}\,\boxed{6}\,\boxed{2}\,\boxed{6}\,\boxed{6}\,\boxed{2}\,\boxed{1}\,\boxed{4}\,\boxed{3}\,\boxed{3}\,\boxed{3}\,\boxed{4}$$

In this case, there are two adjacent triples of the same kind, the three 3's and the three 5's.

(a) Derive a formula for the probability that the 4th, 5th, and 6th consecutive cards will be the same kind—that is, all 1's or all 2's or...all 6's?

(b) Let $p ::= \Pr[\text{4th, 5th and 6th cards match}]$—that is, p is the correct answer to part (a). Write a simple formula for the expected number of matching triples in terms of p.

20   Deviation from the Mean

In the previous chapter, we took it for granted that expectation is useful and developed a bunch of techniques for calculating expected values. But why should we care about this value? After all, a random variable may never take a value anywhere near its expectation.

The most important reason to care about the mean value comes from its connection to estimation by sampling. For example, suppose we want to estimate the average age, income, family size, or other measure of a population. To do this, we determine a random process for selecting people—say, throwing darts at census lists. This process makes the selected person's age, income, and so on into a random variable whose *mean* equals the *actual average* age or income of the population. So, we can select a random sample of people and calculate the average of people in the sample to estimate the true average in the whole population. But when we make an estimate by repeated sampling, we need to know how much confidence we should have that our estimate is OK, and how large a sample is needed to reach a given confidence level. The issue is fundamental to all experimental science. Because of random errors—*noise*—repeated measurements of the same quantity rarely come out exactly the same. Determining how much confidence to put in experimental measurements is a fundamental and universal scientific issue. Technically, judging sampling or measurement accuracy reduces to finding the probability that an estimate *deviates* by a given amount from its expected value.

Another aspect of this issue comes up in engineering. When designing a sea wall, you need to know how strong to make it to withstand tsunamis for, say, at least a century. If you're assembling a computer network, you might need to know how many component failures it should tolerate to likely operate without maintenance for at least a month. If your business is insurance, you need to know how large a financial reserve to maintain to be nearly certain of paying benefits for, say, the next three decades. Technically, such questions come down to finding the probability of *extreme* deviations from the mean.

This issue of *deviation from the mean* is the focus of this chapter.

20.1   Markov's Theorem

Markov's theorem gives a generally coarse estimate of the probability that a random variable takes a value *much larger* than its mean. It is an almost trivial result by itself, but it actually leads fairly directly to much stronger results.

The idea behind Markov's Theorem can be explained by considering the quantity known as *intelligence quotient*, IQ, which remains in wide use despite doubts about its legitimacy. IQ was devised so that its average measurement would be 100. This immediately implies that at most 1/3 of the population can have an IQ of 300 or more, because if more than a third had an IQ of 300, then the average would have to be *more* than $(1/3) \cdot 300 = 100$. So, the probability that a randomly chosen person has an IQ of 300 or more is at most 1/3. By the same logic, we can also conclude that at most 2/3 of the population can have an IQ of 150 or more.

Of course, these are not very strong conclusions. No IQ of over 300 has ever been recorded; and while many IQ's of over 150 have been recorded, the fraction of the population that actually has an IQ that high is very much smaller than 2/3. But though these conclusions are weak, we reached them using just the fact that the average IQ is 100—along with another fact we took for granted, that IQ is never negative. Using only these facts, we can't derive smaller fractions, because there are nonnegative random variables with mean 100 that achieve these fractions. For example, if we choose a random variable equal to 300 with probability 1/3 and 0 with probability 2/3, then its mean is 100, and the probability of a value of 300 or more really is 1/3.

Theorem 20.1.1 (Markov's Theorem). *If R is a nonnegative random variable, then for all $x > 0$*

$$\Pr[R \geq x] \leq \frac{\text{Ex}[R]}{x}. \tag{20.1}$$

Proof. Let y vary over the range of R. Then for any $x > 0$

$$
\begin{aligned}
\text{Ex}[R] &::= \sum_y y \Pr[R = y] \\
&\geq \sum_{y \geq x} y \Pr[R = y] \geq \sum_{y \geq x} x \Pr[R = y] = x \sum_{y \geq x} \Pr[R = y] \\
&= x \Pr[R \geq x], \tag{20.2}
\end{aligned}
$$

where the first inequality follows from the fact that $R \geq 0$.

Dividing the first and last expressions in (20.2) by x gives the desired result. ∎

Our focus is deviation from the mean, so it's useful to rephrase Markov's Theorem this way:

Corollary 20.1.2. *If R is a nonnegative random variable, then for all $c \geq 1$*

$$\Pr[R \geq c \cdot \text{Ex}[R]] \leq \frac{1}{c}. \tag{20.3}$$

This Corollary follows immediately from Markov's Theorem(20.1.1) by letting x be $c \cdot \text{Ex}[R]$.

20.1.1 Applying Markov's Theorem

Let's go back to the Hat-Check problem of Section 19.5.2. Now we ask what the probability is that x or more men get the right hat, this is, what the value of $\Pr[G \geq x]$ is.

We can compute an upper bound with Markov's Theorem. Since we know $\text{Ex}[G] = 1$, Markov's Theorem implies

$$\Pr[G \geq x] \leq \frac{\text{Ex}[G]}{x} = \frac{1}{x}.$$

For example, there is no better than a 20% chance that 5 men get the right hat, regardless of the number of people at the dinner party.

The Chinese Appetizer problem is similar to the Hat-Check problem. In this case, n people are eating different appetizers arranged on a circular, rotating Chinese banquet tray. Someone then spins the tray so that each person receives a random appetizer. What is the probability that everyone gets the same appetizer as before?

There are n equally likely orientations for the tray after it stops spinning. Everyone gets the right appetizer in just one of these n orientations. Therefore, the correct answer is $1/n$.

But what probability do we get from Markov's Theorem? Let the random variable R be the number of people that get the right appetizer. Then of course $\text{Ex}[R] = 1$, so applying Markov's Theorem, we find:

$$\Pr[R \geq n] \leq \frac{\text{Ex}[R]}{n} = \frac{1}{n}.$$

So for the Chinese appetizer problem, Markov's Theorem is precisely right!

Unfortunately, Markov's Theorem is not always so accurate. For example, it gives the same $1/n$ upper limit for the probability that everyone gets their own hat back in the Hat-Check problem, where the probability is actually $1/(n!)$. So for Hat-Check, Markov's Theorem gives a probability bound that is way too large.

20.1.2 Markov's Theorem for Bounded Variables

Suppose we learn that the average IQ among MIT students is 150 (which is not true, by the way). What can we say about the probability that an MIT student has an IQ of more than 200? Markov's theorem immediately tells us that no more than 150/200 or 3/4 of the students can have such a high IQ. Here, we simply applied

Markov's Theorem to the random variable R equal to the IQ of a random MIT student to conclude:

$$\Pr[R > 200] \le \frac{\text{Ex}[R]}{200} = \frac{150}{200} = \frac{3}{4}.$$

But let's observe an additional fact (which may be true): no MIT student has an IQ less than 100. This means that if we let $T ::= R - 100$, then T is nonnegative and $\text{Ex}[T] = 50$, so we can apply Markov's Theorem to T and conclude:

$$\Pr[R > 200] = \Pr[T > 100] \le \frac{\text{Ex}[T]}{100} = \frac{50}{100} = \frac{1}{2}.$$

So only half, not 3/4, of the students can be as amazing as they think they are. A bit of a relief!

In fact, we can get better bounds applying Markov's Theorem to $R - b$ instead of R for any lower bound b on R (see Problem 20.3). Similarly, if we have any upper bound u on a random variable S, then $u - S$ will be a nonnegative random variable, and applying Markov's Theorem to $u - S$ will allow us to bound the probability that S is much *less* than its expectation.

20.2   Chebyshev's Theorem

We've seen that Markov's Theorem can give a better bound when applied to $R - b$ rather than R. More generally, a good trick for getting stronger bounds on a random variable R out of Markov's Theorem is to apply the theorem to some cleverly chosen function of R. Choosing functions that are powers of the absolute value of R turns out to be especially useful. In particular, since $|R|^z$ is nonnegative for any real number z, Markov's inequality also applies to the event $[|R|^z \ge x^z]$. But for positive $x, z > 0$ this event is equivalent to the event $[|R| \ge x]$ for , so we have:

Lemma 20.2.1. *For any random variable R and positive real numbers x, z,*

$$\Pr[|R| \ge x] \le \frac{\text{Ex}[|R|^z]}{x^z}.$$

Rephrasing (20.2.1) in terms of $|R - \text{Ex}[R]|$, the random variable that measures R's deviation from its mean, we get

$$\Pr[|R - \text{Ex}[R]| \ge x] \le \frac{\text{Ex}[(|R - \text{Ex}[R]|)^z]}{x^z}. \tag{20.4}$$

When z is positive and even, $(R - \text{Ex}[R])^z$ is nonnegative, so the absolute value on the right-hand side of the inequality (20.4) is redundant. The case when $z = 2$ turns out to be so important that the numerator of the right-hand side has been given a name:

Definition 20.2.2. The *variance* of a random variable R is:

$$\text{Var}[R] ::= \text{Ex}\left[(R - \text{Ex}[R])^2\right].$$

Variance is also known as *mean square deviation*.
The restatement of (20.4) for $z = 2$ is known as *Chebyshev's Theorem*.[1]

Theorem 20.2.3 (Chebyshev). *Let R be a random variable and $x \in \mathbb{R}^+$. Then*

$$\Pr[|R - \text{Ex}[R]| \geq x] \leq \frac{\text{Var}[R]}{x^2}.$$

The expression $\text{Ex}[(R - \text{Ex}[R])^2]$ for variance is a bit cryptic; the best approach is to work through it from the inside out. The innermost expression $R - \text{Ex}[R]$ is precisely the deviation of R above its mean. Squaring this, we obtain $(R - \text{Ex}[R])^2$. This is a random variable that is near 0 when R is close to the mean and is a large positive number when R deviates far above or below the mean. So if R is always close to the mean, then the variance will be small. If R is often far from the mean, then the variance will be large.

20.2.1 Variance in Two Gambling Games

The relevance of variance is apparent when we compare the following two gambling games.

Game A: We win \$2 with probability 2/3 and lose \$1 with probability 1/3.

Game B: We win \$1002 with probability 2/3 and lose \$2001 with probability 1/3.

Which game is better financially? We have the same probability, 2/3, of winning each game, but that does not tell the whole story. What about the expected return for each game? Let random variables A and B be the payoffs for the two games. For example, A is 2 with probability 2/3 and -1 with probability 1/3. We can compute the expected payoff for each game as follows:

$$\text{Ex}[A] = 2 \cdot \frac{2}{3} + (-1) \cdot \frac{1}{3} = 1,$$
$$\text{Ex}[B] = 1002 \cdot \frac{2}{3} + (-2001) \cdot \frac{1}{3} = 1.$$

---

[1] There are Chebyshev Theorems in several other disciplines, but Theorem 20.2.3 is the only one we'll refer to.

The expected payoff is the same for both games, but the games are very different. This difference is not apparent in their expected value, but is captured by variance. We can compute the Var[A] by working "from the inside out" as follows:

$$A - \text{Ex}[A] = \begin{cases} 1 & \text{with probability } \frac{2}{3} \\ -2 & \text{with probability } \frac{1}{3} \end{cases}$$

$$(A - \text{Ex}[A])^2 = \begin{cases} 1 & \text{with probability } \frac{2}{3} \\ 4 & \text{with probability } \frac{1}{3} \end{cases}$$

$$\text{Ex}[(A - \text{Ex}[A])^2] = 1 \cdot \frac{2}{3} + 4 \cdot \frac{1}{3}$$

$$\text{Var}[A] = 2.$$

Similarly, we have for Var[B]:

$$B - \text{Ex}[B] = \begin{cases} 1001 & \text{with probability } \frac{2}{3} \\ -2002 & \text{with probability } \frac{1}{3} \end{cases}$$

$$(B - \text{Ex}[B])^2 = \begin{cases} 1,002,001 & \text{with probability } \frac{2}{3} \\ 4,008,004 & \text{with probability } \frac{1}{3} \end{cases}$$

$$\text{Ex}[(B - \text{Ex}[B])^2] = 1,002,001 \cdot \frac{2}{3} + 4,008,004 \cdot \frac{1}{3}$$

$$\text{Var}[B] = 2,004,002.$$

The variance of Game A is 2 and the variance of Game B is more than two million! Intuitively, this means that the payoff in Game A is usually close to the expected value of \$1, but the payoff in Game B can deviate very far from this expected value.

High variance is often associated with high risk. For example, in ten rounds of Game A, we expect to make \$10, but could conceivably lose \$10 instead. On the other hand, in ten rounds of game B, we also expect to make \$10, but could actually lose more than \$20,000!

20.2.2   Standard Deviation

In Game B above, the deviation from the mean is 1001 in one outcome and -2002 in the other. But the variance is a whopping 2,004,002. The happens because the "units" of variance are wrong: if the random variable is in dollars, then the expectation is also in dollars, but the variance is in square dollars. For this reason, people often describe random variables using *standard deviation* instead of variance.

Definition 20.2.4. The *standard deviation* σ_R of a random variable R is the square root of the variance:

$$\sigma_R ::= \sqrt{\text{Var}[R]} = \sqrt{\text{Ex}[(R - \text{Ex}[R])^2]}.$$

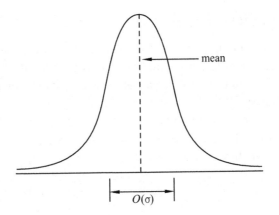

Figure 20.1 The standard deviation of a distribution indicates how wide the "main part" of it is.

So the standard deviation is the square root of the mean square deviation, or the *root mean square* for short. It has the same units—dollars in our example—as the original random variable and as the mean. Intuitively, it measures the average deviation from the mean, since we can think of the square root on the outside as canceling the square on the inside.

Example 20.2.5. The standard deviation of the payoff in Game B is:

$$\sigma_B = \sqrt{\text{Var}[B]} = \sqrt{2,004,002} \approx 1416.$$

The random variable B actually deviates from the mean by either positive 1001 or negative 2002, so the standard deviation of 1416 describes this situation more closely than the value in the millions of the variance.

For bell-shaped distributions like the one illustrated in Figure 20.1, the standard deviation measures the "width" of the interval in which values are most likely to fall. This can be more clearly explained by rephrasing Chebyshev's Theorem in terms of standard deviation, which we can do by substituting $x = c\sigma_R$ in (20.1):

Corollary 20.2.6. *Let R be a random variable, and let c be a positive real number.*

$$\Pr[|R - \text{Ex}[R]| \geq c\sigma_R] \leq \frac{1}{c^2}. \tag{20.5}$$

Now we see explicitly how the "likely" values of R are clustered in an $O(\sigma_R)$-sized region around $\text{Ex}[R]$, confirming that the standard deviation measures how spread out the distribution of R is around its mean.

The IQ Example

The standard standard deviation of IQ's regularly turns out to be about 15 even across different populations. This additional fact along with the national average IQ being 100 allows a better determination of the occurrence of IQ's of 300 or more.

Let the random variable R be the IQ of a random person. So $\mathrm{Ex}[R] = 100$, $\sigma_R = 15$ and R is nonnegative. We want to compute $\mathrm{Pr}[R \geq 300]$.

We have already seen that Markov's Theorem 20.1.1 gives a coarse bound, namely,

$$\mathrm{Pr}[R \geq 300] \leq \frac{1}{3}.$$

Now we apply Chebyshev's Theorem to the same problem:

$$\mathrm{Pr}[R \geq 300] = \mathrm{Pr}[|R - 100| \geq 200] \leq \frac{\mathrm{Var}[R]}{200^2} = \frac{15^2}{200^2} \approx \frac{1}{178}.$$

So Chebyshev's Theorem implies that at most one person in 178 has an IQ of 300 or more. We have gotten a much tighter bound using additional information—the variance of R—than we could get knowing only the expectation.

20.3   Properties of Variance

Variance is the average *of the square* of the distance from the mean. For this reason, variance is sometimes called the "mean square deviation." Then we take its square root to get the standard deviation—which in turn is called "root mean square deviation."

But why bother squaring? Why not study the actual distance from the mean, namely, the absolute value of $R - \mathrm{Ex}[R]$, instead of its root mean square? The answer is that variance and standard deviation have useful properties that make them much more important in probability theory than average absolute deviation. In this section, we'll describe some of those properties. In the next section, we'll see why these properties are important.

20.3.1   A Formula for Variance

Applying linearity of expectation to the formula for variance yields a convenient alternative formula.

Lemma 20.3.1.

$$\mathrm{Var}[R] = \mathrm{Ex}[R^2] - \mathrm{Ex}^2[R],$$

for any random variable R.

Here we use the notation $\text{Ex}^2[R]$ as shorthand for $(\text{Ex}[R])^2$.

Proof. Let $\mu = \text{Ex}[R]$. Then

$$
\begin{aligned}
\text{Var}[R] &= \text{Ex}[(R - \text{Ex}[R])^2] && \text{(Def 20.2.2 of variance)} \\
&= \text{Ex}[(R - \mu)^2] && \text{(def of } \mu) \\
&= \text{Ex}[R^2 - 2\mu R + \mu^2] \\
&= \text{Ex}[R^2] - 2\mu \, \text{Ex}[R] + \mu^2 && \text{(linearity of expectation)} \\
&= \text{Ex}[R^2] - 2\mu^2 + \mu^2 && \text{(def of } \mu) \\
&= \text{Ex}[R^2] - \mu^2 \\
&= \text{Ex}[R^2] - \text{Ex}^2[R]. && \text{(def of } \mu)
\end{aligned}
$$

∎

A simple and very useful formula for the variance of an indicator variable is an immediate consequence.

Corollary 20.3.2. *If B is a Bernoulli variable where* $p ::= \Pr[B = 1]$, *then*

$$
\text{Var}[B] = p - p^2 = p(1 - p). \tag{20.6}
$$

Proof. By Lemma 19.4.2, $\text{Ex}[B] = p$. But B only takes values 0 and 1, so $B^2 = B$ and equation (20.6) follows immediately from Lemma 20.3.1. ∎

20.3.2 Variance of Time to Failure

According to Section 19.4.6, the mean time to failure is $1/p$ for a process that fails during any given hour with probability p. What about the variance?

By Lemma 20.3.1,

$$
\text{Var}[C] = \text{Ex}[C^2] - (1/p)^2 \tag{20.7}
$$

so all we need is a formula for $\text{Ex}[C^2]$.

Reasoning about C using conditional expectation worked nicely in Section 19.4.6 to find mean time to failure, and a similar approach works for C^2. Namely, the expected value of C^2 is the probability p of failure in the first hour times 1^2, plus the probability $(1 - p)$ of non-failure in the first hour times the expected value of

$(C+1)^2$. So

$$\text{Ex}[C^2] = p \cdot 1^2 + (1-p)\,\text{Ex}[(C+1)^2]$$

$$= p + (1-p)\left(\text{Ex}[C^2] + \frac{2}{p} + 1\right)$$

$$= p + (1-p)\,\text{Ex}[C^2] + (1-p)\left(\frac{2}{p}+1\right), \quad \text{so}$$

$$p\,\text{Ex}[C^2] = p + (1-p)\left(\frac{2}{p}+1\right)$$

$$= \frac{p^2 + (1-p)(2+p)}{p} \quad \text{and}$$

$$\text{Ex}[C^2] = \frac{2-p}{p^2}$$

Combining this with (20.7) proves

Lemma 20.3.3. *If failures occur with probability p independently at each step, and C is the number of steps until the first failure,[2] then*

$$\text{Var}[C] = \frac{1-p}{p^2}. \tag{20.8}$$

20.3.3   Dealing with Constants

It helps to know how to calculate the variance of $aR + b$:

Theorem 20.3.4. *[Square Multiple Rule for Variance] Let R be a random variable and a a constant. Then*

$$\text{Var}[aR] = a^2\,\text{Var}[R]. \tag{20.9}$$

Proof. Beginning with the definition of variance and repeatedly applying linearity of expectation, we have:

$$\text{Var}[aR] ::= \text{Ex}[(aR - \text{Ex}[aR])^2]$$

$$= \text{Ex}[(aR)^2 - 2aR\,\text{Ex}[aR] + \text{Ex}^2[aR]]$$

$$= \text{Ex}[(aR)^2] - \text{Ex}[2aR\,\text{Ex}[aR]] + \text{Ex}^2[aR]$$

$$= a^2\,\text{Ex}[R^2] - 2\,\text{Ex}[aR]\,\text{Ex}[aR] + \text{Ex}^2[aR]$$

$$= a^2\,\text{Ex}[R^2] - a^2\,\text{Ex}^2[R]$$

$$= a^2\left(\text{Ex}[R^2] - \text{Ex}^2[R]\right)$$

$$= a^2\,\text{Var}[R] \qquad\qquad\qquad\qquad \text{(Lemma 20.3.1)}$$

---

[2]That is, C has the geometric distribution with parameter p according to Definition 19.4.6.

It's even simpler to prove that adding a constant does not change the variance, as the reader can verify:

Theorem 20.3.5. *Let R be a random variable, and b a constant. Then*

$$\text{Var}[R + b] = \text{Var}[R]. \tag{20.10}$$

Recalling that the standard deviation is the square root of variance, this implies that the standard deviation of $aR + b$ is simply $|a|$ times the standard deviation of R:

Corollary 20.3.6.

$$\sigma_{(aR+b)} = |a|\,\sigma_R.$$

20.3.4 Variance of a Sum

In general, the variance of a sum is not equal to the sum of the variances, but variances do add for *independent* variables. In fact, *mutual* independence is not necessary: *pairwise* independence will do. This is useful to know because there are some important situations, such as Birthday Matching in Section 17.4, that involve variables that are pairwise independent but not mutually independent.

Theorem 20.3.7. *If R and S are independent random variables, then*

$$\text{Var}[R + S] = \text{Var}[R] + \text{Var}[S]. \tag{20.11}$$

Proof. We may assume that $\text{Ex}[R] = 0$, since we could always replace R by $R - \text{Ex}[R]$ in equation (20.11); likewise for S. This substitution preserves the independence of the variables, and by Theorem 20.3.5, does not change the variances.

But for any variable T with expectation zero, we have $\text{Var}[T] = \text{Ex}[T^2]$, so we need only prove

$$\text{Ex}[(R + S)^2] = \text{Ex}[R^2] + \text{Ex}[S^2]. \tag{20.12}$$

But (20.12) follows from linearity of expectation and the fact that

$$\text{Ex}[RS] = \text{Ex}[R]\,\text{Ex}[S] \tag{20.13}$$

since R and S are independent:

$$
\begin{aligned}
\text{Ex}[(R + S)^2] &= \text{Ex}[R^2 + 2RS + S^2] \\
&= \text{Ex}[R^2] + 2\,\text{Ex}[RS] + \text{Ex}[S^2] \\
&= \text{Ex}[R^2] + 2\,\text{Ex}[R]\,\text{Ex}[S] + \text{Ex}[S^2] \qquad \text{(by (20.13))} \\
&= \text{Ex}[R^2] + 2 \cdot 0 \cdot 0 + \text{Ex}[S^2] \\
&= \text{Ex}[R^2] + \text{Ex}[S^2].
\end{aligned}
$$

■

It's easy to see that additivity of variance does not generally hold for variables that are not independent. For example, if $R = S$, then equation (20.11) becomes $\text{Var}[R + R] = \text{Var}[R] + \text{Var}[R]$. By the Square Multiple Rule, Theorem 20.3.4, this holds iff $4\,\text{Var}[R] = 2\,\text{Var}[R]$, which implies that $\text{Var}[R] = 0$. So equation (20.11) fails when $R = S$ and R has nonzero variance.

The proof of Theorem 20.3.7 carries over to the sum of any finite number of variables (Problem 20.18), so we have:

Theorem 20.3.8. *[Pairwise Independent Additivity of Variance] If $R_1, R_2, \ldots, R_n$ are* pairwise *independent random variables, then*

$$\text{Var}[R_1 + R_2 + \cdots + R_n] = \text{Var}[R_1] + \text{Var}[R_2] + \cdots + \text{Var}[R_n]. \qquad (20.14)$$

Now we have a simple way of computing the variance of a variable J that has an (n, p)-binomial distribution. We know that $J = \sum_{k=1}^{n} I_k$ where the I_k are mutually independent indicator variables with $\Pr[I_k = 1] = p$. The variance of each I_k is $p(1 - p)$ by Corollary 20.3.2, so by linearity of variance, we have

Lemma 20.3.9 (Variance of the Binomial Distribution). *If J has the (n, p)-binomial distribution, then*

$$\text{Var}[J] = n\,\text{Var}[I_k] = np(1 - p). \qquad (20.15)$$

20.3.5   Matching Birthdays

We saw in Section 17.4 that in a class of 95 students, it is virtually certain that at least one pair of students will have the same birthday. In fact, several pairs of students are likely to have the same birthday. How many matched birthdays should we expect, and how likely are we to see that many matches in a random group of students?

Having matching birthdays for different pairs of students are *not* mutually independent events. If Alice matches Bob and Alice matches Carol, it's certain that Bob and Carol match as well! So the events that various pairs of students have matching birthdays are not even three-way independent.

But knowing that Alice's birthday matches Bob's tells us nothing about who Carol matches. This means that the events that a pair of people have matching birthdays are pairwise independent (see Problem 19.2). So pairwise independent additivity of variance, Theorem 20.3.8, will allow us to calculate the variance of the number of birthday pairs and then apply Chebyshev's bound to estimate the liklihood of seeing some given number of matching pairs.

In particular, suppose there are n students and d days in the year, and let M be the number of pairs of students with matching birthdays. Namely, let $B_1, B_2, \ldots, B_n$ be the birthdays of n independently chosen people, and let $E_{i,j}$ be the indicator variable for the event that the ith and jth people chosen have the same birthdays, that is, the event $[B_i = B_j]$. So in our probability model, the B_i's are mutually independent variables, and the $E_{i,j}$'s are pairwise independent. Also, the expectations of $E_{i,j}$ for $i \neq j$ equals the probability that $B_i = B_j$, namely, $1/d$.

Now the number M of matching pairs of birthdays among the n choices is simply the sum of the $E_{i,j}$'s:

$$M = \sum_{1 \leq i < j \leq n} E_{i,j}. \tag{20.16}$$

Linearity of expectation make it easy to calculate the expected number of pairs of students with matching birthdays.

$$\mathrm{Ex}[M] = \mathrm{Ex}\left[\sum_{1 \leq i < j \leq n} E_{i,j}\right] = \sum_{1 \leq i < j \leq n} \mathrm{Ex}[E_{i,j}] = \binom{n}{2} \cdot \frac{1}{d}.$$

Similarly, pairwise independence makes it easy to calculate the variance.

$$\begin{aligned}
\mathrm{Var}[M] &= \mathrm{Var}\left[\sum_{1 \leq i < j \leq n} E_{i,j}\right] \\
&= \sum_{1 \leq i < j \leq n} \mathrm{Var}[E_{i,j}] && \text{(Theorem 20.3.8)} \\
&= \binom{n}{2} \cdot \frac{1}{d}\left(1 - \frac{1}{d}\right). && \text{(Corollary 20.3.2)}
\end{aligned}$$

In particular, for a class of $n = 95$ students with $d = 365$ possible birthdays, we have $\mathrm{Ex}[M] \approx 12.23$ and $\mathrm{Var}[M] \approx 12.23(1-1/365) < 12.2$. So by Chebyshev's Theorem

$$\Pr[|M - \mathrm{Ex}[M]| \geq x] < \frac{12.2}{x^2}.$$

Letting $x = 7$, we conclude that there is a better than 75% chance that in a class of 95 students, the number of pairs of students with the same birthday will be within 7 of 12.23, that is, between 6 and 19.

20.4   Estimation by Random Sampling

Democratic politicians were astonished in 2010 when their early polls of sample voters showed Republican Scott Brown was favored by a majority of voters and so would win the special election to fill the Senate seat that the late Democrat Teddy Kennedy had occupied for over 40 years. Based on their poll results, they mounted an intense, but ultimately unsuccessful, effort to save the seat for their party.

20.4.1   A Voter Poll

Suppose at some time before the election that p was the fraction of voters favoring Scott Brown. We want to estimate this unknown fraction p. Suppose we have some random process for selecting voters from registration lists that selects each voter with equal probability. We can define an indicator variable K by the rule that $K = 1$ if the random voter most prefers Brown, and $K = 0$ otherwise.

Now to estimate p, we take a large number n of random choices of voters[3] and count the fraction who favor Brown. That is, we define variables $K_1, K_2, \ldots$, where K_i is interpreted to be the indicator variable for the event that the ith chosen voter prefers Brown. Since our choices are made independently, the K_i's are independent. So formally, we model our estimation process by assuming we have mutually independent indicator variables $K_1, K_2, \ldots$, each with the same probability p of being equal to 1. Now let S_n be their sum, that is,

$$S_n ::= \sum_{i=1}^{n} K_i. \tag{20.17}$$

The variable S_n/n describes the fraction of sampled voters who favor Scott Brown. Most people intuitively, and correctly, expect this sample fraction to give a useful approximation to the unknown fraction p.

So we will use the sample value S_n/n as our *statistical estimate* of p. We know that S_n has a binomial distribution with parameters n and p; we can choose n, but

---

[3] We're choosing a random voter n times *with replacement*. We don't remove a chosen voter from the set of voters eligible to be chosen later; so we might choose the same voter more than once! We would get a slightly better estimate if we required n *different* people to be chosen, but doing so complicates both the selection process and its analysis for little gain.

p is unknown.

How Large a Sample?

Suppose we want our estimate to be within 0.04 of the fraction p at least 95% of the time. This means we want

$$\Pr\left[\left|\frac{S_n}{n} - p\right| \le 0.04\right] \ge 0.95. \tag{20.18}$$

So we'd better determine the number n of times we must poll voters so that inequality (20.18) will hold. Chebyshev's Theorem offers a simple way to determine such a n.

S_n is binomially distributed. Equation (20.15), combined with the fact that $p(1-p)$ is maximized when $p = 1 - p$, that is, when $p = 1/2$ (check for yourself!), gives

$$\text{Var}[S_n] = n(p(1-p)) \le n \cdot \frac{1}{4} = \frac{n}{4}. \tag{20.19}$$

Next, we bound the variance of S_n/n:

$$\text{Var}\left[\frac{S_n}{n}\right] = \left(\frac{1}{n}\right)^2 \text{Var}[S_n] \quad \text{(Square Multiple Rule for Variance (20.9))}$$

$$\le \left(\frac{1}{n}\right)^2 \frac{n}{4} \quad \text{(by (20.19))}$$

$$= \frac{1}{4n} \tag{20.20}$$

Using Chebyshev's bound and (20.20) we have:

$$\Pr\left[\left|\frac{S_n}{n} - p\right| \ge 0.04\right] \le \frac{\text{Var}[S_n/n]}{(0.04)^2} \le \frac{1}{4n(0.04)^2} = \frac{156.25}{n} \tag{20.21}$$

To make our our estimate with 95% confidence, we want the right-hand side of (20.21) to be at most 1/20. So we choose n so that

$$\frac{156.25}{n} \le \frac{1}{20},$$

that is,

$$n \ge 3,125.$$

Section 20.6.2 describes how to get tighter estimates of the tails of binomial distributions that lead to a bound on n that is about four times smaller than the one above. But working through this example using only the variance illustrates an approach to estimation that is applicable to arbitrary random variables, not just binomial variables.

20.4.2   Pairwise Independent Sampling

The reasoning we used above to analyze voter polling and matching birthdays is very similar. We summarize it in slightly more general form with a basic result called the Pairwise Independent Sampling Theorem. In particular, we do not need to restrict ourselves to sums of zero-one valued variables, or to variables with the same distribution. For simplicity, we state the Theorem for pairwise independent variables with possibly different distributions but with the same mean and variance.

Theorem 20.4.1 (Pairwise Independent Sampling). *Let $G_1, \ldots, G_n$ be pairwise independent variables with the same mean μ and deviation σ. Define*

$$S_n ::= \sum_{i=1}^{n} G_i. \tag{20.22}$$

Then

$$\Pr\left[\left| \frac{S_n}{n} - \mu \right| \geq x \right] \leq \frac{1}{n} \left(\frac{\sigma}{x} \right)^2.$$

Proof. We observe first that the expectation of S_n/n is μ:

$$\mathrm{Ex}\left[\frac{S_n}{n} \right] = \mathrm{Ex}\left[\frac{\sum_{i=1}^{n} G_i}{n} \right] \qquad \text{(def of } S_n\text{)}$$

$$= \frac{\sum_{i=1}^{n} \mathrm{Ex}[G_i]}{n} \qquad \text{(linearity of expectation)}$$

$$= \frac{\sum_{i=1}^{n} \mu}{n}$$

$$= \frac{n\mu}{n} = \mu.$$

The second important property of S_n/n is that its variance is the variance of G_i divided by n:

$$\mathrm{Var}\left[\frac{S_n}{n} \right] = \left(\frac{1}{n} \right)^2 \mathrm{Var}[S_n] \qquad \text{(Square Multiple Rule for Variance (20.9))}$$

$$= \frac{1}{n^2} \mathrm{Var}\left[\sum_{i=1}^{n} G_i \right] \qquad \text{(def of } S_n\text{)}$$

$$= \frac{1}{n^2} \sum_{i=1}^{n} \mathrm{Var}[G_i] \qquad \text{(pairwise independent additivity)}$$

$$= \frac{1}{n^2} \cdot n\sigma^2 = \frac{\sigma^2}{n}. \tag{20.23}$$

This is enough to apply Chebyshev's Theorem and conclude:

$$\Pr\left[\left|\frac{S_n}{n} - \mu\right| \geq x\right] \leq \frac{\text{Var}\left[S_n/n\right]}{x^2}. \qquad \text{(Chebyshev's bound)}$$

$$= \frac{\sigma^2/n}{x^2} \qquad \text{(by (20.23))}$$

$$= \frac{1}{n}\left(\frac{\sigma}{x}\right)^2.$$

∎

The Pairwise Independent Sampling Theorem provides a quantitative general statement about how the average of independent samples of a random variable approaches the mean. In particular, it proves what is known as the Law of Large Numbers:[4] by choosing a large enough sample size, we can get arbitrarily accurate estimates of the mean with confidence arbitrarily close to 100%.

Corollary 20.4.2. *[Weak Law of Large Numbers] Let $G_1, \ldots, G_n$ be pairwise independent variables with the same mean μ, and the same finite deviation, and let*

$$S_n ::= \frac{\sum_{i=1}^n G_i}{n}.$$

Then for every $\epsilon > 0$,

$$\lim_{n \to \infty} \Pr[|S_n - \mu| \leq \epsilon] = 1.$$

20.5 Confidence in an Estimation

So Chebyshev's Bound implies that sampling 3,125 voters will yield a fraction that, 95% of the time, is within 0.04 of the actual fraction of the voting population who prefer Brown.

Notice that the actual size of the voting population was never considered because *it did not matter*. People who have not studied probability theory often insist that the population size should influence the sample size. But our analysis shows that polling a little over 3000 people people is always sufficient, regardless of whether there are ten thousand, or a million, or a billion voters. You should think about an intuitive explanation that might persuade someone who thinks population size matters.

---

[4]This is the *Weak* Law of Large Numbers. As you might suppose, there is also a Strong Law, but it's outside the scope of 6.042.

Now suppose a pollster actually takes a sample of 3,125 random voters to estimate the fraction of voters who prefer Brown, and the pollster finds that 1250 of them prefer Brown. It's tempting, **but sloppy**, to say that this means:

False Claim. *With probability 0.95, the fraction p of voters who prefer Brown is* $1250/3125 \pm 0.04$. *Since* $1250/3125 - 0.04 > 1/3$, *there is a 95% chance that more than a third of the voters prefer Brown to all other candidates.*

As already discussed in Section 18.9, what's objectionable about this statement is that it talks about the probability or "chance" that a real world fact is true, namely that the actual fraction p of voters favoring Brown is more than 1/3. But p is what it is, and it simply makes no sense to talk about the probability that it is something else. For example, suppose p is actually 0.3; then it's nonsense to ask about the probability that it is within 0.04 of 1250/3125. It simply isn't.

This example of voter preference is typical: we want to estimate a fixed, unknown real-world quantity. But *being unknown does not make this quantity a random variable*, so it makes no sense to talk about the probability that it has some property.

A more careful summary of what we have accomplished goes this way:

> We have described a probabilistic procedure for estimating the value of the actual fraction p. The probability that *our estimation procedure* will yield a value within 0.04 of p is 0.95.

This is a bit of a mouthful, so special phrasing closer to the sloppy language is commonly used. The pollster would describe his conclusion by saying that

> At the 95% *confidence level*, the fraction of voters who prefer Brown is $1250/3125 \pm 0.04$.

So confidence levels refer to the results of estimation procedures for real-world quantities. The phrase "confidence level" should be heard as a reminder that some statistical procedure was used to obtain an estimate. To judge the credibility of the estimate, it may be important to examine how well this procedure was performed. More important, the confidence assertion above can be rephrased as

> **Either** the fraction of voters who prefer Brown is $1250/3125 \pm 0.04$
> **or** something unlikely (probability 1/20) happened.

If our experience led us to judge that having the preference fraction actually be in this particular interval was unlikely, then this level of confidence would justifiably remain unconvincing.

20.6 Sums of Random Variables

If all you know about a random variable is its mean and variance, then Chebyshev's Theorem is the best you can do when it comes to bounding the probability that the random variable deviates from its mean. In some cases, however, we know more—for example, that the random variable has a binomial distribution—and then it is possible to prove much stronger bounds. Instead of polynomially small bounds such as $1/c^2$, we can sometimes even obtain exponentially small bounds such as $1/e^c$. As we will soon discover, this is the case whenever the random variable T is the sum of n mutually independent random variables $T_1, T_2, \ldots, T_n$ where $0 \leq T_i \leq 1$. A random variable with a binomial distribution is just one of many examples of such a T.

20.6.1 A Motivating Example

Fussbook is a new social networking site oriented toward unpleasant people. Like all major web services, Fussbook has a load balancing problem: it receives lots of forum posts that computer servers have to process. If any server is assigned more work than it can complete in a given interval, then it is overloaded and system performance suffers. That would be bad, because Fussbook users are *not* a tolerant bunch. So balancing the work load across mutliple servers is vital.

An early idea was to assign each server an alphabetic range of forum topics. ("That oughta work!", one programmer said.) But after the computer handling the "*p*rivacy" and "*p*referred text editor" threads melted from overload, the drawback of an *ad hoc* approach was clear: it's easy to miss something that will mess up your plan.

If the length of every task were known in advance, then finding a balanced distribution would be a kind of "bin packing" problem. Such problems are hard to solve exactly, but approximation algorithms can come close. Unfortunately, in this case task lengths are not known in advance, which is typical of workload problems in the real world.

So the load balancing problem seems sort of hopeless, because there is no data available to guide decisions. So the programmers of Fussbook gave up and just randomly assigned posts to computers. Imagine their surprise when the system stayed up and hasn't crashed yet!

As it turns out, random assignment not only balances load reasonably well, but also permits provable performance guarantees. In general, a randomized approach to a problem is worth considering when a deterministic solution is hard to compute or requires unavailable information.

Specifically, Fussbook receives 24,000 forum posts in every 10-minute interval. Each post is assigned to one of several servers for processing, and each server works sequentially through its assigned tasks. It takes a server an average of 1/4 second to process a post. Some posts, such as pointless grammar critiques and snide witticisms, are easier, but no post—not even the most protracted harangues—takes more than one full second.

Measuring workload in seconds, this means a server is overloaded when it is assigned more than 600 units of work in a given 600 second interval. Fussbook's average processing load of $24{,}000 \cdot 1/4 = 6000$ seconds per interval would keep 10 computers running at 100% capacity with perfect load balancing. Surely, more than 10 servers are needed to cope with random fluctuations in task length and imperfect load balance. But would 11 be enough? ... or 15, 20, 100? We'll answer that question with a new mathematical tool.

20.6.2   The Chernoff Bound

The Chernoff[5] bound is a hammer that you can use to nail a great many problems. Roughly, the Chernoff bound says that certain random variables are very unlikely to significantly exceed their expectation. For example, if the expected load on a processor is just a bit below its capacity, then that processor is unlikely to be overloaded, provided the conditions of the Chernoff bound are satisfied.

More precisely, the Chernoff Bound says that *the sum of lots of little, independent, random variables is unlikely to significantly exceed the mean of the sum.* The Markov and Chebyshev bounds lead to the same kind of conclusion but typically provide much weaker bounds. In particular, the Markov and Chebyshev bounds are polynomial, while the Chernoff bound is exponential.

Here is the theorem. The proof will come later in Section 20.6.6.

Theorem 20.6.1 (Chernoff Bound). *Let $T_1, \ldots T_n$ be mutually independent random variables such that $0 \leq T_i \leq 1$ for all i. Let $T = T_1 + \cdots + T_n$. Then for all $c \geq 1$,*

$$\Pr[T \geq c\,\mathrm{Ex}[T]] \leq e^{-\beta(c)\,\mathrm{Ex}[T]} \qquad (20.24)$$

where $\beta(c) ::= c \ln c - c + 1$.

The Chernoff bound applies only to distributions of sums of independent random variables that take on values in the real interval $[0, 1]$. The binomial distribution is the most well-known distribution that fits these criteria, but many others are possible, because the Chernoff bound allows the variables in the sum to have differing,

---

[5]Yes, this is the same Chernoff who figured out how to beat the state lottery—this guy knows a thing or two.

arbitrary, or even unknown distributions over the range [0, 1]. Furthermore, there is no direct dependence on either the number of random variables in the sum or their expectations. In short, the Chernoff bound gives strong results for lots of problems based on little information—no wonder it is widely used!

20.6.3 Chernoff Bound for Binomial Tails

The Chernoff bound can be applied in easy steps, though the details can be daunting at first. Let's walk through a simple example to get the hang of it: bounding the probability that the number of heads that come up in 1000 independent tosses of a coin exceeds the expectation by 20% or more. Let T_i be an indicator variable for the event that the ith coin is heads. Then the total number of heads is

$$T = T_1 + \cdots + T_{1000}.$$

The Chernoff bound requires that the random variables T_i be mutually independent and take on values in the range [0, 1]. Both conditions hold here. In this example the T_i's only take the two values 0 and 1, since they're indicators.

The goal is to bound the probability that the number of heads exceeds its expectation by 20% or more; that is, to bound $\Pr[T \geq c \operatorname{Ex}[T]]$ where c = 1.2. To that end, we compute $\beta(c)$ as defined in the theorem:

$$\beta(c) = c \ln(c) - c + 1 = 0.0187 \ldots.$$

If we assume the coin is fair, then $\operatorname{Ex}[T] = 500$. Plugging these values into the Chernoff bound gives:

$$\Pr\left[T \geq 1.2 \operatorname{Ex}[T]\right] \leq e^{-\beta(c) \cdot \operatorname{Ex}[T]}$$
$$= e^{-(0.0187\ldots) \cdot 500} < 0.0000834.$$

So the probability of getting 20% or more extra heads on 1000 coins is less than 1 in 10,000.

The bound rapidly becomes much smaller as the number of coins increases, because the expected number of heads appears in the exponent of the upper bound. For example, the probability of getting at least 20% extra heads on a million coins is at most

$$e^{-(0.0187\ldots) \cdot 500000} < e^{-9392},$$

which is an inconceivably small number.

Alternatively, the bound also becomes stronger for larger deviations. For example, suppose we're interested in the odds of getting 30% or more extra heads in 1000 tosses, rather than 20%. In that case, $c = 1.3$ instead of 1.2. Consequently, the parameter $\beta(c)$ rises from 0.0187 to about 0.0410, which may not seem significant, but because $\beta(c)$ appears in the exponent of the upper bound, the final probability decreases from around 1 in 10,000 to about 1 in a billion!

20.6.4   Chernoff Bound for a Lottery Game

Pick-4 is a lottery game in which you pay $1 to pick a 4-digit number between 0000 and 9999. If your number comes up in a random drawing, then you win $5,000. Your chance of winning is 1 in 10,000. If 10 million people play, then the expected number of winners is 1000. When there are exactly 1000 winners, the lottery keeps $5 million of the $10 million paid for tickets. The lottery operator's nightmare is that the number of winners is much greater—especially at the point where more than 2000 win and the lottery must pay out more than it received. What is the probability that will happen?

Let T_i be an indicator for the event that the ith player wins. Then $T = T_1 + \cdots + T_n$ is the total number of winners. If we assume[6] that the players' picks and the winning number are random, independent and uniform, then the indicators T_i are independent, as required by the Chernoff bound.

Since 2000 winners would be twice the expected number, we choose $c = 2$, compute $\beta(c) = 0.386\ldots$, and plug these values into the Chernoff bound:

$$\begin{aligned}
\Pr[T \geq 2000] &= \Pr\left[T \geq 2\,\mathrm{Ex}[T]\right] \\
&\leq e^{-k\,\mathrm{Ex}[T]} = e^{-(0.386\ldots)\cdot 1000} \\
&< e^{-386}.
\end{aligned}$$

So there is almost no chance that the lottery operator pays out more than it took in. In fact, the number of winners won't even be 10% higher than expected very often. To prove that, let $c = 1.1$, compute $\beta(c) = 0.00484\ldots$, and plug in again:

$$\begin{aligned}
\Pr\left[T \geq 1.1\,\mathrm{Ex}[T]\right] &\leq e^{-k\,\mathrm{Ex}[T]} \\
&= e^{-(0.00484)\cdot 1000} < 0.01.
\end{aligned}$$

So the Pick-4 lottery may be exciting for the players, but the lottery operator has little doubt as to the outcome!

---

[6]As we noted in Chapter 19, human choices are often not uniform and they can be highly dependent. For example, lots of people will pick an important date. The lottery folks should not get too much comfort from the analysis that follows, unless they assign random 4-digit numbers to each player.

20.6.5   Randomized Load Balancing

Now let's return to Fussbook and its load balancing problem. Specifically, we need to determine a number m of servers that makes it very unlikely that any server is overloaded by being assigned more than 600 seconds of work in a given interval.

To begin, let's find the probability that the first server is overloaded. Letting T be the number of seconds of work assigned to the first server, this means we want an upper bound on $\Pr[T \geq 600]$. Let T_i be the number of seconds that the first server spends on the ith task: then T_i is zero if the task is assigned to another machine, and otherwise T_i is the length of the task. So $T = \sum_{i=1}^{n} T_i$ is the total number of seconds of work assigned to the first server, where $n = 24,000$.

The Chernoff bound is applicable only if the T_i are mutually independent and take on values in the range $[0, 1]$. The first condition is satisfied if we assume that assignment of a post to a server is independent of the time required to process the post. The second condition is satisfied because we know that no post takes more than 1 second to process; this is why we chose to measure work in seconds.

In all, there are 24,000 tasks, each with an expected length of 1/4 second. Since tasks are assigned to the m servers at random, the expected load on the first server is:

$$\text{Ex}[T] = \frac{24{,}000 \text{ tasks} \cdot 1/4 \text{ second per task}}{m \text{ servers}}$$
$$= 6000/m \text{ seconds.} \tag{20.25}$$

So if there are fewer than 10 servers, then the expected load on the first server is greater than its capacity, and we can expect it to be overloaded. If there are exactly 10 servers, then the server is expected to run for $6000/10 = 600$ seconds, which is 100% of its capacity.

Now we can use the Chernoff bound based on the number of servers to bound the probability that the first server is overloaded. We have from (20.25)

$$600 = c \, \text{Ex}[T] \qquad \text{where } c ::= m/10,$$

so by the Chernoff bound

$$\Pr[T \geq 600] = \Pr[T \geq c \, \text{Ex}[T]] \leq e^{-(c \ln(c) - c + 1) \cdot 6000/m},$$

The probability that *some* server is overloaded is at most m times the probability that the first server is overloaded, by the Union Bound in Section 17.5.2. So

$$\Pr[\text{some server is overloaded}] \le \sum_{i=1}^{m} \Pr[\text{server } i \text{ is overloaded}]$$

$$= m \Pr[\text{the first server is overloaded}]$$

$$\le m e^{-(c \ln(c) - c + 1) \cdot 6000/m},$$

where $c = m/10$. Some values of this upper bound are tabulated below:

$$m = 11 : 0.784\ldots$$
$$m = 12 : 0.000999\ldots$$
$$m = 13 : 0.0000000760\ldots$$

These values suggest that a system with $m = 11$ machines might suffer immediate overload, $m = 12$ machines could fail in a few days, but $m = 13$ should be fine for a century or two!

20.6.6   Proof of the Chernoff Bound

The proof of the Chernoff bound is somewhat involved. In fact, *Chernoff himself couldn't come up with it:* his friend, Herman Rubin, showed him the argument. Thinking the bound not very significant, Chernoff did not credit Rubin in print. He felt pretty bad when it became famous![7]

Proof. (of Theorem 20.6.1)

For clarity, we'll go through the proof "top down." That is, we'll use facts that are proved immediately afterward.

The key step is to exponentiate both sides of the inequality $T \ge c \operatorname{Ex}[T]$ and then apply the Markov bound:

$$\Pr[T \ge c \operatorname{Ex}[T]] = \Pr[c^T \ge c^{c \operatorname{Ex}[T]}]$$

$$\le \frac{\operatorname{Ex}[c^T]}{c^{c \operatorname{Ex}[T]}} \qquad\qquad \text{(Markov Bound)}$$

$$\le \frac{e^{(c-1)\operatorname{Ex}[T]}}{c^{c \operatorname{Ex}[T]}} \qquad\qquad \text{(Lemma 20.6.2 below)}$$

$$= \frac{e^{(c-1)\operatorname{Ex}[T]}}{e^{c \ln(c) \operatorname{Ex}[T]}} = e^{-(c \ln(c) - c + 1) \operatorname{Ex}[T]}.$$

∎

---

[7]See "A Conversation with Herman Chernoff," *Statistical Science* 1996, Vol. 11, No. 4, pp 335–350.

Algebra aside, there is a brilliant idea in this proof: in this context, exponentiating somehow supercharges the Markov bound. This is not true in general! One unfortunate side-effect of this supercharging is that we have to bound some nasty expectations involving exponentials in order to complete the proof. This is done in the two lemmas below, where variables take on values as in Theorem 20.6.1.

Lemma 20.6.2.

$$\mathrm{Ex}\left[c^T\right] \le e^{(c-1)\,\mathrm{Ex}[T]}.$$

Proof.

$$
\begin{aligned}
\mathrm{Ex}\left[c^T\right] &= \mathrm{Ex}\left[c^{T_1+\cdots+T_n}\right] && \text{(def of } T) \\
&= \mathrm{Ex}\left[c^{T_1}\cdots c^{T_n}\right] \\
&= \mathrm{Ex}\left[c^{T_1}\right]\cdots\mathrm{Ex}[c^{T_n}] && \text{(independent product Cor 19.5.7)} \\
&\le e^{(c-1)\,\mathrm{Ex}[T_1]}\cdots e^{(c-1)\,\mathrm{Ex}[T_n]} && \text{(Lemma 20.6.3 below)} \\
&= e^{(c-1)(\mathrm{Ex}[T_1]+\cdots+\mathrm{Ex}[T_n])} \\
&= e^{(c-1)\,\mathrm{Ex}[T_1+\cdots+T_n]} && \text{(linearity of Ex}[\cdot]) \\
&= e^{(c-1)\,\mathrm{Ex}[T]}.
\end{aligned}
$$

The third equality depends on the fact that functions of independent variables are also independent (see Lemma 19.2.2). ∎

Lemma 20.6.3.

$$\mathrm{Ex}[c^{T_i}] \le e^{(c-1)\,\mathrm{Ex}[T_i]}$$

Proof. All summations below range over values v taken by the random variable T_i, which are all required to be in the interval $[0, 1]$.

$$
\begin{aligned}
\mathrm{Ex}[c^{T_i}] &= \sum c^v \Pr[T_i = v] && \text{(def of Ex}[\cdot]) \\
&\le \sum (1 + (c-1)v)\Pr[T_i = v] && \text{(convexity—see below)} \\
&= \sum \Pr[T_i = v] + (c-1)v\Pr[T_i = v] \\
&= \sum \Pr[T_i = v] + (c-1)\sum v\Pr[T_i = v] \\
&= 1 + (c-1)\,\mathrm{Ex}[T_i] \\
&\le e^{(c-1)\,\mathrm{Ex}[T_i]} && \text{(since } 1 + z \le e^z).
\end{aligned}
$$

The second step relies on the inequality

$$c^v \leq 1 + (c-1)v,$$

which holds for all v in $[0, 1]$ and $c \geq 1$. This follows from the general principle that a convex function, namely c^v, is less than the linear function $1 + (c-1)v$ between their points of intersection, namely $v = 0$ and 1. This inequality is why the variables T_i are restricted to the real interval $[0, 1]$. ∎

20.6.7   Comparing the Bounds

Suppose that we have a collection of mutually independent events $A_1, A_2, \ldots, A_n$, and we want to know how many of the events are likely to occur.

Let T_i be the indicator random variable for A_i and define

$$p_i = \Pr[T_i = 1] = \Pr\left[A_i\right]$$

for $1 \leq i \leq n$. Define

$$T = T_1 + T_2 + \cdots + T_n$$

to be the number of events that occur.

We know from Linearity of Expectation that

$$\mathrm{Ex}[T] = \mathrm{Ex}[T_1] + \mathrm{Ex}[T_2] + \cdots + \mathrm{Ex}[T_n]$$
$$= \sum_{i=1}^{n} p_i.$$

This is true even if the events are *not* independent.

By Theorem 20.3.8, we also know that

$$\mathrm{Var}[T] = \mathrm{Var}[T_1] + \mathrm{Var}[T_2] + \cdots + \mathrm{Var}[T_n]$$
$$= \sum_{i=1}^{n} p_i(1 - p_i),$$

and thus that

$$\sigma_T = \sqrt{\sum_{i=1}^{n} p_i(1 - p_i)}.$$

This is true even if the events are only pairwise independent.

Markov's Theorem tells us that for any $c > 1$,

$$\Pr[T \geq c\,\mathrm{Ex}[T]] \leq \frac{1}{c}.$$

Chebyshev's Theorem gives us the stronger result that

$$\Pr[|T - \mathrm{Ex}[T]| \geq c\sigma_T] \leq \frac{1}{c^2}.$$

The Chernoff Bound gives us an even stronger result, namely, that for any $c > 0$,

$$\Pr[T - \mathrm{Ex}[T] \geq c\,\mathrm{Ex}[T]] \leq e^{-(c\ln(c)-c+1)\mathrm{Ex}[T]}.$$

In this case, the probability of exceeding the mean by $c\,\mathrm{Ex}[T]$ decreases as an exponentially small function of the deviation.

By considering the random variable $n - T$, we can also use the Chernoff Bound to prove that the probability that T is much *lower* than $\mathrm{Ex}[T]$ is also exponentially small.

20.6.8 Murphy's Law

If the expectation of a random variable is much less than 1, then Markov's Theorem implies that there is only a small probability that the variable has a value of 1 or more. On the other hand, a result that we call *Murphy's Law*[8] says that if a random variable is an independent sum of 0–1-valued variables and has a large expectation, then there is a huge probability of getting a value of at least 1.

Theorem 20.6.4 (Murphy's Law). *Let A_1, A_2, ..., A_n be mutually independent events. Let T_i be the indicator random variable for A_i and define*

$$T ::= T_1 + T_2 + \cdots + T_n$$

to be the number of events that occur. Then

$$\Pr[T = 0] \leq e^{-\mathrm{Ex}[T]}.$$

---

[8]This is in reference and deference to the famous saying that "If something can go wrong, it probably will."

Proof.

$$\Pr[T = 0] = \Pr[\overline{A}_1 \cap \overline{A}_2 \cap \ldots \cap \overline{A}_n] \qquad (T = 0 \text{ iff no } A_i \text{ occurs})$$

$$= \prod_{i=1}^{n} \Pr[\overline{A}_i] \qquad (\text{independence of } A_i)$$

$$= \prod_{i=1}^{n} (1 - \Pr[A_i])$$

$$\leq \prod_{i=1}^{n} e^{-\Pr[A_i]} \qquad (\text{since } 1 - x \leq e^{-x})$$

$$= e^{-\sum_{i=1}^{n} \Pr[A_i]}$$

$$= e^{-\sum_{i=1}^{n} \text{Ex}[T_i]} \qquad (\text{since } T_i \text{ is an indicator for } A_i)$$

$$= e^{-\text{Ex}[T]} \qquad (\text{linearity of expectation}) \qquad \blacksquare$$

For example, given any set of mutually independent events, if you expect 10 of them to happen, then at least one of them will happen with probability at least $1 - e^{-10}$. The probability that none of them happen is at most $e^{-10} < 1/22000$.

So if there are a lot of independent things that can go wrong and their probabilities sum to a number much greater than 1, then Theorem 20.6.4 proves that some of them surely will go wrong.

This result can help to explain "coincidences," "miracles," and crazy events that seem to have been very unlikely to happen. Such events do happen, in part, because there are so many possible unlikely events that the sum of their probabilities is greater than one. For example, someone *does* win the lottery.

In fact, if there are 100,000 random tickets in Pick-4, Theorem 20.6.4 says that the probability that there is no winner is less than $e^{-10} < 1/22000$. More generally, there are literally millions of one-in-a-million possible events and so some of them will surely occur.

20.7   Really Great Expectations

Making independent tosses of a fair coin until some desired pattern comes up is a simple process you should feel solidly in command of by now, right? So how about a bet about the simplest such process—tossing until a head comes up? Ok, you're wary of betting with us, but how about this: we'll let *you set the odds*.

20.7.1 Repeating Yourself

Here's the bet: you make independent tosses of a fair coin until a head comes up. Then you will repeat the process. If a second head comes up in the same or fewer tosses than the first, you have to start over yet again. You keep starting over until you finally toss a run of tails longer than your first one. The payment rules are that you will pay me 1 cent each time you start over. When you win by finally getting a run of tails longer than your first one, I will pay you some generous amount. Notice by the way that you're certain to win—whatever your initial run of tails happened to be, a longer run will eventually occur again with probability 1!

For example, if your first tosses are TTTH, then you will keep tossing until you get a run of 4 tails. So your winning flips might be

TTTHTHTTHHTTHTHTTTHTHHHTTTT.

In this run there are 10 heads, which means you had to start over 9 times. So you would have paid me 9 cents by the time you finally won by tossing 4 tails. Now you've won, and I'll pay you generously —how does 25 cents sound? Maybe you'd rather have \$1? How about \$1000?

Of course there's a trap here. Let's calculate your expected winnings.

Suppose your initial run of tails had length k. After that, each time a head comes up, you have to start over and try to get $k+1$ tails in a row. If we regard your getting $k+1$ tails in a row as a "failed" try, and regard your having to start over because a head came up too soon as a "successful" try, then the number of times you have to start over is the number of tries till the first failure. So the expected number of tries will be the mean time to failure, which is 2^{k+1}, because the probability of tossing $k+1$ tails in a row is $2^{-(k+1)}$.

Let T be the length of your initial run of tails. So $T = k$ means that your initial tosses were T^kH. Let R be the number of times you repeat trying to beat your original run of tails. The number of cents you expect to finish with is the number of cents in my generous payment minus $\text{Ex}[R]$. It's now easy to calculate $\text{Ex}[R]$ by conditioning on the value of T:

$$\text{Ex}[R] = \sum_{k \in \mathbb{N}} \text{Ex}[R \mid T = k] \cdot \text{Pr}[T = k] = \sum_{k \in \mathbb{N}} 2^{k+1} \cdot 2^{-(k+1)} = \sum_{k \in \mathbb{N}} 1 = \infty.$$

So you can expect to pay me an infinite number of cents before winning my "generous" payment. No amount of generosity can make this bet fair! In fact this particular example is a special case of an astonishingly general one: the expected waiting time for *any* random variable to achieve a larger value is infinite.

Problems for Section 20.1

Practice Problems

Problem 20.1.

The vast majority of people have an above average number of fingers. Which of the following statements explain why this is true? Explain your reasoning.

1. Most people have a super secret extra bonus finger of which they are unaware.

2. A pedantic minority don't count their thumbs as fingers, while the majority of people do.

3. Polydactyly is rarer than amputation.

4. When you add up the total number of fingers among the world's population and then divide by the size of the population, you get a number less than ten.

5. This follows from Markov's Theorem, since no one has a negative number of fingers.

6. Missing fingers are more common than extra ones.

Class Problems

Problem 20.2.

A herd of cows is stricken by an outbreak of *cold cow disease*. The disease lowers a cow's body temperature from normal levels, and a cow will die if its temperature goes below 90 degrees F. The disease epidemic is so intense that it lowered the average temperature of the herd to 85 degrees. Body temperatures as low as 70 degrees, **but no lower**, were actually found in the herd.

(a) Use Markov's Bound 20.1.1 to prove that at most 3/4 of the cows could survive.

(b) Suppose there are 400 cows in the herd. Show that the bound from part (a) is the best possible by giving an example set of temperatures for the cows so that the average herd temperature is 85 and 3/4 of the cows will have a high enough temperature to survive.

(c) Notice that the results of part (b) are purely arithmetic facts about averages, not about probabilities. But you verified the claim in part (a) by applying Markov's bound on the deviation of a random variable. Justify this approach by regarding the temperature T of a cow as a random variable. Carefully specify the probability space on which T is defined: what are the sample points? what are their probabilities? Explain the precise connection between properties of T and average herd temperature that justifies the application of Markov's Bound.

Homework Problems

Problem 20.3.
If R is a nonnegative random variable, then Markov's Theorem gives an upper bound on $\Pr[R \geq x]$ for any real number $x > \mathrm{Ex}[R]$. If b is a lower bound on R, then Markov's Theorem can also be applied to $R - b$ to obtain a possibly different bound on $\Pr[R \geq x]$.

(a) Show that if $b > 0$, applying Markov's Theorem to $R - b$ gives a smaller upper bound on $\Pr[R \geq x]$ than simply applying Markov's Theorem directly to R.

(b) What value of $b \geq 0$ in part (a) gives the best bound?

Exam Problems

Problem 20.4.
A herd of cows is stricken by an outbreak of *hot cow disease*. The disease raises the normal body temperature of a cow, and a cow will die if its temperature goes above 90 degrees. The disease epidemic is so intense that it raised the average temperature of the herd to 120 degrees. Body temperatures as high as 140 degrees, **but no higher**, were actually found in the herd.

(a) Use Markov's Bound 20.1.1 to prove that at most 2/5 of the cows could have survived.

(b) Notice that the conclusion of part (a) is a purely arithmetic facts about averages, not about probabilities. But you verified the claim of part (a) by applying Markov's bound on the deviation of a random variable. Justify this approach by explaining how to define a random variable T for the temperature of a cow. Carefully specify the probability space on which T is defined: what are the outcomes? what are their probabilities? Explain the precise connection between properties of T, average herd temperature, and fractions of the herd with various temperatures, that justify application of Markov's Bound.

Problems for Section 20.2

Exam Problems

Problem 20.5.

There is a herd of cows whose average body temperature turns out to be 100 degrees. Our thermometer produces such sensitive readings that no two cows have exactly the same body temperature. The herd is stricken by an outbreak of *wacky cow disease*, which will eventually kill any cow whose body temperature differs from the average by 10 degrees or more.

It turns out that the *collection-variance* of all the body temperatures is 20, where the *collection-variance* $CVar(A)$ of set A of numbers is

$$CVar(A) ::= \frac{\sum_{a \in A}(a - \mu)^2}{|A|},$$

where μ is the average value of the numbers in A. (In other words, $CVar(A)$ is A's average square deviation from its mean.)

(a) Apply the Chebyshev bound to the temperature T of a random cow to show that at most 20% of the cows will be killed by this disease outbreak.

The conclusion of part (a) about a certain fraction of the herd was derived by bounding the deviation of a random variable. We can justify this approach by explaining how to define a suitable probability space in which, the temperature T of a cow is a random variable.

(b) Carefully specify the probability space on which T is defined: what are the outcomes? what are their probabilities?

(c) Explain why for this probability space, the fraction of cows with any given cow property P is the same as $Pr[P]$.

(d) Show that $Ex[T]$ equals the average temperature of the herd.

(e) Show that $Var[T]$ equals the collection variance of the herd.

Problems for Section 20.3

Practice Problems

Problem 20.6.
Suppose 120 students take a final exam and the mean of their scores is 90. You have no other information about the students and the exam, that is, you should not assume that the highest possible score is 100. You may, however, assume that exam scores are nonnegative.

(a) State the best possible upper bound on the number of students who scored at least 180.

(b) Now suppose somebody tells you that the lowest score on the exam is 30. Compute the new best possible upper bound on the number of students who scored at least 180.

Problem 20.7.
Suppose you flip a fair coin 100 times. The coin flips are all mutually independent.

(a) What is the expected number of heads?

(b) What upper bound does Markov's Theorem give for the probability that the number of heads is at least 70?

(c) What is the variance of the number of heads?

(d) What upper bound does Chebyshev's Theorem give for the probability that the number of heads is either less than 30 or greater than 70?

Problem 20.8.
Albert has a gambling problem. He plays 240 hands of draw poker, 120 hands of black jack, and 40 hands of stud poker per day. He wins a hand of draw poker with

probability 1/6, a hand of black jack with probability 1/2, and a hand of stud poker with probability 1/5. Let W be the expected number of hands that Albert wins in a day.

(a) What is $\text{Ex}[W]$?

(b) What would the Markov bound be on the probability that Albert will win at least 216 hands on a given day?

(c) Assume the outcomes of the card games are pairwise independent. What is $\text{Var}[W]$? You may answer with a numerical expression that is not completely evaluated.

(d) What would the Chebyshev bound be on the probability that Albert will win at least 216 hands on a given day? You may answer with a numerical expression that includes the constant $v = \text{Var}[W]$.

Class Problems

Problem 20.9.
The hat-check staff has had a long day serving at a party, and at the end of the party they simply return the n checked hats in a random way such that the probability that any particular person gets their own hat back is $1/n$.

Let X_i be the indicator variable for the ith person getting their own hat back. Let S_n be the total number of people who get their own hat back.

(a) What is the expected number of people who get their own hat back?

(b) Write a simple formula for $\text{Ex}[X_i \cdot X_j]$ for $i \neq j$.
Hint: What is $\Pr[X_j = 1 \mid X_i = 1]$?

(c) Explain why you cannot use the variance of sums formula to calculate $\text{Var}[S_n]$.

(d) Show that $\text{Ex}[(S_n)^2] = 2$. *Hint:* $(X_i)^2 = X_i$.

(e) What is the variance of S_n?

(f) Show that there is at most a 1% chance that more than 10 people get their own hat back.

Problem 20.10.

For any random variable R with mean μ and standard deviation σ the Chebyshev bound says that for any real number $x > 0$,

$$\Pr[|R - \mu| \geq x] \leq \left(\frac{\sigma}{x}\right)^2.$$

Show that for any real number μ and real numbers $x \geq \sigma > 0$, there is an R for which the Chebyshev bound is tight, that is,

$$\Pr[|R - \mu| \geq x] = \left(\frac{\sigma}{x}\right)^2. \tag{20.26}$$

Hint: First assume $\mu = 0$ and let R take only the values $0, -x$ and x.

Problem 20.11.

A computer program crashes at the end of each hour of use with probability $1/p$, if it has not crashed already. Let H be the number of hours until the first crash.

(a) What is the Chebyshev bound on

$$\Pr[|H - (1/p)| > x/p]$$

where $x > 0$?

(b) Conclude from part (a) that for $a \geq 2$,

$$\Pr[H > a/p] \leq \frac{1-p}{(a-1)^2}$$

Hint: Check that $|H - (1/p)| > (a-1)/p$ iff $H > a/p$.

(c) What actually is

$$\Pr[H > a/p]?$$

Conclude that for any fixed $p > 0$, the probability that $H > a/p$ is an asymptotically smaller function of a than the Chebyshev bound of part (b).

Problem 20.12.

Let R be a positive integer valued random variable.

(a) If $Ex[R] = 2$, how large can $Var[R]$ be?

(b) How large can $Ex[1/R]$ be?

(c) If $R \leq 2$, that is, the only values of R are 1 and 2, how large can $Var[R]$ be?

Problem 20.13.

A man has a set of n keys, one of which fits the door to his apartment. He tries the keys randomly throwing away each ill-fitting key that he tries until he finds the key that fits. That is, he chooses keys randomly from among those he has not yet tried. This way he is sure to find the right key within n tries.

Let T be the number of times he tries keys until he finds the right key. Problem 19.25 shows that

$$Ex[T] = \frac{n + 1}{2}.$$

Write a closed formula for $Var[T]$.

Homework Problems

Problem 20.14.

A man has a set of n keys, one of which fits the door to his apartment. He tries a key at random, and if it does not fit the door, he simply puts it back; so he might try the same ill-fitting key several times. He continues until he finds the one right key that fits.

Let T be the number of times he tries keys until he finds the right key.

(a) Explain why

$$Ex[T] = n \quad \text{and} \quad Var[T] = n(n-1).$$

Let

$$f_n(a) ::= Pr[T \geq an].$$

(b) Use the Chebyshev Bound to show that for any fixed $n > 1$,

$$f_n(a) = \Theta\left(\frac{1}{a^2}\right). \tag{20.27}$$

(c) Derive an upper bound for $f_n(a)$ that for any fixed $n > 1$ is asymptoticaly smaller than Chebyshev's bound (20.27).

You may assume that n is large enough to use the approximation

$$\left(1 - \frac{1}{n}\right)^{cn} \approx \frac{1}{e^c}$$

Problem 20.15.
There is a fair coin and a biased coin that flips heads with probability $3/4$. You are given one of the coins, but you don't know which. To determine which coin was picked, your strategy will be to choose a number n and flip the picked coin n times. If the number of heads flipped is closer to $(3/4)n$ than to $(1/2)n$, you will guess that the biased coin had been picked and otherwise you will guess that the fair coin had been picked.

(a) Use the Chebyshev Bound to find a value n so that with probability 0.95 your strategy makes the correct guess, no matter which coin was picked.

(b) Suppose you had access to a computer program that would generate, in the form of a plot or table, the full binomial-(n, p) probability density and cumulative distribution functions. How would you find the minimum number of coin flips needed to infer the identity of the chosen coin with probability 0.95? How would you expect the number n determined this way to compare to the number obtained in part(a)? (You do not need to determine the numerical value of this minimum n, but we'd be interested to know if you did.)

(c) Now that we have determined the proper number n, we will assert that the picked coin was the biased one whenever the number of Heads flipped is greater than $(5/8)n$, and we will be right with probability 0.95. What, if anything, does this imply about

$$\Pr\left[\text{picked coin was biased} \mid \#\,\text{Heads flipped} \geq (5/8)n\right]?$$

Problem 20.16.
The *expected absolute deviation* of a real-valued random variable R with mean μ, is defined to be

$$\text{Ex}[\,|R - \mu|\,].$$

Prove that the expected absolute deviation is always less than or equal to the standard deviation σ. (For simplicity, you may assume that R is defined on a finite sample space.)

Hint: Suppose the sample space outcomes are $\omega_1, \omega_2, \ldots, \omega_n$, and let

$$\mathbf{p} ::= (p_1, p_2, \ldots, p_n) \quad \text{where } p_i = \sqrt{\Pr[\omega_i]},$$
$$\mathbf{r} ::= (r_1, r_2, \ldots, r_n) \quad \text{where } r_i = |R(\omega_i) - \mu| \sqrt{\Pr[\omega_i]}.$$

As usual, let $\mathbf{v} \cdot \mathbf{w} ::= \sum_{i=1}^{n} v_i u_i$ denote the dot product of n-vectors $\mathbf{v}, \mathbf{w}$, and let $|\mathbf{v}|$ be the norm of $\mathbf{v}$, namely, $\sqrt{\mathbf{v} \cdot \mathbf{v}}$.

Then verify that

$$|\mathbf{p}| = 1, \qquad |\mathbf{r}| = \sigma, \quad \text{and} \quad \text{Ex}[\,|R - \mu|\,] = \mathbf{r} \cdot \mathbf{p}.$$

Problem 20.17.

Prove the following "one-sided" version of the Chebyshev bound for deviation above the mean:

Lemma (One-sided Chebyshev bound).

$$\Pr[R - \text{Ex}[R] \geq x] \leq \frac{\text{Var}[R]}{x^2 + \text{Var}[R]}.$$

Hint: Let $S_a ::= (R - \text{Ex}[R] + a)^2$, for $0 \leq a \in \mathbb{R}$. So $R - \text{Ex}[R] \geq x$ implies $S_a \geq (x + a)^2$. Apply Markov's bound to $\Pr[S_a \geq (x + a)^2]$. Choose a to minimize this last bound.

Problem 20.18.

Prove the pairwise independent additivity of variance Theorem 20.3.8: If $R_1, R_2, \ldots, R_n$ are pairwise independent random variables, then

$$\text{Var}[R_1 + R_2 + \cdots + R_n] = \text{Var}[R_1] + \text{Var}[R_2] + \cdots + \text{Var}[R_n]. \qquad (*)$$

Hint: Why is it OK to assume $\text{Ex}[R_i] = 0$?

Exam Problems

Problem 20.19.

You are playing a game where you get n turns. Each of your turns involves flipping a coin a number of times. On the first turn, you have 1 flip, on the second turn you have two flips, and so on until your nth turn when you flip the coin n times. All the flips are mutually independent.

The coin you are using is biased to flip Heads with probability p. You *win* a turn if you flip all Heads. Let W be the number of winning turns.

(a) Write a closed-form (no summations) expression for $\text{Ex}[W]$.

(b) Write a closed-form expression for $\text{Var}[W]$.

Problem 20.20.
Let K_n be the complete graph with n vertices. Each of the edges of the graph will be randomly assigned one of the colors red, green, or blue. The assignments of colors to edges are mutually independent, and the probability of an edge being assigned red is r, blue is b, and green is g (so $r + b + g = 1$).

A set of three vertices in the graph is called a *triangle*. A triangle is *monochromatic* if the three edges connecting the vertices are all the same color.

(a) Let m be the probability that any given triangle T is monochromatic. Write a simple formula for m in terms of r, b, and g.

(b) Let I_T be the indicator variable for whether T is monochromatic. Write simple formulas in terms of m, r, b, and g for $\text{Ex}[I_T]$ and $\text{Var}[I_T]$.

Let T and U be distinct triangles.

(c) What is the probability that T and U are both monochromatic if they do not share an edge?... if they do share an edge?

$$\textbf{Now assume } r = b = g = \frac{1}{3}.$$

(d) Show that I_T and I_U are independent random variables.

(e) Let M be the number of monochromatic triangles. Write simple formulas in terms of n and m for $\text{Ex}[M]$ and $\text{Var}[M]$.

(f) Let $\mu ::= \text{Ex}[M]$. Use Chebyshev's Bound to prove that

$$\Pr[|M - \mu| > \sqrt{\mu \log \mu}] \leq \frac{1}{\log \mu}.$$

(g) Conclude that

$$\lim_{n \to \infty} \Pr[|M - \mu| > \sqrt{\mu \log \mu}] = 0$$

Problem 20.21.

You have a biased coin which flips Heads with probability p. You flip the coin n times. The coin flips are all mutually independent. Let H be the number of Heads.

 (a) Write a simple expression in terms of p and n for $\mathrm{Ex}[H]$, the expected number of Heads.

 (b) Write a simple expression in terms of p and n for $\mathrm{Var}[H]$, the variance of the number of Heads.

 (c) Write a simple expression in terms of p for the upper bound that Markov's Theorem gives for the probability that the number of Heads is larger than the expected number by at least 1% of the number of flips, that is, by $n/100$.

 (d) Show that the bound Chebyshev's Theorem gives for the probability that H differs from $\mathrm{Ex}[H]$ by at least $n/100$ is

$$100^2 \frac{p(1-p)}{n}.$$

 (e) The bound in part (d) implies that if you flip at least m times for a certain number m, then there is a 95% chance that the proportion of Heads among these m flips will be within 0.01 of p. Write a simple expression for m in terms of p.

Problem 20.22.

A classroom has sixteen desks in a 4×4 arrangement as shown below.

If two desks are next to each other, vertically or horizontally, they are called an *adjacent pair*. So there are three horizontally adjacent pairs in each row, for a total of twelve horizontally adjacent pairs. Likewise, there are twelve vertically adjacent pairs. An adjacent pair D of desks is said to have a *flirtation* when there is a boy at one desk and a girl at the other desk.

(a) Suppose boys and girls are assigned to desks in some unknown probabilistic way. What is the Markov bound on the probability that the number of flirtations is at least 33 1/3% more than expected?

Suppose that boys and girls are actually assigned to desks mutually independently, with probability p of a desk being occupied by a boy, where $0 < p < 1$.

(b) Express the expected number of flirtations in terms of p.

Hint: Let I_D be the indicator variable for a flirtation at D.

Different pairs D and E of adjacent desks are said to *overlap* when they share a desk. For example, the first and second pairs in each row overlap, and so do the second and third pairs, but the first and third pairs do not overlap.

(c) Prove that if D and E overlap, and $p = 1/2$, then I_D and I_E are independent.

(d) When $p = 1/2$, what is the variance of the number of flirtations?

(e) What upper bound does Chebyshev's Theorem give on the probability that the number of heads is either less than 30 or greater than 70?

(f) Let D and E be pairs of adjacent desks that overlap. Prove that if $p \neq 1/2$, then F_D and F_E are *not* independent.

(g) Find four pairs of desks D_1, D_2, D_3, D_4 and explain why $F_{D_1}, F_{D_2}, F_{D_3}, F_{D_4}$ are *not* mutually independent (even if $p = 1/2$).

Problems for Section 20.5

Class Problems

Problem 20.23.
A recent Gallup poll found that 35% of the adult population of the United States believes that the theory of evolution is "well-supported by the evidence." Gallup polled 1928 Americans selected uniformly and independently at random. Of these, 675 asserted belief in evolution, leading to Gallup's estimate that the fraction of Americans who believe in evolution is $675/1928 \approx 0.350$. Gallup claims a margin of error of 3 percentage points, that is, he claims to be confident that his estimate is within 0.03 of the actual percentage.

(a) What is the largest variance an indicator variable can have?

(b) Use the Pairwise Independent Sampling Theorem to determine a confidence level with which Gallup can make his claim.

(c) Gallup actually claims greater than 99% confidence in his estimate. How might he have arrived at this conclusion? (Just explain what quantity he could calculate; you do not need to carry out a calculation.)

(d) Accepting the accuracy of all of Gallup's polling data and calculations, can you conclude that there is a high probability that the percentage of adult Americans who believe in evolution is 35 ± 3 percent?

Problem 20.24.
Let $B_1, B_2, \ldots, B_n$ be mutually independent random variables with a uniform distribution on the integer interval $[1..d]$. Let $E_{i,j}$ be the indicator variable for the

event $[B_i = B_j]$.

Let M equal the number of events $[B_i = B_j]$ that are true, where $1 \le i < j \le n$. So

$$M = \sum_{1 \le i < j \le n} E_{i,j}.$$

It was observed in Section 17.4 (and proved in Problem 19.2) that $\Pr[B_i = B_j] = 1/d$ for $i \ne j$ and that the random variables $E_{i,j}$, where $1 \le i < j \le n$, are pairwise independent.

(a) What are $\text{Ex}[E_{i,j}]$ and $\text{Var}[E_{i,j}]$ for $i \ne j$?

(b) What are $\text{Ex}[M]$ and $\text{Var}[M]$?

(c) In a 6.01 class of 500 students, the youngest student was born 15 years ago and the oldest 35 years ago. Show that more than half the time, there will be will be between 12 and 23 pairs of students who have the same birth date. (For simplicity, assume that the distribution of birthdays is uniform over the 7305 days in the two decade interval from 35 years ago to 15 years ago.)

Hint: Let D be the number of pairs of students in the class who have the same birth date. Note that $|D - \text{Ex}[D]| < 6$ IFF $D \in [12..23]$.

Problem 20.25.

A defendent in traffic court is trying to beat a speeding ticket on the grounds that—since virtually everybody speeds on the turnpike—the police have unconstitutional discretion in giving tickets to anyone they choose. (By the way, we don't recommend this defense :-).)

To support his argument, the defendent arranged to get a random sample of trips by 3,125 cars on the turnpike and found that 94% of them broke the speed limit at some point during their trip. He says that as a consequence of sampling theory (in particular, the Pairwise Independent Sampling Theorem), the court can be 95% confident that the actual percentage of all cars that were speeding is $94 \pm 4\%$.

The judge observes that the actual number of car trips on the turnpike was never considered in making this estimate. He is skeptical that, whether there were a thousand, a million, or 100,000,000 car trips on the turnpike, sampling only 3,125 is sufficient to be so confident.

Suppose you were were the defendent. How would you explain to the judge why the number of randomly selected cars that have to be checked for speeding *does not depend on the number of recorded trips*? Remember that judges are not trained to understand formulas, so you have to provide an intuitive, nonquantitative explanation.

Problem 20.26.

The proof of the Pairwise Independent Sampling Theorem 20.4.1 was given for a sequence $R_1, R_2, \ldots$ of pairwise independent random variables with the same mean and variance.

The theorem generalizes straighforwardly to sequences of pairwise independent random variables, possibly with *different* distributions, as long as all their variances are bounded by some constant.

Theorem (Generalized Pairwise Independent Sampling). *Let $X_1, X_2, \ldots$ be a sequence of pairwise independent random variables such that* $\mathrm{Var}[X_i] \leq b$ *for some* $b \geq 0$ *and all* $i \geq 1$. *Let*

$$A_n ::= \frac{X_1 + X_2 + \cdots + X_n}{n},$$

$$\mu_n ::= \mathrm{Ex}[A_n].$$

Then for every $\epsilon > 0$,

$$\Pr[|A_n - \mu_n| \geq \epsilon] \leq \frac{b}{\epsilon^2} \cdot \frac{1}{n}. \tag{20.28}$$

(a) Prove the Generalized Pairwise Independent Sampling Theorem.

(b) Conclude that the following holds:

Corollary (Generalized Weak Law of Large Numbers). *For every $\epsilon > 0$,*

$$\lim_{n \to \infty} \Pr[|A_n - \mu_n| \leq \epsilon] = 1.$$

Exam Problems

Problem 20.27.

You work for the president and you want to estimate the fraction p of voters in the entire nation that will prefer him in the upcoming elections. You do this by random sampling. Specifically, you select a random voter and ask them who they are going to vote for. You do this n times, with each voter selected with uniform probability and independently of other selections. Finally, you use the fraction P of voters who said they will vote for the President as an estimate for p.

(a) Our theorems about sampling and distributions allow us to calculate how confident we can be that the random variable P takes a value near the constant p. This calculation uses some facts about voters and the way they are chosen. Indicate the true facts among the following:

1. Given a particular voter, the probability of that voter preferring the President is p.

2. The probability that some voter is chosen more than once in the random sample goes to one as n increases.

3. The probability that some voter is chosen more than once in the random sample goes to zero as the population of voters grows.

4. All voters are equally likely to be selected as the third in the random sample of n voters (assuming $n \geq 3$).

5. The probability that the second voter in the random sample will favor the President, given that the first voter prefers the President, is greater than p.

6. The probability that the second voter in the random sample will favor the President, given that the second voter is from the same state as the first, may not equal p.

(b) Suppose that according to your calculations, the following is true about your polling:

$$\Pr[|P - p| \leq 0.04] \geq 0.95.$$

You do the asking, you count how many said they will vote for the President, you divide by n, and find the fraction is 0.53. Among the following, Indicate the legitimate things you might say in a call to the President:

1. Mr. President, $p = 0.53$!

2. Mr. President, with probability at least 95 percent, p is within 0.04 of 0.53.

3. Mr. President, either p is within 0.04 of 0.53 or something very strange (5-in-100) has happened.

4. Mr. President, we can be 95% confident that p is within 0.04 of 0.53.

Problem 20.28.

Yesterday, the programmers at a local company wrote a large program. To estimate the fraction b of lines of code in this program that are buggy, the QA team will take a small sample of lines chosen randomly and independently (so it is possible, though unlikely, that the same line of code might be chosen more than once). For each line chosen, they can run tests that determine whether that line of code is buggy, after which they will use the fraction of buggy lines in their sample as their estimate of the fraction b.

The company statistician can use estimates of a binomial distribution to calculate a value s for a number of lines of code to sample which ensures that with 97% confidence, the fraction of buggy lines in the sample will be within 0.006 of the actual fraction b of buggy lines in the program.

Mathematically, the *program* is an actual outcome that already happened. The *random sample* is a random variable defined by the process for randomly choosing s lines from the program. The justification for the statistician's confidence depends on some properties of the program and how the random sample of s lines of code from the program are chosen. These properties are described in some of the statements below. Indicate which of these statements are true, and explain your answers.

1. The probability that the ninth line of code in the *program* is buggy is b.

2. The probability that the ninth line of code chosen for the *random sample* is defective is b.

3. All lines of code in the program are equally likely to be the third line chosen in the *random sample*.

4. Given that the first line chosen for the *random sample* is buggy, the probability that the second line chosen will also be buggy is greater than b.

5. Given that the last line in the *program* is buggy, the probability that the next-to-last line in the program will also be buggy is greater than b.

6. The expectation of the indicator variable for the last line in the *random sample* being buggy is b.

7. Given that the first two lines of code selected in the *random sample* are the same kind of statement—they might both be assignment statements, or both be conditional statements, or both loop statements,...—the probability that the first line is buggy may be greater than b.

8. There is zero probability that all the lines in the *random sample* will be different.

Problem 20.29.
Let $G_1, G_2, G_3, \ldots$, be an infinite sequence of pairwise independent random variables with the same expectation μ and the same finite variance. Let

$$f(n, \epsilon) ::= \Pr\left[\left| \frac{\sum_{i=1}^{n} G_i}{n} - \mu \right| \le \epsilon \right].$$

The Weak Law of Large Numbers can be expressed as a logical formula of the form:

$$\forall \epsilon > 0 \; Q_1 \, Q_2 \ldots [f(n, \epsilon) \ge 1 - \delta]$$

where $Q_1 Q_2 \ldots$ is a sequence of quantifiers from among:

$$\forall n \qquad \exists n \qquad \forall n_0 \qquad \exists n_0 \qquad \forall n \geq n_0 \quad \exists n \geq n_0$$
$$\forall \delta > 0 \quad \exists \delta > 0 \quad \forall \delta \geq 0 \quad \exists \delta \geq 0$$

Here the n and n_0 range over nonnegative integers, and δ and ϵ range over real numbers.

Write out the proper sequence $Q_1 Q_2 \ldots$

Problems for Section 20.6

Practice Problems

Problem 20.30.
A gambler plays 120 hands of draw poker, 60 hands of black jack, and 20 hands of stud poker per day. He wins a hand of draw poker with probability 1/6, a hand of black jack with probability 1/2, and a hand of stud poker with probability 1/5.

(a) What is the expected number of hands the gambler wins in a day?

(b) What would the Markov bound be on the probability that the gambler will win at least 108 hands on a given day?

(c) Assume the outcomes of the card games are *pairwise*, but possibly *not* mutually, independent. What is the variance in the number of hands won per day? You may answer with a numerical expression that is not completely evaluated.

(d) What would the Chebyshev bound be on the probability that the gambler will win at least 108 hands on a given day? You may answer with a numerical expression that is not completely evaluated.

(e) Assuming outcomes of the card games are *mutually* independent, show that the probability that the gambler will win at least 108 hands on a given day is much smaller than the bound in part (d). *Hint:* $e^{1-2\ln 2} \leq 0.7$

Class Problems

Problem 20.31.

We want to store 2 billion records into a hash table that has 1 billion slots. Assuming the records are randomly and independently chosen with uniform probability of being assigned to each slot, two records are expected to be stored in each slot. Of course under a random assignment, some slots may be assigned more than two records.

(a) Show that the probability that a given slot gets assigned more than 23 records is less than e^{-36}.

Hint: Use Chernoff's Bound, Theorem 20.6.1,. Note that $\beta(12) > 18$, where $\beta(c) ::= c \ln c - c + 1$.

(b) Show that the probability that there is a slot that gets assigned more than 23 records is less than e^{-15}, which is less than $1/3,000,000$. *Hint:* $10^9 < e^{21}$; use part (a).

a

Problem 20.32.

Sometimes I forget a few items when I leave the house in the morning. For example, here are probabilities that I forget various pieces of footwear:

left sock	0.2
right sock	0.1
left shoe	0.1
right shoe	0.3

(a) Let X be the number of these that I forget. What is $\text{Ex}[X]$?

(b) Give a tight upper bound on the probability that I forget one or more items when no independence assumption is made about forgetting different items.

(c) Use the Markov Bound to derive an upper bound on the probability that I forget 3 or more items.

(d) Now suppose that I forget each item of footwear independently. Use the Chebyshev Bound to derive an upper bound on the probability that I forget two or more items.

(e) Use Murphy's Law, Theorem 20.6.4, to derive a lower bound on the probability that I forget one or more items.

(f) I'm supposed to remember many other items, of course: clothing, watch, backpack, notebook, pencil, kleenex, ID, keys, etc. Let X be the total number of items I remember. Suppose I remember items mutually independently and $\mathrm{Ex}[X] = 36$. Use Chernoff's Bound to give an upper bound on the probability that I remember 48 or more items.

(g) Give an upper bound on the probability that I remember 108 or more items.

Problem 20.33.
Reasoning based on the Chernoff bound goes a long way in explaining the recent subprime mortgage collapse. A bit of standard vocabulary about the mortgage market is needed:

- A **loan** is money lent to a borrower. If the borrower does not pay on the loan, the loan is said to be in **default**, and collateral is seized. In the case of mortgage loans, the borrower's home is used as collateral.

- A **bond** is a collection of loans, packaged into one entity. A bond can be divided into **tranches**, in some ordering, which tell us how to assign losses from defaults. Suppose a bond contains 1000 loans, and is divided into 10 tranches of 100 bonds each. Then, all the defaults must fill up the lowest tranche before the affect others. For example, suppose 150 defaults happened. Then, the first 100 defaults would occur in tranche 1, and the next 50 defaults would happen in tranche 2.

- The lowest tranche of a bond is called the **mezzanine tranche**.

- We can make a "super bond" of tranches called a **collateralized debt obligation (CDO)** by collecting mezzanine tranches from different bonds. This super bond can then be itself separated into tranches, which are again ordered to indicate how to assign losses.

(a) Suppose that 1000 loans make up a bond, and the fail rate is 5% in a year. Assuming mutual independence, give an upper bound for the probability that there are one or more failures in the second-worst tranche. What is the probability that there are failures in the best tranche?

(b) Now, do not assume that the loans are independent. Give an upper bound for the probability that there are one or more failures in the second tranche. What is an upper bound for the probability that the entire bond defaults? Show that it is a tight bound. *Hint:* Use Markov's theorem.

(c) Given this setup (and assuming mutual independence between the loans), what is the expected failure rate in the mezzanine tranche?

(d) We take the mezzanine tranches from 100 bonds and create a CDO. What is the expected number of underlying failures to hit the CDO?

(e) We divide this CDO into 10 tranches of 1000 bonds each. Assuming mutual independence, give an upper bound on the probability of one or more failures in the best tranche. The third tranche?

(f) Repeat the previous question without the assumption of mutual independence.

Homework Problems

Problem 20.34.

We have two coins: one is a fair coin, but the other produces heads with probability $3/4$. One of the two coins is picked, and this coin is tossed n times. Use the Chernoff Bound to determine the smallest n which allows determination of which coin was picked with 95% confidence.

Problem 20.35.

An infinite version of Murphy's Law is that if an infinite number of mutually independent events are expected to happen, then the probability that only finitely many happen is 0. This is known as the first *Borel-Cantelli Lemma*.

(a) Let $A_0, A_1, \ldots$ be any infinite sequence of mutually independent events such that

$$\sum_{n \in \mathbb{N}} \Pr[A_n] = \infty. \tag{20.29}$$

Prove that $\Pr[\text{no } A_n \text{ occurs}] = 0$.

Hint: B_k the event that no A_n with $n \leq k$ occurs. So the event that no A_n occurs is

$$B ::= \bigcap_{k \in \mathbb{N}} B_k.$$

Apply Murphy's Law, Theorem 20.6.4, to B_k.

(b) Conclude that $\Pr[\text{only finitely many } A_n\text{'s occur}] = 0$.

Hint: Let C_k be the event that no A_n with $n \geq k$ occurs. So the event that only finitely many A_n's occur is

$$C ::= \bigcup_{k \in \mathbb{N}} C_k.$$

Apply part (a) to C_k.

Problems for Section 20.7

Practice Problems

Problem 20.36.
Let R be a positive integer valued random variable such that

$$\text{PDF}_R(n) = \frac{1}{cn^3},$$

where

$$c ::= \sum_{n=1}^{\infty} \frac{1}{n^3}.$$

(a) Prove that $\text{Ex}[R]$ is finite.

(b) Prove that $\text{Var}[R]$ is infinite.

A joking way to phrase the point of this example is "the square root of infinity may be finite." Namely, let $T ::= R^2$; then part (b) implies that $\text{Ex}[T] = \infty$ while $\text{Ex}[\sqrt{T}] < \infty$ by (a).

Class Problems

Problem 20.37.
You have a biased coin with nonzero probability $p < 1$ of tossing a Head. You toss until a Head comes up. Then, similar to the example in Section 20.7, you keep tossing until you get another Head preceded by a run of consecutive Tails whose length is within 10 of your original run. That is, if you began by tossing k tails followed by a Head, then you continue tossing until you get a run of at least $\max\{k - 10, 0\}$ consecutive Tails.

(a) Let H be the number of Heads that you toss until you get the required run of Tails. Prove that the expected value of H is infinite.

(b) Let $r < 1$ be a positive real number. Instead of waiting for a run of Tails of length $k - 10$ when your original run was length k, just wait for a run of length at least rk. Show that in this case, the expected number of Heads is finite.

Exam Problems

Problem 20.38.

You have a random process for generating a positive integer K. The behavior of your process each time you use it is (mutually) independent of all its other uses. You use your process to generate an integer, and then use your procedure repeatedly until you generate an integer as big as your first one. Let R be the number of additional integers you have to generate.

(a) State and briefly explain a simple closed formula for $\mathrm{Ex}[R \mid K = k]$ in terms of $\Pr[K \geq k]$.

Suppose $\Pr[K = k] = \Theta(k^{-4})$.

(b) Show that $\Pr[K \geq k] = \Theta(k^{-3})$.

(c) Show that $\mathrm{Ex}[R]$ is infinite.

21   Random Walks

Random Walks are used to model situations in which an object moves in a sequence of steps in randomly chosen directions. For example, physicists use three-dimensional random walks to model Brownian motion and gas diffusion. In this chapter we'll examine two examples of random walks. First, we'll model gambling as a simple 1-dimensional random walk—a walk along a straight line. Then we'll explain how the Google search engine used random walks through the graph of world-wide web links to determine the relative importance of websites.

21.1   Gambler's Ruin

Suppose a gambler starts with an initial stake of n dollars and makes a sequence of \$1 bets. If he wins an individual bet, he gets his money back plus another \$1. If he loses the bet, he loses the \$1.

We can model this scenario as a random walk between integer points on the real line. The position on the line at any time corresponds to the gambler's cash-on-hand, or *capital*. Walking one step to the right corresponds to winning a \$1 bet and thereby increasing his capital by \$1. Similarly, walking one step to the left corresponds to losing a \$1 bet.

The gambler plays until either he runs out of money or increases his capital to a target amount of T dollars. The amount $T - n$ is defined to be his *intended profit*.

If he reaches his target, he will have won his intended profit and is called an overall *winner*. If his capital reaches zero before reaching his target, he will have lost n dollars; this is called *going broke* or being *ruined*. We'll assume that the gambler has the same probability p of winning each individual \$1 bet, and that the bets are mutually independent. We'd like to find the probability that the gambler wins.

The gambler's situation as he proceeds with his \$1 bets is illustrated in Figure 21.1. The random walk has boundaries at 0 and T. If the random walk ever reaches either of these boundary values, then it terminates.

In an *unbiased game*, the individual bets are fair: the gambler is equally likely to win or lose each bet—that is, $p = 1/2$. The gambler is more likely to win if $p > 1/2$ and less likely to win if $p < 1/2$; these random walks are called *biased*. We want to determine the probability that the walk terminates at boundary T—the probability that the gambler wins. We'll do this in Section 21.1.1. But before we

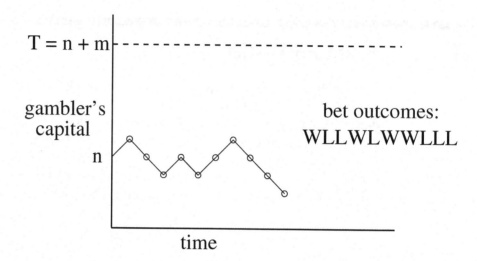

Figure 21.1 A graph of the gambler's capital versus time for one possible sequence of bet outcomes. At each time step, the graph goes up with probability p and down with probability $1 - p$. The gambler continues betting until the graph reaches either 0 or T. If he starts with \$$n$, his intended profit is \$$m$ where $T = n + m$.

derive the probability, let's examine what it turns out to be.

Let's begin by supposing the gambler plays an unbiased game starting with \$100 and will play until he goes broke or reaches a target of 200 dollars. Since he starts equidistant from his target and bankruptcy in this case, it's clear by symmetry that his probability of winning is 1/2.

We'll show below that starting with n dollars and aiming for a target of $T \geq n$ dollars, the probability the gambler reaches his target before going broke is n/T. For example, suppose he wants to win the same \$100, but instead starts out with \$500. Now his chances are pretty good: the probability of his making the 100 dollars is 5/6. And if he started with one million dollars still aiming to win \$100 dollars he almost certain to win: the probability is $1M/(1M + 100) > .9999$.

So in the unbiased game, the larger the initial stake relative to the target, the higher the probability the gambler will win, which makes some intuitive sense. But note that although the gambler now wins nearly all the time, when he loses, he loses *big*. Bankruptcy costs him \$1M, while when he wins, he wins only \$100. The gambler's average win remains zero dollars, which is what you'd expect when making fair bets.

Another useful way to describe this scenario is as a game between two players. Say Albert starts with \$500, and Eric starts with \$100. They flip a fair coin, and every time a Head appears, Albert wins $1 from Eric, and vice versa for Tails. They play this game until one person goes bankrupt. This problem is identical to the Gambler's Ruin problem with $n = 500$ and $T = 100 + 500 = 600$. The probability of Albert winning is $500/600 = 5/6$.

Now suppose instead that the gambler chooses to play roulette in an American casino, always betting $1 on red. Because the casino puts two green numbers on its roulette wheels, the probability of winning a single bet is a little less than 1/2. The casino has an advantage, but the bets are close to fair, and you might expect that starting with $500, the gambler has a reasonable chance of winning $100—the 5/6 probability of winning in the unbiased game surely gets reduced, but perhaps not too drastically.

This mistaken intuition is how casinos stay in business. In fact, the gambler's odds of winning $100 by making $1 bets against the "slightly" unfair roulette wheel are less than 1 in 37,000. If that's surprising to you, it only gets weirder from here: 1 in 37,000 is in fact an upper bound on the gambler's chance of winning *regardless of his starting stake*. Whether he starts with $5000 or $5 billion, he still has almost no chance of winning!

21.1.1 The Probability of Avoiding Ruin

We will determine the probability that the gambler wins using an idea of Pascal's dating back to the beginnings probability theory in the mid-seventeenth century.

Pascal viewed the walk as a two-player game between Albert and Eric as described above. Albert starts with a stack of n chips and Eric starts with a stack of $m = T - n$ chips. At each bet, Albert wins Eric's top chip with probability p and loses his top chip to Eric with probability $q ::= 1 - p$. They play this game until one person goes bankrupt.

Pascal's ingenious idea was to alter the worth of the chips to make the game fair regardless of p. Specifically, Pascal assigned Albert's bottom chip a worth of $r ::= q/p$ and then assigned successive chips *up* his stack worths equal to $r^2, r^3, \ldots$ up to his top chip with worth r^n. Eric's top chip gets assigned worth r^{n+1}, and the successive chips *down* his stack are worth $r^{n+2}, r^{n+3}, \ldots$ down to his bottom chip worth r^{n+m}.

The expected payoff of Albert's first bet is worth

$$r^{n+1} \cdot p - r^n \cdot q = \left(r^n \cdot \frac{q}{p} \right) \cdot p - r^n \cdot q = 0.$$

so this assignment makes the first bet a fair one in terms of worth. Moreover, whether Albert wins or loses the bet, the successive chip worths counting up Albert's stack and then down Eric's remain $r, r^2, \ldots, r^n, \ldots, r^{n+m}$, ensuring by the same reasoning that every bet has fair worth. So, Albert's expected worth at the end of the game is the sum of the expectations of the worth of each bet, which is 0.[1]

When Albert wins all of Eric's chips his total gain is worth

$$\sum_{i=n+1}^{n+m} r^i,$$

and when he loses all his chips to Eric, his total loss is worth $\sum_{i=1}^{n} r^i$. Letting w_n be Albert's probability of winning, we now have

$$0 = \text{Ex[worth of Albert's payoff]} = w_n \sum_{i=n+1}^{n+m} r^i - (1 - w_n) \sum_{i=1}^{n} r^i.$$

In the truly fair game when $r = 1$, we have $0 = m w_n - n(1 - w_n)$, so $w_n = n/(n + m)$, as claimed above.

In the biased game with $r \neq 1$, we have

$$0 = r \cdot \frac{r^{n+m} - r^n}{r - 1} \cdot w_n - r \cdot \frac{r^n - 1}{r - 1} \cdot (1 - w_n).$$

Solving for w_n gives

$$w_n = \frac{r^n - 1}{r^{n+m} - 1} = \frac{r^n - 1}{r^T - 1} \tag{21.1}$$

We have now proved

Theorem 21.1.1. *In the Gambler's Ruin game with initial capital n, target T, and probability p of winning each individual bet,*

$$\text{Pr[\textit{the gambler wins}]} = \begin{cases} \dfrac{n}{T} & \text{for } p = \dfrac{1}{2}, \\[2ex] \dfrac{r^n - 1}{r^T - 1} & \text{for } p \neq \dfrac{1}{2}, \end{cases} \tag{21.2}$$

where $r ::= q/p$.

---

[1] Here we're legitimately appealing to infinite linearity, since the payoff amounts remain bounded independent of the number of bets.

21.1.2   A Recurrence for the Probability of Winning

Fortunately, you don't need to be as ingenuious Pascal in order to handle Gambler's Ruin, because linear recurrences offer a methodical approach to the basic problems.

The probability that the gambler wins is a function of his initial capital n his target $T \geq n$ and the probability p that the wins an individual one dollar bet. For fixed p and T, let w_n be the gambler's probability of winning when his initial capital is n dollars. For example, w_0 is the probability that the gambler will win given that he starts off broke and w_T is the probability he will win if he starts off with his target amount, so clearly

$$w_0 = 0, \tag{21.3}$$

$$w_T = 1. \tag{21.4}$$

Otherwise, the gambler starts with n dollars, where $0 < n < T$. Now suppose the gambler wins his first bet. In this case, he is left with $n + 1$ dollars and becomes a winner with probability w_{n+1}. On the other hand, if he loses the first bet, he is left with $n - 1$ dollars and becomes a winner with probability w_{n-1}. By the Total Probability Rule, he wins with probability $w_n = pw_{n+1} + qw_{n-1}$. Solving for w_{n+1} we have

$$w_{n+1} = \frac{w_n}{p} - rw_{n-1} \tag{21.5}$$

where r is q/p as in Section 21.1.1.

This recurrence holds only for $n + 1 \leq T$, but there's no harm in using (21.5) to define w_{n+1} for all $n + 1 > 1$. Now, letting

$$W(x) ::= w_0 + w_1 x + w_2 x^2 + \cdots$$

be the generating function for the w_n, we derive from (21.5) and (21.3) using our generating function methods that

$$W(x) = \frac{w_1 x}{rx^2 - x/p + 1}. \tag{21.6}$$

But it's easy to check that the denominator factors:

$$rx^2 - \frac{x}{p} + 1 = (1 - x)(1 - rx).$$

Now if $p \neq q$, then using partial fractions we conclude that

$$W(x) = \frac{A}{1 - x} + \frac{B}{1 - rx}, \tag{21.7}$$

for some constants A, B. To solve for A, B, note that by (21.6) and (21.7),

$$w_1 x = A(1 - rx) + B(1 - x),$$

so letting $x = 1$, we get $A = w_1/(1 - r)$, and letting $x = 1/r$, we get $B = w_1/(r - 1)$. Therefore,

$$W(x) = \frac{w_1}{r - 1} \left(\frac{1}{1 - rx} - \frac{1}{1 - x} \right),$$

which implies

$$w_n = w_1 \frac{r^n - 1}{r - 1}. \tag{21.8}$$

Finally, we can use (21.8) to solve for w_1 by letting $n = T$ to get

$$w_1 = \frac{r - 1}{r^T - 1}.$$

Plugging this value of w_1 into (21.8), we arrive at the solution:

$$w_n = \frac{r^n - 1}{r^T - 1},$$

matching Pascal's result (21.1).

In the unbiased case where $p = q$, we get from (21.6) that

$$W(x) = \frac{w_1 x}{(1 - x)^2},$$

and again can use partial fractions to match Pascal's result (21.2).

21.1.3   A simpler expression for the biased case

The expression (21.1) for the probability that the Gambler wins in the biased game is a little hard to interpret. There is a simpler upper bound which is nearly tight when the gambler's starting capital is large and the game is biased *against* the gambler. Then $r > 1$, both the numerator and denominator in (21.1) are positive, and the numerator is smaller. This implies that

$$w_n < \frac{r^n}{r^T} = \left(\frac{1}{r} \right)^{T-n}$$

and gives:

Corollary 21.1.2. *In the Gambler's Ruin game with initial capital n, target T, and probability $p < 1/2$ of winning each individual bet,*

$$\Pr[\textit{the gambler wins}] < \left(\frac{1}{r}\right)^{T-n} \tag{21.9}$$

where $r ::= q/p > 1$.

So the gambler gains his intended profit before going broke with probability at most $1/r$ raised to the intended profit power. Notice that this upper bound does not depend on the gambler's starting capital, but only on his intended profit. This has the amazing consequence we announced above: *no matter how much money he starts with*, if he makes \$1 bets on red in roulette aiming to win \$100, the probability that he wins is less than

$$\left(\frac{18/38}{20/38}\right)^{100} = \left(\frac{9}{10}\right)^{100} < \frac{1}{37,648}.$$

The bound (21.9) decreases exponentially as the intended profit increases. So, for example, doubling his intended profit will square his probability of winning. In this case, the probability that the gambler's stake goes up 200 dollars before he goes broke playing roulette is at most

$$(9/10)^{200} = ((9/10)^{100})^2 < \left(\frac{1}{37,648}\right)^2,$$

which is about 1 in 1.4 billion.

Intuition

Why is the gambler so unlikely to make money when the game is only slightly biased against him? To answer this intuitively, we can identify two forces at work on the gambler's wallet. First, the gambler's capital has random upward and downward *swings* from runs of good and bad luck. Second, the gambler's capital will have a steady, downward *drift*, because the negative bias means an average loss of a few cents on each \$1 bet. The situation is shown in Figure 21.2.

Our intuition is that if the gambler starts with, say, a billion dollars, then he is sure to play for a very long time, so at some point there should be a lucky, upward swing that puts him \$100 ahead. But his capital is steadily drifting downward. If the gambler does not have a lucky, upward swing early on, then he is doomed. After his capital drifts downward by tens and then hundreds of dollars, the size of the upward swing the gambler needs to win grows larger and larger. And as the

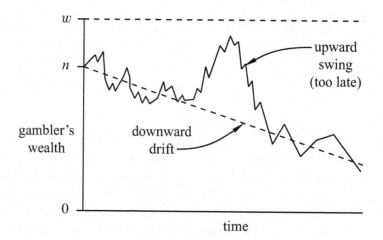

Figure 21.2   In a biased random walk, the downward drift usually dominates swings of good luck.

size of the required swing grows, the odds that it occurs decrease exponentially. As a rule of thumb, *drift dominates swings* in the long term.

We can quantify these drifts and swings. After k rounds for $k \leq \min(m, n)$, the number of wins by our player has a binomial distribution with parameters $p < 1/2$ and k. His expected win on any single bet is $p - q = 2p - 1$ dollars, so his expected capital is $n - k(1 - 2p)$. Now to be a winner, his actual number of wins must exceed the expected number by $m + k(1 - 2p)$. But from the formula (20.15), the binomial distribution has a standard deviation of only $\sqrt{kp(1 - p)}$. So for the gambler to win, he needs his number of wins to deviate by

$$\frac{m + k(1 - 2p)}{\sqrt{kp(1 - 2p)}} = \Theta(\sqrt{k})$$

times its standard deviation. In our study of binomial tails, we saw that this was extremely unlikely.

In a fair game, there is no drift; swings are the only effect. In the absence of downward drift, our earlier intuition is correct. If the gambler starts with a trillion dollars then almost certainly there will eventually be a lucky swing that puts him $100 ahead.

21.1.4   How Long a Walk?

Now that we know the probability w_n that the gambler is a winner in both fair and unfair games, we consider how many bets he needs on average to either win or go broke. A linear recurrence approach works here as well.

For fixed p and T, let e_n be the expected number of bets until the game ends when the gambler's initial capital is n dollars. Since the game is over in zero steps if $n = 0$ or T, the boundary conditions this time are $e_0 = e_T = 0$.

Otherwise, the gambler starts with n dollars, where $0 < n < T$. Now by the conditional expectation rule, the expected number of steps can be broken down into the expected number of steps given the outcome of the first bet weighted by the probability of that outcome. But after the gambler wins the first bet, his capital is $n + 1$, so he can expect to make another e_{n+1} bets. That is,

$$\text{Ex[\#bets starting with \$n \mid gambler wins first bet]} = 1 + e_{n+1}.$$

Similarly, after the gambler loses his first bet, he can expect to make another e_{n-1} bets:

$$\text{Ex[\#bets starting with \$n \mid gambler loses first bet]} = 1 + e_{n-1}.$$

So we have

$$e_n = p\,\text{Ex[\#bets starting with \$n \mid gambler wins first bet]} + q\,\text{Ex[\#bets starting with \$n \mid gaml}$$
$$= p(1 + e_{n+1}) + q(1 + e_{n-1}) = pe_{n+1} + qe_{n-1} + 1.$$

This yields the linear recurrence

$$e_{n+1} = \frac{1}{p}e_n - \frac{q}{p}e_{n-1} - \frac{1}{p}. \tag{21.10}$$

The routine solution of this linear recurrence yields:

Theorem 21.1.3. *In the Gambler's Ruin game with initial capital n, target T, and probability p of winning each bet,*

$$\text{Ex[\textit{number of bets}]} = \begin{cases} n(T - n) & \textit{for } p = \dfrac{1}{2}, \\[2ex] \dfrac{w_n \cdot T - n}{p - q} & \textit{for } p \neq \dfrac{1}{2} \\ & \textit{where } w_n = (r^n - 1)/(r^T - 1) \\ & = \Pr[\textit{the gambler wins}]. \end{cases} \tag{21.11}$$

In the unbiased case, (21.11) can be rephrased simply as

$$\text{Ex[number of fair bets]} = \text{initial capital} \cdot \text{intended profit}. \tag{21.12}$$

For example, if the gambler starts with \$10 dollars and plays until he is broke or ahead \$10, then $10 \cdot 10 = 100$ bets are required on average. If he starts with \$500 and plays until he is broke or ahead \$100, then the expected number of bets until the game is over is $500 \times 100 = 50,000$. This simple formula (21.12) cries out for an intuitive proof, but we have not found one (where are you, Pascal?).

21.1.5   Quit While You Are Ahead

Suppose that the gambler never quits while he is ahead. That is, he starts with $n > 0$ dollars, ignores any target T, but plays until he is flat broke. Call this the *unbounded Gambler's ruin* game. It turns out that if the game is not favorable, that is, $p \leq 1/2$, the gambler is sure to go broke. In particular, this holds in an unbiased game with $p = 1/2$.

Lemma 21.1.4. *If the gambler starts with one or more dollars and plays a fair unbounded game, then he will go broke with probability 1.*

Proof. If the gambler has initial capital n and goes broke in a game without reaching a target T, then he would also go broke if he were playing and ignored the target. So the probability that he will lose if he keeps playing without stopping at any target T must be at least as large as the probability that he loses when he has a target $T > n$.

But we know that in a fair game, the probability that he loses is $1 - n/T$. This number can be made arbitrarily close to 1 by choosing a sufficiently large value of T. Hence, the probability of his losing while playing without any target has a lower bound arbitrarily close to 1, which means it must in fact be 1. ∎

So even if the gambler starts with a million dollars and plays a perfectly fair game, he will eventually lose it all with probability 1. But there is good news: if the game is fair, he can "expect" to play forever:

Lemma 21.1.5. *If the gambler starts with one or more dollars and plays a fair unbounded game, then his expected number of plays is infinite.*

A proof appears in Problem 21.2.

So even starting with just one dollar, the expected number of plays before going broke is infinite! This sounds reassuring—you can go about your business without worrying about being doomed, because doom will be infinitely delayed. To illustrate a situation where you really needn't worry, think about mean time to failure with a really tiny probability of failure in any given second—say 10^{-100}. In this case you are unlikely to fail any time much sooner than many lifetimes of the estimated age of the universe, even though you will eventually fail with probability one.

But in general, you shouldn't feel reassured by an infinite expected time to go broke. For example, think about a variant Gambler's Ruin game which works as follows: run one second of the process that has a 10^{-100} of failing in any second. If it does *not* fail, then you go broke immediately. Otherwise, you play a fair, unbounded Gambler's Ruin game. Now there is an overwhelming probability, namely,

$1 - 10^{-100}$, that you will go broke immediately. But there is a 10^{-100} probability that you will wind up playing fair Gambler's Ruin, so your overall expected time will be at least 10^{-100} times the expectation of fair Gambler's Ruin, namely, it will still be infinite.

For the actual fair, unbounded Gambler's Ruin gain starting with one dollar, there is a a 50% chance the Gambler will go broke after the first bet, and a more than 15/16 chance of going broke within five bets, for example. So infinite expected time is not much consolation to a Gambler who goes broke quickly with high probability.

21.2 Random Walks on Graphs

The hyperlink structure of the World Wide Web can be described as a digraph. The vertices are the web pages with a directed edge from vertex x to vertex y if x has a link to y. A digraph showing part of the website for MIT subject 6.042, *Mathematics for Computer Science*, is shown in Figure 21.3.

The web graph is an enormous graph with trillions of vertices. In 1995, two students at Stanford, Larry Page and Sergey Brin, realized that the structure of this graph could be very useful in building a search engine. Traditional document searching programs had been around for a long time and they worked in a fairly straightforward way. Basically, you would enter some search terms and the searching program would return all documents containing those terms. A relevance score might also be returned for each document based on the frequency or position that the search terms appeared in the document. For example, if the search term appeared in the title or appeared 100 times in a document, that document would get a higher score.

This approach works fine if you only have a few documents that match a search term. But on the web, there are many billions of documents and millions of matches to a typical search. For example, on May 2, 2012, a search on Google for " 'Mathematics for Computer Science' text" gave 482,000 hits! Which ones should we look at first? Just because a page gets a high keyword score—say because it has "Mathematics Mathematics ... Mathematics" copied 200 times across the front of the document—does not make it a great candidate for attention. The web is filled with bogus websites that repeat certain words over and over in order to attract visitors.

Google's enormous market capital in part derives from the revenue it receives from advertisers paying to appear at the top of search results. That top placement would not be worth much if Google's results were as easy to manipulate as keyword frquencies. Advertisers pay because Google's ranking method is consistently good

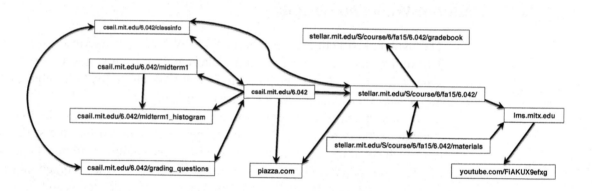

Figure 21.3   Website digraph for MIT subject 6.042

at determining the most relevant web pages. For example, Google demonstrated its accuracy in our case by giving first rank[2] to our 6.042 text.

So how did Google know to pick our text to be first out of 482,000?—because back in 1995 Larry and Sergey got the idea to allow the digraph structure of the web to determine which pages are likely to be the most important.

21.2.1 A First Crack at Page Rank

Looking at the web graph, do you have an idea which vertex/page might be the best to rank first? Assume that all the pages match the search terms for now. Well, intuitively, we should choose x_2, since lots of other pages point to it. This leads us to their first idea: try defining the *page rank* of x to be indegree(x), the number of links pointing to x. The idea is to think of web pages as voting for the most important page—the more votes, the better the rank.

Unfortunately, there are some problems with this idea. Suppose you wanted to have your page get a high ranking. One thing you could do is to create lots of dummy pages with links to your page.

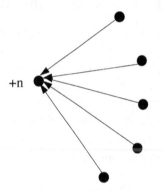

There is another problem—a page could become unfairly influential by having lots of links to other pages it wanted to hype.

---

[2]First rank for some reason was an early version archived at Princeton; the Spring 2010 version on the MIT Open Courseware site ranked 4th and 5th.

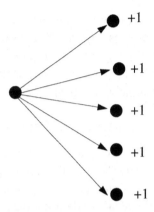

So this strategy for high ranking would amount to, "vote early, vote often," which is no good if you want to build a search engine that's worth paying fees for. So, admittedly, their original idea was not so great. It was better than nothing, but certainly not worth billions of dollars.

21.2.2   Random Walk on the Web Graph

But then Sergey and Larry thought some more and came up with a couple of improvements. Instead of just counting the indegree of a vertex, they considered the probability of being at each page after a long random walk on the web graph. In particular, they decided to model a user's web experience as following each link on a page with uniform probability. For example, if the user is at page x, and there are three links from page x, then each link is followed with probability $1/3$. More generally, they assigned each edge $x \to y$ of the web graph with a probability conditioned on being on page x:

$$\Pr\left[\text{follow link } \langle x \to y \rangle \mid \text{at page } x\right] ::= \frac{1}{\text{outdeg}(x)}.$$

The simulated user experience is then just a random walk on the web graph.

We can also compute the probability of arriving at a particular page y by summing over all edges pointing to y. We thus have

$$
\begin{aligned}
\Pr[\text{go to } y] &= \sum_{\text{edges } \langle x \to y \rangle} \Pr\left[\text{follow link } \langle x \to y \rangle \mid \text{at page } x\right] \cdot \Pr[\text{at page } x] \\
&= \sum_{\text{edges } \langle x \to y \rangle} \frac{\Pr[\text{at } x]}{\text{outdeg}(x)} \quad\quad (21.13)
\end{aligned}
$$

For example, in our web graph, we have

$$\Pr[\text{go to } x_4] = \frac{\Pr[\text{at } x_7]}{2} + \frac{\Pr[\text{at } x_2]}{1}.$$

One can think of this equation as x_7 sending half its probability to x_2 and the other half to x_4. The page x_2 sends all of its probability to x_4.

There's one aspect of the web graph described thus far that doesn't mesh with the user experience—some pages have no hyperlinks out. Under the current model, the user cannot escape these pages. In reality, however, the user doesn't fall off the end of the web into a void of nothingness. Instead, he restarts his web journey. Moreover, even if a user does not get stuck at a dead end, they will commonly get discouraged after following some unproductive path for a while and will decide to restart.

To model this aspect of the web, Sergey and Larry added a *supervertex* to the web graph and added an edge from every page to the supervertex. Moreover, the supervertex points to every other vertex in the graph with equal probability, allowing the walk to restart from a random place. This ensures that the graph is strongly connected.

If a page had no hyperlinks, then its edge to the supervertex has to be assigned probability one. For pages that had some hyperlinks, the additional edge pointing to the supervertex was assigned some specially given probability. In the original versions of Page Rank, this probability was arbitrarily set to 0.15. That is, each vertex with outdegree $n \geq 1$ got an additional edge pointing to the supervertex with assigned probability 0.15; its other n outgoing edges were still kept equally likely, that is, each of the n edges was assigned probability $0.85/n$.

21.2.3 Stationary Distribution & Page Rank

The basic idea behind page rank is finding a stationary distribution over the web graph, so let's define a stationary distribution.

Suppose each vertex is assigned a probability that corresponds, intuitively, to the likelihood that a random walker is at that vertex at a randomly chosen time. We assume that the walk never leaves the vertices in the graph, so we require that

$$\sum_{\text{vertices } x} \Pr[\text{at } x] = 1. \tag{21.14}$$

Definition 21.2.1. An assignment of probabilities to vertices in a digraph is a *stationary distribution* if for all vertices x

$$\Pr[\text{at } x] = \Pr[\text{go to } x \text{ at next step}]$$

Sergey and Larry defined their page ranks to be a stationary distribution. They did this by solving the following system of linear equations: find a nonnegative number $\text{Rank}(x)$ for each vertex x such that

$$\text{Rank}(x) = \sum_{\text{edges } \langle y \to x \rangle} \frac{\text{Rank}(y)}{\text{outdeg}(y)}, \qquad (21.15)$$

corresponding to the intuitive equations given in (21.13). These numbers must also satisfy the additional constraint corresponding to (21.14):

$$\sum_{\text{vertices } x} \text{Rank}(x) = 1. \qquad (21.16)$$

So if there are n vertices, then equations (21.15) and (21.16) provide a system of $n + 1$ linear equations in the n variables $\text{Rank}(x)$. Note that constraint (21.16) is needed because the remaining constraints (21.15) could be satisfied by letting $\text{Rank}(x) ::= 0$ for all x, which is useless.

Sergey and Larry were smart fellows, and they set up their page rank algorithm so it would always have a meaningful solution. Strongly connected graphs have *unique* stationary distributions (Problem 21.12), and their addition of a supervertex ensures this. Moreover, starting from *any* vertex and taking a sufficiently long random walk on the graph, the probability of being at each page will get closer and closer to the stationary distribution. Note that general digraphs without supervertices may have neither of these properties: there may not be a unique stationary distribution, and even when there is, there may be starting points from which the probabilities of positions during a random walk do not converge to the stationary distribution (Problem 21.8).

Now just keeping track of the digraph whose vertices are trillions of web pages is a daunting task. That's why in 2011 Google invested \$168,000,000 in a solar power plant—the electrical power drawn by Google's servers in 2011 would have supplied the needs of 200,000 households.[3] Indeed, Larry and Sergey named their system Google after the number 10^{100}—which is called a "googol"—to reflect the fact that the web graph is so enormous.

Anyway, now you can see how this text ranked first out of 378,000 matches. Lots of other universities used our notes and presumably have links to the MIT Mathematics for Computer Science Open Course Ware site, and the university sites themselves are legitimate, which ultimately leads to the text getting a high page rank in the web graph.

---

[3] *Google Details, and Defends, Its Use of Electricity*, New York Times, September 8, 2011.

Problems for Section 21.1

Practice Problems

Problem 21.1.

Suppose that a gambler is playing a game in which he makes a series of $1 bets. He wins each one with probability 0.49, and he keeps betting until he either runs out of money or reaches some fixed goal of T dollars.

Let $t(n)$ be the expected number of *bets* the gambler makes until the game ends, where n is the number of dollars the gambler has when he starts betting. Then the function t satisfies a linear recurrence of the form

$$t(n) = a \cdot t(n+1) + b \cdot t(n-1) + c$$

for real constants a, b, c, and $0 < n < T$.

(a) What are the values of a, b and c?

(b) What is $t(0)$?

(c) What is $t(T)$?

Class Problems

Problem 21.2.

In a gambler's ruin scenario, the gambler makes independent $1 bets, where the probability of winning a bet is p and of losing is $q ::= 1 - p$. The gambler keeps betting until he goes broke or reaches a target of T dollars.

Suppose $T = \infty$, that is, the gambler keeps playing until he goes broke. Let r be the probability that starting with $n > 0$ dollars, the gambler's stake ever gets reduced to $n - 1$ dollars.

(a) Explain why
$$r = q + pr^2.$$

(b) Conclude that if $p \leq 1/2$, then $r = 1$.

(c) Prove that even in a fair game, the gambler is sure to get ruined *no matter how much money he starts with*!

(d) Let t be the expected time for the gambler's stake to go down by 1 dollar. Verify that
$$t = q + p(1 + 2t).$$

Conclude that starting with a 1 dollar stake in a fair game, the gambler can expect to play forever!

Problem 21.3.

A gambler is placing \$1 bets on the "1st dozen" in roulette. This bet wins when a number from one to twelve comes in, and then the gambler gets his \$1 back plus \$2 more. Recall that there are 38 numbers on the roulette wheel.

The gambler's initial stake in \$$n$ and his target is \$$T$. He will keep betting until he runs out of money ("goes broke") or reaches his target. Let w_n be the probability of the gambler winning, that is, reaching target \$$T$ before going broke.

(a) Write a linear recurrence with boundary conditions for w_n. You need *not* solve the recurrence.

(b) Let e_n be the expected number of bets until the game ends. Write a linear recurrence with boundary conditions for e_n. You need *not* solve the recurrence.

Problem 21.4.

In the fair Gambler's Ruin game with initial stake of n dollars and target of T dollars, let e_n be the number of \$1 bets the gambler makes until the game ends (because he reaches his target or goes broke).

(a) Describe constants a, b, c such that

$$e_n = ae_{n-1} + be_{n-2} + c. \qquad (21.17)$$

for $1 < n < T$.

(b) Let e_n be defined by (21.17) for all $n > 1$, where $e_0 = 0$ and $e_1 = d$ for some constant d. Derive a closed form (involving d) for the generating function $E(x) ::= \sum_0^\infty e_n x^n$.

(c) Find a closed form (involving d) for e_n.

(d) Use part (c) to solve for d.

(e) Prove that $e_n = n(T - n)$.

Problems for Section 21.2

Practice Problems

Problem 21.5.
Consider the following random-walk graphs:

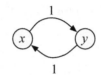

Figure 21.4

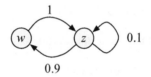

Figure 21.5

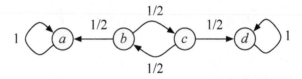

Figure 21.6

(a) Find $d(x)$ for a stationary distribution for graph 21.4.

(b) Find $d(y)$ for a stationary distribution for graph 21.4.

(c) If you start at node x in graph 21.4 and take a (long) random walk, does the distribution over nodes ever get close to the stationary distribution?

(d) Find $d(w)$ for a stationary distribution for graph 21.5.

(e) Find $d(z)$ for a stationary distribution for graph 21.5.

(f) If you start at node w in graph 21.5 and take a (long) random walk, does the distribution over nodes ever get close to the stationary distribution? (*Hint:* try a few steps and watch what is happening.)

(g) How many stationary distributions are there for graph 21.6?

(h) If you start at node b in graph 21.6 and take a (long) random walk, what will be the approximate probability that you are at node d?

Problem 21.6.
A *sink* in a digraph is a vertex with no edges leaving it. Circle whichever of the following assertions are true of stable distributions on finite digraphs with exactly two sinks:

- there may not be any

- there may be a unique one

- there are exactly two

- there may be a countably infinite number

- there may be a uncountable number

- there always is an uncountable number

Problem 21.7.
Explain why there are an uncountable number of stationary distributions for the following random walk graph.

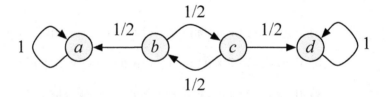

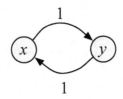

Figure 21.7

Class Problems

Problem 21.8. (a) Find a stationary distribution for the random walk graph in Figure 21.7.

(b) Explain why a long random walk starting at node x in Figure 21.7 will not converge to a stationary distribution. Characterize which starting distributions will converge to the stationary one.

(c) Find a stationary distribution for the random walk graph in Figure 21.8.

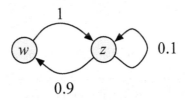

Figure 21.8

(d) If you start at node w Figure 21.8 and take a (long) random walk, does the distribution over nodes ever get close to the stationary distribution? You needn't prove anything here, just write out a few steps and see what's happening.

(e) Explain why the random walk graph in Figure 21.9 has an uncountable number of stationary distributions.

(f) If you start at node b in Figure 21.9 and take a long random walk, the probability you are at node d will be close to what fraction? Explain.

(g) Give an example of a random walk graph that is not strongly connected but has a unique stationary distribution. *Hint:* There is a trivial example.

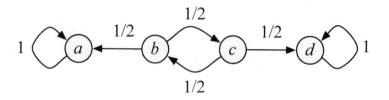

Figure 21.9

Problem 21.9.
We use random walks on a digraph G to model the typical movement pattern of a Math for CS student right after the final exam.

The student comes out of the final exam located on a particular node of the graph, corresponding to the exam room. What happens next is unpredictable, as the student is in a total haze. At each step of the walk, if the student is at node u at the end of the previous step, they pick one of the edges $\langle u \to v \rangle$ uniformly at random from the set of all edges directed out of u, and then walk to the node v.

Let $n ::= |V(G)|$ and define the vector $P^{(j)}$ to be

$$P^{(j)} ::= (p_1^{(j)}, \ldots, p_n^{(j)})$$

where $p_i^{(j)}$ is the probability of being at node i after j steps.

(a) We will start by looking at a simple graph. If the student starts at node 1 (the top node) in the following graph, what is $P^{(0)}$, $P^{(1)}$, $P^{(2)}$? Give a nice expression for $P^{(n)}$.

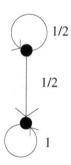

(b) Given an arbitrary graph, show how to write an expression for $p_i^{(j)}$ in terms of the $p_k^{(j-1)}$'s.

(c) Does your answer to the last part look like any other system of equations you've seen in this course?

(d) Let the *limiting distribution* vector π be

$$\lim_{k \to \infty} \frac{\sum_{i=1}^{k} P^{(i)}}{k}.$$

What is the limiting distribution of the graph from part a? Would it change if the start distribution were $P^{(0)} = (1/2, 1/2)$ or $P^{(0)} = (1/3, 2/3)$?

(e) Let's consider another directed graph. If the student starts at node 1 with probability 1/2 and node 2 with probability 1/2, what is $P^{(0)}, P^{(1)}, P^{(2)}$ in the following graph? What is the limiting distribution?

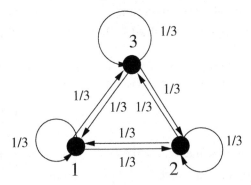

(f) Now we are ready for the real problem. In order to make it home, the poor Math for student is faced with n doors along a long hall way. Unbeknownst to him, the door that goes outside to paradise (that is, freedom from the class and more importantly, vacation!) is at the *very end*. At each step along the way, he passes by a door which he opens up and goes through with probability 1/2. Every time he does this, he gets teleported back to the exam room. Let's figure out how long it will take the poor guy to escape from the class. What is $P^{(0)}, P^{(1)}, P^{(2)}$? What is the limiting distribution?

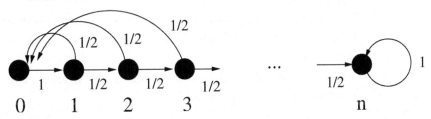

(g) Show that the expected number $T(n)$ of teleportations you make back to the exam room before you escape to the outside world is $2^{n-1} - 1$.

Problem 21.10.

Prove that for finite random walk graphs, the uniform distribution is stationary iff the probabilities of the edges coming into each vertex always sum to 1, namely

$$\sum_{u \in into(v)} p(u, v) = 1, \tag{21.18}$$

where $into(w) ::= \{v \mid \langle v \to w \rangle \text{ is an edge}\}$.

Problem 21.11.

A Google-graph is a random-walk graph such that every edge leaving any given vertex has the same probability. That is, the probability of each edge $\langle v \to w \rangle$ is $1/\text{outdeg}(v)$.

A digraph is *symmetric* if, whenever $\langle v \to w \rangle$ is an edge, so is $\langle w \to v \rangle$. Given any finite, symmetric Google-graph, let

$$d(v) ::= \frac{\text{outdeg}(v)}{e},$$

where e is the total number of edges in the graph.

 (a) If d was used for webpage ranking, how could you hack this to give your page a high rank? ...and explain informally why this wouldn't work for "real" page rank using digraphs?

 (b) Show that d is a stationary distribution.

a

Homework Problems

Problem 21.12.

A digraph is *strongly connected* iff there is a directed path between every pair of distinct vertices. In this problem we consider a finite random walk graph that is strongly connected.

 (a) Let d_1 and d_2 be distinct distributions for the graph, and define the *maximum dilation* γ of d_1 over d_2 to be

$$\gamma ::= \max_{x \in V} \frac{d_1(x)}{d_2(x)}.$$

Call a vertex x *dilated* if $d_1(x)/d_2(x) = \gamma$. Show that there is an edge $\langle y \to z \rangle$ from an undilated vertex y to a dilated vertex z. *Hint:* Choose any dilated vertex x

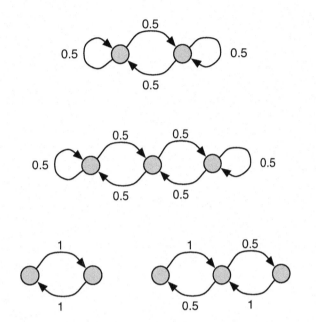

Figure 21.10 Which ones have uniform stationary distribution?

and consider the set D of dilated vertices connected to x by a directed path (going to x) that only uses dilated vertices. Explain why $D \neq V$, and then use the fact that the graph is strongly connected.

(b) Prove that the graph has *at most one* stationary distribution. (There always *is* a stationary distribution, but we're not asking you prove this.) *Hint:* Let d_1 be a stationary distribution and d_2 be a different distribution. Let z be the vertex from part (a). Show that starting from d_2, the probability of z changes at the next step. That is, $\widehat{d_2}(z) \neq d_2(z)$.

Exam Problems

Problem 21.13.
For which of the graphs in Figure 21.10 is the uniform distribution over nodes a stationary distribution? The edges are labeled with transition probabilities. Explain your reasoning.

1

V Recurrences

Introduction

A *recurrence* describes a sequence of numbers. Early terms are specified explicitly, and later terms are expressed as a function of their predecessors. As a trivial example, here is a recurrence describing the sequence $1, 2, 3, \ldots$:

$$T_1 = 1$$
$$T_n = T_{n-1} + 1 \qquad \text{(for } n \geq 2\text{)}.$$

Here, the first term is defined to be 1 and each subsequent term is one more than its predecessor.

Recurrences turn out to be a powerful tool. In this chapter, we'll emphasize using recurrences to analyze the performance of recursive algorithms. However, recurrences have other applications in computer science as well, such as enumeration of structures and analysis of random processes. And, as we saw in Section 14.4, they also arise in the analysis of problems in the physical sciences.

A recurrence in isolation is not a very useful description of a sequence. Simple questions such as, "What is the hundredth term?" or "What is the asymptotic growth rate?" are not in general easy to answer by inspection of the recurrence. So a typical goal is to *solve* a recurrence—that is, to find a closed-form expression for the nth term.

We'll first introduce two general solving techniques: *guess-and-verify* and *plug-and-chug*. These methods are applicable to every recurrence, but their success requires a flash of insight—sometimes an unrealistically brilliant flash. So we'll also introduce two big classes of recurrences, linear and divide-and-conquer, that often come up in computer science. Essentially all recurrences in these two classes are solvable using cookbook techniques; you follow the recipe and get the answer. A drawback is that calculation replaces insight. The "Aha!" moment that is essential in the guess-and-verify and plug-and-chug methods is replaced by a "Huh" at the end of a cookbook procedure.

At the end of the chapter, we'll develop rules of thumb to help you assess many recurrences without any calculation. These rules can help you distinguish promising approaches from bad ideas early in the process of designing an algorithm.

Recurrences are one aspect of a broad theme in computer science: reducing a big problem to progressively smaller problems until easy base cases are reached. This same idea underlies both induction proofs and recursive algorithms. As we'll see, all three ideas snap together nicely. For example, the running time of a recursive algorithm could be described with a recurrence with induction used to verify the solution.

22 Recurrences

22.1 The Towers of Hanoi

There are several methods for solving recurrence equations. The simplest is to *guess* the solution and then *verify* that the guess is correct with an induction proof.

For example, as a alternative to the generating function derivation in Section 16.4.2 of the value of the number T_n of moves in the Tower of Hanoi problem with n disks, we could have tried guessing. As a basis for a good guess, let's look for a pattern in the values of T_n computed above: $1, 3, 7, 15, 31, 63$. A natural guess is $T_n = 2^n - 1$. But whenever you guess a solution to a recurrence, you should always verify it with a proof, typically by induction. After all, your guess might be wrong. (But why bother to verify in this case? After all, if we're wrong, its not the end of the...no, let's check.)

Claim 22.1.1. $T_n = 2^n - 1$ *satisfies the recurrence:*

$$T_1 = 1$$
$$T_n = 2T_{n-1} + 1 \qquad \qquad (for\ n \geq 2).$$

Proof. The proof is by induction on n. The induction hypothesis is that $T_n = 2^n - 1$. This is true for $n = 1$ because $T_1 = 1 = 2^1 - 1$. Now assume that $T_{n-1} = 2^{n-1} - 1$ in order to prove that $T_n = 2^n - 1$, where $n \geq 2$:

$$T_n = 2T_{n-1} + 1$$
$$= 2(2^{n-1} - 1) + 1$$
$$= 2^n - 1.$$

The first equality is the recurrence equation, the second follows from the induction assumption, and the last step is simplification. ∎

Such verification proofs are especially tidy because recurrence equations and induction proofs have analogous structures. In particular, the base case relies on the first line of the recurrence, which defines T_1. And the inductive step uses the second line of the recurrence, which defines T_n as a function of preceding terms.

Our guess is verified. So we can now resolve our remaining questions about the 64-disk puzzle. Since $T_{64} = 2^{64} - 1$, the monks must complete more than 18 billion billion steps before the world ends. Better study for the final.

22.1.1   The Upper Bound Trap

When the solution to a recurrence is complicated, one might try to prove that some simpler expression is an upper bound on the solution. For example, the exact solution to the Towers of Hanoi recurrence is $T_n = 2^n - 1$. Let's try to prove the "nicer" upper bound $T_n \leq 2^n$, proceeding exactly as before.

Proof. (Failed attempt.) The proof is by induction on n. The induction hypothesis is that $T_n \leq 2^n$. This is true for $n = 1$ because $T_1 = 1 \leq 2^1$. Now assume that $T_{n-1} \leq 2^{n-1}$ in order to prove that $T_n \leq 2^n$, where $n \geq 2$:

$$T_n = 2T_{n-1} + 1$$
$$\leq 2(2^{n-1}) + 1$$
$$\not\leq 2^n \qquad \text{IMPLIES Uh-oh!}$$

The first equality is the recurrence relation, the second follows from the induction hypothesis, and the third step is a flaming train wreck. ∎

The proof doesn't work! As is so often the case with induction proofs, the argument only goes through with a *stronger* hypothesis. This isn't to say that upper bounding the solution to a recurrence is hopeless, but this is a situation where induction and recurrences do not mix well.

22.1.2   Plug and Chug

Guess-and-verify is a simple and general way to solve recurrence equations. But there is one big drawback: you have to *guess right*. That was not hard for the Towers of Hanoi example. But sometimes the solution to a recurrence has a strange form that is quite difficult to guess. Practice helps, of course, but so can some other methods.

Plug-and-chug is another way to solve recurrences. This is also sometimes called "expansion" or "iteration." As in guess-and-verify, the key step is identifying a pattern. But instead of looking at a sequence of *numbers*, you have to spot a pattern in a sequence of *expressions*, which is sometimes easier. The method consists of three steps, which are described below and illustrated with the Towers of Hanoi example.

Step 1: Plug and Chug Until a Pattern Appears

The first step is to expand the recurrence equation by alternately "plugging" (applying the recurrence) and "chugging" (simplifying the result) until a pattern appears. Be careful: too much simplification can make a pattern harder to spot. The rule to remember—indeed, a rule applicable to the whole of college life—is *chug in moderation.*

$$
\begin{aligned}
T_n &= 2T_{n-1} + 1 \\
&= 2(2T_{n-2} + 1) + 1 && \text{plug} \\
&= 4T_{n-2} + 2 + 1 && \text{chug} \\
&= 4(2T_{n-3} + 1) + 2 + 1 && \text{plug} \\
&= 8T_{n-3} + 4 + 2 + 1 && \text{chug} \\
&= 8(2T_{n-4} + 1) + 4 + 2 + 1 && \text{plug} \\
&= 16T_{n-4} + 8 + 4 + 2 + 1 && \text{chug}
\end{aligned}
$$

Above, we started with the recurrence equation. Then we replaced T_{n-1} with $2T_{n-2} + 1$, since the recurrence says the two are equivalent. In the third step, we simplified a little—but not too much! After several similar rounds of plugging and chugging, a pattern is apparent. The following formula seems to hold:

$$
\begin{aligned}
T_n &= 2^k T_{n-k} + 2^{k-1} + 2^{k-2} + \cdots + 2^2 + 2^1 + 2^0 \\
&= 2^k T_{n-k} + 2^k - 1
\end{aligned}
$$

Once the pattern is clear, simplifying is safe and convenient. In particular, we've collapsed the geometric sum to a closed form on the second line.

Step 2: Verify the Pattern

The next step is to verify the general formula with one more round of plug-and-chug.

$$
\begin{aligned}
T_n &= 2^k T_{n-k} + 2^k - 1 \\
&= 2^k (2T_{n-(k+1)} + 1) + 2^k - 1 && \text{plug} \\
&= 2^{k+1} T_{n-(k+1)} + 2^{k+1} - 1 && \text{chug}
\end{aligned}
$$

The final expression on the right is the same as the expression on the first line, except that k is replaced by $k + 1$. Surprisingly, this effectively *proves* that the formula is correct for all k. Here is why: we know the formula holds for $k = 1$, because that's the original recurrence equation. And we've just shown that if the formula holds for some $k \geq 1$, then it also holds for $k + 1$. So the formula holds for all $k \geq 1$ by induction.

Step 3: Write T_n Using Early Terms with Known Values

The last step is to express T_n as a function of early terms whose values are known. Here, choosing $k = n - 1$ expresses T_n in terms of T_1, which is equal to 1. Simplifying gives a closed-form expression for T_n:

$$
\begin{aligned}
T_n &= 2^{n-1} T_1 + 2^{n-1} - 1 \\
&= 2^{n-1} \cdot 1 + 2^{n-1} - 1 \\
&= 2^n - 1.
\end{aligned}
$$

We're done! This is the same answer we got from guess-and-verify.

Let's compare guess-and-verify with plug-and-chug. In the guess-and-verify method, we computed several terms at the beginning of the sequence T_1, T_2, T_3, etc., until a pattern appeared. We generalized to a formula for the nth term T_n. In contrast, plug-and-chug works backward from the nth term. Specifically, we started with an expression for T_n involving the preceding term T_{n-1}, and rewrote this using progressively earlier terms T_{n-2}, T_{n-3}, etc. Eventually, we noticed a pattern, which allowed us to express T_n using the very first term T_1 whose value we knew. Substituting this value gave a closed-form expression for T_n. So guess-and-verify and plug-and-chug tackle the problem from opposite directions.

22.2   Merge Sort

Algorithms textbooks traditionally claim that sorting is an important, fundamental problem in computer science. Then they smack you with sorting algorithms until life as a disk-stacking monk in Hanoi sounds delightful. Here, we'll cover just *one* well-known sorting algorithm, *Merge Sort*. The analysis introduces another kind of recurrence.

Here is how Merge Sort works. The input is a list of n numbers, and the output is those same numbers in nondecreasing order. There are two cases:

- If the input is a single number, then the algorithm does nothing, because the list is already sorted.

- Otherwise, the list contains two or more numbers. The first half and the second half of the list are each sorted recursively. Then the two halves are merged to form a sorted list with all n numbers.

Let's work through an example. Suppose we want to sort this list:

10, 7, 23, 5, 2, 8, 6, 9.

Since there is more than one number, the first half (10, 7, 23, 5) and the second half (2, 8, 6, 9) are sorted recursively. The results are 5, 7, 10, 23 and 2, 6, 8, 9. All that remains is to merge these two lists. This is done by repeatedly emitting the smaller of the two leading terms. When one list is empty, the whole other list is emitted. The example is worked out below. In this table, underlined numbers are about to be emitted.

First Half	Second Half	Output
5, 7, 10, 23	2, 6, 8, 9	
5, 7, 10, 23	6, 8, 9	2
7, 10, 23	6, 8, 9	2, 5
7, 10, 23	8, 9	2, 5, 6
10, 23	8, 9	2, 5, 6, 7
10, 23	9	2, 5, 6, 7, 8
10, 23		2, 5, 6, 7, 8, 9
		2, 5, 6, 7, 8, 9, 10, 23

The leading terms are initially 5 and 2. So we output 2. Then the leading terms are 5 and 6, so we output 5. Eventually, the second list becomes empty. At that point, we output the whole first list, which consists of 10 and 23. The complete output consists of all the numbers in sorted order.

22.2.1 Finding a Recurrence

A traditional question about sorting algorithms is, "What is the maximum number of comparisons used in sorting n items?" This is taken as an estimate of the running time. In the case of Merge Sort, we can express this quantity with a recurrence. Let T_n be the maximum number of comparisons used while Merge Sorting a list of n numbers. For now, assume that n is a power of 2. This ensures that the input can be divided in half at every stage of the recursion.

- If there is only one number in the list, then no comparisons are required, so $T_1 = 0$.

- Otherwise, T_n includes comparisons used in sorting the first half (at most $T_{n/2}$), in sorting the second half (also at most $T_{n/2}$), and in merging the two halves. The number of comparisons in the merging step is at most $n - 1$. This is because at least one number is emitted after each comparison and one more number is emitted at the end when one list becomes empty. Since n items are emitted in all, there can be at most $n - 1$ comparisons.

Therefore, the maximum number of comparisons needed to Merge Sort n items is given by this recurrence:

$$T_1 = 0$$
$$T_n = 2T_{n/2} + n - 1 \qquad \text{(for } n \geq 2 \text{ and a power of 2)}.$$

This fully describes the number of comparisons, but not in a very useful way; a closed-form expression would be much more helpful. To get that, we have to solve the recurrence.

22.2.2   Solving the Recurrence

Let's first try to solve the Merge Sort recurrence with the guess-and-verify technique. Here are the first few values:

$$T_1 = 0$$
$$T_2 = 2T_1 + 2 - 1 = 1$$
$$T_4 = 2T_2 + 4 - 1 = 5$$
$$T_8 = 2T_4 + 8 - 1 = 17$$
$$T_{16} = 2T_8 + 16 - 1 = 49.$$

We're in trouble! Guessing the solution to this recurrence is hard because there is no obvious pattern. So let's try the plug-and-chug method instead.

Step 1: Plug and Chug Until a Pattern Appears

First, we expand the recurrence equation by alternately plugging and chugging until a pattern appears.

$$
\begin{aligned}
T_n &= 2T_{n/2} + n - 1 \\
&= 2(2T_{n/4} + n/2 - 1) + (n - 1) &&\text{plug} \\
&= 4T_{n/4} + (n - 2) + (n - 1) &&\text{chug} \\
&= 4(2T_{n/8} + n/4 - 1) + (n - 2) + (n - 1) &&\text{plug} \\
&= 8T_{n/8} + (n - 4) + (n - 2) + (n - 1) &&\text{chug} \\
&= 8(2T_{n/16} + n/8 - 1) + (n - 4) + (n - 2) + (n - 1) &&\text{plug} \\
&= 16T_{n/16} + (n - 8) + (n - 4) + (n - 2) + (n - 1) &&\text{chug}
\end{aligned}
$$

A pattern is emerging. In particular, this formula seems holds:

$$
\begin{aligned}
T_n &= 2^k T_{n/2^k} + (n - 2^{k-1}) + (n - 2^{k-2}) + \cdots + (n - 2^0) \\
&= 2^k T_{n/2^k} + kn - 2^{k-1} - 2^{k-2} \cdots - 2^0 \\
&= 2^k T_{n/2^k} + kn - 2^k + 1.
\end{aligned}
$$

On the second line, we grouped the n terms and powers of 2. On the third, we collapsed the geometric sum.

Step 2: Verify the Pattern

Next, we verify the pattern with one additional round of plug-and-chug. If we guessed the wrong pattern, then this is where we'll discover the mistake.

$$
\begin{aligned}
T_n &= 2^k T_{n/2^k} + kn - 2^k + 1 \\
&= 2^k (2T_{n/2^{k+1}} + n/2^k - 1) + kn - 2^k + 1 \qquad \text{plug} \\
&= 2^{k+1} T_{n/2^{k+1}} + (k+1)n - 2^{k+1} + 1 \qquad \text{chug}
\end{aligned}
$$

The formula is unchanged except that k is replaced by $k + 1$. This amounts to the induction step in a proof that the formula holds for all $k \geq 1$.

Step 3: Write T_n Using Early Terms with Known Values

Finally, we express T_n using early terms whose values are known. Specifically, if we let $k = \log n$, then $T_{n/2^k} = T_1$, which we know is 0:

$$
\begin{aligned}
T_n &= 2^k T_{n/2^k} + kn - 2^k + 1 \\
&= 2^{\log n} T_{n/2^{\log n}} + n \log n - 2^{\log n} + 1 \\
&= nT_1 + n \log n - n + 1 \\
&= n \log n - n + 1.
\end{aligned}
$$

We're done! We have a closed-form expression for the maximum number of comparisons used in Merge Sorting a list of n numbers. In retrospect, it is easy to see why guess-and-verify failed: this formula is fairly complicated.

As a check, we can confirm that this formula gives the same values that we computed earlier:

n	T_n	$n \log n - n + 1$
1	0	$1 \log 1 - 1 + 1 = 0$
2	1	$2 \log 2 - 2 + 1 = 1$
4	5	$4 \log 4 - 4 + 1 = 5$
8	17	$8 \log 8 - 8 + 1 = 17$
16	49	$16 \log 16 - 16 + 1 = 49$

As a double-check, we could write out an explicit induction proof. This would be straightforward, because we already worked out the guts of the proof in step 2 of the plug-and-chug procedure.

22.3   Linear Recurrences

So far we've solved recurrences with two techniques: guess-and-verify and plug-and-chug. These methods require spotting a pattern in a sequence of numbers or expressions. In this section and the next, we'll give cookbook solutions for two large classes of recurrences. These methods require no flash of insight; you just follow the recipe and get the answer.

22.3.1   Climbing Stairs

How many different ways are there to climb n stairs, if you can either step up one stair or hop up two? For example, there are five different ways to climb four stairs:

1. step, step, step, step

2. hop, hop

3. hop, step, step

4. step, hop step

5. step, step, hop

Working through this problem will demonstrate the major features of our first cookbook method for solving recurrences. We'll fill in the details of the general solution afterward.

Finding a Recurrence

As special cases, there is 1 way to climb 0 stairs (do nothing) and 1 way to climb 1 stair (step up). In general, an ascent of n stairs consists of either a step followed by an ascent of the remaining $n - 1$ stairs or a hop followed by an ascent of $n - 2$ stairs. So the total number of ways to climb n stairs is equal to the number of ways to climb $n - 1$ plus the number of ways to climb $n - 2$. These observations define a recurrence:

$$f(0) = 1$$
$$f(1) = 1$$
$$f(n) = f(n - 1) + f(n - 2) \qquad \text{for } n \geq 2.$$

Here, $f(n)$ denotes the number of ways to climb n stairs. Also, we've switched from subscript notation to functional notation, from T_n to f_n. Here the change is cosmetic, but the expressiveness of functions will be useful later.

This is the Fibonaccifamous of all recurrence equations. Fibonacci numbers arise in all sorts of applications and in nature. For example,

- The recurrence was introduced by Fibonacci himself in thirteenth century to model rabbit reproduction.

- The sizes of the spiral patterns on the face of a sunflower grow in proportion to Fibonacci numbers.

- The input values on which Euclid's gcd algorithm requires the greatest number of steps are consecutive Fibonacci numbers.

Solving the Recurrence

The Fibonacci recurrence belongs to the class of linear recurrences, which are essentially all solvable with a technique that you can learn in an hour. This is somewhat amazing, since the Fibonacci recurrence remained unsolved for almost six centuries!

In general, a *homogeneous linear recurrence* has the form

$$f(n) = a_1 f(n-1) + a_2 f(n-2) + \cdots + a_d f(n-d)$$

where $a_1, a_2, \ldots, a_d$ and d are constants. The *order* of the recurrence is d. Commonly, the value of the function f is also specified at a few points; these are called *boundary conditions*. For example, the Fibonacci recurrence has order $d = 2$ with coefficients $a_1 = a_2 = 1$ and $g(n) = 0$. The boundary conditions are $f(0) = 1$ and $f(1) = 1$. The word "homogeneous" sounds scary, but effectively means "the simpler kind." We'll consider linear recurrences with a more complicated form later.

Let's try to solve the Fibonacci recurrence with the benefit centuries of hindsight. In general, linear recurrences tend to have exponential solutions. So let's guess that

$$f(n) = x^n$$

where x is a parameter introduced to improve our odds of making a correct guess. We'll figure out the best value for x later. To further improve our odds, let's neglect the boundary conditions $f(0) = 0$ and $f(1) = 1$ for now. Plugging this guess into the recurrence $f(n) = f(n-1) + f(n-2)$ gives

$$x^n = x^{n-1} + x^{n-2}.$$

Dividing both sides by x^{n-2} leaves a quadratic equation:

$$x^2 = x + 1.$$

Solving this equation gives *two* plausible values for the parameter x:

$$x = \frac{1 \pm \sqrt{5}}{2}.$$

This suggests that there are at least two different solutions to the recurrence, neglecting the boundary conditions.

$$f(n) = \left(\frac{1 + \sqrt{5}}{2}\right)^n \quad \text{or} \quad f(n) = \left(\frac{1 - \sqrt{5}}{2}\right)^n$$

A charming features of homogeneous linear recurrences is that any linear combination of solutions is another solution.

Theorem 22.3.1. *If $f(n)$ and $g(n)$ are both solutions to a homogeneous linear recurrence, then $h(n) = sf(n) + tg(n)$ is also a solution for all $s, t \in \mathbb{R}$.*

Proof.

$$
\begin{aligned}
h(n) &= sf(n) + tg(n) \\
&= s\left(a_1 f(n-1) + \cdots + a_d f(n-d)\right) + t\left(a_1 g(n-1) + \cdots + a_d g(n-d)\right) \\
&= a_1\left(sf(n-1) + tg(n-1)\right) + \cdots + a_d\left(sf(n-d) + tg(n-d)\right) \\
&= a_1 h(n-1) + \cdots + a_d h(n-d)
\end{aligned}
$$

The first step uses the definition of the function h, and the second uses the fact that f and g are solutions to the recurrence. In the last two steps, we rearrange terms and use the definition of h again. Since the first expression is equal to the last, h is also a solution to the recurrence. ∎

The phenomenon described in this theorem—a linear combination of solutions is another solution—also holds for many differential equations and physical systems. In fact, linear recurrences are so similar to linear differential equations that you can safely snooze through that topic in some future math class.

Returning to the Fibonacci recurrence, this theorem implies that

$$f(n) = s\left(\frac{1 + \sqrt{5}}{2}\right)^n + t\left(\frac{1 - \sqrt{5}}{2}\right)^n$$

is a solution for all real numbers s and t. The theorem expanded two solutions to a whole spectrum of possibilities! Now, given all these options to choose from, we can find one solution that satisfies the boundary conditions, $f(0) = 1$ and

$f(1) = 1$. Each boundary condition puts some constraints on the parameters s and t. In particular, the first boundary condition implies that

$$f(0) = s \left(\frac{1 + \sqrt{5}}{2} \right)^0 + t \left(\frac{1 - \sqrt{5}}{2} \right)^0 = s + t = 1.$$

Similarly, the second boundary condition implies that

$$f(1) = s \left(\frac{1 + \sqrt{5}}{2} \right)^1 + t \left(\frac{1 - \sqrt{5}}{2} \right)^1 = 1.$$

Now we have two linear equations in two unknowns. The system is not degenerate, so there is a unique solution:

$$s = \frac{1}{\sqrt{5}} \cdot \frac{1 + \sqrt{5}}{2} \qquad t = -\frac{1}{\sqrt{5}} \cdot \frac{1 - \sqrt{5}}{2}.$$

These values of s and t identify a solution to the Fibonacci recurrence that also satisfies the boundary conditions:

$$f(n) = \frac{1}{\sqrt{5}} \cdot \frac{1 + \sqrt{5}}{2} \left(\frac{1 + \sqrt{5}}{2} \right)^n - \frac{1}{\sqrt{5}} \cdot \frac{1 - \sqrt{5}}{2} \left(\frac{1 - \sqrt{5}}{2} \right)^n$$

$$= \frac{1}{\sqrt{5}} \left(\frac{1 + \sqrt{5}}{2} \right)^{n+1} - \frac{1}{\sqrt{5}} \left(\frac{1 - \sqrt{5}}{2} \right)^{n+1}.$$

It is easy to see why no one stumbled across this solution for almost six centuries. All Fibonacci numbers are integers, but this expression is full of square roots of five! Amazingly, the square roots always cancel out. This expression really does give the Fibonacci numbers if we plug in $n = 0, 1, 2$, etc.

This closed form for Fibonacci numbers is known as Binet's formula and has some interesting corollaries. The first term tends to infinity because the base of the exponential, $(1 + \sqrt{5})/2 = 1.618\ldots$ is greater than one. This value is often denoted ϕ and called the "golden ratio." The second term tends to zero, because $(1 - \sqrt{5})/2 = -0.618033988\ldots$ has absolute value less than 1. This implies that the nth Fibonacci number is:

$$f(n) = \frac{\phi^{n+1}}{\sqrt{5}} + o(1).$$

Remarkably, this expression involving irrational numbers is actually very close to an integer for all large n—namely, a Fibonacci number! For example:

$$\frac{\phi^{20}}{\sqrt{5}} = 6765.000029\cdots \approx f(19).$$

This also implies that the ratio of consecutive Fibonacci numbers rapidly approaches the golden ratio. For example:

$$\frac{f(20)}{f(19)} = \frac{10946}{6765} = 1.618033998\ldots.$$

22.3.2   Solving Homogeneous Linear Recurrences

The method we used to solve the Fibonacci recurrence can be extended to solve any homogeneous linear recurrence; that is, a recurrence of the form

$$f(n) = a_1 f(n-1) + a_2 f(n-2) + \cdots + a_d f(n-d)$$

where $a_1, a_2, \ldots, a_d$ and d are constants. Substituting the guess $f(n) = x^n$, as with the Fibonacci recurrence, gives

$$x^n = a_1 x^{n-1} + a_2 x^{n-2} + \cdots + a_d x^{n-d}.$$

Dividing by x^{n-d} gives

$$x^d = a_1 x^{d-1} + a_2 x^{d-2} + \cdots + a_{d-1} x + a_d.$$

This is called the *characteristic equation* of the recurrence. The characteristic equation can be read off quickly since the coefficients of the equation are the same as the coefficients of the recurrence.

The solutions to a linear recurrence are defined by the roots of the characteristic equation. Neglecting boundary conditions for the moment:

- If r is a nonrepeated root of the characteristic equation, then r^n is a solution to the recurrence.

- If r is a repeated root with multiplicity k then r^n, nr^n, $n^2 r^n$, $\ldots$, $n^{k-1} r^n$ are all solutions to the recurrence.

Theorem 22.3.1 implies that every linear combination of these solutions is also a solution.

For example, suppose that the characteristic equation of a recurrence has roots s, t and u twice. These four roots imply four distinct solutions:

$$f(n) = s^n \qquad f(n) = t^n \qquad f(n) = u^n \qquad f(n) = nu^n.$$

Furthermore, every linear combination

$$f(n) = a \cdot s^n + b \cdot t^n + c \cdot u^n + d \cdot nu^n \tag{22.1}$$

is also a solution.

All that remains is to select a solution consistent with the boundary conditions by choosing the constants appropriately. Each boundary condition implies a linear equation involving these constants. So we can determine the constants by solving a system of linear equations. For example, suppose our boundary conditions were $f(0) = 0$, $f(1) = 1$, $f(2) = 4$ and $f(3) = 9$. Then we would obtain four equations in four unknowns:

$$
\begin{array}{llll}
f(0) = 0 & \text{implies} & a \cdot s^0 + b \cdot t^0 + c \cdot u^0 + d \cdot 0u^0 = 0 \\
f(1) = 1 & \text{implies} & a \cdot s^1 + b \cdot t^1 + c \cdot u^1 + d \cdot 1u^1 = 1 \\
f(2) = 4 & \text{implies} & a \cdot s^2 + b \cdot t^2 + c \cdot u^2 + d \cdot 2u^2 = 4 \\
f(3) = 9 & \text{implies} & a \cdot s^3 + b \cdot t^3 + c \cdot u^3 + d \cdot 3u^3 = 9
\end{array}
$$

This looks nasty, but remember that s, t and u are just constants. Solving this system gives values for a, b, c and d that define a solution to the recurrence consistent with the boundary conditions.

22.3.3 Solving General Linear Recurrences

We can now solve all linear homogeneous recurrences, which have the form

$$ f(n) = a_1 f(n-1) + a_2 f(n-2) + \cdots + a_d f(n-d). $$

Many recurrences that arise in practice do not quite fit this mold. For example, the Towers of Hanoi problem led to this recurrence:

$$
\begin{aligned}
f(1) &= 1 \\
f(n) &= 2f(n-1) + 1 \qquad\qquad \text{(for } n \geq 2\text{)}.
\end{aligned}
$$

The problem is the extra $+1$; that is not allowed in a homogeneous linear recurrence. In general, adding an extra function $g(n)$ to the right side of a linear recurrence gives an *inhomogeneous linear recurrence*:

$$ f(n) = a_1 f(n-1) + a_2 f(n-2) + \cdots + a_d f(n-d) + g(n). $$

Solving inhomogeneous linear recurrences is neither very different nor very difficult. We can divide the whole job into five steps:

1. Replace $g(n)$ by 0, leaving a homogeneous recurrence. As before, find roots of the characteristic equation.

2. Write down the solution to the homogeneous recurrence, but do not yet use the boundary conditions to determine coefficients. This is called the *homogeneous solution*.

3. Now restore $g(n)$ and find a single solution to the recurrence, ignoring boundary conditions. This is called a *particular solution*. We'll explain how to find a particular solution shortly.

4. Add the homogeneous and particular solutions together to obtain the *general solution*.

5. Now use the boundary conditions to determine constants by the usual method of generating and solving a system of linear equations.

As an example, let's consider a variation of the Towers of Hanoi problem. Suppose that moving a disk takes time proportional to its size. Specifically, moving the smallest disk takes 1 second, the next-smallest takes 2 seconds, and moving the nth disk then requires n seconds instead of 1. So, in this variation, the time to complete the job is given by a recurrence with a $+n$ term instead of a $+1$:

$$f(1) = 1$$
$$f(n) = 2f(n - 1) + n \qquad\qquad \text{for } n \geq 2.$$

Clearly, this will take longer, but how much longer? Let's solve the recurrence with the method described above.

In Steps 1 and 2, dropping the $+n$ leaves the homogeneous recurrence $f(n) = 2f(n - 1)$. The characteristic equation is $x = 2$. So the homogeneous solution is $f(n) = c2^n$.

In Step 3, we must find a solution to the full recurrence $f(n) = 2f(n - 1) + n$, without regard to the boundary condition. Let's guess that there is a solution of the form $f(n) = an + b$ for some constants a and b. Substituting this guess into the recurrence gives

$$an + b = 2(a(n - 1) + b) + n$$
$$0 = (a + 1)n + (b - 2a).$$

The second equation is a simplification of the first. The second equation holds for all n if both $a + 1 = 0$ (which implies $a = -1$) and $b - 2a = 0$ (which implies that $b = -2$). So $f(n) = an + b = -n - 2$ is a particular solution.

In the Step 4, we add the homogeneous and particular solutions to obtain the general solution

$$f(n) = c2^n - n - 2.$$

Finally, in step 5, we use the boundary condition $f(1) = 1$ to determine the value of the constant c:

$$f(1) = 1 \quad \text{IMPLIES} \quad c2^1 - 1 - 2 = 1$$
$$\text{IMPLIES} \quad c = 2.$$

Therefore, the function $f(n) = 2 \cdot 2^n - n - 2$ solves this variant of the Towers of Hanoi recurrence. For comparison, the solution to the original Towers of Hanoi problem was $2^n - 1$. So if moving disks takes time proportional to their size, then the monks will need about twice as much time to solve the whole puzzle.

22.3.4   How to Guess a Particular Solution

Finding a particular solution can be the hardest part of solving inhomogeneous recurrences. This involves guessing, and you might guess wrong.[1] However, some rules of thumb make this job fairly easy most of the time.

- Generally, look for a particular solution with the same form as the inhomogeneous term $g(n)$.

- If $g(n)$ is a constant, then guess a particular solution $f(n) = c$. If this doesn't work, try polynomials of progressively higher degree: $f(n) = bn + c$, then $f(n) = an^2 + bn + c$, etc.

- More generally, if $g(n)$ is a polynomial, try a polynomial of the same degree, then a polynomial of degree one higher, then two higher, etc. For example, if $g(n) = 6n + 5$, then try $f(n) = bn + c$ and then $f(n) = an^2 + bn + c$.

- If $g(n)$ is an exponential, such as 3^n, then first guess that $f(n) = c3^n$. Failing that, try $f(n) = bn3^n + c3^n$ and then $an^2 3^n + bn3^n + c3^n$, etc.

The entire process is summarized on the following page.

22.4   Divide-and-Conquer Recurrences

We now have a recipe for solving general linear recurrences. But the Merge Sort recurrence, which we encountered earlier, is not linear:

$$T(1) = 0$$
$$T(n) = 2T(n/2) + n - 1 \qquad \text{(for } n \geq 2\text{)}.$$

---

[1] Chapter 16 explains how to solve linear recurrences with generating functions—it's a little more complicated, but it does not require guessing.

Short Guide to Solving Linear Recurrences

A linear recurrence is an equation

$$f(n) = \underbrace{a_1 f(n-1) + a_2 f(n-2) + \cdots + a_d f(n-d)}_{\text{homogeneous part}} \quad \underbrace{+\, g(n)}_{\text{inhomogeneous part}}$$

together with boundary conditions such as $f(0) = b_0$, $f(1) = b_1$, etc. Linear recurrences are solved as follows:

1. Find the roots of the characteristic equation

   $$x^n = a_1 x^{n-1} + a_2 x^{n-2} + \cdots + a_{k-1} x + a_k.$$

2. Write down the homogeneous solution. Each root generates one term and the homogeneous solution is their sum. A nonrepeated root r generates the term $c\, r^n$, where c is a constant to be determined later. A root r with multiplicity k generates the terms

   $$d_1 r^n \qquad d_2 n r^n \qquad d_3 n^2 r^n \qquad \ldots \qquad d_k n^{k-1} r^n$$

   where $d_1, \ldots d_k$ are constants to be determined later.

3. Find a particular solution. This is a solution to the full recurrence that need not be consistent with the boundary conditions. Use guess-and-verify. If $g(n)$ is a constant or a polynomial, try a polynomial of the same degree, then of one higher degree, then two higher. For example, if $g(n) = n$, then try $f(n) = bn + c$ and then $an^2 + bn + c$. If $g(n)$ is an exponential, such as 3^n, then first guess $f(n) = c3^n$. Failing that, try $f(n) = (bn + c)3^n$ and then $(an^2 + bn + c)3^n$, etc.

4. Form the general solution, which is the sum of the homogeneous solution and the particular solution. Here is a typical general solution:

   $$f(n) = \underbrace{c2^n + d(-1)^n}_{\text{homogeneous solution}} + \underbrace{3n + 1}_{\text{inhomogeneous solution}}.$$

5. Substitute the boundary conditions into the general solution. Each boundary condition gives a linear equation in the unknown constants. For example, substituting $f(1) = 2$ into the general solution above gives

   $$2 = c \cdot 2^1 + d \cdot (-1)^1 + 3 \cdot 1 + 1$$
   $$\text{IMPLIES} \quad -2 = 2c - d.$$

   Determine the values of these constants by solving the resulting system of linear equations.

In particular, $T(n)$ is not a linear combination of a fixed number of immediately preceding terms; rather, $T(n)$ is a function of $T(n/2)$, a term halfway back in the sequence.

Merge Sort is an example of a divide-and-conquer algorithm: it divides the input, "conquers" the pieces, and combines the results. Analysis of such algorithms commonly leads to *divide-and-conquer* recurrences, which have this form:

$$T(n) = \sum_{i=1}^{k} a_i T(b_i n) + g(n)$$

Here $a_1, \ldots a_k$ are positive constants, $b_1, \ldots, b_k$ are constants between 0 and 1, and $g(n)$ is a nonnegative function. For example, setting $a_1 = 2$, $b_1 = 1/2$ and $g(n) = n - 1$ gives the Merge Sort recurrence.

22.4.1 The Akra-Bazzi Formula

The solution to virtually all divide and conquer solutions is given by the amazing *Akra-Bazzi formula*. Quite simply, the asymptotic solution to the general divide-and-conquer recurrence

$$T(n) = \sum_{i=1}^{k} a_i T(b_i n) + g(n)$$

is

$$T(n) = \Theta\left(n^p \left(1 + \int_1^n \frac{g(u)}{u^{p+1}} \, du \right) \right) \tag{22.2}$$

where p satisfies

$$\sum_{i=1}^{k} a_i b_i^p = 1. \tag{22.3}$$

A rarely-troublesome requirement is that the function $g(n)$ must not grow or oscillate too quickly. Specifically, $|g'(n)|$ must be bounded by some polynomial. So, for example, the Akra-Bazzi formula is valid when $g(n) = x^2 \log n$, but not when $g(n) = 2^n$.

Let's solve the Merge Sort recurrence again, using the Akra-Bazzi formula instead of plug-and-chug. First, we find the value p that satisfies

$$2 \cdot (1/2)^p = 1.$$

Looks like $p = 1$ does the job. Then we compute the integral:

$$T(n) = \Theta\left(n\left(1 + \int_1^n \frac{u-1}{u^2}\,du\right)\right)$$

$$= \Theta\left(n\left(1 + \left[\log u + \frac{1}{u}\right]_1^n\right)\right)$$

$$= \Theta\left(n\left(\log n + \frac{1}{n}\right)\right)$$

$$= \Theta(n\log n).$$

The first step is integration and the second is simplification. We can drop the $1/n$ term in the last step, because the $\log n$ term dominates. We're done!

Let's try a scary-looking recurrence:

$$T(n) = 2T(n/2) + (8/9)T(3n/4) + n^2.$$

Here, $a_1 = 2$, $b_1 = 1/2$, $a_2 = 8/9$ and $b_2 = 3/4$. So we find the value p that satisfies

$$2 \cdot (1/2)^p + (8/9)(3/4)^p = 1.$$

Equations of this form don't always have closed-form solutions, so you may need to approximate p numerically sometimes. But in this case the solution is simple: $p = 2$. Then we integrate:

$$T(n) = \Theta\left(n^2\left(1 + \int_1^n \frac{u^2}{u^3}\,du\right)\right)$$

$$= \Theta\left(n^2(1 + \log n)\right)$$

$$= \Theta\left(n^2 \log n\right).$$

That was easy!

22.4.2   Two Technical Issues

Until now, we've swept a couple issues related to divide-and-conquer recurrences under the rug. Let's address those issues now.

First, the Akra-Bazzi formula makes no use of boundary conditions. To see why, let's go back to Merge Sort. During the plug-and-chug analysis, we found that

$$T_n = nT_1 + n\log n - n + 1.$$

This expresses the nth term as a function of the first term, whose value is specified in a boundary condition. But notice that $T_n = \Theta(n\log n)$ for *every* value of T_1. The boundary condition doesn't matter!

This is the typical situation: *the asymptotic solution to a divide-and-conquer recurrence is independent of the boundary conditions.* Intuitively, if the bottom-level operation in a recursive algorithm takes, say, twice as long, then the overall running time will at most double. This matters in practice, but the factor of 2 is concealed by asymptotic notation. There are corner-case exceptions. For example, the solution to $T(n) = 2T(n/2)$ is either $\Theta(n)$ or zero, depending on whether $T(1)$ is zero. These cases are of little practical interest, so we won't consider them further.

There is a second nagging issue with divide-and-conquer recurrences that does not arise with linear recurrences. Specifically, dividing a problem of size n may create subproblems of non-integer size. For example, the Merge Sort recurrence contains the term $T(n/2)$. So what if n is 15? How long does it take to sort seven-and-a-half items? Previously, we dodged this issue by analyzing Merge Sort only when the size of the input was a power of 2. But then we don't know what happens for an input of size, say, 100.

Of course, a practical implementation of Merge Sort would split the input *approximately* in half, sort the halves recursively, and merge the results. For example, a list of 15 numbers would be split into lists of 7 and 8. More generally, a list of n numbers would be split into approximate halves of size $\lceil n/2 \rceil$ and $\lfloor n/2 \rfloor$. So the maximum number of comparisons is actually given by this recurrence:

$$T(1) = 0$$
$$T(n) = T(\lceil n/2 \rceil) + T(\lfloor n/2 \rfloor) + n - 1 \qquad \text{(for } n \geq 2\text{)}.$$

This may be rigorously correct, but the ceiling and floor operations make the recurrence hard to solve exactly.

Fortunately, *the asymptotic solution to a divide and conquer recurrence is unaffected by floors and ceilings.* More precisely, the solution is not changed by replacing a term $T(b_i n)$ with either $T(ceilb_i n)$ or $T(\lfloor b_i n \rfloor)$. So leaving floors and ceilings out of divide-and-conquer recurrences makes sense in many contexts; those are complications that make no difference.

22.4.3   The Akra-Bazzi Theorem

The Akra-Bazzi formula together with our assertions about boundary conditions and integrality all follow from the *Akra-Bazzi Theorem*, which is stated below.

Theorem 22.4.1 (Akra-Bazzi). *Suppose that the function* $T : \mathbb{R} \rightarrow \mathbb{R}$ *is nonnegative and bounded for* $0 \leq x \leq x_0$ *and satisfies the recurrence*

$$T(x) = \sum_{i=1}^{k} a_i T(b_i x + h_i(x)) + g(x) \qquad \text{for } x > x_0, \tag{22.4}$$

where:

1. x_0 *is large enough so that T is well-defined,*

2. $a_1, \ldots, a_k$ *are positive constants,*

3. $b_1, \ldots, b_k$ *are constants between 0 and 1,*

4. $g(x)$ *is a nonnegative function such that $|g'(x)|$ is bounded by a polynomial,*

5. $|h_i(x)| = O(x/\log^2 x).$

Then

$$T(x) = \Theta\left(x^p \left(1 + \int_1^x \frac{g(u)}{u^{p+1}}\, du\right)\right)$$

where p satisfies

$$\sum_{i=1}^{k} a_i b_i^p = 1.$$

The Akra-Bazzi theorem can be proved using a complicated induction argument, though we won't do that here. But let's at least go over the statement of the theorem.

All the recurrences we've considered were defined over the integers, and that is the common case. But the Akra-Bazzi theorem applies more generally to functions defined over the real numbers.

The Akra-Bazzi formula is lifted directed from the theorem statement, except that the recurrence in the theorem includes extra functions, h_i. These functions extend the theorem to address floors, ceilings, and other small adjustments to the sizes of subproblems. The trick is illustrated by this combination of parameters

$$
\begin{array}{lll}
a_1 = 1 & b_1 = 1/2 & h_1(x) = \left\lceil \dfrac{x}{2} \right\rceil - \dfrac{x}{2} \\[2ex]
a_2 = 1 & b_2 = 1/2 & h_2(x) = \left\lfloor \dfrac{x}{2} \right\rfloor - \dfrac{x}{2} \\[2ex]
 & g(x) = x - 1 &
\end{array}
$$

which corresponds the recurrence

$$
\begin{aligned}
T(x) &= 1 \cdot T\left(\frac{x}{2} + \left(\left\lceil \frac{x}{2} \right\rceil - \frac{x}{2}\right)\right) + \cdot T\left(\frac{x}{2} + \left(\left\lfloor \frac{x}{2} \right\rfloor - \frac{x}{2}\right)\right) + x - 1 \\
&= T\left(\left\lceil \frac{x}{2} \right\rceil\right) + T\left(\left\lfloor \frac{x}{2} \right\rfloor\right) + x - 1.
\end{aligned}
$$

This is the rigorously correct Merge Sort recurrence valid for all input sizes, complete with floor and ceiling operators. In this case, the functions $h_1(x)$ and

$h_2(x)$ are both at most 1, which is easily $O(x / \log^2 x)$ as required by the theorem statement. These functions h_i do not affect—or even appear in—the asymptotic solution to the recurrence. This justifies our earlier claim that applying floor and ceiling operators to the size of a subproblem does not alter the asymptotic solution to a divide-and-conquer recurrence.

22.4.4 The Master Theorem

There is a special case of the Akra-Bazzi formula known as the Master Theorem that handles some of the recurrences that commonly arise in computer science. It is called the *Master* Theorem because it was proved long before Akra and Bazzi arrived on the scene and, for many years, it was the final word on solving divide-and-conquer recurrences. We include the Master Theorem here because it is still widely referenced in algorithms courses and you can use it without having to know anything about integration.

Theorem 22.4.2 (Master Theorem). *Let T be a recurrence of the form*

$$T(n) = aT\left(\frac{n}{b}\right) + g(n).$$

Case 1: *If $g(n) = O\left(n^{\log_b(a)-\epsilon}\right)$ for some constant $\epsilon > 0$, then*

$$T(n) = \Theta\left(n^{\log_b(a)}\right).$$

Case 2: *If $g(n) = \Theta\left(n^{\log_b(a)} \log^k(n)\right)$ for some constant $k \geq 0$, then*

$$T(n) = \Theta\left(n^{\log_b(a)} \log^{k+1}(n)\right).$$

Case 3: *If $g(n) = \Omega\left(n^{\log_b(a)+\epsilon}\right)$ for some constant $\epsilon > 0$ and $ag(n/b) < cg(n)$ for some constant $c < 1$ and sufficiently large n, then*

$$T(n) = \Theta(g(n)).$$

The Master Theorem can be proved by induction on n or, more easily, as a corollary of Theorem 22.4.1. We will not include the details here.

22.5   A Feel for Recurrences

We've guessed and verified, plugged and chugged, found roots, computed integrals, and solved linear systems and exponential equations. Now let's step back and look for some rules of thumb. What kinds of recurrences have what sorts of solutions?

Here are some recurrences we solved earlier:

	Recurrence	Solution
Towers of Hanoi	$T_n = 2T_{n-1} + 1$	$T_n \sim 2^n$
Merge Sort	$T_n = 2T_{n/2} + n - 1$	$T_n \sim n \log n$
Hanoi variation	$T_n = 2T_{n-1} + n$	$T_n \sim 2 \cdot 2^n$
Fibonacci	$T_n = T_{n-1} + T_{n-2}$	$T_n \sim (1.618\ldots)^{n+1}/\sqrt{5}$

Notice that the recurrence equations for Towers of Hanoi and Merge Sort are somewhat similar, but the solutions are radically different. Merge Sorting $n = 64$ items takes a few hundred comparisons, while moving $n = 64$ disks takes more than 10^{19} steps!

Each recurrence has one strength and one weakness. In the Towers of Hanoi, we broke a problem of size n into two subproblem of size $n - 1$ (which is large), but needed only 1 additional step (which is small). In Merge Sort, we divided the problem of size n into two subproblems of size $n/2$ (which is small), but needed $(n - 1)$ additional steps (which is large). Yet, Merge Sort is faster by a mile!

This suggests that *generating smaller subproblems is far more important to algorithmic speed than reducing the additional steps per recursive call.* For example, shifting to the variation of Towers of Hanoi increased the last term from $+1$ to $+n$, but the solution only doubled. And one of the two subproblems in the Fibonacci recurrence is just *slightly* smaller than in Towers of Hanoi (size $n - 2$ instead of $n-1$). Yet the solution is exponentially smaller! More generally, linear recurrences (which have big subproblems) typically have exponential solutions, while divide-and-conquer recurrences (which have small subproblems) usually have solutions bounded above by a polynomial.

All the examples listed above break a problem of size n into two smaller problems. How does the number of subproblems affect the solution? For example, suppose we increased the number of subproblems in Towers of Hanoi from 2 to 3, giving this recurrence:

$$T_n = 3T_{n-1} + 1$$

This increases the root of the characteristic equation from 2 to 3, which raises the solution exponentially, from $\Theta(2^n)$ to $\Theta(3^n)$.

Divide-and-conquer recurrences are also sensitive to the number of subproblems. For example, for this generalization of the Merge Sort recurrence:

$$T_1 = 0$$
$$T_n = a T_{n/2} + n - 1.$$

the Akra-Bazzi formula gives:

$$T_n = \begin{cases} \Theta(n) & \text{for } a < 2 \\ \Theta(n \log n) & \text{for } a = 2 \\ \Theta(n^{\log a}) & \text{for } a > 2. \end{cases}$$

So the solution takes on three completely different forms as a goes from 1.99 to 2.01!

How do boundary conditions affect the solution to a recurrence? We've seen that they are almost irrelevant for divide-and-conquer recurrences. For linear recurrences, the solution is usually dominated by an exponential whose base is determined by the number and size of subproblems. Boundary conditions matter greatly only when they give the dominant term a zero coefficient, which changes the asymptotic solution.

So now we have a rule of thumb! The performance of a recursive procedure is usually dictated by the size and number of subproblems, rather than the amount of work per recursive call or time spent at the base of the recursion. In particular, if subproblems are smaller than the original by an additive factor, the solution is most often exponential. But if the subproblems are only a fraction the size of the original, then the solution is typically bounded by a polynomial.

Problems for Section 22.4

Homework Problems

Problem 22.1.
The running time of an algorithm A is described by the recurrence $T(n) = 7T(n/2) + n^2$. A competing algorithm A' has a running time of $T'(n) = aT'(n/4) + n^2$. For what values of a is A' asymptotically faster than A?

Problem 22.2.
Use the Akra-Bazzi formula to find $\Theta()$ asymptotic bounds for the following divide-and-conquer recurrences. For each recurrence, $T(1) = 1$ and $T(n) = \Theta(1)$ for all

constant n. State the value of p you get for each recurrence (which can be left in the form of logs). Also, state the values of the $a_i, b_i,$ and $h_i(n)$ for each recurrence.

1. $T(n) = 3T(\lfloor n/3 \rfloor) + n.$

2. $T(n) = 4T(\lfloor n/3 \rfloor) + n^2.$

3. $T(n) = 3T(\lfloor n/4 \rfloor) + n.$

4. $T(n) = T(\lfloor n/4 \rfloor) + T(\lfloor n/3 \rfloor) + n.$

5. $T(n) = T(\lceil n/4 \rceil) + T(\lfloor 3n/4 \rfloor) + n.$

6. $T(n) = 2T(\lfloor n/4 \rfloor) + \sqrt{n}.$

7. $T(n) = 2T(\lfloor n/4 \rfloor + 1) + \sqrt{n}.$

8. $T(n) = 2T(\lfloor n/4 + \sqrt{n} \rfloor) + 1.$

9. $T(n) = 3T\left(\left\lceil n^{1/3} \right\rceil\right) + \log_3 n.$ (For this problem, $T(2) = 1.$)

10. $T(n) = \sqrt{e}\, T\left(\left\lfloor n^{1/e} \right\rfloor\right) + \ln n.$

Class Problems

Problem 22.3.
We have devised an error-tolerant version of **MergeSort**. We call our exciting new algorithm **OverSort**.

   Here is how the new algorithm works. The input is a list of n distinct numbers. If the list contains a single number, then there is nothing to do. If the list contains two numbers, then we sort them with a single comparison. If the list contains more than two numbers, then we perform the following sequence of steps.

- We make a list containing the first $\frac{2}{3}n$ numbers and sort it recursively.

- We make a list containing the last $\frac{2}{3}n$ numbers and sort it recursively.

- We make a list containing the first $\frac{1}{3}n$ numbers and the last $\frac{1}{3}n$ numbers and sort it recursively.

- We merge the first and second lists, throwing out duplicates.

- We merge this combined list with the third list, again throwing out duplicates.

The final, merged list is the output. What's great is that because multiple copies of each number are maintained, even if the sorter occasionally forgets about a number, **OverSort** can still output a complete, sorted list.

(a) Let $T(n)$ be the maximum number of comparisons that **OverSort** could use to sort a list of n distinct numbers, assuming the sorter never forgets a number and n is a power of 3. What is $T(3)$? Write a recurrence relation for $T(n)$. (*Hint:* Merging a list of j distinct numbers and a list of k distinct numbers, and throwing out duplicates of numbers that appear in both lists, requires $j + k - d$ comparisons, when $d > 0$ is the number of duplicates.)

(b) Now we're going to apply the Akra-Bazzi Theorem to find a Θ bound on $T(n)$. Begin by identifying the following constants and functions in the Akra-Bazzi recurrence (22.4):

- The constant k.
- The constants a_i.
- The constants b_i.
- The functions h_i.
- The function g.
- The constant p. You can leave p in terms of logarithms, but you'll need a rough estimate of its value later on.

(c) Does the condition $|g'(x)| = O(x^c)$ for some $c \in \mathbb{N}$ hold?

(d) Does the condition $|h_i(x)| = O(x/\log^2 x)$ hold?

(e) Determine a Θ bound on $T(n)$ by integration.

Exam Problems

Problem 22.4.
Use the Akra-Bazzi formula to find $\Theta()$ asymptotic bounds for the following recurrences. For each recurrence $T(0) = 1$ and $n \in \mathbb{N}$.

(a) $T(n) = 2T\left(\lfloor n/4 \rfloor\right) + T\left(\lfloor n/3 \rfloor\right) + n$

(b) $T(n) = 4T\left(\lfloor n/2 + \sqrt{n} \rfloor\right) + n^2$

(c) A society of devil-worshipers meets every week in a catacomb to initiate new members. Members who have been in the society for two or more weeks initiate four new members each and members who have been in the society for only one week initiate one new member each. On week 0 there is one devil-worshiper. There are two devil-worshipers on week 1.

Write a recurrence relation for the number of members $D(n)$ in the society on the nth week.

You do NOT need to solve the recurrence. Be sure to include the base cases.

Bibliography

[1] Martin Aigner and Günter M. *Proofs from The Book*. Springer-Verlag, 1999. MR1723092. 4, 19

[2] Eric Bach and Jeffrey Shallit. *Efficient Algorithms*, volume 1 of *Algorithmic Number Theory*. The MIT Press, 1996. 329

[3] John Beam. A powerful method of proof. *College Mathematics Journal*, 48(1), 2017. 83

[4] Edward A. Bender and S. Gill Williamson. *A Short Course in Discrete Mathematics*. Dover Publications, 2005.

[5] Arthur T. Benjamin and Jennifer J. Quinn. *Proofs That Really Count: The Art of Combinatorial Proof*. The Mathematical Association of America, 2003. 637

[6] P. J. Bickell, E. A. Hammell, and J. W. O'Connell1. Sex bias in graduate admissions: Data from berkeley. *Science*, 187(4175):398–404, 1975. 762

[7] Norman L. Biggs. *Discrete Mathematics*. Oxford University Press, second edition, 2002.

[8] Béla Bollobás. *Modern Graph Theory*, volume 184 of *Graduate Texts in Mathematics*. Springer-Verlag, 1998. MR1633290. 478

[9] Miklós Bóna. *Introduction to Enumerative Combinatorics*. Walter Rudin Student Series in Advanced Mathematics. McGraw Hill Higher Education, 2007. MR2359513. 694

[10] Timothy Y. Chow. The surprise examination or unexpected hanging paradox. *American Mathematical Monthly*, pages 41–51, 1998.

[11] Thomas H. Cormen, Charles E. Leiserson, Ronald L. Rivest, and Clifford Stein. *Introduction to Algorithms*. The MIT Press, third edition, 2009.

[12] Antonella Cupillari. *The Nuts and Bolts of Proofs*. Academic Press, fourth edition, 2012. MR1818534. 4, 19

[13] Reinhard Diestel. *Graph Theory*. Springer-Verlag, second edition, 2000. 478

[14] Michael Paterson *et al.* Maximum overhang. *MAA Monthly*, 116:763–787, 2009. 564

[15] Shimon Even. *Algorithmic Combinatorics*. Macmillan, 1973. 637

[16] Ronald Fagin, Joseph Y. Halpern, Yoram Moses, and Moshe T. Vardi. *Reasoning About Knowledge*. MIT Press, 1995. 19

[17] William Feller. *An Introduction to Probability Theory and Its Applications. Vol. I.* John Wiley & Sons Inc., New York, third edition, 1968. MR0228020. 738

[18] Philippe Flajolet and Robert Sedgewick. *Analytic Combinatorics*. Cambridge Univ. Press, 2009. 694

[19] Michael Garey and David Johnson. *tba*. tba, 1970. 66

[20] A. Gelfond. Sur le septième problème de hilbert. *Bulletin de l'Académie des Sciences de l'URSS*, 4:623–634, 1934. 19

[21] Judith L. Gersting. *Mathematical Structures for Computer Science: A Modern Treatement of Discrete Mathematics*. W. H. Freeman and Company, fifth edition, 2003.

[22] Edgar G. Goodaire and Michael M. Parmenter. *Discrete Mathematics with Graph Theory*. Prentice Hall, second edition, 2001. 478

[23] Ronald L. Graham, Donald E. Knuth, and Oren Patashnik. *Concrete Mathematics: A Foundation for Computer Science*. Addison-Wesley, second edition, 1994. 694

[24] Charles M. Grinstead and J. Laurie Snell. *Introduction to Probability*. American Mathematical Society, second revised edition, 1997. 738

[25] Dan Gusfield and Robert W. Irving. *The Stable Marriage Problem: Structure and Algorithms*. MIT Press, Cambridge, Massachusetts, 1989. 179, 478

[26] Gary Haggard, John Schlipf, and Sue Whitesides. *Discrete Mathematics for Computer Science*. Brooks Cole, 2005.

[27] Nora Hartsfield and Gerhard Ringel. *Pearls in Graph Theory: A Comprehensive Introduction*. Dover Publications, 2003. 478

[28] Gregory F. Lawler and Lester N. Coyle. *Lectures on Contemporary Probability*. American Mathematical Society, 1999. 738

[29] Eric Lehman, Tom Leighton, and Albert R Meyer. *Mathematics for Computer Science*. unpublished notes for class MIT 6.042, 2016.

[30] L. Lovász, Pelikán J. and K. Vesztergombi. *Discrete Mathematics: Elementary and Beyond*. Undergraduate Texts in Mathematics. Springer-Verlag, 2003. MR1952453. 490

[31] Burton Gordon Malkiel. *A Random Walk down Wall Street: The Time-tested Strategy for Success*. W. W. Norton, 2003. 738

[32] Yuri V. Matiyasevich. *Hilbert's Tenth Problem*. MIT Press, 1993. 342

[33] Albert R. Meyer. A note on star-free events. *J. Assoc. Comput. Machinery*, 16(2), 1969. 235

[34] John G. Michaels and Kenneth H. Rosen. *Applications of Discrete Mathematics*. McGraw-Hill, 1991.

[35] Michael Mitzenmacher and Eli Upfal. *Probability and Computing: Randomized algorithms and probabilistic analysis*. Cambridge University Press, 2005. MR2144605. 738

[36] Rajeev Motwani and Prabhakar Raghavan. *Randomized Algorithms*. Cambridge University Press, 1995. MR1344451,. 738

[37] G. Polya. *How to Solve It: A New Aspect of Mathematical Method*. Princeton University Press, second edition, 1971.

[38] Kenneth H. Rosen. *Discrete Mathematics and Its Applications*. McGraw Hill Higher Education, fifth edition, 2002.

[39] Sheldon Ross. *A First Course in Probability*. Prentice Hall, sixth edition, 2002. 738

[40] Sheldon M. Ross. *Probability Models for Computer Science*. Academic Press, 2001. 738

[41] Edward A. Scheinerman. *Mathematics: A Discrete Introduction*. Brooks Cole, third edition, 2012.

[42] Victor Shoup. *A Computational Introduction to Number Theory and Algebra*. Cambridge University Press, 2005. 329

[43] Larry Stockmeyer. Planar 3-colorability is polynomial complete. *ACM SIGACT News*, pages 19–25, 1973. 497

[44] Gilbert Strang. *Introduction to Applied Mathematics*. Wellesley-Cambridge Press, Wellesley, Massachusetts, 1986.

[45] Michael Stueben and Diane Sandford. *Twenty Years Before the Blackboard*. Mathematical Association of America, 1998. 22

[46] Daniel J. Velleman. *How To Prove It: A Structured Approach*. Cambridge University Press, 1994. 4, 19, 144

[47] Herbert S. Wilf. *generatingfunctionology*. Academic Press, 1990. 694

[48] David Williams. *Weighing the Odds*. Cambridge University Press, 2001. MR1854128. 738

Glossary of Symbols

symbol	meaning
$::=$	is defined to be
■	end of proof symbol
$\neq$	not equal
$\wedge$	and, AND
$\vee$	or, OR
$\longrightarrow$	implies, if ..., then $\cdots$, IMPLIES
$\longrightarrow$	state transition
$\neg P, \overline{P}$	not P, NOT(p)
$\longleftrightarrow$	iff, equivalent, IFF
$\oplus$	xor, exclusive-or, XOR
$\exists$	exists
$\forall$	for all
$\in$	is a member of, is in
$\subseteq$	is a (possibly =) subset of
$\nsubseteq$	is **not** a (possibly =) subset of
$\subset$	is a proper (not =) subset of
$\not\subset$	is **not** a proper (not =) subset of
$\cup$	set union
$\bigcup_{i \in I} S_i$	union of sets S_i where i ranges over set I of indices
$\cap$	set intersection
$\bigcap_{i \in I} S_i$	intersection of sets S_i where i ranges over set I of indices
$\emptyset$	the empty set, $\{\,\}$
$\overline{A}$	complement of set A
$-$	set difference
$\mathrm{pow}(A)$	powerset of set, A
$A \times B$	Cartesian product of sets A and B
S^n	Cartesian product of n copies of set S
$\mathbb{Z}$	integers
$\mathbb{N}, \mathbb{Z}^{\geq 0}$	nonnegative integers
$\mathbb{Z}^+, \mathbb{N}^+$	positive integers
$\mathbb{Z}^-$	negative integers
$\mathbb{Q}$	rational numbers
$\mathbb{R}$	real numbers
$\mathbb{C}$	complex numbers
$\lfloor r \rfloor$	the *floor* of r: the greatest integer $\leq r$
$\lceil r \rceil$	the *ceiling* of r: the least integer $\geq r$
$\lvert r \rvert$	the absolute value of a real number r

symbol	meaning
$R(X)$	image of set X under binary relation R
R^{-1}	inverse of binary relation R
$R^{-1}(X)$	inverse image of set X under relation R
surj	A surj B iff $\exists f : A \to B$. f is a surjective *function*
inj	A inj B iff $\exists R : A \to B$. R is an injective *total relation*
bij	A bij B iff $\exists f : A \to B$. f is a bijection
$[\leq 1 \text{ in}]$	injective property of a relation
$[\geq 1 \text{ in}]$	surjective property of a relation
$[\leq 1 \text{ out}]$	function property of a relation
$[\geq 1 \text{ out}]$	total property of a relation
$[= 1 \text{ out}, = 1 \text{ in}]$	bijection relation
$\circ$	relational composition operator
λ	the empty string/list
A^*	the finite strings over alphabet A
A^ω	the infinite strings over alphabet A
$\text{rev}(s)$	the reversal of string s
$s \cdot t$	concatenation of strings s, t; append(s, t)
$\#_c(s)$	number of occurrences of character c in string s
$m \mid n$	integer m divides integer n; m is a factor of n
gcd	greatest common divisor
log	the base 2 logarithm, log_2
ln	the natural logarithm, log_e
lcm	least common multiple
$(k..n)$	$\{i \in \mathbb{Z} \mid k < i < n\}$
$[k..n)$	$\{i \in \mathbb{Z} \mid k \leq i < n\}$
$(k..n]$	$\{i \in \mathbb{Z} \mid k < i \leq n\}$
$[k..n]$	$\{i \in \mathbb{Z} \mid k \leq i \leq n\}$
$\sum_{i \in I} r_i$	sum of numbers r_i where i ranges over set I of indices
$\prod_{i \in I} r_i$	product of numbers r_i where i ranges over set I of indices
$\text{qcnt}(n, d)$	quotient of n divided by d
$\text{rem}(n, d)$	remainder of n divided by d
$\equiv \pmod{n}$	congruence modulo n
$\not\equiv$	not congruent
$\mathbb{Z}_n$	the ring of integers modulo n
$+_n, \cdot_n$	addition and multiplication operations in $\mathbb{Z}_n$
$\mathbb{Z}_n^*$	the set of numbers in $[0, n)$ relatively prime to n
$\phi(n)$	Euler's totient function $::= |\mathbb{Z}_n^*|$
$\langle u \to v \rangle$	directed edge from vertex u to vertex v
Id_A	identity relation on set A: $a\text{Id}_A a'$ iff $a = a'$

symbol	meaning
R^*	path relation of relation R; reflexive transitive closure of R
R^+	positive path relation of R; transitive closure of R
$\mathbf{f}\,\widehat{x}\,\mathbf{g}$	merge of walk $\mathbf{f}$ with end vertex x
	and walk $\mathbf{g}$ with start vertex x
$\mathbf{f}\,\widehat{\ }\,\mathbf{g}$	merge of walk $\mathbf{f}$ and walk $\mathbf{g}$
	where $\mathbf{f}$'s end vertex equals $\mathbf{g}$'s start vertex
$\langle u\!-\!v\rangle$	undirected edge connecting vertices $u \neq v$
$E(G)$	the edges of graph G
$V(G)$	the vertices of graph G
C_n	the length-n undirected cycle
L_n	the length-n line graph
K_n	the n-vertex complete graph
H_n	the n-dimensional hypercube
$L(G)$	the "left" vertices of bipartite graph G
$R(G)$	the "right" vertices of bipartite graph G
$K_{n,m}$	the complete bipartite graph with n left and m right vertices
$\chi(G)$	chromatic number of simple graph G
H_n	the nth Harmonic number $\sum_{i=1}^{n} 1/i$
$\sim$	asymptotic equality
$n!$	n factorial $::= n \cdot (n-1) \cdots 2 \cdot 1$
$\binom{n}{m}$	$::= n!/m!((n-m)!$; the binomial coefficient
$o()$	asymptotic notation "little oh"
$O()$	asymptotic notation "big oh"
$\Theta()$	asymptotic notation "Theta"
$\Omega()$	asymptotic notation "big Omega"
$\omega()$	asymptotic notation "little omega"
$\Pr[A]$	probability of event A
$\Pr[A \mid B]$	conditional probability of A given B
$\mathcal{S}$	sample space
I_A	indicator variable for event A
PDF	probability density function
CDF	cumulative distribution function
$\mathrm{Ex}[R]$	expectation of random variable R
$\mathrm{Ex}[R \mid A]$	conditional expectation of R given event A
$\mathrm{Ex}^2[R]$	abbreviation for $(\mathrm{Ex}[R])^2$
$\mathrm{Var}[R]$	variance of R
$\mathrm{Var}^2[R]$	the square of the variance of R
σ_R	standard deviation of R

Index

CPSIA information can be obtained
at www.ICGtesting.com
Printed in the USA
LVOW04*1427141117

556254LV00017B/319/P

9 789888 407064